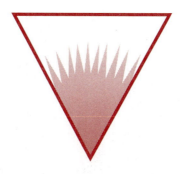

A PRACTICAL REVIEW OF GERMAN GRAMMAR

Second Edition

Gerda Dippmann

Prentice Hall, Englewood Cliffs, New Jersey 07632

Editor-in-Chief: Steve Debow
Director of Development: Marian Wassner
Assistant Editor: María García
Editorial Assistant: Brian Wheel

Managing Editor: Deborah Brennan
Interior Design: Amy Rosen
Cover Design: Chris Wolf
Manufacturing Buyer: Tricia Kenny

Printed in the United States of America
10   9   8   7   6   5   4   3   2   1

0-13-106493-2

Prentice Hall International (UK) Limited, *London*
Prentice Hall of Australia Pty. Limited, *Sydney*
Prentice Hall Canada Inc., *Toronto*
Prentice Hall Hispanoamericana, S. A., *Mexico*
Prentice Hall of India Private Limited, *New Delhi*
Prentice Hall of Japan, Inc., *Tokyo*
Simon & Schuster Asia Pte. Ltd., *Singapore*
Editora Prentice hall do Brasil, Ltda., *Rio de Janeiro*

Contents

Preface

College students enrolled in intermediate or advanced-intermediate courses usually vary in their grasp of German grammar, and there is often limited class time for grammar review. We were delighted by the success of *A Practical Review of German Grammar* and are excited to share this *Second Edition* with you.

A Practical Review of German Grammar is arranged so that the instructor can assign the major portion as work outside of class. Before work on the *Second Edition* was begun, a survey was sent to instructors using or familiar with the *First Edition*. Replies indicated, that the book was in use in a variety of intermediate and post-intermediate courses, generally in combination with reading and conversation or composition materials. Instructors and students underscored the value the "self-study" feature of the book-the more grammar studies can be done outside the classroom, the more class time can be reserved for speaking and reading German.

The sequence and treatment of the grammatical features in *A Practical Review of German Grammar* are based on an empirical approach. The foremost consideration has been to facilitate comprehension by the students. Explanations are basic enough that even students with little formal knowledge of grammar will be able to understand them. Each explanation is followed immediately by exercises to allow students to check their ability to apply what they have just read to practice materials. Summarizing exercises at the end of a section or chapter review larger units of grammar. Students with deficient backgrounds will appreciate the detailed treatment; those with strong backgrounds will be able to work through the review rapidly.

We decided to retain almost all the exercises of the *First Edition*. For the benefit of students in advanced-intermediate or advanced courses, we have added some grammar sections with additional exercises in the *Second Edition*. All exercises are in natural German, frequently in conversational form. Words presumed to be unknown are footnoted for quick reference. Instructors may assign chapters in any sequence as the vocabulary for each chapter is largely self-contained. (This accounts for some duplication in the glossed words.) There is also a glossary in the *Appendix*. We encourage instructors to assign only those sections and exercises which seem necessary and appropriate.

The cassettes for the *First Edition* are no longer available. We expect to publish tutorial software free of charge in the coming months.

Acknowledgments

We are grateful to the many users of the first edition who responded to our questions as we began to prepare for this edition. We thank each of the following colleagues for their suggestions and recommendations.

Elizabeth Bredeck, University of California, San Diego
Lynn R. Eliason, Utah State University
Gerlinde Ulm Sanford, Syracuse University
Frauke A. Harvey, Baylor University
Christa W. Britt, Thunderbird University
Robert B. Youngblood, Washington and Lee University
Ferrel Rose, Grinnell College
Kenneth E. Keeton, Eckerd College
Walke von Reinhart, University of Rhode Island
Nancy Decker, Rollins College
Dinah Dodds, Lewis and Clark College
Jeffrey B. Gardiner, Western Michigan University
Carla J. Love, University of Wisconsin-Madison
Susan M. Johnson, Susquehanna University
Frauke Loewensen, Monterey Institute of International Studies
Gudrun Tabbert-Jones, Santa Clara University
Charles J. Kenlan, Washington State University
Astrid Klocke, Indiana University
James F. Hyde, Jr., Ripon College
Kent Hooper, University of Puget Sound
Eberhard Geyer, Hillsdale College
Annemarie Arnold, Wesleyan University
Mary Wauchope, San Diego State University
Karen Six, University of California, Berkeley
Cecile Cazort Zorach, Franklin and Marshall College
Hans K. Musslee, Utah State University
Henning Falkenstein, Valparaiso University
Mark Southern, Carthage College
Peter R. Erspamer, Winona State University
Ruth I. Cape, Skidmore College
Wallace Sue, Michigan State University

We acknowledge the comments and participation of Leo Connally, of Middle Tennesse State University, who generously contributed his time at the final draft phase of the manuscript. His comments greatly strengthened the material.

At Prentice Hall, I extend my thanks to the publishing team: Steve Debow, Editor-in Chief; , Brian Wheel, Editorial Assistant, and Debbie Brennan, Managing Editor. I also thank Petra Hausberger, Project Manager for her expertise in the production process and her diligence in monitoring the project; and to Lev Nisnevitch for his composition and page layout work.

A PRACTICAL REVIEW
OF GERMAN GRAMMAR

Preliminary Remarks about German Word Order

This chapter deals with some basic aspects of German word order. Other aspects will be treated in subsequent chapters.

▽ Word Order in Statements

§1 NORMAL WORD ORDER: SUBJECT — INFLECTED VERB

The inflected (conjugated) verb is the form with the personal endings.

Wir wiederholen die Grammatik.   *We are reviewing grammar.*
SUBJECT   VERB   DIRECT OBJECT

Adding an adverb:

Wir wiederholen **oft** die Grammatik.   *We **often** review grammar.*

In English an adverb may be placed between the subject and the verb. This cannot be done in German. The verb must be the second element.

§2 INVERTED WORD ORDER: INFLECTED VERB — SUBJECT

For emphasis or stylistic reasons an element other than the subject may be in first position.

Heute **wiederholen wir** die Grammatik.
VERB   SUBJ.   DIR. OBJ.

The verb remains in second position: the subject follows the inflected verb. Thus the normal subject-verb sequence is inverted.

1-1   Restate the following sentences, placing the boldface element first.

> MODEL: Ich gehe **heute abend** mit Hans ins Kino.
> **Heute abend gehe ich mit Hans ins Kino.**

1. Du glaubst das **natürlich** nicht.
2. Sie verstehen mich **vielleicht**[1] nicht.
3. Wir spielen **am Montag** Tennis.
4. Mein Kassettenrecorder funktioniert **leider**[2] nicht.
5. Ich fahre nicht wieder **mit dir** in die Stadt.
6. Michael sagt **hoffentlich**[3] die Wahrheit.[4]
7. Wir spielen **manchmal**[5] Karten
8. Es war **gestern** sehr kalt.
9. Helga ist **jetzt** nicht zu Hause.
10. Viele Leute wissen **das** nicht.

ELEMENTS WITH NO EFFECT ON WORD ORDER

The most common elements that do not affect word order are listed below.

a. **Set off by a comma**

ja	**Ja, ich verstehe** Sie.
nein	**Nein, ich verstehe** Sie nicht.
(form of address)	Frau Böhme, **ich verstehe** Sie nicht.

b. **Not set off by a comma**

aber (*but*)	Aber
denn (*for*)	Denn
oder (*or*)	Oder
und (*and*)	Und

> viele Leute wissen das nicht.

Aber, denn, oder, und are coordinating conjunctions that usually connect two clauses (cf. Chapter 12, §1).

> Das Postamt ist heute geschlossen, **aber** viele Leute wissen das nicht.
> *The post office is closed today, **but** many people don't know that.*

§3   DEPENDENT WORD ORDER: INFLECTED VERB STANDS LAST

Dependent word order occurs in dependent clauses. Such clauses cannot stand alone; they are dependent upon other clauses. They are introduced by subordinating conjunctions, such as **daß, weil** (*because*), **wenn** (*when, if*) (cf. Chapter 12, §2).

---

[1] **vielleicht**	*perhaps*
[2] **leider**	*unfortunately*
[3] **hoffentlich**	lit. *hopefully*, generally used in the sense of *I hope*
[4] **die Wahrheit sagen**	*to tell the truth*
[5] **manchmal**	*sometimes*

Es ist möglich, | daß wir heute die Grammatik wiederholen.
└ MAIN CLAUSE ┘ └──── DEPENDENT CLAUSE ────┘

It is possible   that we'll review grammar today.

The subject usually follows the subordinating conjunction immediately. The inflected verb is in final position.

PRACTICE

1-2   Convert the following sentences to dependent clauses by beginning with **Es ist möglich, daß...**

MODEL: Das ist ein Fehler.
Es ist möglich, daß das ein Fehler ist.

1. Das ist Peters Freundin.
2. Müllers[1] sind jetzt zu Hause.
3. Herr Schmidt arbeitet heute nicht.
4. Andreas und Barbara heiraten[2] im Juni.
5. Frau Braun sagt die Wahrheit.
6. Die Hausaufgaben[3] sind zu schwer.
7. Karin hat heute keine Zeit.
8. Es wird morgen kälter.
9. Wir besuchen Sie am Sonntag.
10. Ich bin nicht tolerant genug.

WORD ORDER WITHOUT *daß*

When **daß** is omitted, normal or inverted word order is used.

Ich weiß, **Müllers sind** jetzt nicht zu Hause.
Ich glaube, jetzt **sind Müllers** nicht zu Hause.

THE DEPENDENT CLAUSE PRECEDING THE MAIN CLAUSE.

Wir gehen heute abend nicht ins Kino, weil wir kein Geld haben.
Weil wir kein Geld haben, | **gehen wir** heute abend nicht ins Kino.
└── DEPENDENT CLAUSE ──┘ └──── MAIN CLAUSE ────┘

The main clause has inverted word order when it is preceded by a dependent clause. The latter is treated as the first element of the main clause. Compare:

Wir	**gehen**	heute abend nicht ins Kino.
SUBJ.	VERB	
Heute abend	**gehen**	**wir** nicht ins Kino.
	VERB	SUBJ.
Weil wir kein Geld haben,	**gehen**	**wir** heute abend nicht ins Kino.
	VERB	SUBJ.

---

[1] **Müllers**   *the Müllers* (in German without article)
[2] **heiraten**   *to marry, get married*
[3] **die Hausaufgaben** (pl.)   *homework*

1-3   Restate the following sentences beginning with the dependent clause.

> **MODEL:**   Wir kaufen ein neues Auto, wenn wir genug Geld haben.
> **Wenn wir genug Geld haben, kaufen wir ein neues Auto.**

1. Ich schreibe dir, wenn ich mehr Zeit habe.
2. Er geht heute nicht in die Vorlesung, weil er Fieber hat.
3. Ich werde sehr böse,[1] wenn du nicht pünktlich bist.[2]
4. Inge hat schlechte Laune,[3] weil Heinz nicht anruft.
5. Ich nehme zwei Aspirintabletten,[4] wenn ich Kopfschmerzen habe.

Word Order in Questions

§4   DIRECT QUESTIONS

Direct questions have inverted word order: the inflected verb is in first or second position. Compare the following two types of questions:

Wann **wiederholen wir** die Grammatik?   **Wiederholen wir** heute die Grammatik?
　　　　VERB　　SUBJ　　　　　　　　　　　　　　VERB　　SUBJ

The verb is in second position when the question begins with a question word, such as **wann** (*when*), **warum** (*why*), **wo** (*where*), **wieviel** (*how much*).

When there is no question word, the verb is in first position.

Note that there is no German equivalent for the English auxiliary *do* in questions:

> *Do you understand me?*   **Verstehen Sie mich?**

1-4   Convert the following statements to questions.

A.   Begin with the verb.

> **MODEL:** Das ist ein Fehler.
> **Ist das ein Fehler?**

1. Elke hat einen Job.
2. Andreas sagt die Wahrheit
3. Neumanns sind nicht zu Hause.
4. Es wird morgen kälter.
5. Der Kassettenrecorder funktioniert nicht.
6. Ich bin nicht tolerant genug.

---

[1] **böse werden**　　　　　　　　　　*to become angry*
[2] **pünktlich sein**　　　　　　　　　*to be on time*
[3] **die Laune**　　　　　　　　　　　*mood*
　　gute/schlechte Laune haben　　*to be in a good/bad mood*
[4] **die Aspirintablette, -n**　　　　*aspirin*

B. Begin with the indicated question word.

MODEL: Das ist ein Fehler (warum)
Warum ist das ein Fehler?

1. Schmidts sind zu Hause. (wann)
2. Anita fährt in die Stadt. (wann)
3. Andreas hat schlechte Laune. (warum)
4. Du glaubst das nicht. (warum)
5. Dieter und Elke heiraten. (wann)
6. Monika und Renate spielen Tennis (wo)

§5   INDIRECT QUESTIONS

Indirect questions have dependent word order: the inflected verb stands last. They depend on an introductory clause, such as **Ich weiß nicht... Ich möchte wissen**.... (*I would* or *I'd like to know* ...). Compare the following two types of indirect questions:

Wann wiederholen wir die Grammatik?
Ich möchte wissen, **wann wir** die Grammatik **wiederholen**.
*I would like to know **when** we'll review the grammar.*

Wiederholen wir heute die Grammatik?
Ich möchte wissen, **ob wir** heute die Grammatik **wiederholen**.
*I'd like to know **whether (if)** we'll review grammar today.*

In an indirect question the question word functions as a subordinating conjunction, hence the dependent word order.

If the direct question has no question word, the subordinating conjunction **ob** (*whether, if*) is used to introduce the indirect question.

PRACTICE

1-5   Convert the following direct questions to indirect questions using the introductory clause of the model.

A. Direct questions with question word.

MODEL: Was ist das?
Ich weiß nicht, was das ist.

1. Wo wohnen Bergers?
2. Wo ist die Toilette?[1]
3. Warum lachen die Leute?
4. Wann kommt Klaus nach Hause?
5. Wieviel kostet dieser Ring?
6. Warum ist Frau Köhler so schockiert?[2]
7. Wo sind die Autoschlüssel?[3]
8. Was kostet das?

---

[1] **die Toilette, -n**   *toilet* (commonly used as the equivalent of *ladies' room, men's room, lavatory*)
[2] **schockiert sein**   *to be shocked*
[3] **der Autoschlüssel, -**   *car key*

B. Direct questions without a question word

MODEL: Hat Andreas eine Freundin?
> **Ich möchte wissen, ob Andreas eine Freundin hat.**

1. Sind Schmidts jetzt zu Hause?
2. Ist das ein Fehler?
3. Sagt Rita die Wahrheit?
4. Bin ich tolerant genug?
5. Hat der Chef[1] gute order schlechte Laune?
6. Ist die Chefin in ihrem Büro?[2]
7. Liebst du mich wirklich?[3]

The introductory clause may be a question, such a **Weißt du . . .?, Wisssen Sie...?, Können Sie mir sagen ...?, Kannst du mir sagen...?**

DIRECT QUESTION	INDIRECT QUESTION
Was ist das?	**Weißt du, was das ist?**
	Do you know what that is?
Sind Schmidts zu Hause?	**Wissen Sie, ob Schmidts zu Hause sind?**
	Do you know whether the Schmidts are at home?
Wo wohnen Bergers?	**Können Sie mir sagen, wo Bergers wohnen?**
	Can you tell me where the Bergers live?

Remember:
> An indirect question depends on an introductory clause (statement or question) and may be regarded as a "dependent question" requiring dependent word order.

PRACTICE

▼ 1-6   The following questions begin with or without a question word. Convert them to indirect questions, using the indicated introductory clauses.

MODEL: Wo ist der Bahnhof? (Können Sie mir sagen)
> **Können Sie mir sagen, wo der Bahnhof ist?**

1. Wo ist die nächste Tankstelle?[4] (Können Sie mir sagen)
2. Wann beginnt das Konzert? (Wissen Sie)
3. Wieviel kostet dieser Kassettenrecorder? (Weißt du)
4. Wo wohnt Helga? (Wissen Sie)
5. Wohnt Helga bei ihren Eltern? (Wissen Sie)
6. Hat Andreas einen Job? (Weißt du)
7. Ist Professor Wagner jetzt in seinem Büro? (Wissen Sie)

---

[1] der Chef, -s	*male boss*
die Chefin, -nen	*female boss*
[2] das Büro, -s	*office*
[3] wirklich	*real(ly)*
[4] die Tankstelle, -n	*gas station*

8. Wo ist sein Büro? (Können Sie mir sagen)
9. Hat Renate die Grippe?[1] (Weißt du)
10. Was bedeutet[2] dieses Wort? (Kannst du mir sagen)

§6 SUMMARY

The following patterns illustrate the normal word order, the inverted word order and the dependent word order.

a. Normal word order

	INFLECTED VERB	
Wir	**wiederholen**	die Grammatik.

b. Inverted word order

		INFLECTED VERB	
STATEMENT	Heute	**wiederholen**	**wir** die Grammatik
DIRECT QUESTION WITH QUESTION WORD	Wann	**wiederholen**	**wir** die Grammatik?
WITHOUT QUESTION WORD		**Wiederholen**	**wir** die Grammatik?

The inflected verb is in second position except indirect questions that do not begin with a question word, in which case it is in first position.

c. Dependent word order

			INFLECTED VERB
STATEMENT	Es ist möglich,	**daß** wir die Grammatik	**wiederholen.**
INDIRECT QUESTION	Ich weiß nicht,	**wann** wir die Grammatik	**wiederholen.**
	Ich weiß nicht,	**ob** wir die Grammatik	**wiederholen.**
	Weißt du,	**wann** wir die Grammatik	**wiederholen?**

The inflected verb is in final position.

▼ **1-7**   Express in German.

MODEL: a. She is in a good mood.   **Sie hat gute Laune.**
         b. I hope she's in a good mood.   **Hoffentlich hat sie gute Laune.**
         c. Is she in a good mood?   **Hat sie gute Laune?**
         d. Do you (**du**) know whether   **Weißt du, ob sie gute**
            she is in a good mood?   **Laune hat?**

1. a. He has a car.   **Er hat einen Wagen.**
    b. I hope he has a car.
    c. Does he have a car?
    d. Do you (**du**) know whether he has a car?

[2] die Grippe, -n   *flu*
[3] bedeuten   *to mean*

2. a. She believes that.   Sie glaubt das.
    b. I hope she believes that.
    c. Does she believe that?
    d. I don't know whether she believes that.

3. a. She is Dieter's girlfriend.   Sie ist Dieters Freundin.
    b. Perhaps she is Dieter's girlfriend.
    c. Is she Dieter's girlfriend?
    d. I'd like to know whether she is Dieter's girlfriend.
    e. It is possible that she is Dieter's girlfriend.

4. a. I am not tolerant enough.   Ich bin nicht tolerant genug.
    b. Perhaps I am not tolerant enough.
    c. Am I not tolerant enough?
    d. It is possible that I am not tolerant enough.

5. a. The Neumanns live in Munich.   Neumanns wohnen in München.
    b. Do the Neumanns live in Munich?
    c. Where do the Neumanns live?
    d. I'd like to know where the Neumanns live.

6. a. She is not at home.   Sie ist nicht zu Hause.
    b. Is she not at home?
    c. Why isn't she at home?
    d. I don't know why she isn't at home.

7. a. He's in a bad mood.   Er hat schlechte Laune.
    b. Perhaps he's in a bad mood.
    c. Why is he in a bad mood?
    d. Do you (Sie) know why he is in a bad mood?

 # The Position of *nicht*

A distinction has to be made between normally accented negation and strong negation of a particular element.

§7   NORMALLY ACCENTED NEGATION

Nicht follows the inflected verb, pronoun objects, and most noun objects.

INFLECTED VERB	Sein Bruder raucht **nicht.**
PRONOUN OBJECT	Ich kenne ihn **nicht.**
NOUN OBJECT	Ich kenne seinen Bruder **nicht.**

Nicht precedes most other elements, such as:

a. predicate adjectives and predicate nouns
    (they follow the main verbs **sein, werden, heißen**):

Ich bin **nicht** nervös.
Ich werde **nicht** nervös.
Sabine wird **nicht** Lehrerin.
Er heißt **nicht** Martin.

b.   most adverbs:

Sie sprechen **nicht** laut genug.
Wir fahren **nicht** zu schnell.

but **nicht** follows most adverbs of time:

Er kommt heute **nicht.**
Dieser Kassettenrecorder funktioniert manchmal **nicht.**

c.   most prepositional phrases:

Dieser Brief ist **nicht** für mich.
Susanne wohnt **nicht** bei ihren Eltern.

If several of the above elements occur in a sentence, **nicht** usually precedes the first one:

Sie ist **nicht** freundlich zu mir.
Schmidts fliegen **nicht** mit uns nach Europa.

The position of **nicht** is the same in questions:

Ist sie **nicht** freundlich zu dir?
Warum fliegen Schmidts **nicht** mit uns nach Europa?

When negating dependent clauses, keep in mind that the inflected verb stands last. Compare:

Frau Weber kennt meinen Vater **nicht.**
Es ist möglich, daß Frau Weber meinen Vater **nicht** kennt.

Otherwise the position of **nicht** follows the same rules that are valid for main clauses.

§8   STRONG NEGATION OF A PARTICULAR ELEMENT

If one element is strongly negated, nicht precedes that particular element. Such an emphatic negation is often part of a contrast.

Ulrich kauft **nicht diesen Wagen**; er kauft einen anderen.
Nicht Mathias kauft diesen Wagen; seine Schwester kauft ihn.

PRACTICE

1-8   **A.** Explain the position of **nicht** in the following sentences.

MODEL: Sie is nicht nett¹ zu mir.
                Nicht precedes the predicate adjective *nett.*

---

¹ **nett**   *nice*

1. Helga ist nicht meine Freundin.
2. Dieser Ring gefällt mir nicht.
3. Klaus weiß, daß der Ring Annette nicht gefällt.
4. Ich verstehe die Hausaufgaben nicht.
5. Warum fragen Sie ihn nicht?
6. Ich möchte wissen, warum Sie ihn nicht fragen.
7. Das ist nicht mein Hobby.
8. Martin fliegt nicht mit seinen Eltern nach Florida.
9. Ich gehe mit Peter nicht ins Kino; wir gehen in die Disko.
10. Fräulein Schiller arbeitet nicht bei dieser Firma.
11. Warum glauben Sie mir nicht?
12. Nicht Schmidts, sondern (*but rather*) Bergers besuchen uns morgen.
13. Schmidts besuchen uns morgen nicht.
14. Es ist schade,[1] daß sie uns morgen nicht besuchen.
15. Hoffentlich wird es nicht kälter.
16. Monikas Freund heißt nicht Thomas.

B. Negate the following sentences according to the rules for normally accented negation. (Do not negate the boldface introductory clauses.)

1. Meine Eltern fliegen nach Paris.
2. Margot ist meine Freundin.
3. Ich bezahle diese Rechnung.[2]
4. **Es ist möglich**, daß er die Rechnung bezahlt.
5. Peter arbeitet in der Bibliothek.
6. Meine Noten[3] werden besser.
7. Arbeiten Sie heute?
8. Sind Zimmermanns zu Hause?
9. **Ich weiß**, daß Zimmermanns heute zu Hause sind.
10. Der italienische Film gefällt meiner Freundin.
11. **Es ist möglich**, daß der italienische Film meiner Freundin gefällt.
12. Vielleicht weiß Astrid seinen Namen.
13. **Es ist möglich**, daß unsere Fußballmannschaft[4] morgen gewinnt.
14. Das ist gut für die Nerven.
15. **Wissen Sie**, daß das gut für die Nerven ist?
16. Verstehen Sie mich?
17. **Ich weiß**, daß er mich versteht.

(For the position of **nicht** in sentences that contain verb complements, see Chap. 19, §4 [Note].)

---

[1] **es ist schade** — *it is a pity*
[2] **die Rechnung, -en** — *bill*
[3] **die Note, -n** — *grade*
[4] **die Fußballmannschaft, -en** — *soccer team*

§9   USING *nicht wahr?*

Du hast eine Schwester, **nicht wahr?**
*You have a sister, **don't you?***

Du hast keinen Bruder, **nicht wahr?**
*You don't have a brother, **do you?***

Hans und Margot haben geheiratet, **nicht wahr?**
*Hans and Margot got married, **didn't they?***

Du kannst mich verstehen, **nicht wahr?**
*You can understand me, **can't you?***

Nicht wahr? (lit. *not true?*) is used like English *don't you?, do you?, didn't they?, can't you?*, and the like to seek confirmation of what was just said. **Nicht wahr?** is often shortened to **nicht?**

Du hast eine Schwester, **nicht?**

PRACTICE

1-9   Express in English.

1. Helga ist deine Freundin, nicht wahr?
2. Sie hat einen Wagen, nicht wahr?
3. Du verstehst mich, nicht wahr?
4. Renate und Frank spielen Tennis, nicht?

CHAPTER

2

Verbs in the Present Tense
The Imperative

 Verbs in the Present Tense

§1   BASIC FORMS OF THE PRESENT TENSE

The infinitive is the form of the verb you will find in a dictionary. It usually has
the ending **-en**. A small group of verbs has the ending **-n**, such as **sammeln** *(to
collect)*, **bewundern** *(to admire)*, **tun** *(to do)*. The verb stem may be obtained by
dropping the ending **-en** or **-n**.

INFINITIVE:	gehen	STEM:	geh-
	studieren		studier-
	sammeln		sammel-
	bewundern		bewunder-
	tun		tu-

The inflectional endings of the present tense are added to the stem. They are as
follows:

INFINITIVE ENDING **-en**

SINGULAR	1st person	ich	gehe	I	go	ich ___ e		
	2nd (familiar)	du	gehst	you	go	du ___ st		
	3rd	er		he		er		
		sie }	geht	she }	goes	sie } ___ t		
		es		it		es		
PLURAL	1st person	wir	gehen	we	go	wir ___ [en]		
	2nd (familiar)	ihr	geht	you	go	ihr ___ t		
	3rd	sie	gehen	they	go	sie ___ [en]		
	2nd (polite sing. + pl.)	Sie	gehen	you	go	Sie ___ [en]		

Note that the three marked forms have the same endings as the infinitive.

infinitive ending **-n**

The three marked forms add **-n** instead of **-en**, making them identical to the infinitive.

ich	samm(e)le*	ich	bewund(e)re*	ich	tue	ich ___ e
du	sammel**st**	du	bewunder**st**	du	tu**st**	du ___ st
er ⎫		er ⎫		er ⎫		er ⎫
sie ⎬	sammel**t**	sie ⎬	bewunder**t**	sie ⎬	tu**t**	sie ⎬ ___ t
es ⎭		es ⎭		es ⎭		es ⎭
wir	sammel**n**	wir	bewunder**n**	wir	tu**n**	wir ___ [n]
ihr	sammel**t**	ihr	bewunder**t**	ihr	tu**t**	ihr ___ t
sie	sammel**n**	sie	bewunder**n**	sie	tu**n**	sie ___ [n]
Sie	sammel**n**	Sie	bewunder**n**	Sie	tu**n**	Sie ___ [n]

*Verbs ending in **-eln** or **-ern** often drop the **e** of the stem in the first person singular.

There are three German equivalents to the English you:

you ⟵
- **du** familiar address singular
- **ihr** familiar address plural
- **Sie** formal address singular and plural

The familiar form **du** and its plural counterpart **ihr** are used when addressing relatives, close friends, children up to about the age of 15, pets, or the deity. Young people usually also say **du** to one another. Otherwise, **Sie** is used.

2-1   A. Substitute the appropriate forms of the verbs in the parentheses.

MODEL: Helga lernt es nicht. (studieren, tun).
Helga studiert es nicht.
Helga tut es nicht.

1. Frank sagt das nicht. (glauben, sammeln, bewundern, tun, organisieren)
2. Warum glaubst du das nicht? (lernen, studieren, tun)
3. Warum raucht ihr? (lachen, lächeln¹, applaudieren)
4. Warum verstehen Sie das nicht? (glauben, korrigieren, tun)
5. Ich frage ihn. (lieben, bewundern, kritisieren, manipulieren, irritieren)

B. Restate the following sentences, using the subjects in parentheses.

1. Wir lernen Deutsch. (ich, sie [she], sie [they])
2. Meine Schwester studiert in Bonn. (ich, wir)
3. Warum lachen Sie? (du, er, ihr)

---

¹² **lächeln**   *to smile*

4.   Warum applaudieren Sie? (du, ihr)
5.   Er bewundert Sie. (ich, wir)
6.   Meine Freundin sammelt Briefmarken.[1] (ich, wir, sie [they])
7.   Ich tue das nicht. (er, wir, viele Leute)
8.   Warum tun sie das nicht? (du, ihr)
9.   Diese Musik irritiert mich. (diese Kinder)
10.   Thomas sagt nichts, er lächelt nur. (ich, wir, sie [they])

A note on the German equivalents of *to study*

Studieren is used

a.   to refer to enrollment at a college or university:

> Klaus studiert an der Universität Bonn.
> or: Klaus studiert in Bonn.

b.   to indicate a student's major:

> Anita studiert Chemie. (Meaning: Anita's major is chemistry.)

c.   to mean *gaze at intently*:

> Ich studiere den Fahrplan.   *I'm studying the time table.*
> Wir studieren die Speisekarte.   *We're studying the menu.*

Lernen is used to render *to study* in the sense of studying for a test, an exam, or of learning something:

> *I'm studyng for an exam.*   Ich lerne für eine Prüfung.
> *Barbara studies German and*   Barbara lernt Deutsch und Spanish.
> *Spanish.*   Meaning: *Barbara is taking German and Spanish courses.* (Neither German nor Spanish is her major.)

§2   VERBS WITH STEMS ENDING IN *-d*, *-t*, OR CONSONANT CLUSTERS

To facilitate pronunciation, an **e** is inserted between the stem and the endings of the 3rd pers. sing. and the **du** and **ihr**-forms of:

a.   verbs whose stems end in -d or -t, such as antworten, (*to answer*) arbeiten (*to work*), bedeuten (*to mean*), beneiden (*to envy*), finden (*to find*), heiraten (*to marry*), reden (*to talk*):

b.   verbs whose stems end in certain consonant clusters, i.e.

> a single **m** or **n** that is preceded by a consonant other than l or r.

Few verbs belong to this group. Some common ones are **atmen** (*to breathe*), **öffnen** (*to open*), **regnen** (*to rain*), **zeichnen** (*to draw*).

---

[1] **die Briefmarke, -n**   *stamp*

ich	rede	ich	antworte	ich	öffne	ich ___ e	
du	red**est**	du	antwort**est**	du	öffn**est**	du ___ est	
er		er		er		er	
sie }	red**et**	sie }	antwort**et**	sie }	öffn**et**	sie } ___ et	— **e** added
es		es		es		es	
wir	reden	wir	antworten	wir	öffnen	wir ___ en	
ihr	red**et**	ihr	antwort**et**	wir	öffn**et**	ihr ___ et	
sie	reden	sie	antworten	sie	öffnen	sie ___ en	
Sie	reden	Sie	antworten	Sie	öffnen	Sie ___ en	

All endings begin with **e**.

PRACTICE

2-2

A. Supply the appropriate forms of the verbs in parentheses.

MODEL: Barbara _____ .(reden, zeichnen)
          Barbara redet.
          Barbara zeichnet.

1. Rainer _____ nicht. (arbeiten, antworten, warten)
2. _____ du mich? (beneiden, heiraten, bitten)
3. Warum _____ ihr nicht? (warten, antworten, reden, zeichnen)
4. _____ du den Brief nicht? (finden, öffnen)
5. Es _____ viel. (regnen, kosten, bedeuten)

B. Restate the following sentences, using the subjects in parentheses.

1. Wir arbeiten zuviel. (du)
2. Sie atmen nicht tief genug. (der Patient)
3. Warten Sie auf mich? (du)
4. Ich rede zuviel. (meine Freundin)
5. Warum beneiden Sie mich? (ihr)
6. Ich bitte um Verzeihung.[1] (Klaus)
7. Ich zeichne gern.[2] (Helga)
8. Finden Sie diesen Film wirklich interessant? (du)

§3   VERBS WITH STEMS ENDING IN -s, -ss, -ß, -tz, or -z

These verbs add only -t to the stem of the **du**- form; thus the 2nd and 3rd person singular are identical.

Some common verbs that belong to this group are **hassen** (*to hate*), **heißen** (*to be called*), **reisen** (*to travel*), **schließen** (*to close*), **schwänzen** (*to skip class*), **sitzen** (*to sit*), **tanzen** (*to dance*), **übersetzen** (*to translate*).

---

[1] **um Verzeihung bitten**   *to apologize*
[2] **etwas gern tun**   *to like doing something*

reisen	hassen	heißen	sitzen	schwänzen
ich reise	ich hasse	ich heiße	ich sitze	ich schwänzt
du reist	du haßt*	du heißt	du sitzt	du schwänzt

er		er		er		er		er	
sie } reist		sie } haßt		sie } heißt		sie } sitzt		sie } schwänzt	
es		es		es		es		es	

* Note that **ss** becomes **ß** when followed by a consonant (cf. Appendix, §1).

PRACTICE

2-3   Restate the following sentences using **du** as the subject.

1. Sitzen Sie immer in der ersten Reihe?[1]
2. Reisen Sie viel?
3. Warum hassen Sie diese Frau?
4. Warum übersetzen Sie diesen Satz nicht?
5. Warum schließen Sie die Tür nicht?
6. Wie heißen Sie?
7. Monika schwänzt jeden Freitag.
8. Susanne tanzt sehr gut.

§4   VERBS WITH STEM VOWEL CHANGES

Many strong verbs (cf. chap. 3, §5) change their stem vowels in the 2nd and 3rd pers. sing. In addition, the verbs **nehmen** and **treten** also change stem consonants.

1. Change from *e* to *ie* or *i*

sehen	lesen	essen	geben	nehmen (*to take*)
ich sehe	ich lese	ich esse	ich gebe	ich nehme
du **siehst**	du **liest**	du **ißt**	du **gibst**	du **nimmst**
er	er	er	er	er
sie } **sieht**	sie } **liest**	sie } **ißt**	sie } **gibt**	sie } **nimmt**
es	es	es	es	es
wir sehen	wir lesen	wir essen	wir geben	wir nehmen
ihr seht	ihr lest	ihr eßt	ihr gebt	ihr nehmt
sie sehen	sie lesen	sie essen	sie geben	sie nehmen
Sie sehen	Sie lesen	Sie essen	Sie geben	Sie nehmen

Note that the forms **du liest** and **du ißt** add -**t**, rather than -**st**, because of the stem ending in **s** or **ß**.

---

[1] **die Reihe, -n**   *row*

2. Change from *a, au, o* to *ä, äu, ö*

fahren		**schlafen**		**laufen** (*to run*)		**stoßen** (*to push*)	
ich	fahre	ich	schlafe	ich	laufe	ich	stoße
du	**fährst**	du	**schläfst**	du	**läufst**	du	**stößt**
er		er		er		er	
sie }	**fährt**	sie }	**schläft**	sie }	**läuft**	sie }	**stößt**
es		es		es		es	
wir	fahren	wir	schlafen	wir	laufen	wir	stoßen
etc.		etc.		etc.		etc.	

Verbs whose stems end in **-d** or **-t** do not add the usual **e** when the vowel changes:

laden (*to load*)		**halten** (*to hold, stop*)		**raten** (*to advise*)		**treten** (*to step*)	
ich	lade	ich	halte	ich	rate	ich	trete
du	**lädst**	du	**hältst**	du	**rätst**	du	**tri_tt_st**
er		er		er		er	
sie }	**lädt**	sie }	**hält**	sie }	**rät**	sie }	**tri_tt_**
es		es		es		es	
wir	laden	wir	halten	wir	raten	wir	treten
ihr	lad**et**	ihr	halt**et**	ihr	rat**et**	ihr	tret**et**
sie	laden	sie	halten	sie	raten	sie	treten
Sie	laden	Sie	halten	Sie	raten	Sie	treten

Note that **halten** and **raten** do not add an ending in the 3rd pers. sing.

Verbs with a stem change in the singular are listed in this book showing their 3rd pers. sing. form as follows:

helfen (hilft)	*to help*
sprechen (spricht)	*to speak*
vergessen (vergißt)	*to forget*

PRACTICE

2-4 Restate the following sentences, using the subjects in parentheses.

1. Wir laufen sehr schnell. (du, ihr, Anita)
2. Sehen Sie den Fehler nicht? (du, er, ihr)
3. Essen Sie gern Eis?[1] (du, deine Freundin, ihr)
4. Ich vergesse das vielleicht. (Karin, du, ihr)
5. Lesen Sie deutsche Zeitungen? (du, ihr)
6. Sie sprechen zu schnell. (du, er)
7. Warum fahren Sie nicht mit dem Bus? (ihr, du)
8. Die Busse halten hier nicht. (der Bus)
9. Warum nehmen Sie kein Taxi? (du, ihr, Astrid)

---

[1] **das Eis**   *ice, ice cream*

10. Warum laden Sie das Gepäck[1] nicht ins Auto? (er, du, ihr)
11. Warum treten Sie nicht auf die Bremse?[2] (du)
12. Was raten Sie mir? (du, ihr)
13. Warum stoßen Sie mich? (du)
14. Schlafen die Kinder? (das Baby)
15. Helfen Sie mir bei den Hausaufgaben? (du)
16. Ich gebe Monika einen Kuß. (er)

§5   IRREGULAR CONJUGATION OF *haben, sein, werden*

haben (*to have*)	sein (*to be*)	werden (*to become, get*)
ich habe	ich bin	ich werde
du hast	du bist	du wirst
er ⎫	er ⎫	er ⎫
sie ⎬ hat	sie ⎬ ist	sie ⎬ wird
es ⎭	es ⎭	es ⎭
wir haben	wir sind	wir werden
ihr habt	ihr seid	ihr werdet
sie haben	sie sind	sie werden
Sie haben	Sie sind	Sie werden

§6   IRREGULAR CONJUGATION OF *wissen*

wissen (*to know*)

ich weiß
du weißt
er ⎫
sie ⎬ weiß
es ⎭
wir wissen
ihr wißt
sie wissen
Sie wissen

Note: The stem vowel changes throughout the singular to **ei**; the 1st and 3rd pers. sing. do not have an inflectional ending.

PRACTICE

▽ 2-5   Restate the following sentences, using the subjects in parentheses.

1. Andreas ist sehr nervös. (ich, Sie, du, ihr)
2. Warum werden Sie so nervös? (du, ihr)
3. Sie haben recht.[3] (du, Anita, ich)

---

¹ das Gepäck   *luggage*
² die Bremse, -n   *brake*
³ recht haben   *to be right*

4. Wissen Sie das nicht? (er, du, ihr)
5. Ich werde zu dick.¹(das Baby, die Kinder)
6. Sie haben es immer eilig.² (du, er, ihr)
7. Warum sind Sie so unfreundlich? (du, ihr)
8. Klaus ist ein Miesepeter.³ (ich, sie [she])

§7   USES OF THE PRESENT TENSE

1. German has neither a progressive nor an emphatic form; a single present tense
   form may therefore have any of three English equivalents:

   Sie raucht.   *She smokes.*
                                                 She is smoking. (progressive form)
                                                 She does smoke. (emphatic form)

   The context generally indicates which meaning is applicable. If it is necessary to
   make absolutely clear in German that an action is in progress, an adverb is added
   or the sentence is paraphrased.

   Er kommt gerade.   *He is coming this very moment.*

   Ich bin gerarde dabei,   *I am in the process of*
       einen Brief zu schreiben.   *writing a letter.*

   Emphasis may be expressed by intonation or by adding the flavoring particle
   doch (cf. Appendix, §4).

   Er weiß das doch.   *He does know that.*

2. The present tense often has future meaning, when used with adverbs of time,
   such as **morgen, nächste Woche, bald** (*soon*).

   Morgen gehe ich ins Kino.   *Tomorrow I'm going to the movies.*

PRACTICE

2-6   Express in German, using the present tense.

1. I am going home.
2. Are they going to the movies?
3. Is he sleeping?
4. What are you eating? (fam. sing.)
5. Renate will visit us next week.
6. I won't work tomorrow.
7. We are going to buy the house in Waldheim.

---

¹ **dick werden**   *to get fat*
² **es eilig haben**   *to be in a hurry*
³ **ein Miesepeter sein** *to be a grouch, sourpuss*
                                (lit. *grouchy Peter; also used for*
                                 a female: Sie ist ein Miesepeter.)

3. The present tense is also used to express a stretch of time that began in the past and continues into the present. English uses the present perfect in such instances, as the following examples illustrate.

Wie lange lernen Sie schon Deutsch?	*How long have you been studying German?*
Ich lerne seit einem Jahr Deutsch.	*I have been studying German for a year.*
Wie lange kennen Sie Herrn Berger schon?	*How long have you known Mr. Berger?*
Ich kenne ihn schon seit Oktober.	*I have known him since October.*

This use of the present tense can easily be recognized by time expressions introduced with **schon** (*already*), **seit** (*since*), or **schon seit. Schon** usually remains untranslated. Note that in German the time element generally precedes the place element.

Wir wohnen **schon fünf Jahre** in Hamburg.	*We have been living in Hamburg **for five years.***
Ich arbeite **schon seit April** dort.	*I've been working there **since April.***

PRACTICE

2-7   Express the following questions and answers in English.

1.   X: Wie lange arbeiten Sie schon im Supermarkt?
      Y: Ich arbeite schon ein Jahr dort.
2.   X: Seit wann lernt Barbara Deutsch?
      Y: Sie lernt es schon seit drei Jahren.
3.   X: Seit wann studiert Frank an der Universität Heidelberg?
      Y: Er studiert seit November dort.
4.   X: Wohnen Sie schon lange in Bremen?
      Y: Wir wohnen schon viele Jahre dort.
5. a. X: Wie lange ist Herr Köhler schon im Krankenhaus?[1]
      Y: Er ist seit Sonntag dort.
   b. X: Wie lange weißt du das schon?
      Y: Ich weiß das schon seit Montag.

 Verbs With Prefixes

There are two basic types of verb prefixes: inseparable and separable prefixes.

§8   VERBS WITH INSEPARABLE PREFIXES

These verbs pose few problems. Some of the verbs have already appeared in the exercises. The following prefixes always remain attached to the verb:

---

[1] **das Krankenhaus, ¨er**   *hospital*

be-	**bekommen**	*to get, receive*
emp-	**empfehlen** (empfiehlt)	*to recommend*
ent-	**entlassen** (entläßt)	*to dismiss, fire*
er-	**erklären**	*to explain*
ge-	**gewinnen**	*to win*
miß-	**mißverstehen**	*to misunderstand*
ver-	**verkaufen**	*to sell*
zer-	**zerreißen**	*to tear up*

These prefixes always remain unstressed with the exception of **miß-**where the stress varies. It carries the stress in **míßverstehen** whereas the verb **mißáchten** (to disregard) may be pronounced **mißáchten** or **míßachten.**

2-8   Supply the appropriate forms of the verbs in parentheses.

1. Warum _____ Bergmanns ihr schönes Haus? (verkaufen)
2. Dr. Winkler _____ diese Hautcreme.[1] (empfehlen)
3. Vielleicht _____ du diese Geste.[2] (mißverstehen)
4. Unsere Nachbarn _____ alle Warnungen.[3] (mißachten)
5. Wir _____ zu wenig Geld für unsere Arbeit. (bekommen)
6. Wann _____ Sie uns dieses Experiment? (erklären)
7. Wir alle hoffen, daß du den ersten Preis _____ (gewinnen)
8. Ich verstehe nicht warum du Peters Brief _____ (zerreißen)
9. Ich glaube nicht,[4] daß er seine Sekretärin _____ (entlassen)
10. Herr Schulze, Sie _____ uns. (beleidigen[5])

The following verbs are often confused:

verkaufen	*to sell*		**bekommen**	*to get, in the sense of to receive*
kaufen	*to buy*		**werden**	*to get, in the sense of to become*

2-9   Insert in the blanks the German equivalents of the English verb forms.

1. Mr. Zimmermann is selling his car.
   Herr Zimmermann _____ seinen Wagen.
2. Why are you not buying his car?
   Warum _____ du seinen Wagen nicht?
3. Mrs. Schulze buys and sells stamps.
   Frau Schulze _____ Briefmarken.

---

[1] **die Hautcreme**	*skin cream*
[2] **die Geste, -n**	*gesture*
[3] **die Warnung, -en**	*warning*
[4] **ich glaube nicht**	*I don't believe . . . frequently used*
	as the German equivalent of I don't think . . .
[5] **beleidigen**	*to insult*

4. The days are getting longer.
   Die Tage _____ länger.
5. I hope I'll get a scholarship.
   Hoffentlich _____ ich ein Stipendium.
6. How often do you get mail from home?
   Wie oft _____ du Post von zu Hause?
7. The matter is getting complicated.
   Die Sache _____ kompliziert.
8. This term I am getting better grades.
   In diesem Semester _____ ich bessere Noten.
9. My grades are getting better.
   Meine Noten _____ besser.

§9   VERBS WITH SEPARABLE PREFIXES

In English there are a number of verbs that complete their meanings by using complements:

to give:	to give up, give in
to turn:	to turn on, turn off, turn down, turn in, turn out

The position of these complements may vary:

	They turned down our offer.
or:	They turned our offer down.

In German such a complement is attached to the front of the infinitive:

nach•geben	*to give in, yield*
auf•geben	*to give up*
an•geben	*to show off, brag*

These complements are called *separable prefixes* because they are separated from the verb under certain conditions. (The dot is not part of the spelling of the infinitive; it is used in this book to identify separable prefixes.) The separable prefix is always accented: nách•geben, aúf•geben, án•geben.

USE OF VERBS WITH SEPARABLE PREFIXES IN MAIN CLAUSES AND QUESTIONS

The prefix stands last.

a. Peter gibt **an.**   *Peter is showing off.*
b. Peter gibt **an.**   *Peter is showing off today.*
       heute
c. Peter gibt **an.**   *Peter is showing off today with his new motorcycle.*

heute mit seinem neuen Motorrad

Sentence a. consists of the bare minimum of words. The additions in sentences b. and c. are not tacked on at the end, as in English, but are inserted between the verb and the prefix.

This also applies to questions:

>Warum gibt Peter heute so sehr **an**?

These common verbs with separable prefixes occur in the exercises:

ab•holen	*to pick up*
ab•nehmen (nimmt ab)	*to decrease; lose weight*
an•fangen (fängt an)	*to begin, start*
an•geben (gibt an)	*to show off, brag, put on airs*
an•nehmen (nimmt an)	*to accept, assume*
an•rufen	*to phone, call*
auf•geben (gibt auf)	*to give up*
auf•hören	*to stop, end, cease*
auf•machen	*to open*
auf•passen	*to pay attention, watch, keep an eye on*
aus•gehen	*to go out*
aus•sehen (sieht aus)	*to appear, look*
ein•laden (lädt ein)	*to invite*
mit•bringen	*to bring along*
mit•kommen	*to come along*
mit•nehmen (nimmt mit)	*to take along*
nach•geben (gibt nach)	*to give in, yield*
übel•nehmen (nimmt übel)	*to take amiss, resent, take offense*
vor•haben	*to plan, have plans*
weiter•lesen (liest weiter)	*to continue reading, go on reading*
weiter•machen	*to continue (doing something)*
weiter•sprechen (spricht weiter)	*to continue talking, go on talking*
zu•hören	*to listen*
zu•machen	*to close*
zu•nehmen (nimmt zu)	*to increase, gain weight*
zurück•bringen	*to bring back, take back, return*
zurück•fahren (fährt zurück)	*to drive back, return*
zurück•geben(gibt zurück)	*to give back, return*
zurück•gehen	*to go back, return*

Note that verbs with prefixes have the same stem changes as their unprefixed forms.

PRACTICE

2-10   A. Restate the following sentences, using subjects indicated in parentheses.

1. Sie sehen müde aus. (du, er)
2. Paßt du auf meine Sachen auf?[1] (Sie, ihr)
3. Ich gebe zuviel an. (du, ihr, Renate)

---

[1] auf meine Sachen auf•passen   *to keep an eye on my things*

4. Ich gebe die Hoffnung noch nicht[1] auf. (wir, er)
5. Hoffentlich geben Sie nicht nach. (du, Margot)
6. Ich nehme das übel. (Dieter, wir)
7. Nehmen Sie mich mit? (du, ihr)
8. Hoffentlich nehme ich nicht zu. (du, Andreas)
9. Wann geben Sie mir das Geld zurück? (du, ihr)
10. Haben Sie heute abend etwas vor? (du, ihr)
11. Warum sprechen Sie nicht weiter? (du)

B. Supply the appropriate forms of the verbs in parentheses.

MODEL: Monika _____ heute abend mit Volker _____ .(aus•gehen)

Monika geht heute abend mit Volker aus.

1. Herr Kaufmann _____ mich um 7 Uhr _____ . (ab•holen)
2. Margot _____ nächsten Monat nach Wien _____ .
     (zurück•fahren)
3. Michael _____ auf meine Sachen _____ . (auf•passen)
4. Ellen _____ heute ein bißchen _____ . (an•geben)
5. Ich _____ dich vielleicht heute nachmittag _____ . (an•rufen)
6. Dein neuer Wagen _____ sehr schick _____ . (aus•sehen)
7. Frau Krause _____ mich in ihrem Wagen _____ .
     (mit•nehmen)
8. Hoffentlich _____ ich etwas _____ . (ab•nehmen)
9   Vielleicht _____ Gisela diese Bemerkung[2] _____ .
     (übel•nehmen)
10. Wann _____ das Postamt _____ ? (auf•machen)
11. Warum _____ ihr nicht _____ ? (mit•kommen)
12. Warum _____ du nicht _____ ? (weiter•lesen)
13. Wann _____ das neue Semester _____ ? (an•fangen)
14. Hoffentlich _____ er mich wieder _____ . (ein•laden)
15. Warum _____ du ihn nicht _____ ? (ein•laden}
16. _____ ihr mich auch _____ ? (ein•laden}
17. _____ Sie mir _____ ? (zu•hören)
18. _____ du schon wieder[3] _____ ? (zu•nehmen)
19. Was _____ Sie morgen abend _____ ? (vor•haben}
20. Warum _____ du Peters Einladung nicht _____ ? (an•nehmen)
21. Er weiß es nicht genau;[4] er _____ es nur _____ . (an•nehmen)

---

[1] **noch nicht**   *not yet*
[2] **die Bemerkung, -en**   *remark*
[3] **schon wieder**   *again (emphatic)*
[4] **genau**   *exact{ly}, precise(ly)*
    etwas genau wissen   *to know something for sure*

Verbs with separable prefixes in dependent clauses

Compare:

> Karin **kommt** nicht **mit**.
> Es ist schade, daß Karin nicht **mitkommt**.

In dependent clauses the inflected verb is at the end and is attached to the prefix.

PRACTICE

2-11   Restate the following sentences, using the indicated introductory clauses.

MODEL: Ich rufe Markus heute abend an.
Ich weiß noch nicht, ob ich Markus heute abend anrufe.

1. Elke bringt ihren Freund mit.
    Ich glaube nicht, daß…
2. Sie gibt mir das Geld zurück.
    Ich nehme an, daß…
3. Er lädt mich nicht wieder ein.
    Es ist möglich, daß…
4. Margot hat heute abend etwas vor.
    Ich habe keine Ahnung,[1] ob…
5. Herr Schumann geht nicht zu seiner Familie zurück.
    Es ist schade[2], daß…
6. Die Bank macht schon um 4 Uhr zu.
    Schade,[3] daß…
7. Jörg und Elke gehen heute abend aus.
    Ich weiß nicht, ob…
8. Er bringt ein paar Bücher zur Bibliothek zurück.
    Ich nehme an, daß…
9. Du siehst etwas müde aus.
    Ich finde, daß…

§10 The Use of *her* and *hin* as Separable Prefixes

Her suggests "this way, here" and **hin** suggests "that way, there"

her•kommen to come here (motion toward the speaker or the perspective of the narrator)	**hin•gehen** to go there (motion away from the speaker or the perspective of the narrator)
Er **kommt** zu mir **her**.	Ich **gehe** zu ihm **hin**.

Her and **hin** are frequently combined with other adverbs and prepositions:

herauf•kommen to come up (*here*)	**hinunter•gehen** to go down (there)
Sie **kommt** die Treppe **herauf**.	Sie **geht** die Treppe **hinunter**.

---

[1] **keine Ahnung haben**   *to have no idea*
[2] **es ist schade**   *it is a pity*
[3] **schade**   *too bad*

herein·kommen to come in (*here*)   **hinein·gehen** to go in (**there**)

Warum **kommen** Sie nicht **herein**?   Warum **gehen** Sie nicht **hinein**?

Idiom: **Herein!** *Come in.*

REMEMBER:

> **her** denotes **coming**, motion toward the speaker
>
> **hin** denotes **going**, motion away from the speaker

PRACTICE

2-12   Insert **her-** or **hin-** according to context.

1. Das Wasser im Schwimmbad ist heute zu kalt. Da geht niemand
   _____ ein.
2. Bauers sind unsere Nachbarn. Wir gehen oft zu ihnen _____ über, und sie
   kommen oft zu uns _____ über.
3. Ich mache ein Fenster auf und hänge eine Fahne[1] _____ aus.
4. Der Ball liegt auf dem Dach.[2] Klaus holt[3] eine Leiter[4] und steigt _____ auf.
   Ich habe Angst, daß Klaus _____ unterfällt.
5. Diese Autotür schließt nicht gut. Hoffentlich falle ich nicht _____ aus.

Her and **hin** are also used in several idioms in which the directional distinction
does not apply.

Examples:

herein·fallen	*to be taken in*
hinein·ziehen	*to drag in, involve, implicate*
hin·richten	*to execute*

Wo... *hin*? wo... *her*?

In spoken German, the question words **wohin** and **woher** are often separated: **wo** is
placed at the start of the question, while **hin** and **her** are treated as separable prefixes.

Wohin geht Renate?
or: **Wo** geht Renate **hin**?
} *Where is Renate going?*

Ich weiß nicht, **wohin** Renate geht.
or: Ich weiß nicht, **wo** Renate **hingeht.**
} *I don't know where Renate is going.*

Woher kommt Andreas?
or: **Wo** kommt Andreas **her**?
} *Where is Andreas coming from?*

Ich weiß nicht, **woher** Andreas kommt.
or: Ich weiß nicht, **wo** Andreas **herkommt.**
} *I don't know where Andreas is
coming from.*

---

[1] **die Fahne, -n**		*flag*
[2] **das Dach, ̈er**		*roof*
[3] **holen**		*to fetch, (go and) get*
[4] **die Leiter, -n**		*ladder*

§11 PREFIXES THAT ARE USED SEPARABLY AND INSEPARABLY

Some prefixes, such as **durch- über-, um-, wieder-,** are used both separably and inseparably with different meanings. The verb with the separable prefix is usually used in its literal sense, whereas its couterpart with the inseparable prefix often has a figurative meaning.

SEPARABLE	INSEPARABLE
	durch-
dúrch·fahren *to go nonstop*	**durchfáhren** *to run through, go through*
Der Zug **fährt** bis Hamburg durch.	Ein großer Schreck **durchfährt** die Menge.
The train goes nonstop (through)	*A (feeling of) great horror is running*
to Hamburg.	*through the crowd.*
	über-
über·setzen *to ferry across*	**übersétzen** *to translate*
Hier ist keine Brücke. Ein Boot	
setzt die Leute **über.**	Wie übersetzt man das?
There is no bridge here. A boat	*How does one translate that?*
ferries the people across.	
	um-
úm·gehen *to go around, circulate*	**umgéhen** *to circumvent, dodge, evade,*
	bypass
Dumme Gerüchte **gehen um.**	Sie **umgehen** meine Frage.
Stupid rumors are circulating.	*You are dodging my question.*
	wieder-
wíeder·holen *to (go and) get*	**wiederhólen** *to repeat, to review*
(something or someone) back	
Die Zeitung ist im Mülleimer. Ich	Ich wiederhole meine Frage.
hole sie **wieder.**	*I repeat my question*
The newspaper is in the garbage can.	Wir **wiederholen** die Grammatik.
I'll (go and) get it back.	*We are reviewing the grammar.*

When in doubt about the use of a prefix, consult a good dictionary. It will indicate possible uses and meanings.

PRACTICE

2-13 Summarizing exercises.

    A. Supply the appropriate forms of the verbs in parentheses.

    1. X: _____ du an dieser Tankstelle? (halten)
        Y: Nein. Wir _____ bis München _____ . (durch·fahren)
    2. X: Wo _____ dein Kassettenrecorder? (sein)
        Y: In Barbaras Zimmer. Ich _____ ihn gleich _____ .
        (wieder·holen)

3.   X: _____ du mir bei den Hausaufgaben? (helfen)

      Y: Natürlich. Vielleicht _____ wir zuerst[1] die Grammatik. (wiederholen)

4.   X: Die ganze Familie Baumann _____ die Grippe. (haben)

      Y: Kein Wunder. Die Grippe _____ jetzt _____ . (um•gehen)

5.   X: Herr Schubert _____ keine Steuern.[2] (bezahlen)

      Y: Wie _____ er das Gesetz?[3] (umgehen)

6.   X: Helga _____ einen netten Freund. (haben)

      Y: _____ du sie? (beneiden)

7.   X: _____ ihr es eilig? (haben)

      Y: Wir _____ es immer eilig. (haben)

8.   X: _____ du schlechte Laune? (haben)

      Y: Nein, aber meine Nachbarin _____ mich. (irritieren)

9.   X: _____ du heute abend etwas _____ ? (vor•haben)

      Y: Bis jetzt[4] _____ ich noch nichts _____ .(vor•haben)

10.   X: Warum _____ du so schnell? (laufen)

      Y: Weil es sehr spät _____ . (sein)

11.   X: Hoffentlich _____ du uns nicht, wenn du in Europa _____ . (vergessen; sein)

      Y: Und ihr? Hoffentlich _____ ihr mich nicht. (vergessen)

12.   X: Rainer _____ nicht gut _____ .(aus•sehen) Hoffentlich _____ er nicht krank. (werden)

      Y: Er _____ zuviel und _____ zu wenig. (arbeiten; schlafen)

13.   X: Du _____ nie _____ wenn man mit dir _____ . (zu•hören; sprechen)

      Y: Es ist nicht wahr, daß ich nie _____ .(zu•hören)

14.   a. X: Wann _____ ihr? (heiraten)

      Y: Wir _____ vielleicht im Juni. (heiraten)

   b. X: _____ ihr mich zur Hochzeit _____ ?(ein•laden)

      Y: Natürlich _____ wir dich _____.(ein•laden)

15.   a. X: Heinz _____ zuviel. (reden)

      Y: Du _____ auch manchmal zuviel. (reden)

   b. X: Du _____ sehr unhöflich[5]. (sein)

      Y: Ich _____ nur die Wahreit. (sagen)

16.   a. X: Dietmar _____ oft frech. (werden)

      Y: Du _____ auch manchmal frech. (werden)

   b. X: Du _____ mich. (beleidigen)

      Y: Ich _____ um Verzeihung. (bitten)

17.   a. X: Warum _____ du soviel? (essen)

      Y: Weil ich zu dünn[5] _____ . (sein)

---

[1] zuerst   *first*
[2] die Steuer -n   *tax*
[3] das Gesetz, -e   *law*
[4] bis jetzt   *so far*
[5] unhöflich (höflich)   *impolite (polite)*
[6] dünn   *thin*

   b. X: Zu dünn? Du _____ zu dick. (meinen[1])
      Y: Warum _____ du mir immer so nette Komplimente?
         (machen)
   c. X: Weil ich…
      Y: Warum _____ du nicht _____? (weiter•sprechen)
   d. X: Ich fürchte, die Sache _____ zu kompliziert. (werden)

   B. Express in German. (Use **Ich glaube nicht** for *I don't think*)

   1. a. Helga is going back to the dormitory. **Helga geht ins Studentenheim
         zurück.**
      b. Why is she going back to the dormitory?
      c. I have no idea why she is going back to the dormitory.
   2. a. That is impolite. **Das ist unhöflich.**
      b. Why are you so impolite? (fam. sing., fam. pl., formal)
      c. Too bad that they are so impolite.
   3. a. He is picking me up. **Er holt mich ab.**
      b. Are you picking me up? (fam. sing.)
      c. I don't think that they are picking me up.
   4. a. I apologize. **Ich bitte um Verzeihung.**
      b. Why are you apologizing? (fam. sing. , formal)
      c. It is not necessary[2] that she apologize.
   5. a. She is not right. **Sie hat nicht recht.**
      b. You are not right. (fam. sing., fam. pl.)
      c. You know that you are not right. (formal)
   6. a. They are getting nervous. **Sie werden nervös.**
      b. Are you getting nervous? (fam. sing., formal)
      c. I am not getting nervous, I am already nervous.
   7. a. He often skips class. **Er schwänzt oft.**
      b. Why do you skip class so often? (fam. sing.)
      c. I'd like to know why you skip class so often. (formal)
   8. a. I envy Andreas. **Ich beneide Andreas.**
      b. Why do you envy Andreas? (fam. sing., fam. pl.)
      c. I don't understand why you envy Andreas. (formal)
   9. a. I am not inviting Helga. **Ich lade Helga nicht ein.**
      b. Are you inviting Karin? (fam. sing.)
      c. Frank is inviting Karin.
      d. I don't think that he is inviting Karin.
  10. a. She is always in a hurry. **Sie hat es immer eilig.**
      b. You are always in a hurry. (fam. sing., fam. pl.))
      c. Too bad that you are always in a hurry. (formal)
  11. a. I don't know it for sure. **Ich weiß es nicht genau.**
      b. We don't know it for sure.
      c. Do you know it for sure? (fam. sing., formal)

---

[1] **meinen**   *to mean*
[2] **nötig**   *necessary*

12. a. I am only assuming it. **Ich nehme es nur an.**
     b. She is only assuming it.
     c. Are you only assuming it? (fam. sing.)
     d. Do you know it for sure or are you only assuming it?(fam. sing., formal)

The Imperative

Imperatives express commands, requests, or directives. German has three imperative forms corresponding to the three words for *you*:

1. **Sie**-address   **Bitte kommen Sie!**
2. **du**-address   **Bitte komm(e)!**   *Please come.*
3. **ihr**-address   **Bitte kommt!**

Imperative sentences end with an exclamation mark or, if there is no special emphasis, with a period.

§12   BASIC PATTERN OF THE IMPERATIVE

1. The **formal** (*Sie*-address) **imperative** is identical to the present tense **Sie**-form except that it has inverted word order.

PRESENT TENSE	IMPERATIVE	
Sie stören	**Stören Sie** mich nicht!	*Don't disturb me.*
Sie tun	**Tun Sie** das nicht!	*Don't do that.*
Sie haben	**Haben Sie** keine Angst!	*Don't be afraid.*
Sie rufen an	**Rufen Sie** Herrn Köhler an!	*Phone Mr. Köhler.*

2. **The familiar singular (du-address) imperative** consists of the stem of the verb with the optional ending **-e**. The pronoun **du** is omitted.

Stör(e) mich nicht!
Tu(e) das nicht!
Hab(e) keine Angst!
Ruf(e) Herrn Köhler an!

The final **-e** is obligatory if the stem ends in

a.   -d, -t, or certain consonant clusters (cf. §2):

Bade nicht zu lange!
Arbeite schneller!
Öffne die Tür!

b.   -ig, as in erledigen (*to take care of, settle*), beleidigen (*to insult*) entschuldigen (*to excuse*):

Erledige das sofort!   *Take care of that immediately.*
Beleidige mich nicht!   *Don't insult me.*
Entschuldige!   *Excuse me. (me added in English)*

3. The familiar plural (**ihr**-address) imperative is identical to the **ihr**-form of the present tense except that **ihr** is omitted.

PRESENT TENSE	IMPERATIVE
ihr stört	**Stört** mich nicht!
ihr tut	**Tut** das nicht!
ihr habt	**Habt** keine Angst!
ihr ruft an	**Ruft** Herrn Köhler an!
ihr wartet	**Wartet** hier!

THE USE OF *doch* OR *doch mal* IN IMPERATIVES

Doch is frequently added for emphasis:

> Komm doch mit! *Do come along. Do join us.*

When **doch** is followed by **mal**, it has a more casual tone:

> Komm doch mal mit!

A note on the position of *bitte*

> **Bitte** rufen Sie mich an.
> Rufen Sie mich an, **bitte**.

When final, **bitte** is set off by a comma except after very short sentences, such as:

> **Warten Sie bitte. Warte bitte.**

Bitte may also be placed in the middle of the sentence. It then generally follows pronoun objects but precedes all other elements.

> Rufen Sie mich **bitte** an.
> Rufen Sie **bitte** Frau Krause an.

PRACTICE

▽ 2-14   Add the two familiar forms of the following formal imperatives.

> MODEL: Kommen Sie bitte herein!
> **Komm(e) bitte herein!**
> **Kommt bitte herein!**

1. Hören Sie bitte zu!
2. Gehen Sie doch zum Arzt!
3. Besuchen Sie uns doch mal!
4. Bitte tun Sie das nicht!
5. Bitte warten Sie einen Augenblick![1]
6. Beleidigen Sie mich nicht!
7. Entschuldigen Sie bitte.
8. Machen Sie ein Fenster auf, bitte.
9. Rufen Sie doch mal an!
10. Bitte stören Sie uns nicht!

---

[1]**einen Augenblick warten**   *to wait a moment or a minute*

11. Bitte erledigen Sie das sofort!
12. Sagen Sie doch nicht immer nein zu mir!

§13 VARIATIONS AND IRREGULARITIES IN IMPERATIVE FORMS

1. The familiar singular form of verbs with vowel change from **e** to **i** or **ie**

helfen (hilft)	Helfen Sie mir!	
	Hilf mir!	Help me.
	Helft mir!	
essen (ißt)	Essen Sie das nicht!	
	Iß das nicht!	Don't eat that.
	Eßt das nicht!	
übel•nehmen	Nehmen Sie es nicht übel!	
(nimmt übel)	**Nimm** es nicht übel!	Don't take offense.
	Nehmt es nicht übel!	

The familiar singular form has the same stem changes that occur in the present tense singular. The ending **-e** is never added.

EXCEPTION:

werden (wird)	Werden Sie nicht krank!	
	Werde nicht krank!	Don't get sick.
	Werdet nicht krank!	

The fam. sing. form has no vowel change and adds the ending **-e**.
Note that the changes from **a** to **ä**, **au** to **äu**, and **o** to **ö** in the present tense do not occur in the imperative:

schlafen (schläft)	**Schlaf(e)** gut!
ein•laden (lädt ein)	**Lade** auch Margot **ein!**
laufen (läuft)	**Lauf(e)** doch nicht so schnell!
stoßen (stößt)	**Stoß(e)** mich doch nicht so!

2. The imperative forms of **sein**

formal	**Seien** Sie still!	
fam. sing.	**Sei** still!	Be quiet.
fam. pl.	**Seid** still!	

In the formal address the ending **-en** is added to the stem **sei-**.
The fam. sing. address never has the ending **-e**.
The fam. pl. address ends in **-d**; it is identical to the **ihr-** form of the present tense: **(ihr) seid**.

PRACTICE

2-15   Add the two familiar forms of the following formal imperatives.

1. Seien Sie vorsichtig![1]
2. Werden Sie nicht frech!

---

[1] **vorsichtig**   *careful*

3. Sprechen Sie etwas lauter, bitte!
4. Schlafen Sie gut!
5. Fahren Sie doch nicht so schnell!
6. Bitte laden Sie auch meinen Freund ein!
7. Essen Sie doch nicht so viel!
8. Vergessen Sie das nicht!
9. Nehmen Sie mich bitte mit!
10. Halten Sie bitte an der nächsten Tankstelle!
11. Seien Sie doch ein bißchen nett zu mir!

§14 THE GERMAN EQUIVALENT OF ENGLISH *let's*...

Let's go home.	**Gehen wir** nach Hause.
Let's begin.	**Fangen wir an.**
Let's stop (come to an end).	**Hören wir auf.** or: **Machen wir Schluß.**
Let's be fair.	**Seien wir** doch fair.

Note the inverted word order of the present tense **wir**-form and the use of **seien wir**.

PRACTICE

2-16 Answer in German.

MODEL: Wollen wir es noch einmal versuchen? OK, let's try it again.
O.K., versuchen wir es noch einmal.

1. Wollen wir in die Disko gehen?	*OK, let's go to the disco.*
2. Wollen wir im Juni heiraten?	*OK, let's get married in June.*
3. Wollen wir eine Pause machen?[1]	*OK, let's take a break.*
4. Wollen wir die Sache begraben?[2]	*OK, let's bury the matter.*
5. Wollen wir mal vernüftig[3] sein?	*OK, let's be sensible.*
6. Wollen wir aufhören?	*OK, let's stop.*

§15 USING INFINITIVES

Commands directed to the public are often expressed with the infinitive.

Bitte **weitergehen**!	*Please keep moving.*
(instead of: Bitte gehen Sie weiter!)	
Bitte **einsteigen**!	*All aboard, please.*
(instead of: Bitte steigen Sie ein!)	
Bitte nicht **rauchen**!	*Please don't smoke.*
(instead of: Bitte rauchen Sie nicht!)	

---

[1] die Pause, -n   *recess, break*
   eine Pause machen   *to take a break*
[2] begraben (begräbt)   *to bury*
[3] vernünftig   *sensible, reasonable*

Summarizing exercises for the imperative.

PRACTICE

2-17   Express in German.

1. Please come in. (formal, fam. sing., pl.)
2. Drive carefully. (formal, fam. sing., pl.)
3. Please don't disturb me. (formal, fam. sing., pl.)
4. Please be quiet. (formal, fam. sing., pl.)
5. Don't get nervous. (formal, fam. sing., pl.)
6. Let's begin.
7. Let's bury the matter.
8. Excuse me please. (formal, fam. sing.)
9. Please help me. (formal, fam. sing.)
10. Don't be afraid. (formal, fam. sing., pl.)
11. Don't eat so much. (fam. sing., pl.)
12. Don't forget that. (fam. sing., pl.)
13. Please don't take offense. (formal, fam. sing.)
14. Please take care of that. (fam. sing.)
15. Please wait a minute. (fam. sing.)
16. Let's be fair.
17. Let's take a break.
18. Let's stop.

Verbs in the Past and Future Tenses

Introduction

There are six tenses in English:

Present tense		*she sings (is singing, does sing)*

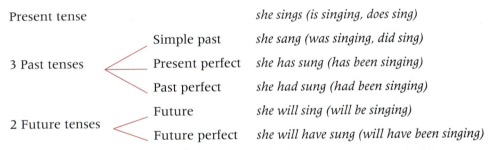

3 Past tenses
- Simple past — *she sang (was singing, did sing)*
- Present perfect — *she has sung (has been singing)*
- Past perfect — *she had sung (had been singing)*

2 Future tenses
- Future — *she will sing (will be singing)*
- Future perfect — *she will have sung (will have been singing)*

These tenses can be derived from three basic verb forms, the so-called "principal parts" of a verb:

	INFINITIVE	PAST	PAST PARTICIPLE
REGULAR VERB	to ask	asked	asked
IRREGULAR VERB	to sing	sang	sung

Ordinarily the principal parts are stated only for irregular verbs, because the forms of the regular verbs are predictable and need not be learned.

As in English, there are six tenses in German, but they do not have progressive or emphatic forms (cf. Chap. 2, §7, 1). German distinguishes between weak verbs (corresponding to English regular verbs) and strong verbs (corresponding to English irregular verbs). In addition, there are a third group of verbs that fit neither pattern; they are called *irregular*.

The Simple Past and Present Perfect of Weak Verbs

§1   THE SIMPLE PAST TENSE

FORMATION

The personal endings are added to the stem as shown here:

Infintive **lachen**	ich	lachte	*I laughed*	ich ____te
	du	lachtest		du ____test
	er			er
	sie	lachte		sie}____te
	es			es
	wir	lachten		wir ____ten
	ihr	lachtet		ihr ____tet
	sie	lachten		sie ____ten
	Sie	lachten		Sie ____ten

PRACTICE

3-1   Substitute the appropriate past-tense forms of the verbs in the parentheses.

1. Helga glaubte es nicht. (erklären, lernen, sammeln, studieren)
2. Die Leute fragten nicht. (rauchen, lachen, lächeln, kritisieren)
3. Er haßte mich. (lieben, bewundern, irritieren, ignorieren)

Verbs with stems ending in *-d, -t,* or certain consonant clusters (cf. Chap. 2 §2) insert an **e** between the stem and the personal endings:

ich	antwortete	*I answered*	ich ____ete
du	antwortetest		du ____etest
er			er
sie	antwortete		sie}____ete
es			es
wir	antworteten		wir ____eten
ihr	antwortetet		ihr ____etet
sie	antworteten		sie ____eten
Sie	antworteten		Sie ____eten

PRACTICE

3-2   Substitute the appropriate past-tense forms of the verbs in parentheses.

1. Ich antwortete nicht. (arbeiten, warten, reden)
2. Sie zeichneten es. (öffnen, landen)
3. Es regnete viel. (kosten, bedeuten)

▼ 3-3   Supply the appropriate forms of the simple past tense.

1. Wir _____ viel, aber leider _____ wir nicht viel Geld.
   (arbeiten)   (verdienen)[1]

2. Martin _____ die Verkäuferin[2], aber sie _____ ihm nicht.
   (fragen)   (antworten)

3. Alle _____ ,aber der Redner _____ es nicht.
   (gähnen)[3]   (merken)[4]

4. Frau Zimmermann _____ ,und das _____ den Chef.
   (lachen)   (irritieren)

5. Ich _____ Gisela und _____ sie auch ein wenig.
   {bewundern)   (beneiden)

6. Bergers _____ ihr Haus und _____ eine Wohnung.[6]
   (verkaufen)   (mieten)[5]

7. Mathias _____ einen Ring und _____ ihn seiner Freundin.
   (kaufen)   (schenken)[7]

USE OF THE SIMPLE PAST

In German the simple past tense commonly expresses connected past actions. It is used mainly in written descriptions and narratives and is therefore also called *narrative past*. Thus we might read in a report of a meeting:

> "Der Redner merkte nicht, daß die Zuhörer gähnten. Er redete und redete. Als er endlich aufhörte, applaudierten nur seine höflichen Freunde."

> *"The speaker did not notice that the audience was yawning. He talked and talked. When he finally stopped, only his polite friends applauded."*

§2   THE PRESENT PERFECT TENSE

THE BASIC DIFFERENCE BETWEEN THE ENGLISH AND GERMAN USE OF THE PRESENT PERFECT

Compare the following two sentences:

> a. I paid the bill yesterday.
> b. I haven't paid the bill yet.

Sentence a. expresses an act completed at a point of time in the past, i.e. yesterday. There is no relation to the present; the simple past is used. Sentence b. relates to the present and is expressed in the present perfect.

---

[1] **verdienen**   *to earn (make money)*
[2] **die Verkäuferin, -nen**   *saleslady*
[3] **gähnen**   *to yawn*
[4] **merken**   *to notice*
[5] **mieten**   *to rent*
[6] **die Wohnung, -en**   *apartment*
[7] **schenken**   *to give (as a gift)*

The German equivalents of the two sentences above are:

a. **Ich habe** die Rechnung gestern **bezahlt**.
b. **Ich habe** die Rechnung noch nicht **bezahlt**.

In contrast to English, sentence a. is in the present perfect tense. As mentioned in §1, in German the simple past is also called "narrative past," because it mainly occurs in written descriptions and narratives. Not being part of a narrative, sentence a. is expressed in the so-called "conversational past," i.e. the present perfect, which is commonly used in spoken German and informal writing, such as notes, personal letters, diaries.

As the following examples illustrate, sentences in the present perfect used as "conversational past" are rendered into English by the simple past tense.

X: Was **hast** du gestern **gemacht**?
*What **did** you do **yesterday**?*
Y: Ich **habe** Tennis **gespielt**.
*I **played** tennis.*

Am Samstag **hat** mich mein Freund **abgeholt**. Wir **haben** Geschenke für den Muttertag **gekauft**. Dann **haben** wir einen lustigen Film in einem kleinen Kino **gesehen**.
*On Saturday my friend **picked** me up. We **bought** presents for Mother's Day. Then we **saw** a funny film in a little moviehouse.*

FORMATION OF THE PRESENT PERFECT

The present perfect is formed with an auxiliary verb (in most cases **haben**) and the past participle of the main verb.

Conjugation:
ich	**habe** gefragt
du	**hast** gefragt
er sie es	**hat** gefragt
wir	**haben** gefragt
ihr	**habt** gefragt
sie	**haben** gefragt
Sie	**haben** gefragt

The auxilliary verb **haben** is inflected. The past participle **gefragt** remains unchanged. It is formed as follows:

1. The prefix **ge-** and the ending **-t** are added to the stem of the verb.

lernen	**gelernt**	wandern	**gewandert**
lachen	**gelacht**	schneien[1]	**geschneit**
lächeln	**gelächelt**		

2. Past participles of verbs whose stems end in **-d, -t,** or certain consonant clusters add **-et** to the stem.

---

[1] **schneien**   *to snow*

antworten	**geantwortet**	öffnen	**geöffnet**
kosten	**gekostet**	regnen	**geregnet**
reden	**geredet**		

3. No **ge-** is added to

   a. verbs that end in **-ieren**

studieren	**studiert**	passieren	**passiert**
protestieren	**protestiert**	irritieren	**irritiert**

   b. verbs with inseparable prefixes (cf. Chap. 2, §8)

versuchen[1]	**versucht**	beleidigen	**beleidigt**
erledigen	**erledigt**	beneiden	**beneidet**

4. Verbs with separable prefixes insert **ge-** between prefix and stem.

auf•räumen[2]	**aufgeräumt**
aus•lachen[3]	**ausgelacht**
zu•hören	**zugehört**

PRACTICE

3-4   State the past participles of the following verbs

1. lachen	10. antworten	19. versuchen	28. auf•räumen
2. aus•lachen	11. arbeiten	20. verdienen	29. irritieren
3. machen	12. mieten	21. kaufen	30. lächeln
4. auf•machen	13. heiraten	22. verkaufen	31. wandern
5. zu•machen	14. landen	23. schenken	32. bewundern
6. hören	15. studieren	24. schneien	33. beneiden
7. zu•hören	16. ignorieren	25. folgen	34. marschieren
8. holen	17. beleidigen	26. regnen	35. stören
9. ab•holen	18. bezahlen	27. kosten	36. warten

WORD ORDER IN MAIN CLAUSES AND QUESTIONS

Haben occupies the position of the inflected verb; the past participle is in final position.

Main clause:	NORMAL WORD ORDER	Du glaubst das nicht.
		Du **hast** das nicht **geglaubt**.
	INVERTED WORD ORDER	Natürlich glaubst du das nicht.
		Natürlich **hast** du das nicht **geglaubt**.
Question:	WITHOUT A QUESTION WORD	Glaubst du das nicht?
		Hast du das nicht **geglaubt**?
	WITH A QUESTION WORD	Warum glaubst du das nicht?
		Warum **hast** du das nicht **geglaubt**?

---

[1] **versuchen**   *to try*
[2] **auf•räumen**   *to tidy up, to straighten up*
[3] **aus•lachen**   *to laugh at*

A. Form sentences in normal and inverted word order.

MODEL: a. Helga / diese Sache / erledigen
Helga hat diese Sache erledigt.
   b. vielleicht / Helga / diese Sache / erledigen
Vielleicht hat Helga diese Sache erledigt.

1. a. ich / Dietmar / beleidigen
    b. vielleicht / ich / Dietmar / beleidigen
2. a. du / mir / nicht / antworten
    b. leider / du / mir / nicht / antworten
3. a. es / mir / Spaß / machen[1]
    b. natürlich / es / mir / Spaß / machen
4. a. es / nicht / schneien
    b. hoffentlich / es / nicht / regnen
5. a. wir / ein Wohnung / mieten
    b. am Montag / wir / unser Haus / verkaufen
6. a. mein Freund / diese Frage / ignorieren
    b. vielleicht / diese Frage / meinen Freund / irritieren
7. a. Helga / auf einer Tankstelle / arbeiten
    b. leider / sie / sehr wenig Geld / verdienen
8. a. wir / dich / bewundern
    b. natürlich / wir / dich / auch / beneiden

B. Form questions in the present perfect tense.

MODEL: a. ihr / für die Prüfung /lernen?
Habt ihr für die Prüfung gelernt?
   b. wann / ihr / für die Prüfung / lernen?
Wann habt ihr für die Prüfung gelernt?

1. a. ihr / heiraten?
    b. wann / ihr / heiraten?
2. a. du / Margot / nicht / ab•holen?
    b. warum / du / Margot / nicht / ab•holen?
3. a. du / das Fenster / auf•machen?
    b. warum / Udo / das Fenster / zu•machen?
4. a. du / lachen?
    b. warum / du / mich / aus•lachen?
5. a. ihr / die Musik / hören?
    b. warum / ihr / nicht / zu•hören?
6. a. du / Rainer / eine Schallplatte[2] / schenken?
    b. wo / du / die Platte / kaufen?
7. a. das Motorrad / viel Geld / kosten?
    b. wieviel / Sie / für das Motorrad / bezahlen?

---

[1] **Spaß machen**   *to be fun*
   expression: **Es macht mir Spaß.**   *I like it a lot. / I enjoy it.*
[2] **die Schallplatte, -n**   *record*
   short: **die Platte, -n**

C. Form questions and answers in the present perfect tense.

MODEL: X: du / Andreas / manipulieren?
              Hast du Andreas manipuliert?
        Y: nein, / ich / ihn / nicht / manipulieren
              Nein, ich habe ihn nicht manipuliert.

1. X: du / die Post / ab•holen?
    Y: nein, / ich / sie / noch nicht / ab•holen
2. X: du / dein Zimmer / auf•räumen?
    Y: nein, / ich / es / noch nicht / auf•räumen
3. X: ich / Sie / stören?
    Y: natürlich / Sie / mich / stören
4. X: dein Freund / diese Sache / erledigen?
    Y: hoffentlich / er / sie / erledigen
5. X: was / Herr Schreiber / sagen?
    Y: er / viel Unsinn[1] / reden
6. X: ihr / zu•hören?
    Y: niemand / zu•hören
7. X: Sie / mich / aus•lachen?
    Y: ich / nur / lächeln
8. X: was / du / Barbara / zum Geburtstag / schenken?
    Y: ich / ihr / mein Herz / schenken / / das / nichts / kosten

USE OF THE AUXILIARY *sein* INSTEAD OF *haben*

Sabine **ist** durch ganz Europa **gereist.**
Sabine has traveled through all of Europe.
or: *Sabine traveled through all of Europe.*

Intransitive verbs (verbs not followed by an accusative object) and verbs of motion use the auxiliary **sein** instead of **haben**:

folgen	*to follow*	**passieren**	*to happen*
landen	*to land*	**reisen**	*to travel*
marschieren	*to march*	**wandern**	*to wander, to hike*

These verbs are conjugated as the example **reisen**:

ich **bin** gereist   *I have traveled, I traveled*
du **bist** gereist
er
sie } **ist** gereist
es
wir **sind** gereist
ihr **seid** gereist
sie **sind** gereist
Sie **sind** gereist

---

[1]der Unsinn   *nonsense*

PRACTICE

3-6   Form sentences in the present perfect tense.

> **MODEL:** das / selten / passieren
> **Das ist selten passiert.**

1. ich / durch ganz Europa / reisen
2. ein / Polizeiwagen / uns / folgen
3. wir / nach Lichtenwalde / wandern
4. die Soldaten / zum Flugplatz / marschieren
5. wann / das Flugzeug / landen
6. wo / der Unfall[1] / passieren

DEPENDENT WORD ORDER

Compare the two sentences:

> Sie **hat** die Wahrheit **gesagt**.
> Ich nehme an, daß sie die Wahreit **gesagt hat**.

As the inflected verb, the auxiliary is in last position. It is preceded by the past participle.

PRACTICE

3-7   Restate the following sentences, using the indicated introductory clauses.

> **MODEL:** Das ist am Montag oder Dienstag passiert.
> **Ich weiß nicht genau, ob das am Montag oder Dienstag**
> **passiert ist.**

1. Baumanns sind durch ganz Deutschland gereist.
   Ist es wahr, daß…
2. Meine Frage hat den Chef irritiert.
   Ich bin überzeugt[2], daß…
3. Wieviel hat er für das Motorrad bezahlt?
   Ich habe keine Ahnung, wieviel…
4. Er hat es nicht gemerkt.
   Es ist gut, daß…
5. Was ist passiert?
   Wissen Sie, was…
6. Wann hat Erika die neue Wohnung gemietet?
   Ich weiß nicht mehr,[3] wann…

---

[1] **der Unfall, ⸚e**	*accident*
[2] **überzeugt sein**	*to be convinced*
[3] **Ich weiß nicht mehr …**	*I don't remember…* (lit. *I don't know anymore*)
	Nicht mehr wissen *is often used*
	in the sense of not remembering something.

§3   PATTERNS FOR THE WORD ORDER IN THE PRESENT PERFECT TENSE

The patterns stated in Chapter 1, §6, may be applied to sentences in the present perfect tense:

		INFLECTED VERB		UNIFLECTED VERB
a. normal word order	Helga	**hat**	die Grammatik	**wiederholt.**
b. inverted word order				
STATEMENT	Heute	**hat**	Helga die Grammatik	**wiederholt.**
DIRECT QUESTION				
WITH QUESTION WORD	Wann	**hat**	Helga die Grammatik	**wiederholt?**
WITHOUT QUESTION WORD		**Hat**	Helga die Grammatik	**wiederholt?**

The inflected verb is in second or first position; the uninflected verb (past participle) is in final position.

				UNINFLECTED VERB	INFLECTED VERB
c. dependent word order					
STATEMENT	Es ist möglich,	daß	Helga die Grammatik	**wiederholt**	**hat.**
INDIRECT QUESTION	Ich weiß nicht,	wann	Helga die Grammatik	**weiderholt**	**hat.**
	Weißt du,	ob	Helga die Grammatik	**wiederholt**	**hat?**

The inflected verb is in last position; it is preceded by the uninflected verb.

PRACTICE

3-8   Express in German using the present perfect for the English past tense.

MODEL: a. She doesn't notice it   **Sie merkt es nicht.**
        b. She didn't notice it.   **Sie hat es nicht gemerkt.**
        c. It is possible that she didn't **Es ist möglich, daß**
           notice it.   **sie es nicht gemerkt hat.**

1. a. I am trying it again.   **Ich versuche es noch einmal.**
   b. I tried it again.
   c. I am glad[1] that you tried it again. (fam. sing.)
2. a. I don't make a lot of money.   **Ich verdiene nicht viel Geld.**
   b. I didn't make a lot of money.
   c. Did you make a lot of money? (fam. sing.)
   d. Is it true that you made a lot of money? (fam. sing.)
3. a. Where is the plane going to land?   **Wo landet das Flugzeug?**
   b. Where did the plane land?
   c. I don't know where the plane landed.

---

[1] **froh**   *glad*

4. a. We travel a lot.   Wir reisen viel.
    b. We have traveled a lot.
    c. I am glad that we have traveled a lot.
5. a. The boss is straightening up his desk.   Der Chef räumt seinen
                                                 Schreibtisch auf.
    b. He was straightening up his desk.
    c. When was he straightening up his desk?
    d. Do you know when he straightened up his desk? (formal)
6. a. Peter is laughing at me.   Peter lacht mich aus.
    b. Perhaps he was laughing at me.
    c. Why was he laughing at me?
    d. I don't understand why he was laughing at me.
7. a. That happens often.   Das passiert oft.
    b. That happened often.
    c. When did that happen?
    d. I don't remember when that happened.
8. a. Are you waiting for him?   Wartest du auf ihn?
    b. Were you waiting for him?
    c. Why were they waiting for him?
    d. I have no idea why they were waiting for him.
9. a. Nobody is listening.   Niemand hört zu.
    b. Nobody was listening.
    c. Were they listening?
    d. Too bad that they weren't listening.
10. a. Don't you notice it?   Merkst du es nicht?
    b. Didn't you notice it?
    c. I noticed it.
    d. It is good that you noticed it. (formal)

The Simple Past and Present Perfect of Strong Verbs

§4   THE PRINCIPAL PARTS OF STRONG VERBS

As in English, all tenses can be derived from three basic verb forms called "principal parts," i.e. the infinitive, the simple past, and the past participle.
Compare:

WEAK VERBS	STRONG VERBS
Barbara **lernt** Deutsch.	Der Tenor **singt** gut.
Barbara **lernte** Deutsch.	Der Tenor **sang** gut.
Barbara hat Deutsch **gelernt**.	Der Tenor hat gut **gesungen**.

PRINCIPAL PARTS

lernen	lernte	gelernt
	-te ending	-t ending

The verb stem remains unchanged.

PRINCIPAL PARTS

singen	sang	gesungen
	no ending	-en ending

The stem vowel changes.

The principal parts of strong verbs are not predictable. They have to be learned.

The strong verbs are divided into seven classes according to their vowel changes. It is helpful to learn the principal parts of strong verbs in association with other members of the same class. The following table lists some common examples of each class which will occur in the exercises. A more complete listing (in alphabetical order) appears in the Appendix §2. **Ist** before a past participle indicates that the auxiliary **sein** is required.

CLASS	STEM VOWELS	INFINITIVE	SIMPLE PAST	PAST PARTICIPLE	MEANING
I	ei – ie – ie	bleiben	blieb	ist geblieben	to stay, remain
		schreiben	schrieb	geschrieben	to write
		steigen	stieg	ist gestiegen	to climb, go up
		ein•steigen	stieg ein	ist eingestiegen	to climb in, get on, board a vehicle
		aus•steigen	stieg aus	ist ausgestiegen	to get off
	ei – i – i	reiten	ritt	ist geritten	to ride, go on horseback
II	ie – o – o	fliegen	flog	ist geflogen	to fly
		verlieren	verlor	verloren	to lose
	e – o – o	heben	hob	gehoben	to raise, lift
III	i – a – u	finden	fand	gefunden	to find
		singen	sang	gesungen	to sing
		trinken	trank	getrunken	to drink
	i – a – o	beginnen	begann	begonnen	to begin
		gewinnen	gewann	gewonnen	to win
IV	e – a – o	brechen (bricht)	brach	gebrochen	to break
		unterbrechen (unterbricht)	unterbrach	unterbrochen	to interrupt
		helfen (hilft)	half	geholfen	to help
		nehmen (nimmt)	nahm	genommen	to take
		ab•nehmen (nimmt ab)	nahm ab	abgenommen	to decrease; lose weight
		zu•nehmen (nimmt zu)	nahm zu	zugenommen	to increase; gain weight
		übel•nehmen (nimmt übel)	nahm übel	übelgenommen	to take amiss, take offense, resent

CLASS	STEM VOWELS	INFINITIVE	SIMPLE PAST	PAST PARTICIPLE	MEANING
		sprechen (spricht)	sprach	gesprochen	*to speak*
		versprechen (verspricht)	versprach	versprochen	*to promise*
		sterben (stirbt)	starb	ist gestorben	*to die*
V	e – a – e	essen (ißt)	aß	gegessen	*to eat*
		vergessen (vergißt)	vergaß	vergessen	*to forget*
		geben (gibt)	gab	gegeben	*to give*
		auf•geben (gibt auf)	gab auf	aufgegeben	*to give up*
		nach•geben (gibt nach)	gab nach	nachgegeben	*to give in*
		lesen (liest)	las	gelesen	*to read*
		vor•lesen (liest vor)	las vor	vorgelesen	*to read to (someone)*
		sehen (sieht)	sah	gesehen	*to see*
	i – a – e	bitten	bat	gebeten	*to ask for, request*
		sitzen	saß	gesessen	*to sit*
	ie – a – e	liegen	lag	gelegen	*to lie, be situated*
VI	a – u –a	fahren (fährt)	fuhr	ist gefahren	*to drive, go (by locomotion)*
		mit–fahren (fährt mit)	fuhr mit	ist mitgefahren	*to ride with (someone)*
		laden (lädt)	lud	geladen	*to load*
		ein•laden (lädt ein)	lud ein	eingeladen	*to invite*
		tragen (trägt)	trug	getragen	*to carry*
VII	a– ie –a	fallen (fällt)	fiel	ist gefallen	*to fall*
		durch•fallen (fällt durch)	fiel durch	ist durchgefallen	*to fall through, flunk (exam)*
		gefallen (gefällt)	gefiel	gefallen	*to please, like*
		halten (hält)	hielt	gehalten	*to hold, stop*
		lassen (läßt)	ließ	gelassen	*to let, leave*
		schlafen (schläft)	schlief	geschlafen	*to sleep*
		ein•schlafen (schläft ein)	schlief ein	ist eingeschlafen	*to fall asleep*
	au– ie –au	laufen (läuft)	lief	ist gelaufen	*to run, walk*
	ei – ie – ei	heißen	hieß	geheißen	*to be called*
	u – ie – u	rufen	rief	gerufen	*to call, shout*
		an•rufen	rief an	angerufen	*to phone*
	o– ie – o	stoßen (stößt)	stieß	gestoßen	*to push*
	a – i – a	fangen (fängt)	fing	gefangen	*to catch*
		an•fangen (fängt an)	fing an	angefangen	*to begin start*

All verbs in this class change the stem vowel to ie or i in the past.
The past participles retain the stem vowel.

Some common verbs that do not fit in the seven classes are:

tun	tat	getan	*to do*
stehen	stand		gestanden	*to stand*
auf•stehen	stand auf	ist aufgestanden	*to rise, get up*
bestehen	bestand	bestanden	*to pass (exam)*
verstehen	verstand	verstanden	*to understand*
gehen	ging	ist gegangen	*to go*
spazieren•gehen	ging spazieren	ist spazierengegangen	*to go for a walk*
kommen	kam	ist gekommen	*to come*
mit•kommen	kam mit	ist mitgekommen	*to come along, join*
bekommen	bekam	bekommen	*to receive, get*

§5 VERBS REQUIRING THE AUXILIARY *sein*

Verbs requiring the auxiliary **sein** are intransitive (they do not take an accusative object) and denote a change of location (**gehen, kommen, reisen, wandern**) or condition (**ein•schlafen, sterben, explodieren, platzen** (*to burst*). There are exceptions to this, the most common of which are **bleiben** (*to stay, remain*) and **sein** (*to be* [cf. §9]) which take the auxiliary **sein** despite their meanings.

§6 THE SIMPLE PAST TENSE OF STRONG VERBS

The personal endings are added to the stem of the simple past (the second principal part).

sprechen (spricht) - sprach - gesprochen

ich	sprach	*I spoke, I was speaking*	**ich** ___
du	sprachst		**du** ___ st
er			**er**
sie }	sprach		**sie** } ___
es			**es**
wir	sprachen		**wir** ___ en
ihr	spracht		**ihr** ___ t
sie	sprachen		**sie** ___ en
Sie	sprachen		**Sie** ___ en

Note that the first and third pers. sing. have no personal endings. When the stem ends in **d, t, s,** or **ß,** an **e** is inserted in the **du** and **ihr** forms:

ich fand	ich hielt	ich ließ
du fandest	du hieltest	du ließest
ihr fandet	ihr hieltet	ihr ließet or ließt (**e** may be omitted in the **ihr** form after **ß/s**)

§7   THE PRESENT PERFECT TENSE OF STRONG VERBS

The auxiliaries **haben** and **sein** are conjugated; the past participle does not change.

ich	**habe** gesprochen	ich	**bin** gefahren
du	**hast** gesprochen	du	**bist** gefahren
er		er	
sie	**hat** gesprochen	sie	**ist** gefahren
es		es	
wir	**haben** gesprochen	wir	**sind** gefahren
ihr	**habt** gesprochen	ihr	**seid** gefahren
sie	**haben** gesprochen	sie	**sind** gefahren
Sie	**haben** gesprochen	Sie	**sind** gefahren

PRACTICE

3-9   **A.** In this exercise the verbs of classes I, II, III and IV will be practiced. Learn their principal parts before proceeding; then express the following sentences in the simple past and present perfect tenses.

MODEL: Der Tenor singt sehr gut.
          Der Tenor sang sehr gut.
          Der Tenor hat sehr gut gesungen.

1.   Der Redner spricht zu schnell.
2.   Du versprichst zuviel.
3.   Ein Student unterbricht den Redner.
4.   Ihr trinkt zuviel.
5   Das Konzert beginnt um 8 Uhr.
6   Leider findet ihr den Film langweilig.[1]
7   Warum hebt Dieter die Hand?
8   Er schreibt uns nicht.
9   In diesem Fluß[2] sterben viele Fische.
10   Wir reiten durch den Park.
11.   Schmidts fliegen nach Rom.
12.   Sie bleiben drei Wochen in Italien.
13.   Niemand hilft mir.
14.   Mein Nachbar nimmt das übel.
15.   Du nimmst ab, und ich nehme zu.
16.   Wir gewinnen, und sie verlieren.
17.   Wir steigen in Köln aus dem Bus aus, und ihr steigt dort ein.

B. In this exercise the verbs of classes V, VI, VII, and the verbs that do not fit in the seven classes will be practiced. Learn their principal parts before proceeding, then express the following sentences in the simple past and present perfect tenses.

1.   Ich gehe zu Fuß.[3]

---

[1] langweilig   *boring*
[2] der Fluß, ¨-sse   *river*
[3] zu Fuß gehen   *to go on foot*

2. Wir gehen spazieren.
3. Maria kommt nicht mit.
4. Monika bekommt ein Telegramm.
5. Niemand versteht mich.
6. Das tut mir leid.
7. Klaus steht am Fenster.
8. Meine Eltern stehen um 6 Uhr auf.
9. Nicht alle Studenten bestehen die Prüfung.
10. Ein paar¹ Studenten fallen durch.
11. Das gefällt meinen Eltern nicht.
12. Das Baby schläft schon.
13. Ich schlafe schnell ein.
14. Das Fußballspiel fängt um 2 Uhr an.
15. Klaus ruft seine Freundin an.
16. Wir lassen das Gepäck im Auto.
17. Margot läuft zum Briefkasten.²
18. Wie heißt das Hotel?
19. Der Bus hält an der Ecke.
20. Er ißt zuviel.
21. Helga vergißt nichts.
22. Sie bittet mich um Verzeihung.
23. Karin liest die Zeitung.
24. Leider gibt Peter nicht nach.
25. Martin sitzt in der ersten Reihe.
26. Deine Brille liegt auf dem Schreibtisch.
27. Andreas lädt alle seine Freunde ein.
28. Klaus trägt meinen Koffer.
29. Zimmermanns fahren nach Düsseldorf.
30. Hannelore fährt auch mit.

PRACTICE

3-10 Express the dependent clauses in the present perfect tense.

MODEL: Sie fürchtet, daß sie die Prüfung nicht besteht.
Sie fürchtet, daß sie die Prüfung nicht bestanden hat.

1. Sie fürchtet, daß sie in der Prüfung durchfällt.
2. Entschuldigen Sie bitte, daß ich zu spät komme.
3. Schade, daß ihr schon die Hoffnung aufgebt.
4. Ich möchte wissen, warum du mich stößt.
5. Ich verstehe nicht, warum Sie das tun.
6. Ich glaube nicht, daß er den Fehler sieht.
7. Es ist möglich, daß Frau Schmidt die Stelle³ bekommt.
8. Ich bin überzeugt, daß Martin einen Job⁴ findet.

---

¹ **ein paar**   *a few*
² **der Briefkasten, ⁻**   *mailbox*
³ **die Stelle, -n**   *job, position*
⁴ **der Job, -s**   *job (colloquially used by younger people)*

THE SIMPLE PAST AND PRESENT PERFECT OF IRREGULAR VERBS

§8   MIXED VERBS

A small group of verbs have the endings of weak verbs but the vowel change of strong verbs. They are therefore often referred to as mixed verbs. Their principal parts are listed below.

brennen	brannte	gebrannt	*to burn, be on fire*
bringen	bra<u>ch</u>te	gebra<u>ch</u>t	*to bring*
denken	da<u>ch</u>te	geda<u>ch</u>t	*to think*
kennen	kannte	gekannt	*to know, be familiar with*
nennen	nannte	genannt	*to call, name*
rennen	rannte	ist gerannt	*to run*
senden	sandte	gesandt	*to send*
(rarely)	sendete	gesendet	
wenden	wandte	gewandt	*to turn*
(rarely)	wendete	gewendet	
wissen (weiß)	wußte	gewußt	*to know* (a fact)

Note that **bringen** and **denken** also change consonants in the simple past and past participle.

PRACTICE

3-11   Express the following sentences in the simple past and present perfect.

1. Ich denke an die Sommerferien.
2. Sie kennt mich nicht.
3. Sie wendet schnell den Kopf.
4. Unsere Nachbarn senden uns Grüße aus Heidelberg.
5. Alle nennen mich beim Vornamen.[1]
6. Ich bringe Renate nach Hause.[2]
7. Niemand weiß das.
8. Es brennt[3] in der Garage.
9. Wir rennen schnell zur Garage.

A NOTE ON THE USE OF *kennen* AND *wissen*

The English equivalent of both **kennen** and **wissen** is *to know.*

a.   The verb **kennen** is used in the sense of *to be acquainted or familiar with* (persons, places, books, films, etc.). It must have a noun or a pronoun as direct object.

---

[1] **der Vorname, -n**   *first name*
[2] **nach Hause bringen**   *to take someone home*
[3] **es brennt**   *idiom . there is a fire (lit. it burns)*

Kennst du meine Freundin?
Kennen Sie Berlin?
Kennen Sie diesen Roman?[1]
Kennst du diese Komposition von Beethoven?

b.   The verb **wissen** means to *know something* as a fact, or *to have information about something*. Its object is often **es, das,** (refering to facts), or a clause.

Er weiß es vielleicht nicht.
Warum wissen Sie das nicht?
Du weißt doch, daß ich kein Geld habe.

PRACTICE

3-12   Supply the German equivalent of *to know.*

1. _____ Sie diesen Fußballspieler?
2. _____ du, daß wir morgen keine Schule haben?
3. _____ Sie Frankfurt?
4. _____ ihr diesen Schlager?[2]
5. _____ du, wie Peters neue Freundin heißt?
6. Niemand _____ mich hier.
7. Ich _____ , was du jetzt denkst, denn ich _____ dich sehr gut.

§9   IRREGULAR FORMS OF *haben, sein,* AND *werden*

a.   The principal parts of **haben** are | haben - hatte - gehabt |

Note the slight irregularity in the simple past tense:

PRESENT	SIMPLE PAST	PRESENT PERFECT	
ich habe *I have*	ich hatte *I had*	ich habe gehabt	*I have had, I had*
du hast	du hattest	du hast gehabt	
er	er	er	
sie }hat	sie }hatte	sie }hat gehabt	
es	es	es	
wir haben	wir hatten	wir haben gehabt	
ihr habt	ihr hattet	ihr habt gehabt	
sie haben	sie hatten	sie haben gehabt	
Sie haben	Sie hatten	Sie haben gehabt	

REMEMBER:

er hat   *he has*

er hatte   *he had*

b.   The principal parts of **sein** are | sein - war - ist gewesen |

Sein is a highly irregular verb.

---

¹ **der Roman, -e**   *novel*
² **der Schlager, -**   *pop song*

PRESENT	SIMPLE PAST	PRESENT PERFECT
ich bin *I am*	ich war *I was*	ich bin gewesen *I have been, I was*
du bist	du warst	du bist gewesen
er	er	er
sie } ist	sie } war	sie } ist gewesen
es	es	es
wir sind	wir waren	wir sind gewesen
ihr seid	ihr wart	ihr seid gewesen
sie sind	sie waren	sie sind gewesen
Sie sind	Sie waren	Sie sind gewesen

c.   The principal parts of **werden** are | **werden (wird) - wurde - ist geworden** |

Note that **werden** has an **-e** ending in the 1st and 3rd person singular of the simple past.

PRESENT	SIMPLE PAST	PRESENT PERFECT
ich werde *I become*	ich wurde *I became*	ich bin geworden *I have become* / *I became*
du wirst	du wurdest	du bist geworden
er	er	er
sie } wird	sie } wurde	sie } ist geworden
es	es	es
wir werden	wir wurden	wir sind geworden
ihr werdet	ihr wurdet	ihr seid geworden
sie werden	sie wurden	sie sind geworden
Sie werden	Sie wurden	Sie sind geworden

PRACTICE

3-13   Restate the following sentences, using the subjects indicated in parentheses.

1. Ich war pleite.[1] (wir, er, du, ihr, Sie)
2. Ich bin schon oft bei Winklers gewesen. (du, ihr, Sie, wir)
3. Frank hatte recht. (wir, du, ihr, Sie, ich)
4. Haben Sie Lampenfieber[2] gehabt? (du, ihr)
5. Ich wurde böse. (er, du, Sie)
6. Warum sind Sie so böse geworden? (du, Martin)

THE USE OF THE SIMPLE PAST TENSE OF *sein* AND *haben*

Contrary to the general practice in conversational German of using the present perfect to refer to past events, sentences with **sein** as the main verb frequently use the simple past. This occurs less often with **haben**.

Habt ihr gestern Karten **gespielt**?   Nein, wir **waren** im Kino.
Ist Rainer auch **mitgekommen**?   Nein, er **hatte** keine Zeit.

---

[1] **pleite sein**   *to be broke*
[2] **das Lampenfieber**   *stage fright*

The following exercise contains strong and irregular verbs. Express the sentences in German, using the present perfect for the English past tense except where otherwise indicated.

MODEL: a. Sabine isn't coming back.   **Sabine kommt nicht zurück.**
          b. She didn't come back.   **Sie ist nicht zurückgekommen.**
          c. Too bad that she didn't   **Schade, daß sie nicht**
             come back.   **zurückgekommen ist.**

1. a. We are late again.   **Wir kommen schon wieder zu spät.**
     b. We were late again.
     c. Why were you late again? (fam. sing.)
     d. I'd like to know why you were late again.

2. a. I hope you get the scholarship. **Hoffentlich bekommst**
       (fam. sing.)   **du das Stipendium.**
     b. I hope she got the scholarship.
     c. I'm glad that she got the scholarship.

3. a. I'm not going to do that.   **Ich tue das nicht.**
     b. I didn't do that.
     c. Who did that?
     d. Nobody knows who did that.

4. a. I am shocked.   **Ich bin schockiert.**
     b. I was shocked. (past)
     c. They were shocked. (past)
     d. Why were you so shocked? (fam. sing., past)
     e. I'd like to know why you were so shocked. (formal, past)

5. a. We are lucky.   **Wir haben Glück.**
     b. We were lucky. (past, pres. perf.)
     c. I hope they were lucky. (past, pres. perf.)

6. a. I hope I'll lose some weight.   **Hoffentlich nehme ich etwas ab.**
     b. I hope I lost some weight.
     c. Did you lose some weight? (formal)
     d. I am very glad that I lost some weight.

7. a. I hope I pass the exam.   **Hoffentlich bestehe ich die Prüfung.**
     b. I hope I passed the exam.
     c. Did you pass the exam? (fam. sing.)
     d. I assume that she passed the exam.

8. a. Perhaps I'll flunk the exam.   **Vielleicht falle ich in der Prüfung**
                                   durch.
     b. Perhaps I flunked the exam.
     c. Who flunked the exam?
     d. I don't know who flunked the exam.

9. a. Do you know him?   **Kennst du ihn?**
     b. Nobody knew him.
     c. I don't think that she knew him.

10. a. Don't you know that?   **Weißt du das nicht?**
      b. Didn't you know that?

       c. I assume that he didn't know that.

11.   a. I resent that.   **Ich nehme das übel.**

       b. He resented that.

       c. Did you resent that? (formal)

       d. It is possible that she resented that.

12.   a. I hope I won't lose the key.   **Hoffentlich verliere ich den Schlüssel nicht.**

       b. I hope I didn't lose the key.

       c. Where did you lose the key? (fam. sing.)

       d. I have no idea where I lost the key.

13.   a. I hope you won't become angry. (formal)   **Hoffentlich werden Sie nicht böse.**

       b. He became very angry.

       c. I don't understand why he became so angry.

14.   a. She is not inviting the Bergmanns.   **Sie lädt Bergmanns nicht ein.**

       b. They did not invite the Bergmanns.

       c. I'd like to know why they did not invite the Bergmanns.

The Past Perfect, Future, and Future Perfect of Weak, Strong, and Irregular Verbs.

§10   THE PAST PERFECT TENSE

The past perfect expresses a past event that occurred previous to some other past event. It corresponds to the same tense in English.

> Ein Polizist **gab** Klaus einen Strafzettel, weil er den Wagen auf der
>   (past)
> falschen Straßenseite **geparkt hatte.**
>   (past perfect)
> *A policeman **gave** Klaus a ticket because he **had parked** the car on the wrong side of the street.*

In this sentence two past events are expressed which did not occur simultaneously. First Klaus parked on the wrong side of the street, then the policeman gave him a ticket. The first event is in the past perfect tense, the other is in the simple past tense.

The forms of the past perfect differ from the present perfect only in that the auxiliary verb **haben** or **sein** is in the simple past tense rather than in the present tense. Compare:

PRESENT PERFECT	PAST PERFECT
Sie **hat** mich nicht **angerufen.**	Sie **hatte** mich nicht **angerufen.** *She had not called me.*
Wir **sind** nach Hause **gefahren.**	Wir **waren** nach Hause **gefahren.** *We had gone home.*

PRACTICE

3-15   Restate the following sentences in the past perfect tense.

1. Ich habe Ihre Frage nicht verstanden.
2. Die Kinder sind zu Hause geblieben.
3. Er hat zuviel Geld ausgegeben.[1]
4. Wir haben Ellen gewarnt.[2]
5. Es ist kälter geworden.
6. Helga hat meinen Geburtstag vergessen.

WORD ORDER IN DEPENDENT CLAUSES:

>Wir gingen spazieren, nachdem wir gegessen **hatten.**
>*We went for a walk after we had eaten.*

The inflected verb is in last position.

PRACTICE

3-16   Express the dependent clauses in the past perfect, using the indicated words.

MODEL: Ich bat Erika um Verzeihung, weil / ich / eine dumme
Bemerkung / machen
**Ich bat Erika um Verzeihung, weil ich eine dumme Bemerkung
gemacht hatte.**

1. Sie hatte einen Nervenzusammenbruch[3] weil / sie / zuviel / arbeiten
2. Wir räumten die Wohnung auf, nachdem / alle Gäste / nach Hause / gehen
3. Ich wurde sehr böse, weil / Klaus / sein Versprechen / nicht / halten[4]
4. Annerose bekam einen Strafzettel, weil / sie / zu schnell / fahren

§11 THE FUTURE TENSE

FORMATION

>PRESENT   Barbara hilft mir bei den Hausaufgaben.
>FUTURE   Barbara **wird** mir bei den Hausaufgaben **helfen.**
>*Barbara will help me with the homework.*

The future tense is formed with the present tense of the auxiliary **werden** and the
infinitive of the main verb.

---

[1] **Geld aus•geben**   *to spend money*
  (gibt aus), gab aus, ausgegeben
[2] **warnen**   *to warn*
[3] **der Nervenzusammenbruch, ⸚e**   *nervous breakdown*
[4] **das Versprechen halten**   *to keep the promise*
  (hält), hielt, gehalten

Conjugation: ich **werde** helfen   *I will help*
     du **wirst** helfen
     er
     sie } **wird** helfen
     es
     wir **werden** helfen
     ihr **werdet** helfen
     sie **werden** helfen
     Sie **werden** helfen

| **werden** + infinitive | **will** + infinitive |

In main clauses and questions **werden** takes the position of the inflected verb; the infinitive is in last position. Compare these present and future tense sentences:

Sie fährt nach Hause.   Fährt sie nach Hause?

Sie **wird** nach Hause **fahren.**   **Wird** sie nach Hause **fahren?**

Sie ist zu Hause.   Wann ist sie zu Hause?

Sie **wird** zu Hause **sein.**   Wann **wird** sie zu Hause **sein?**

Sie hat kein Geld.   Warum hat sie kein Geld?

Sie **wird** kein Geld **haben.**   Warum **wird** sie kein Geld **haben?**

Sie wird nervös.   Wird sie nervös?

Sie **wird** nervös **werden.**   **Wird** sie nervös **werden?**

(auxiliary) (infinitive of main verb)

When the infinitive has a separable prefix, it is attached to the verb:

Sie ruft ihn an.   Ruft sie ihn an?

Sie wird ihn **anrufen.**   Wird sie ihn **anrufen?**

PRACTICE

3-17 Express the following sentences in the future tense.

MODEL: Ich komme nicht zurück.
      Ich werde nicht zurückkommen.

1. Dietmar holt mich ab.
2. Wann holt er dich ab?
3. Wir verkaufen unseren Wagen.
4. Verkaufen Sie Ihren Wagen?
5. Du lachst mich aus.
6. Lachst du mich aus?
7. Er hält sein Versprechen.

8. Hält er sein Versprechen?
9. Helga hat keine Zeit für mich.
10. Hast du Zeit für mich?
11. Es wird noch kälter.
12. Wird es wirklich noch kälter?
13. Ist die Prüfung schwer?

WORD ORDER IN DEPENDENT CLAUSES

Er **wird** es mir nicht **sagen**.
Ich bin überzeugt, daß er es mir nicht **sagen wird**.
I am convinced that he won't tell me.

In dependent clauses the inflected auxiliary **werden** is in last position; it is preceded by the infinitive of the main verb.

PRACTICE

3-18   Restate the following sentences beginning with **Ich bin überzeugt, daß...**

MODEL: Er wird es nicht übelnehmen.
          Ich bin überzeugt, daß er es nicht übelnehmen wird.

1   Du wirst nicht nachgeben.
2. Schmidts werden auch meine Freundin einladen.
3. Ihr werdet mich nicht verstehen.
4. Annette wird ihr Versprechen nicht halten.
5. Dieter wird sein Zimmer nicht aufräumen.
6. Du wirst das vergessen.
7. Diese Firma wird großen Erfolg[1] haben.

USE OF THE FUTURE TENSE

The present tense is often used to express future time if an adverb or the context indicates that the future is referred to (cf. Chap. 2, §7, 2).

Ich rufe dich morgen an.   *I'll call you tomorrow.*
Ich rufe dich bestimmt an.   *I'll certainly call you.*

The future tense has to be used if futurity is not otherwise indicated. Compare:

Sie **unterstützt** ihre Eltern.   *She **supports** her parents.*
Sie **wird** ihre Eltern **unterstützen**.   *She **will support** her parents.*

The future tense is also used to express assumption. Adverbs such as **wohl** (most commonly used), **wahrscheinlich, vielleicht** often enhance this notion. Compare:

Klaus ist wahrscheinlich krank.
Klaus **wird wohl** (wahrscheinlich) **krank sein.**   *Klaus is probably ill.*

Helga kommt wahrscheinlich nicht mit.
Helga **wird wohl** (wahrscheinlich) nicht **mitkommen.**   *Helga is probably not coming along.*

---

[1] **der Erfolg, -e**   *success*

PRACTICE

3-19
Restate the following sentences expressing an assumption by using the future tense and **wohl.**

MODEL: Fräulein Schmidt erkennt mich wahrscheinlich nicht.
        Fräulein Schmidt wird mich wohl nicht erkennen.

1. Michael arbeitet wahrscheinlich in der Bibliothek.
2. Du vergißt mich wahrscheinlich sehr schnell.
3. Maria hat vielleicht Lampenfieber.
4. Das ist vielleicht nicht wahr.
5. Es wird vielleicht kälter.
6. Ich bleibe wahrscheinlich zu Hause.
7. Renate ruft mich wahrscheinlich nicht an.
8. Herr Kästner gibt vielleicht nicht nach.

§12 THE FUTURE PERFECT TENSE

FUTURE   Wir **werden** unser Haus im Sommer **verkaufen.**
FUTURE PERFECT   Wir **werden** es hoffentlich bis Ende des Sommers **verkauft haben.**
                       *We hope we **will have sold** it by the end of the summer.*

In the example above the future perfect tense expresses the anticipated conclusion of an action by a certain time in the future. It is formed with the auxiliary **werden** + the perfect infinitive **verkauft haben** in the example above.

Compare the future and the future perfect:

FUTURE	FUTURE PERFECT	FUTURE FUTURE	PERFECT
er wird verkaufen	er wird **verkauft haben**	he will sell	he will *have sold*
er wird bezahlen	er wird **bezahlt haben**	he will pay	he will *have paid*
er wird gehen	er wird **gegangen sein**	he will go	he will *have gone*
er wird haben	er wird **gehabt haben**	he will have	he will *have had*
er wird sein	er wird **gewesen sein**	he will be	he will *have been*
er wird werden	er wird **geworden sein**	he will become	he will *have become*
werden + inf.	werden + perf. inf.	will + inf.	will + perf. inf.

In German the perfect infinitve consists of the past participle followed by the infinitive of the auxiliary **haben** or **sein,** depending on the past participle. In English the auxiliary *have* precedes the past participle.

PRACTICE

3-20
Express in English.

1. Nächsten Freitag werden wir dieses Projekt beendet haben.
2. Bis dahin[1] werden wir unsere Schulden[2] bezahlt haben.

---

[1] **bis dahin**   *by then*
[2] **die Schuld, -en**   *debt*

3. Ich werde diese Sache bis Mittwoch erledigt haben.
4. Ende dieses Jahres wird Frau Schramm drei Jahre bei dieser Firma gewesen sein.

THE FUTURE PERFECT TENSE EXPRESSING A SUPPOSITION OR PROBABILITY

The future perfect tense is more commonly used to express a supposition or probability referring to a past event. Compare:

a. Sie **haben** wahrscheinlich Tennis **gespielt.**
b. Sie **werden** wohl Tennis **gespielt haben.** } *They probably played tennis.*

Sentence a. uses the present perfect and sentence b. the future perfect. Both sentences are rendered by the English past tense.

PRACTICE

3-21   Express the following sentences in English.

MODEL: Ich werde wohl in der Prüfung durchgefallen sein.
I probably flunked the exam.

1   Der Lärm wird wohl meine Nachbarn gestört haben.
2. Anita wird wohl zum Arzt gegangen sein.
3. Du wirst wohl zu spät aufgestanden sein.
4. Es wird wohl in der Nacht geregnet haben.
5. Schuberts werden wohl nicht zu Hause gewesen sein.
6. Der Chef wird wohl nervös geworden sein.

§13 REFERENCE CHART: SYNOPSIS OF THE TENSES

Verbs selected as examples:

fragen   weak verb
mit·kommen strong verb with separable prefix, using **sein**
haben
sein   ——→ functioning as main verbs
werden

MAIN CLAUSES	DEPENDENT CLAUSES
PRESENT	
Er **fragt** (nicht).	daß er (nicht) **fragt.**
Er **kommt** (nicht) **mit.**	daß er (nicht) **mitkommt.**
Er **hat** (kein) Geld.	daß er (kein) Geld **hat.**
Er **ist** (nicht)nervös.	daß er (nicht) nervös **ist.**
Er **wird** (nicht) nervös.	daß er (nicht) nervös **wird.**
PAST	
Er **fragte** (nicht).	daß er (nicht) **fragte.**
Er **kam** (nicht) mit.	daß er (nicht) **mitkam.**
Er **hatte** (kein) Geld.	daß er (kein) Geld **hatte.**
Er **war** (nicht) nervös.	daß er (nicht) nervös **war.**
Er **wurde** (nicht) nervös.	daß er (nicht) nervös **wurde.**

PRESENT PERFECT

Er **hat** (nicht) **gefrafgt**.	daß er (nicht) **gefragt hat**.
Er **ist** (nicht) **mitgekommen**.	daß er (nicht) **mitgekommen ist**.
Er **hat** (kein) Geld **gehabt**.	daß er (kein) Geld **gehabt hat**.
Er **ist** (nicht) nervös **gewesen**.	daß er (nicht) nervös **gewesen ist**.
Er **ist** (nicht) nervös **geworden**.	daß er (nicht) nervös **geworden ist**.

PAST PERFECT

Er **hatte** (nicht) **gefragt**.	daß er (nicht) **gefragt hatte**.
Er **war** (nicht) **mitgekommen**.	daß er (nicht) **mitgekommen war**.
Er **hatte** (kein) Geld **gehabt**.	daß er (kein) Geld **gehabt hatte**.
Er **war** (nicht) nervös **gewesen**.	daß er (nicht) nervös **gewesen war**.
Er **war** (nicht) nervös **geworden**.	daß er (nicht) nervös **geworden war**.

FUTURE

Er **wird** (nicht) **fragen**.	daß er (nicht) **fragen wird**.
Er **wird** (nicht) **mitkommen**.	daß er (nicht) **mitkommen wird**.
Er **wird** (kein) Geld **haben**.	daß er (kein) Geld **haben wird**.
Er **wird** (nicht) nervös **sein**.	daß er (nicht) nervös **sein wird**.
Er **wird** (nicht) nervös **werden**.	daß er (nicht) nervös **werden wird**.

FUTURE PERFECT

Er **wird** (nicht) **gefragt haben**.	daß er (nicht) **gefragt haben wird***.
Er **wird** (nicht) **mitgekommen sein**.	daß er (nicht) **mitgekommen sein wird**.
Er **wird** (kein) Geld **gehabt haben**.	daß er (kein) Geld **gehabt haben wird**.
Er **wird** (nicht) nervös **gewesen sein**.	daß er (nicht) nervös **gewesen sein wird**.
Er **wird** (nicht) nervös **geworden sein**.	daß er (nicht) nervös **geworden sein wird**.

The present and the simple past are formed without auxiliary; they are so-called *simple tenses*. The other four tenses are formed with the auxiliary **haben, sein,** or **werden**; they are compound tenses.

§14 THE POSITION OF SEPARABLE PREFIXES

The separable prefix is separated when the verb to which it belongs is in first or second position. This occurs in the following instances:

	MAIN CLAUSE	DIRECT QUESTION	IMPERATIVE
PRESENT	Sie kommt **mit**.	Kommt sie **mit**?	Komm **mit**!
PAST	Sie kam **mit**.	Wer kam **mit**?	

In all other instances the prefix is attached to the verb, i.e. in infinitives, past participles, and in dependent clauses (including indirect questions):

* The future perfect hardly ever occurs in dependent clauses.

Sie wird nicht **mitkommen.**
Sie ist nicht **mitgekommen.**
Schade, daß sie nicht **mitkommt.**
Ich möchte wissen, warum sie nicht **mitkommt.**

3-22   Summarizing exercises.

A. Express the following sentences in the past, present perfect, past perfect and future.

1. Das ist ein Skandal.
2. Irene ruft micht nicht an.
3. Sie wird böse.
4   Frank hat Lampenfieber.

B. Express the following sentences in the tenses indicated in parentheses. (Do not change the boldface introductory clauses.)

1. Rita hat recht. (past, past perf.)
2   Niemand hilft uns. (pres. perf., past perf., future)
3. Das ist nicht leicht. (past, future)
4. Udo weiß das nicht. (past, past perf.)
5. Die Sache wird problematisch. (past, pres. perf.)
6. Margot vergißt das bestimmt. (future, pres. perf.)
7. Wir haben Hunger und auch Durst. (past)
8. **Ich glaube nicht**, daß er Angst vor mir hat. (past)
9. Der Redner spricht zu leise und zu schnell. (past perf.)
10. Wir mieten eine kleine Wohnung. (future)
11. Kennen Sie Helgas Mann? (pres. perf)
12. Ihr lacht mich vielleicht aus. (future)
13. Ich esse sehr wenig, und trotzdem[1] nehme ich nicht ab. (pres. perf.)
14. Frau Krause gibt dieses Mal nicht nach. (future)
15. **Ich glaube auch**, daß sie dieses Mal nicht nachgibt. (future)
16. Er wartet und wartet, aber sie kommt nicht. Kein Wunder, daß er böse wird. (past)
17. **Ist es wahr**, daß ihr im August in die Schweiz fliegt? (pres. perf.)
18. **Ich bin überzeugt**, daß er sein Versprechen hält. (future)
19. Meine Nachbarn stehen schon um 6 Uhr auf. (past perf.)
20. Diese Übung macht mir Spaß. (pres. perf.)
21. Das ist wohl nicht wahr. (future)

---

[1] trotzdem   *nevertheless*

Modal Auxiliaries

Introduction

Compare:

a. Ich **helfe** Inge bei den Hausaufgaben. *I am helping Inge with the homework.*

b. Ich **kann** Inge bei den Hausaufgaben **helfen.** *I can help Inge …*
Ich **muß** Inge bei den Hausaufgaben **helfen.** *I must help Inge …*
Ich **soll** Inge bei den Hausaufgaben helfen. *I am supposed to help Inge …*

Sentence a. simply states the act of helping: it is modified in the three following sentences by the use of **können**, **müssen**, and **sollen**. These modal auxiliaries, commonly called *modals*, are inflected whereas the accompanying verb **helfen** is in the infinitive. This accompanying verb is referred to as *dependent infinitive*.

In German there are six modals:

dürfen	*may*	*expression of:*	permission
	to be allowed to		
	to be permitted to		
können	*can*		ability, possibility
	to be able to		
mögen	*to like to*		liking
	to care to		
müssen	*must*		necessity
	to have to		
sollen	*to be expected to*		obligation
	to be supposed to		
wollen	*to want to*		wish, desire, intention
	to intend to		

All German modals take the dependent infinitive without **zu**.

Wir dürfen hier parken.	*We may park here.*
	We are allowed to park here.
Wir können das nicht bezahlen.	*We cannot pay that.*
	We are not able to pay that.
Wir mögen jetzt nicht Tennis spielen.	*We don't care to play tennis now.*
Wir müssen auf Barbara warten.	*We must wait for Barbara.*
	We have to wait for Barbara.
Wir sollen den Fall der Polizei melden.	*We are expected to report the case to the police.*
	We are supposed to report the case to the police.
Wir wollen ein Haus kaufen.	*We want to buy a house.*
	We intend to buy a house.

 The Modals in the Simple Tenses

§1 THE PRESENT TENSE

FORMATION

dürfen	können	mögen	müssen	sollen	wollen
ich darf	ich kann	ich mag	ich muß	ich soll	ich will
du darfst	du kannst	du magst	du mußt	du sollst	du willst
er	er	er	er	er	er
sie } darf	sie } kann	sie } mag	sie } muß	sie } soll	sie } will
es	es	es	es	es	es
wir dürfen	wir können	wir mögen	wir müssen	wir sollen	wir wollen
ihr dürft	ihr könnt	ihr mögt	ihr müßt	ihr sollt	ihr wollt
sie dürfen	sie können	sie mögen	sie müssen	sie sollen	sie wollen
Sie dürfen	Sie können	Sie mögen	Sie müssen	Sie sollen	Sie wollen
I may, I am allowed to, etc.	*I can, I am able to, etc.*	*I like to, I care to, etc.*	*I must, I have to, etc.*	*I am expected, I am supposed to, etc.*	*I want to, I intend to, etc.*

Note: a. The 1st and 3rd pers. sing. are identical.

      b. The vowel change occurs throughout the singular but never in the plural; **sollen,** however, has no vowel change.

PRACTICE
4-1

A. Supply the correct form of the modals in parentheses.

1. Ich _____ nicht rauchen. (wollen, sollen, dürfen)
2. Du _____ Thomas helfen. (können, sollen, müssen)
3. Hannelore _____ das nicht essen. (mögen, wollen, dürfen)
4. Wir _____ jetzt nach Hause gehen. (müssen, wollen, sollen, können)
5. Ihr _____ hier parken. (können, dürfen)
6. Meine Eltern _____ das bezahlen. (sollen, müssen)

B. Express the following sentences in English.

1. Niemand kann mir helfen.
2. Maria will mitkommen.
3. Ich mag ihn nicht fragen.
4. Du mußt das heute erledigen.
5. Hier dürft ihr nicht rauchen.
6. Darf ich Sie zu einer Tasse Kaffee einladen?
7. Was soll das bedeuten?

C. Complete the following sentences in German, using the English cues in parentheses.

1. Die Chefin _____ das Geld investieren. (*to want to, intend to*)
2. Ich _____ jetzt die Hausaufgaben machen. (*to have to*)
3. Wir _____ ihn um Erlaubnis bitten.[1] (*to be supposed to*)
4. Hier _____ du nicht überholen.[2] (*to be allowed to*)
5. Ihr _____ mich nicht überreden[3] (*can*)
6. Ich _____ das nicht trinken. (*to like to*)

INTRODUCING MODALS IN MAIN CLAUSES AND QUESTIONS

When modals are introduced, the following changes occur in the structure of main clauses and questions:

Main clause

Ich glaube das nicht.

Ich kann das nicht glauben.

The inflected verb becomes the dependent infinitive and goes to the end of the sentence, while the modal becomes the inflected verb and thus occupies the second position.

Question   a. beginning with a question word—modal in second position:

Warum glaubst du das nicht?

Warum **kannst** du das nicht **glauben**?

---

[1] **um Erlaubnis bitten**   *to ask for permission*
[2] **überholen**   *to overtake, pass*
[3] **überreden**   *to persuade*

b. without a question word – modal in first position:

> Glaubst du das nicht?
>
> **Kannst** du das nicht **glauben**?

PRACTICE

4-2   Restate the following sentences, using the modals indicated in parentheses.

MODEL: a. Wir fahren in die Stadt. (wollen)
Wir wollen in die Stadt fahren.

b. Wann fahrt ihr in die Stadt? (wollen)
Wann wollt ihr in die Stadt fahren?

1. a. Ich sage es dir nicht. (dürfen)
    b. Warum sagst du es mir nicht? (dürfen)
2. a. Meine Eltern verstehen das nicht. (können)
    b. Verstehen sie das wirklich nicht? (können)
3. a. Ich gehe jetzt nach Hause. (müssen)
    b. Gehst du wirklich schon nach Hause? (müssen)
4. a. Andreas bezahlt das. (sollen)
    b. Wer bezahlt das? (sollen)
5. a. Ich esse diesen Fisch nicht. (mögen)
    b. Warum essen Sie diesen Fisch nicht? (mögen)
6. a. Wir fliegen nach Alaska. (wollen)
    b. Fliegt ihr wirklich nach Alaska? (wollen)

Note the use of **haben**, **sein**, and **werden** as dependent infinitives:

> Ich bin still.   Sie hat viel Geduld[1] mit mir.
>
> Ich **soll** still **sein**.   Sie **muß** viel Geduld mit mir **haben**.
>
> Er wird reich.
>
> Er will reich **werden**.

Do not confuse **will** … **werden** (*want to get* or *become*) with
wird … **werden** (*will get* or *become* [future tense]).

PRACTICE

4-3   Restate the following sentences using German modals.

1. Meine Noten werden besser. (*must/ have to*)
2. Neumanns haben keine Kinder. (*to want to*)
3. Wann ist die Arbeit fertig? (*to be supposed to*)
4. Heute hat niemand schlechte Laune. (*to be allowed to*)
5. Sabine wird nicht dick. (*to want to*)
6. Dietmar ist nicht treu.[2] (*can*)

---

[1] **die Geduld**   *patience*
[2] **treu**   *faithful*

Verbs with separable prefix as dependent infinitives:

Hans ruft mich heute nicht an.

Hans **kann** mich heute nicht **anrufen.**

Warum **kann** er dich heute nicht **anrufen**?

Kann er dich heute nicht **anrufen**?

The separable prefix is attached to the infinitive.

PRACTICE

4-4   Restate the following sentences using the modals in parentheses.

MODEL: Lädst du Rainer ein? (wollen)
Willst du Rainer einladen?

1. Holst du Annerose ab? (wollen)
2. Wann fängt das Konzert an? (sollen)
3. Warum fahrt ihr nach Bonn zurück? (wollen)
4. Ich bringe die Bücher zur Bibliothek zurück. (müssen)
5. Bei diesem Wetter gehen wir nicht spazieren. (können)
6. Reicht Hannelore die Semesterarbeit[1] später ein?[2] (dürfen)
7. Wann stehst du morgen auf? (müssen)
8. Warum lädst du ihn nicht ein? (wollen)
9. Nehmen Sie die Einladung an?[3] (können)
10. Jörg räumt seinen Schreibtisch auf. (sollen)

DEPENDENT WORD ORDER

Barbara **kann** nicht mitkommen.

Ich weiß, daß Barbara nicht mitkommen **kann.**

In dependent clauses the conjugated modal is in last position; the dependent infinitive precedes it.

PRACTICE

4-5   Restate the following sentences, using the indicated introductory clauses.

MODEL: Wer kann dieses Problem lösen?
Ich möchte wissen, **wer dieses Problem lösen kann.**

1. Will Manfred seine Freundin mitbringen?
Ich weiß nicht, ob…
2. Muß Astrid für eine Prüfung lernen?
Ich nehme an, daß …
3. Dürfen wir hier über die Straße gehen?[4]
Ich glaube nicht, daß…

---

[1] die Semesterarbeit, -en   *term paper*
[2] ein•reichen   *to hand in*
[3] die Einladung an•nehmen   *to accept the invitation*
[4] über die Straße gehen   *to cross the street*

4. Ihr sollt den Chef um Erlaubnis bitten.
   Wißt ihr nicht, daß …
5. Ich muß am Wochenende die Nase ins Buch stecken.[1]
   Schade, daß …
6. Du sollst nicht soviel klatschen.[2]
   Du weißt doch, daß …

USE OF MODALS WITHOUT A DEPENDENT INFINITIVE

Kannst du mir helfen?	Nein, ich kann nicht.	*No, I can't.*
	Nein, ich kann es nicht.	*No, I can't do it.*
	Nein, ich kann das nicht.	*No, I can't do that.*

Dependent infinitives need not be repeated in such sequences. They may be either omitted completely or replaced by **es** or **das**.

The verbs **fahren**, **gehen**, **machen**, and **tun** are often omitted because they are clearly understood from the context.

Ich muß in die Bibliothek.	*I must go to the library.*
Wo willst du hin?	*Where do you want to go?*
Was soll ich mit diesen Sachen?	*What am I supposed to do with these things?*

PRACTICE

4-6   A. Express the following questions and answers in idiomatic English.

1. X: Müssen Sie schon nach Hause?
   Y: Leider ja. Unsere Kinder müssen jetzt ins Bett.
2. X: Wo willst du hin?
   Y: Ich muß ins Studentenheim[3] zurück. Ich habe meine Brille[4] vergessen.
3. X: Was macht ihr heute nachmittag?
   Y: Hans und Udo wollen zum Fußballspiel; Maria und ich wollen in den Zirkus.
4. a. X: Warum hast du mir diesen Katalog gegeben? Was soll ich damit?
      Y: Ein Geschenk bestellen. Jemand[5] hat bald Geburtstag.
   b. X: Ach so,[6] ein leiser Wink.[7] Und wer soll es bezahlen?
      Y: Du natürlich. Du kannst es doch.
   c. X: Wenn ich es aber nicht will?
      Y: Ich weiß, du kannst es, und du willst es auch.

---

[1] **die Nasse ins Buch stecken**	*to hit the books*	
[2] **klatschen**	*to gossip*	
[3] **das Studentenheim, -e**	*dormitory*	
[4] **die Brille, -n**	*eyeglasses*	
[5] **jemand somebody,**	*someone*	
[6] **ach so**	*generally used in the sense of "oh, I see"*	
[7] **ein leiser Wink**	*a subtle hint*	

B.   Respond in German, adding *es* to the modal.

1.   X: Willst du wirklich am Wochenende arbeiten?
     Y: (*I have to.*)
2.   X: Warum essen Sie keine Schlagsahne?[1]
     Y: (*I'm not allowed to.*) Der Arzt hat es mir verboten.[2]
3.   X: Du kannst doch mitfahren.
     Y: (*Yes, but I don't want to.*)
4.   X: Wer soll diesen schweren Koffer tragen?
     Y: (*I'm supposed to, but I can't*)
5.   X: Niemand darf ihn jetzt bei der Arbeit stören
     Y: (*I'm allowed to*), denn ich bin ein Jemand[3] kein Niemand.*

PRACTICE

4-7   Summarizing exercises for the present tense.

A.   Form questions.

MODEL: du / wollen / mit•kommen / wirklich nicht
          Willst du wirklich nicht mitkommen?

1.   du / wollen / versuchen / es noch einmal?
2.   Sie / können / lösen[4] / dieses Problem?
3.   wir / sollen / warten / auf Marlene?
4.   ihr / wollen / spazieren•gehen / heute nachmittag?
5.   du / können / helfen / mir / bei den Hausaufgaben?
6.   Sie / müssen / bitten / den Chef um Erlaubnis?
7.   du / wollen / ab•holen / die Post?
8.   wir / dürfen / parken / hier?
9.   warum / du / können / mit•kommen / nicht?
10. warum / ihr / wollen / ein•laden / Bergmanns / nicht?
11. wann / Sie / können / reparieren / meinen Wagen?
12. was / du / wollen / schenken / deiner Freundin zum Geburtstag?
13. du / wollen / heiraten / mich?

B.   Form answers.

MODEL: X: Warum haben Sie diese Wohnung nicht gemietet?
          Y: weil / wir / wollen / kaufen / ein Haus
          Weil wir ein Haus kaufen wollen.

1.   X: Warum fährst du zum Flughafen?
     Y: weil / ich / sollen / ab•holen / Volker
2.   X: Warum überholst du den Wagen vor uns nicht?
     Y: weil / man / dürfen / über•holen / hier nicht
3.   X: Warum gehst du nicht mit uns schwimmen?
     Y: weil / ich / müssen / stecken / die Nase ins Buch

---

[1] die Schlagsahne   *whipped cream*
[2] der Artz hat es mir verboten   *doctor's order (lit.: The doctor has forbidden it to me.)*
[3] ein Jemand   *a somebody*
[4] lösen   *to solve*

*Jemand and **niemand** are capitalized when preceded by a **der-** word or **ein-** word.

4. X: Warum erzählst du mir nicht, was du über Bergers gehört hast?
    Y: weil / ich / sollen / klatschen / nicht

5. X: Warum gehst du schon nach Hause?
    Y: weil / ich / müssen / sein / vor Mitternacht[1] zu Hause

6. X: Warum läufst du so schnell?
    Y: weil / ich / wollen / kommen / nicht zu spät

7. X: Warum heiratest du nicht?
    Y: weil / ich / können / sein / nicht treu

C. Express the following sentences in German.

1. a. Frank is studying for an exam.   **Frank lernt für eine Prüfung.**
    b. He has to study for an exam.
    c. He has to, but he doesn't want to.

2. a. Helga doesn't know (it).   **Helga weiß es nicht.**
    b. She wants to know (it).
    c. I assume that she wants to know (it).

3. a. They are not telling me.   **Sie sagen es[2] mir nicht.**
    b. They don't want to tell me.
    c. You don't want to tell me. (fam. sing.)
    d. I want to, but I am not allowed to.

4. a. When are you going to straighten   **Wann räumst du**
       up your room?   **dein Zimmer auf?**
    b. You have to straighten up your room.
    c. I'm supposed to, but I don't want to.

5. a. When are you handing in the   **Wann reichst du die**
       term paper?   **Semesterarbeit ein?**
    b. When do we have to hand in the term paper?
    c. I don't know when we have to hand in the term paper.

6. a. Who is taking care of that?   **Wer erledigt das?**
    b. Who wants to take care of that?
    c. Who is supposed to take care of that?
    d. You have to take care of that. (fam. sing.)
    e. I can't take care of that.

7. a. I'm not losing weight. On the   **Ich nehme nicht ab. Im**
       contrary, I'm gaining weight.   **Gegenteil, ich nehme zu.**
    b. Do you want to gain weight? (formal)
    c. On the contrary, I want to lose weight.
    d. Ute wants to gain weight.
    e. I can't believe (it) that she wants to gain weight.

8. a. My grades are getting worse.   **Meine Noten werden schlechter.**
    b. They have to get better.
    c. How can they get better?
    d. You have to hit the books. (fam. sing.)
    e. I have to hit the books so that[3] my grades get better.

---

[1] vor Mitternacht   *before midnight*
[2] es sagen (sagen + dir. obj.)   *to tell*
[3] damit   *so that*

§2   THE SIMPLE PAST TENSE

FORMATION

The modals are conjugated in the simple past as follows:

dürfen	können	mögen	müssen	sollen	wollen
ich durfte	ich konnte	ich mochte	ich mußte	ich sollte	ich wollte
du durftest	du konntest	du mochtest	du mußtest	du solltest	du wolltest
er ⎫ sie ⎬ durfte es ⎭	er ⎫ sie ⎬ konnte es ⎭	er ⎫ sie ⎬ mochte es ⎭	er ⎫ sie ⎬ mußte es ⎭	er ⎫ sie ⎬ sollte es ⎭	er ⎫ sie ⎬ wollte es ⎭
wir durften	wir konnten	wir mochten	wir mußten	wir sollten	wir wollten
ihr durftet	ihr konntet	ihr mochtet	ihr mußtet	ihr solltet	ihr wolltet
sie durften	sie konnten	sie mochten	sie mußten	sie sollten	sie wollten
Sie durften	Sie konnten	Sie mochten	Sie mußten	Sie sollten	Sie wollten
I was allowed to, etc.	*I could, I was able to, etc.*	*I liked to, etc.*	*I had to, etc.*	*I was expected, I was supposed to, etc.*	*I wanted to I intended to, etc.*

Note: a. Modals take the same endings in the simple past as weak verbs.
 b. Modals have no umlaut in the past.
 c. **Mochte** has a change of consonants.

THE USE OF MODALS IN THE SIMPLE PAST TENSE

Modals generally use the simple past even in coversational German where most other verbs are in the present perfect tense (cf. Chap. 3,§2).

> X: Warum **sind** Sie nur zwei Tage in München **geblieben**?
> *Why did you stay in Munich only two days?*

> Y: Mein Freund **konnte** nicht länger bleiben.
> *My friend **could** not stay any longer.*

This parallels the English use of the simple past tense.

PRACTICE

4-8   **A.** Supply the past tense forms of the infinitives in parentheses.

1. Wir _____ das tun. (müssen, sollen, wollen, können, dürfen)
2. Hannelore _____ es mir sagen. (wollen, sollen, können, müssen)
3. _____ du das nicht? (können, wollen, dürfen, sollen, mögen)
4. _____ ihr mitfahren? (wollen, können, dürfen)

B. Change the sentences to the past tense. (*Do not change the boldface introductory clauses.*)

1. Kannst du Klaus nicht anrufen?
2. Warum wollen Sie nicht zum Arzt gehen?

3. Leider darf man da nicht parken.
4. Niemand mag den Pudding essen.
5. Wir sollen am Montag einen Vertrag[1] unterschreiben.[2]
6. Können Sie die Unterschrift[3] lesen?
7. Andreas will das Formular[4] nicht ausfüllen.[5]
8. **Es tut mir leid**, daß ich dich enttäuschen[6] muß.
9. **Ich glaube nicht**, daß Körners wirklich nach Afrika fliegen wollen.
10. **Niemand weiß**, ob der Chef es nicht kann oder nicht will.

 # The Modals in Compound Tenses

§3   THE PRESENT PERFECT TENSE

FORMATION

A distinction has to be made between the form of modals with and without an accompaning infintive.

WITHOUT ACCOMPANING INFINITIVE

Ich habe (es) nicht gekonnt.
gedurft.
gemußt.
gewollt.
gemo<u>ch</u>t.
(past participle)

WITH ACCOMPANING INFINITIVE

Ich habe nicht **mitfahren können.**
mitfahren dürfen.
mitfahren müssen.
mitfahren wollen.
mitfahren mögen.
(double infinitive)

The past participle of the modal follows the pattern of weak verbs. It has no umlaut. **Mögen** has a change of consonants: **gemocht.**

When an accompanying infinitive is present, the modal verbs form the present perfect with the infinitive instead of the past participle. It stands at the end of a clause. This produces the so-called *double-infinitive construction.*

Modals use the auxiliary haben even if the accompanying infinitive requires **sein** when occuring without a modal.

Er **ist** noch nie mitgefahren.
but: Er **hat** noch nie mitfahren **können.**

---

[1] der Vertrag, ⸚e   *contract*
[2] unterschreiben   *to sign*
  unterschrieb, unterschrieben
[3] die Unterschrift, -en   *signature*
[4] das Formular, -e   *form (not formula!)*
[5] aus·füllen   *to fill out*
[6] enttäuschen   *to disappoint*

THE USE OF MODALS IN THE PRESENT PERFECT TENSE

The present perfect tense of the modals tends to be used in contexts where English would also use the present perfect rather than the simple past. This occurs, for example, with the time expressions **noch nie, schon oft, schon immer.**[1]

Frau Berger hat das noch nie zugeben wollen.
Mrs. Berger has never wanted to admit that.

Ich habe ihm schon oft bei den Hausaufgaben helfen müssen.
I've often had to help him with the homework.

Wir haben schon immer hier parken dürfen.
We've always been allowed to park here.

Note the position of these time expressions: they normally follow pronoun objects but precede all other elements.

PRACTICE

4-9   Change the sentences to the present perfect tense, using the time expressions in parentheses.

MODEL: a. Ich kann meine Schulden nicht bezahlen. (schon oft)
Ich habe schon oft meine Schulden nicht bezahlen können.

b. Ich kann es nicht. (schon oft)
Ich habe es schon oft nicht gekonnt.

1. a. Helga kann ihren Vater überreden. (schon oft)
    b. Sie kann es. (schon oft)
2. a. Wir müssen auf Dietmar warten. (schon oft)
    b. Wir müssen es. (schon oft)
3. a. Ich darf mit seinem Wagen fahren. (schon oft)
    b. Ich darf es. (schon oft)
4. a. Du kannst mich verstehen. (noch nie)
    b. Du kannst es. (noch nie)
5. a. Klaus will arbeiten. (noch nie)
    b. Klaus will es. (noch nie)
6. a. Ich muß nachgeben. (schon immer)
    b. Ich muß es. (schon immer)
7. a. Ich will deinen Freund kennenlernen.[2] (schon immer)
    b. Ich will es. (schon immer)
8. a. Martina mag keinen Käse essen. (schon immer)
    b. Sie mag keinen Käse. (schon immer)

§4   THE PAST PERFECT TENSE

The past perfect tense of modals is identical to the present perfect except that the past tense of **haben** is used as the auxiliary.

---

[1] **noch** and **schon** stand for added emphasis.
[2] **kennen•lernen**   *to get to know, meet (for the first time).*

Ich **hatte** (es) nicht **gekonnt.**   Ich **hatte** nicht **mitfahren können.**
I had not been able to do it.   *I had not been able to come along.*

4-10   Change the following sentences to the past perfect tense.

1. Niemand kann Anita helfen.
2. Wir können es auch nicht.
3. Ich muß ihn leider enttäuschen.
4. Rainer will drei Tage bei uns bleiben.
5. Seine Freundin will es aber nicht.
6. Man darf ihm nicht widersprechen.[1]
7. Helga muß das zugeben.[2]

§5   THE FUTURE TENSE

Compare:

Er kann es nicht.   Er kann nicht mitkommen.

Er **wird es** nicht **können.**   Er **wird** nicht **mitkommen können.**
He will not be able to.   *He will not be able to come along.*

The future tense is formed with the auxiliary **werden**; the modal appears as an infinitive at the end of a clause. If there is an accompanying infinitive, it precedes the modal (another instance of a *double-infinitive construction*).

If the future is to express supposition or probability, adverbs such as **wohl,** **wahrscheinlich,** or **vielleicht** are usually added (cf. Chap. 3, $11).

Sie werden mir wohl nicht helfen können.
I suppose you won't be able to help me.

4-11   Restate the following sentences in the future tense.

MODEL: Frank will wahrscheinlich den Vertrag nicht unterschreiben.
Frank wird wahrscheinlich den Vertrag nicht unterschreiben wollen.

1. Frau Braun muß wahrscheinlich eine hohe Strafe[3] bezahlen.
2. Sie kann das wahrscheinlich nicht.
3. Andreas darf keinen Alkohol trinken.
4. Er will es auch nicht.
5. Diesen Kaffee mag wohl niemand.
6. Barbara kann wohl nicht treu sein.
7. Ich muß Sie leider enttäuschen.

---

[1] widersprechen (widerspricht),   *to contradict*
  widersprach, widersprochen
[2] zu•geben (gibt zu), gab zu, zugegeben   *to admit*
[3] die Strafe, -n   *fine*

§6   THE FUTURE PERFECT TENSE

Modals with a dependent infinitive very rarely appear in the future perfect tense. Modals without a dependent infinitive are used occasionally in the future perfect expressing a past supposition or probability (cf. Chap. 3 §12).

Er wird es wohl nicht **gekonnt haben**.   *He probably was not able to do it.*
(perfect infinitive)

§7   DEPENDENT WORD ORDER IN COMPOUND TENSES

WITHOUT DEPENDENT INFINITIVE	WITH DEPENDENT INFINITIVE
Ich weiß,	Ich weiß,
daß er es nicht **gekonnt hat.**	daß er nicht hat **mitkommen können.**
daß er es nicht **gekonnt hatte.**	daß er nicht **hatte mitkommen können.**
daß er es nicht **können wird.**	daß er nicht **wird mitkommen können.**

The inflected auxiliary stands last in accordance with the general rule for dependent word order.

A double infinitive always has absolute right to final position in its clause.

PRACTICE

4-12   Restate the following sentences, using the indicated introductory clauses.

A. Without a dependent infinitive

MODEL: Er hat das nicht gekonnt.
Warum denken Sie, **daß er das nicht gekonnt hat**?

1. Sie hat es nicht gedurft.
   Warum denkst du, daß…
2. Sie hatte es nicht gewollt.
   Es ist möglich daß…
3. Er wird das können.
   Ich nehme an, daß…

B. With a dependent infinitive

MODEL: Ich habe ihm schon oft helfen können.
Ich bin froh, **daß ich ihm schon oft habe helfen können.**

1. Ich habe ihn noch nie verstehen können.
   Ich gebe zu, daß…
2. Sie hatte schon um 5 Uhr morgens aufstehen müssen.
   Monika hatte schlechte Laune, weil…
3. Man hatte das Problem nicht lösen können.
   Es war sehr schade, daß…
4. Du wirst ihn überreden können.
   Ich bin überzeugt, daß…
5. Ich werde Sie enttäuschen müssen.
   Es tut mir leid, daß…

§8   REFERENCE CHART: SYNOPSIS OF THE TENSES OF MODALS AND THEIR BASIC MEANINGS

Keep in mind: With modals the use of the simple past and present perfect in German parallels the English use of these tenses (§2 and §3).

DÜRFEN

PRESENT	ich darf es	ich darf anrufen	*I may,*	*I am allowed to*
PAST	ich durfte es	ich durfte anrufen		*I was allowed to*
PRES. PERF.	ich habe es **gedurft**	ich habe **anrufen dürfen**		*I have been allowed to*
PAST PERF.	ich hatte es **gedurft**	ich hatte **anrufen dürfen**		*I had been allowed to*
FUTURE	ich werde es dürfen	ich werde anrufen dürfen		*I will be allowed to*

KÖNNEN

PRESENT	ich kann es	ich kann anrufen	*I can,*	*I am able to*
PAST	ich konnte es	ich konnte anrufen	*I could,*	*I was able to*
PRES. PERF.	ich habe es **gekonnt**	ich habe **anrufen können**		*I have been able to*
PAST PERF.	ich hatte es **gekonnt**	ich hatte **anrufen können**		*I had been able to*
FUTURE	ich werde es können	ich werde anrufen können		*I will be able to*

MÖGEN

PRESENT	ich mag es nicht	ich mag nicht anrufen	*I do not like to*
PAST	ich mochte es nicht	ich mochte nicht anrufen	*I did not like to*
PERF. PERF.	ich habe es nicht **gemocht**	ich habe nicht **anrufen mögen**	*I have not liked to*
PAST PERF.	ich hatte es nicht **gemocht**	ich hatte nicht **anrufen mögen**	*I had not liked to*
FUTURE	ich werde es nicht mögen	ich werde nicht anrufen mögen	*I will not like to*

MÜSSEN

PRESENT	ich muß es	ich muß anrufen	*I must,*	*I have to*
PAST	ich mußte es	ich mußte anrufen		*I had to*
PRES. PERF.	ich habe es **gemußt**	ich habe **anrufen müssen**		*I have had to*
PAST PERF.	ich hatte es **gemußt**	ich hatte **anrufen müssen**		*I had had to*
FUTURE	ich werde es müssen	ich werde anrufen müssen		*I will have to*

SOLLEN

PRESENT	ich soll es	ich soll anrufen	*I am expected to,*
			I am supposed to
PAST	ich sollte es	ich sollte anrufen	*I was expected to*
PRES. PERF.	ich habe es **gesollt**	ich habe **anrufen sollen**	*I have been expected to*
PAST PERF.	ich hatte es **gesollt**	ich hatte **anrufen sollen**	*I had been expected to*
FUTURE	ich werde es sollen	ich werde anrufen sollen	*I will be expected to*

WOLLEN

PRESENT	ich will es	ich will anrufen	*I want to*
PAST	ich wollte es	ich wollte anrufen	*I wanted to*
PRES. PERF.	ich habe es **gewollt**	ich habe **anrufen wollen**	*I have wanted to*
PAST PERF.	ich hatte es **gewollt**	ich hatte **anrufen wollen**	*I had wanted to*
FUTURE	ich werde es wollen	ich werde anrufen wollen	*I will want to*

§9   SUMMARY OF WORD ORDER IN DEPENDENT CLAUSES

Ich weiß
    daß er es nicht **kann.**
    daß er es nicht **konnte.**
    daß er es nicht gekonnt **hat.**
    daß er es nicht gekonnt **hatte.**
    daß er es nicht können **wird.**

Ich weiß
    daß er nicht anrufen **kann.**
    daß er nicht anrufen **konnte.**
    daß er nicht **hat** anrufen können.
    daß er nicht **hatte** anrufen können.
    daß er nicht **wird** anrufen können.

4-13   Summarizing exercises

A. Change the following sentences to the past, present perfect, past perfect, and future tenses. (*Do not change the boldface introductory clauses.*)

1. Sie darf es mir nicht sagen.
2. Sie will es nicht.
3. **Ich glaube nicht**, daß er das Projekt aufgeben will.
4. **Ich nehme an**, daß er es nicht darf.

B. Form sentences in the indicated tenses.

Simple Past

MODEL: ich / müssen / bitten / die Chefin / um Erlaubnis
Ich mußte die Chefin um Erlaubnis bitten.

1. der Chef / müssen / bezahlen / eine hohe Strafe
2. Frau Kästner / sollen / unterschreiben / einen Vertrag
3. ich / wollen / versuchen / es / noch einmal
4. wir / können / lösen / das Problem / nicht
5. die Kinder / dürfen / das nicht

Present Perfect

MODEL: ich / müssen / bezahlen / noch nie / eine Strafe
Ich habe noch nie eine Strafe bezahlen müssen.

1. wir / müssen / aus•füllen / noch nie / so viele Formulare
2. man / wollen / überreden / mich / schon oft
3. ich / wollen / kennen•lernen/ ihn / schon immer
4. du / können / verstehen / mich / noch nie
5. du / wollen / das / noch nie
6. wir / dürfen / das / noch nie
7. er / mögen / das / noch nie
8. ich / können / es / schon immer

Past Perfect

MODEL: Erika / wollen / unterschreiben / den Vertrag / nicht
Erika hatte den Vertrag nicht unterschreiben wollen.

1. man / können / überreden / die Professorin / nicht
2. niemand / können / lesen / meine Unterschrift
3. er / dürfen / trinken / keinen Alkohol
4. ich / dürfen / das / auch nicht
5. wir / wollen / das / wirklich nicht

Future

MODEL: Sie / können / verstehen / mich / wohl
Sie werden mich wohl verstehen können.

1. Sie / können / überreden / mich / wohl
2. du / müssen / zu•geben / das / wohl

3. ich / können / das / wohl / nicht
4. wir / dürfen / es / wahrscheinlich / nicht
5. ich / müssen / stecken / die Nase ins Buch

Mixed Tenses

1. ich / können / helfen / dir / wohl / nicht (future)
2. wir / müssen / auf•stehen / um 5 Uhr (simple past)
3. ich / müssen / auf•stehen / noch nie / so früh (pres. perf.)
4. Erika / wollen / sagen / es / mir / nicht (past perf.)
5. ich / wollen / warnen / ihn (simple past)
6. ich / müssen / warnen / ihn / wohl (future)
7. Klaus / wollen / zu•geben / das / noch nie (pres. perf.)
8. wir / dürfen / widersprechen / ihm / nicht (simple past)
9. man / dürfen / widersprechen / ihm / noch nie (pres. perf.)
10. niemand / wollen / stören / dich (past perf.)
11. ich / müssen / enttäuschen / Sie / wohl (future)
12. Elke / mögen / das / nicht (simple past)
13. wir / dürfen / es / nicht (past perf.)

C. Express in German using the same tenses as the English sentences.

1. a. She doesn't understand that.   **Sie versteht das nicht.**
   b. She can't understand that.
   c. Nobody was able to understand that.
   d. I've never been able to understand that.
2. a. I'm warning you.   **Ich warne dich.**
   b. I must warn you.
   c. I didn't want to warn Dieter, but I had to.
   d. Nobody had wanted to warn Dieter.
   e. We'll have to warn Dieter.
3. a. When are you signing the contract?   **Wann unterschreiben Sie den Vertrag?**
   b. You have to sign the contract. (formal)
   c. You'll have to sign the contract.
   d. She didn't want to sign the contract.
4. a. I'm trying it again.   **Ich versuche es noch einmal.**
   b. May I try it again?
   c. They wanted to try it again.
   d. They had wanted to try it again.
5. a. Who's going to solve the problem?   **Wer löst dieses Problem?**
   b. Who can solve this problem?
   c. We weren't able to solve this problem.
   d. It's a pity that we weren't able to solve this problem.
   e. We will not be able to solve this problem.
   f. Will you be able to solve this problem? (fam. sing.)
6. a. He doesn't admit it.   **Er gibt es nicht zu.**
   b. He has to admit it.

c. He'll have to admit it.
d. He doesn't want to admit it.
e. He didn't want to admit it.
f. He has never wanted to admit it.

 # Additional Meanings and Uses of Modal Auxiliaries

Modal auxiliaries may express various shades of meanings which largely depend on the context in which they occur. The preceding section focused on the basic meanings of modals. Here are some additional connotations.

§10 *nicht dürfen*

Sie müssen das tun. <
    a. You have to do that.
    b. You must do that.

Both English sentences express the same thing as their German counterpart, i.e. the necessity of doing something. But notice the difference in meaning of the respective negative forms of the two English sentences:

a. *You don't have to do that.*   no obligation
b. *You mustn't do that.*   strong warning or prohibition

This distinction is expressed in German by **nicht müssen** and **nicht dürfen**:

a. *You don't have to do that.*   Sie **müssen** das **nicht** tun.
b. *You mustn't do that.*   Sie **dürfen** das **nicht** tun.

REMEMBER: *must not* = nicht dürfen

PRACTICE

4-14 Express in German.

1. We must not forget that.   Wir **dürfen** das **nicht** vergessen.
2. I mustn't drink that.
3. You mustn't say that. (fam. sing.)
4. You mustn't disturb Mrs. Körner. (formal)
5. You mustn't be so stubborn.[1] (fam. pl.)
6. I must not gossip.

§11 *können*

a. Just as English speakers often use *can* instead of *may*, Germans often use **können** instead of **dürfen**:

        Du kannst das Geld behalten
instead of
        Du darfst das Geld behalten.   *You may keep the money.*

---

[1] **stur**   *stubborn*

b.   Another meaning of **können** is *to know how to do something*:

Kannst du schwimmen?	*Do you know how to swim?*
Können Sie Deutsch?	*Do you know German? Do you speak German?*
Sie kann kein Englisch.	⎰ *She doesn't know English.*
	⎱ *She doesn't speak English.*

c.   **Können** is used in the idiomatic expression: **Ich kann nicht anders.**
I can't help it.

Ich konnte nicht anders, ich mußte lachen.
I couldn't help it, I had to laugh.
I couldn't help laughing.

§12   *sollen*

a.   **Sollen** may have the meaning of *shall*, principally in questions expressing a suggestion:

Soll ich Ihnen einen Stuhl bringen?   ***Shall** I bring you a chair?*

b.   **Sollen** is frequently used in the sense of *should*, expressing an obligation:

Ich weiß nicht, ob ich es ihm sagen **soll**. *I don't know whether I **should** tell him.*

§13   *wollte gerade* **or** *wollte eben*

In conversational German **wollte gerade** or **wollte eben** is frequently used in the
sense of *was on the point of or was (just) about to.*

Ich wollte Sie gerade anrufen.	*I wanted (was about) to call you.*
Wir wollten eben wegfahren.	*We were (just) about to leave.*

PRACTICE

▼ 4-15   Express in German.

1. Shall I close the door?
2. I don't know whether I should call Dr. Krämer.
3. Dr. Krämer was just about to go home.
4. Does he know English?
5. Mary knows German.
6. Frank doesn't know German.
7. I couldn't help it, I had to protest.

§14   *mögen*

Mögen is used principally with **nicht** or some other negative to express dislike or
reluctance.

Ich **mag** es ihm **nicht** sagen.	*I don't like to tell him that.*
Ich **mag** das **nicht**.	*I don't like that.*

It also occurs without **nicht**, mainly in questions about food, drink, persons, places:

Mögen Sie Fisch?	*Do you like fish?*
Magst du diesen Tee?	*Do you like this tea?*
Mögt ihr eure Nachbarn?	*Do you like your neighbors?*
Mögen Ihre Kinder die neue Schule?	*Do your children like the new school?*

The subjunctive form **möchte** (*would like*) is frequently used in both positive and negative sentences.

Ich **möchte** es ihm (nicht) sagen.	*I would (not) like to, (don't) want to tell him.*
Was **möchtest** du?	*What would you like?*
Ich **möchte** eine Tasse Kaffee.	*I would like a cup of coffee.*

Möchte is conjugated as follows:

ich möchte
du möchtest
er möchte   The same endings as the past tense **mochte.**
wir möchten
ihr möchtet
sie möchten
Sie möchten

PRACTICE

4-16   Express in English; then reproduce the German from your translation.

1. Ich möchte mehr Geld haben.
2. Meine Eltern möchten dich kennenlernen.
3. Möchtest du meine Frau[1] werden?
4. Möchtet ihr fernsehen?[2]
5. Wer möchte ein Plätzchen?[3]
6. Was möchten Sie?

§15   THE USE OF *nicht brauchen* INSTEAD OF *nicht müssen*

Sie **müssen** es mir **nicht** sagen.   ⎫
                                   ⎬ You don't have to tell me.
Sie **brauchen** es mir **nicht zu** sagen. ⎭

Nicht müssen having the meaning of *don't / doesn't have to* is frequently expressed by **nicht brauchen** (lit. *need not*). It takes the dependent infinitive with **zu** in contrast to the modal auxiliaries.

Verb with separable prefix:

Sie brauchen die Platte nicht zurück**zu**geben. *You don't have to return the record.*

zu is inserted between the prefix and the verb

---

[1] **meine Frau**   *my wife*
  (mein Mann)   *(my husband)*
[2] **fern•sehen (sieht fern),**   *to watch television*
  sah fern, ferngesehen
[3] **das Plätzchen,-**   *cookie*

PRACTICE
4-17 Substitute **nicht brauchen** for **nicht müssen**.

MODEL: Er muß mir nicht in der Küche helfen.
Er braucht mir nicht in der Küche zu helfen.

1. Wir müssen heute nicht arbeiten.
2. Sie müssen ihn nicht um Erlaubnis bitten.
3. Du mußt nicht bar bezahlen.[1]
4. Diesen Stoff[2] muß man nicht bügeln.[3]
5. Sie müssen mein Angebot[4] nicht annehmen.
6. Ihr müßt Schreibers nicht einladen.

The use of **nicht brauchen** in the simple past and present perfect:

Wir **brauchten** das nicht **zu übersetzen**.   *We didn't have to*
Wir **haben** das nicht **zu übersetzen brauchen**.   *translate that*
                 INF.   INF.

Sie **brauchten** mein Angebot nicht **anzunehmen**.   *You didn't have to*
Sie **haben** mein Angebot nicht **anzunehmen brauchen**.   *accept my offer.*
                       INF.   INF.

In compound tenses a double infinitive with **zu** is used.

PRACTICE
4-18 Restate each sentence first in the simple past, then in the present perfect.

MODEL: Sie brauchen das nicht noch einmal zu erklären.
Sie brauchten das nicht noch einmal zu erklären.
Sie haben das nicht noch einmal zu erklären brauchen.

1. Ich brauche die Rechnung nicht zu bezahlen.
2. Wir brauchen Helga nicht zu helfen.
3. Karin braucht das Formular nicht auszufüllen.
4. Wir brauchen nicht um Erlaubnis zu bitten.
5. Er braucht die Platte nicht zurückzugeben.

PRACTICE
4-19 Summarizing exercises for §10 to §15.

A.   The following sentences illustrate various uses of the modals. Render them into acceptable English.

_____

[1] **bar bezahlen**   *to pay cash*
[2] **der Stoff, -e**   *material, fabric*
[3] **bügeln**   *to iron, press*
[4] **das Angebot, -e**   *offer*
  das Angebot an•nehmen (nimmt an),   *to accept the offer*
  nahm an, angenommen

1. X: Herr Bauer, Sie wollten eben etwas sagen.
    Y: Ich weiß nicht mehr[1], was ich eben sagen wollte.
2. X: Hier ist ein Stück Kuchen für dich.
    Y: Ich mache eine Schlankheitskur[2]. Du darfst mich nicht in
    Versuchung führen[3].
3. X: Es ist sehr warm in diesem Zimmer.
    Y: Soll ich ein Fenster aufmachen?
4. X: Warum brummst[4] du soviel?
    Y: Ich kann einfach[5] nicht anders, ich muß brummen.
5. a. X: Sie brauchen mir meinen alten Plattenspieler nicht zurückzugeben.
    Y: Kann ich ihn wirklich behalten?[6]
    b. X: Sie können und dürfen es.
6. a. X: Können Sie Italienisch?
    Y: Ich kann etwas Spanisch, aber kein Italienisch.
    b. X: Können Sie auch Deutsch?
    Y: Ein wenig. Wenn mich ein Deutscher sprechen hört, weiß er nicht,
    ob er lachen oder weinen soll.

B. Express in German. (Use **nicht brauchen** for **not have to**.)

1. a. I'm paying the bill.
    b. I have to pay the bill.
    c. You don't have to pay the bill. (fam. sing.)
    d. We didn't have to pay the bill. (past, pres. perf)
2. a. Would you like a cookie? (formal)
    b. Would you like to meet my parents? (fam. sing.)
    c. I'd like to be in Hawaii.
3. a. I mustn't disappoint Monika.
    b. Ruth mustn't eat that because she's on a diet.
    c. We mustn't lead Ruth into temptation.
4. a. I was just about to call Martin.
    b. I was just about to protest.
    c. We are just about to go home.
    d. I don't remember what I was about to say.
5. a. She simply can't help it, she has to grumble.
    b. I simply can't help it, I have to gossip.
    c. They simply couldn't help it, they had to protest.

(The subjective use of modals is explained in Chapter 20, §2.)

---

[1] **ich weiß nicht mehr**	*I don't remember* (lit. *I don't know anymore*)
[2] **eine Schlankheitskur machen**	*to be or go on a diet*
[3] **in Versuchung führen**	*to lead into temptation*
[4] **brummen**	*to grumble*
[5] **einfach**	*simple, simply*
[6] **behalten (behält),**	*to keep*
behielt, behalten	

CHAPTER 5

The Nouns

Gender and Plural

§1 GENDER

The definite article indicates the gender of the noun that follows it:

der (masculine)	der Vater
die (feminine)	die Mutter
das (neuter)	das Kind

In English, nouns referring to inanimate things and abstracts are neuter. In German, however, the so-called *grammatical gender* of such nouns is masculine, feminine or neuter. It is imperative to learn German nouns with the corresponding definite article, since the gender of a noun is often the most important clue to the function of the noun in the sentence.

Here are a few useful guidelines for determining the gender of a noun.

Masculine

1. Nouns referring to male persons, their professions, nationalities:

> der Vater, der Bruder, der Junge, der Freund, der Lehrer, der Professor, der Arzt (*doctor*) der Chef (*boss*), der Polizist, der Komponist (*composer*), der Präsident, der Engländer, der Amerikaner, der Franzose, der Deutsche, der Ausländer (*foreigner*), der Verkäufer (*salesman*)

2. Names of all seasons, months, days of the week:

> der Frühling, der Sommer, der Herbst, der Winter;
> der Januar, der Februar, der März, etc.
> der Montag, der Dienstag, der Mittwoch, etc.

3. Most nouns ending in **-en:**

> der Wagen, der Regen, der Garten, der Osten, der Süden, der Westen, der Norden

Feminine

1. Nouns referring to female persons:

> die Mutter, die Frau, die Tante, etc.

Many feminine nouns are formed from masculine nouns by adding the suffix **-in:**

> die Freundin die Lehrerin, die Professorin, die Assistentin, die Ärztin, die Sekretärin, die Amerikanerin, die Ausländerin

2. Most nouns ending in unstressed **-e:**

> die Liebe, die Frage, die Straße, die Karte, die Reise, die Schule

Common exceptions:

> der Name, der Käse, das Ende, das Auge

3. All nouns ending in **-ei, -ie, -ik, -ion, -heit, -keit, -schaft, -tät, -ung:**

> die Bäckerei (*bakery*), die Polizei (*police*), die Philosophie, die Musik, die Religion, die Freiheit (*freedom liberty*), die Möglichkeit (*possibility*), die Freundschaft (*friendship*), die Universität, die Meinung (*opinion*)

Neuter

1. Nouns referring to the young of animals and human beings:

> das Kalb (*calf*), das Fohlen (*foal, colt, filly*), das Lamm, das Kind, das Baby

2. Nouns with the diminutive suffix **-chen** or **-lein:**

> das Mädchen, das Fräulein

All nouns become neuter and usually add an umlaut (if possible) when they take on the diminutive form:

> die Stadt (*town, city*)   das Städtchen (*small town*)
> der Hund (*dog*)   das Hündchen (*small dog, puppy*)
> die Katze (*cat*)   das Kätzchen (*kitten*)

The diminutive of names is sometimes used for children or simply for endearment:

> Hans—Hänschen.

The ending **-chen** is more common than **-lein.**

3. Most metals:

> das Gold, das Silber, das Eisen (*iron*), das Blei (*lead*), das Kupfer, das Metall

4. Infinitives used as nouns:

> das Rauchen (*smoking*), das Trinken (*drinking*), das Essen (*meal*)

5. Letters when used as nouns:

> das A, das B, das C

PRACTICE

5-1   Add the definite article to the following nouns.

1. _____ Frage
2. _____ Platte
3. _____ Lüge (lie)
4. _____ Rauchen
5. _____ Essen
6. _____ A
7. _____ F
8. _____ Arzt
9. _____ Ärztin
10. _____ Verkäufer
11. _____ Verkäuferin
12. _____ Polizist
13. _____ Polizistin
14. _____ Polizei
15. _____ Konditorei
    (*pastry shop*)
16. _____ Religion
17. _____ Operation
18. _____ Million
19. _____ Vorlesung
20. _____ Warnung
21. _____ Erkältung (*cold*)
22. _____ Musik
23. _____ Grammatik
24. _____ Fabrik (*factory*)
25. _____ Republik

26. _____ Winter
27. _____ Sonntag
28. _____ Schwester
29. _____ Schwesterchen
30. _____ Wagen
31. _____ Garten
32. _____ Osten
33. _____ Kind
34. _____ Baby
35. _____ Universität
36. _____ Spezialität
37. _____ Gold
38. _____ Silber
39. _____ Freiheit
40. _____ Krankheit
41. _____ Möglichkeit
42. _____ Freundlichkeit
    (*friendliness*)
43. _____ Held (*hero*)
44. _____ Heldin
45. _____ C
46. _____ Liebe
47. _____ Information
48. _____ Meinung (*opinion*)
49. _____ Bruder
50. _____ Brüderchen

GENDER OF COMPOUND NOUNS

das Semester
die Arbeit
→ **die** Semesterarbeit (*term paper*)

Compound nouns have the gender of their element.

§2   THE PLURAL

The plural of the definite article is the same for all genders: **die**.

die Väter, die Mütter, die Kinder.

English ordinarily adds an **-s** to the singular of a noun to form the plural. There are a few exceptions, such as *child - children, foot - feet, man, men, etc.*

In German, nouns form their plural in several different ways.
Some add an ending: **-e, -er, -en, -n,** or **-s.**

Examples:

Listed in the vocabulary
of this book:

der Tag	die Tage	der Tag, -e
das Lied	die Lieder	das Lied, -er
die Nation	die Nationen	die Nation, -en
die Frage	die Fragen	die Frage, -n
das Hotel	die Hotels	das Hotel, -s

Some nouns add no ending to form the plural:

der Lehrer	die Lehrer	der Lehrer

Some umlaut the stem vowel in the plural:

der Gast	die Gäste	der Gast, ⸚e

Because of the many ways German plurals are formed, it is very important to learn
the plural (along with the gender) of each noun. You may find it helpful to study the
following charts which provide an overview of the most common patterns of the plural formation. There are often exceptions to these patterns, however, and while these
charts can help you to guess a plural, they are no substitute for the learning of indi-
vidual plural forms.

MONOSYLLABICS
(nouns of one syllable)

The majority of masculine and feminine nouns add **-e;** neuter nouns ad **-er,** less
frequently **-e.**

MASCULINE	NEUTER	FEMININE
add **-e** some also add umlaut	add **-er** and umlaut if possible or **-e**	add **-e** and umlaut if possilbe

der Punkt	**die Punkte**	das Buch	**die Bücher**	die Nacht	**die Nächte**
der Hund	**die Hunde**	das Haus	**die Häuser**	die Stadt	**die Städte**
der Satz	**die Sätze**	das Licht	**die Lichter**	die Hand	**die Hände**
der Baum	**die Bäume**	das Rad	**die Räder**	die Wurst	**die Würste**
der Saal	**die Säle**	(*wheel*)		but: die Frau	**die Frauen**
(*hall*)		das Ding	**die Dinge**	die Tür	**die Türen**
but: der Mann	**die Männer**	das Jahr	**die Jahre**		
der Wald	**die Wälder**	das Stück	**die Stücke**		

Keep in mind: **a, o, u,** and **au** umlaut to **ä, ö, ü,** and **äu; aa** umlauts to **ä.**

POLYSYLLABICS
(nouns of more than one syllable)

MASCULINE AND NEUTER	FEMININE

1. add no ending to nouns that end in -el, -en, -er, -chen, -lein; some masculine nouns take umlaut

der Mantel	**die Mäntel**
der Wagen	**die Wagen**
der Lerher	**die Lehrer**
das Mädchen	**die Mädchen**
das Fräulein	**die Fräulein**

2. ending -e added to most other nouns; some masculine nouns also add umlaut

der Anzug (*suit*)	**die Anzüge**
der Versuch	**die Versuche**
der Vertrag	**die Verträge**
das Paket	**die Pakete**
das Problem	**die Probleme**
das Gefängnis (*prison*)	**die Gefängni**ss**e**
der Autobus	**die Autobu**ss**e**
short: der Bus	**die Bu**ss**e**

Note: Nouns with the ending -nis and -us double the s when a declensional ending is added.

add -n to nouns ending in -e, -el, -er; add -en to all others

die Familie	**die Familien**
die Stande	**die Stunden**
die Vokabel	**die Vokabeln**
die Schwester	**die Schwestern**
die Antwort	**die Antworten**
die Arbeit	**die Arbeiten**
die Nation	**die Nationen**
die Universität	**die Universitäten**
die Rechnung	**die Rechnungen**
die Studentin	**die Studentinnen**

Note: Feminine nouns with the ending -in have double n in the plural.

Mutter does not add a plural ending; it umlauts the stem vowel:
die Mutter   **die Mütter**

For masculine nouns adding -(e)n, see "Special Declensions" §5,1.
For foreign nouns that add the plural ending -s, §5, 3.

PRACTICE

5-2 The following nouns form the plural in accordance with the above guidelines. (The neuter monosyllabics listed here add the ending -er.) State the plural forms of these nouns and add umlaut where indicated.

MODELS:		
	der Freund	**die Freunde**
	das Glas (umlaut)	**die Gläser**
	der Koffer	**die Koffer**
	das Programm	**die Programme**
	die Straße	**die Straßen**

1. der Tag
2. der Schuh
3. der Kopf (umlaut)
4. der Film
5. der Saal (umlaut)
6. die Stadt (umlaut)
7. die Wand (*wall*) (umlaut)
8. das Haus (umlaut)
9. das Kleid
10. das Dorf (*village*) (umlaut)
11. der Mantel (umlaut)
12. der Löffel (*spoon*)
13. das Kapitel (*chapter*)
14. der Lehrer
15. der Reporter
16. der Ausländer
17. der Erfinder (*inventor*)
18. das Mädchen
19. das Märchen (*fairy tale*)
20. der Wagen
21. die Stunde
22. die Vase
23. die Chance
24. die Frage
25. die Freundin
26. die Reporterin
27. die Ausländerin
28. die Prüfung
29. die Sendung (*broadcast*)
30. die Erfindung
31. die Schwester
32. die Nummer
33. die Arbeit
34. die Religion
35. die Zigarette
36. die Serviette (*napkin*)
37. das Problem
38. das Experiment
39. das Paket
40. das Programm
41. das Kompliment
42. das Regal (*shelf*)
43. der Roman
44. der Anzug (umlaut)
45. das Rad (umlaut)
46. der Feind (*enemy*)
47. die Warnung
48. der Arbeiter (*worker*)
49. der Trainer (*coach*)
50. das Gefängnis
51. das Geheimnis (*secret*)
52. der Katalog
53. der Brief
54. der Faulenzer (*lazybones*)
55. die Faulenzerin

COMPOUND NOUNS IN THE PLURAL

The last element, which determines the gender of the compound noun, also determines its plural form. The other elements remain unchanged.

das Haus
die Frau   **die Hausfrau**   PLURAL: **die Hausfrauen**

der Motor
das Rad   **das Motorrad**   **die Motorräder**
              (*motorcycle*)

PRACTICE

5-3   Give the plurals of the following compound nouns.

1. der Geburtstag
2. die Mathematikprüfung
3. die Telefonnummer
4. der Fußballtrainer
5. das Sommerkleid
6. der Handschuh (glove)
7. das Weinglas
8. das Bücherregal
9. das Krankenhaus
10. die Semesterarbeit
11. der Konzertsaal
12. der Wintermantel

The Cases

§3 GENERAL PATTERN FOR DECLINING GERMAN NOUNS

There are four cases in German: nominative, accusative, dative, and genitive. The following paradigm shows a typical masculine, neuter, and feminine noun in all its singular and plural forms.

		MASCULINE		NEUTER		FEMININE	
SINGULAR	NOM.	der	Freund	das	Mädchen	die	Stadt
	ACC.	den	Freund	das	Mädchen	die	Stadt
	DAT.	dem	Freund(e)	dem	Mädchen	der	Stadt
	GEN.	des	Freundes	des	Mädchens	der	Stadt
PLURAL	NOM.	die	Freunde	die	Mädchen	die	Städte
	ACC.	die	Freunde	die	Mädchen	die	Strädte
	DAT.	den	Freunden	den	Mädchen	den	Städten
	GEN.	der	Freunde	der	Mädchen	der	Städte

Note: a. The nominative and accusative are identical in form except for the masculine singular, where the article is different.

b. The dative masculine and neuter of monosyllabics may add **-e** in the singular. In present-day German, however, it is generally omitted.

In some fixed expressions the dative **-e** is still retained: **nach (zu) Hause, auf dem Lande** (*in the country*), **im Jahre** (*in the year of*). In colloquial speech, however, the **-e** may be omitted.

c. The dative plural adds **-n** to all nouns unless the plural ends in **-n** or **-s**.

d. The genitive masculine and neuter may add **-es** or **-s**:
   -es is usually added to monosyllabics (des Buch**es**, des Tisch**es**).
   It is mandatory with all nouns that end in
   -s, -ß, -z, -x (des Glas**es**, Gruß**es**, Gesetz**es**, Reflex**es**).
   -s is added in all other instances.

e. Feminine nouns never take an ending in the singular.

PATTERN:	MASCULINE	NEUTER	FEMININE	PLURAL
NOM. ACC.	der — den —	das — das —	die — die —	die — die —
DAT. GEN.	dem — (e) des — (e)s	dem — (e) des — (e)s	der — der —	den — n der —

PRACTICE

5-4   Change the following nominatives to the cases indicated.

MODEL: a. der Hund   b. die Katze   c. das Auto
        gen. sing.   **des Hundes   der Katze   des Autos**

    1. a. der Koffer   b. die Schule   c. das Wetter
acc. sing. _____   _____   _____

    2. a. das Kind   b. die Frau   c. der Mann
dat. sing. _____   _____   _____

    3. a. die Häuser   b. die Leute   c. die Wagen
dat. pl. _____   _____   _____

    4. a. die Prüfung   b. das Mädchen   c. der Lehrer
gen. sing. _____   _____   _____

    5. a. die Freunde   b. die Freundinnen   c. die Mädchen
gen. pl. _____   _____   _____

§4   THE MAIN USES OF THE CASES

1. The nominative

a. The nominative is the case of the subject of the sentence.

> **Der Katalog** liegt auf meinem Schreibtisch.
> **Die Studentin** heißt Margot Bauer.
> **Das Mädchen** kennt mich vielleicht nicht.
> **Die Leute** glauben das nicht.

b. The nominative is the case of the predicate noun, also called *predicate nominative*. It is a noun that completes the meaning of the verbs **sein, werden, bleiben** (*to remain*), **heißen.**

> Die Feier ist **der Höhepunkt** ihres Lebens. *The celebration is the high point of her life.*
>
> Das wird **der Höhepunkt** seines Lebens.
> Das bleibt **der Höhepunkt** meines Lebens.
> Der Direktor heißt **Herr Bachmann**.

2. The accusative

The accusative is the case of the direct object of the verb. The direct object is the noun (or pronoun) that receives the direct action implied in the meaning of the verb.

> Bitte fragen Sie **den Chef!**
> Kennen Sie den **Musiklehrer**?

Do not confuse:

> Inge hat **den Katalog**. (direct object)
> Das ist **der Katalog**. (predicate nominative)

PRACTICE

5-5   Insert the appropriate form of each noun in parentheses.

1. Das ist _____ für Renate. (der Scheck, das Paket, die Zeitung)
2. Peter hat _____ für Renate. (der Scheck, das Packet, die Zeitung)

3. Herr Wolf ist _____ des Reporters. (der Freund)
4. Wissen Sie, wo _____ ist? (der Chef, die Chefin)
5. Fragen Sie doch _____ ! (der Chef, die Chefin)
6. Kennen Sie _____ ? (der Ausländer, die Ausländerin, die Ausländer, die Ausländerinnen)
7. Wollen Sie_____ kaufen? (die Kamera, der Kalender, das Bild, die Bilder)
8. Wann bringst du _____ in die Reinigung?[1] (das Kleid, die Kleider, der Anzug, die Anzüge)

3. The dative

a. The dative is the case of the indirect object: often the person to whom something is given or said, or for whom something is done.

> Bitte geben Sie **dem Chef die Post!** Please give the boss the mail.
>   INDIRECT   DIRECT
>   OBJ.   OBJ.

When both objects are nouns, the indirect object (often a person) normally precedes the direct object (usually a thing).

PRACTICE
5-6   Insert the appropriate forms in the direct and indirect objects.

1. Wer hat _____ _____ geschenkt?
        (die Reporterin) (die Kamera)
2. Wer hat _____ _____ erzählt?
        (der Reporter) (der Klatsch[2])
3. Wer hat _____ _____ erzählt?
        (die Kinder) (die Geschichte)
4. Haben Sie _____ _____ gezeigt?
        (die Polizistin) (der Führerschein[3])
5. Wer hat _____ _____ gegeben?
        (der Gepäckträger[4]) (das Trinkgeld[5])
6. Wer hat _____ _____ gegeben?
        (die Polizei) (der Tip[6])
7. Geben Sie doch _____ _____ !
        (der Mann) (die Chance)

---

[1] die Reinigung — *cleaning*
  in die Reinigung bringen — *to take to the cleaners*
[2] der Klatsch — *gossip*
[3] der Führerschein, -e — *driver's licence*
[4] der Gepäckträger, - — *porter*
[5] das Trinkgeld, -er — *tip, gratuity*
[6] der Tip, -s — *tip, hint, clue*

8. Haben Sie _____ _____ zum Bahnhof gezeigt?
        (die Ausländerin) (der Weg)
9. Können Sie _____ _____ erklären?
            (die Ausländer) (die Grammatik)

b.   Some verbs have only a dative object without an accusative object. These
      include:

antworten	*to answer*
danken	*to thank*
folgen	*to follow*
gefallen (gefällt),	*to please, like*
gefiel, gefallen	
gehören	*to belong to*
gratulieren	*to congratulate*
helfen (hilft),	*to help*
half, geholfen	
trauen	*to trust*
widersprechen (widerspricht),	*to contradict*
widersprach, widersprochen	

PRACTICE

5-7   Insert the dative forms of the nouns in parentheses.

1. Warum antworten Sie _____ nicht? (der Professor, die Dame)
2. Die Kamera gehört _____. (die Reporterin, der Reporter)
3. Matthias hat _____ nicht widersprochen. (der Dekan[1], die Chefin)
4. Bitte folgen Sie _____! (der Reiseleiter,[2] die Reiseleiterin)
5. Haben Sie schon _____ zum Geburtstag gratuliert? (die Assistentin,
        der Hausmeister[3])
6. Warum hilfst du _____ nicht? (die Kinder, die Leute)
7. Wir möchten_____ danken. (der Schauspieler,[4] die Schauspielerin,
        die Schauspieler, die Schauspielerinnen)
8. Warum traust du _____ nicht? (der Mann, die Männer, die Frau, Frauen)

Note the use of *gefallen*:

Der Protest gefällt dem Bürgermeister nicht.

lit: *The protest does not please the mayor.*

idiom.: *The mayor does not like the protest.*

---

[1] der Dekan,-e	*dean*
[2] der Reiseleiter, -	*male travel guide*
die Reiseleiterin, -nen	*female travel guide*
[3] der Hausmeister, -	*janitor*
[4] der Schauspieler,-	*actor*
die Schauspielerin, -nen	*actress*

In German the person or thing liked or disliked is the subject of the sentence. The person who does the liking or disliking is the dative object of the verb.

PRACTICE

5-8   Translate into English, then recall the German from your English translation.

1. Das Regenwetter gefällt den Fußballspielern nicht.
2. Die Werbesendungen[1] haben den Leuten nicht gefallen.
3. Das Hotel Continental hat den Ausländern gefallen.
4. Die Arbeit (*job*) hat Fräulein Neumann nicht gefallen.
5. Das Theaterstück[2] hat Martin gefallen.

Frequently the dative is in first position:

> Dem Bürgermeister hat der Protest nicht gefallen.
> *The mayor did not like the protest.*

PRACTICE

5-9   Translate into English, then recall the German from your English translation.

1. Den Kindern gefällt Disneyland.
2. Den Arbeitern gefällt der Direktor nicht.
3. Der Dame hat das Motel nicht gefallen.
4. Dem Chef hat der Reporter gefallen.
5. Den Fußballspielern hat der Trainer nicht gefallen.

4. The genitive

The genitive case is used in German to show the possessive relationship or the relationship of belonging together. In English it is expressed by *of* or *'s*, as seen in the following examples:

Das ist der Vorname **des Vaters**.	*That's the first name of **the father**.*
	or: *That's **the father's** first name.*
Das ist der Vorname **des Kindes**.	*That's the first name of **the child**.*
	or: *That's **the child's** first name.*
Das ist die Verantwortung **der Mutter**.	*That's the responsibility of **the mother**.*
	or: *That's **the mother's** responsibility.*
Das ist die Pflicht **der Eltern**.	*That's the duty of **the parents**.*
	or: *That's **the parents'** duty.*

Except with proper names (see below), German normally uses the word order resembling the English of-construction.

---

[1] **die Werbesendung,-en**   *commercial (radio, television)*
[2] **das Theaterstück,-e**   *stage play*

A. Insert the genitive of the nouns in parentheses.

MODEL: Das ist der Anfang _____ . (das Semester)
Das ist der Anfang des Semesters.

1. Das ist der Anfang _____ . (der Roman, die Geschichte)
2. Das ist das Ende _____ . (die Übung, die Übungen)
3. Das ist der Wagen _____ . (der Bürgermeister, die Journalistin)
4. Das ist der Name _____ . (die Musiklehrerin, der Hausmeister)
5. Das ist das Problem _____ . (der Lehrer, die Lehrer)
6. Das ist der Titel _____ . (das Buch, die Biographie)
7. Das ist die Telefonnummer _____ . (der Dekan)
8. Das ist der Mann _____ . (die Schauspielerin)
9. Das ist die Frau _____ . (der Schauspieler)
10. Das ist der Höhepunkt _____ . (das Konzert)

B. Express in German.

1. That's the janitor's daughter.
2. That's the lady's son.
3. That's the mayor's brother.
4. That's the dean's car.
5. That's the reporter's (female) telephone number.
6. That's the reporter's (male) name.
7. That's the beginning of the semester.
8. That's the end of the story.
9. That's the title of the novel.

In spoken German, **von** + dative is often used instead of the genitive:

Das ist der Wagen **von der Sekretärin.**

The use of the genitive with proper names:

Das ist **Barbaras** Hund.   *That's Barbara's dog.*
but: Das ist der Hund **des Hausmeisters.**   *That's the janitor's dog.*

The genitive -s is added to the name regardless of gender; it is not separated by an apostrophe. This form is commonly used with proper names, seldom with other nouns.

When the proper name ends in an **s**-sound (**-s, -ß, -z, -tz**), no **-s** is added to the name. The omission is indicated by an apostrophe:

Das ist **Thomas'** Wagen.

However, in these instances the construction with **von** is generally preferred:

Das ist der Wagen **von Thomas.**

Express in German.

1. a. That's Barbara's car.
    b. That's the janitor's car.

2. a. That's Dieter's telephone number.
    b. That's the dean's telephone number.
3. a. That's Renate's sister.
    b. That's the lady's sister.
4. a. That's Werner's friend.
    b. That's the mayor's friend.
5. a. That's Mathias' camera. (2 ways)
    b. That's the reporter's (female) camera.

§5 SPECIAL DECLENSIONS OF NOUNS

1. Some masculine nouns add **-(e)n** in all cases except in the nominative singular.
    They are usually referred to as weak nouns.

SINGULAR	NOM.	der Student	der Junge	der Herr
	ACC.	den Studenten	den Jungen	den Herrn
	DAT.	dem Studenten	dem Jungen	dem Herrn
	GEN.	des Studenten	des Jungen	des Herrn
PLURAL	NOM.	die Studenten	die Jungen	die Herren
	ACC.	die Studenten	die Jungen	die Herren
	DAT.	den Studenten	den Jungen	den Herren
	GEN.	der Studenten	der Jungen	der Herren

These nouns do not take the customary **-s** in the genitive singular. Note that **Herr**
adds **-n** in the singular and **-en** in the plural. When used with a name, **Herr** is
declined in accordance with its function in the sentence:

> Wo ist Herr Berger?
> Haben Sie Herr**n** Berger gesehen?

In this group are:

a. many nouns of foreign origin that are accented on the last syllable, such as
    **der Assistént, der Demokrát, der Komponíst, der Philosóph, der Polizíst,
    der Präsidént, der Studént, der Touríst;**
b. masculine noun that end in an unstressed **-e**, such as **der Junge, der
    Kunde** (*customer*), **der Löwe;**
c. a few monosyllabic nouns, such as **der Mensch, der Christ, der Held, der Herr.**

2. A very few masculine nouns, such as **der Buchstabe** (*letter*), **der Friede** (*peace*),
    der Gedanke (*thought*), **der Glaube** (*faith*), **der Name, der Wille,** have the end-
    ings of the weak noun declension and an additional **-s** in the genitive.

    One neuter noun, **das Herz**, adds the same endings except in the accusative singular.

SINGULAR	der Name	das Herz
	den Namen	das Herz
	dem Namen	dem Herzen
	des Namen**s**	des Herzen**s**

PLURAL	die	Namen	die	Herzen

die	Namen	die	Herzen
den	Namen	den	Herzen
der	Namen	der	Herzen

3. Nouns of foreign origin that form the plural by adding -s have ending -s in all cases of the plural.

		MASCULINE		NEUTER		FEMININE	
SINGULAR	NOM.	der	Scheck	das	Auto	die	Party
	ACC.	den	Scheck	das	Auto	die	Party
	DAT.	dem	Scheck	dem	Auto	der	Party
	GEN.	des	Schecks	des	Autos	der	Party
PLURAL	NOM.	die	Schecks	die	Autos	die	Partys
	ACC.	die	Schecks	die	Autos	die	Partys
	DAT.	den	Schecks	den	Autos	den	Partys
	GEN.	der	Schecks	der	Autos	der	Partys

Other common nouns of this group are: **das Baby — die Babys, der Chef — die Chefs, das Hobby — die Hobbys, das Hotel —- die Hotels, die Kamera — die Kameras, das Kino — die Kinos, das Restaurant — die Restaurants, der Tip — die Tips.**

Keep in mind: Only with these nouns may the declensional ending **-s** be a plural form: otherwise it signals the genitive singular case.

4.   Some nouns of foreign origin have special plurals.

SING.	NOM.	das	Thema[1]	das Drama	das Datum	das Museum	das Stipendium[2]
	ACC.	das	Thema				
	DAT.	dem	Thema				
	GEN.	des	Themas				
PL.	NOM.	die	Themen	die Dramen	die Daten	die Museen	die Stipendien
	ACC.	die	Themen				
	DAT.	die	Themen				
	GEN.	die	Themen				

PRACTICE

5-12   Insert the German equivalents.

1. In unserer Stadt haben wir _____ , _____
      two museums, ten movie theaters

   und viele _____ .
      restaurants

---

[1] **das Thema**   *topic, theme*
[2] **das Stipendium**   *stipend, scholarship*

2. Leider hat man _____ nicht erhöht.[1]
   (the scholarships)

3. Diese _____ interessieren mich nicht.
   (topics)

4. Ich habe _____ von Schiller gelesen.
   (two dramas)

5. Diese Statue ist ein Symbol _____ .
   (of peace)

6. Das ist eine Frage _____ , nicht des Verstandes.[2]
   (of the heart)

7. Leider habe ich seinen _____ vergessen.
   (name)

8. Kennen Sie _____ da drüben?
   (the gentlemen)

9. Ich kenne nur _____ .
   (Mr. Schreiber)

10. Zeigen Sie doch _____ Ihren Ausweis![3]
    (the policeman)

11. Mein Vater hat viele _____ .
    (hobbies)

12. Ich muß in diesem Monat _____ geben.
    (two parties)

13. Das ist das Privileg _____ .
    (of the president)

14. Haben Sie _____ gefragt?
    (the assistant)

15. Alle haben_____ gratuliert.
    (the hero)

16. Ich habe _____ bei den Hausaufgaben geholfen.
    (the boy)

17. Warum haben Sie _____ widersprochen?
    (the customer)

18. Wissen Sie _____ ?
    (the name of the customer)

19. Wer hat Ihnen diese _____ gegeben?
    (hints)

20. Ich vergesse Geburtstage und andere _____ sehr schnell.
    (dates)

21. Das kann man nicht beweisen[4], denn das ist eine Sache _____ .
    (of faith)

---

[1] erhöhen   *to raise*
[2] der Verstand   *eason, mind*
[3] der Ausweis, -e   *identification card*
[4] beweisen, bewies, bewiesen   *to prove*

§6   FOR REFERENCE: THE DECLENSION OF NOUNS

1. Most masculine nouns and all neuter nouns add **-s** or **-es** to the genitive singular.
2. A small group of masculine nouns add **-n** or **-en** in all forms except in the nominative singular. This is the *weak declension*.
3. All nouns add **-n** to the dative plural unless the nominative plural ends in **-n** or **-s**.
4. Feminine nouns never take an ending in the singular.
5. The last word of a compound noun is declined.
6. Similar to the principal parts of verbs, from which all tenses can be derived, there are principal parts of nouns from which all cases and be derived. They are:
   a. the nominative singular (the case in which all nouns are listed in vocabularies and dictionaries)
   b. the genitive singular
   c. the nominative plural

Good dictionaries list them in some form or other. Examples taken from one of them:

Film *m* (-[e]s/-e)	which means:		
	nominative sing.	der	**Film** *(m.* = masculine)
	genitive sing.		**Filmes** or **Films**
	nominative pl.		**Filme**
Student *m.* (-en/en)	which means:		
	nominative sing.	der	**Student**
	genitive sing.		**Studenten**
	nominative pl.		**Studenten**
Studentin *f.* (-/-nen)	which means:		
	nominative sing.	die	**Studentin** *(f* = feminine)
	genitive sing.		**Studentin**
	nominative pl.		**Studentinnen**
Drama *n.* (-s/Dramen)	which means:		
	nominative sing.	das	**Drama** *(n.* = neuter)
	genitive sing.		**Dramas**
	nominative pl.		**Dramen**

The principal parts of compound nouns that are not listed as such in a dictionary can be found by looking up the last element of the compound.

In this book, the nominative singular and plural of each noun are given, since the genitive singular for most nouns is predictable:
a. feminine nouns never add an ending,
b. masculine and neuter nouns add **-(e)s** with the exception of weak nouns, which add **-(e)n**. The latter are marked weak in this book.

The genitive is only stated in those rare instances when it has the weak ending plus **-s**, as in **der Name** (*weak; gen.* **-ns**), **-n**.

For the use of nouns with **der**-words and **ein**-words, see Chapter 6; with prepositions, see Chapter 7; in time expressions, see Chapter 11.

CHAPTER 6

der-Words and *ein*-Words; Personal Pronouns

der-Words

§1 FORMS

Compare the boldface words in the following sentences:

> **Der** Wagen gefällt mir nicht.
> **Dieser** Wagen gefällt mir nicht.

> Ich kaufe **den** Wagen.
> Ich kaufe **diesen** Wagen.

Dieser is one of several words that are called **"der-words"** because their declensional endings resemble those of the definite article. The most common **der**-words are listed below.

dieser	*this*
jener	*that*
jeder	*every*
mancher	*many a/*pl. *some, a few* (not: *many!*)
solcher	*such a/*pl. *such*
welcher	*which*
alle	*all*
beide	*both*

DECLENSION OF *der*-WORDS

Compare the declension of the definite article and the **der**-word **dieser**:

	MASCULINE	NEUTER	FEMININE	PLURAL
NOM.	der dieser	das dieses	die diese	die diese
ACC.	den diesen	das dieses	die diese	die diese
DAT.	dem diesem	dem diesem	der dieser	den diesen
GEN.	des dieses	des dieses	der dieser	der dieser

The boldface endings of the **der**-words are slightly different from the endings of the definite article.

PRACTICE

6-1   **A.** Restate the following sentences, substituting the German equivalents of the words in parentheses for the boldface definite articles.

1. **Der** Lehrer weiß das. *(this, every)*
2. Hoffentlich können Sie **die** Frage beantworten. *(every, this)*
3. **Das** Kompliment gefällt mir nicht. *(this)*
4. Er macht **der** Frau Komplimente. *(every)*
5. **Den** Unsinn¹ glaube ich nicht. *(this)*
6. Ich traue **dem** Hausmeister nicht. *(this)*
7. Rainer, **der** Faulenzer², will nicht arbeiten. *(this)*
8. Fragen Sie doch **die** Polizistin! (this)
9. Ich glaube, meine Antwort hat **der** Polizistin nicht gefallen. *(this)*
10. **Die** Studenten haben Probleme. *(some, such, all, both)*
11. Das sind die Probleme **der** Studenten. *(of these, of all)*
12. Das ist das Problem **der** Studentin. *(of this)*
13. Das ist das Problem **des** Studenten. *(of this)*
14. Das ist das Ende **der** Liebesgeschichte. *(of this)*

B. Insert the appropriate **der**-words.

1. _____ Lehrer weiß das nicht? *(which)*
2. _____ Frage können Sie nicht beantworten? *(which)*
3. _____ Unsinn glauben Sie nicht? *(which)*
4. _____ Mann trauen Sie nicht? *(which)*
5. _____ Studenten haben Probleme? *(which)*
6. _____ Plattenspieler³ gehört meiner Freundin. *(this)*
7. _____ Plattenspieler meinst du? *(which)*
8. Warum haben Sie _____ Warnung ignoriert? *(every)*
9. Er hat _____ Warnungen ignoriert. *(all)*
10. Das Picknick hat _____ Gästen gefallen. *(all)*
11. Ich habe _____ Reporterinnen nicht gekannt. *(both)*
12. Das ist der Höhepunkt _____ Romans. *(of this)*

---

¹ der Unsinn   *nonsense*
². der Faulenzer,-   *lazybones*
³ der Plattenspieler,-   *record player*

13. Kennen Sie den Erfinder[1] _____ Maschinen? (*of these*)
14. Das war der Höhepunkt im Leben _____ Erfinderin.[2] (*of this*)
15. Das ist das Ende _____ Übungen. (*of these*)

§2   THE USE *dieser* AND *jener*

> Zuerst müssen wir **dieses** und nicht **jenes** Problem besprechen.
> *First we have to discuss this problem, not that one.*

The **der**-words **dieser** and **jener** are sometimes used together to express a contrast, as in the example above. **Jener** is rarely used otherwise. When no contrast is expressed, **dieser** is used as the equivalent of both *this* and *that*.

Nobody can answer this/that question.	Niemand kann **diese** Frage beantworten.
Nobody knows these/those people.	Niemand kennt **diese** Leute.

§3   THE DEFINITE ARTICLE MEANING *this/these* OR *that/those*

In conversational German the definite article, when spoken with heavy stress, is often the equivalent of English *this/these* or *that/those*. In print the letters are sometimes spaced to indicate this stress. Compare:

Dieser Wagen ist mein Traum. Der Wagen ist mein Traum.	*This/That car is my dream.*
Diesen Wagen möchte ich haben. Den Wagen möchte ich haben.	*I'd like to have this/that car.*
Dieses Mädchen möchte ich kennenlernen. Das Mädchen möchte ich kennenlernen.	*I'd like to meet this/that girl.*
Diese Mädchen sind sehr nett. Die Mädchen sind sehr nett.	*These/Those girls are very nice.*

PRACTICE

6-2   Substitute the appropriate form of the definite article for **dies-**.

MODEL: **Diesem** Mann traue ich nicht.
Dem Mann traue ich nicht.

1. **Diesen** Erfinder kenne ich.
2. **Dieser** Plattenspieler gehört Erika.
3. **Diesen** Witz[3] verstehe ich nicht.
4. **Diese** Frage ist zu persönlich.
5. **Dieses** Problem müssen wir lösen.
6. **Diese** Probleme kann niemand lösen.

---

[1] **der Erfinder, -**   male inventor
[2] **die Erfinderin, -nen**   female inventor
[3] **der Witz, -e**   joke

§4   THE GERMAN EQUIVALENTS OF *this/that is* AND *these/those are*

Compare:

a. **Diese** Schallplatte ist großartig.   *This record is great.*

b. **Dies** ⟶ **ist** die beste Schallplatte.   *This* ⟶ *is the best record.*
   Das   *That*

c. **Dies** ⟶ **sind** die besten Schallplatten.   *These* ⟶ *are the best records.*
   Das   *Those*

In sentence a.   **diese** is a demonstrative adjective preceding the noun **Schallplatte.**
                  It is declined and its ending agrees with **Schallplatte.**

In sentence b.   **dies** does not take an ending since it does not precede the noun. It is
                  a demonstrative pronoun pointing out **Schallplatte.** In conversa-
                  tional German it is more common to use **das** than **dies.**

In sentence c.   the noun being pointed out, **Schallplatten,** is in the plural. In contrast
                  to the English use of the plural forms *these* and *those,* the German
                  dies and **das** do not change when pointing out a plural noun.

PRACTICE

6-3   Insert German equivalents. (Use **das** as demonstrative pronoun.)

   1. Ich glaube _____ Unsinn nicht. (*this*)
   2. _____ ist Unsinn. (*this*)
   3. _____ Sendungen[1] sind interessant. (*these*)
   4. _____ sind interessante Sendungen. (*these*)
   5. _____ Sachen gehören Margot. (*these*)
   6. _____ sind Margots Sachen. (*those*)
   7. _____ ist Dieters Kugelschreiber.[2] (*this*)
   8. _____ Kugelschreiber gehört Dieter. (*this*)
   9. _____ ist der Katalog der Firma Schönemann. (*this*)
  10. _____ Katalog ist neu. (*this*)

 ein-Words

The **ein**-words take the endings of the indefinite article **ein.** Including the indefinite
article, **ein**-words are **ein, kein,** and the possesives **mein, dein, sein, ihr, unser, euer,
ihr, Ihr.**

---

[1] **die Sendung, -en**   *broadcast (radio, television)*
[2] **der Kugelschreiber,-**   *ballpoint pen*

§5 Ein - kein

Compare the declension of **der** and **(k)ein:**

	MASCULINE		NEUTER		FEMININE	
NOM.	der Mann	(k)ein Mann	das Kind	(k)ein Kind	die Frau	(k)eine Frau
ACC.	den Mann	(k)einen Mann	das Kind	(k)ein Kind	die Frau	(k)eine Frau
DAT.	dem Mann	(k)einem Mann	dem Kind	(k)einem Kind	der Frau	(k)einer Frau
GEN.	des Mannes	(k)eines Mannes	des Kindes	(k)eines Kindes	der Frau	(k)einer Frau

PLURAL

NOM.	die/keine	Männer,	Frauen,	Kinder
ACC.	die/keine	Männer,	Frauen,	Kinder
DAT.	den/keinen	Männern,	Frauen,	Kindern
GEN.	der/keiner	Männer,	Frauen,	Kinder

Note: a. **Ein,** naturally, does not have a plural, but its negation **kein** does.

b. The **ein**-words have the same endings as the definite article with the exception of the three singular forms (boxed above) which take no ending:

nom. masc. **(k)ein Mann**   nom. neuter **(k)ein Kind**

acc. neuter   **(k)ein Kind**

PRACTICE

6-4   Insert German equivalents.

1. a. Ist das _____? (*a novel*)
    b. Sie schreibt _____ . (*a novel*)
    c. Ist das der Titel _____? (*of a novel*)
2. a. Das ist _____ . (*a hobby*)
    b. Haben Sie _____? (a *hobby*)
    c. Ich habe _____. (*no hobbies*)
3. a. Das ist _____ (*a love story*)
    b. Liest du _____? (*a love story*)
    c. Das ist das Ende _____ . (*of a love story*)
4. a. Das ist _____ . (*a success*[1])
    b. Leider hatten wir _____ . (*no sucess*)
5. a. Bitte fragen Sie _____ . (*a policeman*)
    b. Wo ist _____? (*a policeman*)
6. a. Geben Sie doch dem Mann _____! (*a chance*)
    b. Man hat uns _____ gegeben.(*no chance*)
7. a. Haben Sie _____ der Firma Bauer? (*a catalogue*)
    b. Hier ist _____ dieser Firma. (*a catalogue*)
8. a. Das ist _____ . (*a secret*[2])
    b. Ich habe _____ . (*no secrets*)

---

1 der Erfolg, -e   *success*
2 das Geheimnis, -se   *secret*

THE USE OF *kein*

When preceding a noun, **kein** may mean no, not a, not any.

Ich habe kein Auto. ⟨ *I have no car.*
I don't have a car.

Sie hat keine Geduld. ⟨ *She has no patience.*
She doesn't have any patience.

PRACTICE

6-5   Express in German.

1. I don't have a catalogue.
2. I don't have any money.
3. She doesn't have a ballpoint pen.
4. He doesn't have a career.[1]
5. The Neumanns don't have any enemies.[2]
6. She doesn't make any mistakes.
7. I am not a lazybones.

Nicht ein is used instead of **kein** when **ein** is emphasized (often having the meaning of **one**).

Ordinary stress:

Ich habe kein Wort verstanden.   *I did not understand a word.*

Ein emphasized:

Ich habe nicht **ein** Wort verstanden.   *I did not understand **one** word.*

PRACTICE

6-6   Express in German.

1. Not one child was sick.
2. Not one broadcast was interesting.
3. Not one student protested. (pres. perf.)
4. She didn't make one mistake. (pres. perf.)
5. He didn't say one word. (pres. perf.)

USES OF *manch ein, solch ein,* AND *welch ein*

a.   **manch ein** (*many a*)

The singular inflected forms of **mancher** mean many a. **Manch ein** is sometimes used instead. Note that **manch** remains uninflected and **ein** is inflected to agree with the noun that follows it.

Mancher
Manch ein } Vater hat zu wenig Zeit für seine Kinder.

Many a father has too little time for his children.

---

¹ **die Karriere, -n**   *career*
² **der Feind, -e**   *enemy*

$$\left.\begin{array}{l}\textbf{Manche}\\\textbf{Manch eine}\end{array}\right\}$$ Mutter hat zuviel Verantwortung.

Many a mother has too much responsibility.

b. **solch ein** (*such a*)

More common than the inflected singular forms of **solcher** is the use of **solch ein**. Even more prevalent in conversational German is the expression of **so ein** as the equivalent of *such a.*

$$\left.\begin{array}{l}\textbf{Solch ein}\\\textbf{So ein}\end{array}\right\}$$ Haus möchte ich haben.

I'd like to have such a house.

$$\left.\begin{array}{l}\textbf{Solch eine}\\\textbf{So eine}\end{array}\right\}$$ Mutter verstehe ich nicht.

I don't understand such (that kind of) a mother.

$$\left.\begin{array}{l}\textbf{Solch einen}\\\textbf{So einen}\end{array}\right\}$$ Film habe ich noch nie gesehen.

I have never seen such a film.

c. **welch ein** (*what a*)

Welch ein is used mainly in exclamations. It is often replaced by **was für ein**, particularly in conversational German.

$$\left.\begin{array}{l}\textbf{Welch ein}\\\textbf{Was für ein}\end{array}\right\}$$ Dummkopf!   *What a blockhead! What a dummy!*

$$\left.\begin{array}{l}\textbf{Welch eine}\\\textbf{Was für eine}\end{array}\right\}$$ Zeitverschwendung!   *What a waste of time!*

PRACTICE

6-7   **A.** Insert the appropriate German equivalents. Give both possibilities for each.

1. _____ Erfinder ist arm gestorben. (*many a*)
2. _____ Erfindung ist großartig. (*such a*)
3. _____ Überraschung![1] (*what a*)
4. _____ Tortur[2] ist grausam.[3] (*such a*)

B. Translate expressing *such a* by **so ein** and *what a* by **was für ein**.

1. a. What a mother!
    b. What a lawyer!
    c. What a compliment!
    d. What a torture!
2. Such a car is a status symbol.[4]
3. I would like to have such a car.
4. I hate such a waste of time.

---

[1] **die Überraschung, -en**   *surprise*
[2] **die Tortur, -en**   *torture*
[3] **grausam**   *cruel*
[4] **das Statussymbol, -e**   *status symbol*

THE USE OF *was für (ein)* IN QUESTIONS

Was für (ein) introducing a question has the meaning *of what kind of (a)*.

Was für ein Hund ist das?	*What kind of (a) dog is that?*
Was für einen Hund haben Sie?	*What kind of (a) dog do you have?*
Was für Musik gefällt Ihnen?	*What kind of music do you like?*
Was für Filme gefallen Ihnen?	*What kind of films do you like?*

PRACTICE

6-8   Insert the correct forms of **was für (ein)**.

1. _____ Wagen haben Sie?
2. _____ Kamera hast du gekauft?
3. _____ Haus wollt ihr bauen?
4. _____ Freunde hast du?
5. _____ Experimente haben Sie gemacht?

§6   THE POSSESSIVES

The possessives are

mein	*my*
dein	*your* (fam. sing.)
sein	*his, its*
ihr	*her, its*
unser	*our*
euer	*your* (fam. pl.)
ihr	*their*
Ihr	*your* (formal)

When preceding a noun the possessive takes the ending of **ein/kein**. This ending is determined by the gender, number (singular or plural), and case of the noun that follows it.

Das ist **mein** Vater.
Das ist **meine** Mutter.
Das sind **meine** Eltern.

THE NOMINATIVE CASE

	MASCULINE		NEUTER		FEMININE		PLURAL	
(*my*)	mein	Freund	mein	Auto	meine	Freundin	meine	Hobbys
(*your*)	dein	Freund	dein	Auto	deine	Freundin	deine	Hobbys
(*his*)	sein	Freund	sein	Auto	seine	Freundin	seine	Hobbys
(*her*)	ihr	Freund	ihr	Auto	ihre	Freundin	ihre	Hobbys
(*our*)	unser	Freund	unser	Auto	uns(e)re	Freundin	uns(e)re	Hobbys
(*your*)	euer	Freund	euer	Auto	eu(e)re	Freundin	eu(e)re	Hobbys
(*their*)	ihr	Freund	ihr	Auto	ihre	Freudin	ihre	Hobbys
(*your*)	Ihr	Freund	Ihr	Auto	Ihre	Freundin	Ihre	Hobbys

Note: a. **unser, euer:** -er is part of the stem, not a declensional ending.

b. **uns(e)re, eu(e)re:** The **e** before the **r** may be omitted when a declensional ending is added.

c. your
- **dein** (sing. fam.) — referrring to someone addressed as **du;**
- **euer** (plur. fam.) — referring to two or more addressed as **ihr;**
- **Ihr** (formal) — referring to one or more persons addressed as **Sie.**

d. **ihr:** may have the meaning of *her* and *their.*

ihr Hobby
- *her* hobby
- *their* hobby

The English meaning of **ihr** has to be derived from the context.

PRACTICE

6-9   Express in German, repeating the nouns for each possessive in items 1 to 6.

1. my father	2. my mother	3. my parents	4. my house
his	our	her	his
her	her	our	their
our	his	their	her
their	their	your (fam. sing., fam. pl. formal)	your (fam. sing., fam. pl. formal)

5. my brother and my sister
his   his
her   her

6. my son and my daughter
our   our
your   your (three forms)

7. his girlfriend   8. her boyfriend   9. our friends

10. your child (three forms)   11. their secret   12. her mistake

DECLENSION OF THE POSSESSIVES

As mentioned before, the possessives preceding nouns have the same case ending as **ein** and **kein.**

	MASCULINE	NEUTER	FEMININE	PLURAL
NOM.	mein	mein	meine	meine
ACC.	meinen	mein	meine	meine
DAT.	meinem	meinem	meiner	meinen
GEN.	meines	meines	meiner	meiner

Note the three forms without endings (boxed).

PRACTICE

6-10   Insert the German possessives.

1. Das ist _____ Wagen. (*my, his, her, your* [three forms])
2. Wollen Sie _____ Wagen kaufen? (*my, his, her, our, their*)
3. Haben Sie _____ Frage nicht verstanden? (*my, her, his*)

4. Dieses Fahrrad[1] gehört _____ Freund. (*my, her, your* [fam. sing., formal])
5. Schäfers sind _____ Nachbarn. (*my, our, their*)
6. Sind das _____ Sachen? (*your* [three forms])
7. Das ist _____ Führerschein. (*my, his, her*)
8. Das ist der Führerschein _____ Bruders. (*of my, of your* [fam. sing., formal])
9. Das ist der Anfang _____ Karriere. (*of my, of his, of her*)
10. Ich werde _____ Versprechen halten[2] (*my*)
11. Helga hat _____ Versprechen nicht gehalten. (her)
12. Haben Sie _____ Freund zum Geburtstag gratuliert? (*your*)
13. Hast du _____ Freundin einen Ring geschenkt? (*your*)
14. Fragen sie doch _____ Rechtsanwalt! (*your*)
15. Was ist _____ Hauptfach?[3] (*your* [fam. sing.]
16. Soziologie ist _____ Nebenfach.[4] (*his, her*)
17. _____ Deutsch (*neut.*) ist besser geworden. (*your* [fam. sing., formal])
18. Dieses Haus ist _____ Traum.[5] (*my, our*)
19. Du bist die Frau _____ Träume. (*of my, of his*)

THE GERMAN EQUIVALENT OF ENGLISH *its*

The German equivalent of *its* is **sein-** or **ihr-**:

    a. **der** Staat und **seine** Einwohner
      the state and its inhabitants
    b. **das** Dorf und **seine** Einwohner
      the village and its inhabitants
    c. **die** Stadt und **ihre** Einwohner
      the city and its inhabitants

In *a.* and *b.* the possessors (**Staat/Dorf**) are masculine and neuter; the possessive **sein-** is used. In *c.* the possessor (**Stadt**) is feminine; the possessive **ihr-** is used.

PRACTICE

6-11   Insert the German equivalent of **its**.

1. die Universität und _____ Professoren
2. das Krankenhaus und _____ Ärzte
3. der Klub und _____ Mitglieder [6]
4. die Maschine und _____ Erfinder
5. das Bild und _____ Rahmen[7]
6. die Eskapade und _____ Folgen[8]

---

[1] **das Fahrrad, ⸚er,**   *bicycle*
[2] **das Versprechen halten** *to keep the promise*
   (hält), hielt, gehalten
[3] **das Hauptfach, ⸚er**   *major*
[4] **das Nebenfach, ⸚er**   *minor*
[5] **der Traum, ⸚e**   *dream*
[6] **das Mitglied, -er**   *member*
[7] **der Rahmen,-**   *frame*
[8] **die Folge, -n**   *consequence*

Uses of the Articles

§7   USES OF THE DEFINITE ARTICLE

1. Most names of countries are neuter. They are used without an article except
    when preceded by an adjective.

Deutschland	**in Deutschland**	but: **das** alte Deutschland
Schweden	**in Schweden**	**das** liberale Schweden
Italien	**in Italien**	**das** schöne Italien

The names of feminine, masculine, and plural countries require the definite article.

a. **Feminines**

> die Schweiz
> die Tschechoslowakei
> die Türkei
> die Budesrepublik Deutschland (die BRD)

b. **Masculines**

> der Irak
> der Iran
> der Libanon

c. **Plurals**

> die Niederlande (*The Netherlands*)
> die Vereinigten Staaten von Amerika (die USA)

Note the use of the definite article with these countries:

> Wir fahren **in die Schweiz.**
> **in die Türkei.**
> **in die BRD.**
> **in die USA.**
> **in den Libanon.**

2. German normally uses the definite article rather than the possessive with parts of
    the body and articles of clothing where reference to the subject of the sentence
    may be assumed.

> Sie können den Nachtisch[1] mit **den** Fingern essen.
> *You can eat the dessert with **your** fingers.*
>
> Er hat immer **die** Hände in **den** Taschen.
> *He always has **his** hands in **his** pockets.*
>
> Ich verliere den Verstand.
> *I'm losing **my** mind.*

---

[1] **der Nachtisch, -e**   *dessert*

Sie hat **den** Kopf verloren.
*She has lost **her** head.*

3. In prepositional phrases with verbs of motion, the article is used in German but not in English:

in die Stadt gehen	*to go to town*
in die Schule gehen	*to go to school*
mit dem Auto fahren }	*to go by car*
mit dem Wagen fahren	
mit dem Bus fahren	*to go by bus*
mit der Bahn fahren }	*to go by train*
mit dem Zug fahren	
mit der U-Bahn[1] **fahren**	*to go by subway*

4. The article is used in English but not in German to express:

a. playing an instrument

Klavier spielen	*to play the piano*
Violine/Geige spielen	*to play the violin*
Trompete spielen	*to play the trumpet*

but: **ein** Musikinstrument spielen   *to play a musical instrument*

b. the German equivlaents of *the Wagners, at the Winkers'*, etc.

Wagners haben Gäste.	**The Wagners** have guests.
Wir waren **bei Winklers**.	We were **at the Winklers'**.

§8   USES OF THE INDEFINITE ARTICLE

Unlike English, German does not use the indefinite article after the verbs **sein**, **bleiben**, and **werden** when the following noun denotes a profession or social status.

Andreas ist Student.	Andreas is **a** student.
Karin ist Studentin.	Karin is **a** student.
Barbara wird Ärztin.	Barbara is going to be **a** doctor.
Herr Schmidt will nicht	Mr. Schmidt does not want to remain
Rechtsanwalt bleiben.	**a** lawyer.
Er ist Witwer.	Her is **a** widower.
Sie ist Witwe.	She is **a** widow.

However, the article is used when the noun is modified by an adjective:

Ich bin **ein fauler Student**.
Du wirst bestimmt **ein guter Arzt** werden.

---

[1] **die U-Bahn, -en** (*short for:* **die Untergrundbahn**) *subway*

PRACTICE

6-12   Translate into German

1. Are you a student? (formal, male, female)
2. Mrs. Bachmann is a widow.
3. Where do the Zimmermans live?
4. Their children go to school.
5. Do you play the violin? (fam. sing.)
6. I play the piano.
7. Are you going by car or by train? (fam. pl.)
8. The Schmidts are going by subway.
9. Is Mr. Schreiber a lawyer?
10. He is going to be a teacher.
11. Is Helga at the Bergers'?
12. We are going to Turkey and Lebanon.
13. Germany and Switzerland are neighbors.
14. I am losing my mind.
15. Have you lost your mind?
16. He has lost his had.

6-13   Summarizing Exercises

A.   Insert German equivalents.

1. a. X: Was ist _____ Hauptfach? (*your* [fam. sing.]
      Y: Psychologie ist _____ Hauptfach. (*my*)
   b. X: Hast du auch _____ Nebenfach? (*a*)
      Y: Nein, ich habe _____ Nebenfach. (*not a*)
2. a. X: Spielen Sie _____ Musikinstrument? (*a*)
      Y: Ich nicht, aber die Kinder _____ Nachbarin spielen
         _____ und _____ .(*of my, the piano, the trumpet*)
   b. X: Üben die Kinder viel?
      Y: Leider ja. Ich fürchte, ich verliere noch _____. (*my mind*)
3.   X: Hier ist _____ Paket für Andreas. (*a*)
      Y: Schon wieder für Andreas? Warum bekomme ich ____Pakete.(*no*)
4.   X: Was hast du Inge erzählt?
      Y: Nichts. Ich habe _____ Wort mit ihr gesprochen. (*not one*)
5.   X: Kann man _____ Mann trauen? (*this*)
      Y: Das weiß ich nicht. Ich weiß nur, daß man _____ Frau nicht
         trauen kann.(*his*)
6.   X: Wem gehört _____ Kugelschreiber? (*this*).
      Y: Ich glaube, er gehört _____ Freundin. (*my*)
7.   X: Warum ist Karin so deprimiert?
      Y: _____ Noten sind nicht besser geworden. (*her*)
8.   X: Herr Winkler hat mir _____ Kompliment gemacht. (*a*)
      Y: _____ Mann macht _____ Frau Komplimente. (*this, every*)
9.   X: Ich habe heute _____ Zigarette (*fem.*) geraucht. (*not one*)
      Y: Du bist der Held _____ Tages. (*of the*)

10.   X: Fahren Sie _____ zur Arbeit? (*by bus*)

Y: Nein. Meistens fahre ich _____. (*by subway*)

11.   X: Schenken Sie doch _____ Freundin _____ Diamantring! (your, this)

Y: Ausgeschlossen! ¹ Ich bin doch _____ Millionär. (no)

12.   X: Warum bist du so böse auf ² Andreas?

Y: Weil er _____ Versprechen nicht gehalten hat. (*his*)

13.   X: Wo werden Sie die Flitterwochen verbringen?³

Y: Das ist _____ Geheimnis. (*our*)

14.   X: Ich glaube, ich bekomme _____ Glatze.⁴ (*a*)

Y: Ach, das macht nichts.⁵ Du gefällst _____ Frau auch mit Glatze. (*your*)

B. Express in German, using **so ein** for *such a* and **was für ein** for *what a*.

1.   a. That's a surprise.
     b. That's no surprise.
     c. What a surprise!
2.   a. Is that a secret?
     b. That's no secret.
     c. I don't have any secrets.
     d. That's his secret.
3.   a. This suggestion is very good.
     b. Which suggestion do you mean? (formal)
     c. Do you have a suggestion?
     d. That's only a suggestion.
     e. What a suggestion!
4.   a. That's my record player.
     b. This record player belongs to my friend Dietmar.
     c. Helga, do you have a record player?
     d. Andreas has such a record player.
5.   a. Miss Winkler, do you have a driver's license?
     b. That's my driver's license.
     c. That's the driver's license of my girlfriend.
6.   a. Elke, is that your ring?
     b. Which ring do you mean?
7.   a. Are you my friend or my enemy? (formal)
     b. I am not your enemy.
     c. You don't have any enemies.
     d. What kind of friends do you have?

---

¹ **Ausgeschlossen!**   *That's out of the question!*
² **böse sein auf** (acc.)   *to be angry with*
³ **die Flitterwochen verbringen, verbrachte, verbracht**   *to spend the honeymoon*
⁴ **die Glatze, -n**   *bald head*
  eine Glatze bekommen, bekam, bekommen   *to go bald*
⁵ **Das macht nichts.**   *That doesn't matter.*

8. a. Mr. Bayer is the inventor of this machine.
   b. Do you know this inventor? (fam. plural)
   c. This machine is his invention.
   d. What an invention!

9. a. Is that a warning?
   b. Why do you ignore the warning of a friend? (fam. sing.)
   c. Why do you ignore the warnings of your friends?

10. a. That's a torture.
    b. What a torture!
    c. Such a torture is cruel.
    d. That's the end of this torture.

C. Using the cues, form sentences that fit the context.

MODEL: Barbara war im Sommer in Deutschland. Der Deutschprofessor
          sagt zu ihr:
              "Deutsch / besser / werden (pres. perf.)
              "Ihr Deutsch ist besser geworden."

1. Ich habe heute gute Laune. Warum?
   Noten / besser / werden (pres. perf.)

2. Ich brauche einen Koffer. Vielleicht bestelle ich ihn bei Schönemann.
   Ich frage Helga:
       "haben / Katalog / von Schönemann?"

3. Ich warte schon 20 Minuten auf den Bus und sage:
       "Zeitverschwendung!!"

4. Das ist nicht meine Schreibmaschine.
       Freundin / gehören

5. Martin war in Europa. Er hatte versprochen, mir zu schreiben. Ich habe
   keine Post von ihm bekommen. Ich sage:
       "Versprechen / nicht halten" (pres. perf.)

6. Mein Bruder hat Schulden. Trotzdem (*in spite of this*) hat er heute ein
   neues Motorrad gekauft. Ich sage:
       "du / Verstand / verlieren?" (pres. perf.)

7. Dieter macht Hannelore ein Kompliment. Sie lacht und sagt:
       "du / jede Frau / Komplimente"

8. Herr Köhler ist Direktor der Firma Krause geworden. Er sagt zu seiner
   Frau:
       "Höhepunkt / Karriere"

9. Mein Haar wird dünn. Ich denke:
       hoffentlich / Glatze / bekommen

10. Gestern haben Andreas und Brigitte Schluß gemacht (*broke up*).
    Brigitte sagt:
        "Ende / Liebesgeschichte"

Personal Pronouns

§9   THE CASES OF PERSONAL PRONOUNS AND THEIR USES

The personal pronouns are declined as follows:

	1ST PERS.	2ND PERS. FAM.	3RD PERS. MASC.	3RD PERS. FEM.	3RD PERS. NEUT.
SINGULAR NOM.	ich	du	er	sie	es
ACC.	mich	dich	ihn	sie	es
DAT.	mir	dir	ihm	ihr	ihm

	1ST PERS.	2ND PERS. FAM.	3RD PERS.	FORMAL SING + PL.
PLURAL NOM.	wir	ihr	sie	Sie
ACC.	uns	euch	sie	Sie
DAT.	uns	euch	ihnen	Ihnen

Note: All cases of the formal address **Sie** are capitalized. The forms are the same as those of the 3rd pers. pl. **sie** except for the capitalization.

The genitive forms, which are rare and occur only in literary German, are:

SINGULAR	meiner	deiner	seiner	ihrer seiner	
PLURAL	unser	euer	ihrer		Ihrer

Examples: Gedenke meiner!   *Think of me.*
(commonly: Denke an mich!)
Erbarme dich unser!   *Have mercy on us.*
(used in prayers)

PRACTICE

6-14   A. Insert the correct German equivalents in the accusative.

Frau Mensing haßt (*me, you* [fam. sing.]*, him, her, it.
us, you* [fam. pl.]*, them, you* [formal]

B. Insert the correct German equivalents in the dative.

Das gehört (*to me, to you* [fam. sing.]*, to him, to her, to it.
to us, to you* [fam. pl.] *to them, to you* [formal])

C. Insert the correct German equivalents in the accusative or dative.

1. Verstehst du (*me, us him, her, them*)?
2. Er hilft (*me, him, us, them, her*).

3. Ich beneide (*you*, [fam, sing., fam. pl., formal])
4. Ich danke (*you* [fam. sing., fam. pl., formal]).

D. Substitute pronouns for the boldface noun subjects and objects.

MODEL: Kennen Sie **Herrn Krause?**
         Kennen Sie ihn?

1. Liebst du **Helga?**
2. **Helga** liebt **Klaus.**
3. Ich kenne deine **Eltern.**
4. **Elke** bringt **Bergers** zum Flughafen.
5. **Herr Berger** hat **seinen Rechtsanwalt** angerufen.
6. Hast du **den Kindern** bei den Hausaufgaben geholfen?
7. Haben Sie **der Chefin** zum Geburtstag gratuliert?
8. Ich weiß nicht, ob ich **dem Hausmeister** trauen kann.
9. Haben Sie **der Reporterin** die Wahrheit gesagt?
10. Hast du **dem Taxifahrer** ein Trinkgeld gegeben?

PERSONAL PRONOUNS REFERRING TO INANIMATE OBJECTS

Since in German inanimate objects are masculine, feminine, or neuter (according to their grammatical gender, cf. Chap. 5, §1), they are referred to by masculine, feminine, or neuter personal pronouns.

Dieser Wagen	ist nicht zu teuer.	Vielleicht kaufe ich	**diesen Wagen.**
Er	ist nicht zu teuer.	Vielleicht kaufe ich	**ihn.**
It	*is not too expensive.*	*Maybe I'll buy*	*it.*

PRACTICE

6-15   Substitute pronouns for the boldface subjects and objects.

1. Ich verstehe **diese Frage** nicht.
2. **Dieser Fernseher** ist kaputt.
3. Können Sie **den Fernseher** reparieren?
4. Bitte bringen Sie **diesen Anzug** in die Reinigung!
5. Sind **die Hausaufgaben** immer so leicht?
6. Hast du **die Dias**[1] gesehen?
7. Haben Sie **die Notiz**[2] gefunden?
8. Wann haben Sie **das Paket** bekommen?
9. Hast du **den Brief** gelesen?

PRACTICE

6-16   Answer the following questions in the negative, substituting pronouns for the nouns.

MODEL: Hast du die Post abgeholt? **Nein, ich habe sie noch nicht[3] abgeholt.**

---

[1] das Dia, -s   *slide*
    short for: das Diapositiv, -e
[2] die Notiz, -en   *note, memo*
[3] noch nicht   *not yet*

1. Hast du den Scheck eingelöst?[1]
2. Haben Sie Ihre Eltern angerufen?
3. Haben Sie die Rechnung bezahlt?
4. Hast du den Koffer gepackt?
5. Hast du das Paket bekommen?
6. Hast du Hannelore gratuliert?
7. Haben Sie dem Hausmeister gedankt?
8. Hast du den Brief geschrieben?
9. Haben Sie die Hausaufgaben gemacht?
10. Hast du dein Zimmer aufgeräumt?
11. Hast du die Autoschlüssel gefunden?

A NOTE ON THE USE OF PERSONAL PRONOUNS REFERRING TO *das Mädchen* AND *das Fräulein*

The nouns **Mädchen** and **Fräulein** are neuter. Normally personal pronouns must be in the same gender as the nouns to which they refer; however, for these two nouns the feminine **sie** is often used instead.

> Das Mädchen da drüben wohnt im Studentenheim. **Es/Sie** ist sehr nett.
> Kennst du das Fräulein da drüben? **Es/Sie** sieht wie Dieters Schwester aus.

When the name is mentioned, the feminine form has to be used:

> Das Mädchen ⎫
> Das Fräulein ⎭ heißt Maria Schreiber. **Sie** studiert in Köln.

THE USE OF PERSONAL PRONOUNS WITH *gefallen*

	Dieser Anzug	gefällt	**meinem Vater**	sehr gut.
	Er	gefällt	**ihm**	sehr gut.
lit.	*It*	*pleases*	*him*	*very much.*
idiom.	*He*	*likes*	*it*	*very much*

As mentioned in Chapter 5, §4, the person or thing liked or disliked is the subject of the German sentence. The person who does the liking or disliking is the dative object of the verb.

PRACTICE

6-17   Express in German, following the models of sentences a.

1. a. My brother likes this record player very much.
      Dieser Plattenspieler gefällt meinem Bruder sehr gut.
   b. He likes it very much.
   c. I like it very much.
   d. We like it very much
   e. They like it very much.
2. a. My sister doesn't like this motorcycle.
      Dieses Motorrad gefällt meiner Schwester nicht.
   b. She doesn't like it.

---

[1] **den Scheck ein·lösen**   *to cash the check*

    c. I don't like it.
    d. He doesn't like it.
    e. They don't like it.
    f. We don't like it.

3. a. Marlene didn't like the reporter.
      Der Reporter hat Marlene nicht gefallen.
    b. She didn't like him.
    c. I didn't like him.
    d. You didn't like him, (fam. sing., formal)
    e. Why didn't you like him? (fam. sing., formal)
    f. Did you like him? (fam. plur.)

§10 POSITION OF PERSONAL PRONOUN OBJECTS

1. One personal pronoun object and one noun object

Compare the following three sentences:

a. Sie hat **meinem Bruder diesen Koffer** geschenkt. *She gave my brother the suitcase.*

             INDIRECT OBJECT   DIRECT OBJECT
           (dat./person)   (acc./thing)

b. Sie hat   **ihm**   **diesen Koffer** geschenkt. *She gave him this suitcase.*

c. Sie hat   **ihn**   **meinem Bruder** geschenkt. *She gave it **to** my brother.*

When there are two noun objects, the indirect object usually precedes the direct object, as in sentence a.

Personal pronoun objects precede noun objects regardless of which one is the direct or indirect object, as in sentences b and c.

In English the indirect object is preceded by *to* when it follows the direct object as in sentence c.

PRACTICE

6-18   Substitute personal pronouns for the boldface nouns and change the word order if necessary.

1. Frau Berger hat **ihrem Sohn** ein Paket geschickt.
2. Hast du deinem Freund **die Dias** gezeigt?
3. Ich habe dem Polizisten **meinen Ausweis**[1] gezeigt.
4. Der Polizist hat **dem Fahrer** einen Strafzettel gegeben.
5. Wer hat **deiner Freundin** diesen Witz erzählt?
6. Wer hat **den Kindern** das Märchen[2] vorgelesen?[3]
7. Ich habe **meinen Eltern** mein Ehrenwort gegeben.
8. Sie hat ihrem Freund **ihr neues Kleid** gezeigt.

---

[1] der Ausweis, -e   *identity card*
[2] das Märchen, -   *fairy tale*
[3] vor•lesen (liest vor), las vor, vorgelesen   *to read to*

9. Wer hat den Touristen **das Hotel** empfohlen?[1]
10. Bitte sagen Sie **der Reporterin** die Wahrheit!
11. Bitte gib der Sekretärin **diese Notiz**!
12. Bitte geben Sie **diesem Mann** eine Chance!

2. Two personal pronoun objects

When there are two personal pronoun objects, the accusative precedes the dative.

Barbara hat   Martin diesen Koffer   geschenkt.

Barbara hat   **ihn**   **ihm**   geschenkt.
Barbara gave   *it*   *to him.*

PRACTICE

6-19   Substitute personal pronouns for the boldface nouns.

Model: Hast du **Margot das Geld** zurückgegeben?
Hast du es ihr zurückgegeben?

1. Kannst du **Barbara diese Sache** erklären?
2. Hast du **Udo die Hausaufgaben** erklärt?
3. Bitte geben Sie **dem Gepäckträger das Trinkgeld**!
4. Bitte geben Sie **den Kindern dieses Märchenbuch**!
5. Ich habe **meiner Frau diesen Witz** erzählt.
6. Ich habe **Herrn Baumann das Gerücht**[2] erzählt.
7. Ich habe **Dieter meine Dias** gezeigt.
8. Wir haben **den Touristen dieses Hotel** empfohlen.
9. Ich habe **meiner Freundin das Geld** noch nicht zurückgegeben.

3. A personal pronoun object and a noun subject

Personal pronoun objects commonly precede noun subjects in sentences with inverted word order as in the following sentences *a.* and *b.* or dependent word order as in sentence *c.*

Inverted word order
Statement   a. Hoffentlich hat der Film meinem Freund gefallen.

Hoffentlich hat der Film   ihm   gefallen.

more common: Hoffentlich hat **ihm der Film** gefallen

Question   b. Hat der Film deiner Freundin gefallen?

Hat der Film   ihr   gefallen?

more common: Hat **ihr der Film** gefallen?

Dependent word order
c. Ich glaube nicht, daß der Film meinen Freunden gefallen hat.

Ich glaube nicht, daß der Film   ihnen   gefallen hat.

more common: Ich glaube nicht, daß **ihnen der Film** gefallen hat.

---

[1] **empfehlen (empfiehlt), empfahl, empfohlen**   *to recommend*
[2] **das Gerücht, -e**   *rumor*

PRACTICE
6-20

Replace the boldface noun objects with pronouns and change the word order accordingly.

MODEL: Leider hat der Ring **meiner Freundin** nicht gefallen.
Leider hat ihr der Ring nicht gefallen.

1. Leider hat der Koffer **meinem Freund** nicht gefallen.
2. Hoffentlich kann Udo **das Radio** reparieren.
3. Vielleicht hat Frau Krause **den Ausländer** nicht richtig verstanden.
4. Ich nehme an, daß Herr Zimmermann **die Rechnung** bezahlt hat.
5. Es ist möglich, daß meine Frau **den Anzug** in die Reinigung gebracht hat.
6. Hat Klaus **das Paket** schon aufgemacht?
7. Wie gefällt der Ring **deiner Freundin**?
8. Wann hat Monika **den Reisescheck** eingelöst?

PRACTICE
6-21

Summarizing exercises for §9 to §10

A. Express the answers in German, using the present perfect for the English simple past.

1. X: Wer hat dir diese Schallplatte geschenkt?
   Y: Renate gave it to me.
2. X: Wer hat Ihnen dieses Paket geschickt?
   Y: My parents sent it to me.
3. X: Wer hat dir diesen Witz erzählt?
   Y: You told it to me.
4. X: Hast du Frank dein neues Kleid gezeigt?
   Y: Yes, I showed it to him.
5. X: Haben Sie der Polizistin Ihren Führerschein gezeigt?
   Y: Of course, I showed it to her.
6. X: Haben Sie den Kindern dieses Märchen vorgelesen?
   Y: No, Annerose read it to them.
7. X Hast du die Notiz von Renate gelesen?
   Y: Yes, I read it.
8. X: Haben Sie meine Frage verstanden?
   Y: No, I didn't understand it.
9. X: Habt ihr das Problem schon gelöst?
   Y: No, we haven't solved it yet.
10. X: Hast du den Reisescheck schon eingelöst?
    Y: No, I haven't cashed it yet.
11. X: Hast du meinen Geburtstag vergessen?
    Y: Of course, I haven't forgotten it.
12. X: Ist mein Deutsch (*neuter*) besser geworden?
    Y: Of course, it has improved (= *become better*).
13. X: Wer hat Margot zum Flughafen gebracht?
    Y: Thomas and Elke took her to the airport.

14. X: Wer hat deine Eltern am Flughafen abgeholt?
    Y: My brother picked them up.
15. X: Wirst du die Sache sofort erledigen?
    Y: Yes, I am giving you my word of honor.
16. X: Wer hat den Vertrag unterschrieben?
    Y: My wife signed it.
17. X: Wie gefällt Ihnen diese Sendung?
    Y: I don't like it.
18. X: Wie hat Ihnen die Reporterin gefallen?
    Y: I didn't like her.
19. X: Wie gefällt dir mein neuer Anzug?
    Y: I like it very much.
20. X: Und wie gefalle ich dir?
    Y: You are the man of my dreams.

B. Form sentences that fir the context, using the present perfect except where otherwise indicated.

MODEL: Ich habe viele Dias von meiner Europareise.
          ich / Freunde / zeigen
          Ich habe sie meinen Freunden gezeigt.

1. Ich bin zu schnell gefahren.
   Polizist / Strafzettel / geben
2. Ich frage Inge, warum sie so lacht. Sie antwortet:
   Klaus / Witz / erzählen
3. Herr Krause wollte nicht glauben, daß ich 20 Jahre alt bin.
   ich / Ausweis / zeigen
4. Ich habe Rainer 200 Mark geliehen (lent). Er gibt mir das Geld bestimmt zurück.
   er / Ehrenwort / geben
5. Gestern waren die Hausaufgaben in Mathematik sehr kompliziert. Ich bin zu Margot gegangen, denn sie ist in Mathematik besser als ich.
   sie / Hausaufgaben in Mathematik / erklären
6. Ich habe Müllers zum Flughafen gebracht.
   sie / nicht / danken
7. Ich habe heute Geburtstag.
   Freundin / noch nicht / gratulieren
8. Frank zeigt mir seine neue Kamera. Ich sage:
   diese Kamera / gefallen (present tense)
9. Frank war gestern im Konzert. Er sagt:
   Konzer / nicht gefallen
10. Ich habe Margots Freund kennengelernt. Sie fragt mich:
    wie / mein Freund / gefallen? (present tense)

CHAPTER 7

Prepositions

Introduction

A preposition usually precedes a noun or pronoun, called its *object*. The preposition and its object constitute a phrase, called a *prepositional phrase*, e.g. **with a friend, for my friends, without them.** The use of prepositions is highly idiomatic. It is therefore imperative to pay close attention to these tricky words.

German prepositions are commonly divided into four groups:
prepositions that govern the dative case,
prepositions that govern the accusative case,
prepositions that govern the dative or accusative case,
prepositions that govern the genitive case.

In our treatment of these groups we shall consider only the most commonly used prepositions and their meanings. (For a fuller treatment of the use of prepositions in time expressions, see Chapter 11.)

§1 Prepositions that Govern the Dative Case

1. **aus**

   a. *out of* (expressing motion)

   > Sie kommt gerade **aus dem Haus.**
   > *She's just coming out of the house.*
   > Ich komme gerade **aus einer Vorlesung.**
   > *I'm just coming from a lecture.*

   b. *from* (being, coming from a place)

   > Schreibers kommen **aus Deutschland.**
   > *The Schreibers come from Germany.*

   c. *made of* (a certain material)

   > **Aus welchem Stoff** ist dieser Anzug?
   > *What material is this suit made of?*
   > Das Denkmal ist **aus Marmor.**
   > *The monument is made of marble.*

   d. expression: **aus diesem Grund** *for this/that reason*

   > **Aus diesem Grund** haben wir die Einladung nicht angenommen.
   > *For this/that reason we did not accept the invitation.*

2.   außer *except for, besides*

> **Außer meiner Schwester waren alle gekommen.**
> *Except for my sister everybody had come.*
> **Außer diesem Paket** habe ich noch einen Scheck bekommen.
> *Besides this parcel I also received a check.*

3.   bei

a.   *at, near*

> Wir haben das Auto **beim Postamt** geparkt. (*at/near the post office*)
> Das ist eine Stadt **bei Nürnberg.** (*near Nuremberg*)

b.   *at, with* (someone's home, business, or office)

> Er wohnt **bei seinen Eltern.** (*with his parents*)
> Ich war gestern **bei Schmidts.** (*at the Smiths'*)
> Sie arbeitet **bei der Firma Köhler.** (*at the Köhler company*)
> Andreas ist **beim Arzt.** (*at the doctor's*)
>   (bei dem)
> Inge hat die Handschuhe **bei Hertie** gekauft. (*at Hertie's*)

c.   *in* (when used in connection with the weather)

> **bei diesem Wetter**   *in this weather*
> **bei diesem Regen**   *in this rain*
> **bei dieser Kälte**   *in this cold*
> **bei dieser Hitze**   *in this heat*

4.   gegenüber *opposite, across from*

> Das Postamt ist **dem Bahnhof gegenüber.**
> or: Das Postamt ist **gegenüber dem Bahnhof.**
> *The post office is across from the railway station.*

Gegenüber may precede or follow a noun, but it must follow a pronoun.

> Herr Schmidt saß **mir gegenüber.**
> *Mr. Schmidt was sitting across from me.*

5.   mit

a. *with*

> Wir fliegen **mit Freunden** nach Europa. (*with friends*)
> Haben Sie **mit ihm** gesprochen? (*with him*)

Mit corresponds very closely to English *with*.

b. *by* (with means of transportation)

> Wir fahren **mit dem Wagen.**   *We are going by car.*
> **mit dem Bus.**   *by bus.*
> **mit dem Zug/mit der Bahn.**   *by train.*

Note the use of the definite article in German (cf. Chap. 6, §7, 3).

6. **nach**

a. *after* (in connection with time)

nach einer Stunde	*after an hour*
nach der Vorlesung	*after the lecture*
nach der Deutschstunde	*after German class*
nach dieser Stunde	*after this class*

b. *to* (with names of villages, towns, countries, islands, continents)

Wir fahren **nach Wien.**(*to Vienna*)
Wir fliegen **nach England.**(*to England*)
but: Wir fahren **in die Schweiz**. (*to Switzerland*)

Place names that are used with the definite article use the preposition **in** (cf. Chap. 6,§7,1)

expression: **nach Hause gehen** *to go home*

c. *according to*

Man kann nicht nur **nach dem Aussehen** urteilen.
One cannot judge by appearances only.

expression: **meiner Meinung nach**	*in my opinion*
seiner	*his*
ihrer	*her*

Note that the presposition in this expression normally follows the noun.

7. **seit** *since, for a period of time*

Käte schwäntzt **seit Montag.**	*Käte has skipped class since Monday.*
Klaus schwänzt **seit einer Woche.**	*Klaus has skipped class for a week.*

Note the use of the present tense in German and the present perfect in English to express a stretch of time that began in the past and continues into the present (cf. Chap. 2, §7, 3)

8. **von**

a. *from,* (indicating the starting point of some action or state of things)

Wir sind mit dem Wagen **von Hamburg nach Berlin** gefahren.
We drove from Hamburg nach Berlin.

Ich komme **von zu Hause.**
I am coming from home.

Dieser Brief kommt **von meinen Eltern.**
This letter is coming from my parents.

Das alles kommt **von meiner Vergeßlichkeit**.
All that comes from my forgetfulness.

b. *of,* (used figuratively)

Das ist sehr nett **von Ihnen.**
That is very nice of you.

Das war sehr dumm **von mir.**
That was very stupid of me.

used in phrases that substitute for the genitive case
(cf. Chap. 5, §4, 4). Compare:

Das ist die Adresse **eines Freundes.**
Das ist die Adresse **von einem Freund.**
That is the address of a freind.

c. by (author)

Das ist ein Roman **von Thomas Mann.**
Das ist eine Komposition **von Beethoven.**

9. **zu** *to*

a. direction, goal (cf. §6)

Ich gehe **zum Arzt.** *I am going to the doctor.*
        (zu dem)
Sie geht **zum Briefkasten.** *She's going to the mail box.*
Wir gehen **zur Bushaltestelle.** *We are going to the bus stop.*
        (zu der)

b. attitude

Er ist sehr nett **zu mir.** *He is very nice to me.*

c. idiomatic expressions

(keine) Lust haben zu *(not) to be in the mood to …*
                (not) to feel like …
Ich habe (keine) Lust **zur Arbeit.** *I am (not) in the mood to work.*
        (zu der)   *I (don't) feel like working.*
zu Fuß gehen *to go on foot, walk*
zu Hause *at home*

REMEMBER:

The following prepositions may be contracted with the definite article:

bei dem = **beim**   Ich war **beim Arzt.**
von dem = **vom**   Ich komme **vom Arzt.**
zu dem = **zum**   Ich gehe **zum Arzt.**
zu der = **zur**   Ich gehe **zur Bushaltestelle.**

A. Complete the following sentences with the German equivalents of the English words in parentheses.

1. _____ Sonntag habe ich Zahnschmerzen. (*since*)
2. Frank hat schon _____ Woche Zahnschmerzen. (*for a*)
3. Er geht heute _____ Zahnarzt. (*to the* [contract])
4. Ich war gestern _____ Zahnarzt. (*at the* [contract])
5. Gehst du _____ U-Bahn? [1] (*to the* [contract])
6. Ich fahre _____ Freundin. (*to my*)
7. Haben Sie _____ Dekan gesprochen? (*with the*)
8. Wohnt Margot noch _____ Großeltern? (*with her*)
9. Hast du den Anzug _____ Neckermann gekauft? (*at*)
10. Meine Mutter arbeitet _____ Firma in Frankfurt. (*at a*)
11. Kommen Sie _____ (*from home*)?
12. Das ist eine Oper _____ Verdi. (*by*)
13. _____ Freund Mathias haben alle getanzt. (*except for my*)
14. _____ Aktentasche [2] haben mir meine Eltern auch eine Brieftasche[3] geschenkt. (*besides a*)
15. Hast du Lust _____ Spaziergang?[4] (*for a*)
16. _____ Kälte gehe ich nicht gern spazieren. (*in this*)
17. Barbara ist nicht Amerikanerin. Sie kommt _____ Österreich. (*from*)
18. Diese Figur ist _____ Holz. (*made of*)
19. Wann fliegen Sie _____ München? (*to*)
20. _____ Deutschstunde gehe ich in die Sporthalle.[5] (*after the*)
21. Anita und Jörg kommen gerade _____ Sporthalle. (*out of the*)
22. Martins Eltern wohnen in einem Dorf _____ Heidelberg. (*near*)
23. _____ Augen, _____ Sinn.[6] (*out of the; out of the*)

B. Complete the sentences, using German equivalents of the prepositional phrases in parentheses.

1. Warum sprichst du nicht _____? (*with me, with him, with her, with your girlfriend*)
2. Dieses Paket ist _____. (*from my brother, from my sister, from my grandparents*)
3. Schmidts sind sehr freundlich _____. (*to me, to their neighbors*)
4. Das war sehr nett _____ .(*of you* [fam. sing., pl., formal])

---

[1] die U-Bahn, -en   *subway*
  short for: **die Untergrundbahn**
[2] **die Aktentasche, -n**   *briefcase*
[3] **die Brieftasche, -n**   *wallet*
[4] **der Spaziergang, ⸚e**   *walk*
[5] **die Sporthalle, -n**   *gymnasium*
[6] **der Sinn**   *sense, mind*
                      Here used in a German proverb which corresponds to English "Out of sight, out of mind."

5. Wir fliegen morgen _____. (*to England, to Switzerland*)
6. Ich habe _____ gesessen. (*across from him, across from her, across from them*)
7. Das Postamt ist _____ .(*across from the department store*[1])
8. _____ gehen wir nicht einkaufen.[2] (*in this rain*)
9. Sind diese Schuhe _____ ? (*made of leather*[3])
10. _____ war niemand zu Hause. (*except for the dog*)
11. _____ haben alle die Prüfung bestanden. (*except for him and her*)
12. _____ sind wir in die Disko gegangen. (*after the concert*)
13. Wir sind _____ gefahren. (*by train to Bremen*)
14. _____ habe ich Sie nicht angerufen. (*for this/that reason*)
15. _____ haben Sie einen großen Fehler gemacht. (*in my opinion*)
16. Wir können _____ in die Stadt gehen. (*on foot*)
17. Haben Sie den Mantel _____ gekauft? (*at Stern's*)
18. _____ ist es gefährlich[4] zu fliegen. (*in this weather*)
19. Hannelore ist _____ krank. (*since Wednesday*)
20. Ich lerne schon _____ Deutsch. (*for a year*)
21. Was machst du _____? (*after this class*[5])
22. Ich war den ganzen Sonntag _____. (*at home*)
23. Wollen Sie schon _____? (*go home*)

§2 Prepositions that Govern the Accusative Case

1. bis

a. *till, until, by* (time)

> Ich bin **bis Ende August** in Stuttgart.
> *I'll be in Stuttgart until the end of August.*

> Die Arbeit soll **bis nächste Woche** fertig sein.
> *The work is to be finished by next week.*

b. *as far as, to, up to* (location)

> Ich fahre nur **bis Köln.**
> *I'm only going to /as far as Cologne.*

> Ich habe den Roman **bis Seite 200** gelesen.
> *I read the novel up to page 200.*

Bis is frequently used with a numeral or a place name and then the accusative case of the object is not evident. When **bis** ocurrs with another preposition, the latter one determines the case of the noun:

> Wir haben **bis zur Kaffeepause** auf Sie gewartet.
> *We waited for you until coffee break.*

---

[1] **das Warenhaus, ̈er**   *department store*
[2] **einkaufen gehen**   *to go shopping*
[3] **das Leder**   *leather*
[4] **gefährlich**   *dangerous*
[5] **die Stunde, -n**   *class (instruction)*

Wir sind **bis zu einem** Dorf bei Stuttgart gefahren.
We went as far as a village near Stuttgart.

2. durch *through*

Wir sind **durch die Stadt** gelaufen.
We walked through the town.

Ich habe den Job **durch einen Freund** bekommen.
I got the job through a friend.

3. entlang *along*

Wir fuhren **die Straße entlang**.
We were driving along the street.

Entlang generally follows its noun object. Occasionally it precedes; it then governs the dative case:

Entlang der Straße standen viele Zuschauer.
Many onlookers were standing along the street.

4. für *for*

Hier ist ein Brief **für dich.**
Here is a letter for you.

5. gegen *against*

a. *denoting opposition, adversity*

Die ganze Welt ist **gegen mich.**
The whole world is against me.

Haben Sie etwas **gegen mich?**
Do you have something against me?

b. *denoting impact*

Ich bin **gegen einen Baum** gefahren.
I ran/crashed into a tree.

6. ohne *without*

Ich kann nicht **ohne dich** leben.
I can't live without you.

7. um *around*

Wir sind **um den See (herum)** gefahren.
We drove around the lake.

The adverb **herum** is frequently added.

The following prepositions may be contracted with **das:**

durch das	= **durchs**	Der Dieb ist **durchs Feld** gelaufen.
für das	= **fürs**	Diese Milch ist **fürs Baby.**
um das	= **ums**	Der Hund ist **ums Haus** gerrant.

7-2   **A.** Complete the following sentences.

1. Man macht viel Reklame[1] _____ Zigaretten. (*for these*)
2. Ich bin _____ Vorschlag. (*against this*)
3. Herr Helbig kann nicht _____ Briefmarken leben. (*without this*)
4. Wir sind _____ Marktplatz[2] gefahren. (*around the*)
5. Ich bin _____ Ende Juli in der Schweiz geblieben. (*until*)
6. Wir sind nur _____ München gefahren. (*as far as*)
7. Ich habe die Stelle _____ Dekan bekommen. (*through the*)

B. Complete the sentences with the German equivalents of the prepositional phrases in parentheses.

1. Warum sind alle _____? (*against me, against us, against him, against her*)
2. Sind Sie _____? (*for or against this suggestion*)
3. Das ist ein Geschenk _____. (*for my girlfriend, for my boyfriend, for him, for her, for you* [fam. sing., formal])
4. Wir haben einen Bummel[3] _____ gemacht. (*through the village* [contract])
5. Ich kann nicht _____ leben. (*without my husband, without my wife*)
6. Möchten Sie eine Reise _____ machen? (*around the world[4]*)
7. Wir sind _____ gelaufen. (*along the river[5]*)
8. Sind Sie wirklich _____ gefahren? (*into a tree*)

§3   PREPOSITIONS THAT GOVERN BOTH THE DATIVE AND THE ACCUSATIVE

Some prepositions govern the dative or accusative, depending on meaning. The following rules will help you determine the appropriate case.

a.   **Motion to a place: The preposition governs the accusative.**

Peter und Linda gehen **in den** Park.
(*into/to the*)

---

[1] die Reklame, -n	*advertising, advertisement*
Reklame machen	*to advertise*
[2] der Marktplatz, ¨e	*city square, marketplace*
[3] der Bummel, -	*stroll*
einen Bummel machen	*to go for or take a stroll*
[4] die Welt, -en	*world*
[5] der Fluß, ¨sse	*river*

Answers the question: **Wohin** gehen Peter und Linda?
or: **Wo** gehen Peter und Linda **hin**?

Wohin or **wo … hin** are used in the sense of **where to** … asking for the direction of a motion.

b. **Being in a place:** The preposition governs **the dative.**

Peter und Linda sind **im** Park.
(in dem)

Answers the question: **Wo** sind Peter und Linda? (*where/in what place?*)

c. **Motion at or within a place:** The preposition governs **the dative.**

Peter und Linda laufen **im Park** herum.
Peter and Linda are walking around in the park.
Sie gehen **im** Park spazieren.
They are taking a walk in the park.

Answers the questions: **Wo** laufen Peter und Linda herum?
Wo gehen sie spazieren?

REMEMBER:

> **Accusative:**
> motion to a place
> answering **wohin** (*where to*) questions
> **Dative:**
> being somewhere or motion within a place
> answering **wo** (*where/in* or *at what place*) questions

Complete the answers using the preposition **in** with the dative or accusative.

PRACTICE
7-3

1. X: Ist Werner in der Schule?
    Y: Nein, aber er geht jetzt _____. (*to school*)
2. X: Ist Inge in der Buchhandlung?
    Y: Nein, aber sie geht jetzt _____. (*to the bookstore*)
3. X: Warum gehst du so oft in die Bibliothek?
    Y: Ich arbeite doch _____. (*in the library*)
4. X: Gehst du jetzt in die Deutschstunde?

Y: Nein, aber ich war heute morgen _____. (*in the German class*)

5. X: Ist Professor Schiller jetzt in seinem Büro? (*neut.*)

Y: Nein, aber ich glaube, er geht jetzt _____. (*to his office*)

6. X: Sind Astrid und Dietmar in der Disko?

Y: Nein, aber ich glaube, die zwei wollen _____ gehen. (*to the disco*)

7. X: Was habt ihr in diesem Warenhaus gekauft?

Y: Nichts. Wir sind nur _____ herumgelaufen. (*in this department store*)

The following prepositions use the dative or the accusative case, depending on meaning. They are often called two-way prepositions.

ACCUSATIVE	DATIVE
wohin? (*where to?*)	**wo?** (*where? in* or *at what place?*)

1. **an**

   a. **an** *on* (verticle surface)

Ich hänge das Bild **an die** Wand.	Jetzt hängt das Bild **an der** Wand.
I am hanging the picture on the wall.	*Now the picture is hanging on the wall.*

   b. **an** (*to go*) *to* or (*to be*) *at* (something)

Ich gehe **ans** Fenster.	Jetzt stehe ich **am** Fenster.
(an das)	(an dem)
I am going to the window.	*Now I am standing at the window.*
Der Kellner kommt **an den** Tisch.	Jetzt steht er **am** Tisch.
The waiter is coming to the table.	*Now he is standing at the table.*
Ich gehe **an die** Straßenecke.	Jetzt stehe ich **an der** Straßenecke.
I am going to the street corner.	*Now I am standing at the street corner.*
Wir fahren **an den** Rhein.	Jetzt sind wir **am** Rhein.
We are going to the Rhine.	*Now we are at the Rhine.*

2. **auf**

   a. **auf** *on* (horizontal surface)

Ich stelle die Lampe **auf den** Tisch.	Die Lampe steht **auf dem** Tisch.
I am putting the lamp on the table.	*The lamp is standing on the table.*

   b. **auf** *to*, *in*, and *at*

Ich gehe **auf den** Fußballplatz.	Jetzt bin ich **auf dem** Fußballplatz.
I am going to the soccer field.	*Now I am on the soccer field.*
auf den Marktplatz.	**auf dem** Marktplatz.
to the city square.	*on the city square.*

auf den Bahnof.
to the railway station

auf dem Bahnof.
at/in the railway station.

aufs Postamt.
(auf das)
to the post office.

auf dem Postamt.
at/in the post office.

3. hinter *behind*

Ich habe den Mülleimer **hinter die** Garage gestellt.
I put the garbage can behind the garage.

Der Mülleimer steht **hinter der** Garage.

The garbage can is standing behind the garage.

4. in *in, into, to*

Wir gehen **ins** Auditorium.
(in das)
We are going to the auditorium.

Jetzt sind wir **im** Auditorium.

Now we are in the auditorium.

5. neben *next to, beside*

Ich habe die Schlüssel **neben die** Brille gelegt.
I laid the keys next to the glasses.

Die Schlüssel liegen **neben der** Brille.

The keys are lying next to the glasses.

6. über *above, over, across*

Heute sind viele Flugzeuge **über die** Stadt **geflogen**.
Today many planes flew over the city.

Jetzt kreist ein Flugzeug **über der** Stadt.

Now a plane is circling over the city.

7. unter *under*

Bitte stellen Sie den Papierkorb **unter den** Schreibtisch!
Please put the wastebasket under the desk.

Der Papierkorb steht **unter dem** Schreibtisch.
The wastebasket is standing under the desk.

8. vor *in front of, before*

Ich habe das Fahrrad **vor die** Tür gestellt.
I put the bicycle in front of the door

Das Fahrrad steht **vor der** Tür.

The bicylce is standing in front of the door.

9. zwischen *between*

Ich habe das Lesezeichen **zwischen** die Seiten 10 und 11 gelegt.
I put the bookmark between pages 10 and 11.

Das Lesezeichen liegt aber nicht mehr **zwischen den** Seiten 10 und 11.
But the bookmark isn't between pages 10 and 11 anymore.

Note that *parking, landing,* and *arriving* are done within an area. Thus two-way prepositions used with the verbs **parken, landen,** and **an•kommen** require the dative.

Ich habe den Wagen auf **dem** Marktplatz geparkt.
I parked the car on the town square.

Das Privatflugzeug kann nicht auf **diesem** Flugplatz landen.
The private plane cannot land on this airfield.

Wir sind um 10 Uhr in **der** Schweiz angekommen.
We arrived in Switzerland at 10 o'clock.

Contractions of two-way prepositions with the definite article:

DATIVE

an dem = **am**
in dem = **im**

ACCUSATIVE

an das = **ans**
auf das = **aufs**
in das = **ins**

PRACTICE

7-4   **A.** Insert the dative or accusative of the words in parentheses.

1. Helga hat den Wagen hinter _____ geparkt. (das Studentenheim)
2. Wir sind um 3 Uhr in _____ angekommen. (das Hotel Excelsior)
3. Mein Mantel liegt auf _____ . (das Bett)
4. Wer hat meinen Mantel auf _____ gelegt? (das Bett [contract])
5. Deine Brille liegt auf _____. (der Tisch)
6. Du hast deine Brille auf _____ gelegt. (der Tisch)
7. Frau Schubert hat mit uns an _____ gesessen. (der Tisch [contract])
8. Bitte stellen Sie den Sessel[1] in _____! (die Ecke)
9. Wer sitzt dort in _____? (die Ecke)
10. An _____ ist ein Zeitungsstand.[2] (die Ecke)
11. Mein Mantel hängt da drüben an _____. (der Haken[3] [contract])
12. Wollen Sie Ihre Jacke an _____ hängen? (der Haken)
13. Was liegt dort unter _____ ? (der Tisch)
14. Mein Serviette ist unter _____ gefallen. (der Tisch)
15. Das neue Restaurant ist zwischen _____ . (eine Bäckerei und eine Fleischerei)
16. Wir können hier nicht über _____ gehen. (die Straße)
17. Wir haben eine kleine Wohnung über _____. (eine Buchhandlung)
18. Siehst du nicht, daß deine Handschuhe auf _____ liegen? (der Boden[4])
19. Warum stehen so viele Studenten vor _____ ? (die Sporthalle)
20. Ich habe vor_____ gesessen. (er und seine Freundin)

---

[1] **der Sessel, -**   *armchair*
[2] **der Zeitungestand, ⸚e**   *newsstand*
[3] **der Haken, -**   *hook*
[4] **der Boden, ⸚**   *floor*

21.   Helga hat hinter _____ gestanden. (mein Freund und ich)
22.   Warum gehst du nicht an _____? (das Telefon¹ [contract])
23.   Marlene hängt die ganze Zeit an _____ . (das Telefon [contract])
24.   Ein Spatz in _____ ist besser als eine Taube auf _____*.
       (die Hand, das Dach)

  B.   Insert German equivalents of the English prepositional phrases in
       parentheses.

   1.   X: Warum hast du den Wagen nicht _____ gefahren?
         (*into the garage*)
         Y: _____ ist kein Platz mehr. (*in the garage*)
   2.   X: Was liegt da _____? (*under the table*)
         Y: Das ist eine Notiz. Sie ist _____ gefallen. (*under the table*)
   3.   X: Warum haben Sie den Sessel _____ gestellt? (*in this corner*)
         Y: Ich sitze gern _____. (*in this corner*)
   4. a. X: Wie heißt das Restaurant da _____? (*on the corner*)
         Y: Meinen Sie das Restaurant _____? (*next to the newsstand*)
       b. X: Nein. Ich meine das Restaurant _____. (*between the bank
          and the hotel Excelsior*)
         Y: Es heißt "Goldner Schwan". _____ ißt man sehr gut.²
         (*in this restaurant*)
   5.   X: Wo sitzt Helga?
         Y: Dort _____ Rainer. (*next to*) Siehst du sie nicht? Renate
         sitzt _____ (*in front of her*), und Barbara und Frank sitzen
         _____. (*behind her*)
   6.   X: Ist Klaus _____? (*on the soccer field*)
         Y: Nein. Er sitzt mit Renate da _____. (*at the table* [contract])
   7.   X: Bitte stellen Sie die Lampe _____! (*on the table*)
         Y: Sie steht doch schon _____. (*on the table*)
   8.   X: Warum legst du die Mappen³ _____? (*on the floor*)
         Y: Ich habe nicht genug Platz _____. (*on my desk*)
   9.   X: Wo ist deine Semesterarbeit?
         Y: _____. (*in this folder*)
  10.   X: Geht ihr _____ , oder wart ihr _____?
         (*to the movies* [contract]; *at the movies* [contract])
         Y: Wir waren _____ und gehen jetzt _____. (*in the
         dormitory* [contract]; *to the auditorium* [contract])
  11.   X: Wie lange willst du noch _____ bleiben? (*on the tennis
         court*)
         Y: Nicht mehr lange. Um 3 Uhr gehe ich _____. (*to the library*)

---

¹ **ans Telefon gehen**   *to go to or answer the phone*
² **Dort ißt man gut**   *idiomatic: The food is good there.*
³ **die Mappe, -n**   *folder*

*Proverb – literal: *"A sparrow in the hand is better than a dove on the roof."*
*idiomatic: *"A bird in the hand is worth two in the bnush."*

12.   X: Hängt dein Mantel _____ ? (*on the hook*[contract])
      Y: Nein: ich habe ihn _____ gelegt. (*on the bed* [contract])
13.   X: Rainer hängt schon wieder _____ . (*on the phone* [contract])
      Y: Du weißt doch, er hat die Telefonitis.

§4   PREPOSITIONS THAT GOVERN THE GENITIVE CASE

1.   anstatt, statt *instead of*

> **Anstatt des Wagens** hat er das Motorrad repariert.
> or: **Statt des Wagens ...**
> *Instead of the car he repaired the motorcycle.*

Nouns immediately following the preposition have no genitive ending:

> **Statt Fisch** haben wir Sauerkraut mit Bratwurst gegessen.
> *Instead of fish we ate sauerkraut with bratwurst (fried sausage)*

> **Statt Dieter** habe ich Frank eingeladen.
> *Instead of Dieter I invited Frank.*

2.   trotz *in spite of*

> **Trotz des Gewitters** sind wir in die Stadt gefahren.
> *In spite of the thunderstorm we went downtown.*

3.   während *during*

> **Während des Vortrags** habe ich die Zeitung gelesen.
> *During the address I read the newspaper.*

4.   wegen *because of*

> **Wegen meiner Eltern** haben wir die Reise verschoben.
> *Because of my parents we postponed the trip.*

In elevated speech, **wegen** sometimes follows the noun:

> **Meiner Eltern wegen** haben wir die Reise verschoben.

When used with pronouns, two forms are possible:

combination of genitive + **wegen**	**wegen** + dat.	
meinetwegen	wegen mir	*because of me, for my sake*
deinetwegen	wegen dir	*because of you, for your sake*
seinetwegen	wegen ihm	*because of him, for his sake*
ihretwegen	wegen ihr	*because of her, for her sake*
seinetwegen	wegen ihm	*because of it, for it's sake*
unsertwegen	wegen uns	*because of us, for our sake*
euretwegen	wegen euch	*because of you, for your sake*
ihretwegen	wegen ihnen	*because of them, for their sake*
Ihretwegen	wegen Ihnen	*because of you, for your sake*

Idiomatic expression:

> **meinetwegen** *for all I care, as far as I am concerned*
> Meinetwegen kannst du machen, was du willst.
> *For all I care, you can do what you want.*

Colloquially, the preceding prepositions that normally govern the genitive are often used with the dative:

> statt **dem** Wagen, während **dem** Vortrag, wegen **meinen** Eltern

5. The following prepositions are less frequently used:

diesseits (*on this side of*)	**diesseits**	
jenseits (*on the other side of*)	**jenseits**	der Grenze,[1] **des** Rheins
oberhalb (*above, upstream*)	**oberhalb**	
unterhalb (*below, downstream*)	**unterhalb**	der Stadt, **des** Mississippis
innerhalb (*inside of, within*)	**innerhalb**	
außerhalb (*outside of*)	**außerhalb**	der Stadt, **der** Bürostunden[2]

The preceding prepositions are often used with **von** + dative:

> **diesseits vom Rhein, innerhalb von** einem Jahr
> **außerhalb von** Fußballplatz

7-5   Supply the German equivalents

1. Dieses Dorf liegt _____ (*on this side of the border*), nicht _____ (*on the other side of the border.*)
2. Waldenweil liegt _____ (*above my hometown*[3]) und nicht _____ (*below my hometown*).
3. Ist der Unfall _____ (*within the office hours*) oder _____ (*outside the office hours*) passiert?
4. Dr. Kästners Praxis ist nicht im Stadtzentrum, sondern[4] etwas _____ (*outside of the town*).
5. Wir haben alles _____ (*within one hour*) erledigt.
6. _____ sind wir zu Hause geblieben. (*because of the weather*)
7. Ich bin _____ nicht mitgefahren. (*because of him* [two forms])
8. Er hat das nur _____ getan. (*because of her* [two forms])
9. _____ kann er mitkommen. (*as far as I'm concerned*)
10. _____ haben wir keinen Hund mehr. (*because of the neighbors*)
11. _____ mußten wir unseren Hund weggeben. (*because of them* [two forms])
12. Wo waren Sie _____? (*during the thunderstorm*)
13. Die Leute haben _____ viel geschrien[5]. (*during the soccer game*[6])

---

[1] die Grenze, -n	*border*
[2] die Bürostunde, -n	*office hour*
[3] die Heimatstadt, ¨e	*hometown*
[4] sondern but,	*rather*
[5] schreien, schrie, geschrie(e)n	*to scream*
[6] das Fußballspiel, -e	*soccer game*

14. _____ haben wir einen kleinen Spaziergang gemacht. (*in spite of the rain*)

15. _____ habe ich ihm eine Brieftasche geschenkt. (*instead of a briefcase*)

16. _____ hat sie Italienish gelernt.(*instead of Spanish*)

17. Der Kellner hat uns Tee _____ gebracht. (*instead of coffee*)

§5   SUMMARY OF COMMON PREPOSITIONS AND THEIR BASIC MEANINGS

DATIVE	ACCUSATIVE	DATIVE OR ACCUSATIVE	GENITIVE
aus *out of, from*	**bis** *until,*	**an** *on (vertically) by,*	**anstatt** ⎫ *instead*
außer *except,*	*to, as*	*at the edge of*	**statt** ⎭
besides	*far as*	**auf** *on (horizontally)*	**trotz** *in spite of*
bei *at, near,*	**durch** *through*	**hinter** *behind*	**während** *during*
at someone's	**entlang** *along*	**in** *in, into, to*	**wegen** *because of*
place	**für** *for*	**neben** *next to, beside*	**diesseits** *on this side of*
gegenüber	**gegen** *against*	**über** *above, over, across*	**jenseits** *on the other*
across from	**ohne** *without*	**unter** *under*	*side of*
mit *with, by*	**um** *around*	**vor** *in front of, before*	**oberhalb** *above*
nach *after, to*		**zwischen** *between*	**unterhalb** *below*
according to			**innerhalb** *inside of,*
seit *since*		Use the **accusative**	*within*
von *from, of, by*		when the verb denotes	**außerhalb** *outside of*
zu *to, toward*		**motion toward a place**	
		(answering the question	
		"where to?").	
		Use the **dative** when	
		the verb denotes either	
		position in a place or	
		motion within a place	
		(answering the questions	
		"where?" " in or at	
		what place".	

Common contractions of the preposition with the definite article:

preposition + das = **ans, aufs, durchs, fürs, ins, ums**
preposition + dem = **am, beim, im, vom, zum**
preposition + der = **zur**

Contractions are not used

a. when the article is stressed:

Wir gehen ins Kino. but: In **das** Kino gehen wir nicht wieder.
*We won't go to **that** moviehouse again.*

b. when the noun is modified:

> Wir gehen in das Kino da drüben. *We are going to the little moviehouse over there.*

§6   THE GERMAN COUNTERPARTS OF *to* WITH VERBS OF MOTION.

Various German prepositions correspond to English *to* with verbs of motion.

1. *to* = **nach**

This is the normal preposition used with names of towns, cities, regions, countries, or continents. It is not used when the name is accompanied by the article.

> Wir fahren **nach Bettendorf.**
> **nach Frankfurt.**
> **nach England.**
> **nach Europa.**
> but: Wir fahren **in die Schweiz.**
> **in die Vereinigten Staaten.**

2. *to* = **zu**

This is the most generally acceptable word, and the only one possible if the object is a person.

a. Going to a person's home or business:

> Ich gehe **zum Arzt.**
> Er fährt **zu seiner Schwester.**
> Wir gehen **zu Neumanns.**

b. Used with names of stores:

> Wir gehen **zu Hertie.**

c. Going to places other than cities, regions, countries:

> Sie geht **zum Briefkasten.**
> Ich gehe **zur Bushaltestelle.**
> Wir fahren **zum Flughafen.**

3. In many instances **in, auf,** or **an** with the accusative either may or must be used. This is especially true for public buildings and events in them.

a. *to* = **in** meaning *into a place, into a building*:

> Wir gehen **in die Stadt.**   We are going *to town, downtown, uptown.*
> **in die Vorlesung.**   *to the lecture.*
> **in die Deutschstunde.**   *to the German class.*
> **ins Kino.**   *to the movies.*
> **ins Konzert.**   *to the concert.*
> **ins Theater.**   *to the theater.*

b. *to* = **auf** meaning *onto a surface, base of operation:*

Wir gehen **auf den Fußballplatz.**	*We are going to the football field.*
auf den Tennizplatz.	*to the tennis court.*
auf den Marktplatz.	*to the town square.*

idiomatic:

Wir gehen **auf die Bank.**	*We are going to the bank.*
or: **zur Bank.**	
Wir gehen **aufs Postamt.**	*to the post office.*
or: **zum Postamt.**	
Wir gehen **auf den Bahnhof.**	*to the railway station.*
or: **zum Bahnhof.**	
Wir gehen **auf eine Party.**	*to a party.*
or: **zu einer Party.**	

c. *to* = **an** *meaning up to, to the edge of*:

Ich gehe **ans Fenster.**	*I am going to the window.*
an den Tisch.	*to the table.*
an die Tafel.	*to the blackboard.*
an die Wandtafel.	

PRACTICE

7-6   Insert German equivalents.

1. Gehst du heute _____ Vorlesung?
         (to the)
2. Sie fährt _____ Freundin.
      (to her)
3. Er ging _____ Fenster.
        (to the)
4. Wollen Sie _____ Bergmanns gehen?
         (to)
5. Bitte gehen Sie _____ Tafel!
          (to the)
6. Gehen Sie heute _____ Bank? (two ways)
          (to the)
7. Wann fahren Sie _____ Heidelberg?
         (to)
8. Der Kellner kam _____ Tisch.
          (to our)
9. Gehen Sie _____ Briefkasten?
        (to the)
10. Am Wochenende fahre ich _____ Freundin.
              (to my)
11. Wollen Sie _____ Postamt gehen? (two ways)
         (to the)

12. Käte fährt _____ Flughafen (*masc.*)
        (*to the*)

13. Gehst du _____ Party bei Schneiders? (two ways)
        (*to the*)

14. Vielleicht gehen wir heute abend _____ Theater.
                      (*to the*)

15. Wir bringen dich _____ Bushaltestelle.
        (*to the*)

PRACTICE

7-7   Summarizing exercises.

A. Insert German equivalents.

1. X: Ist Maria _____ gefahren? (*home*)
   Y: Ja. Sie ist wahrscheinlich schon _____ . (*at home*)

2. X: Wohnst du _____ ? (*with your parents*)
   Y: Meine Eltern sind geschieden.[1] Ich wohne _____ , und meine
      Schwester wohnt _____ . (*with my father, with my mother*)

3. X: Warst du gestern _____ ? (*at the Bergers'*)
   Y: Ja. Ich gehe oft _____ . (*to the Bergers*) Sie sind immer sehr nett
      _____ . (*to me*)

4. X: Wer hat deinen Koffer _____ getragen? (*to the bus stop*)
   Y: Peter. Das war sehr nett _____. (*of him*)

5. X: Hast du diese Brieftasche _____ bekommen? (*from your girlfriend*)
   Y: Nein. Das ist ein Geschenk _____ . (*from my parents*)

6. X: Hast du diesen Roman _____ gelesen. (*by him*)

7. X: Die ganze Stadt war _____ . (*on the soccer field*)
   Y: Die ganze Stadt _____ . (*except me*)

8. X: Bist du _____ mitgekommen? (*because of your girlfriend.*)
   Y: Ja, nur _____ . (*because of her* [two forms])

9. X: Hast du Karin _____ kennengelernt? (*through your brother*)
   Y: Nein, ich habe sie _____ kennengelernt. (*through a friend*
      [*masc.., fem.*])

10. X: Wann gehst du _____? (*to the dentist*)
    Y: Ich war doch schon _____ . (*at the dentist's*)

11. X: Wohnen Adreas und Frank auch _____? (*in this dormitory*)
    Y: Ja. Andreas wohnt _____ , und Frank wohnt _____ . (*above
       me, below me*)

12. X: Seid ihr _____ gefahren? (*to Düsseldorf*)
    Y: Nein. Wir sind nur _____ gefahren. (*as far as Bonn*)

13. X: Was hast du _____? (*against my friend* [*masc.*])
    Y: Ich habe nichts _____ . (*against him*)

14. X: Was habt ihr _____ gekauft? (*in the town*)
    Y: Nichts. Wir haben nur einen Bummel _____ gemacht. (*through
       the town*)

15. X: Wollen Sie allein _____ fliegen? (*to Alaska*)

---

[1] **geschieden sein**   *to be divorced*

Y: Natürlich nicht. Ich fliege _____ . (*with my wife but perhaps without our son*)

16.　X: Margot studiert schon _____ in Bonn. (*for a year*)

Y: Ja. Leider schreibt sie mir nicht mehr _____ . (*"Out of sight, out of mind."*)

17.　X: Ich verstehe nicht, warum Müllers den Vertrag so schnell unter-schrieben haben.

Y: Vielleicht haben sie gedacht:

_____

(*"A bird in the hand is worth two in the bush."*)

18.　X: _____ gehen wir nicht spazieren. (*in this weather*)

Y: Und wir sind _____ spazierengegangen. (*in spite of the weather*)

19.　X: _____ bin ich ein Dummkopf. (*in his opinion*)

Y: Und _____ bist du ein Schlaukopf.[1] (*in my opinion*)

20.　a. X: Ihr Mann hat eine wunderbare Briefmarkensammlung.

Y: Das stimmt.[2] Er kann nicht _____ leben. (*without his stamp collection*)

　　b. X: Sagen wir,[3] er kann nicht _____ leben. (*with you and his stamp collection*)

Y: Hoffentlich in dieser Reihenfolge![4]

B.　Using the cues, form sentences that fit the context. Express them in the present tense except where otherwise indicated.

MODEL:　Karin fliegt heute nachmittag nach Berlin.
Martin/bringen/Flughafen
Martin bringt sie zum Flughafen.

1.　Werner Seifert wohnt nicht im Studentenheim.
er / wohnen / Eltern

2.　Ich sehe zuviel fern.
ich / können / leben / nicht / ohne Fernseher

3.　Ich habe lange meine Semersterarbeit gesucht. Endlich (finally) habe ich sie gefunden.
sie / sein / Mappe / Schreibtisch (past)

4.　Mein Bruder hat morgen Geburtstag.
heute nachmittag / ich / fahren / Stadt / /
ich / wollen / kaufen / Geschenk / für / Bruder

5.　Ich bin müde und gähne die ganze Zeit.
gestern abend / ich / sein / Party (past) / /
heute abend / ich / gehen / wieder / Party

---

[1] **der Schlaukopf, -** (male or female)　　*whizz kid, smarty*
[2] **stimmen**　　*to be correct*
[3] **Sagen wir...**　　*Let's say...*
[4] **die Rehenfolge, -n**　　*order, sequence*

6.   Unsere Nachbarn sind reich.
                sie / machen / Reise / um Welt
7.   a. Ich frage Klaus, wo Maria ist. Er antwortet:
                „vielleicht / sie / sein/Tennisplatz"
     b. Dann sagt er:
                „Das stimmt nicht. sie/gehen/mit/Freund/Fußballplatz"
                (pres. perf.)
8.   a. Ich frage Sabine, wo sie gestern abend war. Sie antwortet:
                „ich / sein / mit / Freund Andreas / Konzert" (past)
     b. Ich frage sie, wie ihr das Konzert gefallen hat. Sie antwortet:
                „Meinung nach / das Konzert / sein / nicht sehr gut" (past)

8

Verbs and Adjectives Used with Prepositions; *da*-Compounds; Interrogatives *wer* and *was; wo-* Compounds

 ## Verbs and Adjectives Used with Prepositions

§1 VERBS USED WITH PREPOSITIONS

Many verbs complete their meanings with prepositional phrases. Some common ones are listed below.

1. Verbs with dative prepositions

gratulieren **zu**	*to congratulate on*
handeln **von**	*to deal with, be about*
sprechen **mit**	*to talk with or to*
(spricht), sprach, gesprochen	
sprechen **von**	*to talk of or about*

2. Verbs with accusative prepositions

bitten **um,**	*to ask for, to request*
bat, gebeten	
danken **für**	*to thank for*

3. Verbs with two-way prepositions

antworten **auf** + *acc.*	*to answer something*
arbeiten **an** + *dat.*	*to work on*
denken **an** + *acc.*	*to think of or about*
lachen **über** + *acc.*	*to laugh at or about*
reagieren **auf** + *acc.*	*to react to*
warten **auf** + *acc.*	*to wait for*

Note that in these combinations the rules governing the use of the dative and the accusative with two-way prepositions do not apply, and the case for each must be learned individually. Most such constructions use the accusative.

PRACTICE

8-1   **A.** Change the boldface prepositional phrases, using the dative or accusative of the words in parentheses.

MODEL: Hast du ihm **zum Geburstag** gratuliert? (sein Erfolg)
Hast du ihm zu seinem Erfolg gratuliert?

1. Er hat noch nicht **auf meinen Brief** geantwortet. (meine Frage)
2. Arbeitest du noch **an deinem Referat?**[1] (der Aufsatz)
3. Haben Sie **mit der Chefin** gesprochen? (der Chef)
4. Eva hat nie **von ihrem Vater** gesprochen. (ihre Zukunftspläne[2])
5. Ich habe gerade **an meine Freundin** gedacht. (mein Freund)
6. Ich habe ihm noch nicht **für seinen Brief** gedankt. (sein Paket)
7. Der film handelt von **der Französischen Revolution.** (ein Erfinder)
8. Ich habe den Chef **um Erlaubnis** gebeten. (eine Gehaltserhöhung[3])
9. Klaus hat nicht **über meinen Witz** gelacht. (sein Bruder)
10. Ich habe ihnen **zur Verlobung**[4] gratuliert. (die Hochzeit)
11. Wartest du **auf deine Freundin?** (der Bus)
12. Wie hat der Dekan **auf Ihren Brief** reagiert? (der Protest)

B. Express the responses in German. (Use the pres. perf. for the English past tense.)

MODEL: Denkst du oft an deinen Freund in Berlin?
I think of him very often.
Ich denke sehr oft an ihn.

1. X: Arbeiten Sie noch an diesem Projekt?
Y: No, I'm working on a seminar paper.
2. X: Hast du schon mit Herrn Köhler gesprochen?
Y: I talked with his wife but not with him.
3. X: Haben Sie den Chef um Erlaubnis gebeten?
Y: Of course I asked him for permission.
4. X: Hast du Herrn Baumann für seine Hilfe gedankt?
Y: Not yet, but I thanked Mrs. Baumann for her help.
5. X: Wie hat Frau Klinger auf Ihren Vorschlag reagiert?
Y: Unfortunately she has not yet reacted to my suggestion.
6. X: Handelt dieser Roman vom Krieg?
Y: No, it deals with a family in Alaska.

---

[1] **das Referat, -e**   *seminar paper (oral presentation)*
[2] **der Zukunftsplan, ⁻e**   *plan for the future*
[3] **die Gehaltserhöhung, -en** *salary raise*
[4] **die Verlobung, -en**   *engagement*

7. X: Warum antwortest du nicht auf meine Frage?
   Y: Because you have not yet answered my question.
8. X: Hast du meiner Freundin zu ihrem Erfolg gratuliert?
   Y: Not yet, but I congratulated her brother on his success.
9. X: Wartest du auf Post von zu Hause?
   Y: I'm waiting for a letter with a check from home.
10. X: Du hörst nicht zu. Denkst du schon wieder an das Fußballspiel?
    Y: No, I'm thinking of my girlfriend.
11. X: Warum lachst du über mich?
    Y: I'm not laughing at you. I'm laughing at a joke.
    X: Und dieser Witz bin ich?
    Y: Of course not, my darling.[1]

§2   ADJECTIVES USED WITH PREPOSITIONS

The following frequently used adjectives complete their meanings with prepositional phrases:

begeistert sein **von** + *dat.*	*to be enthusiastic about*
böse sein **auf** + *acc.*	*to be angry with*
or: **mit** + *dat.*	
froh sein **über** + *acc.*	*to be glad about*
glücklich sein **über** + *acc.*	*to be happy about*
stolz sein **auf** + *acc.*	*to be proud of*
verliebt sein **in** + *acc.*	*to be in love with*
verlobt sein **mit** + *dat.*	*to be engaged to*
verheiratet sein **mit** + *dat*	*to be married to*
verrückt sein **auf** + *acc.*	*to be crazy about*
verwandt sein **mit** + *dat.*	*to be related to*
zufrieden sein **mit** + *dat.*	*to be satisfied, content with*

Example:

Ich bin **von diesem Film** begeistert.
or: Ich bin begeistert **von diesem Film.**
> *I am enthusiastic about this film.*

Begeistert functions as a predicate adjective (following the verb **sein**; cf. Chap. 1, §7). Predicate adjectives may precede or follow prepositional phrases.

PRACTICE

8-2   Express the responses in German.

1 X: Alle sind verrückt auf diesen Popstar.
   Y: I'm not crazy about him.
2. X: Sind Sie froh über diese Nachricht?[2]
   Y: Of course, I'm glad about this news.

---

[1] **der Liebling, -e**   *darling*
   (the same form used for male and female)
[2] **die Nachricht, -en**   *news*

3. X: Sind Sie mit dieser Dame verwandt?
   Y: Yes, I'm related to her. She's my mother.
4. X: Ich bin von Professor Klein begeistert.
   Y: Many students are enthusiastic about him.
5. X: Ist deine Schwester mit Dieter verlobt?
   Y: No, she's not engaged to him.
6. X: Bist du verliebt in Karin?
   Y: I don't know whether I'm in love with her.
7. X: Schuberts sind sehr stolz auf ihre Tochter.
   Y: And we are very proud of our son.
8. X: Meine Eltern sind sehr glücklich über meinen Erfolg.
   Y: We all are very happy about your success. (fam. sing.)
9. X: Ist Rainer mit Marias Schwester verheiratet?
   Y: No, he's not married to her.
10. X: Ich bin mit meinem Schicksal[1] zufrieden.
    Y: Not many people are satisfied with their destiny.
11. X: Ich bin sehr böse auf Manfred.
    Y: Why are you so angry with him? (formal)
12: X: Bist du böse mit Monika?
    Y: Why do you think that I am angry with her?

Using a dictionary

We have treated only a few common verbs and adjectives that complete their meanings with prepositional phrases. There are, of course, many more. A good dictionary will tell you what prepositions and cases are used with those verbs and adjectives.

da-Compounds

§3 *da*-AS PRONOUN SUBSTITUTE

Compare:

a.	Haben Sie etwas **gegen Herrn Klein?** Haben Sie etwas **gegen ihn?**	*Do you have something against Mr. Klein?*
b.	Haben Sie etwas **gegen den Vorschlag?**	*Do you have something against him?* *Do you have something against the suggestion?*
	Haben Sie etwas **dagegen?**	*Do you have something against it?*

When referring to beings, the appropriate dative or accusative pronoun is used as the object of preposition as in sentence *a*. When referring to things or concepts as in sentence *b*., a **da**-compound replaces the preposition plus pronoun: **da-(dar-** before vowels) is attached as a prefix to the preposition.

---

[1] **das Schicksal, -e**   *destiny, fate*

Commonly used **da**-compounds:

dabei	daran
dadurch	darauf
dafür	daraus
dagegen	darin
damit	darüber
danach	darum
davon	
davor	
dazu	

Since the **da-** does not change, this construction does not reflect the gender, number (sing. or pl.) or case of the noun it replaces.

Ich weiß nichts **von dieser Sache.**
von diesen Dingen.
von seinen Plänen.

Ich weiß nichts **davon.**
I know nothing about it/them.

Ich habe keine Lust **zur Arbeit.**
zum Lernen.
zum Kochen.

Ich habe keine Lust **dazu.**
I'm not in the mood for it.

Normally the accent is on the preposition: **dazú, damít, davón,** etc. When the **da**-compound is emphasized, the accent shifts to da: **dázu, dámit, dávon,** etc.

Dázu habe ich keine Lust.
Dávon weiß ich nichts.

The emphatic **da**-compound is generally in first position.

Frequently used expression:

Es kommt darauf an.   *It depends.*
Es kommt ganz darauf an.   *It all depends.*

8-3   A. Substitute **da**-compounds for the boldface prepositional phrases.

Model: Klaus hat viele Aufnahmen[1] **von dem Picknick** gemacht.
Klaus hat viele Aufnahmen davon gemacht.

1. Ich habe viel Geld **für diese Brille** bezahlt.
2. Was machst du **mit diesen Sachen?**
3. Du kannst stolz **auf dein Zeugnis[2]** sein.
4. Ich bitte Sie **um einen Gefallen.**[3]

---

[1] **die Aufnahme, -n**   *picture, photograph*
   Aufnahmen machen   *to take pictures*
[2] **das Zeugnis, -se**   *report card*
[3] **der Gefallen,-**   *favor*
   um einen Gefallen bitten *to ask for a favor*

5. Er hat Schwierigkeiten[1] **mit seinem Führerschein.**
6. Ich habe keine Lust **zum Saubermachen.**[2]
7. Hast du Angst **vorm Fliegen?**
8. Die ganze Stadt spricht **von diesem Skandal.**
9. Arbeitest du noch **an dem Projekt?**
10. Barbara ist ganz verrückt **auf diese Schallplatte.**
11. Ich bin sehr froh **über diese Nachricht.**
12. Wer hat dir **bei diesen Hausaufgaben** geholfen?
13. Wie haben Sie **auf seinen Vorschlag** reagiert?
14. **Nach dem Konzert** sind wir in ein Cafe gegangen.
15. Herr Krause ist neutral: Er ist weder **für diesen Vorschlag** noch[3] **gegen diesen Vorschlag.**

B. The boldface prepositional phrases refer to persons, things, or concepts. Complete the answers, using either the preposition and a personal pronoun or a **da**-compound.

1. X: Sprecht ihr **von Frau Becker?**
   Y: Nein, wir sprechen nicht _____ .
2. X: Herr Schulze spricht immer nur **von seiner Arbeit.**
   Y: Warum spricht er denn[4] soviel _____ ?
3. X: Bist du **mit deinem Zeugnis** zufrieden?
   Y: Ja, aber meine Eltern sind nicht _____ zufrieden.
4. X: Sind Sie **mit Ihrer neuen Sekretärin** zufrieden?
   Y: Sie ist eine Perle.[5] Ich bin mehr als zufrieden _____ .
5. X: Ist Annerose verliebt in oder verlobt **mit Thomas?**
   Y: Beides,[6] und bald wird sie verheiratet _____ sein.
6. X: Haben Sie Angst **vor Prufungen?**
   Y: Es kommt darauf an. Manchmal habe ich Angst _____ , und manchmal habe ich keine Angst _____ .
7. X: Ich habe Angst **vorm Fliegen.**
   Y: _____ habe ich auch Angst. (emphatic)
8. X: Ich bin stolz **auf meine Note** in Chemie.
   Y: _____ können sie sehr stolz sein. (emphatic)
9. X: Hoffentlich hast du heute Lust **zum Saubermachen.**
   Y: _____ habe ich nie Lust. (emphatic)

---

[1] die Schwierigkeit, -en   *difficulty*
   Schwierigkeiten haben mit   *to have trouble with*
[2] das Saubermachen   *cleaning (generally housecleaning*
[3] weder ... noch   *neither ... nor*
[4] denn   *here used as a flavoring particle*
                                   implying a special interest on the part of the
                                   speaker (cf. Appendix, §4)
[5] die Perle, -n   *pearl; here used in th sense of gem*
[6] beides   *both*

10. X: Was haben Sie **auf seine Frage** geantwortet?
     Y: Ich weiß nicht mehr, was ich _____ geantwortet habe.
11. X: Frau Helbig ist böse **auf ihre Nachbarin**.
     Y: Weißt du, warum sie böse _____ ist?
12. X: Hat sie dich um **diesen Gefallen** gebeten?
     Y: Sie hat nicht _____ gebeten; sie hat ihn einfach befohlen.[1]
13. X: Niemand hat **über deinen Witz** gelacht.
     Y: Aber ich habe _____ gelacht, und das genügt.[2]

§4   PREPOSITIONS THAT DO NOT FORM *da*-COMPOUNDS

Da-compounds cannot be formed with the following prepositions:

ohne, seit, außer,

and all prepositions governing the genitive case (cf. Chap. 7 §4).

Pronouns or set expressions which convey the idea to be expressed are used instead.

ohne seine Hilfe	*without his help*
ohne sie	*without it*
seit seiner Krankheit	*since his illness*
seitdem	*since then*
außer seinem Geld	*except for or aside from his money*
außerdem	*aside from that, besides*
wegen seines Fleißes	*because of his diligence*
deswegen, deshalb	*because of that, therefore*
trotz meiner Faulheit	*in spite of my laziness*
trotzdem	*in spite of that*
statt eines Erfolgs	*instead of a success*
statt dessen	*instead of that*

PRACTICE

8-4   Supply the German equivalents of the phrases in parentheses.

1. X: Seit der Party bei Köhlers spricht Helga nicht mehr mit Andreas.
    Y: _____ spricht sie auch nicht mehr mit mir. (*since then*)
2. X: Wegen der großben Kälte sind wir am Wochenende nicht weggefahren.
    Y: _____ sind wir auch zu Hause geblieben. (*because of that*)
3. X: Meine Schwester liebt ihren Mann trotz seiner Trunksucht.[3]
    Y: Ich weiß selbst, daß man einen Mann _____ lieben kann.
    (*in spite of that*)
4. X: Winklers haben ein wunderbares Haus.
    Y: Und _____ haben sie noch ein Wochenendhaus[4] in den Bergen.
    (*aside from that*)

---

[1] befehlen (befiehlt),   *to order*
   befahl, befohlen
[2] genügen   *to suffice, to enough*
[3] die Trunksucht   *alcoholism*
[4] das Wochenendhause, ⸚er   *(weekend) cottage*

5. X: Du wolltest doch ein Motorrad kaufen.

    Y: Ja, das wollte ich. _____ mußte ich armer Mann ein

        Fahrrad kaufen.   (*instead of that*)

6. X: Ich habe deinen Großvater noch nie ohne Pfeife[1] gesehen.

    Y: _____ ist er nervös und unsicher.[2] (*without it*)

§5 ANTICIPATORY *da*-COMPOUNDS

Compare the following three sentences:

> Renate ist stolz **auf ihre Aussprache.**
> Renate ist stolz **darauf.**
> Renate ist stolz **darauf,** daß sie so eine gute Aussprache hat.
> *Renate is proud (of the fact) that she has such a good pronunciation.*
> or: *Renate is proud of having such a good pronunciation.*

In the third sentence the **da**-compound anticipates what is expressed in the
following clause. It is an *anticipatory* **da**-compound. Depending on the context,
the English translation of such a construction either disregards the **da**-compound or
uses a prepositional phrase or gerund, as shown above.

PRACTICE

8-5   Express the sentences in acceptable English.

1. Ich habe nicht an deinen Geburstag gedacht.
   Ich habe nicht daran gedacht.
   Ich habe nicht daran gedacht, daß du heute Geburtstag hast.
2. Wir danken Ihnen für Ihre Hilfe.
   Wir danken Ihnen dafür.
   Wir danken Ihnen dafür, daß Sie uns geholfen haben.
3. Helga spricht nie von ihren Zukunftsplänen.
   Helga spricht nie davon.
   Helga spricht nie davon, welche Zukunftspläne sie hat.
4. Ich bin sehr dankbar dafür daß Sie mir diese Chance gegeben haben.
5. Es kommt darauf an, was man im Leben erreichen[3] will.
6. Hoffentlich können wir Andreas davon überzeugen, daß er nachgeben muß.
7. Ich bin sehr froh darüber, daß Helga meine dumme Bemerkung nicht
   übelgenommen hat.
8. Herr König ist dadurch berühmt[4] geworden, daß er diese Maschine
   erfunden hat.

§6 THE POSITION OF PREPOSITIONAL PHRASES AND *da*-COMPOUNDS

Prepositional phrases and **da**-compounds tend to stand toward the end of
the sentence.

[1] **die Pfeife, -n**	*pipe*
[2] **unsicher**	*insecure*
[3] **erreichen**	*to achieve*
[4] **berühmt**	*famous*

PERSONAL PRONOUN		NOUN	PREP.+ NOUN OR PRONOUN, DA-COMPOUND	
Margot	hat		Renate	**bei den Hausaufgaben**	geholfen.
Sie	hat	ihr		**dabei**	geholfen.
Ich	habe		die Uhr	**von meinen Eltern**	bekommen.
Ich	habe	sie		**von ihnen**	bekommen.

 # The Interrogative Pronouns *wer* and *was*

§7   THE INTERROGATIVE PRONOUN *wer*

The interrogative **wer** is used to refer to beings of any gender in the singular and plural. Its forms are as follows:

NOM.	**wer**	*who*
ACC.	**wen**	*who(m)*
DAT.	**wem**	*to whom, who(m)*
GEN.	**wessen**	*whose*

Examples:

Herr Schmidt hat Peter angerufen.
   NOM.
  (subj.)

Wer hat Peter angerufen?
NOM.   *Who called Peter?*
(subj.)

Herr Schmidt hat **Peter** angerufen.
      ACC.
    (dir. obj.)

Wen hat Herr Schmidt angerufen?
ACC.   *Who(m) did Mr. Schmidt call?*
(dir. obj.)

Die Platte gehört **meinen Eltern.**
        DAT.

Wem gehört diese Platte?
DAT.   *To whom does this record belong?*

Das sind **Barbaras** Kinder.
    GEN.

Wessen Kinder sind das?
GEN.   *Whose children are these?*

The genitive **wessen** is often replaced with some other construction, such as:

Whose umbrella is that?

Wem gehört dieser Regenschirm?
(*To whom does this umbrella belong ?*)

PRACTICE
8-6 Translate the questions into German. (Use the present perfect for the English past tense.)

MODEL: Klaus hat Ute angerufen. **Wen hat Klaus angerufen?**
          Whom did Klaus call?

1. Werner hat Ingrid eingeladen. _____
    Whom has Werner invited?

2. Sabine haßt Ulrich.   _____

Who hates Ulrich?

3. Frau Kunze hat ihm geholfen.   _____

Whom did Mrs. Kunze help?

4. Astrid hat viele Aufnahmen gemacht.   _____

Who took a lot of pictures?

5. Dieser Koffer gehört meinem Freund.   _____

To whom does this suitcase belong ?

6. Annerose hat ihm nicht geantwortet.   _____

Whom did Annerose not answer?

7. Rainer hat mich nicht erkannt.[1]   _____

Who didn't recognize you?
(fam. sing.)

8. Ich habe meiner Freundin
   für das Geschenk gedankt.   _____

Whom did you thank for the gift?
(formal)

USING *wer* WITH PREPOSITIONS

Das Geschenk is für einen Freund.   } **Für wen** ist das Geschenk?
                    eine Freundin.   }   For whom is the present?
                    Herrn und Frau Becker. } or: Who is the present for?

Das Geschenk ist von einem Freund.   } **Von wem** ist das Geschenk?
                    einer Freundin.   }   From whom is the present?
                    Herrn und Frau Becker. } or: *Who is the present from?*

In the German the preposition always precedes the interrogative and determines its case.

PRACTICE

8-7 Express the questions in German. (Use the present perfect for the English past tense.)

MODEL: Karin arbeit mit   **Mit wem arbeitet Karin im Labor?**
        Maria im Labor.   Who is Karin working with in the lab?

1. Die Leute haben über den
   Clown gelacht.   _____

Who did the people laugh at?

2. Ich habe Angst vor diesem
   Zahnarzt.   _____

Who are you afraid of? (fam. sing.)

---

[1] **erkennen, erkannte, erkannt**   *to recognize*

3. Ich warte auf meine Freundin.

_____
Who are you waiting for? (formal)

4. Ich habe diese Blumen
   von Mathias bekommen.

_____
Who did you get these flowers from?
(fam. sing.)

5. Volker ist in Margot
   verliebt.

_____
Who is Volker in love with?

6. Meine Schwester ist mit
   Rainer Stern verheiratet.

_____
Who is your sister married to?
(fam. sing.)

7. Wir sprechen von deinem
   Freund Martin.

_____
Who are you talking of?
(fam. plural)

8. Ich gehe mit ein paar
   Freunden kegeln.
   (formal)

_____
Who are you going bowling with?

§8   THE INTERROGATIVE PRONOUN *was*

The interrogative **was** refers to things and concepts of any gender in the singular and plural. It has only one form, which is both nominative and accusative.

Was ist nicht richtig?   *What is not correct?*
 |
NOM.
(subj.)

Was verstehen Sie nicht?   *What don't you understand?*
 |
ACC.
(dir. obj.)

USING *was* WITH PREPOSITIONS

Compare:

STATEMENT   Ich habe Angst **vorm Fliegen.**   *I am afraid of flying.*
            Ich habe Angst **davor.**   *I am afraid of it.*
QUESTION   **Wovor** hast du Angst.   *What are you afraid of?*

Wo- is added as a prefix to the preposition **vor: wovor.**
In colloquial German, the preposition is followed by **was: Vor was** hat du Angst?

Compare the following **da**-compounds and **wo**-compounds:

da-compounds (used in statements)		**wo**-compounds (used in questions)	
damit	*with it/them*	**womit?**	*with what?*
dafür	*for it/them*	**wofür?**	*for what?*
davon	*of it/them*	**wovon?**	*of what?*

r is inserted when the preposition begins with a vowel:

da<u>r</u>in	*in it/them*	wo<u>r</u>in?	*in what?*
da<u>r</u>an	*on or of it/them*	wo<u>r</u>an?	*on or of what?*
da<u>r</u>aus	*from it/them*	wo<u>r</u>aus?	*from what?*
da<u>r</u>auf	*on it/them*	wo<u>r</u>auf?	*on what?*

Examples:

Ich denke **daran.**   **Woran** denkst du?
colloquial: **An was** denkst du?   *What are you thinking of?*

Ich warte **darauf.**   **Worauf** warten Sie?
colloquial: **Auf was** warten Sie?   *What are you waiting for?*

The genitive prepositions and **außer, ohne, seit** form no **wo**-compounds, just as they form no **da**-compounds.

Ich kann nicht ohne Fernseher leben.
Ich kann nicht ohne **ihn** leben.   **Ohne was** kannst du nicht leben?

PRACTICE

8-8   Express the questions in German using **wo**-compounds.

MODEL: Ich denke an die Ferien.   **Woran denkst du?**

What are you thinking of? (fam. sing.)

1. Ich warte auf eine Antwort von Udo.

_____

What are you waiting for? (fam. sing.)
2. Margot arbeitet an einem Referat.

_____

What is she working on?
3. Wir haben Angst vor der Prüfung.

_____

What are you afraid of? (fam. pl.)
4. Klaus ist ganz stolz auf sein Motorrad.

_____

What is he so proud of?
5. Ich bin mit dieser Gehaltserhöhung nicht zufrieden.

_____

What are you not satisfied with? (fam. sing.)
6. Der Film handelt von einer Liebesgeschichte.

_____

What does the film deal with? What is the film about?
7. Wir lachen über unsere Dummheit.

_____

What are you laughing about? (fam. pl.)
8. Ich danke dir für das Geschenk.

_____

What are you thanking me for?

9. Ich denke an die Olympischen Spiele.

_____

What are you thinkng of? (formal)

10. Uwe hat Schwierigkeiten mit seinem Führerschein.

_____

What is he having trouble with?

11. Wir sind begeistert von diesem Theaterstück.

_____

What are you so enthusiastic about? (fam. pl.)

PRACTICE

8-9   Summarizing exercises

A. Express in German.

1. a. She's having trouble with the boss.
    b. Are you having trouble with him? (fam. sing.)
    c. Who are you having trouble with?
2. a. I'm having trouble with my seminar paper.
    b. Are you having trouble with it? (formal)
    c. What are you having trouble with?
3. a. Are you working on this project? (formal)
    b. No, I'm not working on it.
    c. What are you working on?
4. a. I'm angry with Peter. (two forms)
    b. Why are you angry with him? (fam. sing., two forms)
    c. Who are you angry with? (two forms)
5. a. Martin is crazy about soccer.
    b. I know that he's crazy about it.
    c. What are you crazy about? (fam. sing)
6. a. She's in love with Frank.
    b. Is she in love with him?
    c. Who are you in love with? (fam. sing.)
7. a. He's proud of his report card.
    b. He can be proud of it.
    c. What can you be proud of? (fam. sing.)
8. a. I'm thanking you for the gift. (formal)
    b. It is not necessary[1] that you thank me for it.
    c. What are you thanking me for?
9. a. Are you satisfied with your destiny? (fam. sing.)
    b. Yes and no. It depends.

_____

[1] **nötig**   *necessary*

B. Form sentences that fit the context.

MODEL: Martins Vater hat den Nobelpreis bekommen.
            stolz sein / Vater
            Martin ist stolz auf seinen Vater.
      or: **Martin kann stolz auf seinen Vater sein.**

1. Mein Freund wollte mich gestern anrufen. Er hat es nicht getan.
        böse sein/ Freund
2. Ich esse Kaviar sehr gern.
        verrückt sein/ Kaviar
3. In diesem Brief steht, daß ich ein Stipendium (*scholarship*)
    bekomme.
        sehr froh sein/ Nachricht
4. Ich weiß nicht, ob Peter und Andreas Freunde oder Verwandte
        (*relatives*) sind. Ich frage Peter:
        „verwandt sein/ Andreas?"
5. Ich arbeite an einem Experiment.
        Schwierigkeiten/ haben
6. Meine Freundin studiert in Hamburg.
        denken/ oft
7. Heute abend gehe ich ins Kino.
        Film/ handeln/ eine Raumfahrt (*space trip*)
    Elke hat den Film gestern gesehen.
        begeistert sein/ Film
8. Der Chef bezahlt nicht gut. Ich will mehr Geld verdienen.
        bitten/ Gehaltserhöhung
9. Klaus ist mein Schwager (*brother-in-law*).
        er/ verheiratet sein/ Schwester
10. Meine Mutter hat mir am Telefon gesagt, daß sie mir einen Scheck
    schicken wird.
        warten/ Scheck
11. Meine Freundin hat keine Angst vorm Fliegen.
        ßich/ Angst haben
12. Manchmal habe ich Lust zur Arbeit and manchmal habe ich keine.
        darauf an kommen

CHAPTER 9

Adjectives

Introduction

Note the use of **vorsichtig** in the following sentences:

a. Herr Kästner ist **vorsichtig**.   *Mr. Kästner is careful.*
b. Herr Kästner fährt **vorsichtig**.   *Mr. Kästner drives carefully.*
c. Herr Kästner ist ein **vorsichtiger** Fahrer.   *Mr. Kästner is a careful driver.*

In sentence a. **vorsichtig** is a predicate adjective with the verb **sein**; in sentence b, it is an adverb modifying **fahren.** In both situations the base form **vorsichtig** is used with no ending. German does not distinguish between the base forms of adverbs and adjectives.

In sentence c. **vorsichtig** is an attribute adjective directly preceding the noun **Fahrer**, which it modifies. Attributive adjectives have endings which are determined by the gender, number (singular or plural), and case of the nouns they modify.

In this chapter we shall consider only attributive adjectives, which we shall simply call "adjectives".

 ## The Declension of Adjectives

There are three basic groups:

    adjectives that are not preceded by **der**-words or **ein**-words, referred to as unpreceded adjectives,
adjectives preceded by **der**-words,
adjectives preceded by **ein**-words.

§1 UNPRECEDED ADJECTIVES

SINGULAR   PLURAL

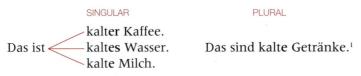

Das ist — kalt**er** Kaffee.
        kalt**es** Wasser.   Das sind kalt**e** Getränke.[1]
        kalt**e** Milch.

---

1 das Getränk, -e *beverage*

Unpreceded adjectives are declined almost exactly like **der**-words.

Review of the declension of the **der**-word **dieser:**

	MASCULINE	NEUTER	FEMININE	PLURAL
NOM.	dieser Kaffee	dieses Wasser	diese Milch	diese Getränke
ACC.	diesen Kaffee	dieses Wasser	diese Milch	diese Getränke
DAT.	diesem Kaffee	diesem Wasser	dieser Milch	diesen Getränken
GEN.	dieses Kaffees	dieses Wassers	dieser Milch	dieser Getränke

The endings attached to the **der**-words are known as strong endings. Compare them with the endings of the unpreceded adjectives below.

	MASCULINE	NEUTER	FEMININE PLURAL	
NOM.	kalter Kaffee	kaltes Wasser	kalte Milch	kalte Getränke
ACC.	kalten Kaffee	kaltes Wasser	kalte Milch	kalte Getränke
DAT.	kaltem Kaffee	kaltem Wasser	kalter Milch	kalten Getränken
GEN.	kalt [en] Kaffees	kalt [en] Wassers	kalter Milch	kalter Getränke

The difference between the two sets of endings occurs in the genitive singular masculine and neuter: the attributive adjective has the ending **-en** instead of **-es.**

PRACTICE

9-1   **A.** Replace the boldface **der**-words with the appropriate forms of the adjectives in parentheses.

MODEL: Trinken Sie **diesen** Tee gern? (englisch)
Trinken Sie **englischen Tee gern**?

1. Wo verkauft man **diesen** Käse? (holländisch)
2. **Dieser** Kaviar ist wirklich gut. (russisch)
3. Auf **solche** Fragen antworte ich nicht. (peinlich[1])
4. In dieser Bibliothek finden Sie **alle** Zeitungen. (ausländisch)
5. Ich habe **diese** Eier[2] bei Schneider gekauft. (frisch)
6. Wo ist **der** Zucker? (braun)
7. Bei **solchem** Wetter gehen wir nicht spazieren. (schlecht)
8. **Manche** Leute gehen mir auf die Nerven. (neugierig[3])
9. **Solches** Brot ist gut für die Gesundheit. (schwarz)
10. Ich liebe das Aroma **dieses** Kaffees. (frisch)

---

[1] peinlich   *embarassing*
[2] das Ei, -er   *egg*
[3] neugierig   *curious, nosy*

B.   Insert adjective endings.

1.   X: Ist dieser Kaffee gut?
     Y: Ja, das ist gut ___ Kaffee.
2.   X: Ist dieser Kaffee zu stark für Sie?
     Y: Nein. Ich trinke stark ___ Kaffee sehr gern.
3.   X: Kommt dieser Wein aus Spanien?
     Y: Ja, das ist spanisch ___ Wein.
4.   X: Haben Sie diesen Tee in England gekauft?
     Y: Nein. Man kann englisch ___ Tee auch hier kaufen.
5.   X: Essen Sie diesen Käse gern?
     Y: Ja, denn das ist amerikanisch ___ Käse. Wir essen meistens[1]
        amerikanisch ___ Käse.
6.   X: Hast du Hunger?
     Y: Ich habe sogar groß ___ Hunger. (masc.)
7.   X: War die Prüfung schwer?
     Y: Ja, aber ich habe groß __ Glück (neut.) gehabt.
8.   X: Wie war das Wetter in Italien?
     Y: Wir hatten meistens schön ___ Wetter.
9.   X: Was für Laune hat der Chef?
     Y: Ich glaube, er hat schlecht ___ Laune.
10. X. Sind diese Methoden noch modern, oder sind sie schon altmodisch[2]
     Y: Meiner Meinung nach sind es altmodisch ___ Methoden.
11. X: Ich finde dieses Theaterstück sehr interessant.
     Y: Ich auch.Dieser Autor schreibt meistens interessant ___ Theater-
        stücke.
12. X: Sind Ihre Nachbarn nett?
     Y: Zum Glück[3] haben wir nett ___ Nanchbarn.
13. X: Gisela denkt, sie hat die Prüfung nicht bestanden.
14. X: In Ihrer Wohnung riecht[4] es wunderbar. Haben Sie Brot gebacken?
     Y: Ja, das ist der Geruch[5] frisch ___ Brotes.
15. X: Hannelores Kleid ist sehr schick.
     Y: Dieses Mädchen hat gut ___ Geschmack.[6]
16. X: Deine Idee ist großartig.[7]
     Y: Ich habe immer großartig ___ Ideen.

---

[1] meistens   *mostly, usually*
[2] altmodisch   *old-fashioned*
[3] zum Glück   *luckily*
[4] riechen, roch, gerochen   *to smell*
[5] der Geruch, -e   *smell*
[6] der Geschmack   *taste*
[7] größartig   *great*

§2   Adjectives Preceded by *der-* Words

Including the definite article, the **der-**words are **der, dieser, jeder, jener, mancher, solcher, welcher, alle,** and **beide** (cf. Chap. 6, §1). Adjectives preceded by **der-** words have weak endings. The following table shows the combinations of **der** and **dieser** + weak adjective + noun.

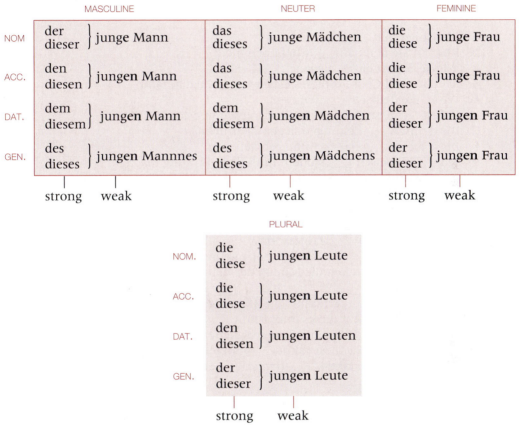

	MASCULINE	NEUTER	FEMININE
NOM	der / dieser } junge Mann	das / dieses } junge Mädchen	die / diese } junge Frau
ACC.	den / diesen } jungen Mann	das / dieses } junge Mädchen	die / diese } junge Frau
DAT.	dem / diesem } jungen Mann	dem / diesem } jungen Mädchen	der / dieser } jungen Frau
GEN.	des / dieses } jungen Mannnes	des / dieses } jungen Mädchens	der / dieser } jungen Frau

strong   weak   strong   weak   strong   weak

PLURAL

	PLURAL
NOM.	die / diese } jungen Leute
ACC.	die / diese } jungen Leute
DAT.	den / diesen } jungen Leuten
GEN.	der / dieser } jungen Leute

strong   weak

The weak adjective endings are either **-e** or **-en**:

> **-e** in the nominative masculine singular.
> the nominative and accusative neuter singular.
> the nominative and accusative feminine singular:
> **-en** in all other cases.

The following key shows the distribution of the endings **-e** and **-en** of adjectives preceded by **der-** words.

	MASC.	NEUT.	FEM.	PLURAL
NOM.	-e	-e	-e	-en
ACC.	-en	-e	-e	-en
DAT.	-en	-en	-en	-en
GEN.	-en	-en	-en	-en

The strong declension of **der-** words has a greater variety of endings which help to identify the gender, number, and case of the noun that follows. The weak declension with the two endings **-e** and **-en** is less distinctive. Remember that weak adjective endings do not occur unless preceded by a strong ending.

PRACTICE

9-2   Insert the appropriate adjective endings.

  1. Wo ist der neu ___ Chef?
  2. Kennen Sie den neu ___ Chef noch nicht?
  3. Wieviel kostet dieses elegant ___ Kleid?
  4. Ich habe viel Geld für dieses elegant ___ Kleid bezahlt.
  5. Wo ist die deutsch ___ Zeitung?
  6. Haben Sie diese deutsch ___ Zeitung schon gelesen?
  7. Die deutsch ___ Zeitungen liegen da drüben.
  8. Diese braun ___ Handschuhe gefallen mir.
  9. Jeder ausländisch ___ Student muß diese Prüfung machen.
 10. Alle ausländisch ___ Studenten wohnen in diesem Studentenheim.
 11. Beide französisch ___ Studenten sind meine Freunde.
 12. Wer hat diese genial ___ [1]Idee gehabt?
 13. Dieser neugierig ___ Mensch geht mir auf die Nerven.
 14. Wie heißt die neu ___ Professorin?
 15. Die neu ___ Professoren haben noch keine Büros.
 16. Auf dieser Liste stehen die Namen der neu ___ Professoren und Professorinnen.
 17. Haben Sie diesen interessant ___ Roman gelesen?
 18. Wie heißt der Autor dieses interessant ___ Romans?
 19. Mancher jung ___ Artz hat Schwierigkeiten mit seinen Patienten.
 20. Bitte ignorieren Sie diese taktlos ___ [2]Bemerkung!
 21. Ich versuche, alle taktlos ___ Bemerkungen zu ignorieren.

OMISSION OF THE NOUN

Welche Handshuhe willst du kaufen?   Vielleicht kaufe ich **die braunen Handschue.**
or: Vielleicht kaufe ich **die braunen**.
Perhaps I'll buy the brown ones.

The fact that the noun **Handschuhe** is not repeated in the second sentence does not affect the adjective ending: **die braunen** is used in both sentences. In English *one(s)* is added when the noun is omitted.

PRACTICE

9-3   Insert the appropriate adjective endings

  1. X: Haben Sie den Chef gesehen?
      Y: Meinen Sie den jung ___ oder den alt ___ ?

---

[1] genial   *ingenious*
[2] taktlos   *tactless*

2. X: Welches Kleid willst du anziehen?[1]

   Y: Ich weiß nicht, ob das grün ___ oder das rot ___ anziehen soll.

3. X: Wie gefällt dir der Mantel?

   Y: Meinst du den schwarz ___ ?

4. X: Welcher Fernseher ist kaputt?

   Y: Der kaputt ___ steht im Nebenzimmer.[2]

5. X: Welches Restaurant haben Steins gekauft?

   Y: Ich glaube, sie haben das klein ___ da an der Ecke gekauft.

6. X: Sind diese Formulare hier neu?

   Y: Ja, das sind die neu ___ .

7. X: Welche Formulare haben Sie schon ausgefüllt?

   Y: Ich habe alle neu ___ ausgefüllt.

§3   ADJECTIVES PRECEDED BY *ein*- WORDS

The **ein-** words are **ein, kein,** and the possessives (cf. Chap. 6, §5 and §6).

The declension of **(k)ein** + adjective + noun is as follows:

	MASCULINE	NEUTER	FEMININE
NOM.	(k)ein junger Mann	(k)ein junges Mädchen	(k)eine junge Frau
ACC.	(k)einen jungen Mann	(k)ein junges Mädchen	(k)eine junge Frau
DAT.	(k)einem jungen Mann	(k)einem jungen Mädchen	(k)einer jungen Frau
GEN.	(k)eines jungen Mannnes	(k)eines jungen Mädchens	(k)einer jungen Frau

	PLURAL
NOM.	keine jungen Leute
ACC.	keine jungen Leute
DAT.	keinen jungen Leuten
GEN.	keiner jungen Leute

The **ein-** words have the same strong endings as the **der-** words except in three cases where they have no ending at all: see boxed forms above.

If an **ein-** word has an ending, the adjective has the same weak ending as after a **der-** word. But if the **ein-** word has no ending, the adjective has a strong ending: **-er** (masculine} or **-es** (neuter}.

The following key shows the endings of adjectives preceded by **ein**-words.

	MASC.	NEUT.	FEM.	PLURAL
NOM.	-er	-es	-e	-en
ACC.	-en	-es	-e	-en
DAT.	-en	-en	-en	-en
GEN.	-en	-en	-en	-en

---

[3] **an·ziehen, zog an, angezogen**   *to put on*

[2] **das Nebenzimmer**   *adjoining room*

Examples of possessive + adjective + noun combinations:

> Ist das dein neu**es** Auto?
> Ist das Ihr neu**er** Wagen?
> Das ist seine neu**e** Freundin?
> Das ist unser neu**es** Haus.
> Ist das euer neu**es** Hobby?

Keep in mind that **-er** of **unser** and **euer** is not a declensional ending (cf. Chap. 6, §6). The **e** before **r** may be omitted when the strong endings are added.

> Das ist **uns(e)re** neue Nachbarin.
> Wir haben **uns(e)rer** neuen Nachbarin geholfen.
> Ist das **eu(e)re** neue Nachbarin?
> Helft ihr **eu(e)rer** neuen Nachbarin?

PRACTICE

9-4   A. Insert the appropriate adjective endings.

MODEL: a. Das ist ein gut**er** Film.
      b. Ich habe gestern einen gut**en** Film gesehen.
      c. In dieser Woche laufen hier keine gut**en** Filme.

1.   a. Das ist ein nett ____ Brief von Dietmar.
     b. Helga hat einen nett ____ Brief von ihrem Freund bekommen.
     c. Warum bekomme ich keine nett ____ Briefe von meinem Freund?
2.   a. Das ist ein groß ____ Problem.
     b. Das sind keine groß ____ Problem.
     c. Ich habe ein groß ____ Problem.
     d. Das ist unser groß ____ Problem.
3.   a. Ist das ein neu ____ Kleid?
     b. Hast du mein neu ____ Kleid schon gesehen?
     c. Ich kann mir keine neu ____ Kleider kaufen.
4.   a. Hast du eine neu ____ Freundin?
     b. Margot hat einen neu ____ Freund.
     c. Rainer ist ihr neu ____ Freund.
5.   a. Wir haben eine modern ____ Wohnung gemietet.
     b. Neumanns wohnen auch in einer modern ____ Wohnung.
     c. In unserer Straße gibt es[1] keine modern ____ Wohnungen.
6.   a. Wir haben einen altmodisch ____ Fernseher
     b. Unser altmodisch ____ Fernseher funktioniert noch sehr gut.
     c. Wir sind mit unserem altmodisch ____ Fernseher sehr zufrieden.
7.   a. Mein kein ____ Bruder ist in der Prüfung durchgefallen.
     b. Warum hilfst du deinem klein ____ Bruder nicht?
     c. Kennen Sie meinen klein ____ Bruder?
     d. Ich kenne nur Ihre klein ____ Schwester.

---

[1] **es gibt** (+ acc.)   *there is or are*

B. Insert the appropriate adjective endings

1. X: Ich habe einen lang ___ Brief von zu·Hause bekommen.
    Y: Und ich habe ein groß ___ Paket von zu Hause bekommen.
    2. X: Das war keine leicht ___ Mathematikprüfung.
    Y: In Mathematik gibt es keine leicht ___ Prüfungen.
3. X: Das ist ein interessant ___ Theaterstück.
    Y: Wir haben am Freitag ein langeweilig ___ Theaterstück gesehen.
4. X: Dieser Fall[1] ist hoffnungslos.[2]
    Y: Ja, leider ist das ein hoffnungslos ___ Fall.
5. X: Haben Sie meine neu ___ Adresse?
    Y: Nein. Ich habe auch Ihre neu ___ Telefonnummer nicht.
6. X: Ist das dein neu ___ Auto?
    Y: Das ist unser neu ___ Auto, denn meine Frau fährt es natürlich auch.
7. X: Ist Andreas dein fest ___ Freund.[3]
    Y: Nein. Ich habe keinen fest ___ Freund.
8. X: Können Sie meine genial ___ Handschrift[4] lesen?
    Y: Natürlich nicht. Sie haben eine schrecklich ___ Handschrift.
9. X: Herr Neumann hat viel Unsinn geredet.
    Y: Dieser Mann hat keinen gesund ___ Menschenverstand.[5]
10. X: Ich bin heute deprimiert.[6] Kannst du mir einen gut ___ Witz erzählen?
    Y: Muß es ein gut ___ Witz sein? Ich weiß keine gut ___ Witze.
11. X: Du hast eine charmant ___ [7] Freundin.
    Y: Stimmt.[8] Und ich bin ihr charmant ___ Freund.

§4   SLIGHTLY IRREGULAR FORMS OF ADJECTIVES

a. **hoch** (*high*)   Das Gebäude ist hoch.
                                    das **hohe** Gebäude/ein **hohes** Gebäude
The c is omitted when an ending is added.

b. **dunkel** (*dark*)   Das Zimmer ist dunkel.
                                    das **dunkle** Zimmer/ein **dunkles** Zimmer

   miserabel (*miserable*)   Das Wetter ist miserabel.
                                    das **miserable** Wetter/ein **miserables** Wetter
Adjectives ending in **-el** when an ending is added.

---

[1] **der Fall, -ë**   *case*
[2] **hoffnungslos**   *hopeless*
[3] **der feste Freund**   *steady boyfriend*
[4] **die Handschrift, -en**   *handwriting*
[5] **der gesunde Menschenverstand** *common sense*
[6] **deprimiert**   *depressed*
[7] **charmant**   *charming*
[8] **stimmt** (*short for:* **das stimmt**)   *that's correct or right*

c. **teuer** (*expensive*)   Die Bücher sind **teuer.**
                                      die **teuren** Bücher

   sauer (*sour*)   Die Milch ist **sauer.**
                                      die **saure** Milch

Adjectives ending in **-er** after **eu** and **au** omit **e** before **r** when an ending is added.

§5   ADJECTIVES DERIVED FROM CITY NAMES

City names used as adjectives add **-er** regardless of the gender, number, or case of the following noun. These adjectives are capitalized.

> Das Flugzeug ist auf dem **Berlinder** Flughafen gelandet.
> *The plane landed at the Berlin airport.*
> Das ist ein Bild vom **Kölner** Dom.
> *That's a picture of the cathedral of Cologne.*
> Wo haben Sie diese **Frankfurter** Würstchen gekauft?
> *Where did you buy these frankfuters?*

§6   SEVERAL ADJECTIVES MODIFYING THE SAME NOUN

> Das ist ein schön**er** Sommertag.
> Das ist ein schön**er**, warm**er** Sommertag.
> Das ist ein schön**er**, warm**er** und klar**er** Sommertag.

Since **schön, warm,** and **klar** all modify the same noun, they must have the same adjective ending.

§7   *alle* FOLLOWED BY A *der-* WORD OR *ein-* WORD

> all**e** dies**e** Sachen
> all**e** mein**e** Freunde

Alle may be followed by a d**er**-word or **ein**-word; both have the same strong ending. Added adjectives have weak endings:

> alle meine gut**en** Freunde
> alle meine gut**en** alt**en** Freunde

PRACTICE

9-5   Complete the responses.

1.   X: Herr Schubert ist wirklich sehr nett.
     Y: Stimmt. Er ist ein _____ Mann. (*nice young*)
2.   X: Warum hast du schon wieder kein Geld?
     Y: Weil ich _____ Schulden bezahlt habe. (*all my old*)
3.   X: Mein Zimmer im Studentenheim ist etwas dunkel.
     Y: Leider habe ich auch ein _____ Zimmer. (*dark*)
4.   X: Ist diese Milch sauer?
     Y: Ja, das ist _____ Milch. (*sour*)
5.   X: Möchtest du etwas essen?
     Y: Hast du _____ ? (*frankfurters*)

6. X: Das Wetter ist heute miserabel.

Y: Dieses _____ Wetter geht mir auf die Nerven. (*miserable*)

7. X: Dieser Mantel ist bestimmt sehr teuer.

Y: Nein, das ist kein _____ Mantel. (*expensive*)

8. X: Wo ist dein Gepäck?

Y: Ich habe es auf dem _____ gelassen. (*Berlin airport*)

9. a. X: Was für eine Wohnung haben Schmidts?

Y: Sie haben eine _____ Wohnung. (*large and modern*)

b. X: Sicher ist die Miete[1] sehr hoch.

Y: Die _____ Miete ist wohl das einzige[2] Minus an dieser Wohnung. (*high*)

§8   SUMMARY OF THE MAIN FEATURES

1. Two sets of endings have to be kept in mind:

the strong endings of the **der-** words

	MASC.	NEUT.	FEM.	PLURAL
NOM.	-er	-es	-e	-e
ACC.	-en	-es	-e	-e
DAT.	-em	-em	-er	-en
GEN.	-es	-es	-er	-er

the weak endings of the adjectives

	MASC.	NEUT.	FEM.	PLURAL
NOM.	-e	-e	-e	-en
ACC.	-en	-e	-e	-en
DAT.	-en	-en	-en	-en
GEN.	-en	-en	-en	-en

2. In the sequence (article)-adjective-noun, at least one strong ending must be present to signal gender, number, and case. Thus we find the following patterns:

a. Unpreceded adjectives have the strong **der-** word endings.

jung**er** Mann	jung**es** Mädchen	jung**e** Frau	jung**e** Leute
(NOM.)	(NOM./ACC.)	(NOM./ACC.)	(NOM./ACC.)

Exception: In the singular, the genitive masculine and neuter have the weak ending **-en** instead of the strong **-es**.

---

[1] **die Miete, -n**   *rent*

[2] **einzig**   *single, only*

b. Adjectives preceded by **der**-words have weak endings, i.e.

-**e** in the following five cases of the singular:

der junge Mann	das junge Mädchen	die junge Frau
(NOM.)	(NOM./ACC.)	(NOM. ACC.)

-**en** in all other cases.

c. Adjectives preceded by **ein**-words

When the **ein**-word has a strong ending, the adjective has a weak ending.
When the **ein**-word has no ending, the adjective has the strong ending -**er** or -**es**.

ein jun**ger** Mann	ein jung**es** Mädchen	eine junge Frau
(NOM.)	(NOM./ACC.)	(NOM. ACC.)

-**en** in all other cases.

3. Adjectives in a series

Adjectives modifying the same noun take the same endings.

ein nett**er**, lang**er** Brief   ein hübsch**es**, aber almodisch**es** Kleid

9-6   Summarizing exercises.

A. Insert the appropriate adjective endings.

Model: a. Das ist ein dumm**er** Fehler
          b. Ich habe einen dumm**en** Fehler gemacht.
          c. Das sind dumm**e** Fehler.
          d. Das sind keine dumm**en** Fehler.

1. a. Das ist ein gut __ Witz.
    b. Wer hat Ihnen diesen gut __ Witz erzählt?
    c. Frau Zimmermannn erzählt meistens gut __ Witze.
    d. Das sind keine gut __ Witze.
2. a. Das ist ein groß __ Problem.
    b. Von welchem groß __ Problem sprechen Sie?
    c. Wir haben groß __ Problem.
    d. Das sind doch keine groß __ Probleme.
3. a. Kennst du dieses deutsch __ Lied?
    b. Das ist kein deutsch __ Lied.
    c. Singt ihr manchmal deutsch __ Lieder?
    d. Kennt ihr keine deutsch __ Lieder?
4. a. Das ist eine großartig __ Idee.
    b. Wer hat diese großartig __ Idee gehabt?
    c. Barbara hat oft großartig __ Ideen.
    d. Warum habe ich keine großartig __ Ideen?

5. a. Das war eine taktlos ___ Bemerkung.
    b. Es tut mir leid, daß ich diese taktlos ___ Bemerkung gemacht habe.
    c. Ich mache oft taktlos ___ Bemerkungen.
    d. Bitte vergessen Sie meine taktlos ___ Bemerkungen.

B.   Insert the appropriate adjective endings.

1.   X: Dieser Anzug ist altmodisch.
     Y: Aber dieser altmodisch ___ Anzug hat Stil.
2.   X: Soll ich den hell ___ [1] Anzug kaufen?
     Y: Der dunkl ___ gefällt mir besser.
3.   X: Diese Kritik ist nicht fair.
     Y: Ich finde auch, daß es eine unfair ___ Kritik ist.
4.   X: Können Sie mir einen gut ___ Rechtsanwalt empfehlen?
     Y: Herr Krause ist ein ausgezeichnet ___ [2] Rechtsanwalt.
5.   X: Ist das der neu ___ Katalog?
     Y: Nein, das ist ein alt ___ Katalog. Die neu ___ Kataloge sind noch
        nicht herausgekommen.
6.   X: Warum hast du dieses teur ___ Kleid gekauft?
     Y: Weil es mir gefällt. Ich möchte wissen, warum mir nur teur ___
        Kleider gefallen.
7.   X: Sie haben schon wieder Ihr Versprechen nicht gehalten.
     Y: Sie sehen, ich bin ein hoffnungslos ___ Fall.
8.   X: Bist du mit deinem Zeugnis zufrieden?
     Y: Ja, Ich habe gut ___ Noten. Nur in Mathematik habe ich keine gut
        ___ Note.
9.   X: Deine Geschwister[3] sind sehr nett.
     Y: Und ich? Bin ich kein nett ___ Mensch? Ach ja, ich bin das schwarz
        ___ Schaf in der Familie.
10. X: Die Preise in diesem Restaurant sind viel zu hoch für meinen
        Geldbeutel.[4]
     Y: Ich kann diese hoh ___ Preise auch nicht bezahlen.
11. X: Wie kommt es,[4] daß du immer so gut ___ Ideen hast?
     Y: Ach, das ist nur gesund ___ Menschenverstand.
12. X: Wie kommt es,[5] daß du so beliebt[6] bist?
     Y: Hm…Das ist mein natürlich ___ Charme (masc.).
13. X: Mein Fräulein, ich finde Sie sehr attraktiv.
     Y: Mein Herr, Sie haben gut ___ Geschmack.
14. a. X: Ich war mit Martin im Kino.
        Y: Mit Martin? Rainer ist doch dein fest ___ Freund.

---

[1] **hell**   *light-colored*
[2] **ausgezeichnet**   *excellent*
[3] **die Geschwister (pl.)**   *brothers and sisters, siblings*
[4] **der Geldbeutel -**   *purse, pocketbook*
[5] **wie kommt es**   *how come*
[6] **beliebt**   *popular*

   b. X: Nicht mehr.[1] Das ist eine lang __ Geschichte.
15.   a. X: Deine Handschrift ist miserabel.
       Y: Miserabel __ Handschriften sind genial.
   b. X: Und du bist doch so ein genial __ Mensch.
       Y: Stimmt. Ich bin ein neu __ Weltwunder (neut.).
16.   a. X: Wo sind die ausländisch __ Zeitungen?
       Y: Alle ausländisch __ Zeitungen liegen da drüben.
   b. X: Verkaufen Sie auch portugiesisch __ Zeitungen?
       Y: Dei portugiesisch __ Zeitungen liegen neben den französisch __
       und spanisch __ .
17.   a. X: Ich glaube, Andreas hat einen neu __ Wagen.
       Y: Sein schick __ rot __ Sportwagen steht hinter der Bibliothek.
   b. X: Hast du auch ein schick __ Auto?
       Y: Natürlich. Dort steht mein alt __ Klapperkasten.[2]

C.   Form sentences using the following cues.

Model: das / sein / ein / großartig /Idee

   Das ist eine großartige Idee.

1.   das / sein / ein / taktlos / Bemerkung
2.   das / sein / ein / langweilig / Theaterstück
3.   das / sein / ein / interessant / Film?
4.   das / sein / ein / unfair / Kritik? (past)
5.   du / haben / ein / fest / Freund?
6.   Frank / sein / mein / fest / Freund
7.   Frau Krause / sein / ein / ausgezeichnet / Rechtsanwältin
8.   ich / haben / ein / miserabel / Handschrift
9.   ich / kaufen / ein / schick / Kleid (pres. perf.)
10.   du / haben / gut / Geschmack
11.   Anita / sein / schwarz / Schaf / in / Familie
12.   mein Wagen / sein / ein / alt / Klapperkasten
13.   ich / schenken / dir / mein / alt / Klapperkasten
14.   dieser Fanatiker / haben / kein / gesund / Menschenverstand
15.   er / sein / ein / hoffnungslos / Fall

Additional Uses of Adjectives

§9   Adjectives Preceded by Uninflected Elements

Adjectives preceded by uninflected elements have strong endings to signal gender, number, and case of the noun that follows.

---

[1] **nicht mehr**   *not anymore*
[2] **der Klapperkasten, ¨e**   *boneshaker*

a. **etwas** *some, a little*

> Wo kann ich etwas heiß**es** Wasser bekommen?

b. **ein wenig** *a little*

> Hier ist noch ein wenig schwarz**er** Kaffee.

> **Etwas** and **ein wenig** are interchangeable.

c. **ein paar** *a few, some* (generally more than two)

> Wir haben ein paar alt**e** Freunde besucht.

d. **genug** *enough*

> Haben wir genug kalt**e** Getränke für unser Picknick?

e. cardinal numbers **zwei, drei, vier,** etc.

With the exception of **ein-,** cardinal numbers remain uninflected:

> drei neu**e** Experimente

When the cardinal number is preceded by a strong **der**-word or **ein**-word, the adjective has a weak ending:

> die   drei   neuen Experimente
> seine   drei   neuen Experimente
> strong un-   weak
>   inflected

f. **manch, solch, welch**

In literary German, **mancher, solcher,** and (in exclamations) **welcher** occur with out endings.

manch gut**er** Freund	solch gut**er** Freund	Welch gut**er** Freund!
or: manch ein gut**er** Freund	solch ein gut**er** Freund	Welch ein gut**er** Freund!
many a good friend	*such a good friend*	*What a good friend!*

In informal German (everyday speech and informal writing) **so (ein)** is used in place of **solch (ein)** and **was für (ein)** is used instead of **welch (ein).** (Cf. Chap. 6, §5.)

So ein gut**er** freund ist unbezahlbar.	*Such a good friend is prizeless.*
So gut**e** Freunde habe ich leider nicht.	*Unfortunately, I don't have such good friends.*
Was für ein gut**er** Freund!	*What a good friend!*
Was für gut**e** Freunde!	*What good friends!*

PRACTICE

9-7 Insert the adjective endings, following the model of sentence 1.

1. Im Kühlschrank¹ ist noch ein wenig grün**er** Salat.

2. Ist das genug heiß __ Wasser?

---

¹der **Kühlschrank, -e**   *refrigerator*

3. Hast du noch etwas kalt __ Milch für mich?
4. Wir haben ein paar nett __ Nachbarn eingeladen.
5. Köhlers haben zwei klein __ Kinder.
6. Haben Sie die zwei klein __ Kinder gesehen?
7. Welch schön __ Sonnenuntergang!¹
8. Was für ein herrlich __ Wetter!
9. So ein __ gut __ Lehrerin habe ich nicht wieder gehabt.
10. So leicht __ Hausaufgaben sind eine Beleidigung² für meine Intelligenz.

§10 ADJECTIVES PRECEDED BY *andere, einige, mehrere, viele, wenige*

Like attributive adjectives, the indefinite numerals **andere** (*other*), **einige** (*some, a few*),
mehrere (*several*), **viele** (*many*), and **wenige** (*few, not many*) may occur with either
strong or weak endings, depending on whether or not they are preceded.

unpreceded:		preceded:	
viele Studenten		die vielen Studenten	
andere Projekte	strong endings	keine anderen Projekte	weak endings
wenige Freunde		meine wenigen Freunde	

When another adjective is added, it has the same strong or weak ending:

unpreceded:	preceded:
viele neue Studenten	die vielen neuen Studenten
andere große Projekte	keine anderen großen Projekte
wenige gute Freunde	meine wenigen guten Freunde

When used in the singular, unpreceded **viel** and **wenig** are usually not inflected;
adjectives that follow them have strong endings:

viel/wenig Geld   viel/wenig ausländisches Geld

For the use of **ander-** in the singular, see Chapter 20, §1.

PRACTICE

9-8   Insert the appropriate adjective endings.

1. Ich esse viel frisch __ Obst.³
2. Wir haben viel __ gut __ Freunde.
3. Einig __ ausländisch __ Studenten wohnen im Studentenheim.
4. Die ander __ ausländisch __ Studenten wohnen in der Stadt.
5. Mehrer __ neu __ Studenten suchen einen Job.
6. Es gibt zu viel __ Bewerber⁴ für die wenig __ Jobs.
7. Ich habe viel __ dumm __ Fehler gemacht.
8. Meine viel __ dumm __ Fehler sind schockierend.

---

¹ der Sonnenuntergang, -e   *sunset*
² die Beleidigung, -en   *insult*
³ das Obst   *fruit*
⁴ der Bewerber   *applicant*

§11 FORMS AND USE OF *derselbe* (the same)

singular: **derselbe** Mann   plural:

Das ist   **dasselbe** Mädchen   Das sind **dieselben** Leute.

           dieselbe Frau

The English expression *the same* corresponds to German **der + selbe,** which is written as one word. **Der** has a strong ending, **selbe** a weak one.

d e r s e l b e

strong weak

The full declension is as follows:

	MASC.	NEUTER	FEM.	PLURAL
NOM.	derselbe	dasselbe	dieselbe	dieselben
ACC.	denselben	dasselbe	dieselbe	dieselben
DAT.	demselben	demselben	derselben	denselben
GEN.	desselben	desselben	derselben	derselben

Any additional adjective takes the same ending as **selbe.**

Das ist derselbe junge Mann.

strong weak weak

PRACTICE

9-9   Translate the sentences into German.

1. That's the same mistake.
2. That's the same stupid mistake.
3. Is that the same young man?
4. That's not the same young lady.
5. I talked with the same janitor. (pres. perf.)
6. Barbara and Frank have the same teachers.
7. That's the same old story.
8. He's telling the same old stories.

§12 ADJECTIVAL NOUNS

Adjectives referring to persons, things, or abstractions may assume the function of nouns.

1. Referrring to persons

Das ist ein Programm für Blind**e**.
That's a program for the blind.
Ein Blind**er** und eine Blind**e** haben gestern im Konzert gesungen.
A blind man and a blind woman sang in the concert yesterday.
Diese Blind**en** haben in unserem Chor gesungen.
These blind people sang in our choir.

Adjectival nouns are capitalized. They follow the rules for the declension of adjectives and hence may have either strong or weak endings. They are frequently rendered into English by adding man, woman, or people.

SINGULAR		PLURAL	
male	**female**	**male and female**	
der Arme	die Arme	die Armen	viele Arme
ein Armer	eine Arme	keine Armen	
		alle Armen	
der Fremde	die Fremde	die Fremden	einige Fremde
the stranger			
ein Fremder	eine Fremde	keine Fremden	
		alle Fremden	
der Deutsche	die Deutsche	die Deutschen	
ein Deutscher	eine Deutsche	keine Deutschen	mehrere Deutsche
		alle Deutschen	
Unpreceded:			
Sind Sie Deutscher? (male)		Sind diese Touristen Deutsche?	
Sind Sie Deutsche (female)			

An attributive adjective has the same ending as the adjectival noun:

ein mysteriöser Fremder   viele junge Deutsche
eine freundliche Blinde

PRACTICE

9-10   Insert the appropriate endings.

   1. a. In unserer Stadt gibt es viele Arm ___.
      b. Ein Arm ___ hat mich um Geld gebeten.
   2. a. Kennen Sie den Blind ___ da drüben?
      b. Mein Bruder ist mit einer Blind ___ verheiratet.
      c. Das ist eine Schule für Blind ___ .
   3. a. Eine Fremd ___ hat mich nach dem Weg zum Bahnhof gefragt.
      b. Als ich die Tür aufmachte, stand ein Fremd ___ vor mir.
      c. Der Fremd ___ war sehr höflich.
      d. Heute sind viele Fremd ___ in unserer Stadt.
   4. a. Unsere Nachbarn sind Deutsch ___ .
      b. Hier wohnen viele Deutsch ___ .
      c. Barbara ist mit einem Deutsch ___ verlobt.
      d. Ich habe gestern mehrere jung ___ Deutsch ___ kennengelernt.

2. Referring to things or abstractions

The neuter forms of adjectives used as nouns are generally collectives or abstractions.

das Neue	*the new, the new stuff, that which is new*
das Alte	*the old, etc.*
das Gute	*the good, etc.*
das Böse	*the evil, etc.*

Das Gute an der Sache ist, daß ich jetzt mehr Zeit für meine Familie habe.
The good thing (or part) about the matter is that I now have more time for my family.

These neuter forms are frequently preceded by **etwas, nichts, viel, wenig, alles.**

etwas Schönes	*something beautiful*	alles Schöne	all that is beautiful
un- strong		strong weak	
inflected			
wenig Neues	*little that is new*	alles Neue	all that is new
	little news	all news	
nichts Interessant**es**	*nothing interesting*	alles Interassante	all that is interesting
viel Gut**es**	*much that is good*	alles Gute	*all that is good*
	many good things	idiom: **Alles Gute!**	*All the best!*
			or: Good luck!

PRACTICE

9-11   Insert the appropriate endings.

1. Weißt du etwas Neu __ ?
2. Erika wird dir alles Neu __ erzählen.
3. Ich habe schon viel Gut __ über Sie gehört.
4. Wir wünschen Ihnen alles Gut __.
5. Ist etwas Interessant __ passiert?
6. Hier passiert nichts Interessant __ .

§13 PARTICIPLES USED AS ADJECTIVES AND NOUNS

There are two types of participles: present participles and past participles.

1. Present participles

lachend	*laughing*	bellend	*barking*
weinend	*crying*	folgend	*following*

In English the present participle has the ending **-ing**; in German a **d** is added to the infinitive.

When the participle is used as an adjective preceding a noun, it follows the rules for the adjective declension.

der folgend**e** Satz	die folgend**en** Sätze	folgend**e** Sätze
das folgend**e** Beispiel[1]	die folgend**en** Beispiele	folgend**e** Beispiele
ein weinend**es** Kind	die weinend**en** Kinder	weinend**e** Kinder

Some present participles are commonly used as nouns. They follow the pattern of adjectival nouns explained in the preceding section.

der/ die Reisend**e**	die Reisend**en**	Reisend**e**
the traveler (male/female)	the travelers	travelers
ein Reisend**er** (male)		
eine Reisend**e** (female)		

---

[1]**das Beispiel, -e**   *example*

der/die Überlebende	die Überlebenden	Überlebende
the survivor (male/female)	*the survivors*	*survivors*
ein Überlebender (male)		
eine Überlebende (female)		
der/die Streikende	die Streikenden	Streikende
the striker (male/female)	*the strikers*	*strikers*
ein Streikender (male)		
eine Streikende (female)		

PRACTICE

9-12   Insert the appropriate endings, following the model of sentence 1.

1. Bei dem Flugzeugunglück hat es keine Überlebenden gegeben.
2. Es gibt nur einen Überlebend __ .
3. Wissen Sie den Namen des Überlebend __ ?
4. Das folgend __ Beispiel spricht für sich selbst.
5. Folgend __ Beispiele sprechen für sich selbst.
6. Bitte übersetzen Sie den folgend __ Satz!
7. Die streikend __ Arbeiter marschieren vor der Fabrik auf und ab.
8. Werden die Streikend __ den neuen Vertrag unterschreiben?
9. Man hat dem Reisand __ eine falsche Auskunft[1] gegeben.
10. Ein Reisand __ hat laut protestiert.
11. Bellend __ Hunde beißen nicht.*

2. Past participles

When a past participle precedes a noun, it has normal adjective endings.

INFINITIVE	PAST PARTICIPLE
verdienen	**verdient**
(*to earn, deserve*)	das verdiente Geld (*the earned money*)
	eine verdiente Strafe (*a deserved punishment*)
gebrauchen	**gebraucht**
(to use)	die gebrauchten Bücher (*the used or second-hand books*)
stehlen	**gestohlen**
(*to steal*)	der gestohlene Wagen (*the stolen car*)

Several past participles have come to be used as nouns. Like other adjectival nouns, they may have strong or weak adjective endings, depending on their usage. Here are some common examples:

der/die Angestellte (the employee)	der/die Gelehrte (*the scholar*)
ein Angestellter	ein Gelehrter
eine Angestellte	eine Gelehrte

---

[1] **Auskunft geben**   *to give information*
* The literal translation is, "Barking dogs don't bite," which corresponds to the English saying, "His bark is worse than his bite."

der/die Erwachsene (*the adult*)	der/die Verlobte (*the fiance*[e])
ein Erwachsen**er**	ein Verlobt**er**
eine Erwachsen**e**	eine Verlobt**e**

When another adjective is added, it has the same ending as the participle:

der/die neu**e** Angestellt**e**	plural: die neu**en** Angestellt**en**
ein neu**er** Angestellt**er**	neu**e** Angestellt**e**
eine neu**e** Angestellt**e**	viele neu**e** Angestellt**e**

PRACTICE

9-13   Insert the appropriate endings.

1. Das ist eine verdient __ Medaille.
2. Das sind keine verdient __ Medaillen.
3. Warum kaufen Sie keine gebraucht __ Bücher?
4. Wo kann man gebraucht __ Bücher kaufen?
5. Er ist mit einem gestohlen __ Wagen nach Nürnberg gefahren.
6. Karin ist meine Verlobt __ .
7. Klaus ist mein Verlobt __ .
8. Dr. Herzog ist ein berühmt __ Gelehrt __ .
9. Seine Frau ist auch eine berühmt __ Gelehrt __ .
10. Die Angestellt __ der Firma Körner streiken.
11. Fragen Sie doch einen Angestellt __ !
12. Ein freundlich __ Angestellt __ hat mir diese Auskunft gegeben.
13. Hier im Bus ist nur noch Platz für einen Erwachsen __ und ein Kind.
14. Dieser Film ist nur für Erwachsen __ .

§14 SUMMARY OF ADDITIONAL USES OF ADJECTIVES

1. Adjectives have strong endings when preceded by uninflected elements, such as **etwas, ein wenig, ein paar, genug,** cardinal numbers (except **ein-**), and **manch, solch, welch.**

2. Adjectives following **andere, einige, mehrere, viele, and wenige** have the same strong or weak endings as these forms.

3. **Derselbe** combines the strong declension of **der** and the weak declension of **selbe** in one word. Additional adjectives take weak endings.

4. Participles preceding nouns follow the rules for the declension of adjectives.

5. Adjectives and participles used as nouns have the usual adjective endings. They are listed as follows:

> **der/die Fremde** (adj. noun) *stranger*
> **der/die Verwandte** (adj. noun) *relative*

PRACTICE

9-14   Summarizing exercises

A. Insert the appropriate endings.

1. X: Diese Gebäude sind schon sehr alt.
   Y: In dieser Stadt gibt es viel __ alt __ Gebäude.

2. X: Hat er denn diese Strafe wirklich verdient?
    Y: Meiner Meinung nach ist das eine verdient ___ Strafe.
3. X: Sind diese Bücher neu oder gebraucht?
    Y: Das sind gebraucht ___ Bücher.
4. X: Käte, ist das dein Verlobt ___ ?
    Y: Kennst du denn meinen Verlobt ___ noch nicht?
5. X: Hoffentlich wird das Wetter etwas besser.
    Y: Ja, wir haben genug schlecht ___ Wetter gehabt.
6. X: Ich glaube, ein amerikanisch ___ Gelehrt ___ arbeitet an diesem Projekt.
    Y: Soviel ich weiß, arbeiten zwei amerikanisch ___ Gelehrt ___ daran.
7. X: Das war nicht fair von Ihrem Chef. Warum haben Sie nicht protestiert?
    Y: Ach, ich bin doch nur ein klein ___ Angestellt ___ .
8. X: Hat ein Fremd ___ Ihnen diese Auskunft gegeben?
    Y: Ich habe den Deutsch ___ da drüben gefragt.
9. X: Wer hat das Glas zerbrochen? Ein Kind oder ein Erwachsen ___ ?
    Y: Es war eine Erwachsen ___ . – Ich.
10. X: Haben Sie viele Verwandt ___ in Berlin?
    Y: Ich habe nur einen Verwandt ___ dort: meinen Vater.
11: X: Was ist denn passiert?
    Y: Es ist etwas Schrecklich ___ passiert.
12. X: Vergessen Sie doch Alles Schlecht ___ in Ihrem Leben und denken Sie
        nur an das Gut ___ !
    Y: Und es gibt viel Gut ___ in meinem Leben.
13. X: Jetzt fahren wir in die Ferien.
    Y: Na, dann alles Gut ___ !
14. X: Warum denkst du, daß ich in Hannelore verliebt bin?
    Y: Ach, das sieht doch ein Blind ___ .
15. X: Was ist der Titel Ihrer Biographie?
    Y: "Ich und meine viel ___ dumm ___ Fehler."

B. Translate into German. (Use the present perfect for the English past tense.)

1. I made many stupid mistakes.
2. We visited a few (ein paar) good friends.
3. They told us something interesting.
4. We saw two interesting films.
5. These films are only for adults.
6. Here is some hot coffee.
7. Many Germans play soccer.
8. Her father is a famous scholar.
9. I asked an employee (fem.).
10. An employee (masc.) gave me this information.
11. That's the same old story.
12. I bought three second-hand books.
13. His bark is worse than his bite.
14. All the best.

10 Comparison of Adjectives and Adverbs

Forms of Comparison

§1 BASIC PATTERN

There are three degrees of comparison:

the positive degree (base form)	**fast**	My car is fast.
the comparative degree	**faster**	Your car is faster.
the superlative degree	**fastest**	Her car is the fastest.

In English short adjectives form the comparative and superlative by adding the endings -*er* and -*est* to the base form, whereas longer adjectives use more and most: more elegant, most elegant.

The German forms are:

POSITIVE	schnell	elegant	_____
COMPARATIVE	schnell**er**	elegant**er**	_____ **er**
SUPERLATIVE	schnell**st-**	elegant**est-**	_____ **(e)st-**

Regardless of length, German adjectives add **-er** to form the comparative and **-st** or **-est** to form the superlative. For the sake of pronunciation, **-est** is added to adjectives ending in **-d, -t, -s, -sch, -ß, or -z:**

mild	laut	hübsch (*pretty*)	heiß
milder	lauter	hübscher	heißer
mild**est-**	laut**est-**	hübsch**est-**	heiß**est-**

Polysyllabic adjectives ending in **-d, -t,** or **-sch** add **-st** in the superlative when the last syllable is unstressed:

interessant	but: dringend (*urgent*)	praktisch
interessanter	dringender	praktischer
interessant**est-**	dringend**st-**	praktisch**st-**

§2   Variations and Irregularities

a.   Most monsyllabic adjectives with the stem vowels **a, o,** or **u** require an umlaut in the comparative and superlative:

alt	kalt	lang	warm	groß	jung	kurz (short)	dumm
älter	kälter	länger	wärmer	größer	jünger	kürzer	dümmer
ältest-	kältest-	längst-	wärmst-	größt-	jüngst-	kürzest-	dümmst-

Note the irregular form **größt-**: only **-t** is added to the stem in the superlative. §3 of the Appendix offers a list of adjectives that add an umlaut in the comparative and superlative.

b.   Adjectives ending in **-e, -el,** and **-er** show a variation in the comparative:

leise (soft)	dunkel (dark)	teuer (*expensive*)
leiser	dunkler	teurer
(only **r** added)	(e omitted)	
leisest-	dunkelst-	teuerst-

c.   **Hoch** drops **c** in the comparative; **nahe** adds **c** in the superlative:

hoch	nahe (close, near)
höher	näher
höchst-	nächst-

d.   The comparative and superlative of **gut** and **viel** are irregular, as are the forms of their English counterparts:

gut	(*good*)	**viel**	(*much, many*)
besser	(*better*)	**mehr**	(*more*)
best-	(*best*)	**meist-**	(*most*)

Note that in contrast to their English equivalents the comparative and superlative of **schlecht** and **wenig** are regular:

schlecht	(*bad*)	wenig	(*little*)
schlechter	(*worse*)	weniger	(*less*)
schlechtest-	(*worst*)	wenigst-	(*least*)

 # Using the Forms of Comparison

In German all three forms of adjectives – positive, comparative, and superlative – may function as a predicate adjective, an adverb, or an attributive adjective.

§3   Comparison of Predicate Adjectives and Adverbs

Heute ist es **kalt.**	Inge fährt **schnell.**	_____
kälter.	schneller.	_____ er
am kältesten.	am schnellsten.	am _____ (e)sten

The comparative has the ending **-er**, the superlative **-(e)sten**. The superlative is preceded by **am**. These forms do not change.

10-1   **A.** Complete the sentences with comparative forms.

MODEL: Das ist _____. (interessant)
Das ist interessanter.

1.   Das ist _____. (dringend, praktisch, elegant, modern, hoch, nahe, gut, schlecht, viel, wenig)
2.   Hannelore ist _____. (nett, freundlich, intelligent)
3.   Ulrich ist _____. (jung, alt, unfreundlich, egoistisch)
4.   Unsere Nachbarn sind __. (neugierig, tolerant)
5.   Diese Sache ist _____. (wichtig,[1] kompliziert, einfach[2])
6.   Bitte fahren Sie _____. (langsam, vorsichtig[3])
7.   Welches Kleid ist _____? (billig,[4] teuer)
8.   Diese Farbe ist _____. (dunkel, hell)
9.   Die Tage werden _____. (lang, kurz)
10.   Bitte sprechen Sie _____! (laut, leise)

B. Complete the sentences with superlative forms.

MODEL: Das ist _____. (interessant)
Das ist am interessantesten.

1.   Das ist _____. (schwer, leicht, praktisch, gut, schlecht, langweilig,[5] einfach, wichtig, billig, teuer hoch, nahe)
2.   Klaus arbeitet _____. (schnell, langsam, viel, wenig)
3.   Frau Büchner ist _____. (nett, tolerant, höflich,[6] neugierig)
4.   Hier ist es _____. (warm, heiß, kalt)
5.   Du gefällst mir _____. (gut)

PHRASES OF COMPARISON EXPRESSING EQUALITY AND INEQUALITY

In phrases of comparison, the positive degree is expressed with **so... wie** and the comparative degree with **als**:

Marlene ist **so groß wie** ich.
Marlene is as tall as I (am).   so _____ wie   *as _____ as*

Klaus ist **größer als** ich.
Klaus is taller than I (am).

Helga ist **intelligenter als** ich.   _____ er als   _____ er than
Helga is more intelligent than I (am).   *more _____ than*

---

[1] **wichtig**   *important*
[2] **einfach**   *simple*
[3] **vorsichtig**   *careful(ly)*
[4] **billig**   *cheap, inexpensive*
[5] **langweilig**   *boring*
[6] **höflich**   *polite*

Note that in comparisons

> **wie** = *as*
> **als** = *than*

10-2   Supply the German equivalents of the English phrases in parentheses.

Model: X: Ich finde, daß Andreas sehr tolerant ist.
   Y: Er ist _____ seine Eltern. (*as tolerant as*)
   Er ist so tolerant wie seine Eltern.

1. X: Deine Schwester ist wirklich sehr hübsch.
   Y: Das stimmt. Sie ist _____ ich. (*as pretty as*)
2. X: Sind die neuen Schuhe bequem?[1]
   Y: Sie sind nicht _____ die alten. (*as comfortable as*)
3. X: Klaus ist immer sehr höflich.
   Y: Stimmt. Er ist _____ du. (*more polite than*)
4. X: Bist du dicker[2] geworden?
   Y: Nein. Ich bin _____ immer. (*as slim[3] as*)
5. X: Margot fährt _____ ich. (*more slowly than*)
   Y: Und sie fährt auch _____ du. (*more carefully than*)
6. X: Meine Noten sind nicht _____ deine. (*as good as*)
   Y: Aber meine Note in Biologie ist _____ deine. (*worse than*)
7. X: Du ißt _____ ich. (*more than*)
   Y: Das stimmt nicht. Ich esse _____ du. (*less than*)
8. X: Ist Margot _____ du? (*shorter[4] than*)
   Y: Nein. Sie ist _____ ich (*as tall[5] as*)
9. X: Bist du ordentlich[6] oder liederlich?[7]
   Y: Sagen wir, ich bin _____ meine Schwester und _____ mein Bruder. (*neater than, sloppier than*)

STRENGTHENING THE COMPARISON

Certain words or prefixes may be added to strengthen a comparison.

a.   **So** may be replaced by **ebenso** or **genauso**:

> Walter ist **ebenso/genauso groß wie** ich.
> *Walter is just as tall as I (am).*

---

[1] **bequem**	*comfortable*
[2] **dick**	*fat, heavy*
[3] **schlank**	*slim*
[4] **klein**	*short* ⎱ (*a person's height*)
[5] **groß**	*tall* ⎰
[6] **ordentlich**	*orderly, neat*
[7] **liederlich**	*sloppy*

b. The comparative form may be preceded by **noch, etwas,** or **viel:**

Dieter ist **noch fauler als** ich.   *Dieter is even lazier than I (am).*
Helga ist **etwas dicker als** du.   *Helga is somewhat (a little) heavier than you.*
Ich bin **viel kleiner als** er.   *I am much shorter than he (is).*

c. In the superlative **aller-** may be added as a prefix:

Das ist am **allerbesten.**   *That is best of all/ the very best.*

PRACTICE

10-3   Supply the German equivalents.

Model: Astrid spricht jetzt sehr gut Deutsch.
Ja, ihr Deutsch ist __ geworden. (*much better*)
Ja, ihr Deutsch ist viel besser geworden.

1. X: War die Prüfung leicht oder schwer?
    Y: Sehr schwer. Sie war _____ sonst.[1] (*much harder than*)
2. X: Wer ist größer, du oder Thomas?
    Y: Thomas. Ich bin _____ er. (*a little shorter than*)
3. X: Merkst [2] du denn nicht, wie neugierig Rainer ist?
    Y: Ach, ich bin _____ er. (*even noisier than*)
4. X: Warum ist Monika Baumann immer so egoistisch?
    Y: Das liegt in der Familie.[3] Sie ist _____ alle Baumanns. (*just as egotistical as*)
5. X: Hoffentlich ist die neue Methode _____ die alte. (*just as simple as*)
    Y: Ich glaube, die neue ist _____ die alte. (*a little more complicated than*)
6. X: Ich weiß, meine Frage war sehr dumm.
    Y: Und meine Antwort war _____ . (*even dumber*)
7. X: Astrid wiegt[4] _____ ich. (*much more than*)
    Y: Und ich wiege _____ Astrid. (_____)
8. X: Wir alle fahren viel zu schnell.
    Y: Und du fährst _____ . (*fastest of all*)
9. X: Ich glaube, dieser Punkt ist sehr wichtig.
    Y: Er ist _____ . (*most important of all*)

§4   COMPARISON OF ATTRIBUTIVE ADJECTIVES

Used attributively, comparative and superlative adjectives have the same strong or weak endings as any other adjective (cf. Chap. 9). The endings are added to the base forms as given in §1 and §2.

---

[1] **sonst**   *usual(ly)*
[2] **merken**   *to notice*
[3] **etwas liegt in der Familie** *something runs in the family*
[4] **wiegen, wog, gewogen**   *to weigh*

Der große Koffer gehört mir.   Das ist ein großer Koffer.
Der größere Koffer gehört mir.   Das ist kein größerer Koffer.
Der größte Koffer gehört mir.   Das ist mein größter Koffer.

        strong weak   un- strong
                                              inflected

10-4 **A.** Replace the comparatives in the following sentences with appropriate comparative forms of the adjectives in parentheses.

MODEL: Das ist der kürzere Weg. (lang)
          Das ist der längere Weg.

1. Das ist eine nettere Kollegin. (freundlich, jung, alt)
2. Das sind elegantere Schuhe. (bequem, billig, teuer)
3. Das ist ein kleinerer Wagen. (groß, alt, schick)
4. Frank Morgenstern ist ein jüngerer Fußballspieler. (gut, schlecht)
5. Das ist ein längerer Film. (kurz, interessant, langweilig)
6. Er hat ein schöneres Leben als wir. (leicht, schwer, gut)

B. Change the attributive adjectives to the comparative.

MODEL: Das ist ein kleiner Wagen.
          Das ist ein kleinerer Wagen.

1. Das ist ein freundlicher Briefträger.
2. Das ist ein bequemer Sessel.[1]
3. Das ist ein intelligentes Mädchen.
4. Herr Hofmann ist ein guter Pianist.
5. Haben Sie einen guten Vorschlag?
6. Das ist eine wichtige Sache.
7. Hoffentlich finden wir eine einfache Lösung.[2]
8. Ich muß eine praktische Tasche[3] kaufen.

C. Insert superlative forms of the adjectives in parentheses.

MODEL: Das ist das _____ Auto. (teuer)
          Das ist das teuerste Auto.

1. Das ist der _____ Wagen. (klein, groß, billig)
2. Das ist die _____ Übung. (leicht, schwer, einfach, kompliziert)
3. Renate hat den _____ Mann geheiratet. (reich, intelligent, nett, egoistisch)
4. Ich habe den _____ Aufsatz geschrieben. (lang, kurz, gut, schlecht)

----

[1] **der Sessel,-**   *armchair*
[2] **die Lösung, -en**   *solution*
[3] **die Tasche, -n**   *bag*

COMPARATIVE AND SUPERLATIVE FORMS OF *viel* AND *wenig*

viel	SINGULAR:	Sie hat **viel** Zeit.	(much)
		mehr Zeit.	(more)
		die meiste Zeit.	(the most)
	PLURAL:	**Viele** Leute sind dagegen.	(many)
		Mehr Leute	(more)
		Die meisten Leute.	(most)
wenig	SINGULAR:	Sie hat **wenig** Zeit.	(little)
		weniger Zeit.	(less)
		die wenigste Zeit.	(the least)
	PLURAL:	**Wenige** Leute sind dagegen.	(few)
		Weniger Leute	(fewer)
		Die wenigsten Leute	(the fewest)

Note: a. **Viel** and **wenig** usually have endings in the plural but not in the singular.
b. The comparatives **mehr** and **weniger** never add an ending.
c. **Meist-** requires the definite article: **die** meisten Leute (most people).

PRACTICE

10-5 Insert the German equivalents.

MODEL: Ich habe _____ du. (*fewer hobbies than*)
Ich habe weniger Hobbys als du.

1. Du hast _____ ich. (*more stamps than*)
2. Kaufmanns haben _____ wir. (*more money than*)
3. _____ arbeiten im Sommer. (*most students*)
4. Der neue Bürgermeister hat _____ der alte. (*fewer difficulties[1] than*)
5. Ich habe _____ du. (*less willpower[2] than*)
6. Du hast _____ . (*the fewest worries[3]*)

PRACTICE

10-6 Summarizing exercises.

A. Express in German.

1. a. That's a simple solution.   **Das ist eine einfache Lösung.**
   b. That's a simpler solution.
   c. That's the simplest solution.
   d. That's simpler.
   e. That's the simplest.
2. a. That's a good suggestion.   **Das ist ein guter Vorschlag.**
   b. That's a better suggestion.

---

[1] **die Schwierigkeit, -en**   *difficulty*
[2] **die Willenskraft**   *willpower*
[3] **die Sorge, -n**   *worry*

c. Do you have a better suggestion? (formal)

d. That's the best suggestion.

3. a. The brown shoes are very comfortable.   **Die braunen Schuhe sind sehr bequem.**

b. Are the black shoes as comfortable as the brown ones?

c. The black shoes are even more comfortable.

d. These are (**Das sind**) the most comfortable shoes.

4. a. This color isn't dark enough.   **Diese Farbe ist nicht dunkel genug.**

b. This color is a little darker.

c. Do you have a darker color? (formal)

d. That's the darkest color.

5. a. This composition isn't good.   **Dieser Aufsatz ist nicht gut.**

b. My composition is worse.

c. That's the worst composition.

d. Who wrote the worst composition? (pres. perf.)

6. a. This coffee tastes very good.   **Dieser Kaffee schmeckt sehr gut.**

b. Which coffee tastes better?

c. Klaus makes[1] the best coffee.

d. His coffee tastes best of all.

7. a. This bag isn't practical.   **Diese Tasche ist nicht praktisch.**

b. Do you have a more practical bag? (formal)

c. I bought the most practical bag. (pres. perf.)

8. a. That's a big worry.   **Das ist eine große Sorge.**

b. That's my biggest worry.

c. I've more worries than you. (fam. sing.)

d. You have fewer worries than I.

9. a. Margrit is very neat.   **Margrit ist sehr ordentlich.**

b. She's much neater than you. (fam. sing.)

c. I'm a little sloppier than my sister.

d. You're just as sloppy as I. (fam. sing.)

B.   Supply the German equivalents.

1.   X: Das ist ein wichtiger Punkt.

Y: Meiner Meinung nach ist das der _____ Punkt. (*most important*)

2.   X: Hast du einen Job gefunden?

Y: Noch nicht. Das ist jetzt mein _____ Problem. (*biggest*)

3.   X: Haben Sie jetzt _____ Zeit für Ihre Familie? (*more*)

Y: Leider habe ich jetzt _____ Zeit für sie. (*even less*)

4.   X: Ich habe _____ du. (*fewer friends than*)

Y: Aber du hast _____ ich. (*more girlfriends than*)

5.   X: Hoffentlich haben unsere Kinder ein _____ wir. (*better life than*)

Y: Das hoffen _____ . (*most parents*)

6.   X: Wer hat den _____ Aufsatz geschrieben? (*best*)

---

[1] idiom: **Kaffee kochen**   *to make coffee*

Y: Das weiß ich nicht. Ich weiß nur, daß ich den _____ geschrieben habe. (*worst one*)

7.   X: Ich finde, daß du jetzt _____ bist. (*slimmer*)

Y: Leider stimmt das nicht. Ich bin _____ immer. (*as fat as*)

8.   X: Ist dein neuer Freund _____ du? (*as tall as*)

Y: Leider nicht. Er ist _____ ich. (*a little shorter than*)

9.   X: Ich bin sehr liederlich. Bist du _____ ich? (*neater than*)

Y: Nein. Ich bin _____ du. (*even sloppier than*)

10. X: Sind die Hausafgaben wieder so kompliziert?

Y: Meiner Meinung nach sind sie _____ (*even more complicated*)

11. X: Sind deine Noten _____ geworden? (*a little better*)

Y: Leider sind sie _____ geworden. (*even worse*)

12. X: Wer kocht den _____ Kaffee? (*best*)

Y: Ich finde, mein Kaffee schmeckt _____ . (*best*)

13. X: Meine Schwester ißt _____ ich. (*less than*)

Y: Sie hat wahrscheinlich _____ du. (*more willpower than*)

14. a. X: Wieviel wiegst du?

Y: _____ früher.[1] (*less than*)

b. X: Und wieviel hast du früher gewogen?

Y: _____ jetzt. (*more than*)

c. X: Sehr logisch.

Y: _____ immer.[2] (*as logical as*)

C.   Compare yourself with relatives and friends and form sentences expressing equality or inequality. Vary your sentences.

MODEL: schlank sein

_____ (*name*) **ist so schlank wie ich.**

or: **genauso schlank wie ich.**

or: **nicht so schlank wie ich.**

or: **schlanker als ich.**

or: **viel (etwas) schlanker als ich.**

1. dick sein
2. liederlich sein
3. neugierig sein
4. egoistisch sein
5. intelligent sein

6. vorsichtig fahren
7. schnell lernen
8. langsam arbeiten
9. viel essen

D.   Answer the following questions:

1. Wer in Ihrer Familie ißt am meisten?
2. Wer in Ihrer Familie spricht am wenigsten?
3. Wer von Ihren Freunden und Freudinnen hat die meiste Willenskraft?

---

1 früher earlier, before, in the past
2 immer always

4. Wen von Ihren Freunden und Freundinnen finden Sie am nettesten?

5. Welchen Schauspieler und welche Schauspielerin bewundern Sie am meisten?

6. Welche Fersehsendung (TV program) gefällt Ihnen am besten oder hat Ihnen am besten gefallen?

Additional Features of Comparatives and Superlatives

§5   TWO WAYS OF EXPRESSING THE SUPERLATIVE OF PREDICATE ADJECTIVES

Meine Freunde sind sehr nett.	Rainer ist **am nettesten.**
	or: Rainer ist **der netteste** (Freund).
My friends are very nice.	*Rainer is the nicest (one).*

When persons or things of a distinctive group are compared, the superlative predicate adjective frequently appears in the attributive form (in agreement with the noun to which it refers) rather than in the form that requires **am ... (e)sten.**

Additional examples:

Körners Töchter sind sehr intelligent.
Astrid is **am intelligentesten.**
or: Astrid ist **die intelligenteste** (Tochter).
The Körners' daughters are very intelligent.
Astrid is the most intelligent (one).

Sie sehen hier sehr wertvolle Gemälde.
Dieses Gemälde ist **am wertvollsten.**
or: Dieses Gemälde ist **das wertvollste** (Gemälde).
You are seeing here very valuable paintings.
This painting is the most valuable (one).

PRACTICE

10-7   Supply the German attributive forms.

MODEL: Wir haben sehr freundliche Nachbarn.
Kästners sind _____ (Nachbarn).
(the friendliest)
Kästners sind die freundlichtsten.

1. Die Mieter[1] in diesem Haus sind sehr tolerant.
Köhlers sind _____ (Mieter).
(the most tolerant)

2. Meine Schwester hat sehr strenge Lehrer.
Ihr Mathematiklehrer ist _____ (Lehrer).
(the strictest)

---

[1] **der Mieter**   tenant

3. Die Kurzgeschichten in diesem Buch sind interessant.
   Diese hier ist _____ (Kurzgeschichte).
           (*the most interesting*)
4. In diesem Standtteil¹ gibt es viele alte Häuser.
   Das hier ist _____ (Haus).
           (*the oldest*)
5. Ich habe viele dumme Fehler gemacht, und dieser hier ist _____ (Fehler).
                                              (*the most stupid*)
6. Alle Prüfungen waren schwer: die Biologieprüfung war _____ (Prüfung).
                                              (*the hardest*)

§6   THE COMPARATIVES AND SUPERLATIVES OF THE ADVERBS *bald, oft,* AND *gern*

a. **bald**	*soon*	Besuchst du uns **bald?**
eher	*sooner*	Kannst du nicht **eher** kommen?
am ehesten	*(the) soonest*	Er hat **am ehesten** reagiert.
b. **oft**	*often*	Er hat **oft** angerufen.
öfter	*oftener/more often*	Sie hat **öfter** angerufen.
(am öftesten)	*most often*	
am häufigsten	*most frequently*	Du hast **am häufigsten** angerufen.

The superlative **am öftesten** is rare: **am häufigsten** is commonly used instead.

c. **gern(e)**	etwas **gern** tun	*to like to do something*
lieber	etwas **lieber** tun	*to prefer to do something*
am liebsten	etwas **am liebsten** tun	*to like to do something most, best*

Gern(e), lieber, am liebsten are used together with a verb to express various degrees of liking. An **e** may be added to **gern.**

Note the use of **essen** and **trinken** when referring to food and drink:

Er **trinkt gern** Kaffee.	*He likes coffee.*
Ich **trinke lieber** Tee.	*I prefer tea.*
Sie **ißt am liebsten** Hummer.	*She likes lobster the best.*

PRACTICE

10-8 Translate into English, then reproduce the German from your translation.

1. Ich spiele gern Tennis, aber mein Freund spielt Fußball.
2. Ich trinke gern Orangensaft,² aber Apfelsaft trinke ich lieber.
3. Was trinkst du am liebsten?
4. Meine Freundin ißt am liebsten Pizza.
5. Was tust du am liebsten?
6. Ich tue liebsten nichts.
7. Warum hast du mir das nicht eher gesagt?

---

¹der Stadtteil, -e   *part of town*
²der Orangensaft, -ë   *orange juice*

8. Warum schreibst du mir nicht öfter?

9. Von allen meinen Freunden ruft Thomas am häufigsten an.

§7   THE USE OF *immer* + COMPARATIVE

The construction **immer** + comparative indicates a progressive change:

Es wird immer kälter.
It is getting colder and colder. It keeps getting colder. (lit. It is always/ever colder.)
Du wirst immer egoistischer.
You are becoming more and more egotistical.
Immer mehr Arbeiter verlieren ihren Arbeitsplatz.
More and more workers are losing their jobs.

PRACTICE

10-9   Insert German equivalents.

MODEL: _____ Leute sind politisch aktiv. (*fewer and fewer*)
Immer weniger Leute sind politisch aktiv.

1. _____ Studenten suchen einen Job. (*more and more*)
2. _____ Studenten finden einen Job. (*fewer and fewer*)
3. Er ist _____ gefahren. (*faster and faster*)
4. Du wirst _____ . (*prettier and prettier*)
5. Meine Noten werden _____ . (*better and better*)
6. Das Wetter wird _____ .(*worse and worse*)
7. Ich werde _____ . (*fatter and fatter*)
8. Die Sache wird _____ . (*more and more complicated*)
9. Das Benzin wird _____ . (*more and more expensive*)
10. Ich verdiene _____ Geld. (*less and less*)

§8   THE USE OF *je...desto* OR *je...um so*

Je schneller desto besser.
    or: um so besser.   *The faster the better*

Je bequemer, desto besser.
    or: um so besser.   *The more comfortable the better.*

Observe the word order:

Je mehr ich für dich **tue**, desto mehr **verlangst du** von mir.
— DEPENDENT CLAUSE — — MAIN CLAUSE —
    verb at the end   inverted word order
The more I do for you, the more you demand from me.

PRACTICE

10-10   Translate into English, then reproduce the German from your translation.

1. Je eher, desto besser.
2. Je praktischer, um so besser.

3. Je weniger Arbeit, um so besser.
4. Je mehr Geld ich verdiene, desto mehr Geld gebe ich aus.[1]
5. Es ist absurd: Je weniger ich esse, desto dicker werde ich.
6. Je mehr Sie ihn tadeln,[2] um so unsicherer wird er.

§9 ABSOLUTE COMPARATIVES AND SUPERLATIVES

ABSOLUTE COMPARATIVES

In certain expressions a comparative form is used where no comparison is actually implied:

ein **älterer** Herr	*an elderly gentleman*
ein **größerer** Geldbetrag	*a rather large amount of money*
eine **längere** Reise	*a rather long trip*
Neuere Sprachen	*modern languages*

ABSOLUTE SUPERLATIVES

Superlative forms may be used to indicate a very high degree of some quality, As adjectives some superlatives are often unpreceded:

Liebste Barbara!	*Dearest Barbara!*
Liebster Peter!	*Dearest Peter!*
Beste Grüße!	*Best regards!*

As adverbs these superlatives modify an adjective or another adverb; they lack **am** and the ending **-en**:

Das war **höchst** interessant.	*That was most interesting.*
Das ist **äußerst** unangenehm.	*That is extremely unpleasant.*

SPECIAL ADVERBIAL SUPERLATIVES WITH THE ENDING *-ens*

höchstens	*at the most*	Sie ist **höchstens** 20 Jahre alt.
mindestens	*at least*	Er arbeitet **mindestens** 8 Stunden am Tag.
frühestens	*at the earliest*	Ich komme **frühestens** am Freitag zurück.
spätestens	*at the latest*	Wir rufen Sie **spätestens** am Sonnabend an.
meistens }	*mostly, most of*	Ich komme **meistens/meist** zu spät.
meist }	*the time, usually*	*I'm usually late. I'm late most of the time.*

---

[1] **aus·geben (gibt aus)**   *to spend*
gab aus, ausgegeben
[2] **tadeln**   *to reprimand*

10-11   Insert German equivalents.

1. Ich muß _____ die Drekarbeit[1] machen. (*most of the time*)
2. Wenn wir Pizza essen wollen, gehen wir _____ in dieses Restaurant. (*usually*)
3. Klaus wiegt _____ 200 Pfund. (*at least*)
4. Wir haben _____ zehn Minuten gewartet. (*at the most*)
5. Ich kann dich _____ um 7 Uhr abholen. (*at the earliest*)
6. Ich gebe dir das Geld _____ am Freitag zurück. (*at the least*)
7. Das war eine _____ peinliche Frage. (*most*)
8. Das ist ein _____ kompliziertes Problem. (*extremely*)
9. Frau Krause ist eine _____ Dame. (*elderly*)
10. Renate studiert _____ in Hamburg. (*modern languages*)
11. Alle unsere Nachbarn haben _____ Familien. (*rather large*)
12. Wir senden Dir,*_____ , _____ aus München. (*dearest Karin, best regards*)

§10   COMPARATIVES AND SUPERLATIVES USED AS NOUNS

Like other adjectives, comparatives and superlatives may be used as nouns. They
retain their usual adjective endings. (cf. Chap. 9, §12)

COMPARATIVES

der/die/das Stärkere	*the stronger one*
die Stärkeren	*the stronger ones*
nichts Leichteres	*nothing easier*
nichts Schöneres	*nothing more beautiful*
nichts Besseres	*nothing better*
etwas Besseres	*something better*
etwas Billigeres	*something cheaper, something less expensive*
etwas Interessanteres	*something more interesting*
etwas Praktischeres	*something more practical*
etwas Wichtigeres	*something more important*

SUPERLATIVES

Thomas ist **der Beste** in Chemie.	*Thomas is the best (one) in chemistry.*
Er ist **der Allerbeste.**	*He is the best (one) of all.*
Du bist **die Schönste.**	*You are the most beautiful one.*
Du bist **die Allerschöntste**	*You are the most beautiful one of all.*
Der Nächste bitte!	*The next (one) please.*
Das ist **das Schwerste.**	*That is the hardest thing.*
Das ist **das Wichtigste.**	*That is the most important thing.*
Haben Sie **das Neu(e)ste** gehört?	*Have you heard the latest?*
Ich habe **mein Bestes** getan.	*I did my best.*

---

[1]**die Drekarbeit**   *dirty work*
der Dreck   *dirt*
* The familiar address is capitalized in letters, cards, and notes (cf. Appendix §7).

PRACTICE

10-12   Insert the German equivalents.

1. Ich konnte nichts _____ finden. (*better*)
2. Du mußt immer das _____ haben. (*best*)
3. Ich werde mein _____ tun. (*best*)
4. Frau Stern, Sie sind die _____ . (*next one*)
5. Nicht immer gewinnt der _____ . (*stronger one*)
6. Es gibt für ihn nichts _____ als Fußball. (*more intersting*)
7. Haben Sie nicht etwas _____ ? (*more practical*)
8. Werner besucht uns nie. Immer hat er etwas _____ vor. (*more important*)
9. Was ist für dich das _____ ? (*most important thing*)
10. Ich finde, Selbstbeherrschung[1] ist das _____ . (*hardest thing*)
11. Haben Sie Frau Bergmann schon das _____ erzählt? (*latest*)
12. Helga ist die _____ .(*best of all*)

PRACTICE

10-13   Summarizing exercises for §5 to §10.

A.   Express in German.

1. a. That's important.   **Das ist wichtig.**
   b. That's extremely important.
   c. There's[2] nothing more important than that.
   d. That's the most important thing.
2. a. This music is very romantic.   **Diese Musik ist sehr romatisch.**
   b. It's getting more and more romantic.
   c. The more romantic the better.
   d. There's nothing more romantic than that.
3. a. I have to buy something cheap.   **Ich muß etwas Billiges kaufen.**
   b. The cheaper the better.
   c. Do you have something cheaper? (formal)
   d. Do you have something more practical?
   e. Do you have something more interesting?
4. a. Life is hard.   **Das Leben ist schwer.**
   b. Life is becoming harder and harder.
   c. What's the hardest thing for you? (fam. sing)
   d. What's the easiest thing for you?
   e. There's nothing easier than that.
   f. There's nothing better than that.

B.   Insert the German equivalents.

1. a. X: Meine Klavierlehrerin ist sehr streng.
      Y: Meine auch. Ich finde, sie wird _____ . (*stricter and stricter*)

---

[1] **die Selbstbeherrschung**   *self-control*
[2] **es gibt** (+ acc)   *there is or are*

  b. X: Strenge Lehrer sind gut für mich.

    Y: Für mich auch _____ . (*The stricter the better.*)

2. a. X: Die deutsche Grammatik ist sehr schwer.

    Y: Nur am Anfang. Später wird sie _____ . (*easier and easier*)

  b. X: Ich finde, sie wird _____ . (*more and more complicated*)

3. X: Werden deine Noten _____ ? (*better*)

    Y: Leider werden sie _____ . (*worse and worse*)

4. X: Wollt ihr wirklich schon im Mai heiraten?

    Y: Ja _____ . (*The sooner the better.*)

5. X: Ich finde diesen Tanz verrückt.

    Y: Mir gefällt er _____ . (*The crazier the better.*)

6. X: Soll ich Ihnen Kaffee oder Tee bringen?

    Y: Für mich Tee. Meine Freundin _____ . (*prefers coffee*)

7. X: Ist deine Freundin immer so nett?

    Y: Nicht immer, aber _____ . (*most of the time*)

8. X: Was machst du sonnabends?

    Y: Da gehe ich _____ einkaufen. (*usually*)

9. X: Wie lange willst du in Wien studieren?

    Y: _____ zwei Semester. (*at least*)

10. X: Hast du die Prüfung bestanden?

    Y: Hoffentlich. Ich habe _____ getan. (*my best*)

11. X: Ich verstehe nicht, wie du in der Prüfung durchfallen konntest.

    Y: Es gibt _____ als das. (*nothing easier*)

12. X: Ich werde _____ . (*dumber and dumber*)

    Y: Keine Angst![1] Das merkt hier niemand.

13. X: Es ist schrecklich, wie oft Barbara in den Spiegel[2] sieht.

    Y: Und jedesmal[3] fragt sie:

        "Spieglein, Spieglein an der Wand,

        wer ist die _____ im ganzen Land?"* (*most beautiful*)

---

[1] **keine Angst!**   *don't worry* (lit.: no fear)
[2] **der Spiegel, -**   *mirror*
[3] **jedesmal**   *every or each time*

* In English, "Mirror, mirror on the wall, who is the fairest of them all?"

CHAPTER 11

Numerals; Time Expressions

Cardinal and Ordinal Numbers

§1 CARDINAL NUMBERS AND THEIR USES

0 null	80 achtzig
1 eins	90 neunzig
2 zwei	100 (ein)hundert
3 drei	101 hunderteins
4 vier	102 hundertzwei
5 fünf	150 hundertfünfzig
6 sechs	151 hunderteinundfünfzig
7 sieben	199 hundertneunundneunzig
8 acht	200 zweihundert
9 neun	201 zweihunderteins
10 zehn	300 dreihundert
11 elf	400 vierhundert
12 zwölf	500 fünfhundert
13 dreizehn	600 sechshundert
14 vierzehn	700 siebenhundert
15 fünfzehn	800 achthundert
16 **sechzehn**	900 neunhundert
17 **siebzehn**	999 neunhundertneunundneunzig
18 achtzehn	1 000 (ein)tausend
19 neunzehn	2 000 zweitausend
20 zwanzig	10 000 zehntausend
21 **einundzwanzig**	100 000 (ein)hunderttausend
22 zweiundzwanzig	250 320 zweihundertfünfzigtausend-
23 dreiundzwanzig	dreihundertzwanzig
30 **dreißig**	1 000 000 eine Million
31 einunddreißig	10 000 000 zehn Millionen
40 vierzig	100 000 000 hundert Millionen
41 einundvierzig	200 500 000 zweihundert Millionen
50 fünfzig	fünfhunderttausend
60 **sechzig**	1 000 000 000 eine Milliarde (*one billion*)
70 **siebzig**	1 000 000 000 000 eine Billion (*one trillion*)

a.   **Eins** is used in counting. It is the only cardinal number that changes when modifying a noun. It then uses the endings of the **ein**-words (cf. Chap. 6, §5).

> Ich habe nur einen Freund.
> Ich habe zwei Freunde.

b.   **Eins** is written **1**.

> **Sieben** is usually written **7** to distinguish from **eins.**

c.   The boldface numbers are irregular:

> eins but **einundzwanzig** (**s** omitted)
> sechs but **sechzehn, sechzig** (**s** omitted)
> sieben but **siebzehn, siebzig** (**en** omitted)
> **dreißig** (ending -**ßig** instead of -**zig**)

d.   To separate thousands, German leaves a space or inserts a period. It does not insert a comma, as English does.

> 10 570 or 10.570 zehntausendfünfhundertsiebzig

e.   All numbers of less than a million are written with small letters. Numbers of a million or more are feminine nouns; their plural forms end in -**en**:

> **zwei Millionen, Milliarden, Billionen.**

REMEMBER: | **eine Milliarde** = *one billion*
eine Billion　 = *one trillion (one thousand billions)*

PRACTICE

11-1   Read aloud the following figures.

1. 26	5. 126	9. 1 317	13. 431 690
2. 67	6. 247	10. 4 255	14. 919 900
3. 88	7. 739	11. 19 387	15. 1 500 000
4. 94	8. 966	12. 51 674	16. 10 800 750

APPROXIMATE FIGURES

etwa		etwa hundert
rund	*about, approximately, roughly*	rund zwanzig
ungefähr		ungefähr zehn
über	*over, more than*	über fünfzig

DECIMALS

The German equivalent of a decimal point is a comma:

> 0,5   (read: null Komma fünf)
> 2,75   (read: zwei Komma sieben fünf)

AMOUNTS IN *Deutsche Mark* (DM) AND *Pfennig*

Diese Schallplatte kostet DM 30,50 (read: dreißig Mark fünfzig [Pfennig])

Note: a. **Mark** and **Pfennig** are in the singular.
    b. **Pfennig** is generally omitted except, of course, when it is the only currency:

Ich habe nur noch 50 Pfennig.

SIMPLE ARITHMETIC

$12 + 4 = 16$ zwölf und vier ist sechzehn
                or: zwölf plus vier…

$12 - 4 = 8$ zwölf weniger vier ist acht
                or: zwölf minus vier…

$\left.\begin{array}{l} 12 \times 4 \\ \text{or: } 12 \cdot 4 \end{array}\right\} = 48$ zwölf mal vier ist achtundvierzig

$12 : 4 = 3$ zwölf geteilt durch 4 ist drei
                (short: zwölf durch vier ist drei)

German uses a colon to express division.

PRACTICE

11-2   Read aloud the following sentences and equations.

1. Diese Uhr kostet DM 124,95.
2. Bergmanns haben über 100 000 Mark gewonnen.
3. Etwa 20 000 Ausländer haben diese Ausstellung[1] besucht.
4. Unsere Stadt hat rund 600 000 Einwohner.
5. Haben Sie 4,5 oder 5,4 gesagt?
6. $56 + 21 = 77$
7. $75 - 45 = 30$
8. $7 \times 9 = 63$
9. $150 : 10 = 15$

§2   ORDINAL NUMBERS AND THEIR USES

der, das, die 1.   der, das, die **erste**   *the first*
           2.   zweite   *the second*
           3.   **dritte**   *the third*
           4.   vierte
           5.   fünfte
           6.   sechste
           7.   siebente
                or: **siebte**
           8.   **achte**
           9.   neunte

---

[1] die Ausstellung, -en   *exhibition*

10.	zehnte
11.	elfte
12.	zwölfte
13.	dreizehnte
19.	neunzehnte
20.	zwanzigste
21.	einundzwanzigste
22.	zweiundzwanzigste
23.	dreiundzwanzigste
30.	dreißigste
31.	einunddreißigste
40.	vierzigste
50.	fünfzigste
60.	sechzigste
70.	siebzigste
80.	achtzigste
90.	neunzigste
100.	hundertste
200.	zweihundertste
1000.	tausendste
1000000.	millionste

a.   The ordinal numbers **erste, dritte, siebte,** and **achte** are irregular. The others from 2nd to 19th are formed by adding **-te** to the cardinal number. Higher numbers add **-ste**.

b.   Ordinal numbers take normal adjective endings (cf. Chap. 9, §8).

       der erst**e** Sonntag   die erst**e** Frage
       am erst**en** Sonntag   nach der erst**en** Frage

c.   When numerals are used, ordinal numbers are indicated by placing a period after the number.

       Mein Büro ist im 19. Stock.   *My office is on the 19th floor.*

THE USE OF THE ADVERBS *erstens, zweitens, drittens, etc.*

1. **erstens**	*first(ly), in the first place*
2. **zweitens**	*second(ly), in the second place*
3. **drittens**	*third(ly), in the third place*
4. **viertens**	*fourth(ly), in the fourth place*

      Warum willst du nicht mit uns ins Kino gehen?
      Erstens bin ich müde, **zweitens** habe ich keine Zeit, und **drittens** bin ich pleite.

THE USE OF *-mal* AND *MAL* WITH CARDINAL AND ORDINAL NUMBERS

cardinal number + -mal:		ordinal number used as adjective:	
einmal	once	**das erste Mal**	*the first time*
noch einmal	once more	**zum ersten Mal**	*for the first time*

zweimal	*twice, two times*	das zweite Mal	
dreimal	*three times*	das dritte Mal	
zehnmal	*ten times*	das vierte Mal	
hundertmal	*a hundred times*		
tausendmal	*a thousand times*		

FRACTIONS

$\frac{1}{2}$	ein halb-	Das ist **ein halber Kuchen**.	*This is half a cake.*
$\frac{1}{2}$	die Hälfte	**Die Hälfte** gehört mir.	*Half of it is mine.*
$\frac{1}{3}$	ein Drittel		
$\frac{1}{4}$	ein Viertel		
$\frac{2}{5}$	zwei Fünftel		
$\frac{3}{10}$	drei Zehntel		
$\frac{1}{100}$	ein Hundertstel		

With the exception of **ein halb-** and **die Hälfte**, fractions are neuter nouns. They are formed by adding **-l** to the ordinal number. **Ein halb-** takes the normal adjective endings. However, in compounds like **eineinhalb** and **anderthalb** ($1\frac{1}{2}$) no adjective ending is used.

$1\frac{1}{2}$	eineinhalb	Wir haben **eineinhalb (anderthalb) Jahre** in Zürich gewohnt.
or:	anderthalb	
$2\frac{1}{2}$	zweieinhalb	Martin hat **zweieinhalb Jahre** Deutsch gelernt.
$3\frac{1}{2}$	dreieinhalb	Helgas Eltern sind **dreieinhalb Wochen** in Florida geblieben.

PRACTICE

11-3

A. Replace the boldface words with German equivalents of the English words and phrases in parentheses.

1. Wir haben in der **ersten** Reihe gesessen. (*third, fifth, tenth*)
2. Ich habe die **zweite** Frage nicht verstanden. (*fourth, sixth, eighth*)
3. Wir haben das **dritte** Kapitel noch nicht behandelt. (*seventh, seventeenth*)
4. Alle diese Gedichte sind aus dem **sechzehnten** Jahrhundert.[1] (*nineteenth, twentieth*)
5. Du hast nun schon **dreimal** gewonnen. (*five times, nine times*)
6. Sie hat **zum ersten Mal** nachgegeben. (*for the second time*)
7. Ich kann nur **die Hälfte** von meinen Schulden bezahlen. (*one fourth*)
8. Müllers waren **anderthalb** Monate in Europa. (*three and a half*)

B. Insert German equivalents of the English words and phrases in parentheses.

1. X: Wollen Sie es _____ versuchen? (*once more*)
   Y: Ich habe es schon _____ versucht. (*twice*)
2. X: _____ hat Helga gewonnen und _____ Thomas.
   (*the first time, the second time*)
   Y: Und _____ werde ich gewinnen. (*the third time*)

---

[1] das Jahrhundert, -e   *century*

3. X: Warum hast du mich nicht angerufen?

    Y: _____ wollte ich dich nicht bei der Arbeit stören, und _____ dachte ich, du würdest vielleicht später anrufen.

    (in the first place, in the second place)

4. X: Kennst du Herrn Morgensterns _____ Frau? *(first)*

    Y: Ich kenne nur seine jetzige[1] Frau. Ist das seine _____ Frau? *(second)*

    X: Nein, seine _____ . *(third)* Vielleicht lernen wir noch eine _____ kennen. *(fourth)*

    Y: Hoffentlich nicht.

5. X: Du hast nun schon _____ gesagt, daß du Monika nicht leiden kannst.[2] *(ten times)* Wann hörst du endlich damit auf?

    Y: Wenn ich es _____ gesagt habe. *(a hundred times)*

6. X: Möchten Sie eine Tasse Kaffee?

    Y: Bitte nur _____ . *(half a cup)*

7. X: Michael, du vernachlässigst[3] mich. Liebst du mich nicht mehr?

    Y: Unsinn! Du weißt doch, daß du meine _____ bist. *(better half)*

THE USE OF ORDINAL NUMBERS WITH DYNASTIC NAMES

Papst Paul **der Erste**	written: Papst Paul I.
Kaiser Wilhelm **der Zweite**	Kaiser Wilhelm II.
König Ludwig **der Vierzehnte**	König Ludwig XIV.

Here the ordinal numbers are capitalized, since they are regarded as part of a proper name. They have the usual adjective endings.

NOM.	Kaiser Friedrich **der Dritte**	Kaiser Friedrich III, war sein Freund.
ACC.	Kaiser Friedrich **den Dritten**	Er haßte Kaiser Friedrich III.
DAT.	Kaiser Friedrich **dem Dritten**	Sie halfen Kaiser Friedrich III.
GEN.	Kaiser Friedrichs **des Dritten**	Sie war die Tochter Kaiser Friedrichs III.

Note that the genitive **-s** is attached to the name only, not to the title.

PRACTICE

11-4   Read the following sentences aloud:

1. Das war ein großes Problem für Kaiser Friedrich III.
2. Das waren die Kinder Kaiser Karls VI.
3. Sie mußten mit König Ludwig XIV. verhandeln.[4]
4. Papst Gregor VII. bannte[5] König Heinrich IV.

---

[1] **jetzig**   *present, current*
[2] **nicht leiden können**   *to dislike, not like*
[3] **vernachlässigen**   *to neglect*
[4] **verhandeln**   *to negotiate*
[5] **bannen**   *to excommunicate*

Time Expressions

INTRODUCTION

In using time expressions, one must pay particular attention to the gender of the noun. Here is a list of frequently occurring nouns grouped according to gender.

MASCULINE	NEUTER	FEMININE
der Monat, -e	das Jahr, -e	die Sekunde, -n
der Tag, -e	das Wochenende, -n	die Minute, -n
		die Stunde, -n
		die Nacht, ⸚e
		die Mitternacht, ⸚e
		die Zeit, -en
		die Jahreszeit, -en (*season*)
		die Woche, -n
		die Uhr, -en (*clock, watch*)

days of the week
    der Sonntag, -e
    Montag, -e
    Dienstag, -e
    Mittwoch, -e
    Donnerstag, -e
    Freitag, -e
    Sonnabend, -e
or: Samstag, -e

parts of the day
der Morgen, -
    Vormittag, -e
    Mittag, -e
    Nachmittag, -e
    Abend, -e
(but: die Nacht)

REMEMBER:
> **die Stunde** = *hour*
> **die Uhr**   = *clock, watch*

months
der Januar
    Februar
    März
    April
    Mai
    Juni
    Juli
    August
    September
    Oktober
    November
    Dezember

seasons
der Frühling, -e
    Sommer, -
    Herbst, -e
    Winter, -

§3 TIME EXPRESSIONS REFERRING TO SEASONS, MONTHS, DAYS OF THE WEEK, AND PARTS OF THE DAY

Most time expressions that include a preposition are in the dative case.

1. Seasons and months

im Frühling	*in the spring*	**im** Januar	*in January*
im Sommer	*in the summer*	**im** Februar	
im Herbst	*in the fall*	**im** März	
im Winter	*in the winter*		

In contrast to English usage, German names of the months require the definite article.

> Wir heiraten **im Januar**. (contraction of **in + dem**)
> **Der Juli** war dieses Jahr sehr heiß.

2. Days of the week

(am) Sonntag *on Sunday* (Am) Sonntag bin ich in Berlin.
(am) Montag
(am) Dienstag

Note that **am (an + dem)** may be omitted.

3. Parts of the day

am Morgen	*in the (early) morning* Am Morgen war ich zu Hause.
am Vormittag	*in the (late) morning or forenoon (from 10 to noon)*
am Mittag / **zu** Mittag	*at noon*
am Nachmittag	*in the afternoon*
am Abend	*in the evening* / *at night (before bedtime)*
in der Nacht	*at night (after bedtime)*

Note that **at night** (before bedtime) is expressed by **am Abend**.

4. The days of the week combined with parts of the day

(am) Sonntag morgen (Am) Sonntag morgen ist unser Hund davongelaufen.
(am) Montag vormittag
(am) Dienstag mittag
(am) Mittwoch abend (*Wednesday evening/night*)

in der Nacht — vom Donnerstag zum Freitag
vom ersten zum zweiten Mai

(*during the night from…to…*)

With the exception of **Nacht**, the parts of the day are used as adverbs in these combinations and are therefore not capitalized.

11-5   Insert German equivalents of the English phrases in parentheses.

1. Vielleicht mieten wir _____ eine größere Wohnung. (*in the spring; in the fall*)
2. Dieses Jahr fahren wir schon _____ nach Italien. (*in June; in May*)
3. _____ habe ich an meinem Referat[1] gearbeitet. (*on Tuesday, on Thursday*)
4. Ich besuche dich vielleicht _____ . (*on Wednesday, on Saturday*)
5. Wir sind _____ einkaufen gegangen. (*Saturday morning, Friday afternoon, Thursday evening*)
6. Hast du _____ etwas vor? (*Friday night, Sunday afternoon*)
7. Ich war _____ im Supermarkt. (*Monday morning, Tuesday noon*)
8. Das ist _____ passiert. (*during the night from Wednesday to Thursday, during the night from the second to the third of June*)

5. Adverbial forms ending in **-s**

a. Herr Zimmermann arbeitet **am Montag** nicht.
b. Herr Zimmermann arbeitet **montags** nicht.

Sentence a. may mean that Mr. Zimmermann will not work this coming Monday or that he usually does not work on Mondays. The use of **montags** in sentence b. clearly indicates that he does not work on Mondays.

Forms ending in **-s** normally denote repeated occurrences. Because they function as adverbs, they are not capitalized.

sonntags, montags, dienstags, mittwochs, donnerstags, freitags, sonnabends/ samstags
on Sundays, Mondays…

Parts of the day functioning as adverbs:

morgens, vormittags, mittags, nachmittags, abends, nachts
in the morning(s)…

Meistens lerne ich **abends**. *I usually study at night.*

These forms may also refer to one event:

Ich war gestern zu Hause. Nur **am Nachmittag**
or: Nur **nachmittags** } war ich bei Kleins.

I was at home yesterday. Only in the afternoon I was at the Kleins'.

The days of the week combined with parts of the day have two forms:

Frau Berger ist **donnerstags nachmittags** immer in ihrem Büro.
(two adverbs)
or: **Donnerstag nachmittags**
(noun + adverb)

---

[1] **das Referat, -e**   *seminar paper (oral presentation)*

11-6   Insert German equivalents of the English phrases in parentheses, using adverbial **s**-forms.

1. _____ ist Frau Morgenstern meistens zu Hause. (*on Mondays, on Tuesdays*)
2. Meistens gehe ich _____ einkaufen. (*on Fridays, on Thursdays*)
3. Diese Bank ist _____ geschlossen. (*on Saturdays and on Wednesday afternoons*)
4. _____ mache ich die Wohnung sauber. (*on Thursday evenings*)
5. Ich weiß meistens nicht, was ich _____ machen soll. (*on Sunday afternoons*)
6. _____ mache ich immer die Hausaufgaben für Montag. (*on Sunday nights*)

§4   ADDITIONAL TIME EXPRESSIONS

1. Adverbs

vorgestern	**gestern**	**heute**	**morgen**	**übermorgen**
the day before yesterday	*yesterday*	*today*	*tomorrow*	*the day after tomorrow*

The parts of the day used with **heute, gestern,** and **morgen**:

heute morgen **heute früh** }	*this morning*	**gestern morgen** **gestern früh**	**morgen früh** *tomorrow morning* (only this form)
heute vormittag	*this morning* *this afternoon*	**gestern vormittag** *etc.*	**morgen vormittag** *etc.*
heute mittag	*this noon*		
heute nachmittag	*this afternoon*		
heute abend	{ *this evening* *tonight*		
heute nacht	*tonight*		

The adverb **morgen** may have two meanings: *morning or tomorrow*. When it follows another time expression, it has the meaning of *morning*:

> **Heute morgen** habe ich den Wecker nicht gehört.
> ***This morning*** *I didn't hear the alarm clock.*

When it precedes another time expression or stands alone, it has the meaning of *tomorrow*:

> Ich fahre **morgen nachmittag** nach Münster.
> *I'm going to Münster **tomorrow afternoon.***

> Dieter fährt **morgen** auch nach Münster.
> *Dieter is also going to Münster **tomorrow.***

Keep in mind that until bedtime (about 11 P.M.) **abend** corresponds to English night:

tonight	**heute abend**
tomorrow night	**morgen abend**
last night	**gestern abend**

Last night after bedtime is expressed by **letzte Nacht.** Compare:

> Ich habe **gestern abend** in der Bibliothek gearbeitet.
> *I worked in the library last night.*

> Ich habe **letzte Nacht** nicht gut geschlafen.
> *I didn't sleep well last night.*

11-7   Insert the German equivalents of the English phrases in parentheses.

1. Arnold hat _____ an seinem Referat gearbeitet. (*last night*)
2. Vielleicht räume ich _____ mein Zimmer auf. (*tonight, tomorrow night*)
3. Ich habe _____ von dir geträumt. (*last night*)
4. _____ habe ich meinen Wagen gewaschen. (*this noon, yesterday noon*)
5. Wahrscheinlich geht Ursula _____ zum Arzt. (*this afternoon, tomorrow afternoon*)
6. _____ arbeite ich im Labor. (*this morning, tomorrow morning*)
7. _____ habe ich die Deutschstunde geschwänzt. (*this morning, yesterday morning* [use **vormittag**])
8. Ellen ist _____ weggefahren, und _____ kommt sie zurück. (*the day before yesterday, the day after tomorrow*)

2. Time expressions in the accusative case

Most time expressions that do not include a preposition are in the accusative case.

diese Woche	nächste Woche	jede Woche
this week	*next week*	*every week*
dieses Wochenende	näch**stes** Wochenende	je**des** Wochenende
dies**en** Monat	näch**sten** Monat	je**den** Monat
dieses Jahr	nächs**tes** Jahr	je**des** Jahr
	nächs**ten** Freitag	je**den** Freitag
	but: <u>am</u> nächs**ten** Tag	
	the next day	

vorige letzte } Woche		den ganzen Tag
last week		*all day*
voriges letztes } Wochenende		*the whole/entire day* den ganzen Abend
vorigen letzten } Monat		die ganze Nacht den ganzen Monat
voriges letztes } Jahr		das ganze Jahr die ganze Zeit

3.   Time expressions with prepositions + dative case

a. Answering the question **wann?** (when?)

in ein paar Minuten	<u>vor</u> ein paar Minuten	nach einer Weile
in a few minutes	*a few minutes ago*	*after a while*
in **einer** Stunde	vor einer Stunde	nach der Deutschstunde
in **einer** Woche	vor drei Wochen	nach ein paar Tagen
in **einem** Monat	vor fünf Monaten	nach einer Woche
in **einem** Jahr	vor zwei Jahren	nach einem Jahr

heute <u>in</u> **einer** Woche	heute <u>vor</u> einer Woche
a week <u>from</u> today	*a week <u>ago</u> today*
heute <u>in</u> **einem** Monat	heute <u>vor</u> einem Monat
a month <u>from</u> today	*a month <u>ago</u> today*
heute <u>in</u> **einem** Jahr	heute <u>vor</u> einem Jahr
a year <u>from</u> today	*a year <u>ago</u> today*

b. Answering the question **wie oft?** (how often?)

einmal, zweimal, dreimal **am Tag**   *once, twice, three times a day*
                          in der Woche   *a week*
               or: **die Woche**
                  (acccusative)
                          im Monat   *a month*
                          im Jahr   *a year*

c. Exception: preposition + accusative
answering the question **für/auf wie lange?** (for how long?)

Heike und Detlef fahren für einen Tag nach Köln.
                       für eine Woche
                       für einen Monat
                       für ein paar Monate

Heike und Detlef are going to Cologne for one day.
                                  for a week.
                                  for a month.
                                  for a few months.

Der Präsident wird **auf** vier Jahre gewählt.
The president is elected for four years.

Für… is more often used than **auf**…
Note that **ein paar** is not inflected (cf. Chap. 9, §9).
(For the use of **seit** + dative, cf. Chap. 2, §7, 3 and Chap. 7, §1, 7.)

4.   Set expressions in the genitive case denoting indefinite time

Eines Tages ist Frank davongelaufen.		*One day Frank ran away.*
Eines Morgens ⎫		*One morning* ⎫
Eines Abends ⎬ ist er zurückgekommen.		*One evening* ⎬ *he came back.*
Eines Nachts ⎭		*One night* ⎭

Although **Nacht** is of feminine gender, the masculine form **eines Nachts** is used by analogy with **eines Morgens** and **eines Abends**.

PRACTICE

11-8   Insert German equivalents of the English phrases in parentheses.

1. Meine Frau und ich waren _____ in Österreich. (*a week ago, a month ago, a year ago*)
2. _____ waren wir in Wien. (*a week ago today, a month ago today, a year ago today*)
3. Wo werden wir _____ sein? (*a week from today, a month from today, a year from today*)
4. _____ muß diese Arbeit fertig sein. (*in a week, in a month, in a year*)
5. _____ muß ich sehr sparsam[1] sein. (*this week, this month, this year*)
6. Vielleicht sehen wir uns _____ wieder. (*next week, next month, next year*)
7. Erst[2] hat er ja gesagt, aber _____ hat er nein gesagt. (*the next day*)
8. Erst waren wir begeistert von unserem Haus, aber _____ hat es uns nicht mehr gefallen. (*after a few years*)
9. Die ganze Familie Berger war _____ bei uns. (*last Sunday, last weekend, last week*)
10. Käte fährt _____ nach Hause. (*every day, every weekend, every month*)
11. Maria hat mich _____ angerufen. (*a few minutes ago, an hour ago*)
12. Er ruft mindestens _____ an. (*once a day, twice a week, four times a month*)
13. Wir haben _____ Ferien. (*three times a year*)
14. Wir wollen _____ zu meinen Verwandten in Hamburg fahren. (*for a month*)
15. Meine Eltern werden uns _____ besuchen. (*for a few days*)
16. Mein Freund hat _____ vor dem Fernseher gesessen. (*all evening, all the time*)
17. _____ war mein Fahrrad verschwunden.[3] (*one day, one night*)
18. _____ brachte die Polizei mein Fahrrad zurück. (*one morning*)

5. Expressing dates

    a. Heute ist **der elfte Mai.**   written: Heute ist **der 11. Mai.**
    b. Heute haben wir **den elften Mai.**   Heute haben wir **den 11. Mai.**
    c. Ich habe **am elften Mai** Geburtstag.   Ich habe **am 11. Mai** Geburtstag.

In sentence a. **der elfte Mai** is a predicate nominative (after **sein**). In sentence b. **den elften Mai** is in the accusative (direct object). In sentence c. **am elften Mai** is in the dative (prepositional phrase).

Asking about today's date:

> **Welches Datum haben wir heute** ⎫
> or: **Den wievielten haben wir heute?** ⎭   *What is today's date?*

---

[1] **sparsam**   *thrifty, economical*
[2] **erst**   *at first*
[3] **verschwinden,**   *to disappear*
   verschwand, ist verschwunden

Dates in letterheads and documents:

> **Berlin, den 11. Mai 1972**
> (spoken: den elften Mai neunzehnhundertzweiundsiebzig)
> **Bonn, den 31. Oktober 1985**
> (spoken: den einunddreißigsten Oktober neunzehnhundertfünfundachtzig)

The day always precedes the month, even when the month is indicated by an ordinal number:

> 31.10.1985 = 31. Oktober 1985

The English phrase *in 1950* is in German **im Jahr(e) 1950** or simply **1950.**

> Der Komponist starb **im Jahr(e) 1929.** ⎫
> or: Der Komponist starb **1929.**   ⎬ *The composer died in 1929.*
>   ⎭

PRACTICE

▼ 11-9   **A.** Insert German equivalents of the English phrases in parentheses.

MODEL: Dieses Jahr beginnen die Sommerferien _____ . (on May 31)
          Dieses Jahr beginnen die Sommerferien am 31. Mai.

1. Schuberts geben _____ (*on December 2*) eine große Party.
2. Karin hat _____ Geburtstag. (*on July 21*)
3. Ich habe _____ Geburtstag. [insert your birthday]
4. Heute ist _____ .(*April 1*)
5. Haben wir heute _____ ? (*June 5*)
6. _____ hatten wir eine Explosion in unserem Studentenheim. (*in 1979* [two ways])

B. Write the following dates in German, then read them aloud.

1. Hamburg, August 3, 1982
2. Berlin, December 31, 1946
3. Vienna, January 1, 1985

PRACTICE

▼ 11-10   Summarizing exercises for §3 to §5.

A. Complete the sentences in German.

1. X: Welches Datum haben wir heute?
   Y: Ich glaube, heute haben wir _____ [insert today's date].
2. X: In welchem Jahr waren die Olympischen Spiele in München?
   Y: Weißt du das nicht mehr? Das war doch _____ (in 1972 [two ways])
3. X: Fährst du am Wochenende mit Gisela nach Hause?
   Y: _____ sind wir zu ihren Eltern gefahren, und _____ fahren wir zu meinen Eltern. (*last weekend, this weekend*)
4. X: Wann ist dieses Museum geöffnet?
   Y: Das weiß ich nicht genau. Ich weiß nur, daß es _____ geschlossen ist. (*Wednesday afternoons*)

5. X: Weißt du, ob Elke jetzt zu Hause ist?
  Y: _____ ist sie nie zu Hause. (*Friday nights*)

6. X: Wann kann man Sie zu Hause erreichen?[1]
  Y: _____ bin ich meistens zu Hause. (*Sunday noons*)

7. X: Warum gehst du nicht zum Zahnarzt?
  Y: Ich war doch _____ dort. (*yesterday noon*)

8. X: Hat es in der Nacht geregnet?
  Y: Es hat _____ geregnet. (*all night*)

9. X: Wann beginnen die Semesterprüfungen?
  Y: Leider schon _____ . (*tomorrow morning*)

10. X: Wie oft mußt du diese Tabletten einnehmen?[2]
  Y: _____ . (*three times a day*)

11. X: Wie oft geht ihr schwimmen?
  Y: _____ . (*twice a week*)

12. X: Wann haben die Schulferien angefangen?
  Y: _____ . (*three days ago*)

13. X: Wann werden Sie mit dem Studium fertig?[3]
  Y: Hoffentlich _____ . (*in the spring*)

14. X: Was hast du heute gemacht?
  Y: Ich habe _____ die Wohnung saubergemacht. (*all day*)

15. X: Wann hast du Peter das letzte Mal gesehen?
  Y: Er war _____ hier. (*the day before yesterday*)

16. X: Wann hast du Post von Margot bekommen?
  Y: _____ (*a few days ago*)

17. X: Wann haben Frank und Barbara geheiratet?
  Y: _____ . (*a week ago today*)

18. X: Ich möchte wissen, ob dein Bruder jemals[4] gute Laune hat.
  Y: Ich glaube, das passiert nur _____ . (*once or twice a year*)

19. X: Du ißt _____ . (*all the time*)
  Y: Nicht _____ . (*all the time*) Ich esse doch nur _____ .
  (*ten times a day*)

B. Form sentences using the time expressions in the left column.
You may select expressions from the right column or create your own.

MODEL: heute nachmittag
    **Heute nachmittag habe ich meine Freundin zum Flughafen
    gebracht.**

1. gestern abend   mit Professor Zimmermann sprechen
2. heute morgen   Peter Geburtstag haben
3. morgen früh   mein Zimmer sauber•machen

---

[1] erreichen   *to reach, contact*
[2] eine Tablette ein•nehmen,   *to take a tablet, pill*
  (nimmt ein), nahm ein, eingenommen
[3] mit dem Studium fertig werden   *to graduate*
[4] jemals   *ever*

4.	mittwochs nachmittags	einen Job suchen
5.	nächsten Sonnabend	für eine Prüfung lernen
6.	vorgestern	nichts vor•haben
7.	übermorgen	Bank geschlossen
8.	am ersten August	mit meiner Freundin aus•gehen
9.	vorigen Sonntag	zu spät auf•stehen
10.	im Sommer	nur Unsinn reden
11.	voriges Wochenende	einkaufen gehen
12.	jeden Donnerstag	die Semesterferien beginnen
13.	einmal in der Woche	nach Hause fahren
14.	heute abend	zu Hause bleiben
15.	die ganze Zeit	schwimmen gehen

Clock Time

In official statements of time (such as timetables, office hours, performance time) the 24-hour system is used (explained in §6). Otherwise time is expressed according to the 12-hour system.

§5   USING THE 12-HOUR SYSTEM

Wie spät ist es? ⎫
Wieviel Uhr ist es? ⎭   *What time is it?*

Time is most commonly expressed as follows:

3.00   **Es ist drei Uhr.**   *It is three o'clock.*

3.15   **Es ist Viertel nach drei**
     or: **Es ist Viertel vier.**   *It is a quarter past three.*

3.30   **Es ist halb vier.**   *It is half past three.*

3.45   **Es ist Viertel vor vier.**
     or: **Es ist drei Viertel vier.**   *It is a quarter to four.*

In German, hours are separated from minutes by a period rather than a colon. Alternatively, the minutes may be raised:

$$3.15 \text{ or } 3^{15}$$

Note the use of **ein** when it precedes **Uhr**, and **eins** when it stands alone:

1.00	Es ist **ein Uhr.**
1.15	Es ist Viertel nach **eins.**
12.30	Es ist halb **eins.**
12.45	Es ist Viertel vor **eins.**

PRACTICE

11-11   Give the time in German. Use also the options.

MODEL: **8.15 Es ist Viertel nach acht.**
         Es ist Viertel neun.

1. 10.15	5. 6.15	9. 11.45	13. 1.00
2. 10.30	6. 7.15	10. 12.45	14. 2.15
3. 10.45	7. 8.30	11. 1.45	15. 3.45
4. 11.00	8. 9.30	12. 7.00	16. 12.30

FIVE-MINUTE INTERVALS

The most usual forms of five-minute intervals are shown below.

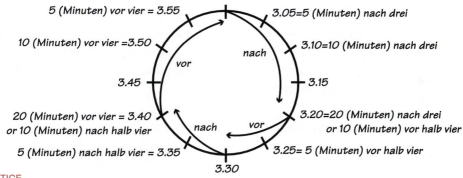

PRACTICE

11-12   Give the time in German following the above pattern.

MODEL: **6.20 Es ist 20 (Minuten) nach sechs.**
         or: Es ist 10 (Minuten) vor halb sieben.

1. 5.20	5. 9.05	9. 12.25	13. 7.50
2. 5.40	6. 9.25	10. 12.35	14. 2.20
3. 11.20	7. 9.35	11. 12.55	15. 9.40
4. 11.40	8. 12.05	12. 1.55	16. 10.35

Other intervals may be expressed the same way.

3.02	Es ist zwei (Minuten) nach drei.
3.32	Es ist zwei (Minuten) nach halb vier.

3.38   Es ist acht (Minuten) nach halb vier.
3.48   Es ist zwölf (Minuten) vor vier.
3.58   Es ist zwei (Minuten) vor vier.

Minute cannot be omitted after **eine.**

3.01   Es ist **eine Minute** nach drei.
3.59   Es ist **eine Minute** vor vier.

PRACTICE

11-13   Give the time in German.

MODEL: 10.04   **Es ist 4 (Minuten) nach zehn.**

1. 10.13	5. 6.09	9. 12.07	13. 2.01
2. 10.29	6. 6.17	10. 12.39	14. 3.29
3. 10.36	7. 6.27	11. 1.06	15. 11.59
4. 10.57	8. 6.54	12. 1.33	

Advice to students: If you don't remember the above ways of expressing the time, you may resort to a simpler way:

5.10   Es ist fünf Uhr zehn.
7.20   Es ist sieben Uhr zwanzig.
1.55   Es ist ein Uhr fünfundfünfzig.
12.33   Es ist 12 Uhr dreiunddreißig.

People will understand you. However, when German-speaking people express the time as explained in this section, you should be able to understand them.

To make clear whether A.M. or P.M. is meant **morgens, vormittags, mittags, nachmittags, abends,** or **nachts** is frequently added.

7:00 A.M. = 7 Uhr morgens   10:00 A.M. = zehn Uhr vormittags
7:00 P.M. = 7 Uhr abends   10:00 P.M. = zehn Uhr abends
                                                1:00 A.M. = ein Uhr nachts
                                                1:00 P.M. = ein Uhr mittags

§6   USING THE 24-HOUR SYSTEM

Official statements of time are based on the 24-hour system.

Der Zug fährt 13:40 (dreizehn Uhr vierzig) ab.
The train leaves at 1:40 P.M.

Das Konzert beginnt 19:30 (neunzehn Uhr dreißig).
The concert begins at 7:30 P.M.

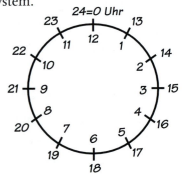

English A.M. = German   1-12 Uhr
P.M. =   13-24 Uhr

1:15 A.M. = 1.15   **ein Uhr fünfzehn**
1:15 P.M. = 13.15   **dreizehn Uhr fünfzehn**
                                    (= English p.m. time + 12)

8:45 A.M. = 8.45	acht Uhr fünfundvierzig
8:45 P.M. = 20.45	zwanzig Uhr fünfundvierzig
11:56 A.M. = 11.56	elf Uhr sechsundfünfzig
11:56 P.M. = 23.56	dreiundzwanzig Uhr sechsundfünfzig
12:15 A.M = 0.15	null Uhr fünfzehn
12:15 P.M. = 12.15	zwölf Uhr fünfzehn

Note: **Viertel, halb, drei Viertel, vor,** and **nach** are not used in the 24-hour system.

PRACTICE

11-14 **A.** Give the time according to the 24-hour system.

MODEL: 4:13 A.M. **vier Uhr dreizehn**
4:13 P.M. **sechzehn Uhr dreizehn**

1.	7:20 A.M.	3.	10:45 A.M.	5.	3:15 A.M.
	7:20 P.M.		10:45 P.M.		3:15 P.M.
2.	9:30 A.M.	4.	6:10 A.M.	6.	12:30 A.M.
	9:30 P.M.		6:10 P.M.		12:30 P.M.

B. Convert to English P.M. time.

MODEL: 14.30 = **2:30 P.M.**

1.	19.00	3.	20.45	5.	23.45
2.	17.15	4.	13.30		

§7 COMMON EXPRESSIONS USED WHEN TELLING TIME

um 1 Uhr **at** *1 o'clock*
Um 1 Uhr esse ich zu Mittag und **um** 7 Uhr zu Abend.
At *1 o'clock I have lunch/dinner (noon meal) and* **at** *7 o'clock supper/dinner (evening meal).*

When telling time, **um** is the German equivalent of English *at.*

Punkt 3 Uhr *3 o'clock sharp*

gegen 3 Uhr
so gegen 3 Uhr } *around 3 o'clock*

von...bis.../*from...to...*	Das Postamt ist **von 9 bis 5** Uhr geöffnet.
vor•gehen (Uhr) *to be fast*	Meine Uhr **geht etwas vor.**
	My watch is a little fast.
	Diese Uhr **geht 5 Minuten vor.**
nach•gehen (Uhr) *to be slow*	Meine Uhr **geht etwas nach.**
	My watch is a little slow.
	Diese Uhr **geht 10 Minuten nach.**
richtig gehen (Uhr) *to be correct*	**Geht** diese Uhr **richtig?**
	Is that clock correct?
	Is that the right time?

nicht gehen *not work, not run*	Meine Uhr **geht nicht.** *My watch doesn't work.*
stehen·bleiben *to stop*	Meine Uhr **ist** schon wieder **stehengeblieben.** *My watch has stopped again.*
die Uhr stellen *to set the clock*	Ich habe vergessen, **den Wecker zu stellen.** *I forgot to set the alarm clock.*
nach meiner Uhr *according to my watch*	**Nach meiner Uhr** ist es 3 Uhr. *According to my watch it is 3 o'clock.*

PRACTICE

11-15   **A.**   Insert German equivalents.

1. X: Warum kommen Sie schon wieder zu spät?
    Y: _____ . (*Because my watch has stopped.*)
2. X: Wissen Sie, wann Dr. Lippert heute Sprechstunde[1] hat?
    Y: Soviel ich weiß, hat er heute _____ Sprechstunde.
    (*from 9 to 12 o'clock*)
3. X: Es kann doch nicht schon zwölf Uhr sein.
    Y: _____ . (*This clock is a little fast.*)
4. X: Geht Ihre Uhr richtig?
    Y: _____ . (*It is two or three minutes slow.*)
5. X: Wann mußt du morgen früh aufstehen?
    Y: _____ . (*At 5 o'clock. I have to set the alarm clock.*)
6. X: Heute morgen habe ich verschlafen.[2]
    Y: _____. (*Did you forget to set the alarm clock?* [fam.; pres. perf.])
7. X: Können Sie mir sagen, wie spät es ist?
    Y: _____ . (*According to my watch it is 7:30.*)
8. X: Wann beginnt das Konzert?
    Y: Soviel ich weiß, beginnt es _____ . (*at 8 o'clock*)
9. X: Wo ist deine Uhr?
    Y: Ich habe sie zu Hause gelassen _____ . (*It doesn't work.*)
10. X: Wann bist du gestern abend ins Bett gegangen?
    Y: Ich glaube, es war _____ . (*around 11 o'clock*)
11. X: Wann ist der Zug abgefahren?
    Y: _____ . (*9 o'clock sharp*)

B.   Form sentences using the following cues.

MODEL: meine Uhr / ein paar Minuten / vor·gehen
         Meine Uhr geht ein paar Minuten vor.

1. diese Uhr / fünf Minuten / nach·gehen
2. leider / meine Uhr / stehen·bleiben (pres. perf.)

---

[1] **Sprechstunde haben**   *to have office hours, consultation*
[2] **verschlafen (verschläft),**   *to oversleep*
   verschlief, verschlafen

3. um 4 Uhr / ich / beim Zahnarzt / müssen / sein
4. von 5 bis 9 Uhr / ich / auf der Tankstelle / arbeiten
5. gegen 2 Uhr / ich/ Margot / ab•holen

C. Ein Tag im Leben einer Studentin.
    State the indicated time and form sentences using the cues.

MODEL: _____ Margot / auf•stehen
                 Um Viertel vor sieben steht Margot auf.

1.   _____ sie / zur Universität / fahren

2.   _____ sie / im Hörsaal / sitzen

3.   _____ sie / zu Mittag / essen

4.   _____ sie / in die Bibliothek / gehen

5.   _____ sie / nach Hause / fahren

6.   _____ sie / zu Abend / essen

7.   _____ sie / Dieter / an•rufen

8.   _____ sie / an einem Referat / arbeiten

9.   _____ sie / ins Bett / gehen

CHAPTER 12

Conjunctions; Infinitive Phrases

 Conjunctions

There are two basic types of conjunctions: coordinating and subordinating.

§1 COORDINATING CONJUNCTIONS

Coordinating conjunctions connect words, phrases, and clauses of equal importance, coordinating them, not subordinating one to the other. The following coordinating conjunctions are used frequently:

aber	*but (however, nevertheless)*
denn	*for, because*
oder	*or*
sondern	*but (rather)*
und	*and*

Coordinating conjunctions have no effect on the word order. Sentences joined by them retain their normal or inverted word order, as the following sentences illustrate.

1. a. Monika spielt gern Tennis. **Ihr Freund spielt** lieber Fußball.
   b. Monika spielt gern Tennis, aber **ihr Freund spielt** lieber Fußball.
   Monika likes to play tennis, but her friend prefers to play soccer.
2. a. Ich rufe Martin um 7 Uhr an. Dann **ist er** bestimmt zu Hause.
   b. Ich rufe Martin um 7 Uhr an, denn dann **ist er** bestimmt zu Hause.
   I'll call Martin at 7 o'clock, because he definitely will be home then.

In sentence 2, *a.* and *b.* the inversion is caused by the adverb **dann.**

Do not confuse: **denn** = *for, because* (coordinating conjunction)
   dann = *then* (adverb)

THE GERMAN EQUIVALENTS OF *but*

but = **sondern** when used in the sense of *but on the contrary* or *but rather* (only after a negative).

Klaus ist **nicht** dumm, **sondern** sehr intelligent.
Klaus is not stupid but (on the contrary) very intelligent.

Wir sprechen **nicht** von dir, **sondern** von Klaus.
We are not talking of you but (rather) of Klaus.

Observe the use of **sondern** in the phrase **nicht nur...sondern auch:**

Diese Transaktion ist **nicht nur** kompliziert, **sondern auch** riskant.
*This transaction is **not only** complicated **but also** risky.*

but = **aber** in all other instances. **Aber** is also used in the sense of *however or neverthe-less*. The preceding clause may or may not be negated.

Ulrich ist nicht dumm, **aber** er hat immer schlechte Noten.
Ulrich is not stupid, but (however, nevertheless) he has always bad grades.

Sabine ist intelligent, **aber** ihre Noten sind nicht gut.
Sabine is intelligent, but (however, nevertheless) her grades are not good.

PRACTICE

12-1

A. Insert **sondern** or **aber** and state the reason for your choice.

1. Wir wohnen in einem kleinen alten Haus, _____ es gefällt uns sehr.
2. Müllers fahren nicht nach Spanien, _____ nach Italien.
3. Dieses Dokument ist nicht das Original, _____ eine Kopie.
4. Ich habe nicht viel Geld, _____ einmal im Monat kaufe ich mir etwas Besonderes.
5. Nicht Lore, _____ Klaus hat das Geschirr gespült.[1]
6. Ich verstehe nicht immer alles, was mein mexikanischer Freund sagt, _____ meistens weiß ich, was er sagen will.

B. Express the responses in German, using the expression **nicht nur... sondern auch.**

MODEL: X: Hast du Hunger?
        Y: I am not only hungry but also thirsty.
           Ich habe nicht nur Hunger, sondern auch Durst.

1. X: Heute ist es wirklich sehr heiß.
   Y: It is not only hot, but also muggy.[2]
2. X: Heinz hat ja[3] eine sehr dumme Bemerkung gemacht.
   Y: His observation was not only stupid but also dangerous.[4]
3. X: Findest du auch, daß die Prüfung zu lang war?
   Y: It was not only too long but also too hard.
4. X: Deine neue Freundin ist wirklich sehr nett.
   Y: She is not only very nice but also very interesting.

---

[1] **das Geschirr spülen** *to do the dishes (lit.: rinse the dishes)*
[2] **schwül** *muggy, close*
[3] **ja** *here used as a flavoring particle (cf. Appendix, §4)*
[4] **gefährlich** *dangerous*

PRACTICE

12-2   Combine the following sentences using German coordinating conjunctions.

1. Sie hat mich nicht erkannt.[1] (*or*) Sie wollte mich nicht erkennen.
2. Ich bin sehr böse auf Klaus. (*for*) Er hat sein Versprechen nicht gehalten.
3. Das ist ein langweiliger Film. (*but*) Meine Freundin will ihn unbedingt[2] sehen.
4. Mein Bruder hat den Motor repariert. (*and*) Jetzt läuft er ausgezeichnet.
5. Wir gehen immer morgens schwimmen. (*for*) Dann ist das Hallenbad[3] nicht so voll.

§2   SUBORDINATING CONJUNCTIONS

Subordinating conjunctions introduce dependent clauses. Compare these sentences:

a. **Ich bin** jetzt oft in der Bibliothek,   denn **ich schreibe** eine Semesterarbeit.
   MAIN CLAUSE   MAIN CLAUSE
b. **Ich bin** jetzt oft in der Bibliothek,   weil **ich** eine Semesterarbeit **schreibe.**
   MAIN CLAUSE   DEPENDENT CLAUSE
c. Weil **ich** eine Semesterarbeit **schreibe,**   bin ich jetzt oft in der Bibliothek.
   DEPENDENT CLAUSE   MAIN CLAUSE

In sentence *b*. the clause introduced by the subordinating conjunction **weil** has dependent word order: the inflected verb is in last position. When the dependent clause precedes the main clause, as in sentence *c.*, the latter has inverted word order (cf. Chap. 1, §3).

Here is a list of subordinating conjunctions that are used frequently.

als	*when*
bevor ⎫ ehe ⎭	*before*
bis	*until*
da	*since* (stating reason), *because*
damit	*so that, in order that*
daß	*that*
indem	*by* (doing something)
nachdem	*after*
ob	*whether, if*
obwohl ⎫ obgleich ⎭	*although*
seit ⎫ seitdem ⎭	*since* (referring to time)
sobald	*as soon as*
solange	*as long as*

---

[1] erkennen, erkannte, erkannt   *to recognize*
[2] unbedingt   *absolutely, by all means*
[3] das Hallenbad, ̈er   *indoor swimming pool*

während	*while*
weil	*because*
wenn	*when, whenever, if*

Observe the use of the following subordinating conjunctions.

1.   Three German equivalents of **when**

a. when = **wann** used in the sense of *at what time* in direct and indirect questions.

Direct question:

Wann kommt Sonja nach Hause?
When (at what time) is Sonja coming home?

Indirect question (preceded by an introductory clause; cf. Chap. 1, §5):

Weißt du, **wann** Sonja nach Hause **kommt**?
Ich weiß nicht, **wann** Sonja nach Hause kommt.

In indirect questions, question word like **wann** functions as subordinating conjunction.

b. when = **als** in clauses that refer to a single past occurrence or state:

Leider hat es gestern geregnet, **als** wir ein Picknick machen wollten.
Unfortunately it rained yesterday when we were planning to have a picnic.

Sie war sehr vorsichtig, **als** sie am Montag mit dem Chef sprach.
She was very careful when she talked with the boss on Monday.

Ich habe mich erkältet, **als** ich gestern in der Stadt war.
I caught a cold when I was in town yesterday.

The occurence or state may cover a period of time:

Sabine hat Peter kennengelernt, **als** sie in München studierte.
Sabine met Peter when she was studying in Munich.

Er hatte viele Freunde, **als** er jung und unternehmungslustig war.
He had many friends when he was young and enterprising.

Als is also used in present-tense summaries of such past events in stories, plays, films, etc.

Als der Held seinen Gegner kommen sieht, stellt er sich tot.
When the hero sees his opponent coming, he pretends to be dead.

c. when = **wenn** in all other instances:

when referring to repeated occurences in the past, (In such cases, English often uses *whenever*.)

Leider hat es immer geregnet, **wenn** wir ein Picknick machen wollten.
Unfortunately, it always rained when (whenever) we wanted to have a picnic.

Sie war immer sehr vorsichtig, **wenn** sie mit dem Chef gesprochen hat.
She was always very careful when (whenever) she talked with the boss.

in all clauses referring to the present and future (single or repeated occurences).

Hoffentlich regnet es nicht, **wenn** ihr morgen ein Picknick macht.
Sie ist immer sehr vorsichtig, **wenn** sie mit dem Chef spricht.

REMEMBER: when

= **wann** (at what time) in direct and indirect questions
= **als** referring to a single past occurence or state
  (including present-tense summaries of such past events)
= **wenn** in all other instances

PRACTICE

12-3   Supply the German equivalent of *when*.

1. Ich habe mich sehr gefreut,[1] _____ ich am Montag die gute Nachricht bekam.
2. Ich habe mich immer gefreut, _____ du mich angerufen hast.
3. _____ rufst du Renate an? Ich weiß noch nicht, _____ ich sie anrufen kann.
4. Natürlich werde ich dir alles erzählen, _____ du morgen zu mir kommst.
5. _____ er mich gestern sah, wurde er verlegen.[2]
6. _____ er mich sieht, wird er immer verlegen.
7. Weißt du noch, _____ du den Brief abgeschickt hast?
8. _____ Sonja in Frankfurt studierte, hatte sie einen französischen Freund.
9. Wir haben Goethes *Faust* gesehen, _____ wir vorige Woche im Theater waren.
   Faust sieht Margarete zum ersten Mal, _____ sie gerade aus der Kirche kommt.

2.   The German equivalents of **if**

   a. *if* = **wenn** in conditional statements.

   Wenn das wahr is, (dann) gibt es bestimmt einen Skandal.
   If that is true, (then) there will certainly be a scandal.

   b. *if* = **ob** in indirect questions. (English also uses *whether* in this context; (cf. Chap,1, §5.)

   Ist das wahr? Ich weiß nicht, **ob** das wahr ist.
   Is that true? I don't know if (whether) that is true.

REMEMBER: *if* = **wenn** unless it is replaceable by *whether*,
             in which case it is **ob.**

PRACTICE

12-4   Supply the German equivalents of *if*.

1. Ich weiß nicht, _____ er die Wahrheit gesagt hat.
2. Sie wird bestimmt sehr böse, _____ er ihr nicht die Wahrheit sagt.
3. Ich möchte wissen, _____ Kästners jetzt zu Hause sind.
4. _____ ich mein Stipendium verliere, muß ich mit dem Studium aufhören.

---

[1] **sich freuen**   *to be happy, glad*
[2] **verlegen**   *embarrassed*

5. Wissen Sie, _____ der Zug aus München Verspätung hat?[1]

6. _____ der Zug pünktlich abfährt, kommen wir um 12 Uhr in Bonn an.

3. The German equivalents of *since*

a. since = **seitdem** or **seit** when it refers to time.

> **Seitdem (seit)** Maria in Bonn studiert, schreibt sie mir nicht mehr.
> *Since Maria has been studying at Bonn, she does not write to me anymore.*

Seitdem and **seit** are used with the present tense if the action is not yet completed, while English since is used with the present perfect (often in the progressive form). (See Chap. 2 §7,3.)

Seitdem and **seit** are used with the present perfect tense if the action was completed in the past:

> Wir haben noch nicht von Alexander gehört, **seitdem (seit)** er nach Bonn gezogen ist.
> *We have not yet heard from Alexander since he moved to Bonn.*

Note that English uses the simple past in this situation.

b. since = **da** when it indicates causal connection (replaceable by **because**).

> Wir können ihn nicht anrufen, **da** wir nicht wissen, wo er jetzt ist.
> *We cannot call him since / because we don't know where he is now.*

PRACTICE

12-5   Supply the German equivalents of *since.*

1. _____ es nicht aufhörte zu regnen, sind wir den ganzen Sonntag zu Hause geblieben.
2. Wir haben nicht wieder von Winklers gehört, _____ sie in Basel wohnen.
3. Leider kann ich Martin nicht schreiben, _____ ich seine Adresse nicht weiß.
4. _____ Maria für eine Prüfung lernen mußte, bin ich mit Sonja ins Kino gegangen.
5. _____ Wagners vom Urlaub[2] zurückgekommen sind, haben sie uns noch nicht wieder besucht.

Both **da** and **weil** indicate causal connection. The following examples show the difference between their uses.

> Ich muß heute zur Bibliothek, **weil** diese zwei Bücher bereits überfällig sind.
> *I have to go to the library today because these two books are overdue.*

> **Da** Katrin in der Nähe von der Bibliothek wohnt, werde ich sie auf dem Heimweg besuchen.
> *Since Katrin lives near the library, I'll visit her on my way home.*

---

[1] **Verspätung haben**   *to be late (train, bus, plane)*
[2] **der Urlaub , -e**   *vacation*

In the first sentence the decisive reason for the trip to the library is expressed in the clause introduced by **weil**: the overdue books must be returned.

In the second sentence there is no compelling reason to visit Katrin. The clause introduced with **da** implies that I want to take advantage of the opportunity, since Katrin lives near the library.

In general, the choice of **weil** or **da** depends on how important the causal connection is. **Weil** is more commonly used than **da.** In particular, **da** cannot be used to answer the question *why*.

> Warum hast du die Bücher nicht zurückgebracht?
> **Weil** ich es vergessen habe.

REMEMBER: **Weil** indicates a strong, definite causal connection.
Da indicates a less definite causal connection.

4.   The use of **indem**

> Wir haben das Problem gelöst, **indem** wir einen Kompromiß geschlossen haben.
> *We solved the problem by making a compromise.*

The German dependent clause introduced by **indem** states a means by which something is, was, or will be done. The English equivalent is usually expressed with **by** plus a gerund.

5.   The use of tenses in clauses introduced by *nachdem*

> a. Er duscht meistens,   **nachdem** er den Rasen **gemäht hat.**
>
> PRESENT   PRES. PERF.
> *He usually takes a shower,*   *after he has mowed the lawn.*
> *or: after he mows the lawn.*
> *or: after mowing the lawn.*
>
> b. Er duschte gestern,   **nachdem** er den Rasen **gemäht hatte.**
>
> PAST   PAST PERF.
> *He took a shower yesterday,*   *after he had mowed the lawn.*
> *or: after he mowed the lawn.*
> *or: after mowing the lawn.*

The clause introduced by **nachdem** expresses an action which preceded that of the main clause. If the verb in the main clause is in the present or future tense, the **nachdem** clause is in the present perfect tense. If the main clause is in the past, present perfect, or past perfect tense, the **nachdem** clause is in the past perfect tense. German lacks the choice of tenses that English has.

6.   Subordinating conjunctions that are frequently confused with other words

The best way to recognize subordinating conjunctions is the position of the inflected verb at the end of the clause.

a. da

since (subordinating conjunction)
there (adverb of place)
then (adverb of time)

Da Martin nicht weit von mir **wohnt,** sehe ich ihn oft (verb last: dependent clause)
Since Martin doesn't live far from me, I often see him.

Da wohnt Martin. (verb second: main clause with inverted word order)
*Martin lives **there**.*

Da war es schon zu spät.
***Then** it was already too late.*

b. während

while (subordinating conjunction)
during (preposition)

Während wir uns **unterhielten** rauchte Dietmar.
***While** we were **talking,** Dietmar was smoking.*

Während unserer Unterhaltung rauchte Dietmar.
***During our conversation** Dietmar was smoking.*

PRACTICE
12-6

The following sentences refer to the preceding items 4, 5, and 6. Render into English:

1. Während des Vortrags habe ich einen Brief an Karola geschrieben.
2. Während der Redner die Dias zeigte, bin ich eingeschlafen.
3. Gestern war ich auf der Bank. Da wollte ich einige Fragen klären.[1]
    Nachdem ich alles erledigt hatte, bin ich einkaufen gegangen.
4. Da ich sowieso[2] einen kleinen Spaziergang machen wollte, bin ich zu Fuß
    zum Postamt gegangen.
5. Meine Noten müssen besser werden, weil ich sonst[3] mein Stipendium[4]
    verliere.
6. Mein Vater hat ja gesagt, indem er mit dem Kopf genickt[5] hat.
    Da war ich sehr erleichtert.[6]

PRACTICE
12-7

A. Combine the sentences, using the appropriate subordinating conjunction.

Model: Ich rufe dich an. (*as soon as*) Ich bin mit der Arbeit fertig.
        Ich rufe dich an, sobald ich mit der Arbeit fertig bin.

1. Ich bin sehr böse auf Dieter. (*because*) Er hat sein Versprechen nicht
    gehalten.
2. Mein Wagen läuft ausgezeichnet. (*since* [time]) Ich habe ihn repariert.

[1] klären	*to clarify*
[2] sowieso	*anyway*
[3] sonst	*otherwise*
[4] das Stipendium	*scholarship*
pl. **Stipendien**	
[5] mit dem Kopf nicken	*to nod*
[6] erleichtert sein	*to be relieved*

3. Wir haben nicht gewartet. (*until*) Das Flugzeug ist abgeflogen.
4. Ich habe nachgegeben. (*in order that*) Es gibt keinen Streit.[1]
5. Ich weiß nicht. (*whether, if*) Ich kann mitfahren.
6. Natürlich können Sie mitfahren. (*if*) Sie haben nichts anderes vor.[2]
7. Leider kann ich nicht mitfahren. (*since* [causal]) Ich habe etwas anderes vor.[3]
8. Ein Reifen[4] ist geplatzt.[5] (*when*) Der Fahrer wollte einen anderen Wagen überholen.[6]
9. Ein Reifen platzte. (*after*) Der Fahrer hatte einen anderen Wagen überholt.
10. Frau Krause hat einen Streit vermieden[7] (*by*) Sie hat geschwiegen.[8]

B. Introduce the first sentence in each pair with the appropriate subordinating conjunction.

MODEL: (*as long as*) Ich habe keinen Job. Ich kann dir das Geld nicht zurückgeben.
Solange ich keinen Job habe, kann ich dir das Geld nicht zurückgeben.

1. (*since* [causal]) Wir konnten keinen Parkplatz finden. Wir sind einfach weitergefahren.
2. (*before*) Sabine fährt nach Hause. Sie ruft mich hoffentlich an.
3. (*if*) Der Kurs wird zu schwer. Ich muß damit aufhören.[9]
4. (*while*) Du spülst das Geschirr. Ich räume die Wohnung auf.
5. (*although*) Ich habe wenig Geld. Ich werde einen Kassettenrecorder kaufen.
6. (*as long as*) Man widerspricht ihm nicht. Man kommt gut mit ihm aus.[10]
7. (*as soon as*) Man widerspricht ihm. Es gibt Streit.

PRACTICE

12-8   Summarizing exercises

A. Combine the following sentences using the appropriate coordinating and subordinating conjunctions.

1. Ich konnte nicht mit Frau Krause sprechen. (*because*) Die Leitung war immer besetzt.[11]

---

[1] der Streit	*quarrel, fight*
[2] nichts anderes vor•haben	*to have nothing else planned*
[3] etwas anderes vor•haben	*to have something else planned*
[4] der Reifen,-	*tire*
[5] platzen (ist)	*to blow out, burst*
[6] überholen	*to overtake, pass*
[7] vermeiden, vermied, vermieden	*to avoid*
[8] schweigen, schwieg, geschwiegen	*to remain silent*
[9] mit einem Kurs auf•hören	*to drop a course*
[10] aus•kommen, kam aus, ist ausgekommen mit (dat.)	*to get along with*
[11] Die Leitung ist besetzt. or simply: Es ist besetzt.	*The line is busy.*

2. Ich habe fünfmal angerufen. (*but*) Es war immer besetzt.

3. Ich mache Überstunden.[1] (*for*) Ich muß unbedingt mehr Geld verdienen.

4. Frank macht auch Überstunden. (*in order that*) Er verdient mehr Geld.

5. (*after*) Ich habe meine Schulden bezahlt. Ich schlafe bestimmt besser.

6. Rita war pleite. (*after*) Sie hatte ihre Schulden bezahlt.

7. Wir können das Problem lösen. (*if*) Wir schließen einen Kompromiß.[2]

8. Ich weiß nicht. (*whether, if*) Annette will einen Kompromiß schließen.

9. Wir haben das Problem gelöst. (*by*) Wir haben einen Kompromiß geschlossen.

10. Helga treibt viel Sport.[3] (*in order that*) Sie bleibt fit.

11. (*if*) Du willst fit bleiben. Du mußt viel Sport treiben.

12. (*since* [causal]) Wir wollten einen Streit vermeiden. Wir haben geschwiegen.

13. Wir haben einen Streit vermieden. (*by*) Wir haben geschwiegen.

14. Ich gehe nicht gern zum Supermarkt. (*when*) Ich habe großen Hunger. (*for*) Dann kaufe ich zuviel.

15. Peter ist eingeschlafen. (*when*) Ich war gestern mit ihm im Kino.

16. Ich habe Peter sehr gern.[4] (*although*) Er schläft oft ein. (*when*) Ich bin mit ihm im Kino.

B. Express in German. (Use the present for the English future and the present perfect for the English simple past except where otherwise in dicated.)

1. a. I hear from Ellen. I call you.
       Ich höre von Ellen. Ich rufe dich an.
    b. When I hear from Ellen, I'll call you.
    c. I'll call you, as soon as I hear from Ellen.
    d. I'll call you, after I have heard from Ellen.
    e. I called Mathias, after I had heard from Ellen.

2. a. I help him. He never thanks me.
       Ich helfe ihm. Er dankt mir nie.
    b. He never thanks me when I help him.
    c. I help him, although he never thanks me.
    d. He always thanked me when I helped him.
    e. He thanked me when I helped him yesterday.

3. a. I am waiting. She is coming back.
       Ich warte. Sie kommt zurück.
    b. I'll wait until she comes back.
    c. I waited but she didn't come back.
    d. Nobody knows when she is coming back.

---

[1] **Überstunden machen**   *to work overtime*

[2] **einen Kompromiß schließen,**   *to make a compromise*
   schloß, geschlossen

[3] **viel Sport treiben, trieb, getrieben** *to do a lot of sport*

[4] **sehr gern haben**   *to be very fond of*

4. a. I am not coming along. I have other plans.
    Ich komme nicht mit. Ich habe etwas anderes vor.
    b. Are you coming along or do you have other plans? (fam. sing.)
    c. I can't come along, because I have other plans.
    d. I couldn't come along, since I had other plans. (past)
    e. Since Elke had other plans, she couldn't come along. (past)

5. a. She is doing the dishes. I am straightening up the room.
    Sie spült das Geschirr. Ich räume das Zimmer auf.
    b. I am straightening up the room while she is doing the dishes.
    c. If you do the dishes, I'll straighten up the room. (fam. sing.)
    d. After I have done the dishes, I'll straighten up the room.
    e. After I had done the dishes, I straightened up the room.

6. a. We'll solve the problem. We'll make a compromise.
    Wir lösen das Problem. Wir schließen einen Kompromiß.
    b. We can solve the problem, if we make a compromise.
    c. We can solve the problem by making a compromise.
    d. If we want to solve the problem, we must make a compromise.
    e. I don't know whether we can solve the problem.

7. a. I am remaining silent. I want to avoid a fight.
    Ich schweige. Ich will einen Streit vermeiden.
    b. I am remaining silent because I want to avoid a fight.
    c. Perhaps I can avoid a fight if I remain silent.
    d. Perhaps we can avoid a fight by remaining silent.

 # Infinitive Phrases

§3   BASIC STRUCTURE

Ich hatte nicht den Mut **zu fragen.**
*I didn't have the courage **to ask**.*

Ich hatte nicht den Mut, ihn **zu fragen.**
*I didn't have the courage **to ask** him.*

Ich hatte nicht den Mut, ihn gestern **zu fragen.**
*I didn't have the courage **to ask** him yesterday.*

Note: a. The German infinitive normally stands at the end. All modifiers and objects
precede it, though in English they would follow.
b. Infinitive phrases are usually set off by commas. However, the bare infinitive
with no modifiers or objects is not set off (as in the first example).

Zu, when accompanying a verb with a separable prefix, stands between the prefix and
verb:

Ich habe vor, dieses Mal nach**zu**geben.
I am planning to give in this time.

PRACTICE

12-9   **A.** Complete the responses in German.

MODEL: X: Hast du die Dias mitgebracht?
         Y: Leider habe ich vergessen, _____ .
         (*to bring them along*)
         Leider habe ich vergessen, sie mitzubringen.

1. X: Hast du Marlene angerufen?
   Y: Ich habe versucht, _____ (*to call her*), aber es war immer besetzt.
2. X: Hat Peter die Post abgeholt?
   Y: Ich glaube, er hat vergessen, _____ . (*to pick up the mail*)
3. X: Hast du dein Zimmer aufgeräumt?
   Y: Ich habe noch keine Zeit gehabt, _____ . (*to straighten it up*)
4. X: Warum ist Dagmar nicht mitgekommen?
   Y: Ich nehme an, daß sie keine Lust hatte[1] _____ . (*to come along*)
5. X: Ich weiß nicht, was ich zu dieser Sache sagen soll.
   Y: Ich glaube, es ist besser, _____ . (*to say nothing*)
6. X: Warum suchst du dir keinen besseren Job?
   Y: Ach, du weißt doch, wie schwer es ist, _____ . (*to find a better job*)
7. X: Hoffentlich hältst du dein Versprechen (neut.).
   Y: Ich werde versuchen, _____ . (*to keep it*)
8. X: Ich weiß nicht, ob ich den Chef um einen Gefallen bitten kann.
   Y: Es hat keinen Zweck,[2] _____ . (*to ask him for a favor*). Er sagt doch immer nein.
9. X: Wollt ihr zu Morgensterns gehen?
   Y: Nein. Wir haben vor, _____ . (*to go to the Seiferts'*)
10. X: Wie kommst du mit Rainer aus?
    Y: Nicht besonders gut. Es ist nicht leicht, _____ . (*to get along with him*)
11. X: Ich habe noch nie gehört, daß jemand dem Chef widersprochen hat.
    Y: Niemand wagt,[3] _____ . (*to contradict him*)
12. X: Hast du auch Frau Dr. Schubert zu deiner Party eingeladen?
    Y: Nein. Ich habe nicht gewagt, _____ . (*to invite her*)
13. X: Will Dietmar den Magister machen?[4]
    Y: Ich glaube, er hat nicht vor, _____ . (*to get his* [the] *Master's*)

B. Express the following sentences in German.

1. I don't feel like playing tennis.
2. It's not easy to remain silent.
3. It's hard to avoid a quarrel.

[1] **ich habe keine Lust**   *I don't feel like, I am not in the mood*
[2] **es hat keinen Zweck**   *it's no use, there is no point*
[3] **wagen**   *to dare*
[4] **den Magister machen**   *to get one's Master's degree*
   (*with the definite article*)

4. It's no use to warn him.
5. I am trying to get along with her.
6. She's planning to get her (the) Master's.
7. She doesn't dare to ask Mrs. Bauer.
8. He doesn't have the courage to contradict the boss.

§4   INFINITIVE PHRASES INTRODUCED WITH *um, ohne, anstatt* OR *statt*

Um introduces infinitive phrases that express a purpose or intention:

> Ich habe das getan, **um** Geld zu sparen.
> *I did this (in order) to save money.*
> **um** nicht in Schulden zu geraten.
> *in order not to run up debts*.

When the infinitive phrase is introduced with **ohne, anstatt** or **statt**, the English equivalents include gerunds:

> Monika legte den Hörer auf, **ohne** ein Wort **zu sagen**.
>
> *Monika put down the receiver* ⎫
> *or: Monika hung up* ⎭ ***without saying** a word*

> Ich bin auf eine Party gegangen, **anstatt/statt** für die Prüfung **zu lernen**.
> *I went to a party **instead of studying** for the exam.*

PRACTICE

12-10

A. Complete the sentences with infinitive phrases.

MODEL: Barbara hat mit meiner Kamera Aufnahmen gemacht.[1]
ohne / bitten / mich / um Erlaubnis
ohne mich um Erlaubnis zu bitten.

1. Hannelore ist einkaufen gegangen, ohne / warten / auf mich
2. Ich mache Überstunden, um / verdienen / mehr Geld
3. Manfred hat uns ausgelacht, anstatt / helfen / uns
4. Die ganze Familie treibt Sport, um / bleiben / fit
5. Renate hat geschwiegen, um / vermeiden / einen Streit
6. Wir können das Problem nicht lösen, ohne / schließen / einen Kompromiß
7. Ich habe den ganzen Abend ferngesehen, anstatt / machen / die Hausaufgaben

B. Express the English sentences in German. (Use the present perfect for the English past tense.)

MODEL: Ich habe geschwiegen. Ich wollte Helga nicht ärgern.
Ich habe geschwiegen, um Helga nicht zu ärgern.
I remained silent in order not to annoy Helga.

1. Wir haben alles getan. Wir wollten einen Streit vermeiden.

_____

We did everything (in order) to avoid a quarrel/fight.

---

[1] **Aufnahmen machen**   *to take pictures*

2. Er treibt viel Sport. Er will fit bleiben.

_____

He does a lot of sport (in order) to stay fit.

3. Ich habe ja gesagt. Ich habe nicht an die Folgen[1] gedacht.

_____

I said yes without thinking of the consequences.

4. Meine Schwester hat meine Kamera mitgenommen. Sie hat mich nicht um Erlaubnis gebeten.

_____

My sister took my camera along without asking me for permission.

5. Thomas hat über meinen Vorschlag gelacht. Er hat ihn nicht ernst genommen.[2]

_____

Thomas laughed at my suggestion instead of taking it seriously.

C. Cover up the German sentences of exercise B and state the German equivalents of the English sentences.

MODEL: I remained silent in order not to annoy Helga.
Ich habe geschwiegen, um Helga nicht zu ärgern.

§5   THE INFINITIVE PHRASE PRECEDING THE MAIN CLAUSE

The main clause has inverted word order when it is preceded by an infinitive phrase. Compare:

Ich habe geschwiegen, um Anita nicht zu ärgern.
Um Anita nicht zu ärgern, **habe ich** geschwiegen.

PRACTICE

▼ 12-11

A. Express the English sentences in German. (Use the present perfect for the English past tense.)

MODEL: Wir haben die Hausaufgaben nicht gemacht.
Wir haben Schach gespielt.
Anstatt die Hausaufgaben zu machen, haben wir Schach gespielt.
Instead of doing homework, we played chess.

1. Sie hat mir nicht geholfen. Sie ist davongelaufen.

_____

Instead of helping me, she ran away.

2. Ich habe mein Zimmer nicht aufgeräumt. Ich habe die ganze Zeit vorm Fernseher gesessen.

_____

Instead of straightening up my room, I sat in front of the TV the whole time.

_____

[1] die Folge, -n   *consequence*
[2] ernst nehmen (nimmt),   *to take seriously*
   nahm, genommen

3. Ich habe kein Wort gesagt. Ich habe den Hörer aufgelegt.

_____

Without saying a word, I put down the receiver. (I hung up.)

4. Ich will nicht dick werden. Ich gehe jeden Tag schwimmen.

_____

In order not to get fat, I go swimming every day.

5. Wir wollten Geld sparen. Wir haben in einem miesen[1] Motel übernachtet.[2]

_____

In order to save money, we stayed overnight in a crummy motel.

B. Cover up the German sentences of exercise A and state the German equivalents of the English sentences.

MODEL: Instead of doing the homework, we played chess.
          Anstatt die Hausaufgaben zu machen, haben wir Schach gespielt.

§6   ENGLISH INFINITIVE CONSTRUCTIONS EXPRESSED IN GERMAN BY DEPENDENT CLAUSES

1.   English infinitives with subjects in the objective case

As the following example illustrates, an English infintive may have a subject in the objective case.

My parents want **me** to continue with my studies.

In this sentence, **me** is not a direct object, since it does not mean *My parents want me,* but rather *My parents want that I should continue with my studies.* **Me** is the implied subject of the infinitive **to continue.**

The above sentence is expressed in German by means of a **daß** clause:

Meine Eltern wollen, **daß ich weiterstudiere.**

Additional examples:

Sie erwartet, **daß ich sie heute abend anrufe.**	*She expects **me to call her tonight.***
Ich galube, **daß er ehrlich ist.**	*I believe **him to be honest.***
Meine Eltern wollen, **daß wir heiraten.**	*My parents want **us to get married.***

PRACTICE

12-13   **A.** Express in German.

1. a. I want you to tell me the truth. **Ich will, daß du mir die Wahrheit sagst.**
    b. He wants me to tell him the truth.
    c. Do you want me to tell you the truth? (formal)
    d. We all want you to tell us the truth. (formal)

2. a. I don't expect him to pay the bill. **Ich erwarte nicht, daß er die Rechnung bezahlt.**

_____

[1] mies   *crummy*
[2] übernachten   *to stay overnight*

    b. They expect me to pay the bill.
    c. Do you expect me to pay the bill? (fam. sing.)
    d. Nobody expects you to pay the bill. (fam. sing.)
3. a. I don't believe him to be reliable. **Ich glaube nicht, daß er zuverlässig ist.**
    b. I don't believe her to be reliable.
    c. Nobody believes them to be reliable.
    d Do you believe them to be reliable? (formal)

B. Express the responses in German.

1. X: Wer holt Käte ab?
    Y: She wants me to pick her up.
2. X: Denkst du, daß sie dir die Wahrheit sagen wird?
    Y: I don't expect her to tell me the truth.
3. X: Soll ich es noch einmal versuchen?
    Y: We all want you to try it again. (formal)
4. X: Ich nehme diese Sache nicht ernst.
    Y: But I want you to take this matter seriously. (fam. sing.)
5. X: Ist Monika deinem Bruder wirklich treu?
    Y: He believes her to be faithful to him.
6. X: Der Chef gibt uns vielleicht eine Gehaltserhöhung.
    Y: I don't expect him to give us a raise.

2. English infintives introduced with a question word

    In English but not in German, infinitives may be introduced with a question word. Compare:

    I don't know   Ich weiß nicht,
        a. *what I am supposed to do.*   ⎫
        b. *what to do*   ⎬   **was ich machen soll.**
                                                             ⎭
    She told me   Sie hat mir gesagt,
        a. *where I should buy the record.* ⎫
        b. *where to buy the record.*   ⎬   **wo ich die Platte kaufen soll.**
                                                             ⎭
    He will tell you   Er wird dir sagen,
        a. *how can you solve this problem.* ⎫
        b. *how to solve this problem.*   ⎬   **wie du dieses Problem lösen kannst.**
                                                             ⎭

    Since German does not permit an infinitive phrase after a question word, the English option *b* in each case has no German counterpart.

PRACTICE

12-14   **A.** Complete the German responses using the modals occurring in the quetions.

    MODEL: X: Weißt du, was du machen sollst?
                 Y: Natürlich weiß ich, _____ . (*what to do*)
             Natürlich weiß ich, was ich machen soll.

    1. X: Weißt du, was du ihm sagen sollst?
        Y: Natürlich weiß ich, _____ . (*what to tell him*)

2. X: Können Sie mir sagen, wo ich meinen Wagen parken kann?
   Y: Nein, aber der Polizist da drüben kann Ihnen sicher sagen,
   _____ . (*where to park it*)

3. X: Wißt ihr, wo ihr übernachten könnt?
   Y: Leider wissen wir noch nicht, _____ . (*where to stay overnight*)

4. X: Weißt du, wie du mehr Geld verdienen kannst?
   Y: Nein, aber du kannst mir vielleicht sagen, _____ . (*how to make more money*)

5. X: Wir wissen nicht, wie wir dieses Theaterstück interpretieren sollen.
   Y: Ich weiß auch nicht, _____ . (*how to interpret it*)

6. X: Du ißt zuviel. Du weißt nie, wann du aufhören mußt.
   Y: Ach, ich weiß genau,[1] _____ : eine Sekunde, bevor ich platze.
   (*when to stop*)

B. Express the following sentences in German, using the modals in parentheses.

MODEL: I don't know who(m) to invite. (sollen)
   Ich weiß nicht, wen ich einladen soll.

1. I don't know who(m) to ask. (sollen)
2. I don't know what to say. (sollen)
3. I can't tell you what to do. (müssen [formal])
4. Peter can tell you how to do that. (müssen [fam. sing.])
5. We know how to handle[2] him. (müssen)
6. I don't know how to convince[3] her. (können)
7. I don't know how to solve this problem. (sollen)

Summarizing exercises containing various types of infintive constructions.

PRACTICE

12-15 **A.** Express the following sentences in German.

1. a. I am doing him a favor.   **Ich tue ihm einen Gefallen.**
   b. It is not easy to do him a favor.
   c. He wants him to do him a favor.
   d. I don't know how to do him a favor. (können)

2. a. I am giving (it) up.   **Ich gebe es auf.**
   b. I am planning to give (it) up.
   c. My friends don't want me to give (it) up.

3. a. I am not trying (it) again.   **Ich versuche es nicht noch einmal.**
   b. It's no use trying (it) again.
   c. They expect me to try (it) again.
   d. She is giving (it) up instead of trying (it) again.

---

[1] **genau wissen**   *to know exactly*
[2] **behandeln**   *to handle, treat*
[3] **überzeugen**   *to convince*

4. a. You must ask the boss for permission. **Sie müssen den Chef um Erlaubnis bitten.**
    b. You cannot do that without asking him for permission.
    c. He expects you to ask him for permission.
    d. I don't know what to say. (**sollen**)
5. a. I am taking a few days vacation. **Ich mache ein paar Tage Urlaub.**
    b. He is trying to take a few days vacation.
    c. Why are you working instead of taking a few days vacation? (formal)
    d. My boss doesn't want me to take a few days vacation.
    e. I don't know what to do. (**sollen**)

B. Using the cues, form sentences that fit the context.

Model: Ich habe zwei Einladugen für Freitag abend.
         nicht wissen — was / sollen / machen
         Ich weiß nicht, was ich machen soll.

1. Dieter schwindelt (*is telling a fib*). Ich sage zu ihm:
    „ich / wollen — mir / sagen / Wahrheit"
2. Ich möchte fit bleiben, und deshalb treibe ich viel Sport.
    ich Sport / treiben — fit / bleiben
3. Ich habe die Hausaufgaben nicht gemacht.
    ich / fern•sehen (pres. perf.) — anstatt / machen / Hausaufgaben
4. Ich möchte mit meiner Freundin ins Kino gehen und frage sie:
    „du / Lust / haben — gehen / ins Kino?"
5. Wenn man Barbara um einen Gefallen bittet, sagt sie immer nein.
    keinen Zweck / haben — sie / bitten / um einen Gefallen
6. Margot ist etwas schwierig. Karin sagt:
    „nicht leicht / sein — aus•kommen / mit ihr"
    Meine Freundin und ich kommen gut mit Margot aus.
    wir / wissen-wie / müssen / behandeln / Margot

The Subjunctive
Part 1

Introduction

Both English and German possess two sets of verb forms which indicate how real or how likely the speaker believes a statement to be. The more usual forms, called *indicative*, indicate that an utterance is either factual or relatively likely:

She is Miss America.	Sie ist…"Miss Amerika".
I am not Mr. Körner.	Ich bin nicht Herr Körner.
Perhaps he'll come tomorrow.	Vielleicht kommt er morgen.

The other set of forms, called *subjunctive*, indicates that a statement is relatively unlikely, implausible, conjectural, or simply contrary to fact:

*If he **were** to come tomorrow, …*	Wenn er morgen **käme**,…
*If I **were** Miss America,…*	Wenn ich "Miss Amerika" **wäre**,…
*If I **were** Mr Körner,…*	Wenn ich Herr Körner **wäre**,…

Were, **wäre**, and **käme** in the sentences above are subjunctive forms. English has few distinct subjunctive forms, whereas German has many recognizable subjunctives.

German distinguishes between a *general subjunctive* (also called *subjunctive II*) and a special *subjunctive* (also called *subjunctive I*). This chapter deals only with the general subjunctive. For convenience sake, we shall refer to it simply as the *subjunctive*. It is used mainly to signal unreal conditions. They are divided into two time categories: those that deal with the present or future and those that deal with the past.

Unreal Conditions Referring to the Present or Future

§1   Unreal Conditions in English

Compare these two sentences:

> When I lived in Vienna, I often went to the opera.
> If I lived in Vienna, I would go to the opera often.

In the first sentence **lived** is the past tense indicative: the speaker once lived in Vienna. In the second sentence **lived** refers to the present and is called *present tense subjunctive*. "If I lived in Vienna" is a hypothesis, an **unreal condition**.

Note the difference between an indicative conditional sentence and a subjunctive (unreal) conditional sentence:

a. If **I have** the money, **I'll go** to Europe.
b. If **I had** the money, **I would go** to Europe.

In sentence *a.* the speaker considers it possible that he/she will have the money. Since the condition may be fulfilled, it is real and hence in the indicative. In sentence *b.* the condition is purely hypothetical. The speaker does not have the money (but if he/she had it…); hence the verb **had** is subjunctive (identical in form, but not in meaning, to the past indicative).

Hypothetical (unreal) conditions are generally accompanied by equally hypothetical conclusions. Observe the verb forms used in the following sentences:

CONDITION	CONCLUSION
If I **had** the money,	I **would go** to Europe.
If she **had** the time,	she **would join** us.
If I **could** pay my debts,	I **would be** very relieved.
If he **became** angry,	I **would become** angry, too.
SUBJUNCTIVE	CONDITIONAL
(usually identical in form to the past indicative)	*would* + verb

The subjunctive and the conditional may refer to either the present or future.

If I had more money, I would not be living in such a small apartment.
PRESENT   PRESENT

If I had the money, I would buy this boat tomorrow.
PRESENT   FUTURE

If I lost my scholarship, I would have to quit school.
FUTURE   FUTURE

PRACTICE

13-1   The following sentences contain real conditions. Change them to unreal conditions.

MODEL: If it is raining, we won't walk to school.
         If it were raining, we would not walk to school.

1. If she invites me, I will not accept.
2. If I can, I'll help you.
3. If you have a fever, you'll have to see a doctor.
4. If that is true, I'll never speak to her again.
5. If we have a choice, we won't sign the contract.
6. If I don't call them, they'll be very angry with me.

7. If she loves me, she'll forgive me.
8. If she does that, she'll make me very happy.

§2   UNREAL CONDITIONS IN GERMAN

	CONDITION	CONCLUSION
Real condition:	Wenn Sie es ihr **sagen,** *If you tell her,*	**ist** sie bestimmt schockiert. *she will certainly be shocked.*
Unreal condition:	Wenn Sie es ihr **sagten,** *If you told her,*	**wäre** sie bestimmt schockiert. *she would certainly be shocked.*

The real condition and conclusion are expressed in the indicative, their unreal counterparts in the subjunctive.

A note on word order:

The conditional clause, or **wenn**-clause, is a dependent clause; hence the verb stands at the end. The conclusion is the main clause. It has inverted word order because it is preceded by a dependent clause (cf. Chap. 12, §2).

§3   FORMS OF THE PRESENT SUBJUNCTIVE

1.   Weak verbs

The forms of the present subjunctive and the past indicative are identical (cf. Chap. 3, §1).

PAST INDICATIVE = PRESENT SUBJUNCTIVE

ich sagte	ich arbeitete
du sagtest	du arbeitetest
er, sie, es, sagte	er, sie, es arbeitete
wir sagten	wir arbeiteten
ihr sagtet	ihr arbeitetet
sie sagten	sie arbeiteten
Sie sagten	Sie arbeiteten
	(An **e** is added when the stem ends in
	-d, -t, or consonant clusters.)

PRACTICE

13-2   Supply the appropriate subjunctive forms of the verbs in parentheses. (Keep in mind that in dependent clauses the separable prefix is attached to the verb.)

MODEL: Wenn er nicht _____... (bezahlen, studieren, auf•passen)
Wenn er nicht bezahlte, ...
Wenn er nicht studierte, ...
Wenn er nicht aufpaßte,...

1. Wenn Alexandra _____ ,... (fragen, schwänzen, warten, zu•hören)
2. Wenn es _____ ,... (stören, regnen, passieren)
3. Wenn wir es _____ , ... (glauben, ab•holen, parken, zu•machen)

4. Wenn sie (*she*) ihn _____ , ... (lieben, heiraten, manipulieren)
5. Wenn du mich _____ ... (fragen, aus•lachen, ignorieren)
6. Wenn die Arbeiter _____ , ... (streiken, protestieren)
7. Wenn ihr es noch einmal _____ , ... (versuchen)
8. Wenn das Motorrad nicht soviel Geld _____ ,... (kosten)
9. Wenn die Leute ihr Geld _____ , ... (investieren)

2. Strong verbs

(Cf. Chap. 3, §4, §6, §7 and Appendix, §2)

The personal endings of the subjunctive are identical to the past-tense endings of weak verbs minus **t**:

ich _____	e
du _____	est
er, sie, es _____	e
wir _____	en
ihr _____	et
sie _____	en
Sie _____	en

These endings are attached to the past-tense stem of strong verbs, i.e. the second principal part:

gehen   ging   ist gegangen

PAST INDICATIVE   PRESENT SUBJUNCTIVE

ich ging		ich ginge
du gingst		du gingest
er, sie, es ging		er, sie, es ginge
wir gingen	(identical)	wir gingen
ihr gingt		ihr ginget
sie gingen	(identical)	sie gingen
Sie gingen	(identical)	Sie gingen

Strong verbs with the vowels **a, o,** and **u** in the past indicative require an **umlaut** in the present subjunctive, such as

	PAST INDICATIVE	PRES. SUBJ.
essen (ißt)	aß	**äße**
fliegen	flog	**flöge**
fahren (fährt)	fuhr	**führe**

A few strong verbs have irregular present subjunctives, such as:

beginnen	begann	**begönne**/also: begänne
helfen (hilft)	half	**hülfe**/also: hälfe
stehen	stand	**stünde**/also: stände

Many present subjunctives are now felt to be stilted or obsolete. Students must, however, recognize these forms when they encounter them in literature. They are shown in parentheses in §2 of the Appendix.

The following verbs occur in PRACTICE 3. Their present subjunctives are still current, including the compound forms, some of which are listed here.

		PAST INDICATIVE	PRES. SUBJ.
finden		fand	**fände**
geben (gibt)		gab	**gäbe**
auf•geben	*to give up*		
zu•geben	*to admit*		
zurück•geben	*to give back, to return*		
gehen		ging	**ginge**
aus•gehen	*to go out*		
zurück•gehen	*to go back, to return*		
halten (hält)	*to hold, to stop*	hielt	**hielte**
behalten	*to keep*		
heißen	*to be named*	hieß	**hieße**
kommen		kam	**käme**
an•kommen	*to arrive*		
bekommen	*to receive, get*		
mit•kommen	*to come along*		
lassen (läßt)	*to let; to leave*	ließ	**ließe**
tun		tat	**täte**

PRACTICE

13-3 ▼ Supply the appropriate German present subjunctives of the English forms stated in parentheses.

Model: Wenn wir jetzt nach Hause _____ ,… (*went*)
Wenn wir jetzt nach Hause gingen, …

1. Wenn Frau Helbig zu ihrem Mann _____ , … (*went back*)
2. Wenn dieser Zug pünktlich _____ , … (*arrived*)
3. Wenn die Expreßzüge in unserer Stadt _____ ,…. (*stopped*)
4. Wenn diese Stadt anders[1] _____ , … (*were named*)
5. Wenn meine Frau und ich öfter _____ , … (*went out*)
6. Wenn man dieser Kandidatin eine Chance _____ , … (*gave*)
7. Wenn wir Ulrich diesen Gefallen[2] _____ , … (*did*)

---

[1] anders   *different(ly)*
[2] der Gefallen,-   *favor*

8. Wenn Sie mich ausreden[1] _____ , (*let*)
9. Wenn das Komitee keine bessere Lösung _____ ,... (*found*)
10. Wenn ich ein Stipendium _____ , ... (*got, received*)
11. Wenn Sie _____ ,... (*came along*)
12. Wenn die Bürgermeisterin diesen Plan _____ , ... (*gave up*)
13. Wenn wir diese Sachen im Schließfach[2] _____ , ... (*left*)

3. Irregular Verbs

a. Mixed verbs (cf. Chap. 3, §8)

	PAST INDICATIVE	PRESENT SUBJUNCTIVE
denken	ich dachte	**ich dächte**
bringen	ich brachte	**ich brächte**
wissen	ich wußte	**ich wüßte**

These verbs form the subjunctive by adding an umlaut to the past indicative form. **Dächte** and **brächte** occur mainly in formal German, whereas **wüßte** is commonly used in both formal and informal German.

The following mixed verbs change the stem vowel to **e** in the subjunctive:

brennen	es brannte	es brennte
kennen	ich kannte	ich kennte
nennen	ich nannte	ich nennte
rennen	ich rannte	ich rennte

These four subjunctives are now obsolete. The use of substitute forms is explained in §6 of this chapter.

b. haben, sein, werden (cf. Chap. 3, §9)

haben	ich hatte	**ich hätte**
sein	ich war	**ich wäre**
werden	ich wurde	**ich würde**

Haben and **werden** form the subjunctive by adding an umlaut to the past indicative forms. The subjunctive forms of **sein** follow the pattern of strong verbs.

Haben, sein, and **werden** are frequently used in the subjunctive. Their conjugations are listed below.

haben	**sein**	**werden**
ich hätte	ich wäre	ich würde
du hättest	du wär(e)st	du würdest
er, sie, es hätte	er, sie, es wäre	er, sie, es würde

---

[1] ausreden lassen   *to let finish (talking)*
[2] das Schließfach, ¨er   *locker*

wir hätten	wir wären	wir würden
ihr hättet	ihr wär(e)t	ihr würdet
sie hätten	sie wären	sie würden
Sie hätten	Sie wären	Sie würden

(The **e** of the fam. sing.
and pl. may be omitted.)

PRACTICE

13-4   Restate the following **wenn**-clauses, substituting the subjects indicated.

1. Wenn ich mehr Zeit hätte,… (er, Sie, du, ihr)
2. Wenn ich nicht so egoistisch wäre, … (du, ihr, wir)
3. Wenn ich krank würde, … (Rita, die Kinder, ihr, du, Sie)
4. Wenn ich es wüßte,… (Sie, er, du, ihr)
5. Wenn ich nicht daran dächte … (die Gelehrten,[1] die Pilotin)
6. Wenn man ein Opfer brächte,[2] … (die Fußballspieler)

4. Modal Auxiliaries

(cf. Chap. 4, §2)

INFINITIVE	PAST INDICATIVE	PRESENT SUBJUNCTIVE	
können	ich konnte	**ich könnte**	⎫
dürfen	ich durfte	**ich dürfte**	(with umlaut)
müssen	ich mußte	**ich müßte**	⎬
mögen	ich mochte	**ich möchte**	⎭
wollen	ich wollte	**ich wollte**	⎫ (without umlaut)
sollen	ich sollte	**ich sollte**	⎭

The present subjunctive of modals is like the past indicative except that those that have umlaut in the infinitive add umlaut in the subjunctive.

REMEMBER: **wollen** and **sollen** never have umlaut

PRACTICE

13-5   Supply the appropriate subjunctive forms of the modals in parentheses.

1. Wenn wir das _____ , … (müssen, wollen, können, dürfen, sollen)
2. Wenn Monika zu Hause bleiben _____ ,… (müssen, mögen, wollen, sollen)
3. Wenn du mitkommen _____ , … (dürfen, mögen, können, wollen)
4. Wenn Sie das bezahlen _____ , … (sollen, können, müssen)
5. Wenn ihr das nicht _____ , … (wollen, mögen, dürfen, können)

---

[1] **der/die Gelehrte** (adj. noun)   *the scholar*
  pl. die Gelehrten (masc. + fem.)   *the scholars*
[2] **ein Opfer** (neuter) **bringen**   *to make a sacrifice*

§4   USE OF THE PRESENT SUBJUNCTIVE IN UNREAL CONDITIONS AND CONCLUSIONS

Real condition and conclusion:

> Wenn er wirklich in Gefahr **ist, müssen** wir ihn warnen.
> *If he is really in danger, we have to warn him.*

Unreal condition and conclusion:

> Wenn er wirklich in Gefahr **wäre, müßten** wir ihn warnen.
> *If he were really in danger, we would have to warn him.*

The conclusion may be introduced by **dann** or **so** (the latter has as a literary flavor):

> Wenn er wirklich in Gefahr wäre, **dann (so)** müßten wir ihn warnen.

PRACTICE

13-6   Convert the following sentences with real conditions to unreal conditions. Render the unreal version into English.

> MODEL: Wenn der Kurs in Physik noch schwerer wird, muß ich damit aufhören.
> **Wenn der Kurs in Physik noch schwerer würde, müßte ich damit aufhören.**
> *If the course in Physics got any harder, I would have to drop it.*

1. Wenn dieses Projekt zu teuer wird, müssen wir es aufgeben.
2. Wenn Margot in die Stadt fahren will, dann kann sie meinen Wagen nehmen.
3. Wenn Egon vor 8 Uhr kommt, ist Renate nicht zu Hause.
4. Wenn er die Stelle beim Konsultat bekommt, hat er großes Glück.[1]
5. Wenn Sie Lisas Adresse wissen, dann können wir ihr eine Karte aus Berlin schicken.
6. Wenn du willst, kannst du es noch einmal versuchen.

§5   USE OF *würde* + INFINITIVE IN THE CONCLUSION

Conclusions with the verbs **haben, sein, werden, wissen,** and the modals are normally expressed in the present subjunctive. With other verbs, however, a form of **würde** (subjunctive of **werden**) + infinitive of the main verb is usually preferred. This corresponds to the English use of **would** + verb.

> Wenn wir hier parken könnten, **sparten** wir Zeit und Geld.
> more common: Wenn wir hier parken könnten, **würden** wir Zeit und Geld **sparen.**
> *If we could park here, we would save time and money.*

Würde plus infinitive of the main verb is structurally the future subjunctive. (cf. Chap. 14, §6, 3); however, it frequently serves as a substitute for the present subjunctive.

---

[1] **großes Glück haben**   to be very lucky

Do not confuse the following two uses of **würde:**

> a. Wenn ich diese Rechnung nicht bezahlen könnte, **würde** ich nervös.
> (main verb)
> b. Wenn ich hier parken könnte, **würde** ich Zeit und Geld **sparen.**
> (auxiliary)   (main verb in the infinitive)

In sentence *a.* **würde** is the main verb, accompanied by the predicate adjective **nervös.**

In sentence *b.* the infinitive **sparen** is the main verb and **würde** functions as its auxiliary. This construction will be referred to as "**würde** + infinitive form."

A. Replace the present subjunctive in the conclusion with **würde** + infinitive forms. (Keep in mind that the separable prefix is attached to the infinitive.)

MODEL: Wenn es nicht schneite, holten wir heute unseren neuen Wagen ab.
Wenn es nicht schneite, würden wir heute unseren neuen Wagen abholen.

1. Wenn ich es könnte, gäbe ich dir das Geld sofort zurück.
2. Wenn Sie noch Platz im Wagen hätten, dann käme ich gern mit.
3. Wenn sie es dürften, dann versuchten sie es noch einmal.
4. Wenn ich immer soviel arbeiten müßte, bekäme ich bestimmt einen Nervenzusammenbruch.[1]
5. Wenn ich an deiner Stelle wäre[2], ließe ich diese Sachen im Schließfach.
6. Wenn du an meiner Stelle wärest,[3] sagtest du wahrscheinlich nein.

B. Convert the following real conditions to unreal conditions, using **würde** + infinitive forms in the conclusions.

MODEL: Wenn ich es kann, tue ich dir diesen Gefallen.
Wenn ich es könnte, würde ich dir diesen Gefallen tun.

1. Wenn meine Noten nicht gut genug sind, bekomme ich kein Stipendium.
2. Wenn sie mich fragt, dann sage ich ihr die Wahrheit.
3. Wenn der Chef uns nicht gut bezahlt, streiken wir.
4. Wenn er kein sicherer Fahrer ist, dann fahre ich nicht mit.
5. Wenn du ein Fenster aufmachst, dann macht er es wieder zu.
6. Wenn sie mich auslacht, dann lache ich sie auch aus.

C. Convert to unreal conditions. In the conclusions, use the present subjunctive with **haben, sein, wissen,** and the modals but **würde** + infinitve forms with other verbs.

---

[1] der Nervenzusammenbruch, ⁼e   *nervous breakdown*
[2] Wenn ich an deiner Stelle wäre   *If I were in your place*
                                          If I were you
[3] Wenn du an meiner Stelle wärest   *If you were in my place*
                                          If you were me

1. Wenn er mich ignoriert, dann ignoriere ich ihn auch.
2. Wenn Frau Schneider das hört, ist sie bestimmt schockiert.
3. Wenn Sie eine Gehaltserhöhung[1] bekommen, dann haben Sie großes Glück.
4. Wenn der Chef gute Laune hat, bitte ich ihn um eine Gehaltserhöhung.
5. Wenn es nicht regnet, gehen wir zu Fuß ins Theater.
6. Wenn meine Noten gut genug sind, studiere ich Medizin.
7. Wenn er ein gutes Gedächtnis[2] hat, dann weiß er den Namen des Hotels noch.
8. Wenn man mich manipulieren will, dann protestiere ich sofort.
9. Wenn er mir einen Heiratsantrag macht[3] dann sage ich nein.
10. Wenn du es wirklich willst, dann kannst du es auch.
11. Wenn ich Martina diesen Gefallen tue, dann muß sie mir auch einen Gefallen tun.

§6   USE OF *würde* + INFINITIVE IN THE *wenn*-CLAUSE

1. The present subjunctive of **haben, sein, werden, wissen,** and the modals is used in the **wenn**-clause just as it is in the conclusion. With other verbs it is necessary to distinguish between formal German usage (literary works, lectures, papers, official documents) and informal German (colloquial speech, informal writing as in personal letters, diaries, etc.)

2. In formal German , **würde** + infinitive was traditionally not supposed to be used in **wenn**- clauses. This rule has now been relaxed. As already mentioned in §3, 2 of this chapter, many present subjunctives are now felt to be stilted or obsolete (placed in parentheses in §2 of the Appendix). **Würde** + infinitive is now used instead.

Here are a few examples:

> Wenn die Regierung **helfen würde**,… instead of **hülfe** or **hälfe**
> Wenn man nicht soviel **stehlen**[4] **würde**, … **stähle** or **stöhle**
> Wenn man die Kandidatin besser **kennen würde**, … **kennte**

It is, however, considered poor practice in formal style to have **würde** + infintive forms in both the **wenn**-clause and the conclusion.

poor style: Wenn die Regierung helfen würde, würde diese Firma nicht bankrott machen.
If the government would help, this company would not go bankrupt.

rephrased: Wenn die Regierung helfen könnte, würde diese Firma nicht bankrott machen.

or: Wenn die Regierung helfen würde, machte diese Firma nicht bankrott.

---

[1] **die Gehaltserhöhung, -en**   *raise (salary)*
[2] **das Gedächtnis**   *memory*
[3] **einen Heiratsantrag machen**   *to propose marriage*
[4] **stehlen (stiehlt)**   *to steal*
  stahl, gestohlen

3. In informal German, few present subjunctive forms are used. Studies have shown that the forms listed in §3 and 2 as current, occur in written German as frequently as the equivalents with **würde** + infintive:

fände	finden würde
gäbe	geben würde
ginge	gehen würde
hielte	halten würde
hieße	heißen würde
käme	kommen würde
ließe	lassen würde
täte	tun würde

The same is true of their compound forms (also stated in §3, 2 of this chapter).

In everyday spoken German, only two of these subjunctives occur with any frequency, viz. **käme** and **täte.** These forms, as well as **wäre, hätte, würde, wüßte,** and the subjunctives of modal verbs, are common in everyday speech. For all other verbs, **würde** + infinitive is used. This means that **würde** often occurs both in the **wenn**-clause and in the conclusion.

> Wenn Peter nicht soviel **angeben würde, würde** ich ihn auch zu meiner Party **einladen.**

Advice to the students:

Always use the present subjunctives of **haben, sein, werden, wissen,** and the modals. In everyday spoken German you can use the **würde** + infinitive forms of virtually all other verbs both in the **wenn**-clause and in the conclusion.

§7   OMISSION OF *wenn*

Compare the following sentences:

> Wenn ich eine Schreibmaschine **hätte,** würde ich dir öfter schreiben.
> **Hätte** ich eine Schreibmaschine, **dann/so** würde ich dir öfter schreiben.

Note: The inflected verb is at the beginning of the condition. The particle **dann** or **so** is commonly added.

Literal translations of such sentences are stilted.

> *Had I a typewriter, then I would write to you more often.*
> idiomatic: *If I had a typewriter, I would write to you more often.*

§8   REVERSAL OF THE *wenn*-CLAUSE AND CONCLUSION

Compare the following two sentences:

> Wenn ich an seiner Stelle wäre, **würde ich** die Rechnung nicht bezahlen.
> **Ich würde** die Rechnung nicht bezahlen, wenn ich an seiner Stelle wäre.
> *I would not pay the bill if I were in his place.*

Note the change to normal word order when the conclusion (main clause) precedes the **wenn**-clause.

13-8   **A.**   Omit **wenn,** change the word order, and insert **dann.** Follow the model of sentence 1.

1. Wenn ich nicht für eine Prüfung lernen müßte, würde ich ins Theater gehen.
   Müßte ich nicht für eine Prüfung lernen, dann würde ich ins Theater gehen.
2. Wenn wir eine größere Wohnung hätten, würden wir mehr Leute einladen.
3. Wenn mein Wagen nicht kaputt wäre, würde ich Erika vom Flughafen abholen.
4. Wenn es nach mir ginge,[1] würden wir aufs Land ziehen.[2]
5. Wenn Hans nicht so egoistisch wäre, hätte er bestimmt mehr Freunde.

B.   Begin each sentence with the conclusion, following the model of sentence 1.

1. Wenn du es wirklich wolltest, könntest du uns helfen.
   Du könntest uns helfen, wenn du es wirklich wolltest.
2. Wenn meine Noten besser wären, würde ich Medizin studieren.
3. Wenn Sie mir diesen Gefallen tun könnten, wäre ich Ihnen sehr dankbar.
4. Wenn ich nicht pleite wäre, würde ich heute abend ins Theater gehen.

§9   UNREAL CONDITIONS WITH QUESTIONS

Unreal conditions may follow questions.

Was würdest du sagen, wenn ich nicht zurückkäme?
What would you say if I didn't come back?
Was würden Sie tun, wenn Sie an ihrer Stelle wären?
What would you do if you were in her place?

13-9   Complete the questions, following the model of sentence 1.

1. Was würdest du sagen,   **wenn ich zu Hause bleiben wollte?**
                                  if I wanted to stay at home?
2. Was würden Sie sagen?   _____
                                  if I could not pay the bill?
3. Was würdest du tun.   _____
                                  if you were in my place?
4. Was würden Sie tun,   _____
                                  if you were in his place?
5. Würden Sie es übelnehmen,   _____
                                  if I said no?

---

[1] *idiom:* **es geht nach mir, dir, ihm,** *etc.*   *it is up to me, you, him, etc.*
[2] **aufs Land ziehen, zog, ist gezogen**   *to move to the country*

6. Könntest du es verstehen, _____

if I wanted to move to the country?

§10 CONCLUSIONS STANDING ALONE

Although an unreal condition is not always expressed, one is often implied. In such instances the main clause (conclusion) stands alone.

Ich würde den Vertrag nicht unterschreiben. (wenn ich an deiner Stelle wäre)
I would not sign the contract. (if I were you)
Ich würde ihm gern helfen. (wenn ich es könnte)
I would gladly help him. (if I could)
Das wäre schade. (wenn das passierte)
That would be a pity. (if that happened)
Das wäre großartig. (wenn wir das tun könnten)
That would be great. (if we could do that)

PRACTICE

13-10   Express the responses in German following the model of sentence 1.

1. X: Ich habe etwas Angst vor ihm.
   Y: **Ich hätte keine Angst vor ihm.**
   _____
   I would not be afraid of him.
2. X: Vielleicht sage ich es ihr nicht.
   Y: _____
   I would tell her.
3. X: Ich weiß nicht, ob ich den Chef um eine Gehaltserhöhung bitten soll.
   Y: _____
   I would ask him for a raise.
4. X: Klaus nimmt es vielleicht übel, wenn wir seine Freundin nicht einladen.
   Y: _____
   He would resent it.
5. X: Vielleicht laden wir auch Helga und Dieter ein.
   Y: _____
   That would be great.
6. X: Vielleicht kann ich nicht mitfahren.
   Y: _____
   That would be a pity.

§11 *wenn*-CLAUSES STANDING ALONE

Wenn ich nur mehr Zeit **hätte!**	
less common: **Hätte** ich nur mehr Zeit!	*If only I had more time.*
Wenn Sie mich nur verstehen **könnten!**	*If only you could*
less common: **Könnten** Sie mich nur verstehen!	*understand me.*
Wenn ich nur ihren Namen **wüßte!**	
less common: **Wüßte** ich nur ihren Namen!	*If only I knew her name.*

These are wishes one does not expect to be fulfilled. In German they end with an exclamation point. Just as English uses the particle *only*, German uses **nur**. In most instances **nur** follows the subject and pronoun objects but precedes all other elements.

PRACTICE

13-11   Express in German following the model of sentence 1.

1. Klaus hat viele Vorurteile.[1]
   Wenn er nur nicht so viele Vorurteile hätte!
   _____
   If only he didn't have so many prejudices.
2. Leider habe ich nicht viel Willenskraft.[2]
   _____
   If only I had more will power.
3. Meine Freundin ist sehr stur. _____
   If only she weren't so stubborn.
4. Leider weiß ich es nicht. _____
   If only I knew it.
5. Ich suche[3] eine bessere Stelle, kann jedoch[4] keine finden. _____
   If only I could find a better job.
6. Ich beneide Annerose. _____
   If only I were in her place.
7. Schade, daß Herr Krause verheiratet ist. _____
   If only he were single.[5]

Unreal Conditions Referring to the Past

§12 IN ENGLISH

	CONDITION	CONCLUSION
PRESENT	If I knew,	I would tell you.
	PRES. SUBJ.	PRESENT CONDITIONAL
PAST	If I had known,	I would have told you.
	PAST SUBJ.	PAST CONDITIONAL

Note: a. The past subjunctive form (**I had known**) in the conditional clause is identical to the past perfect indicative.
b. The conclusion is expressed in the past conditional (**would have told**).

---

[1] **das Vorurteil, -e**   *prejudice*
[2] **die Willenskraft**   *willpower*
[3] **suchen**   *to look for*
[4] **jedoch**   *however*
[5] **ledig**   *single*

PRACTICE

13-12   Change the unreal conditions from the present to the past, following the model of sentence 1.

1. If I told you, you would not believe it.
   If I had told you, you would not have believed it.
2. If they invited me, I would not accept.
3. If they printed that, they would ruin our reputation.
4. If I did not call her, she would become very angry.
5. If they were in trouble, we would help them.
6. If I had the money, I would study abroad for a year.

§13 IN GERMAN

	WENN-CLAUSE	CONCLUSION
PRESENT	Wenn ich es wüßte,	(dann/so) würde ich es dir sagen.
PAST	Wenn ich es **gewußt hätte**,	(dann /so) **hätte** ich es dir **gesagt.**
	PAST.SUBJ.	PAST SUBJ.

Both the **wenn**-clause and the conclusion are expressed in the past subjunctive. The **würde**-substitute is not used when referring to the past.

The forms of the past subjunctive will be practiced first in main clauses (conclusions), then in **wenn**-clauses, and finally in sentences consisting of a **wenn**-clause plus a conclusion.

§ 14 MAIN CLAUSES IN THE PAST SUBJUNCTIVE

1. Using weak, strong, and irregular verbs

   The forms of the past subjunctive are derived from the past perfect indicative (cf. Chap. 3, §10).

PAST PERFECT INDICATIVE	PAST SUBJUNCTIVE	ENGLISH EQUIVALENT
<u>verbs with auxiliary **haben**</u>		
ich hatte gewußt	**ich hätte gewußt**	*I would have known*
ich hatte gefragt	**ich hätte gefragt**	*I would have asked*
ich hatte eingeladen	**ich hätte eingeladen**	*I would have invited*
ich hatte gehabt	**ich hätte gehabt**	*I would have had*
<u>verbs with auxiliary **sein**</u>		
Ich war gegangen	**ich wäre gegangen**	*I would have gone*
ich war geblieben	**ich wäre geblieben**	*I would have stayed*
ich war gewesen	**ich wäre gewesen**	*I would have been*
ich war geworden	**ich wäre geworden**	*I would have become*

Note: The auxiliaries **haben** and **sein** are in the subjunctive; the past participle remains unchanged.

PRACTICE

13-13
Supply the past subjunctive forms of the sentences given in the present subjunctive. Follow the model of sentence 1.

A.   Verbs requiring **haben**

1.   Ich würde ihn um eine Gehaltserhöhung bitten.
     Ich hätte ihn um eine Gehaltserhöhung gebeten.
     _____
     I would have asked him for a raise.

2.   Ich würde es Klaus nicht sagen.
     _____
     I wouldn't have told Klaus.

3.   Wir würden Bergmanns nicht einladen.
     _____
     We wouldn't have invited the Bergmanns.

4.   Annerose würde mir die Wahrheit sagen.
     _____
     Annerose would have told me the truth.

5.   Ich hätte keine Angst davor.
     _____
     I wouldn't have been afraid of that.

6.   Ihr hättet bestimmt Pech.[1]
     _____
     You certainly would have bad luck.

B.   Verbs requiring **sein**

1.   Margot würde sehr böse werden.
     Margot wäre sehr böse geworden.
     _____
     Margot would have become very angry.

2.   Die Sache würde zu kompliziert werden.
     _____
     The matter would have become too complicated.

3.   Ich würde etwas länger in Wien bleiben.
     _____
     I would have stayed in Vienna a little longer.

4.   Ich würde vor Angst sterben.
     _____
     I would have died of fear.

5.   Das würde nicht passieren.
     _____
     That wouldn't have happened.

6.   Das wäre schade.
     _____
     That would have been a pity.

7.   Deine Freunde wären schockiert.
     _____
     Your friends would have been shocked.

---

[1] **Pech haben**   *to have bad luck*

C. Cover up the German sentences of exercises A and B and translate the English sentences.

MODEL: I would have asked him for a raise.
   Ich hätte ihn um eine Gehaltserhöhung gebeten.

2.   Using modals

Modals always use the auxiliary **haben** (cf. Chap. 4, §3 and §4).

a.   Modals with a dependent infinitive

Ich **hätte** ihm **helfen können.**	*I could have helped him.*
	or: *I would have been able to help him.*
Ich **hätte** ihm **helfen sollen.**	*I should have helped him.*
Er **hätte** dort nicht **parken dürfen.**	*He would not have been allowed to park there.*
Sie **hätte** lange **warten müssen.**	*She would have had to wait for a long time.*
Niemand **hätte** das **essen wollen.**	*Nobody would have wanted to eat that.*
Niemand **hätte** das **essen mögen.**	*Nobody would have liked to eat that.*

hätte + _____
                DOUBLE INFINITIVE

b.   Modals without a dependent infinitive

Ich hätte es **gekonnt, gesollt, gedurft, gemußt, gewollt, gemocht**.

hätte + _____
                PAST PARTICIPLE

Note the difference between the German and English constructions:

Ich hätte ihm helfen können.	**Ich hätte es gekonnt.**
I could have helped him.	*I could have* (done it).
Ich hätte ihm helfen sollen.	**Ich hätte es gesollt.**
I should have helped him.	*I should have* (done it).

PRACTICE

13-14   **A.** Supply the past subjunctive forms of the sentences given in the present subjunctive. Follow the model of sentences 1a. and b.

1.   a. Ich könnte es nicht bezahlen.
         Ich hätte es nicht bezahlen können.
         _____
         I couldn't have paid for it.

      b. Ich könnte es nicht.
         Ich hätte es nicht gekonnt.
         _____
         I couldn't have (done it).

2.   a. Niemand könnte das voraussehen.
         _____
         Nobody could have foreseen that.

b. Niemand könnte das.

_____

Nobody could have (done that).

3. a. Ich sollte mehr für die Prüfung lernen.

_____

I should have studied more for the exam.

b. Wir alle sollten das.

_____

We all should have done that.

4. a. Sie wollte ihn nicht heiraten.

_____

She wouldn't have wanted to marry him.

b. Sie wollte das nicht.

_____

She wouldn't have wanted to (do that).

5. a. Niemand dürfte ihm widersprechen.

_____

Nobody would have been allowed to contradict him.

b. Niemand dürfte das.

_____

Nobody would have been allowed to (do that).

6. a. Eigentlich müßte die Versicherungsgesellschaft alle Rechnungen bezahlen.

_____

Actually, the insurance company would have had to pay all the bills.

b. Eigentlich müßte die Versicherungsgesellschaft das.

_____

Actually the insurance company would have had to (do that).

B. Cover up the German sentences of exercise A and translate the English sentences.

MODEL: I couldn't have paid it.
          Ich hätte es nicht bezahlen können.

§15 *wenn*-CLAUSES IN THE PAST SUBJUNCTIVE

The following wishes refer to the past:

Wenn er mich nur **angerufen hätte**!	If only he had called me.
Wenn ich nur mehr Zeit **gehabt hätte**!	If only I had had more time.
Wenn ich nur zu Hause **gewesen wäre**!	If only I had been at home.
Wenn ich nur nicht nervös **geworden wäre**!	If only I had not become nervous.

The **wenn**-clause has dependent word order: the inflected form is in final position.

Exception: The inflected form must precede a double infinitive(cf. Chap. 4, §7).

Wenn ich dir nur **hätte** helfen können!	If only I could have helped you.
but: Wenn ich es nur gekonnt **hätte**!	If only I could have (done it).

PRACTICE

13-15   A. Supply the past subjunctive forms of the sentences given in the present subjunctive. Follow the model of sentence 1.

1. Wenn das nur möglich wäre!
    Wenn das nur möglich gewessen wäre!
    _____
    If only that had been possible.

2. Wenn das Wetter nur besser wäre!
    _____
    If only the weather had been better.

3. Wenn ich nur mehr Geduld hätte!
    _____
    If only I had had more patience.

4. Wenn ich nur nicht soviel Angst hätte!
    _____
    If only I had not been so afraid.

5. Wenn er mich nur verstehen könnte!
    _____
    If only he could have understood me.

6. Wenn ich nur rauchen dürfte!
    _____
    If only I had been allowed to smoke.

7. Wenn ich das nur dürfte!
    _____
    If only I had been allowed to (do that).

B. Cover up the German sentences of exercise A and translate the English sentences.

MODEL: If only that had been possible.
         Wenn das nur möglich gewesen wäre.

§16 *wenn*-CLAUSE + CONCLUSION IN THE PAST SUBJUNCTIVE

The **wenn**-clause precedes the conclusion:

Wenn ich es gewußt hätte, (dann/so) hätte ich es dir gesagt.
If I had known it, I would have told you.

The conclusion precedes the **wenn**-clause:

Ich hätte es dir gesagt, wenn ich es gewußt hätte.

PRACTICE

13-16   Change the following present subjunctive sentences to past subjunctive.

A. The **wenn**-clause preceding the conclusion:

MODEL: Wenn meine Noten besser wären, würde ich nicht mit dem Studium aufhören.
         Wenn meine Noten besser gewesen wären, hätte ich nicht mit dem Studium aufgehört.
         If my grades had been better, I would not have dropped out of school.

1. Wenn es möglich wäre, würde ich dir helfen.

   _____

   If it had been possible, I would have helped you.
2. Wenn ich an deiner Stelle wäre, würde ich es noch einmal versuchen.

   _____

   If I had been in your place, I would have tried it again.
3. Wenn wir Zeit hätten, würden wir Sie am Sonntag besuchen.

   _____

   If we had had time, we would have visited you on Sunday.
4. Wenn sie es wollte, würde ich mit ihr in die Oper gehen.

   _____

   If she had wanted it, I would have gone to the opera with her.
5. Wenn ich es dürfte, würde ich etwas länger bleiben.

   _____

   If I had been allowed to, I would have stayed a little longer.
6. Wenn ich rauchen dürfte, wäre ich nicht so nervös.

   _____

   If I had been allowed to smoke, I would not have been so nervous.

B. The conclusion preceding the **wenn**-clause:

MODEL: Ich würde nicht mit dem Studium aufhören, wenn meine Noten besser wären.
   Ich hätte nicht mit dem Studium aufgehört, wenn meine Noten besser gewesen wären.
   I would not have dropped out of school, if my grades had been better.

1. Ich würde den Fernseher kaufen, wenn er nicht so teuer wäre.

   _____

   I would have bought the TV set, if it hadn't been so expensive.
2. Sie wäre schockiert, wenn sie das hörte.

   _____

   She would have been shocked, if she had heard that.
3. Wir würden etwas länger in Wien bleiben, wenn es nur nach mir ginge.

   _____

   We would have stayed in Vienna a little longer, if it had been only up to me.
4. Er würde vor Neugierde[1] sterben, wenn wir es ihm nicht sagten.

   _____

   He would have died of curiosity, if we hadn't told him.
5. Sie könnten es noch einmal versuchen, wenn Sie es wollten.

   _____

   You could have tried it again, if you had wanted to.

C. Cover up the German sentences of exercises A and B, and translate the English sentences.

MODEL: *If my grades had been better, I would not have dropped out of school.*
   Wenn meine Noten besser gewesen wären, hätte ich nicht mit dem Studium aufgehört.

---

[1] **die Neugierde**   *curiosity*

Omission of *wenn*

> Wenn ich es gewußt hätte, hätte ich es dir gesagt.
> **Hätte** ich es gewußt, **dann/so** hätte ich es dir gesagt.

When the sentence begins with the inflected verb signaling an omitted **wenn,** the particle **dann** or **so** is commonly added.

PRACTICE

13-17   Omit **wenn,** change the word order, and add **dann.**

1. Wenn ich an seiner Stelle gewesen wäre, hätte ich den Chef um eine Gehaltserhöhung gebeten.
2. Wenn es nur nach mir gegangen wäre, wären wir etwas länger in Wien geblieben.
3. Wenn wir nicht so schnell gefahren wären, wäre der Unfall vielleicht nicht passiert.
4. Wenn ich es gekonnt hätte, hätte ich Ihnen den Gefallen getan.

§17 *wenn*-CLAUSE AND CONCLUSION IN DIFFERENT TENSES

Observe the use of the tenses in the **wenn**-clause and conclusion:

  a. Wenn Ute nicht krank wäre, könnten wir jetzt ins Konzert gehen.
       PRESENT   PRESENT
     If Ute weren't sick, we could go to the concert now.

  b. Wenn Ute nicht krank gewesen wäre, wären wir gestern ins Konzert gegangen.
       PAST   PAST
     If Ute hadn't been sick, we would have gone to the concert yesterday.

  c. Wenn Ute nicht krank wäre, wären wir gestern ins Konzert gegangen.
       PRESENT   PAST
     If Ute weren't sick, we would have gone to the concert yesterday.

In sentence *c.* the **wenn**-clause is in the present, since Ute is still sick. The conclusion is in the past tense, since the concert was yesterday.

PRACTICE

13-18   Express the English sentences in German.

  MODEL: Der Roman ist sehr lang. Deshalb habe ich ihn nicht gelesen.
            Wenn der Roman kürzer wäre, hätte ich ihn gelesen.
            If the novel were shorter, I would have read it.

1. Das Benzin ist sehr teuer. Wir haben einen kleinen Wagen gekauft.

   ———————————————————————

  If gasoline weren't so expensive, we would have bought a bigger car.

2. Ich bin sehr kleinlich.[1] Ich habe die Rechnung nicht bezahlt.

   _____

   If I weren't so petty, I would have paid the bill.

3. Ich habe nicht viel Ausdauer.[2] Ich habe mit dem Studium aufgehört.

   _____

   If I had more perserverance, I would not have dropped out of school.

4. Mein Vater hat keine bessere Stelle gefunden. Wir können diese moderne Wohnung nicht mieten.

   _____

   If my father had found a better job, we could rent this modern apartment.

5. Wir haben nicht in der Lotterie gewonnen. Wir machen keine Reise um die Welt.

   _____

   If we had won in the lottery, we would take a trip around the world.

§18 SUMMARY OF THE MAIN FEATURES

Unreal Conditions

1. General pattern:

	WENN-CLAUSE	CONCLUSION
PRES./ FUT.	**Wenn ich es wüßte,** PRES. SUBJ.	(dann/so) würde ich es dir sagen. **würde** + infintive or: pres. subj. (especially with **haben, sein, wissen,** and the modals)
PAST	**Wenn ich es gewußt hätte,** PAST SUBJ.	(dann/so) **hätte** ich es dir **gesagt.** PAST SUBJ.

2. Omission of **wenn:**

   Wüßte ich es, dann **würde** ich es dir sagen.
   Hätte ich es **gewußt,** dann **hätte** ich es dir **gesagt.**

3. The conclusion precedes the **wenn**-clause:

   Ich **würde** es dir **sagen,** wenn ich es **wüßte.**
   Ich **hätte** es dir **gesagt,** wenn ich es **gewußt hätte.**

4. The **wenn**-clause and the conclusion in different tenses:

   Wenn ich es **wüßte,** dann **hätte** ich es dir **gesagt.**

5. The **wenn**-clause standing alone:

   Wenn ich es nur **wüßte!**
   Wenn ich es nur **gewußt hätte!**

---

[1] **kleinlich**   *petty*
[2] **die Ausdauer**   *staying power, perserverence*

6. The main clause (conclusion) standing alone:

> Ich **würde** es dir **sagen.**
> Ich **hätte** es dir **gesagt.**

§19 REFERENCE TABLE

Selected verbs:

fragen	weak verb (using **haben**)
gehen	strong verb (using **sein**)
haben ⎫	
sein ⎬	functioning as main verbs
werden ⎭	
können	modal without dependent infinitive
gehen können	modal with dependent infinitive

WENN-CLAUSES

PRESENT	PAST
Wenn ich…**fragte**	Wenn ich…**gefragt hätte**
If I aked	*If I had asked*
Wenn ich…**ginge**	Wenn ich…**gegangen wäre**
If I went	*If I had gome*
Wenn ich…**hätte**	Wenn ich…**gehabt hätte**
If I had	*If I had had*
Wenn ich…**wäre**	Wenn ich…**gewesen wäre**
If I were	*If I had been*
Wenn ich…**würde**	Wenn ich…**geworden wäre**
If I became	*If I had become*
Wenn ich…**könnte**	Wenn ich…**gekonnt hätte**
If I could	*If I could have*
Wenn ich…**gehen könnte**	Wenn ich…**hätte gehen können**
If I could go	*If I could have gone*

MAIN CLAUSES

PRESENT		PAST	
Ich **würde**…**fragen**	*I would ask*	Ich **hätte**… **gefragt**	
			I would have asked
Ich **würde**…**gehen**	*I would go*	Ich **wäre**… **gegangen**	
			I would have gone
Ich **hätte**	*I would have*	Ich **hätte**… **gehabt**	
			I would have had
Ich **wäre**	*I would be*	Ich **wäre**… **gewesen**	
			I would have been
Ich **würde**…**werden**	*I would become*	Ich **wäre**… **geworden**	
			I would have become

Ich **könnte (es)**	*I could (do it)*	Ich **hätte(es) gekonnt** *I could have (done it)*
Ich **könnte… gehen**	*I could go*	Ich **hätte… gehen können** *I could have gone*

PRACTICE

13-19   Summarizing exercises

A. Express in German

1. a. I can't tell you because I don't know it.   **Ich kann es dir nicht sagen, weil ich es nicht weiß.**
    b. If only I knew it.
    c. If I knew it, I would tell you.
    d. If I had known it, I would have told you.
2. a. She is dying of curiosity.   **Sie stirbt vor Neugierde.**
    b. She would die of curiosity.
    c. She would have died of curiosity.
3. a. He is in a bad mood.   **Er hat schlechte Laune.**
    b. If only he were in a good mood.
    c. If only he had been in a good mood.
4. a. I am asking my boss for a raise.   **Ich bitte meinen Chef um eine Gehaltserhöhung.**
    b. I should ask my boss for a raise.
    c. I should have asked my boss for a raise.
    d. If my boss were in a good mood, I would ask him for a raise.
    e. If my boss had been in a good mood, I would have asked him for a raise.
5. a. Life is hard.   **Das Leben ist schwer.**
    b. If only life were easier.
    c. Life would be easier, if I had more money.
6. a. Karin has found a better job.   **Karin hat eine bessere Stelle gefunden.**
    b. If only I could find a better job.
    c. If only I had found a better job.
    d. Life would be easier, if I had found a better job.
7. a. I can't go with you to the theater because I am broke.   **Ich kann nicht mit euch ins Theater gehen, weil ich pleite bin.**
    b. If only I could go with you to the theater.
    c. If only I had not been broke.
    d. If I had not been broke, I would have gone with you to the theater.
8. a. Is she single?   **Ist sie ledig?**
    b. If only she were single.
    c. If she were single, I would invite her.
    d. If she were single, I would have invited her.
9. a. I'd like to be in her place.   **Ich möchte an ihrer Stelle sein.**
    b. If only I were in her place.
    c. If I were in her place, I would marry Frank.
    d. What would you do, if you were in my place? (fam. sing.)

10. a. Why am I so afraid?   **Warum habe ich soviel Angst?**
     b. If only I weren't so afraid.
     c. If only I had not been so afraid.
     d. I should not be so afraid.
     e. I should not have been so afraid.
     f. I would tell you the truth if I weren't so afraid. (formal)
     g. I would have told you the truth if I had not been so afraid.

B. Complete the responses in German.

1. X: Warum werden deine Noten immer schlechter?
    Y: Weil ich faul bin. _____
                            If only I weren't so lazy.

2. X: Liebst du Renate?
    Y: Ja, sehr. _____
                I could not live without her.

3. X: Hast du die Semesterarbeit getippt? Du hast doch eine
       Schreibmaschine.
    Y: _____
       I would have typed it if I had a typewriter.

4. X: Du warst ja gestern sehr stur.
    Y: Ja, leider. _____
                   If only I had not been so stubborn.

5. X: Bist du immer so kleinlich?
    Y: Nicht immer, aber meistens. _____
                                   I shouldn't be so petty.

6. X: Ist es nicht großartig, daß Sie in der Lotterie gewonnen haben?
    Y: _____
       It would be great if it were true.

7. X: Warum hast du nicht länger gewartet?
    Y: Es war schon spät. _____
                          I could not have waited any longer.

8. X: Fahren wir oder gehen wir zu Fuß?
    Y: Es ist sehr windig. _____
                           If it weren't so windy, we could walk. (go on foot)

9. X: Wie ist denn der Unfall passiert? Ist Frank kein sicherer Fahrer?
    Y: _____
       If Frank were a safe driver, the accident would not have happened.

10. X: Haben Sie die Krise nicht vorausgesehen?
    Y: _____
       Nobody could have foreseen it.

11. X: Es ist schade, daß Hans so viele Vorurteile hat.
    Y: Ja, sehr schade. _____
                        Everything (alles) would be easier, if he did not have
    so many prejudices.

12. X: Wie ich höre, studiert deine Schwester Medizin.
    Y: Ich beneide sie sehr. _____
                             If my grades were better, I would also study medicine.

13.   X: Mußt du das ganze Wochenende lernen?
      Y: Zum Glück nicht. _____
                           It would be very boring if I had to study all weekend.

14.   X: Wollen Sie wirklich Neumanns Haus kaufen?
      Y: Meine Frau will, daß wir es kaufen. _____
                           If it were only up to me, we would not buy it.

15.   X: Warum wollen Sie nicht mit Herrn Körner ausgehen?
      Y: Weil das Goldstück[1] verheiratet ist. _____
                           Of course, I would go out with him if he were single.

C.   Using the cues, make sentences that fit the context.

MODEL: Hannelore klatscht zuviel. Eine Freundin sollte es ihr sagen. Ich
         bin nicht ihre Freundin und kann es deshalb nicht.
         Wenn / Freundin—ihr / sagen
         Wenn ich ihre Freundin wäre, würde ich es ihr sagen.

1.   Mein Freund Thomas will ein Jahr in Frankfurt studieren. Leider kann
     ich das nicht, denn ich habe nicht genug Geld.
     Wenn/mehr Geld—auch in Frankfurt/studieren

2.   Ich habe eine sehr kleine Wohnung und kann nicht viele Leute
     einladen.
     Wenn / größere Wohnung—mehr Leute / ein•laden

3.   Marlene hat mehr Ausdauer als ich.
     Wenn / nur / mehr Ausdauer!

4.   Renate will mit dem Studium aufhören. Ich finde, daß sie das nicht tun
     sollte.
     Wenn / ich / an ihrer Stelle—nicht / mit dem Studium / auf•hören

5.   Mein Bruder ist sehr egoistisch. Wahrscheinlich hat er deshalb nicht
     viele Freunde.
     Er / mehr Freunde—wenn / nicht so egoistisch

6.   Ich soll Karin vom Flughafen abholen, kann es aber nicht, denn mein
     Wagen ist kaputt.
     Ich / ab•holen—wenn / Wagen / nicht kaputt

7.   Meiner Meinung nach ist dieser Film etwas langweilig, weil er zu lang
     ist.
     Film / interessanter—wenn / kürzer

8.   Andreas hat einen Sportwagen und fährt wie der Teufel. Ich fahre nie
     mit ihm.
     Ich / sterben / vor Angst

D.   Sagen Sie in fünf Sätzen, was Sie tun würden, wenn Sie eine Million
     Dollar in der Lotterie gewonnen hätten.

---

[1]das Goldstück, -e   *gem* (lit.: *gold piece*)

CHAPTER 14

The Subjunctive Part II

Various Uses of the Subjunctive

§1 WISHES INTRODUCED BY *ich wollte* OR *ich wünschte*

1. Wishes referring to the present or future

Ich wollte, Ich wünschte,	ich **hätte** mehr Freizeit.	*I wish I had more leisure time.*
	ich **wäre** nicht so schüchtern.	*I weren't so shy.*
	ich **wüßte** es.	*I knew it.*
	ich **könnte** Sie überzeugen.	*I could convince you.*
	er **würde** nicht so schnell fahren.	*he would not drive so fast.*

Note: a. The introductory statement **Ich wollte** or **Ich wünschte** is a form of the present subjunctive. The English counterpart *I wish* is, of course, present indicative.

b. The wish itself is expressed in the present subjunctive with **haben, sein, werden, wissen,** and the modals; with other verbs the **würde** + infinitive forms are commonly used.

PRACTICE

14-1   Complete the responses in German.

MODEL: X: Können Sie Klavier spielen?
Y: **Leider nein, aber <u>ich wollte, ich könnte es.</u>**
I wish I could (do it).

1. X: Sind Ihre Nachbarn immer so laut?
Y: Nicht immer, aber meistens. _____
I wish they weren't so loud.

2. X: Du hast ja nicht viel Ausdauer.
Y: Das stimmt. _____
I wish I had more perseverence.

3. X: Kommst du mit?
Y: Leider kann ich nicht. _____
I wish I could come along.

4. X: Wann kommt Karin zurück?
   Y: Ich habe keine Ahnung. _____

   I wish I knew (it).

5. X: Hat dich Werner angerufen?
   Y: Bis jetzt noch nicht.[1] _____

   I wish he would call soon.[2]

6. X: Bringt dich Gisela zum Bahnhof?
   Y: Leider nein. _____

   I wish she would take me to the railway station.

2. Wishes referring to the past

Ich wollte,
Ich wünschte,   } du **hättest** mich gestern **angerufen.**

  PRES. SUBJ.   PAST SUBJ.

There are two different tenses: A present wish (expressed in the present subjunctive) that something occurred in the past, i.e. yesterday (expressed in the past subjunctive). The English equivalent is:

I wish you had called me yesterday.

Additional examples:

Ich wollte,
Ich wünschte   } ich wäre vorsichtiger   *I wish I had been more careful.*
                   gewesen.

                 ich hätte das im voraus   *I had known that beforehand.*
                   gewußt.

                 ich hätte das voraussehen   *I could have foreseen that.*
                   können.

                 er wäre nicht so schnell   *he had not been driving*
                   gefahren.   *so fast.*

PRACTICE

14-2 Complete the responses in German.

   MODEL: X: Hast du es ihm gesagt?
           Y: **Ja, aber ich wünschte, ich hätte es ihm nicht gesagt.**

           I wish I hadn't told him.

1. X: Hast du Leonores Wagen gekauft?
   Y: Ja, aber _____

   I wish I hadn't bought it.

2. X: Du warst schon wieder in der Stadt. Sicher hast du wieder viel Geld
      ausgegeben.
   Y: Leider ja. _____

   I wish I hadn't spent so much money.

---

[1] **bis jetzt noch nicht**   *not yet so far*
[2] **bald**   *soon*

3.   X: Ulrich hat heute Geburtstag. Hast du daran gedacht?
      Y: Leider nein.
      _____
      I wish I had thought of it.

4. a X: Wie war die Party bei Köhlers?
       Y: Sehr langweilig.
       _____
       I wish I had stayed at home.

    b. X: Wenn man sich langweilt,[1] ißt man meistens zuviel.
       Y: Stimmt.
       _____
       I wish I had not eaten so much.

5.   X: Jemand hat gesagt: „Die Herrschaft über den Augenblick ist die
         Herrschaft über das ganze Leben."*
      Y: Großartig!
      _____
      I wish I had said that.

§2   As if Clauses Introduced by *als ob, als wenn, or als*

As if clauses in English

Compare the use of the tenses in the following examples.

1.   The *as if* clause is expressed in the present subjunctive.

     a. Hans doesn't look well today.

         He **looks** today   as if he **were** ill.
         main clause   as if clause
           PRESENT   PRESENT
           INDICATIVE   SUBJUNCTIVE

     b. Hans didn't look well yesterday.

         He **looked** yesterday   as if he **were** ill.
           PAST   PRESENT
           INDICATIVE   SUBJUNCTIVE

In *a.* the main clause is in the present tense and in *b.* it is in the past tense. However, in both sentences the *as if clause* is in the present subjunctive. Why? The reason is what is called in German **Gleichzeitigkeit** meaning **simultaneity**. Hans looks ill at the time of the statement of the main clause, i.e. today or yesterday. In other words, the action or state of the *as if- clause* is simultaneous with the main clause.

Another example: *She **acts** as if she **were** Miss America.*
                        *She **acted** as if she **were** Miss America.*

2.   The *as if-clause* is expressed in the past subjunctive.

     a. Hans **looks** today as if he **had been** ill.
     b. Hans **looked** yesterday as if he **had been** ill.

_____

[1] **sich langweilen**   *to be bored*
Control over the moment is control over one's entire life.

The *as if-clause* refers to a time prior to the main clause. It is expressed in the past subjunctive (identical in form to the past perfect indicative, cf. Chap. 13, §12). The German term is *Vorzeitigkeit*, meaning *prior occurence*.

Another example: *She **feels** so much better, as if she **had been** in a health spa.*
                   *She **felt** so much better, as if she **had been** in a health spa.*

Note: English often uses the indicative after as if:
            He looks as if he is / was / has been ill.

In German

The German equivalents of the above sentences 1. a + b and 2. a + b are stated below.

1.   The *as if*-clause is in the present subjunctive because of **Gleichzeitigkeit**.

    a. Er **sieht** heute so aus, **als ob er krank wäre.**
    b. Er **sah** gestern so aus, **als ob er krank wäre.**

2.   The *as if*-clause is in the past subjunctive because of **Vorzeitigkeit**.

    a. Er **sieht** heute so aus, **als ob er krank gewesen wäre.**
    b. Er **sah** gestern so aus, **als ob er krank gewesen wäre.**

You will see that the subjunctive is used here just as in English. However, as pointed out before, English often uses the indicative in *as if*-clauses, whereas German sentences as those above are the normal forms.

Rule: 1. The *as if*-clause is expressed in the **present subjunctive**,
          if its action or state **is simultaneous** with the main clause.

      2. The *as if*-clause is expressed in the **past subjunctive**,
          if its action or state **was prior** to the main clause.

In German, the **als ob**-clause may also be introduced by **als wenn** (used less frequently) or the shortened form **als**.

       Er sieht/sah so aus, **als wenn** er krank **wäre.**
           or: **als wäre** er krank.

Note: When the shortened form **als** is used, the inflected verb follows immediately after **als**.

Additional examples:
       Cornelia hat ihr Geld verschwendet, **als ob (wenn) sie Millionärin wäre.**
                   als wäre sie Millionärin.
       Cornelia wasted her money, as if she were a millionaire.

       Krauses tun (taten) so, **als ob (wenn) sie viele Freunde hätten.**
                  als hätten sie viele Freunde.
       The Krauses act (acted), as if they had many friends.

       Katrin tut (tat) so, **als ob (wenn) sie noch nie Angst gehabt hätte.**
               als hätte sie noch nie Angst gehabt.
       Katrin acts (acted) as if she had never been afraid.

Unusual or obsolete present subjunctives are replaced by **würde** + *infinitive forms* (cf. Chap. 13, §6).

> Diese Kinder sehen so aus, **als ob (wenn) sie frieren würden.**
>> (instead of **frören**)
>
> **als würden sie frieren.**
>
> *These children look as if they were freezing.*

> Idioms: **Tun Sie so, als ob (wenn) Sie zu Hause wären.**
>> **als wären Sie zu Hause.**
>
> *Make yourself at home.*
>
> **Sie tut nur so.**
>
> *She is only pretending.*

PRACTICE

14-3 **A.** Using the present subjunctive.

Complete the German responses introducing the **as if**-clause with both **als ob** and **als.**

MODEL: X: Ist Herr Körner wirklich so intelligent, wie er tut?
Y: Ach, das ist nur Angabe.[1]

Er tut immer so, —— **als ob er Dr. Allwissend wäre.**
            —— **als wäre er Dr. Allwissend.**

_____

as if he were Dr. know-it-all.

1. X: Sind Lehmanns wirklich Millionäre?
   Y: Das weiß ich nicht. Sagen wir, sie sehen nicht so aus,

   _____

   as if they were poor.

2. X: Hat die Chefin schlechte Laune?
   Y: Sie sieht nicht so aus,   _____

   as if she were in a bad mood.

3. X: Ist in diesem Satz etwas falsch?
   Y: Wahrscheinlich. Er klingt[2] so,   _____

   as if something were wrong.

4. X: Darf ich die Jacke ausziehen?
   Y: Aber natürlich, Herr Stein. _____

   Make yourself at home.

5. X: Frau Schmidt scheint keine Sorgen zu haben.
   Y: Sie hat schon immer so getan, _____

   as if she had no worries.

6. X: Hat dein Bruder diese großartige Stelle nun bekommen?
   Y: Leider nicht, aber vorige Woche sah es noch so aus,

   _____

   as if he could get it.

---

[1] **die Angabe**   *showing off, bragging*
[2] **klingen, klang, geklungen**   *to sound*

7. X: Helfen dir deine Kinder bei der Gartenarbeit?
    Y: Nicht viel. Manchmal tun sie nur so, _____

    as if they were helping.
    (Use **würde** + infinitive)

8. X: Warum hörst du nicht zu, wenn ich mit dir spreche?
    Y: Weil du so angibst. Du tust so, _____

    as if you were Dr. know-it-all.

9. X: Wie gefällt dir der neue Mathematikprofessor?
    Y: Ich finde ihn sehr eingebildet.[1] Er tut so, _____

    as if he were a combination of[2] *Albert Einstein and Bob Hope.*

10. X: Du hast einen großen Fehler gemacht. Wie kann ein Mensch nur so
    dumm sein?
    Y: Ich bin doch gar nicht so dumm. _____

    I'm only pretending (to be dumb).

B. Using the past subjunctive.

Complete the German responses introducing the **as if**-clause with both **als
ob** and **als**.

MODEL: X: War Barbara beim Friseur?

Y: **Sie sieht so aus,** ⟨ als ob sie beim Friseur gewesen **wäre.**
                          als **wäre** sie beim Friseur gewesen.

as if she had been at the hairdresser's.

1. X: Hat es geregnet?
    Y: Es sieht so aus, _____

    as if it had rained.

2. X: Hast du zugenommen?
    Y: Sehe ich so aus, _____

    as if I had gained weight?

3. X: Warum denkst du, daß Marlene den ersten Preis gewonnen hat?
    Y: Sie hat so gestrahlt,[3] _____

    as if she had won the first prize.

4. X: Wie hast du auf Renates taktlose Bermerkung reagiert?
    Y: Ich habe so getan, _____

    as if I hadn't heard it.

5. X: Hast du diesen Film schon gesehen?
    Y: Es kommt mir so vor,[4] _____

    that (als ob) I have seen it already.

A note on the use of the special subjunctive in *als ob* and *als* clauses.

In literary German these clauses are also expressed in the special subjunctive (cf. §7).

---

[1] **eingebildet**   *conceited*
[2] **eine Kombination von**   *a combination of*
[3] **strahlen**   *to beam*
[4] idiom: **es kommt mir so vor**   *it seems to me*

There is no difference in meaning.

Er sah so aus, — als ob er krank **sei**.
— als **sei** er krank.

Er sah so aus, — als ob er krank **gewesen sei**.
— als **sei** er krank **gewesen**.

§3 *beinah(e)* OR *fast* INDICATING THAT SOMETHING ALMOST OCCURRED

Ich hätte es beinah(e) (fast) vergessen.   *I almost forgot it.*
Ich wäre beinah(e) (fast) gestorben.   *I almost died.*

Note: a. To indicate that something almost happened. German often uses the past subjunctive while English uses the past indicative.

b. The **-e** of **beinahe** may be omitted. **Beinah(e)** and **fast** mean *almost* and are used interchangeably.

Beinah(e) and **fast** normally follow subjects and personal pronoun objects but precede all other elements.

PRACTICE

14-4   Express the responses in German.

MODEL: X: Habt ihr den Zug verpaßt?
Y: **Nein, aber wir hätten ihn beinahe verpaßt.**
No, but we almost missed it.

1. X: Hoffentlich hast du den Vertrag nicht unterschrieben.
Y: _____
I almost signed it.

2. X: Hoffentlich hast du nicht schon wieder den Schlüssel vergessen.
Y: _____
I almost forgot it.

3. X: Warum seid ihr so aufgeregt?[1] Habt ihr einen Autounfall gehabt?
Y: _____
No, but we almost had a car accident.

4. X: Hast du verschlafen?
Y: _____
I almost overslept.

5. X: Bist du in der Vorlesung eingeschlafen?
Y: _____
I almost fell asleep.

6. X: Haben Sie Frau Berger sofort erkannt?
Y: _____
No. I almost didn't recognize her.

7. X: War Klaus wirklich so schwer krank,[2] wie seine Freundin sagt?
Y: _____
Yes. He almost died.

---

[1] **aufgeregt**   *excited, upset*
[2] **schwer krank sein**   *to be seriously ill*

§4   TENTATIVE AND POLITE STATEMENTS AND QUESTIONS

In German the subjunctive is frequently used to make statements and questions more tentative, modest, or polite. Compare:

a. INDICATIVE   Ich rate Ihnen, diese dumme Bemerkung zu ignorieren.
I advise you to ignore the stupid remark.

b. SUBJUNCTIVE   Ich **würde** Ihnen **raten**, diese dumme Bemerkung zu ignorieren.
*I **would advise** you to ignore this stupid remark.*

The use of the subjunctive **würde** + **raten** in sentence *b.* makes the statement more tentative. It expresses the advice with modesty and caution in contrast to the somewhat blunt tone of sentence *a.* This distinction is clear in the two English sentences above. However, subjunctive constructions occur more frequently in German than in English. They often have to be rendered into English with indicative forms, as the following examples illustrate:

Wir **hätten** also wieder einmal Glück **gehabt.**
So we have been lucky again.

Damit **hätte** ich endlich mein Ziel **erreicht.**
With that, I have finally achieved my goal.

Questions are frequently made more polite by using the subjunctive. Compare:

INDICATIVE	SUBJUNCTIVE
Haben Sie einen Zettel für mich?	**Hätten** Sie einen Zettel für mich?
Do you have a piece of paper for me?	*Would you have a piece of paper for me?*
Ist Ihnen das recht?	**Wäre** Ihnen das recht?
Is that OK with you?	*Would that be OK with you?*
Können Sie einen Augenblick warten?	**Könnten** Sie einen Augenblick warten?
Can you wait a moment (minute)?	*Could you wait a moment (minute)?*
Tun Sie mir diesen Gefallen?	**Würden** Sie mir diesen Gefallen tun?
Are you going to do me this favor?	*Would you do me this favor?*

Note that the **würde** + infinitive forms are used with most verbs other than **haben, sein,** and the modals.

PRACTICE

14-5   Express the following questions in a more polite way.

MODEL: Passen Sie ein paar Minuten auf meine Sachen auf?
Würden Sie ein paar Minuten auf meine Sachen aufpassen?

1. Hilfst du mir?
2. Haben Sie Lust mitzufahren?
3. Ist dir das recht?

4. Kannst du mir 100 Mark leihen?[1]
5. Darf ich Sie um einen Gefallen bitten?
6. Hast du etwas Zeit für mich?
7. Ist das möglich?
8. Bringt ihr mich zum Flughafen?
9. Paßt du auf meine Sachen auf?

<table>
<tr><td>PRACTICE</td></tr>
<tr><td>14-6</td></tr>
</table>

PRACTICE

14-6   Summarizing exercises for §1–§4

A.   Express the following sentences in German.

1. a. He should speak a little more slowly. **Er sollte etwas langsamer sprechen.**
    b. I wish he would speak a little more slowly.
    c. I wish he had spoken a little more slowly.
    d. Would you speak a little more slowly? (formal)
    e. Could you speak a little more slowly?
2. a. Nobody wants to do me a favor. **Niemand will mir einen Gefallen tun.**
    b. Would you do me a favor? (fam. sing.)
    c. Could you do me a favor? (formal)
    d. I wish we could do her a favor.
3. a. Who is taking care of that? **Wer erledigt das?**
    b. I wish she would take care of that.
    c. I wish she had taken care of that.
    d. Would you take care of that? (formal)
    e. Could you take care of that? (fam. sing.)
4. a. I don't have a computer. **Ich habe keinen Computer.**
    b. I wish I had a computer.
    c. I wish I had bought a computer.
    d. I almost bought a computer.
5. a. Don't give up hope. **Geben Sie die Hoffnung nicht auf!**
    b. It looks as if they would give up hope. (two ways: **als ob/als**)
    c. It looks as if they had given up hope. (two ways)
    d. We almost gave up hope.
6. a. He is a second Albert Einstein. **Er ist ein zweiter Albert Einstein.**
    b. He acts as if he were a second Albert Einstein. (two ways)
    c. He acts as if he had been Albert Einstein's right hand. (two ways)
7. a. She is shy. **Sie ist schüchtern.**
    b. She pretends to be shy. (two ways)
    c. She is only pretending.

B.   Using the cues, form sentences that fit the context.

1. Hannelore war ein Jahr in Europa. Gestern ist sie zurückgekommen.
    Sie sieht anders aus als vor einem Jahr.
       ich / beinahe / nicht erkennen

---

[1] leihen, lieh, geliehen   _to lend_

2. Der neue Professor gefällt mir nicht.
     so tun, / Dr. Alwissend sein
3. Herberts Eltern feiern die Silberne Hochzeit. Herbert soll eine kleine
     Rede halten. Hat er Lampenfieber? (*stage fright*)
     so aus•sehen / haben / Lampenfieber
4. Frau Klinger hat Gäste. Sie möchte, daß sie sich wie zu Hause fühlen,
     und sagt:
     „so tun, / zu Hause sein" (formal)
5. Gestern war die Vorlesung sehr langweilig.
     beinahe / ein•schlafen
6. Ich bin auf dem Bahnhof und habe einen schweren Koffer. Ich sehe
     einen Zeitungsstand. Neben mir steht eine ältere Dame. Sie sieht
     vertrauenswürdig (*trustworthy*) aus. Ich sage zu ihr:
     „Zeitung / kaufen.// auf Koffer auf•passen?"
7. Der Deutschprofessor hat mich etwas gefragt, aber ich habe seine Frage
     nicht verstanden. Ich sage höflich:
     „Frage / wiederholen?"
8. Ich habe keine Ahnung, wie lange meine Freundin in der Schweiz
     bleiben will.
     wollte, / ich /es/ wissen
9. Ich habe Jürgen einen Lügner (*liar*) genannt. Jetzt tut es mir leid, daß
     ich das gesagt habe.
     wünschte, / das / nicht / sagen
10. Was gefällt Ihnen an Ihren Freunden und Freundinnen nicht? (drei Sätze)
     Ich wollte, er/sie…

Using the Indicative and Subjunctive in Indirect Discourse

INTRODUCTION

Compare the following direct and indirect quotes:

> *Mrs. Stern said*, "**My** husband **is** depressed." (direct quote)
> *Mrs. Stern said* **her** husband **was** depressed. (indirect object)

In indirect discourse, one person reports what another has said without quoting
him/her directly. In the example, the possessive **my** changed to **her**. The verb tense
was also shifted in the indirect quote. If the introductory statement (Mrs. Stern said)
has a past time form, **is** may change to **was** in the indirect quote.

In German, indirect discourse may be expressed in the indicative and in the subjunctive. Native speakers of German choose indicative or subjunctive forms according to
what they want to imply and what they feel would sound right in a given context.
The more refined their *Sprachgefühl* (feeling for the language) is, the more

discriminating they are in the use of these forms. On the other end of the scale are those who use them rather haphazardly.

This can be quite puzzling to those who study German as a foreign language. Not yet being able to resort to a German *Sprachgefühl*, they need some rules and guidelines as a basis to work with. The following detailed explanations are designed to provide it.

Indirect discourse is treated somewhat differently in informal German (everyday speech, informal writing) and in formal German (literary works, lectures, papers, official statements).

§5   INFORMAL GERMAN USING THE INDICATIVE

When speakers use the indicative to report what someone has said, they indicate that they do not doubt the correctness of what they are reporting.

Compare the following German direct and indirect quotes with the English example above:

> Frau Stern sagte: „**Mein** Mann ist deprimiert." (direct quote)
> Frau Stern sagte, **ihr** Mann **ist** deprimiert. (indirect quote)
> or: daß **ihr** Mann deprimiert **ist.**

Note: a.   As in English, the possessive changes: **mein** to **ihr.** But unlike English, the time of the verb is not shifted. In German an indirect quote normally uses the same time as the direct quote, regardless of the tense in the introductory statement.

b.   Indirect quotes in the indicative are often introduced by **daß,** which helps to make clear that the quote is indirect.

c.   A direct quote is preceded by a colon. The opening quotation mark is not raised, but consists of two commas.

Additional examples illustrating that the tense of the direct quote is usually retained in the indirect quote:

> Köhlers sagen: „**Unsere** Kinder arbeiten nicht gern im Garten."
> Köhlers sagen, daß **ihre** Kinder nicht gern im Garten **arbeiten.**
>
> Frau Köhler sagte: „**Mein** Mann **arbeitet** im Garten."
> Frau Köhler sagte, daß **ihr** Mann im Garten **arbeitet.**
>
> Herr Köhler hat gesagt: „**Meine** Frau und **ich haben** im Garten **gearbeitet.**"
> Herr Köhler hat gesagt, daß **seine** Frau und **er** im Garten **gearbeitet haben.**

PRACTICE

14-7   Change the following direct quotations to indirect discourse, using **daß.** (Keep in mind that in dependent clauses the separable prefix is attached to the verb.)

MODEL: Sigrid hat gesagt: „Ich rufe dich Freitag abend an."
Sigrid hat gesagt, daß sie mich Freitag abend anruft.

1. Klaus hat gesagt: „Ich hole Sandra um 7 Uhr ab."
2. Elke sagt: „Ich habe Franks Telefonnummer vergessen."
3. Frau Berger sagte: „Ich bin nur drei Tage in Hamburg geblieben."
4. Zimmermanns sagen: „Wir wollen aufs Land ziehen."
5. Fräulein Klinger hat gesagt: „Der Zug ist pünktlich abgefahren."
6. Uwe sagte: „Ich suche eine neue Stelle."

Questions are quoted indirectly as follows:

DIRECT QUOTE

Herr Schreiber hat Herrn Köhler gefragt:
   a. „Wann arbeiten Sie in Ihrem Garten?"
   b. „Arbeiten Sie oft in Ihrem Garten?"

INDIRECT QUOTE

Herr Schreiber hat Herrn Köhler gefragt,
   a. **wann** er in seinem Garten **arbeitet.**
   b. **ob** er oft in seinem Garten **arbeitet.**

Note: Indirect questions always have dependent word order. They are introduced either by a question word, as in sentence *a.*, or by **ob**, as in sentence *b.* (cf. Chap. 1, §5)

Another example:

Ich habe Andreas gefragt:
   a. „Warum hast du Renate eingeladen?"
   b. „Hast du Renate eingeladen?"

Ich habe Andreas gefragt,
   a. **warum** er Renate eingeladen **hat.**
   b. **ob** er Renate eingeladen **hat.**

PRACTICE

14-8   Change the following direct quotations to indirect discourse, using the introductory clauses indicated.

MODEL: „Kommt Inge auch mit?"
Hans hat mich gefragt, <u>ob Inge auch mitkommt.</u>
„Warum kommst du nicht mit?"
Ich habe Klaus gefragt, <u>warum er nicht mitkommt.</u>

1. „Holst du Annerose ab?"
Ich habe Hartmut gefragt, _____
2. „Rufst du mich heute abend an?"
Ich habe Ruth gefragt, _____
3. „Wo hast du Renate kennengelernt?"
Ich habe Martin gefragt, _____

4. „Wann kommt der Zug in München an?"
   Margot hat einen Beamten[1] gefragt, _____

5. „Wieviel kostet der Kassettenrecorder?"
   Ich habe die Verkäuferin gefragt,_____

6. „Haben Sie das Theaterstück gelesen?"
   Professor Krause hat mich gefragt,_____

§6   INFORMAL GERMAN USING THE SUBJUNCTIVE

The subjunctive tends to be used when the reporter has reservations about the validity of what was said.

In indirect discourse, the subjunctive occurs in three tenses: present, past, and future.

1. The direct quote is in the present tense

Sandra had gesagt: Sandra hat gesagt,
  „Professor Bauer ist nicht fair."   Professor Bauer **wäre** nicht fair.

                                            PRESENT SUBJUNCTIVE

The use of the present subjunctive **wäre** instead of **ist** indicates that the reporter has reservations about the validity of Sandra's statement.

Indirect quotations expressed in the subjunctive are usually not inroduced by **daß**. The subjunctive alone suffices to mark the indirect quote.

Additional examples:

Sie sagte: Sie sagte,
  Ich habe Angst.   sie **hätte** Angst.
  Ich kann das nicht essen.   sie **könnte** das nicht essen.
  Ich werde verrückt.   sie **würde** verrückt.
  Ich weiß seinen Namen nicht mehr.   sie **wüßte** seinen Namen nicht mehr.

PRACTICE

14-9   Change to indirect quotations.

MODEL: Frau Kästner hat gesagt: „Ich kann sehr stur sein."
          Frau Kästner hat gesagt, sie könnte sehr stur sein.

1. Herr Kästner hat gesagt: „Ich muß immer nachgeben."
2. Professor Wagner hat gesagt: „Die Prüfung ist nicht schwer."
3. Margot sagte: „Ich habe nicht genug Willenskraft."
4. Ihr Freund sagte: „Ich weiß nichts davon."
5. Fräulein Schmidt hat gesagt: „Frau Stern will nicht zu ihrem Mann zurückgehen."
6. Herr Stern hat gesagt: „Die Kinder werden immer deprimierter."

---

[1] **der Beamte** (*adj. noun* [Chap. 9, §12])   *official (male)*
   die Beamte, -en   *(female)*

In informal German, few present subjunctives are used other than those of **haben, sein, werden, wissen,** and the modals. As stated in Chapter 13, §6, studies have shown that in **written informal German** (personal letters, diaries, etc.) the following present subjunctives of strong verbs occur as frequently as their **würde** + infinitive substitutes.

fände	and	würde finden
gäbe		würde geben
ginge		würde gehen
hielte		würde halten
hieße		würde heißen
käme		würde kommen
ließe		würde lassen
täte		würde tun

The same is true of their compound forms, such as

gäbe an	würde angeben
ginge aus	würde ausgehen
käme an	würde ankommen
bekäme	würde bekommen

PRACTICE 14-10

Change to indirect quotations introducing them with **Alexandra schrieb** and using a. the present subjunctive and b. the **würde** + infinitive substitute. Follow the model of sentence 1.

Alexandra schrieb:

1. „Die Busse halten dort nicht mehr."
   Alexandra schreib: a. die Busse **hielten** dort nicht mehr.
                        b. die Busse **würden** dort nicht mehr **halten**.

2. „Viele Leute finden diesen Film sehr interessant."
   a.
   b.
3. „Vielleicht heißt die Firma jetzt anders."
   a.
   b.
4. „Die Wunde am Bein tut nicht mehr weh.[1]"
   a.
   b.
5. „Dieser Zug kommt oft mit Verspätung an.[2]"
   a.
   b.
6. „Meine Eltern gehen meistens samstags abends aus."
   a.
   b.
7. „Mein Nachbar gibt gern ein bißchen an."
   a.
   b.

---

[1] **weh tun**	*to hurt*
[2] **mit Verspätung an•kommen**	*to arrive late*

8. „Ich bekomme zu wenig Geld für diese schwerre Arbeit."
a.
b.
9. „Manchmal lasse ich den Papagei¹ aus dem Käfig.²"
a.
b.

With regard to weak verbs, there is a preference for the use of the **würde** + infinitive substitute, as the following example illustrates:

> Frau Schneider schrieb: „Mein Mann bezahlt alle Rechnungen."
> Frau Schneider schrieb, a. ihr Mann **bezahlte** alle Rechnungen.
> past subj. = past indicative
> preferred: b. ihr Mann **würde** alle Rechnungen bezahlen.

Since the present subjunctive of weak verbs is identical in form to the past indicative, the **würde** + infinitive substitute is preferred.

In everyday spoken German, the **würde** + infinitive substitutes are used for virtually all verbs other than **haben, sein, werden, wissen**, and the modals.

2. The direct quote is in the past, present perfect, or past perfect.

> Maria hat gesagt: Maria hat gesagt:
> „Ich **wußte** nichts davon."
> „Ich **habe** nichts davon **gewußt**." }   sie **hätte** nichts davon **gewußt**.
> „Ich **hatte** nichts davon **gewußt**."   (PAST SUBJUNCTIVE)
> *Maria said she had known nothing about it.*

The past subjunctive is used in indirect discourse to replace any past time tense in the original statement.

Additional examples:

> Er hat gesagt: Er hat gesagt,
> „Ich hatte keine Angst."   er **hätte** keine Angst **gehabt**.
> „Das war eine Lüge."   das **wäre** eine Lüge **gewesen**.
> „Der Film hat niemand gefallen."   der Film **hätte** niemand **gefallen**.
> „Viele Leute sind im Kino   viele Leute **wären** im Kino
> eingeschlafen."   **eingeschlafen**.
> „Ich mußte immer nachgeben."   er **hätte** immer **nachgeben müssen**.
> „Ich wollte es nicht."   er **hätte** es nicht **gewollt**.

PRACTICE

14-11   Change the following direct quotations to indirect discourse using the subjunctive.

> MODEL: Peter hat gesagt: „Ich konnte meine Eltern nicht überzeugen."
> **Peter hat gesagt, er hätte seine Eltern nicht überzeugen können.**

1. Margot hat gesagt: „Ich konnte die Rechnung nicht bezahlen."
2. Klaus hat gesagt: „Ich konnte es auch nicht."

---

¹ **der Papagei, -en**   *parrot*
² **der Käfig, -en**   *cage*

3. Herr Körner hat gesagt: „Ich wollte den Vertrag nicht unterschreiben."
4. Frau Körner hat gesagt: „Ich wollte es auch nicht."
5. Renate sagte: „Mein Freund hat gelogen.[1]"
6. Ihr Freund sagte: „Ich habe das nur zum Spaß gesagt.[2]"
7. Meine Nachbarin hatte gesagt: „Herr Schubert ist gestorben."
8. Frau Müller hatte gesagt: „Das war nicht fair von meinem Chef."
9. Bauers sagten: „Wir hatten Schwierigkeiten an der Schweizer Grenze."
10. Sabine sagte: „Thomas hat mir einen Heiratsantrag gemacht."
11. Thomas sagte: „Sabine hat mich mißverstanden."

3. The direct quote is in the future tense

So far we have used **würde** + infinitive of the main verb as a substitute for the present subjunctive; however, as mentioned in Chap. 13, §5, these forms are actually the future subjunctive. They are used as such in indirect discourse.

Frau Morgenstern hat gesagt: „Ich werde das bei der Polizei melden."	Frau Morgenstern hat gesagt, sie **würde** das bei der Polizei **melden.** *Mrs. Morgenstern said she would report that to the police.*

The use of the future subjunctive does not necessarily imply reservations as to what was said. It is virtually required if the event has already happened when reported:

> Rainer und Monika haben im Juni geheiratet. Sie haben mir schon im Februar gesagt, sie **würden** im Juni **heiraten.**

PRACTICE

14-12   Change the following direct quotations to indirect discourse using the future subjunctive.

1. Petra sagte: „Ich werde meine Reise verschieben.[3]"
2. Die Studenten haben gesagt: „Wir werden protestieren."
3. Anita hat gesagt: „Ich werde meine Eltern nicht enttäuschen.[4]"
4. Der Bankdirektor hat gesagt: „Die Firma Schütze wird bankrott machen.[5]"
5. Unsere Fußballmannschaft hat gewonnen. Vor Beginn des Spieles sagte der Trainer[6] siegesbewußt[7] zur Presse: „Wir werden gewinnen."

Keep the following two uses of **würde** + infinitive in mind:

a.   **würde** + infinitive = subjunctive in the future tense
Bettina sagte: „Ich werde Holger bei den Hausaufgaben helfen."
future indicative

---

[1] lügen, log, gelogen	*to lie, tell a lie*
[2] zum Spaß sagen	*to be joking*
[3] verschieben, verschob, verschoben	*to postpone*
[4] enttäuschen	*to disappoint*
[5] bankrott machen	*to go bankrupt*
[6] der Trainer, -	*to coach*
[7] siegesbewußt	*confident of victory*

Bettina sagte, sie **würde** Holger bei den Hausaufgaben **helfen**.
future subjunctive

b.   **würde** + infinitive = substitute for present subjunctive
Bettina sagte: „Ich helfe Holger bei den Hausaufgaben."
present indicative
Bettina sagte, sie **würde** Holger bei den Hausaufgaben **helfen**.
substitute for the obsolete pres. subj. **hülfe**.

REMEMBER: | The **würde** + infinitive forms may refer to the present or future. Their meaning has to be derived from context.

INDIRECT REPORTING OF COMMANDS

Commands are reported in indirect discourse with the modal **sollen**. Either the indicative or the subjunctive may be used, the latter option not implying reservations.

Bitte rufen Sie mich an!
Er hat mir gesagt, ich **soll** ihn anrufen. (indicative)
or: ich **sollte** ihn anrufen. (subjunctive)
He told me I should call him.
or: *He told me to call him.*

In English indirect commands are frequently expressed with the infinitive, as in the example above. German does not have this option.

PRACTICE

14-13   Express the following indirect conmmands in German using indicative and subjunctive forms.

MODEL: „Habt keine Angst!"
Wir haben den Kindern gesagt,
sie sollen/sollten keine Angst haben.
not to be afraid (they shouldn't be afraid).

1. „Bitte seid still!"
Wir haben den Kindern gesagt, _____
to be quiet (they should be quiet).

2. „Versuchen Sie es noch einmal!"
Er hat uns gesagt, _____
to try again (we should try again).

3. „Rauchen Sie nicht soviel!"
Die Ärztin hat ihm gesagt, _____
not to smoke so much (he shouldn't smoke so much).

4. „Gib die Hoffnung nicht auf!"
Wir haben Frau Fischer gesagt, _____
not to give up hope. (she shouldn't give up hope}

5. „Glaube diese Gerüchte nicht!"
Ich habe meinem Verlobten gesagt, _____
not to believe these rumors (he shouldn't believe these rumors).

§7   INDIRECT DISCOURSE IN FORMAL GERMAN

Indirect discourse in formal German is normally a matter of noncommittal reporting requiring the subjunctive. Here the subjunctive forms merely denote indirectness of speech and not reservations as to what is reported.

So far we have used only the forms of the general subjunctive. Formal German uses the forms of the special subjunctive in indirect discourse, but only where they are not identical to indicative forms. If they are identical, the general subjunctive is used, as the following paradigms illustrate.

1.   Present subjunctive

The forms of the special subjunctive are based on the stem of the infinitive.

Example: sprechen (spricht), sprach, gesprochen

SPECIAL SUBJUNCTIVE	GENERAL SUBJUNCTIVE
subjunctive endings added to infintive stem **sprech-**	subjunctive endings added to past tense stem **sprach** + umlaut
ich spreche	ich spräche
du sprechest	du sprächest
er, sie, es spreche	er, sie, es spräche
wir sprechen	wir sprächen
ihr sprechet	ihr sprächet
sie sprechen	sie sprächen
Sie sprechen	Sie sprächen

Some forms of the special subjunctive are identical to present indicative forms and hence cannot be readily recognized as subjunctive. These forms are replaced by forms of the general subjunctive, as indicated by the arrows in the following table.

INDICATIVE		SPECIAL SUBJ.		GENERAL SUBJ.
ich spreche	identical	(ich spreche)	⟶	ich spräche
du sprichst		du sprechest		du sprächest
er spricht		er spreche		er spräche
wir sprechen	identical	(wir sprechen)	⟶	wir sprächen
ihr sprecht		ihr sprechet		ihr sprächet
sie sprechen	identical	(sie sprechen)	⟶	sie sprächen
Sie sprechen	identical	(Sie sprechen)	⟶	Sie sprächen

Example:
Der Konsul sagte: „Meine Frau spricht zwei Fremdsprachen, meine Kinder sprechen sogar drei Fremdsprachen."

Der Konsul sagte, seine Frau **spreche** zwei Fremdsprachen, seine Kinder **sprächen** sogar drei Fremdsprachen.

Roughly 90 percent of the subjunctives used in formal indirect discourse are either third person singular or third person plural. The special subjunctive is used in the third singular, while the general subjunctive replaces it in the third plural.

Examples:

	SPECIAL SUBJUNCTIVE	GENERAL SUBJUNCTIVE
machen	er, sie, es **mache**	sie **machten**
geben	**gebe**	**gäben**
gehen	**gehe**	**gingen**
haben	**habe**	**hätten**
werden	**werde**	**würden**
wissen	**wisse**	**wüßten**
können	**könne**	**könnten**
müssen	**müsse**	**müßten**

stem of inf. + e

Exception: All forms of the special subjunctive of **sein** differ from the indicative forms and are not replaced by the general subjunctive **wäre**.

	PRESENT INDICATIVE		PRESENT SPECIAL SUBJUNCTIVE
	ich **bin**		ich **sei**
	du **bist**		du **sei(e)st**
er, sie, es	**ist**	er, sie, es	**sei**
	wir **sind**		wir **seien**
	ihr **seid**		ihr **seiet**
	sie **sind**		sie **seien**
	Sie **sind**		Sie **seien**

Note: a. ich **sei**
er, sie, es **sei** } no **-e** added to the stem of the infinitive.

b. The **e** in **seiest** is generally omitted.

Example for the use of the special subjunctive of **sein:**

Der Direktor sagte: „Das ist ein großes Problem, aber meine Mitarbeiter[1] sind sehr optimistisch, daß sie es lösen können."

Der Direktor sagte, das **sei** ein großes Problem, aber seine Mitarbeiter **seien** sehr optimistisch, daß sie es lösen könnten.

PRACTICE

14-14 Change the following direct quotations to indirect discourse.
Begin each sentence with **Sie sagte,...**

MODEL: „Man kann die Unzufriedenheit der Arbeiter verstehen."
Sie sagte, man könne die Unzufriedenheit der Arbeiter verstehen.

1. „Man muß dieses Problem lösen."
2. „Der Chef und die Arbeiter müssen zusammenarbeiten."
3. „Es gibt keine andere Lösung."
4. „Der Chef weiß das, und die Arbeiter wissen das auch."

---

[1] **der Mitarbeiter, -**   *collaborator*

5. „Diese Firma hat finanzielle Schwierigkeiten, aber andere Firmen haben noch größere Schwierigkeiten."
6. „Die Spannung[1] zwischen dem Chef und seinen Mitarbeitern wird immer größer, und die Debatten werden immer länger."
7. „Der Chef ist nicht diplomatisch, und seine Mitarbeiter sind es auch nicht."

2.   Past subjunctive

The auxiliary **haben** uses the special subjunctive in the 3rd pers. sing. and the general subjunctive in the 3rd pers. pl. The auxiliary **sein** uses the special subjunctive in both forms.

	3RD PERS. SING.	3RD PERS. PL.
	special subjunctive	**general subjunctive**
verbs requiring **haben**	er, sie, es habe vergessen	sie hätten vergessen
	habe gehabt	hätten gehabt
	habe fahren können	hätten fahren können
	habe gekonnt	hätten gekonnt
		special subjunctive
verbs requiring **sein**	er, sie, es sei gefahren	sie seien gefahren
	sei gewesen	seien gewesen
	sei geworden	seien geworden

Examples:

Direct quote in any past tense	Indirect quote in the past subjunctive
Sie sagten:	Sie sagten,
„Wir waren in großer Gefahr."	sie **seien** in großer Gefahr **gewesen.**
„Niemand konnte uns helfen."	niemand **habe** ihnen **helfen können.**
„Zwei Polizisten haben es versucht."	zwei Polizisten **hätten** es **versucht.**
„Sie hatten kein Glück."	sie **hätten** kein Glück **gehabt.**

PRACTICE

14-15   Change the following direct quotations to indirect discourse.

MODEL: „Man konnte nicht alles verstehen, was der Redner sagte."
Sie hat behauptet[2], man habe nicht alles verstehen können, was der Redner gesagt habe.

1. „Ich mußte diesen Plan aufgeben."
   Sie sagte, _____

2. „Ich wußte nichts davon."
   Er hat behauptet, _____

3. „Die Leser haben mich mißverstanden."
   Die Journalistin sagte, _____

---

[1] die Spannung, -en   *tension*
[2] behaupten   *to claim, assert*

4. „Ich hatte meine Frage nicht gut formuliert.[1]"
   Der Reporter sagte, _____

5. „Die zwei Zeugen[2] haben sich widersprochen.[3]"
   Der Richter[4] erklärte, _____

6. „Ich bin die ganze Zeit in meinem Wagen geblieben."
   Ein Zeuge sagte, _____

7. „Ich bin schnell über die Straße gelaufen."
   Dann sagte er, _____

8. „Der Mann hat eine Sonnenbrille getragen."
   Der andere Zeuge sagte, _____

9. „Ich habe den Mann nur von hinten gesehen."
   Später sagte er, _____

10. „Ich habe den Prozeß verloren,[5] weil die Zeugen ihre Aussagen[6]
    geändert[7] haben."
    Die Rechtsanwältin betonte,[8] _____

3. Future subjunctive

   The auxiliary **werden** uses the special subjunctive in the 3rd pers. sing. and the
   general subjunctive in the 3rd. pers. pl.

SPECIAL SUBJUNCTIVE	GENERAL SUBJUNCTIVE
er, sie, es **werde** fahren	sie **würden** fahren

   Examples:

Die Direktorin sagte:	Die Direktorin sagte
„Ich werde den Fall klären.	sie **werde** den Fall klären.
Meine Mitarbeiter werden	ihre Mitarbeiter **würden** den
den Fall klären."	Fall klären.

PRACTICE

14-16   Change the following direct quotations to indirect discourse.

1. „Ich werde den Vertrag ändern."
   Die Rechtsanwältin sagte, _____

2. „Die arbeiter werden bestimmt streiken."
   Die Journalistin prophezeite,[9] _____

3. „Der Bürgermeister wird wohl zurücktreten.[10]"
   Ein Stadtrat[11] sagte, _____

---

[1] **formulieren**	to phrase
[2] **der Zeuge** (*weak*),**-n**	witness
[3] **sich widersprechen**	to contradict oneself
[4] **der Richter, -**	judge
[5] **den Prozeß verlieren**	to lose the case
[6] **die Aussage, -n**	testimony
[7] **ändern**	to change
[8] **betonen**	to emphasize, stress
[9] **prophezeien**	to prophesy, predict
[10] **zurück-treten (tritt zurück),**	to resign
trat zurück, ist zurückgetreten	
[11] **der Stradtrat, ¨e**	town councilor, councilman

4. „Viele Stadträte werden das begrüßen.[1]"
   Ein anderer sagte, _____

INDIRECT REPORTING OF QUESTIONS

The rules for use of the subjunctive in formal indirect discourse apply to questions as well as to statements. Note that dependent word order is required:

Die Reporterin fragte:	Die Reporterin fragte,
„Wann ist der Unfall[2] passiert?"	wann der Unfall passiert **sei.**
„Hat man die Polizei informiert?"	ob man die Polizei informiert **habe.**
„Ist der Fahrer an dem Unfall schuld?[2]"	ob der Fahrer an dem Unfall schuld **sei.**

Indirect reporting of commands

The special subjunctive of **sollen** is used in the singular and the general subjunctive in the plural.

„Bitte stören Sie mich nicht!"
Sie sagte ihm, **er solle** sie nicht stören.

She told him ⟨ *he should not disturb her.*
not to disturb her.

Sie sagte ihnen, **sie sollten** sie nicht stören.

She told them ⟨ *they should not disturb her.*
not to disturb her.

Lengthy indirect quotations

In German, lengthy statements may be quoted indirectly by using the subjunctive. In English, remarks such as *he continued, he also mentioned, he stated further* have to be added as reminders to the listener or reader that the indirect quotation continues. This is not necessary in German, because the subjunctive itself signals the continuation of the indirect quote.

Example:

A direct quotation by councilman Schmidt:

„Die Sitzung[3] war sehr stürmisch. Der Bürgermeister und die Stadträte führten lange Debatten. Man konnte sich nicht einigen,[4] und der Bürgermeister drohte mit seinem Rücktritt.[5]"

---

[1] **begrüßen** — *to welcome*
[2] **Unfall ,-̈** — *accident*
[3] **die Sitzung, -en** — *session*
[4] **sich einigen** — *to come to an agreement*
[5] **der Rücktritt, -e** — *resignation*

The newspaper quotes:

> Stadtrat Schmidt sagte, die Sitzung **sei** sehr stürmisch **gewesen.** Der Bürgermeister und die Stadträte **hätten** lange Debatten **geführt.** Man **habe** sich nicht einigen **können,** und der Bürgermeister **habe** mit seinem Rücktritt **gedroht.**

14-17   Change to indirect discourse using the introductory clauses provided.

1. „Stadtrat Schubert hatte eine geniale Idee. Sein Vorschlag war ein Kompromiß. Der Bürgermeister und die Stradträte fanden diesen Kompromiß akzeptabel." Die Reporterin sagte, …

2. „Die Debatte mit meinen Mitarbeitern hat mich sehr enttäuscht. Zwei Mitarbeiter sind nicht objektiv geblieben. Ich mußte die Diskussion abbrechen.[1]" Die Chefin sagte, …

3. „Der Vortrag[2] über China war interessant. Die Rednerin sprach über die politischen und wirtschaftlichen[3] Probleme Chinas. Am Schluß stellten einige Zuhörer Fragen. Leider konnte die Rednerin nur kurz darauf antworten." Der Journalist schrieb, …

§8   FINAL REMARKS ON THE USE OF THE INDICATIVE AND SUBJUNCTIVE IN INDIRECT DISCOURSE

1. As discussed, informal indirect discourse is expressed in the indicative when the one providing the account has no doubt about the validity of what is reported. The general subjunctive is used in cautious reporting, usually when the speaker has reservations as to what was said.

2. In formal German, the subjunctive is normally required for indirect discourse. The special subjunctive is used unless it is identical to the indicative, in which case the general subjunctive is substituted.

However, the indicative is used in the following cases:

a. When quoting oneself, since one is usually willing to vouch for one's own claims.

> Ich sagte vor Gericht[4]: „Der Polizist hat mich mißverstanden."
> Ich sagte vor Gericht, **daß** der Polizist mich mißverstanden **hat.**

In order to distinguish the indirect quote from the direct quote, a **daß** clause is normally used.

---

[1] **ab•brechen (bricht ab, brach ab, abgebrochen**   *to break off*
[2] **der Vortrag, e**   *lecture*
[3] **wirtschaftlich**   *economical*
[4] **vor Gericht**   *in court*

b. When reporting something that is undeniably true.
Galilei hat als erster gesagt, **daß** sich die Erde um die Sonne **bewegt**.

3. Subjunctives in original statements are retained in both formal and informal indirect discourse.

Frau Morgenstern sagte:	„Ich **möchte** Architektin werden."
Frau Morgenstern sagte,	sie **möchte** Architektin werden.
Herr Morgenstern sagte:	„Wenn meine Frau Architektin **wäre, würden** wir in einem Palast wohnen."
Herr Morgenstern sagte,	wenn seine Frau Architektin **wäre, würden** sie in einem Palast wohnen.

§9   OTHER USES OF THE SPECIAL SUBJUNCTIVE

The special subjunctive is found chiefly in formal indirect discourse. Otherwise it is rarely used. All of the following examples are in the third person singular, and except for **sei,** they all end in **-e.**

1. Set phrases: **wie dem auch sei**   *be that as it may*

Dieses Problem ist sehr kompliziert und schwer zu lösen. Wie dem auch sei, eine Lösung muß gefunden werden.
This problem is very complicated and hard to solve. Be that as it may, a solution must be found.

es sei denn   *unless*

Sie sollte das nicht tun, es sei denn, sie kann einfach nicht anders.
She shouldn't do that unless she simply can't help it.

Komme, was wolle.   *Come what may.*

Komme, was wolle, ich lasse mich nicht umwerfen.
Come what may, I won't let it throw me.

2. Set wishes:

Es lebe die Freiheit!   *Long live freedom!*
Er lebe hoch!   *Hooray for him!*

3. General imperatives, usually with the indefinite pronoun **man** as subject:

Man täusche sich nicht.   *One shouldn't deceive oneself.*
    Don't deceive yourself.

Beim Einnehmen dieser Tabletten **folge man** den Anweisungen des Arztes.
When taking these tablets, follow your doctor's instructions.

REMEMBER: Apart from formal indirect discourse, the special subjunctive occurs only in a few expressions and in general imperatives with **man.**

CHAPTER 15

der-Words and ein-Words Used as Pronouns; Uses of man, jemand, niemand, irgend, and es

 der-Words and ein-Words Used as Pronouns

§1 der-WORDS USED AS PRONOUNS

The definite article denotes gender, number, and case of nouns; it is a *determiner*. The **der**-words **dieser, jeder, jener, mancher, solcher, welcher, alle,** and **beide** function much like the definite article and are also referred to as *determiners* when they precede nouns. When they stand alone, they function as pronouns. In either case, they have the same endings.

DETERMINER	PRONOUN
Welchen Wagen wollen Sie kaufen?	**Welchen** wollen Sie kaufen?
Which car do you want to buy?	*Which one do you want to buy?*
Jeder Student ist dagegen.	**Jeder** ist dagegen.
Every student is against it.	*Everyone is against it.*

§2 der, das, die USED AS DEMONSTRATIVE PRONOUNS

When used as demonstrative pronouns, **der, das, die** are declined as follows:

	MASCULINE	NEUTER	FEMININE	PLURAL
NOM.	der	das	die	die
ACC.	den	das	die	die
DAT.	dem	dem	der	**denen**
GEN.	**dessen**	**dessen**	**deren**	**deren**

The forms in boldface differ from the forms of the definite article: The genitive singular and plural and the dative plural have the long forms **dessen, deren,** and **denen.**

The demonstrative pronouns **der, das, die** occur frequently in informal German:

1. Pointing out persons and things

Welches Bild gefällt dir besser? **Das hier** oder **das da**?
This one or that one?
Mit welchem Mechaniker hast du gesprochen? **Mit dem hier** oder **mit dem da?**
With this one or with that one?
In welchen Katalogen sind die Preise reduziert? **In denen hier** oder in **denen da**?
In these or in those?

In informal German, **this one** and **that one** (pl.: **these** and **those**) are generally expressed by **der, das, die + hier** (close to the speaker) or **da** (more distant from the speaker). The pronouns are always stressed.

PRACTICE

15-1   Add the appropriate forms of **der, das, die + hier** or **da**.

MODEL: X: In welchem Haus wohnt Frau Rose?
Y: **Das weiß ich nicht genau; vielleicht in
<u>dem hier</u> oder in <u>dem da</u>.**
    this one   *That one*

1. X: Welches Kleid willst du kaufen?
Y: Ich glaube, ich nehme _____ . _____ ist zu teuer.
              this one   *That one*
2. X: Wieviel kosten diese Strümpfe?[1]
Y: _____ kosten 10 Mark das Paar, _____ kosten 12 Mark das Paar.
  These   *those*
3. X: Welches Formular soll ich ausfüllen?
Y: _____ und _____ .
   This one   *that one*
4. X: Von welchen Formularen sprecht ihr?
Y: Von _____ und _____ .
       these   *those*
5. X: Welche Rechnung willst du bezahlen?
Y: Keine, aber ich muß heute _____ bezahlen. _____
                 this one   *That one*
bezahle ich nächsten Monat.
6. X: In welchem Gebäude ist Professor Sterns Büro?
Y: In _____ .
    that one

2. Third-person pronouns

Conversational German frequently uses **der, das, die** as third-person pronouns. They may be stressed or unstressed and are translated into English with the normal third person pronouns. In the following examples stress is indicated by spacing the letters:

---

[1] **der Strumpf, ̈e**   *stocking*

Herr Müller   kann uns nicht helfen.
     Er   kann uns nicht helfen.
    Der
or: D e r   kann uns nicht helfen.
He   *cannot help us.*

Ich spreche nicht mehr mit diesen Leuten.
Ich spreche nicht mehr mit   ihnen.
Ich spreche nicht mehrt mit   denen.
or: Mit d e n e n spreche ich nicht mehr.
I don't talk with **them** *any more.*

The stressed pronouns are frequently placed at the beginning of main clauses.

PRACTICE

15-2   **A.** Add sentences c. and d., following the model of sentence 1.

1.   a. Ich helfe meinen Nachbarn gern.
     b. Ich helfe ihnen gern.
     c. Ich helfe denen gern.
     d. Denen helfe ich gern.
2.   a. Ich habe seine Telefonnummer nicht.
     b. Ich habe sie nicht.
     c.
     d.
3.   a. Wir können diese komplizierten Probleme nicht lösen.
     b. Wir können sie nicht lösen.
     c.
     d.
4.   a. Helga hat diesen Film nicht gesehen.
     b. Helga hat ihn nicht gesehen.
     c.
     d.
5.   a. Ich werde es meinen Freunden nicht sagen.
     b. Ich werde es ihnen nicht sagen.
     c.
     d.

B. Insert the appropriate form of the pronoun **der, das, die**, following the model of sentence 1.a.

1.   a. X: Kann man diesem Mann glauben?
        Y: **Nein, <u>dem</u> kann man nicht glauben.**
     b. X: Aber seiner Frau kann man doch glauben?
        Y: _____ glaube ich auch nicht.
2.   X: Willst du Dagmar anrufen?
       Y: Nein, _____ rufe ich nie wieder an.

3. X: Wie kommst du mit Ruth aus?[1]
    Y: Mit _____ komme ich sehr gut aus.
4. X: Hoffentlich laden Müllers auch meinen Freund Peter ein.
    Y: _____ laden Müllers bestimmt ein.
5. X: Alle Nachbarn haben Schulzes beim Umzug[2] geholfen.
    Y: Schulzes sind nette Leute. _____ hilft jeder gern.
6. X: Hast du Post von Monika?
    Y: Von _____ bekomme ich keine Post mehr.
7. X: Gehst du heute abend mit Udo aus?
    Y: Mit _____ gehe ich nie wieder aus.
8. X: Ich bin ganz begeistert von diesen Fußballspielern.
    Y: Von _____ sind alle begeistert.

3. Alternatives to **da**-compounds

Normally pronoun objects of prepositions which refer to inanimate objects are replaced by **da**-compounds (cf. Chap. 8 §3).

> Er ist **stolz auf seinen Sportwagen.**
> Er ist stolz **darauf.**

However, when speakers wish to emphasize the pronoun, they have two choices. They may stress the **da**-element:

> **Dárauf** ist er stolz

or use a form of **der, das, die** as the object of the preposition:

> **Auf dén** ist er stolz.

The second option is more emphatic than the stressed **da**-compound.

PRACTICE

15-3   Begin the following sentences with the preposition + the appropriate form of the pronouns **der, das, die.**

MODEL: Für diese Briefmarken hat Herr Berger kein Interesse.
          Für díe hat Herr Berger kein Interesse.

1. Für diesen Ring hat Klaus viel Geld bezahlt.
2. Mit diesem Bleistift kann ich nicht schreiben.
3. Auf diesen Scheck mußte ich lange warten.
4. Von diesem Haus ist meine Mutter begeistert.
5. Auf diese Platte ist Udos Freundin ganz verrückt.
6. Aus dieser Tasse hat Einstein getrunken.

---

[1] **aus• kommen mit (dat.)**   *to get along with*
  kam aus, ist ausgekommen
[2] **der Umzug, ⸚e**   *move (change of residence)*

4.   Special use of the genitive forms **dessen** and **deren**

> Hans, sein Freund Peter und **dessen** Schwester Barbara haben uns besucht.
> *Hans, his friend Peter, and the latter's sister Barbara visited us.*

Seine Schwester would leave the question open whether Barbara is the sister of Hans or Peter. **Dessen** (*the latter's*) makes it clear that she is Peter's sister. The gender and number of **dessen** is determined by the possessor, i.e. Peter; thus the masculine singular is used.

Additional examples:

> Helga, Margot und **deren** Schwester /**deren** Bruder
> *Helga, Margot, and the latter's sister / the latter's brother*

Margot is the possessor, thus the feminine singular is used.

> Schmidts, Müllers und **deren** Sohn / **deren** Tochter
> *The Smiths, the Müllers, and the latter's son / the latter's daughter*

The Müllers are the possessors, thus the plural form is used.

The case of the noun that follows has no influence on **dessen** or **deren**:

> Wir sind mit **einer Freundin, einer Nachbarin** und **deren Brüdern**
>   DATIVE   DATIVE   GEN.   DATIVE
> nach Wien gefahren.

PRACTICE

15-4   Translate into German.

1. Helmut, Martin, and the latter's girlfriend went to the movies. (pres. perf.)
2. Barbara, Hannelore, and the latter's dog were in the car.
3. Mrs. Zimmermann, the Körners, and the latter's children are in the park.
4. Mr. Schubert, his brother, and the latter's wife visited us. (pres. perf.)
5. This is a present from Monika, Renate, and the latter's parents.

§3   *ein*-Words Used as Pronouns

The **ein**-words (**ein, kein,** and the possessives) are also determiners when preceding nouns, but pronouns when standing alone.

1.   *ein* and *kein*

DETERMINER	PRONOUN
Ist das **ein** Fehler?	Ja, das ist **einer.** *Yes, that is one.*
	Nein, das ist **keiner.** *No, that isn't one.*
	No, that's none.
Ist das **ein** Problem?	Ja, das ist **ein(e)s.**
	Nein, das ist **kein(e)s.**
Ist das **eine** Warnung?	Ja, das ist **eine.**
	Nein, das ist **keine.**

Used as determiners, the **ein**-words have three forms without endings: the nominative masculine singular and the nominative and accusative neuter singular. All other forms have the same endings as the **der**-words (cf. Chap. 6, §5).

Used as pronouns, the **ein**-words have the same endings as the **der**-words in all forms, including the nominative masculine singular (**-er**) and the nominative and accusative neuter singular (**-es**, usually shortened to **-s**).

The following table combines the declension of the determiner and the pronoun:

	MASCULINE		NEUTER		FEMININE	PLURAL
NOM.	ein	einer	ein	ein(e)s	eine	keine
ACC.	einen		ein	ein(e)s	eine	keine
DAT.	einem		einem		einer	keinen
GEN.	eines		eines		einer	keiner

REMEMBER: The forms of the determiner and pronoun differ only in three cases in the singular.

PRACTICE

15-5   **A.**   Answer the questions, following the model of sentence 1.

1.   Wo ist ein Supermarkt? **Da drüben ist einer.**
2.   Wo ist ein Parkplatz? (masc.)
3.   Wo ist ein Restaurant? (neuter)
4.   Wo ist eine Bank?

B.   Answer the questions positively and negatively, following the model of sentence 1.

1.   Hast du einen Regenschirm? **Ja, ich habe einen. Nein, ich habe keinen.**
2.   Hast du eine Kamera?
3.   Hast du ein Auto?
4.   Hast du einen Fernseher?

2.   The possessives

The possessives take the same endings as **ein** and **kein**, as the following nominative masculine and neuter forms illustrate.

DETERMINERS		PRONOUNS	
Das ist mein Wagen.	(*my car*)	Das ist mein**er.**	(*mine*)
mein Auto.		mein**(e)s.**	
Das ist dein Wagen.	(*your car*)	Das ist dein**er.**	(*yours*)
dein Auto.		dein**(e)s.**	
Das ist sein Wagen.	(*his car*)	Das ist sein**er.**	(*his*)
sein Auto.		sein**(e)s.**	

Das ist ihr Wagen.	(her car)	Das ist ihr**er.**	(hers)
ihr Auto.		ihr(e)**s.**	
Das ist unser Wagen.	(our car)	Das ist uns(e)r**er.**	(ours)
unser Auto.		uns(e)r**es.**	
Das ist euer Wagen.	(your car)	Das ist eu(e)r**er**	(yours)
euer Auto.		eu(e)r**es.**	
Das ist ihr Wagen.	(their car)	Das ist ihr**er.**	(theirs)
ihr Auto.		ihr(e)**s**	
Das ist Ihr Wagen.	(your car)	Das ist Ihr**er**	(yours)
Ihr Auto.		Ihr(e)**s**	

Note: a. German equivalents of *your* and *yours:*

your car ⟨ **dein** Wagen / **euer** Wagen / **Ihr** Wagen

yours ⟨ **deiner** (fam. sing.) / **eu(e)rer** (fam. pl.) / **Ihrer** (formal, sing. + pl.)

b. The **e** of **unser** and **euer** may be omitted when the ending **-e** or an ending beginning with **-e** is added (cf. Chap. 6 §6).

PRACTICE

15-6   **A.** Insert the German equivalents of the pronouns in parentheses.

1. Hier ist Peters Plattenspieler, (masc.)
und da drüben ist auch _____ . (*mine, yours*[three forms])
2. Hier ist Karins Radio, (neut.)
und da drüben ist auch _____ . (*mine, yours* [three forms])
3. Hier ist Herrn Bergers Kamera,
und da drüben ist auch _____ . (*mine, yours* [three forms])
4. Hier sind Helgas Sachen,
und da drüben sind _____ . (*mine, ours, theirs*)
5. Wir sind nicht mit meinem Wagen gefahren;
wir sind mit _____ gefahren. (*his, hers*)

B. Insert the appropriate forms of **ein, kein**, and the possessives.

1. X: Ist das hier mein Glas? (neut.)
Y: Ja, das ist _____ . (*yours* [fam. sing., formal])
2. X: Wir haben sehr nette Nachbarn.
Y: Wir nicht, _____ sind sehr unfreundlich. (*ours*)
3. X: Da drüben ist ein Briefkasten. (masc.)
Y: Hier ist auch _____ . (*one*)
4. X: Wo ist hier eine Tankstelle?
Y: Da an der Ecke ist _____ . (*one*)
5. X: Hast du ein Motorrad? (neut.)
Y: Leider habe ich _____ . (*not one* = **kein**)

6. X: Hat Dieter einen Job gefunden?

 Y: Soviel ich weiß,[1] hat er noch _____ gefunden. (*not one* = **kein**)

7. X: Ich muß in die Stadt, habe aber keinen Wagen. _____ ist kaputt. (*mine*)

 Y: Du kannst _____ nehmen. (*mine*)

8. X: Ist das Ihr Hund, der draußen bellt?

 Y: Nein, das ist nicht _____ . (*ours*)

9. X: Haben Sie mit Ihren Freunden über Ihre Pläne gesprochen?

 Y: Ich habe nur mit _____ darüber gesprochen. (*one*)

10. X: Leider habe ich deinen Geburtstag vergessen.

 Y: Ach, das macht nichts.[2] Ich habe ja bald wieder _____ . (*one*)

3. The German equivalents of the possessive phrases *of mine, of yours,* etc.

German uses the preposition **von** with the dative case of the personal pronoun to express the English possessive phrases of mine, of yours, etc.

He is a friend of mine.	Er ist ein Freund **von mir.**
	(lit.: *He is a friend of me.*)
He is a friend of his.	Er ist ein Freund **von ihm.**
of hers.	**von ihr.**
of ours.	**von uns.**
of theirs.	**von ihnen.**
of yours.	⎧ **von dir.**
(three forms)	⎨ **von euch.**
	⎩ **von Ihnen.**

PRACTICE

15-7 Insert German equivalents.

1. X: Ist Thomas ein Freund von Barbara?

 Y: Ich weiß nicht, ob er ein Freund _____ ist. (*of hers*)

2. X: Sind Schmidts Verwandte[3] _____ . (*of yours* [fam. pl., formal])

 Y: Ja, sie sind Verwandte _____ . (*of ours*)

3. X: Ist sie eine Kollegin _____ ? (*of his*)

 Y: Nein, sie ist eine Kollegin _____ . (*of mine*)

4. X: Sind das Freunde von Brauns?

 Y: Das sind sehr gute Freunde _____ . (*of theirs*)

---

[1] **soviel ich weiß**   *as far as I know*

[2] **das macht nichts**   *that doesn't matter*

[3] **der Verwandte**   *relative*
  (adj. noun [cf. Chap. 9, §12])

Uses of *man, jemand, niemand, irgend,* and *es*

§4 THE INDEFINITE PRONOUNS *man, jemand,* AND *niemand*

1. *man*

The English equivalents of **man** may be *one, you, they,* or *people,* depending on the context.

Man weiß das nicht im voraus.	**One** *doesn't know that beforehand.*
	You *don't know that beforehand.*
Man hat mich gewarnt.	**They** *warned me.*
	People *warned me.*

The form **man** exists only in the nominative case. For the accusative and dative **einen** and **einem** are used.

Diese Unsicherheit macht **einen** nervös.
This insecurity makes one (you, people) nervous.

Fräulein Braun dankt **einem** nie.
Miss Braun never thanks you (anyone).

Sein is used as the possessive of **man.**

Man sollte immer **seine** Meinung sagen.
One should always speak one's mind.

In English, a second occurrence of **man** is sometimes replaced by **he.** This cannot be done in German.

If one wants to help, one/he will find a way.
Wenn **man** helfen will, findet **man** einen Weg.

Expression: **Man kann nie wissen.** *One never knows.*
                                    You never know.

PRACTICE

15-8   Restate the following sentences substituting **man, einen,** or **einem** for the boldface pronouns.

MODEL: **Wir** können auch unsere Kinder mitbringen.
          Man kann auch seine Kinder mitbringen.

1. **Wir** können unsere Sachen in der Bibliothek lassen.
2. Hier müssen **Sie** Ihren Hund an der Leine führen.[1]
3. Wie übersetzen **Sie** das?
4. Wie sagen **Sie** das auf deutsch?
5. Er hilft **mir** nie.

---

[1] an der Leine führen   *to keep on a leash*

6. Das ärgert[1] **mich** natürlich.
7. Wenn **ich** mit Barbara spreche, muß **ich** besonders vorsichtig sein.
8. Wenn **du** zu schnell fährst, bekommst **du** einen Strafzettel.
9. Er tut **mir** leid, wenn **ich** ihn vor Schmerzen schreien[2] höre.

2. *jemand* and *niemand*

Jemand (*somebody, someone, anybody, anyone*) and **niemand** (*nobody, no one*) may remain uninflected or take the ending **-en** in the accusative and **-em** in the dative.

Jemand **Niemand**	hat mich gefragt.	*Somebody* *Nobody*	*asked me.*
Ich habe	**jemand(en)** **niemand(en)** gefragt.	*I asked*	*somebody.* *nobody.*
Ich habe mit	**jemand(em)** **niemand(em)** gesprochen.	*I talked with*	*someone.* *no one.*

Expression: **Das geht niemand(en) etwas an.**
            That is nobody's business.

Note the use of **jemand** and **niemand** with **anders:**

jemand anders (als)   *somebody/someone else (but)*
niemand anders (als)   *nobody/no one else (but)*

Nicht Frank, sondern **jemand anders** hat mir das erzählt.
Not Frank but someone else told me that.
Ich habe mit **niemand anders als** mit Helga darüber gesprochen.
I talked with no one else but with Helga about it.

PRACTICE

15-9   Complete the sentences using the German equivalents of *somebody, nobody* (uninflected forms) and *one.*

1. X: Kennen Sie _____ in Berlin? (*somebody*)
   Y: Leider kenne ich dort _____ . (*nobody*)
2. X: Hast du den Ring von Werner bekommen?
   Y: Nein. Ich habe ihn von _____ bekommen. (*somebody else*)
3. X: Da ist ein Paket für dich.
   Y: Das kann von _____ von meinen Eltern sein. (*nobody else but*)
4. X: Alle möchten gern wissen, warum du Ulrich nicht heiraten willst.
   Y: _____ . (*That is nobody's business.*)
5. X: Er redet und redet, aber in Wirklichkeit[3] sagt er nichts. Warum ist er nicht still?
   Y: Das verstehe ich auch nicht. Wenn _____ nichts zu sagen hat, sollte _____ still sein. (*one, one*)

---

[1] **ärgern**   *to annoy*
[2] **vor Schmerzen schreien, schrie, geschrie(e)n**   *to cry out in pain*
[3] **in Wirklichkeit**   *in reality, in actual fact, actually*

6. X: Frau Winkler hat mich schon wieder unterbrochen[1]

Y: Sie unterbricht _____ oft. (*one*)

7. X: Ingrid wird mich betimmt nicht betrügen.[2]

Y: _____ . (*One never knows.*)

§5   Uses of *irgend*

Irgend expresses indefiniteness. It is often used to intensify an indefinite pronoun. Compare:

a. Jemand hat das bei der Polizei gemeldet.
Someone reported that to the police.
b. **Irgend jemand** hat das bei der Polizei gemeldet.
Someone or other reported that to the police.
a. Ich möchte Monika etwas geben.
I'd like to give Monika something.
b. Ich möchte Monika **irgend etwas** geben.
I'd like to give Monika something or other.

In sentences *b* irgend enhances the indefiniteness of **jemand** and **etwas.**

Irgend may be prefixed to another word:

irgendein *a, some, any* (singular)
irgendwelche *some, any* (plural)

Haben Sie **irgendeinen** Vorschlag?
Do you have any suggestion (at all)?
Haben Sie **irgendwelche** Vorschläge?
Do you have any suggestions (at all)?

irgendwann *some time or other, sometime, anytime*

Irgendwann ist sie zur Vernunft gekommen.
At some time or other she came to her senses.
Hoffentlich sehe ich Sie **irgendwann** mal wieder.
I hope to see you again sometime.

irgendwie *somehow (or other)*

Wir müssen das Problem **irgendwie** lösen.
We have to solve this problem somehow (or other).

irgendwo *somewhere (or other), anywhere* (denoting the place at which)
irgendwohin *somewhere (or other), anywhere* (denoting motion to a place)

Ich habe Hannelore **irgendwo** in der Stadt gesehen.
I saw Hannelore somewhere in town.

---

[1] **unterbrechen (unterbricht),**   *to interrupt*
  unterbrach, unterbrochen
[2] **betrügen,**   *to cheat*
  betrog, betrogen

Martin fährt morgen **irgendwohin.**
Martin is going somewhere tomorrow.

The negation of **irgendwo** is **nirgendwo** or **nirgends** *nowhere, not anywhere* (place at which); the negation of **irgendwohin** is **nirgend(s)wohin** *nowhere, not anywhere* (*motion to a place*).

Wir haben unseren Hund gesucht, konnten ihn aber **nirgends** finden.
We were looking for our dog but couldn't find him anywhere.
Ich fahre dieses Wochenende **nirgendwohin.**
I'm not going anywhere this weekend.

PRACTICE

15-10 Insert German equivalents using combinations with **irgend.**

1. X: Ich weiß nicht, wie ich aus diesem Dilemma herauskommen soll.
   Y: Kann ich dir _____ helfen? (*somehow*)
2. X: Wo sollen wir zu Mittag essen?
   Y: Es ist mir ganz gleich.[1] _____ . (*Anywhere*)
3. X: Ist dein Bruder heute abend zu Hause?
   Y: Ich glaube, er geht heute abend _____ . (*somewhere*)
4. X: Bist du heute abend zu Hause?
   Y: Ja. Heute abend gehe ich _____ (*not anywhere, nowhere*)
5. X: Warum bist du so nervös?
   Y: Ich kann meine Brille _____ finden. (*not anywhere, nowhere*)
6. X: Ich glaube, mein Geschenk gefällt Renate nicht.
   Y: Hat sie _____ Bemerkung gemacht? (*any*)
7. X: Ich glaube, die Chefin ist nicht zufrieden mit meiner Arbeit.
   Y: Warum denkst du das? Hat sie _____ Bemerkungen gemacht? (*any*)
8. X: Wann hat Margot Geburstag?
   Y: _____ im August. (*sometime*)
9. X: Warum ist Rainer so deprimiert?
   Y: _____ ist schiefgegangen.[2] (*something*)

§6 USES OF *es*

1. Impersonal use of verbs

   Verbs used impersonally have **es** as their subject. The inflected verb is always in the third person singular. Compare:

   USED PERSONALLY

   Die Kinder klopfen an die Tür.
   The children are knocking at the door.

   Der Briefträger klingelt (läutet).
   The mailman is ringing.

   USED IMPERSONALLY

   Es klopft.
   There is a knock at the door.

   Es klingelt (läutet).
   Someone is ringing the bell.
   The bell is ringing.

---

[1] **es ist mir ganz gleich**   *it's all the same to me*
[2] **schief• gehen, ging schief, ist schiefgegangen**   *to go wrong*

Die Kerzen brennen.   **Es** brennt.
The candles are burning.   *There is a fire.*

Note the use of the impersonal expression **es gibt** (+ acc.):

Es gibt nur **einen ausländischen Studenten** in unserem Studentenheim.

  SUBJ.   DIRECT OBJECT

There is only one foreign student in our dormitory.

Es gibt nur **zwei ausländische Studenten** in unserem Studentenheim.
There are only two foreign students in our dormitory.

Es gibt is used with both singular and plural accusative nouns. The English equivalent is *there is* or *there are*:

Some idiomatic uses of **es gibt:**

Es gibt heute noch Regen (Schnee, ein Gewitter).
 We are going to have rain (snow, a thunderstorm) today.
Was gibt's (gibt es) heute zu Mittag (zum Abendessen/Abendbrot)?
 What is there (are we having) for lunch (dinner/supper) today?
Gibt's (gibt es) noch Kaffee (Kuchen, etc.)?
 Is there any coffee (cake, etc.) left?
Es gibt keinen Kaffee (Kuchen, etc.) mehr.
 There is no coffee (cake, etc.) left.

2. Introductory *es* in main clauses

For reasons of style or emphasis (cf. Chap. 19, §5, 4), an introductory **es** may be used in main clauses. Compare:

Niemand ist zu Hause geblieben.
 SUBJECT

Es ist niemand zu Hause geblieben.
  SUBJECT

    Nobody stayed at home.

The subject follows the inflected verb.

Note that the verb agrees with the subject, not with **es:**

Drei Studenten fehlen.
Es fehlen drei Studenten. *Three students are absent.*

When another element is placed in first position, **es** may not be used:

Es fehlen drei Studenten.
Heute fehlen drei Studenten.

The introductory **es** cannot be used in questions and dependent clauses.

3. *Es* anticipating a dependent clause or infinitive phrase

German often uses **es** to anticipate a clause or infinitive phrase where English would use nothing.

> Ich kann **es** verstehen, daß er böse auf mich ist.
> *I can understand that he is angry with me.*

> Ich hasse **es,** morgens um 6 Uhr aufzustehen.
> *I hate getting up at 6 o'clock in the morning.*

PRACTICE

15-11   The following sentences illustrate various uses of **es**. Express them in English.

1. X: Hat jemand protestiert?
   Y: Es haben alle protestiert.
2. X: Es schwänzen immer ein paar Studenten.
   Y: Heute hat aber niemand geschwänzt.
3. X: Ich kann es nicht glauben, daß so viele Studenten durchgefallen sind.
   Y: So viele? Es sind nur zwei Studenten durchgefallen.
4. X: Arbeitet Fräulein Kluge auch an dem neuen Projekt?
   Y: Leider hat sie es abgelehnt,[1] an dem neuen Projekt zu arbeiten.
5. X: Brennt es irgendwo?
   Y: Es brennt im Nachbarhaus.
6. X: Hat es geklopft?
   Y: Es hat schon zweimal geklopft. Da klopft es wieder.
7. X: Vielleicht gibt's heute Fisch zu Mittag.
   Y: Ach nein. Gestern hat es doch schon Fisch gegeben.
8. X: Könnte ich ein Stück Kuchen haben?
   Y: Leider gibt's keinen Kuchen mehr, aber es gibt noch ein paar Plätzchen.[2]
9. X: Warum hast du keine Bananen gekauft?
   Y: Im Supermarkt gab es keine mehr.
10. X: Heute gibt es bestimmt Regen.
    Y: Hoffentlich gibt es kein Gewitter.
11. X: Ist die Deutschstunde schon zu Ende?
    Y: Nein, es hat noch nicht geklingelt.

PRACTICE

15-12   Summarizing exercises.
Express the responses in German.

1. X: Gibt es eine Konzerthalle in dieser Stadt?
   Y: There are two concert halls in this city.
2. X: Warum gehst du zur Tür?
   Y: There was a knock at the door. (pres. perf.)

---

[1] **ab•lehnen**   *to decline*
[2] **das Plätzchen,-**   *cookie*

3. X: Hoffentlich ist die Deutschstunde bald zu Ende.
    Y: The bell is ringing in two minutes.

4. X: Ich glaube, wir kommen zu spät ins Labor.
    Y: Yes. The bell rang already. (pres. perf.)

5. X: Was möchtest du? Kaffee und Plätzchen?
    Y: Is there any cake left?

6. X: Welche Kamera gefällt dir am besten?
    Y: This one.

7. X: In welchem Gebäude ist Ihr Büro?
    Y: In that one.

8. X: Hier ist dein Koffer.
    Y: That's not mine.

9. X: Ist das Renates Kassettenrecorder?
    Y: Yes, that's hers.

10. X: Haben viele Studenten gestern geschwänzt?
    Y: No, only one cut class. (pres. perf.)

11. X: Ist diese Dame eine Verwandte oder Freundin von Herrn Krause?
    Y: She's a relative of his.

12. X: Warum sagst du uns nicht, warum du mit Walter Schluß gemacht hast?
    Y: That's nobody's business.

13. X: Mit wem sind Sie in die Ferien gefahren?
    Y: With Thomas, Peter, and the latter's brother.

14. X: Ist dieser Brief von deiner Freundin?
    Y: No, it's from someone else.

15. X: Warum stehen so viele Leute vor dem Auditorium?
    Y: There's a fire in the auditorium.

16. X: Es riecht nach[1] Bratwurst. (fem.)
    Y: Today we are having Bratwurst for lunch.
    X: Ich esse Bratwurst nicht gern.
    Y: May I eat yours? (fam. sing.)

17. X: Wo möchten Sie sitzen?
    Y: It's all the same to me. Anywhere.

18. X: Wann kommen Andrea und Ulrike aus Mexiko zurück?
    Y: Sometime in July.

19. X: Ich glaube nicht, daß wir dieses Problem lösen können.
    Y: We have to solve it somehow or other.

20. X: Weißt du, warum der Chef so schlechte Laune hat?
    Y: I assume that something or other went wrong. (pres. perf.)

---

[1] **riechen nach** (dat.), **roch, gerochen**   *to smell of*

CHAPTER 16

Relative Pronouns and Relative Clauses

§1 RELATIVE PRONOUNS AND RELATIVE CLAUSES IN ENGLISH

The gentleman **who** just came in   is the mayor of this city.
└ ANTECEDENT ┘ └ RELATIVE CLAUSE ┘

The Turn of the Screw, **which** I have read many times, is very interesting.
└ ANTECEDENT ┘ └ RELATIVE CLAUSE ┘

The story **that** you told me   is unbelievable.
└ ANTECEDENT ┘ └ RELATIVE CLAUSE ┘

Note: a. The relative pronouns **who** (referring to person), **which** (referring to things), and **that** (referring to persons or things) introduce dependent clauses, which are called *relative clauses*.

b. Relative clauses commonly modify nouns, less frequently pronouns, by giving further information. The nouns or pronouns modified are called *antecedents*.

Relative pronouns can have various functions within the relative clause:

The student   **who** is talking with Mr. Clark   is my sister.
                SUBJ. of the relative clause

The student   **whom you** see in this picture   is my sister.
              DIR. OBJ. SUBJ. of the relative clause

People   **that**   I   owe **money** keep bothering me.
         INDIR. OBJ.   SUBJ.   DIR. OBJ. of the relative clause

In English the relative pronoun is rarely used as a true indirect object. Instead, it is used as the object of the preposition **to**:

This is the city councilor   **to whom the policeman** gave **a ticket.**
                             OBJ. OF   SUBJ.   DIR. OBJ.
                             PREP. **to**

The preposition often stands at the end of the relative clause:

This is an important point ***that*** *the speaker did not go* ***into.***

OBJ. OF
PREP. **into**

When the relative pronoun expresses possession, it is in the possessive (genitive) case:

The student ***whose*** *name is mentioned in the newspaper is my brother.*

Anyone learning German must be able to recognize the function of a given relative pronoun. As a first step, the following exercise will deal with English relative pronouns.

PRACTICE

16-1   State the function of the boldface relative pronouns.

MODEL: This is a remark **that** I resent.
            The relative pronoun *that* functions as direct object.

1. This is a matter **that** you will never understand.
2. I know the artist **who** painted this picture.
3. The figures **that** she quoted are appalling.
4. The lady **whose** picture is on the front page is our neighbor.
5. Professor Johnson, **who** received the Nobel Prize, is the dean of the college.
6. People **who** do such things must be mentally disturbed.
7. The patient to **whom** the nurse gave the wrong medication is recovering.
8. This is a problem for **which** there is no solution.
9. This is only one of the inconveniences **that** they will have to contend with.

The English relative pronoun is often omitted:

This is a matter you will never understand.
The figures she quoted are appalling.
This is only one of the inconveniences they will have to contend with.

§2   RELATIVE PRONOUNS AND RELATIVE CLAUSES IN GERMAN

Most forms of the relative pronoun are the same as those of the definite article.

1. a. Der junge Mann, **der** mich angerufen hat, ist Lindas Bruder.
        who
        SUBJ.

   b. Der junge Mann, **den** ich angerufen habe, ist Lindas Bruder.
        whom
        DIR. OBJ.

2. a. Der Wagen, **der** da vor der Garage steht, gehört meiner Schwester.
        which/that
        SUBJ.

b. Der Wagen, **den** Sie da vor der Garage sehen, gehört meiner Schwester.
   which/that
   DIR. OBJ.

Note: a. The antecedents in the above examples are masculine nouns: **der junge Mann** and **der Wagen.** The relative pronouns refer to both persons and things.

b. In sentences 1. a. and 2. a. the relative pronoun is the subject of the relative clause and therefore in the nominative case: **der.**

In sentences 1. b. and 2. b. the relative pronoun is the direct object of the relative clause and therefore in the accusative case: **den.**

RULE: The relative pronoun agrees in gender and number (singular or plural) with the antecedent. Its case, however, is determined by its function in the relative clause.

c. The relative clause is a dependent clause; hence, the inflected verb stands at the end.

d. Normally, the relative clause follows the antecedent immediately. It is always set off by commas.

e. In German the relative pronoun cannot be omitted.

The young man I called is Linda's brother.
Der junge Mann, **den** ich angerufen habe, ist Lindas Bruder.

§3   DECLENSION OF THE RELATIVE PRONOUN

	MASC.	NEUT.	FEM.	PLURAL
NOM.	der	das	die	die
ACC.	den	das	die	die
DAT.	dem	dem	der	denen
GEN.	dessen	dessen	deren	deren

Depending on context, English equivalents may be:
who, which, that
whom, which, that, (who)
(to) whom, which, that, (who)
whose, of which

Only the boldface *long* forms differ from the definite article. (The forms of the relative pronoun are the same as those of **der, das, die** functioning as demonstrative pronouns [cf. Chap. 15, §2].)

Examples for all cases:

1. The relative pronoun as the subject of the relative clause (nominative):

   Der Student, **der** da drüben steht, ist mein Bruder.
   Das Mädchen, **das** da drüben steht, ist meine Schwester.
   Die Studentin, **die** da drüben steht, ist meine Freundin.
   Die Leute, **die** da drüben stehen, sind meine Freunde.

2. The relative pronoun as the direct object of the relative clause (accusative):

   Der Student, **den** Sie dort sehen, ist mein Bruder.

Das Mädchen, **das** Sie dort sehen, ist meine Schwester.
Die Studentin, **die** Sie dort sehen, ist meine Freundin.

Die Leute, **die** Sie dort sehen, sind meine Freunde.

3. The relative pronoun as the indirect object of the relative clause (dative):

Der Student, **dem** ich das Geld gegeben habe, ist mein Bruder.
Das Mädchen, **dem** ich das Geld gegeben habe, ist meine Schwester.
Die Studentin, **der** ich das Geld gegeben habe, ist meine Freundin.

Die Leute, **denen** ich das Geld gegeben habe, sind meine Freunde.

4. The relative pronoun showing possession (genitive):

Der Student, **dessen** Name in der Zeitung steht, ist mein Bruder.
Das Mädchen, **dessen** Name in der Zeitung steht, ist meine Schwester.
Die Studentin, **deren** Name in der Zeitung steht, ist meine Freundin.

Die Leute, **deren** Namen in der Zeitung stehen, sind meine Freunde.

REMEMBER:

relative pronoun: a. gender and number determined by
the antecedent;
b. case determined by its function
in the relative clause.

PRACTICE

16-2   State the function and give the case and gender (if singular) or number
(if plural) of each relative pronoun in the following sentences.

MODEL: Ist das die Dame, **die** uns das Museum zeigen soll?
subject, nominative, feminine
Sind das die Leute, **die** das Museum sehen wollen?
subject, nominative, plural

1. Ist das der Herr, **der** uns das Museum zeigen soll?
2. Ist das der Tourist, **dem** wir die Stadt zeigen sollen?
3. Sind das die Touristen, **denen** wir unsere Stadt zeigen sollen?
4. Sind das die Touristen, **die** unsere Stadt sehen wollen?
5. Wie heißen die Leute, **deren** Haus Sie kaufen wollen?
6. Wo ist das Paket, **das** Ihre Eltern geschickt haben?
7. Das große Paket, **das** vor der Tür steht, ist für Hannelore.
8. Wo wohnt Ihre Tochter, **der** Sie dieses Paket schicken wollen?
9. Ist das Mädchen, **das** dich immer anruft, deine feste Freundin?[1]
10. Ist das Mädchen, **das** du immer anrufst, deine feste Freundin?

Note that a relative pronoun referring to **Mädchen** or **Fräulein** must be neuter, though
the personal pronoun would often be feminine rather than neuter (cf. Chap. 6, §9).

---

[1] die feste Freundin   *steady girlfriend*
der feste Freund   *steady boyfriend*

Keep in mind that some verbs have dative objects, such as **helfen, antworten, danken, folgen, gratulieren, trauen** (cf. Chap. 5, §4, 3b).

> Das ist ein Mann, **dem** man nicht trauen kann.
> Das sind Leute, **denen** man nicht trauen kann.

Some of these verbs occur in the next exercise.

PRACTICE

16-3   Replace the boldface antecedents with the words given in parentheses. Change the relative pronouns (and if necessary the verbs) to match the new antecedents.

> MODEL: **Der Student,** der im Zimmer neben mir wohnt, ist krank. (die zwei Studenten)
> **Die zwei Studenten, die im Zimmer neben mir wohnen, sind krank.**

1. **Das Buch**, das ich für den Kurs in Chemie brauche, ist sehr teuer. (die Bücher)
2. **Die Bemerkung**, die Rita gemacht hat, werde ich ignorieren. (die Bemerkungen)
3. Das ist **ein Apparat**, der noch nie funktioniert hat. (eine Maschine)
4. Das ist nicht **die Suppe**, die ich bestellt habe. (der Nachtisch)[1]
5. Hast du **das Radio** gesehen, das ich Monika schenken will? (der Ring)
6. Das ist **ein Punkt**, den wir noch klären[2] müssen. (eine Sache)
7. **Das Theaterstück**, das ich gestern gesehen habe, ist sehr langweilig. (der Film)
8. Das ist **eine Haltung**,[3] die ich nicht verstehe. (ein Problem)
9. Da drüben steht **der Polizist**, dem ich meinen Führerschein zeigen mußte. (die Polizistin)
10. **Die Studentin**, der ich bei den Hausaufgaben geholfen habe, hat die Prüfung bestanden. (der Student)
11. Das ist **der Wagen**, dem wir folgen müssen. (die Limousine)
12. Dort sind **Herr und Frau Schreiber**, denen wir für die schöne Party danken müssen. (Frau Krause)
13. **Der Herr**, dem Frau Berger gratuliert, hat eine Gehaltserhöhung bekommen. (die zwei Damen)
14. **Herr Berger**, dessen Vater gestorben ist, hat viel Geld geerbt.[4] (Frau Schiller)
15. Das ist **die Kamera**, die ich geerbt habe. (der Schreibtisch)

[1.] der Nachtisch, -e   *dessert*
[2.] klären   *to clarify*
[3.] die Haltung, -en   *attitude*
[4.] erben   *to inherit*

16-4   **A.** In the following English sentences, two statements are combined by using a relative clause. Express them in German. (Keep in mind that the relative pronoun may be omitted in English but not in German.)

MODEL: Das ist eine Chance. Man bekommt sie nicht jeden Tag.
   Das ist eine Chance, die man nicht jeden Tag bekommt.
   That's a chance one doesn't get every day.

1. Das ist ein Problem. Ich kann es nicht lösen.

   That's a problem I can't solve.

2. Das ist eine grammatische Konstruktion. Ich verstehe sie nicht.

   That'a grammatical construction I don't understand.

3. Wie gefällt Ihnen der antike Wagen? Ich habe ihn geerbt.

   How do you like the antique car I inherited?

4. Das sind peinliche Fragen. Man muß sie ignorieren.

   These are embarrassing questions that one has to ignore.

5. Da drüben ist der neue Student. Ich möchte ihn kennenlernen.

   Over there is the new student who(m) I'd like to meet.

6. Das ist eine Leistung. Ich bewundere sie.

   That's an achievement I admire.

7. Das ist ein modernes Gedicht. Sie sollten es lesen.

   That's a modern poem you should read.

8. Das ist ein Fehler. Professor Naumann hat ihn übersehen.

   That's a mistake Professor Naumann has overlooked.

9. Rainer gibt heute abend eine Party. Seine Freundin hat den ersten Preis gewonnen.

   Rainer, whose girlfriend has won the first prize, is giving a party tonight.

10. Zimmermanns ziehen nach Köln. Wir haben ihr Haus gekauft.

   The Zimmermanns, whose house we bought, are moving to Cologne.

B. Cover up the German sentences of exercise A. and state the German equivalents of the English sentences.

MODEL: That's a chance one doesn't get every day.
   Das ist eine Chance, die man nicht jeden Tag bekommt.

§4   RELATIVE PRONOUNS AS OBJECTS OF PREPOSITIONS

(For cases governed by prepositions, see Chap. 7, §5, and Chap. 8, §1 and §2.)

> Das ist ein Lehrer, **von dem** ich begeistert bin.
>> *about whom I am enthusiastic.*
>> or: *whom I am enthusiastic about.*
> Das ist eine Lehrerin, **von der** ich begeistert bin.
> Das sind zwei Lehrer, **von denen** ich begeistert bin.

Note: a. In German the preposition always precedes the relative pronoun.

b. As usual, gender and number of the relative pronoun are in agreement with the antecedent. The case of the relative pronoun is determined by the preceding preposition: **von** governs the dative; thus the relative pronouns are in the dative case in the examples above.

c. The genitive case – **dessen, deren** – is not affected by any preceding preposition because the object of the preposition is not the relative pronoun but the noun following it:

> Das ist Herr Schmidt, mit **dessen** Frau wir verwandt sind.
>> *(whose wife we are related to)*

The masculine form of the genitive is used because its antecedent is **Herr Schmidt**, regardless of the fact that it precedes the feminine noun **Frau**. For the same reason, the feminine form **deren** is used in the following example:

> Das ist Frau Schmidt, mit **deren** Mann wir verwandt sind.
>> *(whose husband we are related to)*

PRACTICE

16-5   Replace the boldface antecedents with the words given in parentheses. Change the relative pronouns (and if necessary the verb) to match the new antecedents.

MODEL: Das ist **eine Sache**, von der ich nicht gern spreche. (Sachen)
Das sind Sachen, von denen ich nicht gern spreche.

1. Wie heißt **die Studentin**, mit der Sie in einem Zimmer wohnen?[1] (der Student)
2. Das ist **ein Problem**, für das es keine Lösung gibt. (Probleme)
3. Das ist **ein Punkt**, auf den ich später eingehen[2] werde. (zwei Punkte)
4. Das ist **ein Nachbar**, mit dem wir gut auskommen.[3] (Nachbarn)

---

[1] **in einem Zimmer wohnen mit** (*dat.*)   *to room with*
[2] **ein•gehen auf** (*acc.*)   *to go into*
  ging ein, ist eingegangen
[3] **aus•kommen mit** (*dat.*),   *to get along with*
  kam aus, ist ausgekommen

5. Das ist **der Brief**, auf den ich lange gewartet habe. (das Paket)
6. Kennen Sie **das Ehepaar**,[1] bei dem unsere Tochter in Heidelberg wohnt? (die Familie)
7. **Der Kurs**, mit dem ich aufhören[2] will, ist zu schwer für mich. (die Kurse)
8. Das ist **eine Chance**, an die niemand gedacht hat. (ein Problem)
9. Wo wohnt **die Familie**, zu der Sie am Wochenende fahren? (die Freunde)
10. **Bergmanns**, mit deren Sohn ich befreundet bin,[3] haben mir eine Geburtstagskarte geschickt. (Herr Bergmann, Frau Bergmann)

PRACTICE
16-6

A. Express the following English sentences in German. (Again, keep in mind that the relative pronoun may be omitted in English but not in German.)

MODEL: Das ist ein Erfolg. Sie können auf diesen Erfolg stolz sein.
Das ist ein Erfolg, auf den Sie stolz sein können.
That's a success you can be proud of.

1. Das ist eine Leistung. Du kannst stolz auf diese Leistung sein.

_____

That's an achievement you can be proud of.
2. Das ist ein modernes Theaterstück. Ich bin begeistert von dem Theaterstück.

_____

That's a modern stage play I am enthusiastic about.
3. Das ist der Scheck von zu Hause. Ich habe auf den Scheck gewartet.

_____

That's the check from home I have been waiting for.
4. Kennst du die Studentin? Ich wohne mit ihr in einem Zimmer.

_____

Do you know the student (female) I room with?
5. Wie heißt der junge Mann? Hannelore ist verliebt in den jungen Mann.

_____

What's the name of the young man Hannelore is in love with?
6. Das sind Einzelheiten.[4] Wir können nicht auf diese Einzelheiten eingehen.

_____

These are details we cannot go into.
7. Das ist ein Student. Jeder kommt mit ihm aus.

_____

That's a student everybody gets along with.
8. Das ist ein Problem. Es gibt keine Lösung für das Problem.

_____

That's a problem for which there is no solution.

---

[1] **das Ehepaar, -e**   (married) *couple*
[2] **mit dem Kurs auf·hören**   *to drop the course*
[3] **befreundet sein mit** (dat.) *to be friends with*
[4] **die Einzelheit, -en**   *detail*

9. Erika Stein wird uns im Juli besuchen. Wir sind mit ihrem Bruder durch ganz Europa gereist.

_____

Erika Stein, with whose brother we traveled through all of Europe, will visit us in July.

B. Cover up the German sentences of exercise A and state the German equivalents of the English sentences.

MODEL: *That's a success you can be proud of.*
         Das ist ein Erfolg, auf den Sie stolz sein können.

Other Forms of Relatives

§5 *welcher, welches, welche*

Welcher, welches, welche may function as relative pronouns in the nominative, accusative, and dative cases. These forms have a bookish ring and occur mainly in formal German.

> Der Botschafter, **welcher** die Verhandlungen geführt hat, muß den Vertrag unterschreiben.
> *The ambassador who conducted the negotiations must sign the treaty.*

> Das war eine Niederlage für die Arbeiter, **welche** keinen Kompromiß schließen wollten.
> *That was a defeat for the workers who did not want to compromise.*

§6 *wo*

Compare the following two sentences that refer to a place:

> **a.** Das ist der Vorort, **in dem** meine Großeltern wohnen.
> **b.** Das ist der Vorort, **wo** meine Großeltern wohnen.
>   *That is the suburb **where** my grandparents live.*

In *a.* the preposition **in** and the relative pronoun **dem** are used. In *b.* **wo** is used instead, as is often done when referring to places. This corresponds to the English use of **where**.

PRACTICE

16-7   Complete the responses following the model of sentence 1.

1. X: Ist das Unglück¹ an dieser Stelle² passiert?

_____

¹**das Unglück, -e**   *accident*
²**die Stelle, -n**   *place*

Y: Ich glaube, das ist nicht die Stelle, _an der_

das Unglück passiert ist.   _wo_

2. X: An dieser Kreuzung[1] muß man gut aufpassen.

Y: Ja, das ist eine gefährliche Kreuzung, _____

man gut aufpassen muß.   _____

3. X: Wollt ihr wirklich die Ferien in einem kleinen Dorf verbringen[2]?

Y: Ja. Steinheidel heißt das Dorf, _____ wir die Ferien

verbringen wollen.   _____

4. X: Arbeitet Frau Winkler bei der Firma ELBEO?

Y: Ich glaube, das ist nicht die Firma, _____ sie arbeitet.

_____

5. X: Haben Winklers früher in Halle oder in Leipzig gewohnt?

Y: Ich glaube, Dresden ist die Stadt, _____

sie früher gewohnt haben.   _____

§7   *was*

Was is used as a relative pronoun in the following instances:

1. When the antecedent is a neuter indefinite pronoun, such as **etwas** (*something*), **nichts** (*nothing*), **alles** (*all, everything*), **wenig** (*little*), **viel** (*much*), **vieles** (*many things*).

> Das ist **etwas, was** ich nicht verstehen kann.
> *That is something (that) I cannot understand.*
> Nicht **alles, was** er sagt, ist wahr.
> *Not everything he says is true.*
> Es gibt nicht **viel, was** ihm wirklich gefällt.
> *There is not much he really likes.*
> **Vieles, was** sie sagt, ist übertrieben.
> *Many things she says are exaggerated.*

English uses the relative pronouns *that* and *which* or omits them completely.

Note the distinction between **viel** and **vieles:**

---

[1] **die Kreuzung, -en**   *intersection*
[2] **die Ferien verbringen,**   *to spend, take one's vacation*
  verbrachte, verbracht

viel = much (refers to something as a whole)	**vieles** = *many things* (refers to a number of individual, separate things, not taken together as one quantity)
Er weiß viel. *He knows much, a lot.* (referring to his knowledge as a whole)	**Er weiß vieles nicht.** *There are many things he doesn't know.*
Er sagt nicht viel. *He doesn't say much.*	**Er sagt mir vieles nicht.** *There are many things he doesn't tell me.*

2. When the antecedent is a neuter adjective in the superlative used as a noun, such as **das Beste** (*the best* [thing]), **das Klügste** (*the smartest* [thing]), **das Interessanteste** (*the most interesting* [thing]). (Cf. Chap. 10, §13).

> Das ist **das Beste, was** wir für Sie tun konnten.
> *That's the best we could do for you.*
> Das ist **das Klügste, was** man in so einer Situation tun kann.
> *That's the smartest thing one can do in such a situation.*

3. When the antecedent is a neuter ordinal (such as **das erste** [*the first thing*], **das zweite** [*the second thing*], etc.) or **das letzte** (*the last thing*), **das einzige** (t*he only thing*).

Although these words seem to be used as nouns, they are not capitalized.

> Das war **das erste, was** er sagte.
> *That was the first thing he said.*
> Das ist **das letzte, was** ich tun würde.
> *That's the last thing I would do.*
> **Das einzige, was** mir Sorgen macht, ist meine notorische Faulheit.
> *The only thing that worries me is my notorious laziness.*

4. When the antecedent is an entire clause rather than a single element.

> Er will seinen Wagen vor dem Eingang parken, **was** verboten ist.
> *He wants to park his car in front of the entrance, which is forbidden.*

§8   *wo*-COMPOUND INSTEAD OF PREPOSITION + *was*

> Das ist etwas, ~~über was~~ er sich immer beschwert.
>   **worüber**
> *That is something about which he is always complaining.*
>   or: *That is something he is always complaining about.*

When preceded by a preposition, **was** functioning as relative pronoun must be replaced by **wo** as part of a **wo**-compound.

A. Translate the following sentences into acceptable English and then reproduce the German from your translation.

1. Herr Baumann sitzt jeden Abend vorm Fernseher, was seine Frau schrecklich ärgert.
2. Bernhard war pünktlich, was nicht sehr oft passiert.
3. Das war das erste, was Margot wissen wollte.
4. Das ist das Billigste, was ich finden konnte.
5. Das ist das Dümmste, was ich je¹ gehört habe.
6. Das war das letzte, was wir für ihn tun konnten.
7. Das ist nicht das einzige, was mich stört.
8. Es gibt wenig, worauf ich wirklich stolz sein kann.
9. Das ist etwas, wovor ich wirklich Angst habe.

B. Complete the responses in German, following the model of sentence 1.

1. X: Ich möchte wissen, warum Klaus und Ruth Schluß gemacht haben.²
   Y: Das ist etwas, **was ich auch wissen möchte.**
   I also would like to know.

2. X: Warum sagst du es mir nicht?
   Y: Das ist etwas, _____
   I can't tell you.

3. X: Das verstehe ich wirklich nicht.
   Y: Liebling,³ es gibt vieles, _____
   you don't understand.

4. X: Ich danke dir für deine Hilfe.
   Y: Ach, du brauchst mir nicht zu danken. Es war ja nicht viel,

   _____
   I could do for you.

5. X: Können Sie uns etwas mehr von dem neuen Projekt erzählen?
   Y: Leider nicht. Das ist alles, _____
   I know.

6. X: Ich möchte Dagmar etwas schenken, kann aber nur fünf Dollar dafür ausgeben.
   Y: Da hast du keine große Auswahl.⁴ Es gibt wenig.

   _____
   that costs only five dollars.

7. X: Warum sagst du nichts?
   Y: Alles,   , scheint falsch zu sein.
   I say

8. X: Macht Sie dieser Lärm nicht verrückt?
   Y: Es gibt nichts, _____
   that can drive me crazy.

---

¹ je	*ever*
² Schluß machen	*to break up*
³ der Liebling, -e	(male and female) *darling*
⁴ die Auswahl	*selection, choice*

9. X: Seid ihr stolz auf das Resultat eurer Experimente?
    Y: Natürlich. Das ist etwas, _____

                                we can be proud of.

10. X: Der Redner ist nicht auf diesen Punkt eingegangen.
    Y: Es gibt vieles, _____

                    he didn't go into.

§9   THE RELATIVE PRONOUNS *wer* AND *was* WITH NO ANTECEDENT

The relative pronouns **wer** and **was** are used without an antecedent in the sense of

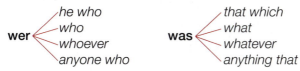

Compare:

wer/was

used as interrogative pronouns (inflected verb in second position)	**used as relative pronouns without antecedents** (inflected verb in last position)
Wer hat einen Wagen? *Who has a car?*	**Wer** einen Wagen **hat,** (der) geht selten zu Fuß. *He who has a car seldom walks.* or: *Anyone who has a car seldom walks.*
Was sagst du? *What are you saying?*	**Was** du **sagst,** (das) ist Unsinn. *What you are saying is nonsense.*

Note: a. **Wer** and **was** functioning as relative pronouns introduce dependent clauses; thus the inflected verb is in final position.

b. In the above examples the demonstratives **der** and **das** are in parentheses because they are generally omitted in sentences with the following combinations:

Wer....   (der)
(nom.)   (nom.)
Was....   (das)
(nom. or acc.)   (nom. or acc.)

In all other instances they must be added.

Wer nicht arbeiten will, **den** sollte man nicht unterstützen.
He who (Whoever) does not want to work should not be supported.
                        (lit. *one should not support*)

Wem das nicht gefällt, **der** kann ja protestieren.
He who (Whoever) does not like it can protest.

The notion of generalization or indefiniteness may be enhanced by adding **immer,**
auch, or **auch immer:**

$$
\left.\begin{array}{l}
\textbf{Wer immer } \text{uns besucht.} \\
\textit{or: } \textbf{Wer } \text{uns } \textbf{auch } \text{besucht,} \\
\textit{or: } \textbf{Wer } \text{uns } \textbf{auch immer } \text{besucht,}
\end{array}\right\}
\text{(der) ist willkommen.}
$$

Whoever visits us is welcome.

$$
\left.\begin{array}{l}
\textbf{Was immer } \text{sie unternimmt,} \\
\textit{or: } \textbf{Was } \text{sie } \textbf{auch } \text{unternimmt,} \\
\textit{or: } \textbf{Was } \text{sie } \textbf{auch immer } \text{unternimmt.}
\end{array}\right\}
\text{(das) ist gut überlegt.}
$$

Whatever she undertakes is well thought out.

The relative pronouns **wer** and **was** frequently occur in advertisements, proverbs, and sayings:

>**Wer gesund bleiben will, trinkt Obstsaft.**
>*Whoever wants to stay healthy drinks fruit juice.*
>
>*or: People who want to ...*
>
>**Wer Qualität liebt, kauft bei Merkur.**
>*Whoever loves quality buys at Merkur.*
>
>*or: People who love quality...*
>
>PROVERB: **Wer im Glashaus sitzt, soll nicht mit Steinen werfen.**
>*People who live in glass houses shouldn't throw stones.*

PRACTICE

16-9 Express in English.

1. Wer zuletzt lacht, lacht am besten. (*proverb*)
2. Was ich nicht weiß, macht mich nicht heiß.[1] (*proverb*)
3. Wer einmal lügt, dem glaubt man nicht, und wenn er auch[2] die Wahrheit spricht. (*proverb*)
4. Wer die Wahl[3] hat, hat die Qual.[4] (*proverb*)
5. Was man auch immer zu ihm sagt, geht zum einen Ohr hinein, zum anderen wieder hinaus.
6. Wen diese Musik stört, der soll es sagen.
7. Wem es Spaß macht,[5] der kann mitsingen.
8. Wem dieser Witz nicht gefällt, der braucht nicht darüber zu lachen.
9. Wer zuviel ißt, begeht Selbstmord[6] mit Messer und Gabel.

§10 SUMMARY OF THE MAIN FEATURES

1. Relative clauses are dependent clauses that ordinarily modify antecedents. They are set off by commas.

---

[1] **heiß**	*hot; here; angry*
[2] **wenn auch**	*even though, even when*
[3] **die Wahl, -en**	*choice*
[4] **die Qual, -en**	*pain; here: pain of having to make a decision*
[5] idiom: **es macht mir Spaß**	*it's fun for me, I enjoy it*
[6] **Selbstmord begehen, beging, begangen**	*to commit suicide*

2. They are introduced by a relative pronoun that cannot be omitted. This pronoun agrees in gender and number with its antecedent, but its case is determined by its function in the relative clause.

3. Relative pronouns usually resemble the definite article.

4. The alternative forms of the relative pronoun **welcher** occur mainly in formal German.

5. When referring to a place, **wo** is often used instead of a preposition and a form of the relative pronoun **der, das,** or **die.**

6. The relative pronoun **was** is used after the following antecedents:
   a. indefinite pronouns, such as **etwas, nichts, alles, wenig, viel, vieles;**
   b. neuter adjectives in the superlative used as nouns, such as **das Beste, das Dümmste;**
   c. neuter ordinals and **das letzte, das einzige;**
   d. entire clauses.

7. **wo**-Compounds must be used in place of a preposition + **was.**

8. **Wer** and **was** are used as relative pronouns when there is no antecedent.

PRACTICE

16-10   Summarizing exercises

   A.   Express in German.[1]

   1.   a. We must clarify this point.   **Wir müssen diesen Punkt klären.**
        b. That's a point we must clarify.
        c. That's something we must clarify.
   2.   a. I cannot understand this attitude.   **Ich kann diese Haltung nicht verstehen.**
        b. That's an attitude I cannot understand.
        c. That's something I cannot understand.
        d. That's not the only thing I cannot understand.
   3.   a. She did that for me.   **Sie hat das für mich getan.**
        b. That's the first thing she did for me.
        c. That's the only thing she did for me.
   4.   a. I would not do that.   **Ich würde das nicht tun.**
        b. That's something I would not do.
        c. That's the last thing I would do.
   5.   a. That worries me.   **Das macht mir Sorgen.**
        b. That's a problem that worries me.

[1.] **Render** | *the first thing* | *by* | **das erste** |
	the last thing	*by*	**das letzte**
	the only thing	*by*	**das einzige**
	many things	*by*	**vieles**
	there is/are	*by*	**es gibt**

   c. That's something that worries me.

   d. That's not the only thing that worries me.

6.   a. I dropped a course. **Ich habe mit einem Kurs aufgehört.**

   b. The course I dropped was too hard for me.

   c. The courses I dropped were too hard for me.

   d. There is nothing that is too hard for you. (formal)

7.   a. I cannot go into details.   **Ich kann nicht auf Einzelheiten eingehen.**

   b. These are (**Das sind**) details I cannot go into.

   c. That is something I cannot go into.

   d. There are many things I cannot go into.

8.   a. She can be proud of this achievement.   **Sie kann auf diese Leistung stolz sein.**

   b. That is an achievement she can be proud of.

   c. That is something she can be proud of.

   d. That is not the only thing she can be proud of.

   e. There is not much I can be proud of.

   f. There are many things you can be proud of. (fam. sing.)

B.   Insert the appropriate relative pronouns.

1.   X: Schuberts haben früher in dieser Villa gewohnt.

   Y: Ich glaube, das ist nicht die Villa, _____ _____
      Schuberts früher gewohnt haben. (two possibilities)

2.   X: Wir haben in einem billigen Hotel übernachtet.

   Y: Billig? Wie heißt das Hotel, _____ _____
      Sie übernachtet haben?   (two possibilities)

3.   X: Ich weiß etwas, _____ du nicht weißt.

   Y: Was könnte das sein? Wahrscheinlich ein Gerücht,[1] _____ du auf
      der Party bei Neumanns gehört hast.

4.   X: Bist du wirklich schon mit dieser Arbeit fertig?

   Y: Ja, _____ mir Spaß macht, tue ich sehr schnell...Hm, meistens.

5.   X: Diese Radiosendung wird nicht allen Leuten gefallen.

   Y: _____ sie nicht gefällt, der kann sie ja abschalten.[2]

6.   X: Ich habe zwei Stellenangebote.[3] Jetzt weiß ich wirklich nicht, welches
      Angebot ich annehmen soll.

   Y: _____ die Wahl hat, hat die Qual. Das ist übrigens[4] eine Qual,
      _____ ich auch haben möchte.

7.   X: Dieter findet, daß du arrogant bist. Er hat gesagt...

   Y: Ach, das will ich gar nicht wissen. _____ ich nicht weiß, macht mich
      nicht heiß.

8.   X: Wie hast du auf seine ironische Bemerkung reagiert?

   Y: Ich bin still geblieben, _____ wirlich nicht leicht für mich ist.

   X: Das ist das Klügste, _____ du tun konntest.

---

[1] das Gerücht, -e   *rumor*
[2] ab•schalten   *to turn off*
[3] das Stellenangebot, -e *job offer*
[4] übrigens   *by the way*

C.   Form sentences that fit the context.

MODEL: Dieter hat eine neue Studentin gesehen. Er möchte sie
             kennenlernen. Ich frage ihn:
             „Wo ist die Studentin—du/kennen•lernen?"
             „Wo ist die Studentin, die du kennenlernen möchtest?"

1. Andreas sagt, daß er ein nettes Mädchen kennen•gelernt hat. Ich frage
    ihn:
        „Wie heißt das Mädchen—du/kennenlernen" (pres. perf.)

2. Helga liest einen Brief. Ich frage sie:
        „Ist das der Brief—du/so lange/ warten" (pres. perf.)

3. In Margots Zimmer steht eine Kuckucksuhr. Ich frage sie:
        „Ist das die Kuckucksuhr—du/erben" (pres. perf.)

4. Ich habe eine großartige Stelle gefunden und sage:
        „Das ist eine Chance—nicht wieder/bekommen"

5. Ich frage Michael, ob es wahr ist, daß er mit dem Kurs in Trigonometrie
    aufgehört hat. Er antwortet:
        „Das ist nicht der Kurs—auf•hören" (pres. perf.)

6. Ich frage Rainer, wie ihm der neue Chemieprofessor gefällt. Er
    antwortet:
        „Das ist ein Professor—alle Studenten/ begeistert"

7. Ich frage Barbara, mit wem sie in einem Zimmer wohnt. Sie antwortet:
        „Dort am Fenster steht die Studentin Zimmer/wohnen"

8. Ich habe den ersten Preis im Hochsprung (high jump) gewonnen.
    Das ist etwas–ich/stolz

9. Fischers haben ihr schönes Haus verkauft. Jetzt finden sie, daß das ein
    großer Fehler war. Herr Fischer sagt:
        „Das war das Dümmste-wir /machen/können" (past)

10. Ich habe zwei Einladungen für Freitag abend. Welche soll ich
    annehmen?
        Wahl – Qual

11. Der Bürgermeister kritisiert zuviel. Ich finde, er sollte vorsichtiger mit
    seiner Kritik sein.
        Glashaus sitzen–nicht werfen

12. Ihr Freund ißt zuviel. Sie warnen ihn:
        „zuviel essen – begehen Selbstmord/Messer und Gabel"

17 Reflexive Pronouns and Reflexive Verbs; Reciprocal Pronouns; Uses of *selbst* (*selber*)

▽ Reflexive Pronouns and Reflexive Verbs

Introduction

Compare the following three sentences:

> a. **John** is defending **his friend**.
> b. **John** is defending **him**.
> c. **John** is defending **himself**.

In sentences *a.* and *b.* the subject and the object are two different persons. In sentence *c.* the subject and object are identical, and the object is expressed with a reflexive pronoun.

In most instances the reflexive pronoun is the direct object, as in the above example, but it may also function as indirect object:

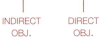

He has to give **himself** more time.

    INDIRECT   DIRECT
      OBJ.   OBJ.

The reflexive pronoun also occurs as the object of a preposition:

> He was **beside himself**.
> He was talking **to himself**.
> He was laughing **at himself**.

There is no difference in form, regardless of whether the reflexive pronoun functions as direct object, indirect object, or object of a preposition.

German reflexive pronouns have the same three functions, but they show some changes in form.

§1   THE REFLEXIVE PRONOUN IN THE ACCUSATIVE CASE

The reflexive pronoun is in the accusative when it functions as a direct object.

Compare: a. **Hans** verteidigt **seinen Freund.**
Hans is defending his friend.

b. **Hans** verteidigt **ihn.** (personal pronoun)
c. **Hans** verteidigt **sich.** (reflexive pronoun)

Here is a complete set of the reflexive pronoun in the accusative case:

Ich verteidige **mich.**	*I am defending myself.*
Du verteidigst **dich.**	*You are defending yourself.*
Er verteidigt **sich.**	*He is defending himself.*
Sie verteidigt **sich.**	*She is defending herself.*
Es verteidigt **sich.**	*etc.*
Wir verteidigen **uns.**	
Ihr verteidigt **euch.**	
Sie verteidigen **sich.**	
Sie verteidigen **sich.** (formal)	

> The reflexive pronouns are identical to the accusative personal pronouns except for the form **sich** in the third person sing. and plural, and in the formal address.

Note that the formal reflexive **sich** is the only formal pronoun not capitalized.

All transitive verbs can be used reflexively, for example:

sich fragen	*to ask oneself*
sich kennen	*to know oneself*
sich loben	*to praise oneself*
sich täuschen	*to deceive oneself*

PRACTICE

17-1   Restate the following sentences, using the subjects in parentheses. Change the reflexive pronoun to match the new subject.

MODEL: Ich frage mich, ob das wahr ist. (Astrid, wir, meine Eltern)
Astrid fragt sich, ob das wahr ist.
Wir fragen uns, ob das wahr ist.
Meine Eltern fragen sich, ob das wahr ist.

1. Er lobt sich zuviel. (ich, du, ihr)
2. Helga täuscht sich vielleicht. (Herr Berger, wir, Sie)
3. Mein Bruder hat sich nicht verteidigt. (die Kinder, ich)
4. Er fragt sich das oft. (ich, wir)
5. Ich kenne mich doch. (du)

Some common verbs that are used reflexively in German but not in English:

sich entschuldigen	*to apologize*
sich erinnern an (acc.)	*to remember*
sich erkälten	*to catch a cold*
sich freuen auf (acc.)	*to look forward to*
sich freuen über (acc.)	*to be happy about*
sich gewöhnen an (acc.)	*to get used or accustomed to*
sich interessieren für (acc.)	*to be interseted in*
sich irren	*to be mistaken*
sich konzentrieren auf (acc.)	*to concentrate on*
sich langweilen	*to be bored, get bored*
sich rasieren	*to shave*
sich setzen	*to sit down*
sich verfahren (verfährt), verfuhr, verfahren	*to lose one's way (driving)*
sich verlaufen (verläuft), verlief, verlaufen	*to lose one's way (walking)*
sich waschen (wäscht), wusch, gewaschen	*to wash (oneself)*

Because they are transitive, verbs used reflexively form the present perfect and the past perfect with the auxilliary **haben,** even if they are derivatives of verbs that employ **sein,** such as **sich verfahren** and **sich verlaufen.** Compare:

Wir **sind** in die Stadt gefahren/gelaufen.   *We drove/walked to town.*
Wir **haben** uns verfahren/verlaufen.   *We lost our way (driving/walking).*

THE POSITION OF THE REFLEXIVE PRONOUNS

The position of the reflexive pronoun is governed by the same rules as the personal pronoun object (cf. Chap. 6, §10).

a. In sentences with **normal word order,** the reflexive pronoun follows the inflected verb form:

Er hat **sich** gestern auf dem Fußballplatz erkältet.

b. In sentences with **inverted** or **dependent word order,** the reflexive pronoun follows the personal pronoun subject:

Vielleicht hat er **sich** gestern auf dem Fußballplatz erkältet.
Es ist möglich, daß er **sich** gestern auf dem Fußballplatz erkältet hat.

It precedes all other elements, usually also noun subjects:

Vielleicht hat **sich** Herr Zimmermann gestern auf dem Fußballplatz erkältet.
Es ist möglich, daß **sich** Herr Zimmermann gestern auf dem Fußballplatz erkältet hat.

REMEMBER: The reflexive pronoun occurs early in the sentence:
It usually <u>follows</u> the inflected verb forms or a personal
pronoun (subject or object), but <u>precedes</u> all other elements.

PRACTICE

17-2   **A.** Express in German.

1. a. I'm bored.   Ich langweile mich.
    b. We are bored.
    c. They are bored.
    d. Are you bored? (fam. sing., pl. formal)
2. a. I'm mistaken.   Ich irre mich.
    b. Perhaps I'm mistaken.
    c. Perhaps you are mistaken. (fam. sing., formal)
    d. We are not mistaken.
3. a. I apologize.   Ich entschuldige mich.
    b. I have to apologize.
    c. I'd like to apologize.
    d. I'm not apologizing.
4. a. Martin is shaving.   Martin rasiert sich.
    b. I'm shaving.
    c. You have to shave. (fam. sing.)
    d. Where can I shave?
5. a. Why aren't we sitting down?   Warum setzen wir uns nicht?
    b. Why aren't you sitting down? (fam. sing., pl., formal)
    c. Would you like to sit down? (formal)
6. a. I hope I won't catch a cold.   Hoffentlich erkälte ich mich nicht.
    b. I hope we won't catch a cold.
    c. I hope you won't catch a cold. (fam. sing., pl. formal)
7. a. I hope we won't lose our way.   Hoffentlich verfahren/verlaufen
                                                 wir uns nicht.

    b. I hope I won't lose my way.
    c. I hope you won't lose your way. (formal, fam. sing., pl.)
8. a. I'm defending myself.   Ich verteidige mich.
    b. I must defend myself.
    c. You must defend yourself. (fam. sing., formal)
    d. She doesn't defend herself.
    e. He can't defend himself.

B. Express the responses in German, using the present perfect for the
English past tense.

1. X: Sie haben sich geirrt.
    Y: No, I wasn't mistaken.
2. X: Habt ihr euch sehr gelangweilt?
    Y: Yes, we were very bored.
3. X: Alle haben sich am Sonntag erkältet.

Y: I didn't catch a cold.

4. X: Haben sich die Kinder heute morgen gewaschen?

    Y: Of course they washed.

5. X: Hat sich Ihre Nachbarin entschuldigt?

    Y: No, she didn't apologize.

6. X: Hast du dich rasiert?

    Y: Of course I shaved.

7. X: Warum hat er sich nicht verteidigt?

    Y: I don't know why he didn't defend himself.

8. X: Maria ist noch nicht zurückgekommen. Hat sie sich verfahren oder verlaufen?

    Y: It is possible that she lost her way.

Particular attention must be paid to verbs associated with a preposition, such as **sich erinnern an** (acc.).

> **Sie erinnert sich noch an meinen Bruder.**
> *She (still) remembers my brother.*
> **Sie erinnert sich noch an ihn.**
> *She (still) remembers him.*
> (**noch** is commonly added)
>
> **Sie erinnert sich nicht mehr an das Picknick.**
> *She doesn't remember the picnic (anymore).*
> **Sie erinnert sich nicht mehr daran.**
> *She doesn't remember it (anymore).*
> (**mehr** is commonly added to **nicht**)

Note the use of the **da**-compound **daran** (cf. Chap. 8, §3).

PRACTICE

17-3   **A.** Express in German.

1. a. I (still) remember this soccer player.   **Ich erinnere mich noch an diesen Fußballspieler.**

    b. I (still) remember him.

    c. My sister (still) remembers him.

    d. Many people (still) remember him.

    e. Do you (still) remember him? (formal, fam. sing., pl.)

2. a. I don't remember this soccer game.   **Ich erinnere mich nicht mehr an dieses Fußballspiel.**

    b. I don't remember it.

    c. Andreas doesn't remember it.

    d. My friends don't remember it.

3. a. I'm happy about this message.   **Ich freue mich über diese Nachricht.**

    b. I'm happy about it.

    c. We are happy about it.

    d. Are you happy about it? (fam. sing., formal)

4. a. I'm looking forward to this trip.   **Ich freue mich auf diese Reise.**
    b. We are looking forward to this trip.
    c. I'm not looking forward to it.
    d. Are you looking forward to it? (fam. sing., pl., formal)
5. a. Margot is interested in karate.   **Margot interessiert sich für Karate.**
    b. Many people are interested in karate.
    c. I'm not interested in it.
    d. Are you interested in it? (fam. sing., formal)
6. a. I have to concentrate more on   **Ich muß mich mehr auf**
       my work.   **meine Arbeit konzentrieren.**
    b. I have to concentrate more on it.
    c. I can't concentrate on it.
7. a. They are getting used to this noise.   **Sie gewöhnen sich an diesen Lärm.**
    b. They are getting used to it.
    c. I'm getting used to it.
    d. I must get used to it.
    e. I can't get used to it.
    f. You have to get used to it. (fam. sing., pl., formal)

B. Express in German, using the present perfect for the English past tense.

1. X: Habt ihr euch an das Leben im Studentenheim gewöhnt?
    Y: Yes, we got used to it.
2. X: Hat sich Herr Lange noch an mich erinnert?
    Y: Yes, he (still) remembered you. (fam. sing.)
3. X: Hat sich Renate über Michaels Geschenk gefreut?
    Y: Of course, she was happy about it.
4. X: Die ganze Familie Wetzel hat sich auf das Wochenende in den Bergen
       gefreut.
    Y: Mrs. Wetzel wasn't looking forward to it.
5. X: Hat sich Herr Rothe für deine Briefmarkensammlung interessiert?
    Y: No, he wasn't interested in it.
6. X: Hast du gehört, was Annerose gesagt hat?
    Y: No, I was concentrating on my work.

§2   THE REFLEXIVE PRONOUN IN THE DATIVE CASE

The reflexive pronoun will be in the dative case if there is a direct object in the sentence.

Example:

sich etwas überlegen   *to think about something*
Ich überlege   **mir die Sache.**   *I am thinking about the matter.*
                  | |
             INDIRECT DIRECT
               OBJ.   OBJ.

Except for the first and second person singular, the dative reflexive pronouns are identical to their accusative counterparts:

Ich überlege **mir** die Sache.
Du überlegst **dir** die Sache.
Er
Sie } überlegt **sich** die Sache.
Es

Wir überlegen **uns** die Sache.
Ihr überlegt **euch** die Sache.
Sie überlegen **sich** die Sache.
Sie überlegen **sich** die Sache. (formal)

Some common verbs with dative reflexive pronouns:

sich etwas an•sehen	*to (take a) look at*
sich etwas an•schauen	
sich etwas leisten	*to treat oneself to something*
sich etwas leisten können	*to be able to afford something*
sich etwas überlegen	*to think about something, think it over*
sich etwas vor•stellen	*to imagine something*

When referring to parts of the body, the dative reflexive pronoun is used in combination with the definite article where English uses the possessive:

Ich wasche **mir die** Hände/**die** Haare.	*I'm washing **my** hands/**my** hair.*
Ich putze **mir die** Zähne.	*I'm brushing **my** teeth.*
Ich habe **mir den** Arm gebrochen.	*I broke **my** arm.*

Verbs requiring a dative object (cf. Chap. 5, §4, 3.b) naturally have a dative rather than an accusative reflexive pronoun:

Ich gefalle **mir** nicht in diesem Kleid.	*I don't like myself in this dress.*
Ich widerspreche **mir.**	*I'm contradicting myself.*

With some verbs, such as **kaufen, bestellen** (*to order*) and **holen** (*to* [go and] *get, fetch*), the use of the dative reflexive pronoun is optional:

Frau Schmidt hat (sich) einen Wagen gekauft.
Mrs. Schmidt bought (herself) a car.

Was hast du (dir) bestellt?
What did you order (for yourself)?

Ich habe (mir) eine Flasche Mineralwasser aus dem Kühlschrank geholt.
I got (myself) a bottle of mineral water from the refrigerator.

PRACTICE

17-4 Restate the following sentences, using the subjects in parentheses.

1. Maria hat sich keinen Nachtisch bestellt. (ich, wir)
2. Martin hat sich widersprochen. (du, ihr)
3. Haben Sie sich die Hand gebrochen? (du)

4. Herr Krause gefällt sich in der Rolle eines Hausmanns.[1] (ich)
5. Sie können sich die Hände im Bad waschen. (du)
6. Käte hat sich eine Morgenzeitung geholt. (ich)
7. Wollen Sie sich die Zähne putzen? (du, ihr)
8. Hast du dir die Sache überlegt? (Sie, ihr)

A NOTE ON WORD ORDER

Compare the following three sentences:

a. Ich kann **mir** diesen Fernseher nicht leisten.   *I can't afford this TV set.*

b. Ich kann **ihn mir** nicht leisten.   *I can't afford it.*
c. Ich kann **mir das** nicht leisten.   *I can't afford that.*

By analogy with the position of personal pronoun objects (cf. Chap. 6, §10) the dative reflexive follows the accusative personal pronoun, as in sentence *b*. However, it precedes other accusative pronouns, for instance, the demonstrative pronoun **das**, as in sentence *c*.

Additional examples:

Ich kann **es mir** vorstellen.   *I can imagine it.*
Ich kann **mir das** vorstellen.   *I can imagine that.*

Ich werde **es mir** überlegen.   *I'll think about it.*
Ich werde **mir das** überlegen.   *I'll think about that.*

PRACTICE

17-5   **A.** Replace the direct object noun with the appropriate form of the personal pronoun; then substitute **das** for the personal pronoun.

MODEL: Hast du dir die Dias angesehen?
Hast du sie dir angesehen ?
Hast du dir das angesehen?

1. Hast du dir diese Fernsehsendung angeschaut?
2. Ich kann mir das Fiasko gut vorstellen.
3. Er hat sich meine Briefmarkensammlung nicht angesehen.
4. Ich habe mir die Sache überlegt.
5. Wir können uns dieses Haus nicht leisten.

B. Express in German.

1. a. I can't imagine it.   **Ich kann es mir nicht vorstellen.**
    b. I can't imagine that.
    c. You can't imagine that. (fam. sing., pl.)
    d. Can you imagine that? (fam. sing., formal)

---

[1]der Hausmann, ̈er   *house husband*

2. a. My parents can't afford it. **Meine Eltern können es sich nicht leisten.**
    b. I can't afford it.
    c. I can't afford that.
    d. Can you afford that? (fam. sing., formal)
3. a. I'm thinking about it.   **Ich überlege es mir.**
    b. I must think about it.
    c. I must think about that.
    d. I thought about that. (pres. perf.)
4. a. They are watching the soccer match on TV. **Sie schauen sich das Fußballspiel im Fernsehen an.**
    b. Are you watching the soccer match on TV? (formal, fam. sing., pl.)
    c. I was watching the soccer match on TV. (pres. perf.)
5. a. We are only window-shopping. **Wir sehen uns nur die Schaufenster[1] an.**
    b. I'm only window-shopping.
    c. I was only window-shopping. (pers. perf.)
    d. They were only window-shopping. (pres. perf.)

§3   THE IMPERATIVE OF REFLEXIVE VERBS

Reflexive verbs must include the appropriate reflexive pronoun in the imperative. (For the formation of the imperative, see Chap. 2, §12 to §14.)

REFLEXIVE IN THE ACCUSATIVE CASE		REFLEXIVE IN THE DATIVE CASE
	fam. sing.	
Wasch(e) **dich** !		Wasch(e) **dir** die Hände!
	fam. pl.	
Wascht **euch!**		Wascht **euch** die Hände!
	formal	
Waschen Sie **sich!**		Waschen Sie **sich** die Hände!
	wir form = *Let's …*	
Waschen wir **uns!**		Waschen wir **uns** die Hände!

Only the familiar singular imperative distinguishes dative and accusative reflexive pronouns.

---

[1] das Schaufenster, -   *shop window*
   sich die Schaufenster an•sehen   *to window-shop*
   (sieht an), sah an, angesehen

PRACTICE

17-6   **A.** Add the familiar singular, plural, and **wir** imperatives.

MODEL: Sehen Sie sich diese Fotos an!
Sieh dir diese Fotos an!
Seht euch diese Fotos an!
Sehen wir uns diese Fotos an!

1. Bestellen Sie sich doch etwas!
2. Stellen Sie sich das mal vor!
3. Setzen Sie sich doch!
4. Täuschen Sie sich nicht!

B. Add the familiar singular and plural imperatives.

1. Erkälten Sie sich nicht!
2. Bitte bedienen Sie sich![1]
3. Schauen Sie sich mal diese Sendung an!
4. Überlegen Sie sich das doch!

§4   THE REFLEXIVE PRONOUN AS THE OBJECT OF A PREPOSITION

Compare the following three sentences:

a. **Ich** habe über **ihn** gelacht.   *I laughed at **him**.*
b. **Ich** habe über **mich** gelacht.   *I laughed at **myself**.*
c. **Er** hat über **sich** gelacht.   *He laughed at **himself**.*

When the reflexive pronoun is the object of a prepsosition, as in *b.* and *c.* its case is determined by the preceding preposition. (For cases governed by prepsositions, see Chap. 7, §5 and Chap. 8, §1 and §2.)

Additional examples:

Du kannst stolz auf **dich** sein.   *You can be proud of **yourself**.*
Bist **du** nun zufrieden mit **dir**?   *Are you now content with **yourself**?*
Ich bin außer **mir**.   *I'm beside **myself**.*

Note that German uses the reflexive pronoun in the expression **bei sich haben** (to have on you, to carry with you):

Haben Sie Ihren Ausweis **bei sich**?   *Do you have your ID card **on you**?*
Ich habe kein Geld **bei mir**.   *I have no money **on me**.*

---

[1]**sich bedienen**   *to help or serve oneself* (lit.: *to wait on oneself*)
   Bitte bedienen Sie sich!   *Please help yourself*

17-7

A. Substitute the indicated subjects and use the appropriate reflexive pronouns.

MODEL: Ich bin nicht zufrieden mit mir. (Helga, wir)
Helga ist nicht zufrieden mit sich.
Wir sind nicht zufrieden mit uns.

1. Er kann stolz auf sich sein. (Sie, du, wir)
2. Lachst du über dich? (Sie, ihr)
3. Ich spreche zuviel von mir. (du, viele Leute)
4. Ich bin außer mir. (wir, Bergers)
5. Ich habe kein Geld bei mir. (Herr Berger, die Kinder)
6. Haben Sie Ihren Ausweis bei sich? (du … deinen)
7. Leonore hat ihren Führerschein[1] nicht bei sich. (ich … meinen)

B. Express in German.

1. I'm not talking of myself.
2. They can be proud of themselves.
3. She was beside herself.
4. He's laughing at himself.
5. I don't have my ID card on me.
6. Do you have your driver's licence on you? (fam. sing.)

Reciprocal Pronouns and Uses of *selbst* (*selber*)

§5   RECIPROCAL PRONOUNS

1. The reciprocal pronoun **einander** (*each other* or *one another*) is never inflected.

Sie helfen **einander.**   *They help each/one another.*

When following a preposition, **einander** is written together with it.

Wir hören oft **voneinander.**   *We often hear from each other.*
Wir sitzen **nebeneinander.**   *We are sitting next to each other.*

2. The reflexive pronouns are often used to express reciprocity.

Sie hassen **sich.** Possible meanings: *They hate themselves.*
They hate each other.

The context must clarify the appropriate meaning.

Normally, **einander** and the reciprocal reflexive pronouns are interchangeable; however, after prespositions only **einander** can be used.

---

[1]der Führerschein, -e   *driver's license*

PRACTICE

17-8   Translate the following sentences, then reproduce the German from your translation.

1. Es ist klar, daß die zwei sich lieben.
2. Wir schreiben uns nicht, aber wir rufen uns manchmal an.
3. Sie küssen sich nicht, sie umarmen[1] sich nur.
4. Markus und Volker grüßen[2] sich nicht. Sie gehen stumm[3] aneinander vorbei.[4]
5. Heidrun und Petra kommen sehr gut miteinander aus.[5]
6. Wir sind nicht miteinander ausgekommen.
7. Wir helfen einander bei den Hausaufgaben.

§6   Uses of *selbst* (*selber*)

Selbst is an intensifier rather than a reflexive pronoun. The form **selber** is preferred in colloquial German.

a. Er glaubt das nicht.	*He doesn't believe that.*
b. Er glaubt das **selbst (selber)** nicht.	*He doesn't believe that **himself.***

In sentence *b.* **selbst (selber)** is used for emphasis. This intensifier has no case endings. English uses the reflexive pronoun as intensifier.

Additional examples:

Waschen Sie Ihren Wagen **selber?**	*Do you wash your car yourself?*
Herr Schreiber macht alle Reparaturen **selbst.**	*Mr. Schreiber does all repair work himself.*
Hast du den Bericht **selber** getippt?	*Did you type the report yourself?*
Kochen Sie **selbst?**	*Do you do your own cooking? (translation!)*
Meine Mutter ist die Güte **selbst.**	*My mother is kindness itself.*

Selbst (selber) may also reinforce reflexives:

Er hat nicht mich, sondern **sich selbst** getäuscht.	*He did not deceive me but himself.*

When **selbst** (never **selber**) precedes the element it qualifies, it means *even*:

Selbst sie hat kein Geld.	***Even she** has no money.*

---

[1] **umarmen**	*to embrace, hug*
[2] **grüßen**	*to greet, say hello*
[3] **stumm**	*silent(ly)*
[4] **vorbei•gehen an** (dat.) **ging vorbei, ist vorbeigegangen**	*to pass by*
[5] **aus•kommen mit** (dat.), **kam aus, ist ausgekommen**	*to get along with*

17-9   Translate the following sentences, then reproduce the German from your translation.

1. Herr Körner hat das selbst zugegeben.
2. Selbst Herr Körner hat das zugegeben.
3. Haben Sie den Kuchen selbst gebacken?
4. Ich gehe nicht oft essen.[1] Meistens koche ich selber.
5. Haben Sie mich gefragt, oder haben Sie mit sich selbst gesprochen?
6. Ich lache nicht über dich, ich lache über mich selber.
7. Selbst der Professor hat es nicht gewußt.
8. Du bist die Bescheidenheit[2] selbst.

§7   SUMMARY OF THE MAIN FEATURES

REFLEXIVE PRONOUNS

1. The reflexive pronouns are identical in form to the personal pronouns except for the form **sich** in the third person singular and plural, and in the formal address.

2. The reflexive pronoun occurs more frequently in the accusative than in the dative. The forms of the accusative and dative differ only in the first and second person singular.

	ACC.	DAT.
ich	mich	mir
du	dich	dir
er		
sie	sich	
es		
wir	uns	
ihr	euch	
sie	sich	
Sie		

3. The forms of the imperative:

Wasch(e) **dich!**   Wasch(e) **dir** die Hände!
Wascht **euch!**   Wascht **euch** die Hände!
Waschen Sie **sich!**   Waschen Sie **sich** die Hände!

Only the familiar singular imperative distinguishes dative and accusative reflexive pronouns.

4. The reflexive pronoun usually follows the inflected verb form or a personal pronoun (subject or direct object), but precedes all other elements.

---

[1]**essen gehen**   *to eat out*
[2]**die Bescheidenheit**   *modesty*

RECIPROCAL PRONOUNS

Each other/one another may be expressed by **einander** or by the appropriate reflexive pronoun (except after prepositions).

USES OF *selbst* (*selber*)

Selbst (selber) is used as intensifier and to strengthen reflexive pronouns. **Selbst** preceding a noun or pronoun corresponds to English **even**.

PRACTICE

17-10   Summarizing exercise

Using the cues, form statements and questions that fit the context.

MODEL: Es ist sehr kalt, und ich trage nur eine dünne Jacke. Ich denke:
„sich erkälten"
„Vielleicht erkälte ich mich."
or: **„Hoffentlich erkälte ich mich nicht."**

1.   Margot sitzt vorm Fernseher.
sich an•schauen / Film
2.   Ich habe Martin beleidigt. Ich denke:
„müssen / sich entschuldigen"
3.   Der Chef ist nicht fair zu Andreas. Warum protestiert Andreas nicht? Ich sage zu ihm:
„müssen / sich verteidigen"
4.   Ich habe Gäste und sage zu ihnen:
„bitte / sich bedienen!" (fam. pl.)
5.   Man hat Dieters Brieftasche (*wallet*) gestohlen. Dieter sagt:
„außer sich sein"
6.   Annerose fragt mich, was ich am Wochenende gemacht habe.
Ich antworte:
„sich langweilen" (pres. perf.)
7.   Mein Freund sagt, daß das Benzin bestimmt billiger wird. Ich sage:
„können / das / sich vor•stellen / nicht"
8.   Ich will einen Scheck einlösen. Leider kann ich es nicht.
Ausweis / nicht / bei sich haben
9.   Ich habe viele alte Münzen (*coins*) und möchte sie meiner Freundin zeigen. Ich frage sie:
„sich interessieren / Münzen?"
10.   Ich niese (*sneeze*) sehr viel. Ich denke:
vielleicht / sich erkälten / am Sonntag (pres. perf.)
11.   Margot und Renate kommen aus der Stadt. Ich frage sie, was sie gekauft haben. Renate sagt:
„Nichts, wir / sich an•sehen / nur die Schaufenster" (pres. perf.)

12. Marlene will ihren Wagen verkaufen. Sie fragt mich, ob ich ihn kaufen will. Ich sage:
    „müssen / sich überlegen"
13. Barbara und Karin haben ein Doppelzimmer im Studentenheim. Im nächsten Semester will Barbara ausziehen (*move out*). Warum? Sie sagt:
    „wir / nicht aus•kommen"
14. Klaus wohnt nicht mehr mit Rainer in einem Zimmer. Helga sagt:
    „sie / nicht aus-kommen" (pres. perf.)
15. Ich bin bei Barbara. Wir trinken Kaffee und essen Kuchen. Ich frage sie:
    „Kuchen / selbst backen?" (pres. perf.)
    Sie antwortet:
    „nur Kaffee / selbst kochen" (pres. perf.)
16. Frank fährt im Sommer nach Kalifornien. Ich frage ihn:
    „sich freuen / Reise?"
    Frank fragt mich, ob ich mitfahren will. Ich habe kein Geld und sage:
    „können / sich leisten / nicht"
17. Andreas Neumann ist ein Freund von mir. Er hat mir eine Karte aus Berlin geschickt. Ich sage zu Käte:
    „du / sich erinnern an? / / diese Karte / bekommen (pres. perf.) / / sich sehr freuen / darüber"

18 The Passive Voice

Basic Differences Between the Active and the Passive Voices

§1 IN ENGLISH

Compare:

       a. The policeman caught the thief.   (ACTIVE VOICE)
       b. The thief was caught by the policeman.   (PASSIVE VOICE)

In sentence *a.* the subject, the policeman, does something; it is active. The sentence is expressed in the active voice.

In sentence *b.* the subject, the thief, is acted upon by someone, i.e. the policeman. Sentences in which the subject is not active but acted upon are expressed in the passive voice. The grammatical term for the element that acts upon the subject of a passive sentence—in the above example, the policeman—is the agent.

When converting a sentence from the active to the passive voice, the following changes occur:

ACTIVE: a. **The policeman** caught **the thief**.
            SUBJECT   DIRECT OBJECT

PASSIVE: b. **The thief** was caught by **the policeman**.
            SUBJECT   AGENT

The direct object of the active voice becomes the subject of the passive, and the subject of the active voice becomes the agent of the passive.

When you compare sentences *a.* and *b.,* you will notice a shift of emphasis: In sentence *a.* the attention focuses on the fact that the policeman caught the thief. In sentence *b.* the focus of attention is the thief and what happened to him.

In many passive sentences the agent is not stated:

       The thief was caught.
       The houses were torn down.
       The Bauers will not be invited.

THE FORMATION OF THE TENSES IN THE ACTIVE AND PASSIVE VOICES

It is very important to keep in mind that the active and the passive voices use different infinitives.

INFINITIVE OF THE ACTIVE VOICE	INFINITIVE OF THE PASSIVE VOICE
to catch	to be caught
to invite	to be invited
to ask	to be asked
to watch	to be watched

The tenses are based on these infinitives, as seen in the following synopsis.

	ACTIVE VOICE	PASSIVE VOICE
infinitive:	**to watch**	infinitive: **to be watched**
PRESENT	he watches/is watching	he is (being) watched
PAST	he watched/was watching	he was (being) watched
PRES. PERF.	he has watched	he has been watched
PAST. PERF.	he had watched	he had been watched
FUTURE	he will watch	he will be watched
FUT. PERF.	he will have watched	he will have been watched

PRACTICE

18-1

A. Express the following sentences in the tenses indicated in parentheses.

1. This project is financed by the government. (past, pres. perf., past perf., future)
2. His name was not mentioned. (future, pres., pres. perf., past perf.)

B. Express the following sentences in the corresponding tenses of the passive voice.

1. Many adolescents are reading his latest book.
2. The speaker did not mention this point.
3. A real estate agent has just sold this house.
4. The police had informed the mayor.
5. The interviewer will ask you to give all your qualifications.

§2 IN GERMAN

Compare:

My car is being repaired by a mechanic.

Note: a. As in English, the direct object of the active voice becomes the subject of the passive voice, which means a switch from the accusative **meinen Wagen** to the nominative **mein Wagen**.

b. The subject of the active voice, **ein Mechaniker**, becomes the agent of the passive, **einem Mechaniker** (the dative object of **von**).

c. English uses the auxiliary *to be* + past participle to express the passive; German uses the auxiliary **werden** + past participle. The past participle is in final position.

d. In the German passive infinitive, **werden** follows the past participle:

repariert werden *to be repaired*

(For the formation of past participles, see Chap. 3, §2 and §4.)

Compare the following infinitives of the active and passive which will occur in the exercises:

	ACTIVE		PASSIVE
absagen	*to call off, cancel*	**abgesagt werden**	*to be called off, be canceled*
ändern	*to change*	**geändert werden**	*to be changed*
aus•nutzen	*to exploit*	**ausgenutzt werden**	*to be exploited*
bedienen	*to serve, wait on*	**bedient werden**	*to be served, be waited on*
behandeln	*to treat, deal with*	**behandelt werden**	*to be treated, be dealt with*
erledigen	*to take care of*	**erledigt werden**	*to be taken care of*
erwähnen	*to mention*	**erwähnt werden**	*to be mentioned*
loben	*to praise*	**gelobt werden**	*to be praised*
manipulieren	*to manipulate*	**manipuliert werden**	*to be manipulated*
unterbrechen	*to interrupt*	**unterbrochen werden**	*to be interrupted*
untersuchen	*to investigate*	**untersucht werden**	*to be investigated*
verwöhnen	*to spoil (someone)*	**verwöhnt werden**	*to be spoiled*

The Tenses in the Passive Voice

§3   THE PRESENT TENSE

Compare the following conjugations:

ACTIVE	PASSIVE
infinitive: **fragen**	infinitive: **gefragt werden**
ich frage *I ask, am asking*	ich **werde** gefragt *I am (being) asked*
du fragst	du **wirst** gefragt
er, sie ,es fragt	er, sie, es **wird** gefragt
wir fragen	wir **werden** gefragt
ihr fragt	ihr **werdet** gefragt
sie fragen	sie **werden** gefragt

ACTIVE

Sie fragen

PASSIVE

Sie **werden** gefragt
werden + past participle
The auxiliary **werden** is conjugated;
the past participle remains the same.

REMEMBER:

In passive sentences, **werden** is rendered by
a form of *to be*.

PRACTICE

18-2   Translate into English.

1. Das wird oft vergessen.
2. Diese Instrumente werden aus Schweden importiert.
3. Du wirst von deinen Großeltern verwöhnt.
4. Wir werden sehr unfair behandelt.
5. Ihr werdet wahrscheinlich ausgenutzt.
6. Dieser Punkt wird im ersten Kapitel erwähnt.
7. Werden Sie schon bedient?
8. Wird dieser Plan geändert?
9. Wie wird das Projekt finanziert?
10. Wie wird das gemacht?

Sometimes the best English equivalent of a German passive construction is in the active voice.

Fräulein Schmidt wird oft angerufen.
lit.: *Miss Schmidt is called often.*
idiom: *Miss Schmidt gets lots of calls.*

Diese Spielzeuge werden gern gekauft.
lit.: *These toys are gladly bought.*
idiom: *People like to buy these toys.*

When stating the English equivalent of a German passive construction, it is advisable to translate it first literally and then make the necessary adjustments to English usage. This sometimes means employing the generalizing *they* or *people* as a subject.

PRACTICE

18-3   Express in English.

1. Ich werde oft von meinen Geschwistern[1] ausgelacht.
2. Barbara wird von uns allen beneidet.
3. Von wem wird diese Sache erledigt?

---

[1] **die Geschwister** (pl.)   *brothers and sisters*

4. Diese Zeitung wird von jungen Leuten sehr gern gelesen.
5. Hier wird viel Obst[1] angebaut[2] und natürlich auch gegessen.

PRACTICE
18-4 Convert the following sentences from the active to the passive voice.

    Model: Diese Verkäuferin bedient uns.
           Wir werden von dieser Verkäuferin bedient.

1. Der Autor erwähnt diesen Punkt.
2. Mein Mann verwöhnt mich.
3. Deine Frau manipuliert dich.
4. Die Regierung finanziert dieses Projekt.
5. Sein Chef lobt ihn oft.
6. Meine Freundin erledigt diese Sache.
7. Helga lacht dich aus.
8. Dieser Chef nutzt die Arbeiter aus.
9. Das FBI untersucht den Fall.

§4   THE PAST, PRESENT PERFECT, PAST PERFECT, FUTURE, AND FUTURE PERFECT

You are familiar with the tenses of **werden** used as the main verb, meaning *to become*.

PRES.	Sie **wird** nervös.	*She is becoming nervous.*
PAST.	Sie **wurde** nervös.	*She became nervous.*
PRES. PERF.	Sie **ist** nervös **geworden.**	*She has become nervous.*
		or: *She became nervous.*
PAST. PERF.	Sie **war** nervös **geworden.**	*She had become nervous.*
FUT.	Sie **wird** nervös **werden.**	*She will become nervous.*
FUT. PERF.	Sie **wird** nervös **geworden sein.**	*She will have become nervous.*

When **werden** functions as the main verb, its principal parts are

    werden (wird), wurde, ist geworden.

In the passive the auxiliary **werden** governs the tense of the sentence, and the form of its past participle is modified from **geworden** to **worden:**

ACTIVE	PASSIVE
infinitive: **fragen**	infinitive: **gefragt werden**

PRESENT

Sie fragt nicht.	Sie wird nicht gefragt.
She does not ask.	*She is not (being) asked.*

---

[2] **das Obst**   *fruit*
[2] **an•bauen**   *to grow, cultivate, plant*

PAST

Sie fragte nicht.	Sie wurde nicht gefragt.
She did not ask.	*She was not (being) asked.*

PRESENT PERFECT

Sie hat nicht gefragt.	Sie ist nicht │ gefragt worden. │
She has not asked.	*She has not been asked.*
or: *She did not ask.*	

PAST PERFECT

Sie hatte nicht gefragt.	Sie war nicht │ gefragt worden. │
She had not asked.	*She had not been asked.*

FUTURE

Sie wird nicht fragen.	Sie wird nicht gefragt werden.
She will not ask.	*She will not be asked.*

FUTURE PERFECT

Sie wird nicht gefragt haben.	Sie wird nicht │gefragt worden│ sein.
She will not have asked.	*She will not have been asked.*

Note: a. The past participle of the main verb, i.e. **gefragt**, does not change.

b. **Werden** requires **sein**; thus the perfect tenses of the passive voice are formed with **sein**.

In the active voice, the present perfect is frequently used as **conversational past** (cf. Chap. 3, §2). This occurs less often in the passive voice. In general, the present perfect tends to be used in contexts where English would use this form.

Examples:

> Die Rechnung *ist* noch nicht **bezahlt worden**.
> The bill **has** not yet **been paid**.
> Die Fernsehsendung *ist* schon wieder **unterbrochen worden**.
> *The TV program* **has been interrupted** again.

c. As in the active voice, the future is formed with **werden** + infinitive of the main verb:

> Sie **wird** nicht **fragen.**   Sie wird nicht **gefragt werden.**
>   active infinitive   passive infinitive

Keep in mind that in German the present tense is commonly used to express future time if an adverb or the context indicates that the future is referred to (cf. Chap. 3, §3).

> Example: Die Sache **wird** morgen **erledigt**.
> The English equivalent is in the future tense:
>
> *This matter* **will be taken care of** *tomorrow.*

d. The future perfect is hardly ever used in the passive. It will therefore not be practiced.

Pattern:

PRES.	sie **wird** _____ (past part).		she is (being) _____ (past part).
PAST	sie **wurde** _____ (past part.)		she was (being) _____ (past part.)
PRES. PERF.	sie **ist** _____ (past part.)	**worden**	she has been _____ (past part.)
PAST PERF.	sie **war** _____ (past part.)	**worden**	she had been _____ (past part.)
FUT.	sie **wird** _____ (past part.)	**werden**	she will be _____ (past part.)

PRACTICE

18-5 Express the following sentences in the tenses indicated and translate them into English.

1. Herr Köhler wird ins Krankenhaus gebracht.   *Mr. Köhler is being taken to the hospital.*

   past
   pres. perf.
   past perf.
   future

2. Wird dieser Fall vom FBI untersucht?   *Is this case being investigated by the FBI?*

   past
   pres. perf.
   past perf.
   future

CONJUGATION OF THE TENSES IN THE PASSIVE

PRESENT

ich werde gefragt   *I am (being) asked*
du wirst
er, sie, es wird
wir werden
ihr werdet
sie werden
Sie werden

PAST

ich wurde gefragt *I was (being) asked*
du wurdest
er, sie, es wurde
wir wurden
ihr wurdet
sie wurden
Sie wurden

	PRESENT PERFECT	ich	bin gefragt worden	*I have been asked*
		du	bist	*I was (being) asked*
	er, sie, es	ist		
		wir	sind	
		ihr	seid	
		sie	sind	
		Sie	sind	

PRESENT PERFECT   ich bin gefragt worden   *I have been asked*
              du bist   *I was (being) asked*
er, sie, es   ist
              wir sind
              ihr seid
              sie sind
              Sie sind

PAST PERFECT   ich war gefragt worden   *I had been asked*
              du warst
er, sie, es   war
              wir waren
              ihr wart
              sie waren
              Sie waren

FUTURE   ich werde gefragt werden   *I will be asked*
              du wirst
er, sie, es   wird
              wir werden
              ihr werdet
              sie werden
              Sie werden

PRACTICE

18-6   Restate the following sentences in the tenses indicated.

1. Du wirst von dieser Firma ausgenutzt. (pres. perf., past perf., fut.)
2. Ihr werdet nicht verwöhnt. (fut., pres. perf.)
3. Wir werden wie Stiefkinder[1] behandelt. (past, pres. perf.)
4. Die Fernsehsendung wird unterbrochen. (past, past perf., future)
5. Wie wird das neue Projekt finanziert? (fut., past)
6. Wird das Programm geändert? (fut.)
7. Warum wird Ulrike nicht gewarnt? (past, pres. perf.)
8. Wo wird Dieters Geburtstag gefeiert? (pres. perf.)
9. Warum wird das Konzert abgesagt? (past perf.)
10. Hoffentlich wird der Junge nicht verhaftet.[2] (pres. perf.)
11. Unser Haus wird am Montag versteigert.[3] (past)
12. Du wirst vielleicht befördert.[4] (fut.)
13. Das Picknick wird verschoben.[5] (past)
14. Hoffentlich werdet ihr nicht betrogen.[6] (pres. perf.)

---

[1] **das Stiefkind, -er**   *stepchild*
[2] **verhaften**   *to arrest*
[3] **versteigern**   *to auction off*
[4] **befördern**   *to promote (to a new position)*
[5] **verschieben, verschob, verschoben**   *to postpone*
[6] **betrügen, betrog, betrogen**   *to cheat*

§5   DEPENDENT WORD ORDER

The inflected verb form is in the final position.

Ich glaube nicht, daß er von seinem Bruder betrogen **wird.**

betrogen **wurde.**

betrogen worden **ist.**

betrogen worden **war.**

betrogen werden **wird.**

PRACTICE

18-7   Restate the following sentences, using dependent word order after the indicated introductory clauses.

MODEL: Das Programm wurde geändert.
Wissen Sie, warum …
Wissen Sie, warum das Programm geändert wurde?

1. Katrin ist befördert worden.
   Weißt du, ob …
2. Wann wird das nächste Kapitel behandelt?
   Können Sie mir sagen, wann …
3. Die Prüfung ist verschoben worden.
   Wir sind überglücklich,[1] daß …
4. Wie wird dieses Fenster aufgemacht?
   Wissen Sie, wie …
5. Ist das Haus schon versteigert worden?
   Peter weiß vielleicht, ob …
6. Von wem wurde das Projekt finanziert?
   Ich habe keine Ahnung, von wem …
7. Ich werde wie ein Stiefkind behandelt.
   Ich möchte wissen, warum …

PRACTICE

18-8   Summarizing exercise.
Express in German.

1. a. Are they being arrested? Werden sie verhaftet?
   b. They were arrested yesterday.
   c. Why were they arrested?
   d. Nobody knows why they were arrested.
2. a. Why is the picnic being postponed? Warum wird das Picknick verschoben?
   b. It has not yet been postponed.
   c. Will it be postponed?
3. a. She is being promoted. Sie wird befördert.
   b. Ralph was not promoted.

---

[1] **überglücklich**   *overjoyed*

       c. Who has been promoted?

       d. Perhaps Sabine knows who has been promoted.

4.   a. The strike is being called off. Der Streik wird abgesagt.

       b. Has the strike been called off?

       c. It has not yet been called off.

       d. It will be called off.

5.   a. This house is being auctioned off. Dieses Haus wird versteigert.

       b. It will be auctioned off.

       c. It has already been auctioned off.

       d. Too bad that it has already been auctioned off.

6.   a. The broadcast is being interrupted again. Die Sendung wird schon wieder[1] unterbrochen.

       b. The broadcast has been interrupted again.

       c. Why has it been interrupted again?

       d. I have no idea why it has been interrupted again.

7.   a. You are being exploited by this company. Sie werden von dieser Firma ausgenutzt.

       b. You will be exploited by this company.

       c. Many people were exploited by this company.

       d. I have never been exploited.

       e. I cannot believe (it) that you have never been exploited. (fam. sing.)

MEANINGS OF *werden*

In order to recognize the meaning of **werden** in a given context, you have to first determine whether it is accompanied by an adjective, a noun, or a verb.

1.   **werden** + predicate adjective or predicate noun

> Es **wird** kälter.   *It is **getting** colder.*
>
> Er **wurde** Präsident.   *He **became** president.*

    Werden is the main verb. The English equivalent is *to become, get*.

2.   **werden** + verb

    When **werden** is an auxiliary, the main verb may be an infinitive or a past participle.

    a.   If the verb is an infinitive, **werden** is the future auxiliary in the active voice.

> Sie **wird** den Fall **untersuchen**. *She **will investigate** the case.*

    b.   If the verb is a past participle, **werden** is the passive auxiliary.

> Der Fall **wird untersucht**. *The case **is being investigated**.*

---

[1] **schon wieder**   *again* (emphatic; lit. *already again*)

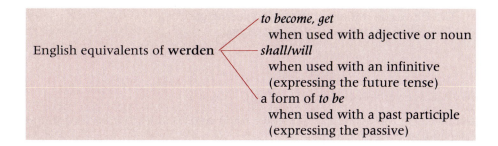

English equivalents of **werden** →

to become, get
when used with adjective or noun

shall/will
when used with an infinitive
(expressing the future tense)

a form of *to be*
when used with a past participle
(expressing the passive)

PRACTICE

18-9

Analyze the use of **werden** in the following sentences and translate them into English.

MODEL: Ich fürchte, Sie werden mich auslachen.
Werden + **infinitive auslachen** express the future tense.
I am afraid you will laugh at me.

1. Niemand wird das glauben.
2. Dein Deutsch wird jeden Tag besser.
3. Das wird anders[1] gemacht.
4. Hoffentlich wirst du das verstehen.
5. Wie werden Sie Ihr Geld investieren?
6. Das Projekt wird von einem Millionär finanziert.
7. Hoffentlich wird es nicht kälter.
8. Ich fürchte, ich werde von Ihnen manipuliert.
9. Das wird nie passieren.
10. Dieses Projekt wird eine Katastrophe.

Additional Features of Passive Sentences

§6   THE AGENT PRECEDED BY *von, durch,* OR *mit*

In most passive sentences the agent is preceded by the preposition **von** (+ dat.). Occasionally **durch** (+ acc.) is used to indicate the intermediary or the inanimate means by which an action is brought about.

Wir wurden **durch einen Boten** benachrichtigt.
We were notified through a messenger.
Die Kirche wurde **durch Bomben** zerstört.
The church was destroyed by bombs.

The preposition **mit** (+ dat.) is used when the reference is to an instrument or a tool. This parallels the English use of *with*.

---

[1] **anders**   *different(ly)*

Die Tür wurde **mit einem Hauptschlüssel** geöffnet.
The door was opened with a master key.

§7   INTRODUCTORY *es* IN PASSIVE SENTENCES

(Its use with active verbs is explained in Chap. 15, §5, 2.)

Es is often placed at the beginning of passive main clauses. It cannot be used in questions or dependent clauses. Compare:

Viele Fabriken werden geschlossen.
SUBJECT

Es werden **viele Fabriken** geschlossen.
SUBJECT

} *Many factories are being closed.*

Naturally, the verb agrees with the subject **viele Fabriken** rather than with **es.**

Es is omitted if another element is placed at the beginning of the sentence. Compare:

Einige Fragen wurden nicht beantwortet.
Es wurden einige Fragen nicht beantwortet.
} *Some questions were not answered.*

Leider wurden einige Fragen nicht beantwortet.
} *Unfortunately, some questions were not answered*

§8   DATIVE OBJECTS IN PASSIVE SENTENCES

1. English permits either the direct or indirect object of an active sentence to become the subject of a passive sentence:

ACTIVE   They awarded **this inventor the Nobel Prize.**
                                    INDIR. OBJ.   DIRECT OBJ.

PASSIVE   a. **The Nobel Prize** was awarded to this inventor.
              SUBJECT

          b. **This inventor** was awarded the Nobel Prize.
              SUBJECT

In German, only the accusative (direct) object of the active sentence may become the subject of the passive voice:

ACTIVE   Sie verliehen **diesem Erfinder den Nobelpreis.**

PASSIVE   a. **Der Nobelpreis** wurde diesem Erfinder verliehen.
              SUBJECT

          b. **Diesem Erfinder** wurde **der Nobelpreis** verliehen.
              INDIRECT OBJ.   SUBJECT

          or: Es wurde **diesem Erfinder der Nobelpreis** verliehen.

In contrast to the English passive sentence *b.*, the subject in the German passive sentence *b.* is **der Nobelpreis**, the direct object of the active sentence.

The indirect object **diesem Erfinder** is retained. It is frequently placed in first position, or it follows the inflected verb when an introductory **es** is used.

Additional examples:

> **Ihm** wurde auch eine französische Medaille verliehen.
> or: Es wurde **ihm** auch eine französische Medaille verliehen.
> *He was also awarded a French medal.*

> **Mir** wurde eine zweite Chance gegeben.
> or: Es wurde **mir** eine zweite Chance gegeben.
> *I was given a second chance.*

> **Uns** wurden nur die Vorteile gezeigt, nicht die Nachteile.
> or: Es wurden **uns** nur die Vorteile gezeigt, nicht die Nachteile.
> *We were shown only the advantages, not the disadvantages.*

2. Dative verbs that lack accusative objects (cf. Chap. 5, §7), such as **danken, drohen** (*to threaten*), **gratulieren, helfen, widersprechen** (*to contradict*), can form only subjectless passives, since there is no accusative object in the active sentence to become the subject in the passive. The verb is in the third person singular. An introductory **es** is frequently added. Compare:

> Active   Man gratuliert ihr.
> Passive   **Ihr** wird gratuliert.
>   or: **Es** wird **ihr** gratuliert.
>   *She* is being congratulated.

> Active   Man dankte ihm nicht dafür.
> Passive   **Ihm** wurde nicht dafür gedankt.
>   or: **Es** wurde **ihm** nicht dafür gedankt.
>   *He* was not thanked for it.

Note that the English equivalents have nominative subjects.

3. In German, the implied subject of a passive verb may be a dependent clause or an infinitive phrase:

> **Mir** wurde gesagt,
> or: **Es** wurde **mir** gesagt, } daß sie Margot Bauer heißt.
> *I was told that her name is Margot Bauer.*

> **Ihm** wurde geraten,
> or: **Es** wurde **ihm** geraten, } weniger aggresiv zu sein.
> *He was advised to be less aggressive.*

PRACTICE

18-10   A. Restate the following sentences in the present and past of the passive. Begin the sentence with the boldface dative pronouns.

MODEL: Man hilft **mir** nicht.
          Mir wird nicht geholfen.
          Mir wurde nicht geholfen.

1. Man dankt **mir** nicht.
2. Man widerspricht **ihr** selten.
3. Man gibt **ihm** eine zweite Chance.
4. Man zeigt **mir** das Geschenk für Marlene nicht.

B.   Translate into English.

1. Mir wurde gesagt, daß ich mehr arbeiten sollte.
2. Es wurde ihr geraten, eine Bewerbung[1] einzureichen.
3. Es wurde mir nicht die Gelegenheit[2] gegeben, mich zu verteidigen.[3]
4. Uns wurde die Erlaubnis erteilt,[4] hier zu zelten.[5]
5. Es wurde den streikenden Arbeitern mit Entlassung gedroht.[6]

§9   PASSIVES WHICH LACK BOTH SUBJECT AND OBJECT

The following sentences illustrate a peculiar passive construction.

Es wurde nicht applaudiert.	*There was no applause (applauding).*
Leider wurde nicht applaudiert.	*Unfortunately, there was no applause (applauding).*

There is neither a subject nor an object; the verb is in the third person singular. The introductory **es** is not used when another element is in the first position.

Passives which lack both subject and object are often difficult to translate into English.

Es wird hier viel gestohlen.
or: **Hier wird viel gestohlen.**
There is a lot of stealing going on around here.

Es wurde viel gegessen und getrunken.
or: **Da wurde viel gegessen und getrunken.**
There was a lot of eating and drinking going on.
They ate and drank a lot.

Heute wird gefaulenzt.[7]
Today we are loafing.
Today I am loafing.

The subject has to be supplied according to the context.

Occasionally, this construction has the force of a command:

Hier wird nicht geraucht!
No smoking here.

---

[1] **die Bewerbung, -en**   *application*
[2] **die Gelegenheit, -en**   *opportunity, chance*
[3] **sich verteidigen**   *to defend oneself*
[4] **die Erlaubnis erteilen**   *to give permission*
[5] **zelten**   *to camp (in a tent)*
[6] **mit Entlassung drohen**   *to threaten with dismissal*
[7] **faulenzen**   *to loaf*

18-11   Express in English.

1. Ihr faulenzt schon wieder. Heute wird gearbeitet!
2. Kinder, warum paßt ihr nicht auf? Hier wird aufgepaßt!
3. Es wird zuviel geschwänzt.
4. Warum ist es so laut im Nachbarhaus?— Ach, da wird heute gefeiert.
5. Wie feiert ihr das Semesterende? — Meistens wird getanzt.
6. Wie wollt ihr gegen die neue Anordnung¹ protestieren? — Es wird einfach gestreikt.

§10 MODAL AUXILIARIES IN PASSIVE SENTENCES

In passive sentences modal auxiliaries usually occur in two tenses: the present and the simple past.

THE PRESENT TENSE

ACTIVE   Detektive **müssen** diesen Fall **untersuchen.**
active infinitive

PASSIVE   Dieser Fall   **muß**   von Detektiven **untersucht werden.**
passive infinitive

This case has to be investigated by detectives.

Note: a. The direct object of the active sentence, **diesen Fall**, becomes the subject of the passive sentence, **dieser Fall**.

b. The modal must agree with the subject, thus **müssen** becomes **muß**.

c. The infinitive **untersuchen** becomes **untersucht werden**, which is the passive infinitive.

Keep in mind: The modal is not in the passive, but it is complemented by a passive infinitive.

Here are some active and passive infinitives which occur in the exercises:

ACTIVE		PASSIVE	
benachrichtigen	*to notify*	**benachrichtigt werden**	*to be notified*
ein·reichen	*to hand in*	**eingereicht werden**	*to be handed in*
klären	*to clarify*	**geklärt werden**	*to be clarified*
lösen	*to solve*	**gelöst werden**	*to be solved*
stören	*to disturb*	**gestört werden**	*to be disturbed*

---

²die Anordnung, -en   *regulation, rule*

übersehen	*to overlook*	**übersehen werden**	*to be overlooked*
vergessen	*to forget*	**vergessen werden**	*to be forgotten*
verm<u>ei</u>den	*to avoid*	**verm<u>ie</u>den werden**	*to be avoided*
voraus•sehen	*to foresee*	**vorausgesehen werden**	*to be foreseen*

PRACTICE

18-12

A. Add the German passive infinitives.

MODEL: Dieser Punkt muß sofort _____ . (*be clarified*)
Dieser Punkt muß sofort geklärt werden.

1. Solche Fehler können leicht _____ . (*be overlooked*)
2. Die Semesterarbeit soll am Freitag _____ . (*be handed in*)
3. Das kann nicht _____ . (*be avoided*)
4. Das darf nicht[1] _____ . (*be forgotten*)
5. Fischers müssen sofort _____ . (*be notified*)
6. Der Chef will nicht _____ . (*be disturbed*)
7. Solche Dinge können nicht _____ . (*be foreseen*)
8. Die Arbeiter wollen nicht _____ . (*be exploited*)

B. Express the following sentences in the passive omitting the agent.

MODEL: Wir müssen ihn sofort benachrichtigen.
Er muß sofort benachrichtigt werden.

1. Wir müssen ihn warnen.
2. Wir müssen dieses Problem lösen.
3. Ich muß diesen Fehler vermeiden.
4. Ich kann diesen Fall sofort klären.
5. Du darfst den Redner nicht unterbrechen.
6. Wir können die Chefin nicht manipulieren.

THE SIMPLE PAST

The modal as the inflected verb is in the past tense (cf. Chap. 4, §2); the passive infinitive remains unchanged. Compare:

ACTIVE	PASSIVE
Ich **mußte** ihn **benachrichtigen.**	Er **mußte benachrichtigt werden.**
	He had to be notified.
Ich **konnte** ihn **benachrichtigen.**	Er **konnte benachrichtigt werden.**
	He could be notified.
Ich **wollte** ihn **benachrichtigen.**	Er **wollte benachrichtigt werden.**
	He wanted to be notified.
Ich **sollte** ihn **benachrichtigen.**	Er **sollte benachrichtigt werden.**
	He was supposed to be notified.

---

[1] **nicht dürfen**   *must not* (cf. Chap. 4, §14)

DEPENDENT WORD ORDER

The inflected modal is in final position.

> Ich nehme an, daß er benachrichtigt werden **muß.**
> Schade, daß er nicht benachrichtigt werden **konnte.**

PRACTICE

18-13   Translate into German.

1. a. They are exploiting us.   Sie nutzen uns aus.
    b. We don't want to be exploited.
    c. We didn't want to be exploited.
2. a. We have to avoid that.   Wir müssen das vermeiden.
    b. That has to be avoided.
    c. That had to be avoided.
3. a. They want to manipulate me.   Sie wollen mich manipulieren.
    b. I don't want to be manipulated.
    c. Nobody wants to be manipulated.
    d. We didn't want to be manipulated.
4. a. We must notify his family.   Wir müssen seine Familie
                                                     benachrichtigen.
    b. His family must be notified.
    c. I assume that his family must be notified.
5. a. We are supposed to hand   Wir sollen die Semesterarbeit
       in the term paper on Monday.   am Montag einreichen.
    b. The term paper is supposed to be handed in on Monday.
    c. It was supposed to be handed in on Monday.
    d. Is it true that it was supposed to be handed in on Monday?
6. a. We have to solve this problem.   Wir müssen dieses Problem lösen.
    b. This problem has to be solved.
    c. It had to be solved.
    d. It cannot be solved.
    e. Unfortunately, it could not be solved.
    f. Too bad that it could not be solved.

THE PRESENT PERFECT, PAST PERFECT, AND FUTURE

As you have seen, passive sentences with modal auxiliaries in the present and simple past parallel their active counterparts. The passive sentences are distinguished merely by the presence of a passive infinitive in place of the active infinitive of the main verb.

This applies also the present perfect, past perfect, and future, as the following table illustrates:

> active infinitive: **fragen**   passive infinitive: **gefragt werden**
> *to ask*   *to be asked*

PRESENT PERFECT

Ich habe ihn nie **fragen müssen.**　　　Er hat nie **gefragt werden müssen.**
　　　(double infinitive)　　　　　　　　　　(double infinitive)
*I have never had **to ask** him.*　　　　*He has never had **to be asked**.*

PAST PERFECT

Ich hatte ihn **fragen müssen.**　　　　Er hatte **gefragt werden müssen.**
　　　(double infinitive)　　　　　　　　　　(double infinitive)
*I had had **to ask** him.*　　　　　　　*He had had **to be asked.***

FUTURE

Ich werde ihn **fragen müssen.**　　　　Er wird **gefragt werden müssen.**
　　　(double infinitive)　　　　　　　　　　(double infinitive)
*I will have **to ask** him.*　　　　　　*He will have **to be asked.***

These awkward passive constructions are rarely used and will therefore not be practiced.

§11   THE STATAL PASSIVE

Ordinarily, passive sentences describe a process: something is, was, or will be taking place. For many passive sentences, there is also a statal counterpart or completed action, as the following examples illustrate.

> 1. a. Die Tür **wird geschlossen.**　　　*The door is being closed.*
>   b. Die Tür **ist geschlossen.**　　　　*The door is closed* (= not open).
> 2. a. Mein Wagen **wird repariert.**　　　*My car is being repaired.*
>   b. Mein Wagen **ist repariert.**　　　　*My car is repaired*
>   　　　　　　　　　　　　　　　　　　　(= *back in working order*).

Sentences *1. a* and *2. a* indicate the process of closing and repairing; sentences *1. b* and *2. b* denote the result of that process, i.e. a state or completed action. The latter, called *statal passives*, employ **sein**: the past participles **geschlossen** and **repariert** function as predicate adjectives.

PRACTICE

18-14　　**A.** Express in English. (**Doch** is used for emphasis; cf. Appendix, §4)

> 1. Der Krieg wird nicht verloren, er ist doch schon verloren.
> 2. Hoffentlich wird die Prüfung verschoben.—Sie ist doch schon verschoben.
> 3. Werde ich zu eurer Hochzeit eingeladen?—Du bist doch schon eingeladen.
> 4. Hoffentlich wird der Streit[1] bald vergessen. - Er ist doch schon vergessen.

B.　Express the responses in German using **doch** for emphasis.

> 1. Wann wird diese Sache erledigt?
>
> 　　‾‾‾‾‾‾‾‾‾‾‾‾‾‾‾‾‾‾‾‾‾‾
> 　　*It is already taken care of.*

---

[1] **der Streit, -e**　　　　*quarrel, fight*

2.   Hoffentlich wird dieses Problem bald gelöst.

_____

It is already solved.

3.   Wann werden diese Rechnungen endlich bezahlt?

_____

They are already paid.

4.   Wird dieses herrliche Schloß[1] wirklich verkauft?

_____

It is already sold.

A NOTE ON THE USE OF *geboren werden* AND *geboren sein*

a.   Wann **wurde** Lincoln **geboren**?   *When **was** Lincoln **born**?*
b.   Wann **sind** Sie **geboren**?   *When **were** you **born**?*
     (lit. *When are you born?*)
c.   Ich **bin** 1960 **geboren**.   *I **was born** in 1960.*

The three English sentences are in the simple past of the passive voice. German uses the simple past of the passive voice for the dead, as in *a.* and the present statal forms for the living, as in *b.* and *c.* However, a living person frequently uses the simple past of the passive voice when listing biographical data in a personal report, such as a curriculum vitae:

Ich **wurde** am 5. Mai 1960 in Düsseldorf **geboren.**

Alternatives to the Passive Voice

The passive voice is used less in German than in English. Here are some German alternative constructions.

§12   THE USE OF *man*

The most common alternative to the passive is the use of **man** as the subject of a sentence in the active voice.

PASSIVE   **Der Autor** wird nicht erwähnt.   *The author is not mentioned.*
ACTIVE   **Man** erwähnt **den Autor** nicht.   *They don't mention the author.*
                                           (lit.: *One doesn't mention the author.*)

The subject of the passive sentence becomes the direct object of the active sentence with **man** as the subject.

---

[1]das Schloß, ̈-sser   *castle*

PRACTICE

18-15   Express the following sentences in the active voice, using **man** as the
subject. Follow the models of sentences 1.

A. PRESENT

1. Ich werde nie gelobt.
    Man lobt mich nie.
2. Ich werde nicht gefragt.
3. Er wird ausgelacht.
4. Wir werden nicht verwöhnt.

B. PAST

1. Sein Vorschlag wurde ignoriert.
    Man ignorierte seinen Vorschlag.
2. Das Geld wurde investiert.
3. Der Fall wurde untersucht.
4. Die Arbeit wurde nicht gut bezahlt.

C. PRESENT PERFECT

1. Ist dieser Fehler übersehen worden?
    Hat man diesen Fehler übersehen?
2. Warum ist dieser Plan schon wieder geändert worden?
3. Ich bin noch nie ausgenutzt worden.
4. Du bist schon oft betrogen worden.

D. PAST PERFECT

1. Alle Studenten waren benachrichtigt worden.
    Man hatte alle Studenten benachrichtigt.
2. Die Kritik war falsch interpretiert worden.
3. Der Scheck war noch nicht eingelöst worden.
4. Er war nicht fair behandelt worden.

E. FUTURE

1. Er wird wohl nicht befördert werden.
    Man wird ihn wohl nicht befördern.
2. Du wirst wohl nicht verwöhnt werden.
3. Ich werde vielleicht ausgenutzt werden.
4. Diese Arbeit wird gut bezahlt werden.

F. VARIOUS TENSES

1. Der Fall wird untersucht.
2. Der Fall wird untersucht werden.
3. Der Fall wurde untersucht.
4. Der Fall ist noch nicht untersucht worden.
5. Cornelia wird wie ein Stiefkind behandelt.
6. Der Autor wurde nicht erwähnt.

7. Ich bin schon wieder manipuliert worden.
8. Ich werde nicht verwöhnt.
9. Wir sind noch nicht eingeladen worden.
10. Mein Vorschlag war zweimal ignoriert worden.

The following alternatives to the passive are far less common than the **man**-construction.

§13 THE USE OF *sein* + *zu* + INFINITIVE

> Hunde **sind** an der Leine **zu führen**.
> *Dogs **are to be kept** on a leash.*
> or: *Dogs **must be kept** on a leash.*

> **Ist** Fräulein Berger telefonisch **zu erreichen**?
> ***Can** Miss Berger **be reached** by phone?*

Such constructions indicate that something is to be done, must be done, or can be done. They also occur in the past tense:

> Die Katastrophe **war** nicht **vorauszusehen**.
> *The catastrophe **could** not **be foreseen**.*

Note that verbs with separable prefixes have **zu** inserted between prefix and verb, as in the example above.

PRACTICE

18-16   Restate the following sentences using **sein** + **zu** + infinitive as alternative to the passive.

MODEL: Diese Rechnungen müssen sofort bezahlt werden.
Diese Rechnungen sind sofort zu bezahlen.

1. Diese zwei Punkte müssen noch geklärt werden.
2. Peters Eltern müssen sofort benachrichtigt werden.
3. Dieser Fehler muß unbedingt vermieden werden.
4. Dieses hohe Ziel[1] kann bestimmt nicht erreicht werden.
5. Diese Entwicklung[2] konnte nicht vorausgesehen werden.
6. Seine Schuld[3] kann nicht bewiesen[4] werden.
7. Frau Neumanns Schuld konnte auch nicht bewiesen werden.
8. Der Rechtsanwalt konnte telefonisch nicht erreicht werden.

§14 THE USE OF REFLEXIVE VERBS

1. **lassen** + **sich** + infinitive is frequently used as a substitute for **können** + passive infinitive.

---

[1] **das Ziel, -e**   *goal*
[2] **die Entwicklung, -en**   *development*
[3] **die Schuld**   *guilt*
[4] **beweisen, bewies, bewiesen**   *to prove*

Das kann nicht vorausgesehen werden.
Das läßt sich nicht voraussehen. } *That cannot be foreseen.*

Das konnte nicht vorausgesehen werden. } *That could not be foreseen.*
Das ließ sich nicht voraussehen.

Idiom:

| **Das/Es läßt sich nicht ändern.** | *That/It cannot be helped.* |
| **Das/Es ließ sich nicht ändern.** | *That/It could not be helped.* |

2. Some other verbs permit the reflexive to substitute for the passive.

Dieses Wort wird anders geschrieben. } *This word is spelled differently.*
Dieses Wort schreibt sich anders.

Wie wird Ihr Name ausgesprochen? } *How is your name pronounced?*
Wir spricht sich Ihr Name aus?

Expression:

Das versteht sich. } *That is understood. That goes*
or: **Das versteht sich von selbst.** } *without saying.*

PRACTICE

18-17   **A.** Restate the following sentences using **lassen + sich +** infinitive as alternative to the passive.

MODEL: Das kann nicht vermieden werden.
          Das läßt sich nicht vermeiden.

1. Das kann nicht bewiesen werden.
2. Das konnte nicht bewiesen werden.
3. Dein Wunsch kann leicht erfüllt werden.
4. Dieser Wunsch konnte nicht erfüllt werden.
5. Meine Enttäuschung[1] kann nicht in Worten ausgedrückt[2] werden.

B. Restate the following sentences, using the reflexive verb as alternative to the passive.

MODEL: Hoffentlich wird bald eine Lösung gefunden.
          Hoffentlich findet sich bald eine Lösung.

1. Hoffentlich wird bald ein Ausweg[3] aus diesem Dilemma gefunden.
2. Dieses Wort wird anders ausgesprochen.
3   Wie wird Ihr Name geschrieben?
4. Diese Tür wird automatisch geschlossen.
5. Solche Gerüchte werden schnell verbreitet[4]

---

[1]**die Enttäuschung, -en**   *disappointment*
[2]**aus·drücken**   *to express*
[3]**der Ausweg, -e**   *way out*
[4]**verbreiten**   *to spread*

A. The following sentences illustrate various features of the passive voice and its alternatives. Express them in English.

1. X: Habe ich Ihren Namen richtig ausgesprochen?
   Y: Nein. Er spricht sich anders aus.
2. X: Die Situation ist hoffnungslos.
   Y: Vielleicht findet sich noch ein Ausweg.
3. X: Willst du wirklich Tierarzt werden?
   Y: Ja. Hoffentlich läßt sich dieser Wunsch erfüllen.
4. X: Von hier aus haben wir einen schönen Blick auf die Stadt.
   Y. Und in der Ferne[1] sind sogar die Alpen zu sehen.
5. X: Bei dem Bankrott[2] der Firma Neubert haben wir viel Geld verloren.
   Y: Wir auch. Dieser Bankrott war nicht vorauszusehen.
6. X: Wie ich höre, haben Sie in der Lotterie gewonnen.
   Y: Ich bin überglücklich. Meine Freude läßt sich nicht in Worten ausdrücken.
7. X: Werden Sie schon bedient?
   Y: Hoffentlich werde ich noch von der Verkäuferin da drüben bedient.
8. X: Passen Sie gut auf Ihre Sachen auf!
   Y: Warum? Wird hier viel gestohlen?
9. X: Hoffentlich schickst du mir eine Ansichtskarte[3] von Berlin.
   Y: Natürlich. Das versteht sich von selbst.
10. X: Hast du schon das Neuste gehört? Ich habe einen Job gefunden.
    Y: Großartig. Das muß unbedingt gefeiert werden.
11. X: Ich glaube nicht, daß Gisela gestern wirklich krank war. Sie ist in der Stadt gesehen worden.
    Y: Hat man sie da wirklich gesehen?
12. X: Kann dieser Stoff[4] gewaschen werden?
    Y: Natürlich läßt er sich waschen.
13. X: Es ist schade, daß du kein Stipendium bekommen hast.
    Y: Ja, das ist schade, aber es läßt sich nicht ändern.
14. X: Spricht man in diesem Laden[5] Deutsch?
    Y: Da ist ein Schild[6] „Hier wird Deutsch gesprochen."
15. X: Wie wird diese Flasche aufgemacht?
    Y: Frag doch Dieter! Er weiß, wie alle Flaschen aufgemacht werden.
16. X: Wissen Sie, wann Schuberts umziehen?
    Y: Mir wurde gesagt, daß sie nächste Woche umziehen.

---

[1] in der Ferne   *in the distance*
[2] der Bankrott   *bankruptcy*
[3] die Ansichtskarte, -n   *picture postcard or simply postcard*
[4] der Stoff, -e   *material*
[5] der Laden, ∹   *store*
[6] das Schild, -er   *sign*

17. a. X: Wann sind Sie geboren?
       Y: Ich bin am 14. August 1950 geboren.
    b. X: Und in welchem Jahr ist Ihr Mann geboren?
       Y: Mein Mann lebt nicht mehr. Er wurde 1940 geboren.

18. a. X: Warum warst du auf der Party bei Zimmermanns so still?
       Y: Mir wurde von einem guten Freund geraten, nicht soviel zu reden.
    b. X: Wir alle reden zuviel und handeln[1] zu wenig.
       Y: Ja, das ist ein altes Problem: Es wird zuviel geredet und nicht
          genug gehandelt.

B. Form sentences that fit the context.

1. Sie sind froh, daß das Semester bald zu Ende ist. Sie sagen zu ihren
   Freunden:
      „das Semesterende / müssen / gefeiert"

2. Annerose sagt, daß sie älter ist als Sie. Sie können das nicht glauben und
   fragen sie:
      „in welchem Jahr / geboren?"

3. Sie sind in einer Buchhandlung und blättern (*leaf*) durch ein paar
   Bücher. Ein Verkäufer kommt und fragt Sie:
      „schon / bedient?"

4. Sie besuchen einen Freund und stellen Ihr Fahrrad hinters Haus. Dann
   fragen Sie Ihren Freund:
      „hier / gestohlen?"

5. Sie haben einen Kanister Farbe (*paint*) gekauft, können ihn aber nicht
   aufmachen. Sie fragen Ihre Schwester:
      „wie / aufgemacht?"

6. Ihr Freund fragt Sie, warum Sie nicht gern zu politischen
   Versammlungen (*meetings*) gehen. Sie antworten
      „zuviel geredet / nicht genug gehandelt"

7. Sie mußten das ganze Wochenende die Nase ins Buch stecken und für
   eine Prüfung lernen. Sie sagen:
      „das / schrecklich / sein, – aber es / sich nicht ändern lassen (past)"

8. Ihr Freund fragt Sie, ob Sie ihn verteidigen würden, wenn jemand etwas
   Schlechtes über ihn sagte. Sie antworten:
      „das / von selbst / sich verstehen"

For the use of subjunctive forms in the passive voice, see Chapter 20, §15 and §16.

---

[1] handeln   *to act*

CHAPTER 19

The Position of Objects, Adverbial Modifiers, and Complements; Variations in the Sequence of Elements

This chapter supplements what has been said about German word order in previous chapters (Chap. 1; 5, §4, 3; 6, §10; 8, §6; 12, §1 to §3; 17, §1 and §2 [Note]).

The Position of Objects

§1 THE SEQUENCE OF DIRECT AND INDIRECT OBJECTS

The indirect object (usually a person) precedes the direct object (usually a thing), unless the latter is a personal pronoun.

	INDIRECT OBJECT (dative/person)	DIRECT OBJECT (accusative/thing)	
Ich habe	**Daniel**	**das Gerücht**	erzählt.
Ich habe	**ihm**	**das Gerücht**	erzählt.
Ich habe	**ihm**	alles etwas nichts das	erzählt.

When the direct object is a personal pronoun, however, the sequence is reversed. (For the cases of pers. pronouns, see Chap. 6, §9)

	DIRECT OBJECT	INDIRECT OBJECT	
Ich habe	**es**	**Daniel**	erzählt.
Ich habe	**es**	**ihm**	erzählt.

Note: Ich habe **es ihm** erzählt.
but: Ich habe **ihm das** erzählt.

Since **das** is a demonstrative pronoun rather than a personal pronoun, it follows the personal pronoun indirect object.

PRACTICE

19-1   Insert the objects in parentheses in the proper sequence.

1. X: Wer hat _____ gesagt? (das / dir)
    Y: Elke hat _____ gesagt. (es / mir)
2. X: Hat die Polizistin _____ gegeben? (einen Strafzettel / dem Fahrer)
    Y: Ich glaube nicht, daß sie _____ gegeben hat. (einen Strafzettel / ihm)
3. X: Hast du _____ erklärt? (deinem Freund / die Hausaufgaben)
    Y: Ich habe versucht, _____ zu erklären. (ihm / sie)
4. X: Bitte erklären Sie _____ ! (diese grammatische Konstruktion / mir)
    Y: Fragen Sie doch den Assistenten! Er wird _____ erklären.(sie / Ihnen)
5. X: Hast du _____ nachgeschickt?[1] (die Post / Dieter)
    Y: Helga hat _____ nachgeschickt. (sie / ihm)
    X: Hat sie _____ nachgeschickt. (ihm / auch die Zeitungen)
    Y: Sie hat _____ nachgeschickt. (alles / ihm)
6. X: Ich möchte _____ zum Geburtstag schenken. (Helga / etwas)
    Y: Ich kann _____ schenken, denn ich bin wieder einmal pleite.
        (nichts / ihr)
7. X: Hat die Chefin _____ gegeben?(eine Gehaltserhöhung / der
        Sekretärin)
    Y: Soviel ich weiß, hat sie _____ gegeben (ihr keine
        Gehaltserhöhung)
8. X: Wollen Sie _____ zeigen? (die Dias / den Studenten)
    Y: Ich habe _____ schon gezeigt. (ihnen sie)
9. X: Wer hat _____ gegeben? (Ihnen / das)
    Y: Meine Nachbarin hat _____ gegeben. (mir / es)

---

[1]**die Post nach schicken**   *to forward the mail*

§2   THE POSITION OF PREPOSITIONAL OBJECTS AND *da*- COMPOUNDS

Prepositional objects and **da**-compounds usually follow pronoun objects and noun objects.

personal or reflexive pronouns	other pronouns or nouns	prepositions + pronouns or nouns. **da**-compounds	
Ich habe		ein Paket	von meinen Eltern	bekommen.
Ich habe	es		von ihnen	bekommen.
Ich habe		das alles etwas nichts	von ihnen	bekommen.
Ich habe	ihnen		dafür	gedankt.
Er hat	sich		über die Einladung	gefreut.

PRACTICE

19-2   Insert the elements in parentheses in the proper sequence.

1. X: Haben Sie _____ besprochen?[1] (mit Ihrer Frau / diesen Plan)
   Y: Natürlich habe ich _____ besprochen. (mit ihr / ihn)
2. X: Hast du _____ gewarnt? (Herrn Berger / vor dieser Gefahr)
   Y: Ich habe versucht, _____ zu warnen. (davor / ihn)
3. X: Hat Barbara den Führerschein bekommen?
   Y: Ja. Du kannst _____ gratulieren. (dazu / ihr)
4. X: Haben Sie _____ entschuldigt? (sich / bei[2] Andreas)
   Y: Ich habe vergessen, _____ zu entschuldigen. (bei ihm / mich)
5. X: Leider habe ich vergessen, _____ mitzubringen. (für Helga / das Geburtstagsgeschenk)
   Y: Und ich habe vergessen, _____ mitzubringen. (für sie / die Geburtstagskarte)
6. X: Michael hat _____ erzählt. (von dieser Sache / nichts / mir)
   Y: Und du? Hast du _____ erzählt? (etwas / davon / ihm)
7. X: Hoffentlich gewöhnen Sie _____ . (sich / an dieses Klima)
   Y: Ich glaube, es ist nicht sehr schwer, _____ zu gewohnen. (daran / sich)

---

[1] **besprechen (bespricht), besprach, besprochen**   *to discuss, talk about*
[2] **sich entschuldigen bei** (dat.)   *to apologize to*

The Position of Adverbial Modifiers and Complements

§3   THE POSITION OF ADVERBIAL MODIFIERS

Adverbial modifiers include simple adverbs, such as **heute, dort, gut,** or phrases, such as **diesen Freitag, in diesem Monat, in der Stadt, mit dem Bus.** For simplicity's sake both will be called *adverbs* here.

An adverb often stands at the beginning of a main clause.

> **Gestern** war ich nicht in der Vorlesung.
> **Dort** steht mein Wagen.

Otherwise adverbs normally have the following positions:

1. **Adverbs of time** (answering the question when?), such as oft, **manchmal, immer, vorher** (*before*), **nachher** (*afterwards*), **heute, nach der Deutschstunde, vor ein paar Minuten** (*a few minutes ago*), occur early in the sentence, following personal pronouns and usually preceding all other elements.

    > Ich rufe dich **nach der Deutschstunde** an.
    > *I am going to call you after German class.*

    > Haben Sie **manchmal** Schwierigkeiten mit Ihren Nachbarn?
    > *Do you sometimes have trouble with your neighbors?*

    > Ich habe vor, Sie **morgen** zu besuchen.
    > *I am planning to visit you tomorrow.*

2. **Adverbs of place** (answering the question *where /at what place?*), such as **dort, da drüben** (*over there*), **vorn** (*in front*), **hinten** (*behind, in the back*), **oben** (*at the top, upstairs*), **unten** (*at the bottom, below, downstairs*), **bei Müllers** (*at the Müllers'*), **auf einer Party** (*at a party*), come toward the end of the sentence and follow adverbs of time. This is unlike English, in which adverbs of place precede adverbs of time.

    > Wir sind nur ein paar Tage **in Hamburg** geblieben.
    > *We stayed in Hamburg only a few days.*

    > Ich war gestern abend **bei Köhlers**.
    > *I was at the Köhlers' last night.*

Do not confuse the following adverbs and prepositions:

ADVERBS

vorn—hinten
Frank sitzt **vorn,** and Käte sitzt **hinten.**
Frank sits in front and Käte sits in the back.

oben—unten
Helga wohnt **oben,** und Ute wohnt **unten.**
Helga lives upstairs, and Ute lives downstairs.

PREPOSITIONS (preceding nouns or pronouns)

vor—hinter

Frank sitzt **vor mir**, und Käte sitzt **hinter mir**.

Frank sits in front of me and Käte sits behind me.

über—unter

Helga wohnt **über mir**, und Ute wohnt **unter mir**.

Helga lives above me, and Ute lives below me.

The prepositional phrases **vor mir, hinter mir, über mir**, and **unter mir** function as adverbs of place.

3. **Other adverbs** generally follow pronouns and nouns. When they occur with adverbs of time and place, they normally follow expressions of time but precede expressions of place. In our examples we shall concentrate on **adverbs of manner** (answering the questions *how? in what way?*). Many such adverbs are identical to adjectives, for instance, **schnell, langsam, gut, schlecht, freundlich, höflich** (*polite*). They also include prepositional phrases, such as **mit dem Bus (Wagen, Zug), zu Fuß** (*on foot*), **mit lauter (leiser) Stimme** (*in a loud* [*low*] *voice*).

Sie hat mich **gestern höflich** gegrüßt.
                TIME   MANNER

She greeted me politely yesterday.

Wir sind **langsam durch den Park** gelaufen.
          MANNER   PLACE

We walked slowly through the park.

Wir sind **heute nachmittag langsam durch den Park** gelaufen.
         TIME   MANNER   PLACE

We walked slowly through the park this afternoon.

PRACTICE

19-3   Insert the adverbs in parentheses in the proper sequence.

1. Wir haben vor, _____ zu bleiben. (im Schwarzwald / eine Woche)
2. Ich habe ihn _____ kennengelernt. (auf einer Party / vor einem Jahr)
3. Meine Freundin hat _____ gestanden. (am Fenster / still)
4. Unser Hund ist _____ gerannt. (bellend / um das ganze Haus)
5. Zwei Studenten haben _____ protestiert. (mit lauter Stimme / gestern)
6. Peter hat _____ gesessen. (vor mir/ oft)
7. Sitzt du _____ ? (vorn / immer)
8. Ich sitze _____ (manchmal / hinten)
9. Ich glaube, Karin hat _____ gesessen. (hinter mir / gestern)
10. Wir wohnen _____ . (oben / seit Montag)
11. Schuberts wohnen _____ . (jetzt / unten)
12. Wir sind _____ gefahren. (mit dem Wagen / um den See)

13. Renate und ich sind _____ gelaufen. (den Fluß entlang / am Sonntag / zu Fuß)

14. Kästners haben uns gebeten, sie _____ zu besuchen. (nächsten Sonnabend / in ihrem Wochenendhaus)

15. Weißt du nicht, daß der Bericht[1] _____ gestanden hat? (in der Zeitung / vorige Woche)

16. Ich habe Lisa _____ gesehen. (beim Friseur / vor ein paar Minuten)

17. Lehmanns wollen _____ fahren. (mit dem Dampfer[2] / auf dem Rhein / morgen)

§4   THE POSITION OF VERB COMPLEMENTS

In this book the term „*verb complements*" is used for certain sentence elements which have a particularly close relationship to the verb and may be said to *complete its meaning*. They stand at the end of a clause, immediately before the final verb elements (if any). The main complement types are listed below.

1.   Predicate adjectives and predicate nouns

(Cf. Chap. 1, §7)

a. Rainer ist **krank.**
b. Rainer ist schon eine Woche **krank.**   *Rainer has been ill for a week.*

a. Sie ist **Journalistin.**
b. Sie ist seit einem Jahr **Journalistin.**   *She has been a journalist for a year.*

a. Er ist **Lehrer** geworden.
b. Er ist vor zwei Jahren **Lehrer** geworden. *He became a teacher two years ago.*

Note that most other sentence elements must precede the predicate adjective or noun. However, prepositional phrases may often stand either before or after a predicate adjective (cf. Chap. 8, §2).

Sie ist **zu mir** sehr nett.
or: Sie ist sehr nett **zu mir.**   *She is very nice to me.*

2.   Necessary adjuncts of verb phrases

a. Many common noun objects, adjectives, adverbs, and prepositional phrases are construed to be verb complements and therefore stand at the end of the clause, followed only by closing verb forms.

Examples:

Tennis (Fußball, Karten, Schach, Klavier) spielen
Wir haben gestern hinter dem Studentenheim **Fußball** gespielt.
We played soccer behind the dormitory yesterday.

---

[1] der Bericht, -e   *report*
[2] der Dampfer, -   *steamship*

zu Mittag (zu Abend) essen *to have lunch (dinner)*
> Wir haben in einem kleinen Restaurant **zu Mittag** gegessen.
> *We had lunch in a little restaurant.*

die Wahrheit sagen *to tell the truth*
> Haben Sie auf der Polizeiwache **die Wahrheit** gesagt?
> *Did you tell the truth at the police station?*

auswendig lernen *to learn by heart, memorize*
> Ich nehme an, daß wir das Gedicht **auswendig** lernen müssen.
> *I assume that we have to memorize the poem.*

ernst nehmen *to take seriously*
> Man kann nicht alles, was er sagt, **ernst** nehmen.
> *One can't take everything he says seriously.*

einen Kompromiß schließen *to compromise, make a compromise*
> Ich werde versuchen, mit meinem Vater **einen Kompromiß** zu schließen.
> *I'll try to make a compromise with my father.*

eine Rede halten *to make a speech*
> Dr. König hat im Auditorium **eine Rede** gehalten.
> *Dr. König made a speech in the auditorium.*

einen Heiratsantrag machen *to propose (marriage)*
> Er hat ihr in Wien **einen Heiratsantrag** gemacht.
> *He proposed to her in Vienna.*

b. **Directionals**

Adverbs of place that merely locate (as in examples above) are not verb complements. However, when adverbs of place denote motion to or from a place, they are called *directionals*. As necessary adjuncts of the verbs of motion, they are verb complements and stand at the end of the clause followed only by final verb forms.

in die Stadt (nach Hause, nach Bremen) fahren
> *to go to town (home, to Bremen)*
> Möchten Sie mit uns **in die Stadt** fahren?
> *Would you like to go to town with us?*

auf eine Party gehen *to go to a party*
> Inge ist vor ein paar Minuten mit Erika **auf eine Party** gegangen.
> *Inge went to a party with Erika a few minutes ago.*

nach oben (nach unten, nach vorn, nach hinten) gehen
> *to go upstairs (downstairs, to the front, to the back)*
> Herr und Frau Berger sind soeben mit ihren Gästen **nach unten** gegangen.
> *Mr. and Mrs. Berger have just gone downstairs with their guests.*

> Bitte kommen Sie mit Ihrem Freund **nach vorn**!
> *Please come to the front with you friend.*

A NOTE ON THE POSITION OF *nicht*

Nicht precedes verb complements in sentences with normally accented negation (cf. Chap. 1, §7):

> Ich habe meinem Freund **nicht** die Wahrheit gesagt.
> Wir haben **nicht** Fußball gespielt.

PRACTICE

19-4   Form sentences arranging the elements in the proper sequence.

MODEL: ich / gehen / in den Zirkus / mit ein paar Freunden / gestern abend (pres. perf.)
Ich bin gestern abend mit ein paar Freunden in den Zirkus gegangen.

1.   Ich / fahren / in die Stadt / mit einer Freundin / gestern nachmittag (pres. perf.)
2.   Ich / gehen / ins Theater / mit Inge / am Sonnabend (pres. perf.)
3.   Helga / gehen / auf eine Party / mit Rainer / gestern abend (pres. perf.)
4.   Wir / spielen / Tennis / nicht (pres. perf.)
5.   Wir / spielen / Fußball / im neuen Stadion / am Freitag nachmittag (pres. perf.)
6.   Renate / spielen / Schach / jeden Mittwoch abend / mit Dietmar
7.   Ich / spielen / Karten / mit meinen Freunden / manchmal
8.   Klaus / gehen / nach unten / mit dem Hund (pres. perf.)
9.   Ich / laufen / nach oben / schnell (pres. perf.)
10.   Inge / gehen / zum Friseur¹ / vor ein paar Minuten / mit Margot (pres. perf.)
11. a. Wir / schließen / einen Kompromiß / mit Dieter
     b. Wir werden versuchen, / zu schließen / einen Kompromiß / mit ihm
12. a. Der Bürgermeister / halten / eine Rede / heute abend / auf dem Marktplatz
     b. Der Bürgermeister hat nicht vor, / zu halten / eine Rede / heute abend / auf dem Marktplatz
13. a. Vielleicht / er / machen / einen Heiratsantrag / in Hollywood / dir
     b. Ich glaube nicht, daß er vorhat, / zu machen / einen Heiratsantrag / in Hollywood / mir
14. a. Wir / essen / zu Mittag /in der Stadt / gestern (pres. perf.)
     b. Es ist möglich, daß / wir / essen / zu Abend / im Hotel / morgen
15. a. Klaus / nehmen / zu ernst / das Leben
     b. Ich glaube nicht, daß, / Andreas / nehmen / ernst / unsere Warnung
     c. Wir bitten dich, / zu nehmen / ernst / unsere Warnung

---

¹der Friseur, -e   *hairdresser*

16. a. Du / sagen / die Wahrheit / nicht (pres. perf.)
    b. Frau Schubert / sagen / die Wahrheit / dem Rechtsanwalt / nicht (pres. perf.)
    c. Hoffentlich / Frau Schubert / sagen / die Wahrheit / vor Gericht[1] (pres. perf.)
    d. Ich bitte dich, / zu sagen / die Wahrheit / vor Gericht

17. a. Ich / lernen / auswendig / dieses Gedicht (pres. perf.)
    b. Meine Freundin denkt, daß es keinen Zweck hat,[2] / zu lernen / auswendig / ein Gedicht

18. a. Dr. Steinbach / sein / Tierarzt / schon seit 20 Jahren
    b. Seine Tochter / werden / Tierärztin / auf eigenen Wunsch[3]

PRACTICE

19-5   Express in German, using the present perfect for the English past tense.

1. a. I am going to the theater.   **Ich gehe ins Theater.**
   b. I am going to the theater tomorrow night.
   c. I am going to the theater with Maria tomorrow night.
   d. I am planning to go to the theater with her tomorrow night.
   e. It is possible that I'll go to the theater with her tomorrow night.
      (pres.)

2. a. We are going to the hairdresser.   **Wir gehen zum Friseur.**
   b. We went to the hairdresser yesterday.
   c. Yesterday I went to the hairdresser with Hannelore.
   d. I am glad that I went to the hairdresser with her yesterday.
   e. I don't have time to go to the hairdresser today.

3. a. He proposed to her.   **Er hat ihr einen Heiratsantrag gemacht.**
   b. Did he propose to her in Bonn?
   c. She proposed to him in Heidelberg.
   d. Is it true that she proposed to him in Heidelberg?

4. a. We have to make a compromise.   **Wir müssen einen Kompromiß**
                                          schließen.
   b. I have to make a compromise with my father.
   c. I am trying to make a compromise with him.

5. a. Are they playing chess?   **Spielen sie Schach?**
   b. They are not playing chess.
   c. They played chess on Monday.
   d. I played chess with Margot on Friday.
   e. I am planning to play chess with her tomorrow.

6. a. I am memorizing a speech.   **Ich lerne eine Rede auswendig.**
   b. I am trying to memorize a speech.
   c. I have to make a speech tomorrow.
   d. Tomorrow I have to make a speech in the auditorium.
   e. I am nervous because I have to make a speech in the auditorium tomorrow.

---

[1] **vor Gericht**   *in court*
[2] **keinen Zweck haben**   *to be of no use or purpose*
[3] **auf eigenen Wunsch**   *at one's own request*

Variations in the sequence of elements

§5   SHIFTING ELEMENTS FURTHER TO THE END OF A SENTENCE

Important elements are placed close to the end of a German sentence. You have already seen that the complement, which is vital, is placed immediately before the final verb forms. Any other element to which in a given context special importance is attached may also be placed unusually close to the end of the sentence, particularly if it represents new information.

1.   Changes in the order of adverbial modifiers

Compare the following two statements:

> X: Monika ist fünf Tage in Hamburg geblieben.
>   TIME   PLACE
>
> *Monika stayed in Hamburg for five days.*
>
> Y: Soviel ich weiß, ist sie in Hamburg **nur drei Tage** geblieben.
>   PLACE   TIME
>
> *As far as I know, she stayed in Hamburg only for three days.*

The statement of X is a sentence with normal intonation, i.e. every element carries its natural stress. No element is given more emphasis than usual, and thus the adverb of time precedes the adverb of place.

In Y's response, the place expression **in Hamburg** is the known element; the time expression **nur drei Tage** is more important, for it provides new information. It is more heavily stressed than usual and moves closer to the end of the sentence. The normal order time before place is reversed.

The same change may occur in questions, dependent clauses, and infinitive phrases.

> Ist sie in Hamburg wirklich **nur drei Tage** geblieben?
> Ich habe gehört, daß sie in Hamburg **nur drei Tage** geblieben ist.
> Sie hatte vor, in Hamburg **nur drei Tage** zu bleiben.

2.   Alternative order of objects

Compare the following two sentences:

> Ich habe meinem Freund einen Kalender gegeben.
>   INDIR. OBJ.   DIR. OBJ.
>
> *I gave my friend a calendar.*
>
> Er hat den Kalender **einer Freundin** gegeben.
>   DIR. OBJ.   INDIR. OBJ.
>
> *He gave the calendar **to** a girl friend.*

The first sentence shows the normal order of noun objects: indirect object before direct object. In the second sentence the direct object represents old information, while the indirect object is new information and is therefore placed toward the end of the sentence. A similar ordering of the objects occurs in English, with the difference that the English indirect object is used with a preposition (*to*, sometimes *for*) when placed after the direct object.

Note the shift from **einen Kalender** in the first sentence to **den Kalender** in the second. Objects preceded by the definite article usually refer to something that is known and have less news value than those preceded by the indefinite article.

3. Alternative order of prepositional phrases

> X: Klaus hat tausend Mark von seinem Vater bekommen.
> Y: Ich glaube, er hat von ihm **nur fünfhundert Mark** bekommen.

Prepositional phrases normally follow direct and indirect objects. But when an object represents new information, it may be placed after a prepositional phrase that communicates old information (as in Y's response) or is less important.

4. Alternative position of subjects

> a. Es ist soeben auf dem Marktplatz **ein schwerer Autounfall** passiert.
> b. Soeben ist auf dem Marktplatz **ein schwerer Autounfall** passiert.
> *A serious car accident happened just now on the marketplace.*

The subject, **ein schwerer Autounfall**, has been moved to the end for greater emphasis. Sentence *a.* begins with an introductory **es**, which is omitted in sentence *b.* because another element is in first position (cf. Chap. 15, §5, 2).

The standard beginning of a fairytale contains such a "delayed" subject:

> Es war einmal **eine schöne Prinzessin** (ein armes Mädchen, ein weiser König).
> *Once upon a time there was a beautiful princess (a poor girl, a wise king).*

PRACTICE
19-6   Form sentences placing the boldface elements toward the end.

> MODEL: X: Ich habe gestern einen Brief an Renate geschrieben.
> Y: du / ab•schicken / **auch gestern** / den Brief an Renate? (pres. perf.)
> **Hast du den Brief an Renate auch gestern abgeschickt?**

1. X: Ich habe vorige Woche jeden Tag in der Bibliothek gearbeitet.
    Y: du / arbeiten / **auch am Sonntag** / da? (pres. perf.)
2. X: Wir sind um 9 Uhr in Frankfurt angekommen.
    Y: ihr / an•kommen / **wirklich schon um 9 Uhr** / in Frankfurt? (pres. perf.)
3. X: Ich glaube, Helga hat vier Semester in Wien studiert.
    Y: sie/ studieren/ **nur zwei Semester** / in Wien (pres. perf.)
4. X: Wer hat Margot das Gerücht erzählt?
    Y: Das war Raine, er / erzählen / **allen Leuten** / das Gerücht. (pres. perf.)
5. X: Wer hat der Polizei den Tip gegeben?
    Y: Unsere Nachbarin: sie / geben / **auch einem Rechtsanwalt** / den Tip
    (pres.perf.)

6. X: Hast du das Paket von deinen Eltern bekommen?
   Y: Ja, und ich / bekommen / **auch einen Scheck** / von ihnen. (pres. perf.)
7. X: Hat der Polizist Renate einen Strafzettel gegeben?
   Y: er / geben/ **Renates Freundin** / den Strafzettel. (pres. perf.)
8. X: Bitte geben Sie der Dame die Speisekarte!
   Y: warum / Sie geben / **dem Herrn und nicht der Dame** / die Speisekarte?
9. X: Bitte sagen Sie dem Polizisten, was gestern abend passiert ist.
   Y: Es war gegen 10 Uhr. Ich ging von der Garage zur Haustür.
   Plötzlich[1] / **ein Mann** / stehen / vor mir. (past)
10. X: Das ist ein Bild von mir, als ich zehn Jahre jünger war.
    Y: Wie im Märchen; es / **ein schöner Prinz** / sein / einmal (past)

A note on the use of stress in spoken German

In spoken German, there is an additional way of indicating unusual importance of a particular element: stressing it without moving it. Thus in spoken German, the example of §5, item 1 could be:

> X: Monika ist fünf Tage in Hamburg geblieben.
> Y: Soviel ich weiß, ist sie nur **drei** Tage in Hamburg geblieben.

§6   PLACING ELEMENTS AFTER THE FINAL VERB FORMS

1.   *Als* and *wie* phrases in comparisons

In comparisons **als** and **wie** phrases (cf. Chap. 10, §3) are normally placed after all other sentence elements, including separable prefixes and final verb forms. Compare:

> a. Ich rufe nicht oft zu Hause **an.**
> b. Ich rufe nicht so oft zu Hause an **wie mein Bruder.**
> c. Er ruft mehr an **als ich.**

In sentence *a.* the separable prefix occupies its normal position at the end of the sentence. In the sentences *b.* and *c.* it is followed by the **als** and **wie** phrases.

Additional examples:

> a. Du kannst sehr schnell laufen.
> b. Du kannst schneller laufen **als ich.**
> c. Du weißt doch, daß du schneller laufen kannst **als ich.**

> a. Ich bin dicker geworden.
> b. Ich bin nicht so dick geworden **wie Renate.**
> c. Ich bin froh, daß ich nicht so dick geworden bin **wie Renate.**

---

[1] **plötzlich**   *suddenly, all of a sudden*

19-7   Express in German, using the present pefect for the English past tense.

1. a. I type faster than you.   **Ich tippe scneller als du.**
    b. I can type faster than you.
    c. I don't think that I can type faster than you.
2. a. He's making more money than I.   **Er verdient mehr Geld als ich.**
    b. He made more money than I.
    c. I assume that he made more money than I.
3. a. She cuts class just as often as he.   **Sie schwänzt genauso oft wie er.**
    b. She cut class just as often as he.
    c. It's not true that she cut class just as often as he.
4. a. Their vacation starts sooner than ours. **Ihre Ferien fangen früher an
                                                    als unsere.**
    b. Their vacation started sooner than ours.
    c. It is possible that their vacation started sooner than ours.

2. Other elements

        a. Wir sind trotz des schlechten Wetters an den Strand gegangen.
        b. Wir sind an den Strand gegangen **trotz des schlechten Wetters.**
            We went to the beach in spite of the bad weather.

In sentence *a.* the past participle is in its usual final position. In sentence *b.* the
prepositional phrase **trotz des schlechten Wetters** has been placed after the past
participle. Such an *extraposition* is sometimes done for special emphasis, but often
the extraposed element (usually a prepositional phrase) is a mere afterthought.

Additional examples:

a. Ich bin aus finanziellen Gründen nicht nach Florida geflogen.
b. Ich bin nicht nach Florida geflogen **aus finanziellen Gründen.**
    I didn't fly to Florida for financial reasons.

a. Mein Vater ist nach vielen Jahren harter Arbeit in den Ruhestand getreten.
b. Mein Vater ist in den Ruhestand getreten **nach vielen Jahren harter Arbeit.**
    My father retired after many years of hard work.

CHAPTER

20

Special Problems

This chapter focuses on several grammatical features that can be treated better separately than in the context of preceding chapters. The discussion of each feature is self-contained to allow instructors to select only those sections that are of particular value for given classes.

The German Equivalent of *another*

§1 **THE GERMAN EQUIVALENT OF** *another* **MAY BE** *ein ander-* **OR** *noch ein:*

  a. Dieser Kaffee ist kalt.   Bitte geben Sie mir **eine andere Tasse Kaffee.**
                                   *Please give me **another cup of coffee.***
  b. Dieser Kaffee ist gut.   Bitte geben Sie mir **noch eine Tasse Kaffee.**
                                   *Please give me **another cup of coffee.***

In sentence *a. another cup of coffee* means "a different cup of coffee." The German equivalent is **eine andere Tasse Kaffe.** In sentence *b. another cup of coffee* means " one more cup" or "an additional cup of coffee." The German equivalent is **noch eine Tasse Kaffee.**

REMEMBER: another < **ein ander-** meaning: a different (one)
                                    noch ein meaning: one more, an additional (one)

In both expressions **ein** has its usual **ein**-word endings; **ander-** has normal adjective endings (cf. Chap. 9, §8).

PRACTICE

20-1   A. Explain the choice of **ein ander-** or **noch ein** in the following sentences.

    1.   Diese Handschuhe gefallen mir. Vielleicht kaufe ich noch ein Paar.

2. Diese Bluse ist schmutzig. Ich muß eine andere anziehen.[1]
3. Der Kuchen schmeckt ausgezeichnet. Könnte ich noch ein Stück haben?
4. Leider habe ich die Stelle nicht bekommen. Sie haben sie einem anderen Studenten gegeben.
5. Dieser Verkäufer hat mich nicht bedient. Es war ein anderer.

B. Insert German equivalents.

1. Ich wollte Herrn Klein meinen Wagen verkaufen. Leider hat er _____ gekauft. (*another car*)
2. Schmidts haben schon zwei Wagen. Wissen Sie, warum sie _____ kaufen wollen? (*another one*)
3. Ich habe schon zwei Semesterarbeiten getippt. Leider muß ich _____ tippen. (*another one*)
4. Diese Fernsehsendung ist ja schrecklich langweilig. Können wir uns nicht _____ anschauen? (*another one*)
5. Wir haben nur einen Sohn und möchten gern _____ haben. (*another child*)

Another with the plural:

another three weeks⟶
= *three more weeks* ⟶ **noch drei Wochen**

PRACTICE

20-2 Insert German equivalents.

1. X: Wie lange wollt ihr noch in Wien bleiben?
   Y: Ich glaube, wir bleiben _____ .(*another five days*)
2. X: Hast du den Bericht schon getippt?
   Y: Ich habe drei Seiten getippt und muß _____ tippen.(*another two*)
3. X: Hast du nun alle Rechnungen bezahlt?
   Y: Nein. Ich muß _____ bezahlen.(*another four*)
4. X: Wieviel Pfund hast du abgenommen?
   Y: 20 Pfund,[2] und ich will _____ abnehmen.(*another 10 pounds*)

German Equivalent of *to like*

§2 To Like Doing Something

1. The most frequent expression uses the adverb **gern** with a verb.

   Ich singe **gern.**   *I like to sing.*

---

[1] an·ziehen, zog an, angezogen   *to put on*
[2] **20 Pfund**   *20 pounds*
  (**Pfund** is in the singular [cf. Appendix, §5])

Ich singe **sehr gern.**	*I like to sing very much.*
Er tanzt **nicht gern.**	*He doesn't like to dance.*

When English adds (*very*) *much*, German uses **sehr**.

2.   The modal **mögen** + infinitive is not common.

Ich **mag** sie nicht um Geld bitten.   *I don't like to ask her for money.*

Only the subjunctive **möchte** (*would like*) is frequently used (cf. Chap. 4, §13).

Ich **möchte** ihr helfen.   *I'd like to help her.*

§3   TO LIKE SOMETHING OR SOMEONE

1.   The verb **gefallen** expresses pleasure or displeasure in a non-emotional fashion.

Dieses Bild **gefällt mir.**	*I like this picture.*
Dieses Bild **gefällt mir sehr.**	
or: Dieses Bild **gefällt mir gut.**	*I like this picture very much.*
or: Dieses Bild **gefällt mir sehr gut.**	
Dieses Bild **gefällt mir nicht.**	*I don't like this picture.*

For emphasis, **sehr, gut,** or **sehr gut** can be added; all correspond to *very much*.

REMEMBER: The verb **gefallen** is used like English to *please*. Its subject is the thing or person that is liked or disliked. Its dative object is the person who has these feelings (cf. Chap. 6, §9).
Das gefällt mir. *I like that.* (*That pleases me.*)

2.   **Mögen** is more emotionally colored than **gefallen.**

Ich **mag** dieses Bild nicht.	*I don't like this picture.*
Wir **mögen** unsere neuen Nachbarn nicht.	*We don't like our new neighbors.*

Used with food or drink:

Mögen Sie Käse?	*Do you like cheese?*
Mögen Sie Tomatensaft?	*Do you like tomato juice?*

It is very common to use **gern** with the verbs **essen** or **trinken** instead:

Essen Sie **gern** Käse?
Trinken Sie **gern** Tomatensaft?

3.   **Gern haben** is used in the sense of *to be fond of.*

Ich **habe** Barbara **sehr gern,** aber ich liebe sie nicht.
I am very fond of Barbara, but I don't love her.

4. People one finds pleasant and likeable are often said to be **sympathisch.**

Sie ist mir sympathisch.	*I like her* (in the sense of *I find her pleasant/likeable*).

> **Sie ist mir nicht sympathisch.**
> or: **Sie ist mir unsympathisch.** } *I don't like her.*

Occasionally **sympathisch** is used with things:

> **Dieser Vorschlag ist mir nicht sympathisch.**
> *I don't like this suggestion.*
> *This suggestion doesn't appeal to me.*

§4   THE POSITION OF *gern*

Gern is an adverb of manner; it is usually follows adverbs of time and precedes adverbs of place (cf. Chap. 19, §3, 3).

> Ich habe vorigen Sommer **gern** im Garten gearbeitet.

It follows pronoun objects:

> Ich helfe Ihnen **gern.**

It follows or precedes noun objects:

> Essen Sie **gern** Fisch?
> Essen Sie Fisch **gern?**

It usually precedes prepositional phrases and verb complements:

> Ich spreche **gern** mit ihm.
> Sie spielt **gern** Tennis.

Exception: With **haben, gern** is a verb complement and stands at the end of the clause followed only by the closing verb forms (cf. Chap. 19, §4):

> Ich habe als Kind diesen Teddybären[1] sehr **gern** gehabt.
> *As a child I was very fond of this teddy bear.*

PRACTICE

20-3   **A.** Translate into German.

1. a. I am fond of my brother.   **Ich habe meinen Bruder gern.**
    b. I am fond of my brother and his girlfriend.
    c. Are you fond of your sister? (formal)
    d. Are you fond of me? (fam. sing.)
2. a. I like this play very much.   **Dieses Theaterstück gefällt mir sehr.**
    b. She likes it very much.
    c. Does she like it?
    d. Do you like it? (fam. sing., formal)
    e. I don't like it.
3. a. I don't like this music.   **Ich mag diese Musik nicht.**
    b. My parents don't like this music.

---

[1] **der Bär** (*weak*), **-en**   *bear*

    c. Why don't they like this music?

4. a. I like pineapple punch.   **Ich trinke gern Ananasbowle.**
    b. My friend likes pineapple punch.
    c. I know that he likes pineapple punch.
    d. Do you like pineapple punch? (fam. sing., formal)

5. a. I like shrimp.[1]   **Ich esse gern Krabben.**
    b. Many people like shrimp.
    c. Do you like shrimp? (formal, fam. sing., fam. pl.)
    d. Do you know whether Hannelore likes shrimp? (fam. sing.)

6. a. I like to play tennis.   **Ich spiele gern Tennis.**
    b. Do you like to play tennis? (fam. sing.)
    c. My girlfriend doesn't like to play tennis.
    d. Too bad that she doesn't like to play tennis.

7. a. I like her.   **Sie ist mir sympathisch.**
    b. I like him.
    c. I like his friends.
    d. I like them.
    e. I don't like this man.
    f. I don't like these people.

8. a. My parents don't like my boyfriend.   **Mein Freund ist meinen Eltern**
                                                   unsympathisch.

    b. They don't like him.
    c. Too bad that they don't like him.

B. Respond using the cues.

MODEL: Wie gefällt dir mein Motorrad?
          Es gefällt mir sehr gut.
         —————————————
         (sehr gut gefallen)

1. Wie gefällt dir mein Freund?
                                    —————————————
                                    sehr gut gefallen)

2. Wie gefällt Ihnen mein neues Kleid?
                                    —————————————
                                    (sehr gefallen)

3. Wie hat dir der Film gefallen?
                                    —————————————
                                    (gut gefallen)

4. Wie hat Ihnen das Konzert gefallen?
                                    —————————————
                                    (nicht gefallen)

5. Wie gefällt Ihnen die neue
Assistentin?
                                    —————————————
                                    (unsympathisch)

6. Haben Sie nette Nachbarn?
                                    —————————————
                                    (sehr sympathisch)

---

[1] **die Krabbe, -n**   *shrimp*
(here used in the plural)

7. Warum lädst du Lore nicht ein? _____
   (nicht mögen)

8. Weißt du, daß du schon fünf Stück _____
   Kuchen gegessen hast? (sehr gern essen)

9. Du hast nicht eine einzige[1] Tasse _____
   Kaffee getrunken. (nicht gern trinken)

10. Spielt dein Freund Fußball? _____
    (sehr gern spielen)

11. Willst du Andreas heiraten? _____
    (sehr gern haben / nicht lieben)

C. Ask yourself the following questions and answer them.

MODEL: Was mache ich gern?
  Ich faulenze gern. Ich esse gern...

1. Was mache ich gern?
2. Was mache ich nicht gern?
3. Wer ist mir sympathisch?
4. Wer ist mir unsympathisch?
5. Wen habe ich gern?
6. Wen habe ich sehr gern?

Uses of *hängen, legen, stellen, setzen,* and *liegen, stehen, sitzen*

§5 *hängen* USED TRANSITIVELY AND INTRANSITIVELY

A transitive verb is capable of taking a direct object in the accusative case.

> Ich schreibe **einen Brief.**
> Sie trinkt **keinen Kaffee.**

An intrasitive verb cannot take a direct object but is often complemented by a prepositional phrase.

> Wir **reisen durch Deutschland.**
> Ich **bleibe in Frankfurt.**

Some verbs are used either transitively or intransitively. One of them is **hängen.**

---

1 einzig *single*

Used transitively: expressing an activity	Used intrasitively: expressing a condition

PRESENT	
Sie hängt **das Bild an die Wand.***	Das Bild hängt **an der Wand.**†
(dir. obj.) (prep. phrase)	(prep. phrase)

PAST	
Sie hängte das Bild an die Wand.	Das Bild hing an der Wand.

PRESENT PERFECT	
Sie hat das Bild an die Wand gehängt.	Das Bild hat an der Wand gehangen.

───────── PRINCIPAL PARTS ─────────

hängen—hängte—gehängt	hängen—hing—gehangen
Used transitively, **hängen** is a <u>weak</u> verb.	Used intransitively, **hängen** is a <u>strong</u> verb.

A good rule of thumb: When **hängen** is used in the sense of *to put*, it is weak; otherwise it is strong.

PRACTICE

20-4 State whether the following sentences express an activity or a condition; then restate them in the simple past and present perfect.

1. Frau Braun hängt die Wäsche auf die Leine.[1]
2. Frau Zimmermanns Wäsche hängt auf der Leine.
3. Klaus hängt seinen Mantel an den Haken.[2]

───────────────────────────

[1] **die Leine, Wäscheleine, -n**   *(clothes)line*
[2] **der Haken, -**   *hook*

   * The two-way preposition **an** requires the accusative because the sentence expresses motion toward a place: the picture is being put someplace it wasn't before.
   † The sentence expresses location; thus the dative case is used **an der Wand**.
(For two-way prepositions, see Chap. 7, §3 and §5.)

4. Mein Mantel hängt am Haken neben der Tür.
5. Ingrids Mantel hängt auf einem Bügel.[1]
6. Dieter hängt den Anzug auf den Bügel.
7. Wo hängt die Fahne?[2]

FORMS OF *hängen* WITH A PREFIX

TRANSITIVE (WEAK)	INTRANSITIVE (STRONG)
erhängen *to hang someone*	**ab·hängen von** (dat.) *to be dependent on*
Sie haben ihn **erhängt.**	Bergers wollen nicht von ihren Kindern **abhängen.**
They hanged him.	*The Bergers don't want to be dependent on their children.*
sich erhängen *to hang oneself*	Sie haben nie von ihren Kindern **abgehangen.**
Er hat **sich erhängt.**	*They have never been dependent on their children.*
He hung himself.	

EXPRESSION:

Das hängt von dir ab. ⟨ *that depends on you.*
That's up to you.

Das hing von dir ab.
Das hat von dir abgehangen.

PRACTICE
20-5   Insert the appropriate past participles of **hängen, erhängen**, or **ab·hängen**.

1. Früher hat man Verbrecher[3] hier _____ .
2. Niemand weiß, warum sich unser Nachbar _____ hat.
3. Herr Schubert hat zu lange finanziell von seinen Eltern _____ .
4. Die Entscheidung[4] hat nicht von mir _____ .
5. Ich habe das Schild[5] „Bitte nicht stören!" an die Tür _____ .
6. Das Schild „Bitte nicht stören!" hat an der Tür _____ .

§6   THE USE OF THE TRANSITIVE VERBS *legen, stellen,* AND *setzen*

English *put* has no good German counterpart. Instead, one uses specialized verbs of placing, such as **hängen**, or the following:

legen   *to put* (in a lying position), *lay, make lie*
Bitte **legen Sie** das Buch auf den Schreibtisch!
Please put (lay) the book on the desk.

---

[1] **der Bügel, Kleiderbügel, -**   *(clothes)hanger*
[2] **die Fahne, -n**   *flag*
[3] **der Verbrecher, -**   *criminal*
[4] **die Entscheidung, -en**   *decision*
[5] **das Schild, -er**   *sign*

stellen   *to put* (in an upright position), *make stand*
Bitte **stellen Sie** das Buch ins Regal!
Please put the book on the shelf.

setzen   *to put, set, make sit*
Bitte **setzen Sie** das Kind auf die Couch!
Please put (set) the child on the couch.

Since these verbs imply motion toward a goal, two-way prepositions used with them require accusative objects.

The three transitive verbs are weak:

legen — legte — gelegt
stellen — stellte — gestellt
setzen — setzte — gesetzt

PRACTICE

20-6   Express the responses in German, using the present perfect. (Remember: **schon** usually follows personal pronouns and precedes all other elements.)

MODEL: X: Bitte stellen Sie die Gläser auf den Tisch!
Y: **Ich habe sie schon auf den Tisch gestellt.**
I already put them on the table.

1. X: Bitte legen Sie Ihre Sachen aufs Bett!
   Y: _____
   We already put them on the bed.
2. X: Bitte stellen Sie den nassen Regenschirm ins Bad!
   Y: _____
   I already put it in the bathroom.
3. X: Bitte legen Sie die Mappe[1] auf den Schreibtisch!
   Y: _____
   I already put it on the desk.
4. X: Warum setzen Sie kein Inserat[2] in die Zeitung?
   Y: _____
   I already put two ads in the newspaper.
5. X: Wir sollten die Milch in den Kühlschrank stellen.
   Y: _____
   Margot has just[3] put it into the refrigerator.
6. X: Vielleicht können Sie die Teller auf den Tisch stellen.
   Y: _____
   Günter has just put them on the table.

---

[1] **die Mappe, -n**   *folder*
[2] **das Inserat, -e**   *ad, advertisement*
ein Inserat in die Zeitung setzen   *to put an ad in the newspaper*
[3] **gerade**   *just (now)*

Note the expression **die Teller auf den Tisch stellen** or **setzen** (*to put the plates on the table*) although it means placing the plates in a horizontal position.

§7   THE USES OF THE INTRANSITIVE VERBS *liegen, stehen,* AND *sitzen*

Just as German uses specialized verbs of putting, it often prefers to use specialized verbs of location. Compare:

transitive verbs (weak): expressing an activity	intransitive counterparts (strong): expressing a condition
legen — legte — gelegt stellen — stellte — gestellt setzen — setzte — gesetzt	liegen — lag — gelegen stehen — stand — gestanden sitzen — saß — gesessen

Examples:

a. Sie legt das Buch auf den Tisch.
     legte
     hat…gelegt
 	
 She lays (laid) the book on the table.
 (principal parts: *to lay—laid—laid*)
 or: *She puts (put) the book on the table.*
	Das Buch **liegt** auf dem Tisch.
	     lag
	     hat…gelegen
	
	 The book lies (lay) on the table.
	 (principal parts: *to lie—lay—lain*)
	 or: *The book is (was) on the table.*

b. Sie stellt die Bücher ins Regal.
     stellte
     hat…gestellt.
 	
 She puts (put) the books on the shelf.
	Die Bücher **stehen** im Regal.
	     standen
	     haben…gestanden.
	
	 The books are (were) on the shelf.

c. Sie setzt das Kind aufs Sofa.
     setzte
     hat…gesetzt.
 	
 She puts (put) the child on the sofa.
	Das Kind **sitzt** auf dem Sofa.
	     saß
	     hat…gesessen.
	
	 The child sits (sat) on the sofa.

two-way prepositions

Note: require the accusative   require the dative

20-7   A. Form sentences expressing a condition in the present, simple past, and present perfect.

MODEL: die Milch / im Kühlschrank / stehen
Die Milch steht im Kühlschrank.
Die Milch stand im Kühlschrank.
Die Milch hat im Kühlschrank gestanden.

1. das Buch / im Regal / stehen
2. die Brille / neben der Zeitung / liegen
3. Rainer / neben seiner Freundin / sitzen
4. das Foto[1] / auf dem Schreibtisch / stehen
5. deine Handschuhe / auf dem Fußboden[2] / liegen

B. State whether the following sentences express an activity or a condition, then express them in the simple past and present perfect.

1. In seinem Zimmer liegen alle Sachen auf dem Boden.
2. Rainer legt alle Sachen auf den Boden.
3. Der Teddybär sitzt auf Helgas Schreibtisch.
4. Helga setzt den Teddybären neben die Schreibtischlampe.
5. Monika stellt den neuen Sessel neben die Couch.
6. Der alte Sessel steht in der Ecke.

20-8   Form sentences that fit the context.

MODEL: Hannelore gibt Ihnen ein Glas Milch. Sie ist lauwarm (*lukewarm*).
Sie denken : Milch / nicht / Kühlschrank (pres. perf.)
Die Milch hat nicht im Kühlschrank gestanden.

1. Ingrid sucht wieder einmal ihre Brille. Sie sehen die Brille und sagen:
„neben / Zeitung"
2. Warum ist Ihr Mantel so zerknittert (*creased*)? Sie sagen:
„nicht / auf Bügel" (pres. perf.)
3. Meine Eltern erwarten Gäste. Ich frage, ob ich irgendwie helfen kann. Meine Mutter sagt:
„du / können / Teller und Gläser / auf Tisch"
Die Gäste wollen nach Hause gehen. Meine Mutter sagt:
„mein Mann / alle Mäntel / auf Bett" (pres. perf.)
4. In Reiners Zimmer liegen die meisten Bücher auf dem Boden. Sie fragen ihn:
„warum / du / Bücher / nicht / Regal"

---

[1] **das Foto, -s**   *photo(graph)*
    short form of **die Fotografie, -n**
    (note the change of gender)
[2] **der Fußboden, ·**   *floor*
    short : **der Boden, ·**

5. Meine neue Freundin hat mir ein Foto geschenkt.
   „ich/ auf Schreibtisch" (pres. perf.)

6. Frank sagt, daß er gestern im Konzert war. Sie haben ihn nicht gesehen.
   Sie fragen:
   „wo / du / sitzen?" (pres. perf.)

7. Sie wollten gestern Sabine etwas fragen, sind aber nicht in ihr Zimmer
   gegangen. Warum nicht?
   Schild   „Bitte nicht stören!" / Tür (pres. perf.)

8. Wenn man mich fragt, ob ich den Magister machen will, antworte ich:
   „das / von Noten / ab•hängen"

9. Ich frage Barbara, wie oder wo sie ihren neuen Freund kennengelernt
   hat. Sie antwortet:
   „ich / Inserat / Zeitung / setzen" (pres. perf.)

The Use of *sein* and *haben* With Some Verbs of Motion

§8 COMPARE THE FOLLOWING TWO USES OF *fahren*:

fahren
— used intransitively: Wir **sind** nach München gefahren.
We drove to Munich.
— used transitively: **Haben** Sie **den Wagen** gefahren?
   DIR. OBJ.
Did you drive the car?

Some verbs that are normally intransitive and take the auxiliary **sein** occasionally
have a direct object. Then, of course, they must use the auxiliary **haben.** Some of the
most common verbs that belong to this class are **fahren, fliegen, landen,** and **reiten.**

Examples:

a. Bergers **sind** mit ihrem Privatflugzeug nach Düsseldorf **geflogen.**
The Bergers flew to Düsseldorf in their private plane.

b. Frau Berger **hat das Flugzeug** zum ersten Mal **geflogen.**
Mrs. Berger flew the plane for the first time.

a. Wann **seid** ihr in Berlin **gelandet?**
When did you land in Berlin?

b. Wo **hat** der Pilot **das Flugzeug gelandet?**
Where did the pilot land the plane?

a. Wir **sind** heute morgen durch die Felder **geritten.**
We rode on horseback through the fields this morning.

b. Welcher Jockei **hat dieses Pferd geritten?**
Which jockey rode this horse?

PRACTICE

20-9   Restate the following sentences in the present perfect.

1. Barbara reitet viel zu schnell.
2. Warum reitet sie immer das schwarze Rennpferd?[1]
3. Fahren Sie mit dem Bus?
4. Wer fährt den Bus?
5. Wann fliegen Sie in die Schweiz?
6. Welcher Pilot fliegt diese Maschine?[2]
7. Hoffentlich landet er nicht im Gefängnis.[3]
8. In meinen schönsten Träumen lande ich ein Raumschiff[4] auf dem Mond.

Double Infinitive Constructions with *sehen, lassen, hören,* and *helfen*

§9   WHEN ACCOMPANIED BY ANOTHER VERB, *sehen, lassen, hören* **AND** *helfen* **OCCUR WITH DOUBLE INFINITIVE CONSTRUCTIONS IN COMPOUND TENSES. THEY FOLLOW THE EXAMPLE OF THE MODAL AUXILIARIES (CF. CHAP. 4, §3 TO §5)**

1. sehen

without a dependent infinitive	with a dependent infinitive
Wir sehen ihn.	Wir sehen ihn kommen
We see him.	*We see him coming.*
Wir sahen ihn.	Wir sahen ihn kommen.
Wir haben ihn **gesehen.**	Wir haben ihn **kommen sehen.**
Wir hatten ihn **gesehen.**	Wir hatten ihn **kommen sehen.**
Wir werden ihn **sehen.**	Wir werden ihn **kommen sehen.**
	The accompanying verb precedes **sehen.**

2. lassen

Wir haben den Koffer im Wagen **gelassen.**	Wir haben Klaus nicht allein **fahren lassen.**
We left the suitcase in the car.	*We didn't let Klaus drive alone.*

---

[1] **das Rennpferd, -e**   *racehorse*
[2] **die Maschine, -n**   *plane*
   (frequently used instead
   of **das Flugzeug**)
[3] **im Gefängnis landen**   *to wind up in prision*
[4] **das Raumschiff, -e**   *spaceship*

3. **hören** and **helfen**

Ich habe ihn nicht **gehört**.
I didn't hear him.

Ich habe ihn nie nie **lachen hören**.
or: Ich habe ihn nie lachen **gehört**.
I have never heard him laugh.

Ich habe ihr **geholfen**.
I helped her.

Ich habe ihr packen **helfen**.
or: Ich habe ihr packen **geholfen**.
I helped her pack.

Careful usage prefers the double infinitive, but the use of the past participle **gehört** or **geholfen** is also considered to be correct.

PRACTICE

20-10   **A.** Restate the following sentences in the present perfect tense.

1. Ich sehe Karin oft im Garten arbeiten.
2. Sehen Sie auch manchmal Peter im Garten?
3. Klaus hilft Andreas umziehen.¹
4. Wir alle helfen ihm.
5. Hören Sie den Hund bellen?
6. Die ganze Nachbarschaft hört ihn.
7. Man läßt mich nicht rauchen.
8. Unser Baby läßt uns nicht schlafen.
9. Ich lasse meine Sachen im Schließfach.²
10. Man läßt mich nicht in Ruhe.³
11. Warum lassen Sie mich nicht ausreden?⁴
12. Wir lassen unsere Kinder nicht gern allein zu Hause.
13. Sehen Sie die zwei Polizisten winken?⁵
14. Ich sehe nur einen Polizisten.

B. Translate into German, using the present perfect for the English past tense.

1. a. I hear the baby crying.   **Ich höre das Baby weinen.**
   b. Do you hear the baby crying? (formal)
   c. Did you hear the baby crying?
   d. I didn't hear it.
2. a. I see her waving.   **Ich sehe sie winken.**
   b. Do you see her waving? (fam. sing.)
   c. Did you see her waving? (fam. plural)
   d. I didn't see that.

---

¹ **um·ziehon, zog um, ist umgezogen**   *to move*
² **das Schließfach, ¨er**   *locker*
³ **in Ruhe lasse (läßt), ließ, gelassen**   *to leave alone*
⁴ **aus·reden lassen**   *to let finish (talking)*
⁵ **winken**   *to wave*

3. a. Let him finish (*talking*). (fam. sing.)   **Laß ihn ausreden!**
    b. Please let me finish (*talking*). (fam. sing., formal)
    c. They didn't let me finish (*talking*).
4. a. Leave her alone. (fam. sing.)   **Laß sie in Ruhe!**
    b. Please leave me alone. (fam. sing., formal)
    c. We left him alone.

THE CAUSATIVE MEANING OF *lassen*

Ich lasse ihn den Wagen waschen.

I let him wash the car. (expressing permission)

or: *I'm having him wash the car.* (expressing causation)

In German **lassen** is used to express both permission and causation; the meaning must be determined from context. The sentences in the preceding section use **lassen** in the sense of *to leave* and *to let*. In this section we shall deal with the causative use of **lassen**.

In German, as in English, the person who actually carries out the action need not be mentioned. When this person is omitted, German continues to use a complementary infinitive, whereas English uses a past participle.

PRESENT	Ich lasse meinen Wagen **waschen**.		*I am having my car **washed**.*
	Ich lasse	ihn	**waschen**.	*I am having it **washed**.*
PRES. PERF.	Ich habe meinen Wagen **waschen lassen**.		*I had my car **washed**.*
	Ich habe	ihn	**waschen lassen**.	*I had it **washed**.*

PRACTICE

20-11   **A.** Express the responses in German using the present tense.

MODEL: X: Kannst du den Fernseher selbst reparieren?
          Y: <u>Nein. Ich lasse ihn reparieren.</u>

            No. I'll have it repaired.

1. X: Kannst du die Bewerbung selbst tippen?
    Y: _____
       No. I'll have it typed.
2. X: Wollen Sie den Rasen selbst mähen?[1]
    Y: _____
       No. I'll have it mowed.
3. X: Wollen Sie das Paket selbst abholen?
    Y: _____
       No. I'll have it picked up.
4. X: Putzen[2] Sie die Fenster selbst?
    Y: _____
       No. I'll have them washed.

---

[1] **den Rasen mähen**   *to mow the lawn*
[2] **die Fenster putzen**   *to clean or wash the windows*

5. X: Entwickeln[1] Sie Ihre Filme selbst?
   Y: _____
      No. I'll have them developed.
6. X: Wollen Sie Ihr Haus selbst streichen?[2]
   Y: _____
      No. We'll have it painted.

B. Express the responses in German using the present perfect tense.

MODEL: X: Wann läßt du den Fernseher reparieren?
         Y: **Ich habe ihn schon reparieren lassen.**

         I already had it repaired.

1. X: Wann läßt du den Film entwickeln?
   Y: _____
      I already had it developed.
2. X: Wann lassen Sie Ihr Haus streichen?
   Y: _____
      We already had it painted.
3. X: Läßt du deine Semesterarbeit tippen?
   Y: _____
      I already had it typed.
4. X: Wann lassen Sie den Rasen mähen?
   Y: _____
      We already had it mowed.
5. X: Wann läßt du deinen Mantel reinigen?[3]
   Y: _____
      I already had it cleaned.

Lassen is also used reflexively: **sich etwas machen lassen** means *to have something done to* or *for oneself.*

sich die Haare schneiden lassen   *to have one's hair cut, get a haircut*

PRESENT   Ich lasse mir die Haare schneiden. ⟨ *I'm having my haircut.*
                                                 I'm getting a haircut.

PRES. PERF.   Ich habe mir die Haare schneiden lassen. ⟨ *I had my haircut.*
                                                           I got a haircut.

sich eine Dauerwelle machen lassen   *to get a permanent*

         Sie läßt **sich** eine Dauerwelle machen.   *She is getting a permanent.*
         Sie hat **sich** eine Dauerwelle machen lassen.   *She got a permanent.*

Note that the reflexive pronoun is in the dative case because the sentences contain a direct object: **die Haare, eine Dauerwelle** (cf. Chap. 17, §2).

---

[1] entwickeln   *to develop*
[2] streichen, strich, gestrichen   *to paint*
[3] reinigen lassen   *to have dry-cleaned*

20-12   Translate into German, using the present perfect for the English past tense.

1. a. I am getting a haircut.   **Ich lasse mir die Haare schneiden.**
    b. She is getting a haircut.
    c. He got a haircut.
    d. Did he get a haircut? (fam. sing., formal)
    e. Did you get a haircut? (fam. sing., formal)
2. a. I am getting a permanent.   **Ich lasse mir eine Dauerwelle machen.**
    b. He is getting a permanent.
    c. She got a permanent.
    d. Did you get a permanent? (fam. sing., formal)

20-13   Form sentences that fit the context.

MODEL: Frank hat gestern wunderbar Flöte (*flute*) gespielt. Ich frage
Margot:
„du / hören / spielen?" (pres. perf.)
„Hast du ihn Flöte spielen hören?"

1. Neumanns haben seit gestern einen Hund. Er hat die ganze Nacht gebellt.
Ulrich fragt mich:
„du / hören / bellen?" (pres. perf.)
2. Ich gehe mit Susanne spazieren. Ihre Schwester fährt an uns vorbei.
Susanne fragt mich:
„du / sehen / winken?" (pres. perf.)
3. Hartmut hat schlechte Laune. Ich will ihn aufheitern (*cheer up*). Er sagt
sehr unfreundlich:
„lassen / in Ruhe!"
4. Martin unterbricht mich immer. Ich sage:
„bitte / lassen / aus•reden!"
5. Brigitte hatte mich mißverstanden. Ich wollte die Sache klären, konnte es
aber nicht.
Brigitte / mich / nicht / lassen / aus•reden. (pres. perf.)
6. Mein Wagen läuft jetzt ausgezeichnet. Warum?
ich / lassen / reparieren (pres. perf.)
7. Wir haben unser Wochenendhaus nicht selbst gestrichen.
wir / lassen / streichen (pres. perf.)
8. Sie fragen Uwe, ob er die Bewerbung selbst getippt hat. Er antwortet:
„Nein, / ich / lassen / tippen." (pres. perf.)
9. Ich frage Anita, ob ihr Mantel neu ist. Sie antwortet:
„Nein, das ist der alte. ich / lassen / reinigen." (pres. perf.)
10. Irene hat eine neue Frisur. (hairdo)
„sie / sich / lassen / machen / Dauerwelle. (pres. perf.)
11. Meine Freundin findet, daß ich heute viel jünger aussehe. Ich sage:
„ich / sich / lassen / schneiden / die Haare" (pres. perf.)

German Equivalents of Two Special Meanings of *would*

§10 *would* Expressing Past Habitual Occurences

Compare the following two sentences:

a. *If she heard such nonsense, she **would laugh** about it.*
   Wenn sie so einen Unsinn hörte, **würde** sie darüber **lachen**.
b. *When she heard such nonsense, she **would laugh** about it.*
                            (used to)
   Wenn sie so einen Unsinn hörte, **lachte** sie **gewöhnlich** darüber.

Sentence *a.* is contrary-to-fact statement using **würde** + infinitive
in the conclusion. (cf. Chap. 13, §5)
Sentence *b.* expresses a past habitual occurence: *would laugh*
means *used to laugh*. German uses the adverb **gewöhnlich** (usually)
and expresses the sentence in the simple past or present perfect.

Additional examples for the expression of past habitual occurances:

My grandfather **would / used to get** very nervous, when he could not find his pipe.
Mein Großvater **wurde gewöhnlich** sehr nervös, wenn er seine Pfeife nicht finden konnte.
*To save money, we **would / used to stay overnight** in cheap motels.*
Um Geld zu sparen, **haben** wir **gewöhnlich** in billigen Motels **übernachtet**.

PRACTICE

20-14   Complete the following sentences in German.

Model: X: Wer in Ihrer Familie hat meistens den Rasen gemäht?
         Y: Ich habe gewöhnlich den Rasen gemäht.
            I would / used to mow the lawn.

1. X: Wer in eurer Familie hat meistens das Geschirr gespült?
   Y: _____
      My sister would / used to do the dishes.
2. X: Wie oft hast du Julia angerufen?
   Y: Sehr oft. _____
      I would / used to call her every day.
3. X: Habt ihr oft einen Spaziergang gemacht?
   Y: _____ , wenn wir uns entspannen[1] wollten.
      We would / used to take a walk

---

[1] sich entspannen   *to relax*

4. X: Hast du manchmal Überstunden gemacht?¹

Y: _____ , wenn ich Geld brauchte.

I would / used to work overtime

5. X: Bist du gut mit Alexander ausgekommen?²

Y: Ja und nein. _____ , wenn er und

I would / used to get along well with him

ich gute Laune hatten.

6. X: Seid ihr oft sonntags zu Hause geblieben?

Y: _____ , wenn wir pleite waren, und das war

We would /used to stay at home   ziemlich oft.³

§11 *would* HAVING THE MEANING OF *was/were willing to*

When *would* has the meaning of *was/were willling to*, it is expressed in German by **wollte**, as the following example illustrates.

> *The case was hopeless, but nobody **would/was willing to** give it up.*
> Der Fall war hoffnungslos, aber niemand **wollte** ihn aufgeben.

For greater emphasis English often adds the adverb *just* in such sentences.

> *We asked Bettina what was bothering her, but she just **wouldn't / wasn't willing to** tell us.*
> Wir fragten Bettina, was ihr Sorgen machte, aber sie **wollte** es uns **einfach** nicht sagen.

Here the German equivalent of *just* is **einfach.**

PRACTICE

20-15   Complete the responses in German.

MODEL: X: Hoffentlich hat sich Tilo entschuldigt.

Y: Er war sehr stur und wollte sich einfach nicht entschuldigen.

just wouldn't / wasn't willing to apologize.

1. X: Wie ich höre, hat Ihr Partner nicht nachgegeben.

Y: Ich habe alles versucht, aber _____

he just wouldn't / wasn't willing to give in.

2. X: Hoffentlich haben die Kinder den Salat gegessen.

Y: Der Salat war sehr gut, aber _____

they just wouldn't / weren't willing to eat it.

3. X: Hat dein Vater den Vertrag unterschrieben?

Y: Nein. Die ganze Familie hat ihn darum gebeten, aber

_____

he just wouldn't / wasn't willing to sign it.

---

¹ **Überstunden machen**   *to work overtime*

² **aus•kommen mit** (dat.)   *to get along with*

   kam aus, ist ausgekommen

³ **ziemlich oft**   *quite often*

4. X: Warum warst du gestern allein im Konzert?

   Y: _____

     Because nobody would / was willing to come along.

5. X: Warum hat Karola die beiden Koffer selbst zum Bus getragen?

   Y: _____

     Because nobody would / was willing to help Karola.

The Subjunctive Use of Modal Auxiliaries

§12   COMPARE THE USE OF *müssen* IN THE FOLLOWING SENTENCES

   a. Thomas sucht eine bessere Stelle. Er **muß** mehr Geld verdienen.
     Thomas is looking for a better job. He must make more money.

   b. Unser Nachbar hat ein großes neues Haus gekauft. Er **muß** viel Geld verdienen.
     Our neighbor bought a big new house. He must make a lot of money.

In *a.* the modal **müssen** expresses the necessity of making more money. In *b.* the speaker concludes that his neighbor is making a lot of money from the fact that he has bought a big new house. That is his judgment, a subjective sizing up of the situation. **Müssen** is used subjectively rather than objectively, as in *a.*

Structurally, the objective and subjective uses look identical. The meaning of the modal must be derived from the context. However, when the subjective modal refers to a past act or state, it differs structurally from the objective modal.

Compare:

     Thomas **mußte** mehr Geld verdienen. *Thomas had to make more money.*

The objective modal is in the simple past.

     Herr Berger hat einige Jahre in Alaska gearbeitet. Als er zurückkam, hat er ein Hotel gekauft.
     Er **muß** viel Geld **verdient haben**, als er in Alaska war.

             perfect infinitive

     Mr. Berger worked in Alaska for a few years. When he came back, he bought a hotel.
     *He **must have made** a lot of money when he was in Alaska.*

          perfect infinitive

This is a present inference about a past situation. Thus in both languages the modal is in the present tense and the accompanying verb in the perfect infinitive (cf. Chap. 3, §12).

Additional examples of the subjective use of **müssen**:

PRESENT   Das **muß** ein Mißverständnis **sein.**
*That **must be** a misunderstanding.*

PAST   Das **muß** ein Mißverständnis **gewesen sein.**
*That **must have been** a misunderstanding.*

PRESENT   Er **muß** Schwierigkeiten in Chemie **haben.**
*He **must have** problems in chemistry.*

PAST   Er **muß** Schwierigkeiten in Chemie **gehabt haben.**
*He **must have had** problems in chemistry.*

Keep in mind: The modal is in the present tense; the dependent infinitive is either a *simple infinitive* (referring to a present action or state) or a *perfect infinitive* (referring to a past action or state).

Examples for the objective and subjective uses of *können, mögen, sollen,* **and** *wollen*

<u>können</u>

objective: a. expressing ability

Ich kann (konnte) das verstehen.
I can (could) understand that.

b. Expressing objective possibility

Wir können (konnten) mit dem Bus vom Flughafen in die Stadt fahren.
We can (could) go by bus from the airport to town.

subjective: expressing a subjectively perceived possibility

PRESENT   Das **kann** wahr **sein.**
That may be true.

PAST   Das **kann** wahr **gewesen sein.**
That may have been true.

<u>mögen</u>

Objective: expressing liking

Ich mag (mochte) ihn nicht fragen.
I don't (didn't) like to ask him.

subjective: expressing a subjectively perceived possibility similar to the use of **können.** (**Mögen** has a more literary connotation.)

PRESENT   Das **mag sein.**
That may be so.

PAST   Das **mag** eine gute Idee **gewesen sein**.
That may have been a good idea.

<u>sollen</u>

objective: expressing obligation

> Der Bürgermeister soll (sollte) eine Rede halten.
> *The mayor is (was) expected to make a speech.*
> or: *The mayor is (was) supposed to make a speech.*

subjective: expressing rumors, hearsay

PRESENT   Sie **soll** sehr reich **sein.**
She is said to be very rich.
or: *She is supposed to be very rich.*

PAST   Sie **soll** sehr reich **gewesen sein**.
They say she was very rich.
or: *She is supposed to have been very rich.*

Note that English **to be supposed to** has similar dual function. It has both objective meaning (*to be expected to*) and subjective meaning (*to be said to*).

<u>wollen</u>

objective: expressing a wish or an intention

> Hannelore will (wollte) das erledigen.
> *Hannelore wants (wanted) to take care of that.*
> or: *Hannelore intends (intended) to take care of that.*

subjective: expressing the speaker's or writer's reservation about someone's claim

PRESENT   Er **will** ein großer Musiker **sein.**
He claims to be a great musician.
(But I have my doubts.)

PAST   Er **will** ein großer Musiker gewesen **sein.**
He claims to have been a great musician.
(But I have my doubts.)
or: *He claims that he was a great musician.*

PRACTICE

20-16   Translate the following sentences into English and then reproduce the German from your translation.

1. Das kann eine Lüge sein.
2. Das kann ein Irrtum[1] gewesen sein.
3. Das mag ein Fehler sein.
4. Das mag eine Ausrede[2] gewesen sein
5. Sabine Richter soll eine gute Schauspielerin sein.
6. Herr Bachmann soll in seiner Jugend ein guter Fußballspieler gewesen sein.

---

[1] **der Irrtum, ̈er**   *error*
[2] **die Ausrede, -n**   *excuse, pretended reason, pretext*

7. Schreibers wollen ein Haus an der Riviera haben, aber das glaubt niemand.
8. Rainer will zwei Jahre in Rom studiert haben, aber ich kann das nicht glauben.
9. Renate schreibt mir nicht mehr. Sie muß mich vergessen haben.
10. Der junge Tenor aus Hamburg hat nicht gut gesungen.
    Er muß Lampenfieber[1] gehabt haben.
11. Petra und Martin wollen eine fliegende Untertasse[2] gesehen haben.

THE MODAL IN THE SUBJUNCTIVE

To make a statement seem more tentative and cautious, the subjective modal may be expressed in the subjunctive mood. This is particularly true with **können.**

PRESENT   Das **könnte** wahr **sein.**
           That might (could) be true.

PAST   Das **könnte** wahr **gewesen sein.**
           That might (could) have been true.

PRACTICE

20-17   Express the responses in German.

1. X: Warum spricht der Redner so leise und so schnell?
   Y: He might be nervous.
2. X: Marlene hat gestottert,[3] als sie sich entschuldigte.
   Y: She might have been nervous.
3. X: Warum sagt Jürgen seinen Eltern nicht die Wahrheit?
   Y: He might be afraid.
4. X: Warum hat mir meine Freundin nicht die Wahrheit gesagt?
   Y: She might have been afraid.
5. X: Ich möchte wissen, warum mich Ruth nicht angerufen hat.
   Y: She might have forgotten it.

PRACTICE

20-18   Express in German.

1. a. That's an error.   **Das ist ein Irrtum.**
   b. That must be an error.
   c. That must have been an error.
2. a. That's a coincidence.   **Das ist ein Zufall.**
   b. That may be a coincidence. (Use **können**)
   c. That may have been a coincidence.

---

[1] das Lampenfieber   *stage fright*
[2] die fliengende Untertasse, -n   *flying saucer*
[3] stottern   *to stutter*

    d. That might be a coincidence.

    e. That might have been a coincidence.

  3. a. She is a child prodigy.   **Sie est ein Wunderkind.**

    b. She is supposed (said) to be a child prodigy.

    c. She is supposed (said) to have been a child prodigy.

  4. a. He's very popular.   **Er ist sehr beliebt.**

    b. He must be very popular.

    c. He must have been very popular.

    d. He claims to be very popular.

    e. He claims to have been very popular.

  5. a. They know many famous artists in Europe. **Sie kennen viele berühmte Künstler in Europa.**

    b. They claim to know many famous artists in Europe.

    c. They are supposed (said) to know many famous artists in Europe.

    d. They must know Janna Hendrik.

    e. They must have known Picasso.

    f. They might have to known your famous grandfather. (fam. sing.)

Appositives

§13 AN APPOSITIVE IS AN EXPLANATORY NOUN PHRASE WHICH FOLLOWS IMMEDIATELY THE NOUN OR PRONOUN IT MODIFIES

Peter Stein, **der berühmte Pianist**, hat den Beethoven-Preis gewonnen.
      | |
   SUBJ.,   NOM
   NOM.

Peter Stein, the famous pianist, won the Beethoven Prize.

The appositive is normally in the same case as the element it modifies. In the above example, the appositive, **der berühmte Pianist**, is in the nominative because it modifies the subject of the sentence, **Peter Stein**.

Examples in other cases:

Wir haben ihm, **dem berühmten Pianisten**, zu seinem Erfolg gratuliert.
        DAT.   DAT.
We congratulated him, the famous pianist, on his success.

Wir haben ihn, **den berühmten Pianisten**, um ein Autogramm gebeten.
        ACC.   ACC.
We asked him, the famous pianist, for an autograph.

Sie ist die Tochter Peter Steins, **des berühmten Pianisten**.
               GEN.   GEN.
She is the daughter of Peter Stein, the famous pianist.

Sie kommt aus Rossau, **einem kleinen Dorf** in Sachsen.

DAT.   DAT.

She comes (is) from Rossau, a little village in Saxony.

Diese Blumen sind für meine Großmutter, **die Mutter** meines Vaters.

ACC.   ACC.

These flowers are for my grandmother, the mother of my father (my father's mother).

PRACTICE

20-19 The elements in parentheses are stated in the nominative. Insert them as appositives in the appropiate cases.

MODEL: Wir haben Herrn Bauer, _____ , in der Stadt getroffen.
(ein guter Freund meiner Eltern)
Wir haben Herrn Bauer, einen guten Freund meiner Eltern, in der Stadt getroffen.

1. Frau Zimmermann, _____ , hat mich gestern angerufen. (eine gute Freundin meiner Mutter)
2. Das ist ein Geschenk für meinen Onkel Werner, _____ (der Bruder meines Vaters)
3. Kennen Sie Ulf Schreiber, _____ ? (der erste Preisträger[1])
4. Das ist Andreas Krause, _____ . (der zweite Preisträger)
5. Ich habe mit Thomas Köhler, _____ gesprochen. (der dritte Preisträger)
6. Erika hat mir viel von Berlin, _____ , erzählt (ihre Heimatstadt)
7. Wir wollen mit Körners, _____ , in die Stadt fahren. (unsere Nachbarn)
8. Maria kommt aus Villingen, _____ . (eine kleine Stadt im Schwarzwald)
9. Wir sprechen von Hannelore, _____ . (die jüngste Tochter von Schmidts)
10. Mit Herrn Winkler, _____ , möchte ich nicht verheiratet sein. (dieser Schürzenjäger[2])

---

[1] **der Preisträger, -**　　　*prize winner*
[2] **der Schürzenjäger, -**　　*womanizer* (lit.: *apron hunter*)

Extended Adjective Constructions

§14 ADJECTIVES PRECEDING NOUNS MAY BE EXTENDED BY ADDITIONAL MODIFIERS

> Herr Krause hat die **schon lange überfällige** Entschädigung noch nicht erhalten.
> *Mr. Krause has not yet received the **long overdue** compensation.*

In this sentence, the adjective **überfällig** is modified by a time expression, **schon lange**. Because this expression is relatively short, both English and German permit the modified adjective to precede the noun. But if the modification of the adjective is more extensive, only German permits the construction to precede the noun. English requires that the adjective construction be placed after the noun often as part of a relative clause.

> Herr Krause hat die **schon seit mehr als drei Monaten fällige** Entschädigung noch nicht erhalten.
> *Mr. Krause has not yet received the compensation **due for more than three months.***
> or: *Mr. Krause has not yet received the compensation **which has been due for more than three months.***

These *extended adjective constructions* occur frequently in written German (literary and scientific texts, newspapers and periodicals). In most instances the adjective is a present or past participle (cf. Chap. 9, §13).

Present participle:

> Der schon seit Monaten **steigende** Preis für Benzin hat zu wirtschaftlichen Schwierigkeiten geführt.
> *The price of gas, which has been rising for months, has led to economic difficulties.*

When preceded by **zu**, the present participle has passive meaning and implies obligation or possibility. There are several English equivalents: *to be, can be, may be, must be, should be* + past participle, depending on the context.

> die heute **zu** bezahlenden Rechnungen
>
> *the bills to be paid today*
> or: *the bills that must be paid today*
> or: *the bills that should be paid today*

Note the position of **zu** if the participle has a separable prefix:

> die nicht voraus**zu**sehenden Schwierigkeiten
>
> *the difficulties that cannot be foreseen*
> or: *the dificulties that may not be foreseen*

Past participle:

> Der im vorigen Jahr so hoch **gestiegene** Preis für Benzin hat zu
> wirtschaftlichen Schwierigkeiten geführt.
>
> *The price of gas, which has climbed so high in the past year, has led to*
> *economic difficulties.*
>
> Alle noch nicht **bezahlten** Rechnungen sind in dieser Mappe.
> *All bills that have not yet been paid are in this folder.*

Rendering extended adjective constructions into idiomatic English often poses considerable problems. Here are a few hints as to how to proceed.

1　　　　　4　　　　　　　3　　　　　　　2

Auf Seite 10 finden wir die bei jungen Leuten sehr beliebten Fernsehsendungen.

First bring together the beginning and the end of the extended adjective construction, i.e. the article **die** (1) and the noun **Fernsehsendungen** (2). Then proceed backwards: Take first the adjective that immediately precedes the noun, i.e. **beliebten** (*popular*). It is modified by the adverb **sehr.** Thus **sehr beliebten** is the third unit. It is preceded by the fourth unit, **bei jungen Leuten.** The result is:

> *On page 10 we find the TV programs that are very popular with young people.*

PRACTICE

20-20   Express in acceptable English.

1. Das ist eine erst neuerdings¹ aufgetauchte² Frage.
2. Die Regierung muß dieses von vielen nicht erkannte Problem lösen.
3. Er ist ein auf der ganzen Welt bekannter Gelehrter.
4. Der Höhepunkt des Konzerts war ein vom Komponisten selbst dirigiertes³ Werk.
5. Die von vielen Gegnern⁴ angegriffene⁵ Journalistin ist ihren Grundsätze⁶ treu geblieben.
6. In diesem 100 km von München entfernt liegenden Dorf gibt es ein reizendes⁷ Gasthaus mit einem ausgezeichneten Koch.

---

¹ **erst neuerdings**	*only recently*
² **auf·tauchen**	*to emerge, come up*
³ **dirigieren**	*to conduct* (music)
⁴ **der Gegner, -**	*opponent*
⁵ **an·greifen,**	*to attack*
griff an, angegriffen	
⁶ **der Grundsatz, ⁻e**	*principle*
⁷ **reizend**	*charming*

7. Die Lohnerhöhungen[1] bleiben hinter den von Monat zu Monat steigenden Lebenshaltungskosten[2] zurück.

8. Der in eine Seitenstraße einbiegende[3] Bus stieß mit einem Lastwagen[4] zusammen.[5]

9. Man hat die bei diesem Unfall verletzten[6] Fahrgäste[7] in das Albert-Schweitzer-Krankenhaus gebracht.

10. Die Bürgermeisterin gab einen Überblick[8] über die in diesem Jahr zu lösenden Probleme.

11. Die Diskussionen über die noch zu klärenden Fragen beginnen am Montag.

12. Die am Anfang des zwanzigsten Jahrhunderts viel gelesenen Romane dieses Autors sind jetzt völlig[9] in Vergessenheit geraten.[10] Das ist eine nicht zu leugnende[11] Tatsache.[12]

More than one extended adjective construction in one sentence

Often there is more than one extended adjective construction in a sentence. If they modify the same noun, translate the first one completely, then add the next one, etc. In the following example, the two constructions *a* and *b* modify the noun **Fernsehsendungen**.

Auf Seite 10 finden wir die bei jungen Leuten sehr beliebten

a

aber von den Eltern oft kritisierten **Fernsehsendungen**.

b

On page 10 we find the TV programs that are very popular with young people, but are often criticized by parents.

If the constructions modify different nouns, each is translated directly after the corresponding noun. In the following sentences, the construction *a*. modifies **Seite 10** and the construction *b*. modifies **Fernsehsendungen**.

Auf der weitere Auskunft erteilenden **Seite 10** finden

a

wir die bei jungen Leuten sehr beliebten **Fernsehsendungen**.

b

---

[1] die Lohnerhöhung, -en	*wage increase*
[2] die Lebenshaltungskosten (pl.)	*cost of living*
[3] ein·biegen, bog ein, ist eingebogen	*to turn into* (a street)
[4] der Lastwagen, -	*truck*
[5] zusammen·stoßen (stößt zusammen), stieß zusammen, ist zusammengestoßen	*to collide*
[6] verletzt	*injured*
[7] der Fahrgast, ⁻e	passenger
[8] der Überblick, -e	*overview*
[9] völlig	*completely*
[10] in Vergessenheit geraten	*to fall into oblivion, be forgotten*
[11] leugnen	*to deny*
[12] die Tatsache, -n	*fact*

On page 10 which gives further information, we find the TV programs that are very popular with young people.

PRACTICE

20-21   Express in English.

1. Die schon seit mehr als drei Monaten fällige und trotz wiederholter Mahnungen[1] noch nicht erhaltene[2] Bezahlung wird durch SUMA kassiert[3] werden.

2. Der bei dem Autounfall vor der Sporthalle schwer verletzte und per Hubschrauber[4] in die Zentralklinik gebrachte Fahrer hat das Bewußtsein noch nicht wiedererlangt.[5]

3. Die schon seit Jahren mit Erfolg auf dem Gebiet[6] der Genetik tätige[7] Forscherin[8] hat jetzt ein sehr kompliziertes und an ihr Können[9] hohe Ansprüche stellendes[10] Projekt in Angriff genommen.[11]

4. Die mit fieberhaftem Eifer[12] und höchster Konzentration arbeitenden Mechaniker tun alles, was menschenmöglich ist,[13] damit die mit den modernsten Geräten[14] ausgestattete[15] Jacht im nächsten Rennen[16] erfolgreich konkurrieren[17] kann.

The Passive in the Subjunctive Mood

Chapters 13 and 14 treated only the active forms of the subjunctive. Passive subjunctive forms also occur, principally in indirect discourse and in unreal conditions and conclusions. They are much less common, since in general the passive voice is far less frequently used than the active voice.

---

[1] die Mahnung, -en   *reminder*
[2] erhalten (erhält)   *to receive*
  erhielt, erhalten
[3] kassieren   *to collect*
[4] der Hubschrauber, -   *helicopter*
[5] das Bewußtsein wiedererlangen   *to regain consciousness*
[6] das Gebiet, -e   *area, field*
[7] tätig sein   *to work, to be active*
[8] die Forscherin, -nen   *research scientist*
[9] das Können   *ability*
[10] Ansprüche stellen an   *to make demands on*
[11] in Angriff nehmen   *to tackle, embark on*
[12] der Eifer   *zeal*
[13] alles, was menschenmöglich ist   *all that is humanly possible*
[14] das Gerät, -e   *device*
[15] aus•statten   *to equip*
[16] das Rennen, -   *race*
[17] konkurrieren   *to compete*

§15 SUBJUNCTIVES IN INDIRECT DISCOURSE

(For their use in the active voice, see Chap. 14, §6 and §7.)

In indirect discourse the subjunctive occurs in three tenses: present, past, and future. The following synopsis shows two different auxiliaries for each tense: the general subjunctive (first form) and the special subjunctive (second form). The two forms have the same meaning.

direct quote	indirect quote
present indicative	present subjunctive
Der Polizist sagte:	Der Polizist sagte,
„Der Fall wird untersucht."	der Fall **würde** untersucht.
	werde
any past indicative	past subjunctive
„Der Fall wurde untersucht."	der Fall **wäre** untersucht worden.
„Der Fall ist untersucht worden"	**sei**
„Der Fall war untersucht worden."	
future indicative	future subjunctive
„Der Fall wird untersucht werden."	der Fall **würde** untersucht werden.
	werde

Note: The auxiliaries **würde/werde** and **wäre/sei** signal the subjunctive.

Examples:

Die Kandidatin sagte: „Mein Name wird nicht erwähnt."
Die Kandidatin sagte, ihr Name **würde/werde** nicht erwähnt.

Der Architekt sagte: „Das Projekt wird von der Regierung finanziert werden."
Der Architekt sagte, das Projekt **würde/werde** von der Regierung finanziert werden.

Die Polizistin sagte: „Der Dieb wurde gestern verhaftet."
Die Polizistin sagte, der Dieb **wäre/sei** gestern verhaftet worden.

PRACTICE
20-22   Change to indirect quotations stating both subjunctives, as in the preceding examples.

1. Eine Beamtin sagte: „Ich werde wohl auch nicht befördert."
2. Eine andere Beamtin sagte: „Ich werde wohl auch nicht befördert werden."
3. Frau Köhler sagte: „Ich wurde nicht gefragt."
4. Herr Köhler sagte: „Meine Frau wird doch immer gefragt."
5. Frau Lange sagte: „Ich bin schon wieder betrogen[1] worden."
6. Ihre Nachbarin sagte: „Leider wurde Frau Lange nicht gewarnt."

---

[1] betrügen, betrog, betrogen   *to cheat*

7. Der Reporter sagte: „Der Redner wird zu oft unterbrochen."
8. Die Zuhörer sagten: „Der Redner ist noch nie so oft unterbrochen worden."
9. Frau Martin sagte: „Der Bürgermeister wurde zuviel kritisiert."
10. Ihr Mann sagte: „Seine Vorgängerin[1] war noch mehr kritisiert worden."
11. Die Agentin sagte: „Diese Reise wird vom Chef bezahlt."
12. Die Chefsekretärin sagte: „Die Reise wird wohl nicht von ihm bezahlt werden."

In the plural, the form **werden** of the special subjunctive is identical to the indicative form **werden** (cf. Chap. 14, §7). It is therefore replaced with the general subjunctive form **würden.** Thus the synopsis for plural forms is as follows:

present indicative	present subjunctive
Der Polizist sagte:	Der Polzist sagte,
„Die Fälle werden untersucht."	die Fälle **würden** untersucht.
any past tense subjunctive	past subjunctive
„Die Fälle wurden untersucht."	
„Die Fälle sind untersucht worden."	die Fälle **wären** untersucht worden
„Die Fälle waren untersucht worden."	**seien**
future indicative	future subjunctive
„Die Fälle werden untersucht werden."	die Fälle **würden** untersucht werden.

REMEMBER: In the plural, only the **würde** forms are used in the present and future.

PRACTICE

20-23   Change to indirect quotations following the models of sentences 1 and 2.

Er/Sie sagte: Er/Sie sagte,
1. „Diese Uhren werden exportiert."   **diese Uhren würden exportiert.**
2. „Viele Fehler wurden übersehen."   **Viele Fehler wären/seien übersehen worden.**

3. „Einige Schecks sind noch nicht eingelöst worden."
4. „Die Arbeiter von MAFRASA werden nicht gut bezahlt."
5. „Die Arbeiter werden wohl ausgenutzt werden."
6. „Diese Sachen sind noch nicht erledigt worden."
7. „Zwei Straßennamen werden geändert."
8. „Die Hausnummern sind schon geändert worden."

---

[1] **der Vorgänger, -**   *predecessor*
(female) **-in, -innen**

§16   SUBJUNCTIVES AND UNREAL CONDITIONS AND CONCLUSIONS

(For their use in the active voice, see Chap. 13)

In unreal conditions and conclusions, only the general subjunctive is used. It occurs in two tenses:

a.   the present subjunctive referring to the present and future,
b.   the past subjunctive referring to the past.

1.   **Wenn**-clauses expressing unreal conditions

a. Wenn der Fall **untersucht würde**...   *If the case **were investigated**...*
present subjunctive

b. Wenn der Fall **untersucht worden wäre**...   *If the case had been*
past subjunctive   ***investigated**...*

Note that the **wenn**-clause is a dependent clause; thus the inflected auxiliary is in last position.

Pattern				
a. present subj.	Wenn... _____ **würde** past part.		*If ... **were** _____* past part.	
b. past subj.	Wenn... _____ **worden wäre** past part.		*If ... **had been** _____* past part.	

PRACTICE

20-24   Add German wenn-clauses following the models of sentences 1.a + b.

1. a. Ich werde nicht gefragt, aber **wenn ich gefragt würde**...
         if I were asked...
    b. Ich wurde nicht gefragt, aber **wenn ich gefragt worden wäre**...
         if I had been asked
2. a. Ich werde nicht ausgenutzt, aber _____ ...
         if I were exploited
    b. Ich wurde nicht ausgenutzt, aber _____ ...
         if I had been exploited
3. a. Mein Name wird nicht erwähnt, aber _____ ...
         if it were mentioned
    b. Mein Name wurde nicht erwähnt, aber _____ ...
         if it had been mentioned
4. a. Diese zwei Projekte werden nicht von der Regierung finanziert, aber
         _____ ...
         if they were financed by the government
    b. Diese zwei Projekte wurden nicht von der Regierung finanziert, aber
         _____ ...
         if they had been financed by the government
5. a. Diese Fehler werden nicht gemacht, aber _____ ...
         if they were made

b. Diese Fehler wurden nicht gemacht, aber _____ ...

if they had been made

6. a. Der Streik wird nicht abgesagt, aber _____ ...

if it were called off

b. Der Streik wurde nicht abgesagt, aber _____ ...

if it had been called off

2. Unreal conclusions

a. referring to the present and future:

Wenn es nach mir **ginge**, (dann) **würde** der Fall **untersucht**.
*If it were up to me, (then) the case **would be investigated**.*

b. referring to the past:

Wenn es nach mir **gegangen wäre**, (dann) **wäre** der Fall **untersucht worden**.
*If it **had been** up to me, (then) the case **would have been investigated**.*

The conclusion (main clause) has inverted word order, because it is preceded by the dependent **wenn**-clause.

Pattern				
a. present subj.	**würde** _____ past part.		would be _____ past part.	
b. past subj.	**wäre** _____ past part.	**worden**	would have been _____ past part.	

PRACTICE

20-25 Complete the sentences in German following the model of sentence 1 (a + b).

1. a. Frau Kästner wird leider nicht eingeladen.
   Wenn es nach mir ginge, dann **würde sie eingeladen**.
   (she would be invited.)
   b. Frau Kästner wurde leider nicht eingeladen.
   Wenn es nach mir gegangen wäre, dann **wäre sie eingeladen worden.**
   (she would have been invited.)
2. a. Herr Böhme wird leider nicht befördert.
   Wenn es nach mir ginge, dann _____
   (he would be promoted.)
   b. Herr Böhme wurde leider nicht befördert.
   Wenn es nach mir gegangen wäre, dann _____
   (he would have been promoted.)
3. a. Das Programm wird leider geändert.
   Wenn es nur nach mir ginge, dann _____
   (it would not be changed.)

    b. Das Programm wurde leider geändert.

      Wenn es nur nach mir gegangen wäre, dann _____

(it would not have been changed.)

4. a. Das Konzert wird leider abgesagt.

      Wenn es nach mir ginge, dann _____

(it would not be called off.)

    b. Das Konzert wurde leider abgesagt.

      Wenn es nach mir gegangen wäre, dann _____

(it would not have been called off.)

5. a. Diese Sachen werden von Claudia erledigt.

      Wenn es nach mir ginge, dann _____

(they would be taken care of by Elke)

    b. Diese Sachen wurden von Claudia erledigt.

      Wenn es ncah mir gegangen wäre, dann

_____

(they would have been taken care of by Elke.)

6. a. Leider wird die Prüfung nicht verschoben.

      Wenn es nach mir ginge, dann _____

(it would be postponed)

    b. Leider wurde die Prüfung nicht verschoben.

      Wenn es nach mir gangangen wäre, dann _____

(it would have been postponed.)

Appendix

§1   ss or ß?

ss is used between two vowels if the preceding vowel is short:

Wasser Flüsse wissen lassen messen essen hassen müssen

ss must also be used in compounds if the two **s's** belong to different parts of the compound:

aussprechen (aus + sprechen) diesseits (dies + Seite)

ß is used in all other cases, for example,

a.   between vowels if the preceding vowel is long or is a diphthong:

grüßen heißen schließen Preußen außer

b.   at the end of a word:

Gruß Fluß Fuß weiß Kongreß Maß bloß

c.   before a consonant:

ihr wißt   sie ißt   er läßt   wir mußten

d.   in compounds if both **s's** belong to the first element:

Mißernte (*crop failure*) (miß + Ernte)
Meßinstrument (*measuring instrument*) (messen + Instrument)
Großstadt (groß + Stadt)

These rules are not always observed. Although **ß** cannot be used where **ss** is required, it is not regarded as wrong to use **ss** instead of **ß.**

§2   Principal Parts of Strong and Irregular Verbs

The third person singular forms of verbs with a vowel change in the present tense are shown in parentheses after the infinitive. The third person singular general subjunctive present is also shown. Note that subjunctive forms which are felt to be stilted or obsolete are placed in parentheses explained in Chap. 13, §6, **würde** + infintive forms are used instead.

For verbs with separable or inseparable prefixes not listed, see the main verb.

infinitive (3rd pers. sing.)	simple past	past participle	subjunctive present	meaning
backen (bäckt)	backte	gebacken	backte	to bake
befehlen (befiehlt)	befahl	befohlen	beföhle or: befähle	to command
beginnen	begann	begonnen	begänne or: begönne	to begin
beißen	biß	gebissen	bisse	to bite
betrügen	betrog	betrogen	betröge	to deceive
beweisen	bewies	bewiesen	bewiese	to prove
biegen	bog	gebogen	böge	to bend
bieten	bot	geboten	böte	to offer
binden	band	gebunden	bände	to bind, tie
bitten	bat	gebeten	bäte	to ask (for), request
blasen (bläst)	blies	geblasen	bliese	to blow
bleiben	blieb	ist geblieben	bliebe	to stay, remain
braten (brät)	briet	gebraten	briete	to roast, fry
brechen (bricht)	brach	gebrochen	bräche	to break
brennen	brannte	gebrannt	brennte	to burn
bringen	brachte	gebracht	brächte	to bring
denken	dachte	gedacht	dächte	to think
empfangen (empfängt)	empfing	empfangen	empfinge	to receive
empfehlen (empfiehlt)	empfahl	empfohlen	empföhle or: empfähle	to recommend
empfinden	empfand	empfunden	empfände	to feel
erlöschen (erlischt)	erlosch	ist erloschen	erlösche	to go out (light, fire)
erschrecken (erschrickt)	erschrak	ist erschrocken	erschräke	to be startled
essen (ißt)	aß	gegessen	äße	to eat
fahren (fährt)	fuhr	ist gefahren	führe	to drive, travel
fallen (fällt)	fiel	ist gefallen	fiele	to fall
fangen (fängt)	fing	gefangen	finge	to catch
finden	fand	gefunden	fände	to find
fliegen	flog	ist geflogen	flöge	to fly
fliehen	floh	ist geflohen	flöhe	to flee
fließen	floß	ist geflossen	flösse	to flow
fressen (frißt)	fraß	gefressen	fräße	to eat (animals)
frieren	fror	gefroren	fröre	to freeze, be cold
geben (gibt)	gab	gegeben	gäbe	to give
gehen	ging	ist gegangen	ginge	to go
gelingen	gelang	ist gelungen	gelänge	to succeed
gelten (gilt)	galt	gegolten	gölte or: gälte	to be valid, carry weight
genesen	genas	ist genesen	genäse	to recover (from illness)
genießen	genoß	genossen	genösse	to enjoy
geschehen (geschieht)	geschah	ist geschehen	geschähe	to happen
gewinnen	gewann	gewonnen	gewönne or: gewänne	to win
gießen	goß	gegossen	gösse	to pour
gleichen	glich	geglichen	gliche	to equal, resemble
gleiten	glitt	ist geglitten	glitte	to glide, slide
graben (gräbt)	grub	gegraben	grübe	to dig
greifen	griff	gegriffen	griffe	to grip, seize

infinitive (3rd. pers. sing.)	simple past	past participle	general subjunctive present	meaning
haben (hat)	hatte	gehabt	hätte	*to have*
halten (hält)	hielt	gehalten	hielte	*to hold, stop*
hängen	hing	gehangen	hinge	*to hang* (intransitive)
heben	hob	gehoben	höbe	*to lift*
heißen	hieß	geheißen	hieße	*to be called*
helfen (hilft)	half	geholfen	hülfe	*to help*
			or hälfe	
kennen	kannte	gekannt	kennte	*to know, to be acquainted with*
klingen	klang	geklungen	klänge	*to sound*
kneifen	kniff	gekniffen	kniffe	*to pinch*
kommen	kam	ist gekommen	käme	*to come*
kriechen	kroch	ist gekrochen	kröche	*to crawl*
laden (lädt)	lud	geladen	lüde	*to load*
lassen (läßt)	ließ	gelassen	ließe	*to leave, let, cause to*
laufen (läuft)	lief	ist gelaufen	liefe	*to run, walk*
lieden	litt	gelitten	litte	*to suffer*
leihen	lieh	geliehen	liehe	*to lend*
lesen (liest)	las	gelesen	läse	*to read*
liegen	lag	gelegen	läge	*to lie, be situated*
lügen	log	gelogen	löge	*to (tell a) lie*
meiden (vermeiden)	mied	gemieden	miede	*to avoid*
messen (mißt)	maß	gemessen	mäße	*to measure*
nehmen (nimmt)	nahm	genommen	nähme	*to take*
nennen	nannte	genannt	nennte	*to name, call*
pfeifen	pfiff	gepfiffen	pfiffe	*to whistle*
preisen	pries	gepriesen	priese	*to praise*
raten (rät)	riet	geraten	riete	*to advise, guess*
reiben	rieb	gerieben	riebe	*to rub*
reißen	riß	ist gerissen	risse	*to tear*
reiten	ritt	ist geritten	ritte	*to ride* (on an animal)
rennen	rannte	ist gerannt	rennte	*to run*
riechen	roch	gerochen	röche	*to smell*
rufen	rief	gerufen	riefe	*to call*
saufen (säuft)	soff	gesoffen	söffe	*to drink* (animal)
scheiden	schied	geschieden	schiede	*to separate*
scheinen	schien	geschienen	schiene	*to shine; seem*
schelten (schilt)	schalt	gescholten	schölte	*to scold*
schieben	schob	geschoben	schöbe	*to shove, push*
schießen	schoß	geschossen	schösse	*to shoot*
schlafen (schläft)	schlief	geschlafen	schliefe	*to sleep*
schlagen (schlägt)	schlug	geschlagen	schlüge	*to hit, beat*
schleichen	schlich	ist geschlichen	schliche	*to creep*
schließen	schloß	geschlossen	schlösse	*to close*
schmelzen (schmilzt)	schmolz	geschmolzen	schmölze	*to melt*
schneiden	schnitt	geschnitten	schnitte	*to cut*
schreiben	schrieb	geschrieben	scriebe	*to write*
schreien	schrie	geschrie(e)n	schree	*to shout, scream*
schreiten	schritt	ist geschritten	schritte	*to stride*

infinitive (3rd. pers. sing.)	simple past	past participle	general subjunctive present	meaning
schweigen	schwieg	geschwiegen	schwiege	*to be silent*
schwimmen	schwamm	ist geschwommen	schwömme	*to swim*
			or: schwämme	
schwingen	schwang	geschwungen	schwänge	*to swing*
schwören	schwor	geschworen	schwöre	*to swear, vow*
sehen (sieht)	sah	gesehen	sähe	*to see*
sein (ist)	war	ist gewesen	wäre	*to be*
senden	sandte	gesandt	sendete	*to send*
singen	sang	gesungen	sänge	*to sing*
sinken	sank	ist gesunken	sänke	*to sink*
sitzen	saß	gesessen	säße	*to sit*
spinnen	spann	gesponnen	spönne	*to spin*
sprechen (spricht)	sprach	gesprochen	spräche	*to speak*
springen	sprang	gesprungen	spränge	*to jump*
stechen (sticht)	stach	gestochen	stäche	*to prick, sting*
stehen	stand	gestanden	stünde	*to stand*
			or: stände	
stehlen (stiehlt)	stahl	gestohlen	stähle	*to steal*
			or: stöhle	
steigen	stieg	ist gestiegen	stiege	*to climb, rise*
sterben (stirbt)	starb	ist gestorben	stürbe	*to die*
stinken	stank	gestunken	stänke	*to stink*
stoßen (stößt)	stieß	gestoßen	stieße	*to push*
streichen	strich	gestrichen	striche	*to paint*
streiten	stritt	gestritten	stritte	*to quarrel*
tragen (trägt)	trug	getragen	trüge	*to carry; wear*
treffen (trifft)	traf	getroffen	träfe	*to meet*
treiben	trieb	getrieben	triebe	*to drive (cattle) pursue (an activity)*
treten (tritt)	trat	ist getreten	träte	*to step, tread*
trinken	trank	getrunken	tränke	*to drink*
tun	tat	ist getan	täte	*to do*
verderben (verdißt)	verdarb	verdorben	verdürbe	*to spoil*
vergessen (verdißt)	vergaß	vergessen	vergäße	*to forget*
verlieren	verlor	verloren	verlöre	*to lose*
verschwinden	verschwand	ist verschwunden	verschwände	*to disappear*
verzeihen	verzieh	verziehen	verziehe	*to pardon*
wachsen (wächst)	wuchs	ist gewachsen	wüchse	*to grow*
waschen (wäscht)	wusch	gewaschen	wüsche	*to wash*
weichen	wich	ist gewichen	wiche	*to yield, give way*
wenden	wandte	gewandt	wendete	*to turn*
werben (wirbt)	warb	geworben	würbe	*to recruit; woo*
werden (wird)	wurde	ist geworden	würde	*to become*
werfen (wirft)	warf	geworfen	würfe	*to throw*
wiegen	wog	gewogen	wöge	*to weigh*
winden	wand	gewunden	wände	*to wind, twist*
wissen (weiß)	wußte	gewußt	wüßte	*to know*
ziehen	zog	gezogen	zöge	*to pull*
zwingen	zwang	gezwungen	zwänge	*to force*

§3   ADJECTIVES THAT ADD UMLAUT IN THE COMPARATIVE AND SUPERLATIVE (CF. CHAP. 10 §2)

The following monosyllabic adjectives add an umlaut in the comparative and superlative:

alt	älter	ältest-
arg (*bad*)	ärger	ärgst-
arm	ärmer	ärmst-
dumm	dümmer	dümmst-
grob (*coarse, rude*)	gröber	gröbst-
groß	größer	größt-
hart	härter	härtest-
hoch	höher	höchst-
jung	jünger	jüngst-
kalt	kälter	kältest-
klug	klüger	klügst-
krank	kränker	kränkst-
kurz	kürzer	kürzest-
lang	länger	längst-
nah	näher	nächst-
oft	öfter	(öftest-) häufigst-
scharf (*sharp*)	schärfer	schärfst-
schwach (*weak*)	schwächer	schwächst-
schwarz	schwärzer	schwärzest-
stark	stärker	stärkst-
warm	wärmer	wärmst-

The following adjectives have comparative and superlative forms with and without umlaut. The boldface forms are more common.

blaß (*pale*)	**blasser**	**blassest-**
	blässer	blässest-
fromm (*religious, devout*)	frommer	frommst-
	frömmer	frömmst-
		(either form)
gesund (*healthy*)	gesunder	gesundest-
	gesünder	**gesündest-**
glatt (*smooth, slippery*)	**glatter**	**glattest-**
	glätter	glättest-
naß (*wet*)	**nasser**	**nassest-**
	nässer	nässest-
rot (*red*)	roter	rotest-
	röter	**rötest-**
schmal (*narrow*)	**schmaler**	**schmalst-**
	schmäler	schmälst-

§4   FLAVORING PARTICLES

Certain adverbs and conjunctions, such as **doch, schon, aber, denn,** are often used as flavoring particles. They express the speaker's attitude toward what is said and are difficult to translate into English in any consistent way. Nevertheless, it is possible to state when, and often why, they are used. Here are some frequently occurring flavoring particles and their most common uses.

aber

Aber merely strenghens the thought expressed.

> **Das hast du aber fein gemacht.**
> *You really did a fine job.*
> *You did a fine job, I must say.*

auch

1. **Auch** may confirm that a possibility or supposition is reality.

    > Köhlers hatten vor, ein Haus zu kaufen.—**Sie haben auch eins gekauft.**
    > *The Köhlers were planning to buy a house—They did buy one.*

    > Frau Schreiber soll sehr nett sein.—**Sie ist auch sehr nett**.
    > *Mrs. Schreiber is supposed to be very nice—She indeed is very nice.*

2. **Auch** used in questions may express a certain doubt.

    > **Hast du mich auch verstanden?**
    > *Did you really understand me? (I wonder.)*

    > **Kann man sich auch auf dich verlassen?**
    > *Can one really rely on you?*

3. **Auch** used in commands reinforces them.

    > **Vergiß das auch nicht!**
    > *Be sure not to forget that.*

    > **Komm auch nicht zu spät!**
    > *Be sure not to be late.*

denn

1. **Denn** used in questions may imply special interest, impatience, or surprise on the part of the speaker.

    > **Wann ist denn der Unfall passiert?**
    > *When did the accident happen? (I'd like to know.)*

    > **Warum kommt denn der Bus nicht?**
    > *Why isn't the bus coming? (We've been waiting at least 15 minutes.)*

    > **Kommst du denn nicht mit?**
    > *Aren't you coming along? (I thought you would.)*

2. **Denn** may make questions less abrupt.

    > **Wieso denn?**   *How so?*
    > **Wo denn?**   *Where?*
    > **Wann denn?**   *When?*

doch

1. **Doch** is frequently used for emphasis.

   > **Das ist doch die Höhe!**
   > *That is the limit.* (stress on *is*)

   > **Das ist doch kaum zu glauben.**
   > *That certainly (indeed) is hard to believe.*

2. **Doch** may express opposition; what is said is opposite to what one would have expected.

   > **Wir haben Müllers doch noch eingeladen.**
   > *We invited the Müllers after all (contrary to what we said or planned to do before).*

   Such a statement is often strengthened by adding **noch**.

einmal, (mal)

1. **Nun einmal (nun mal)** indicates acceptance of something that cannot be helped.

   > **Ich bin nun einmal (nun mal) sehr unbeliebt.**
   > *I am very unpopular (and there is nothing to be done about it).*

   > **Das ist nun einmal (nun mal) so.**
   > *That's how it is. That's how it goes.*

2. **Mal** (seldom **einmal**) usually makes a sentence sound more casual, less abrupt or blunt.

   > **Komm mal her!**
   > *Come here, will you?*

   > **Ich muß mir das mal überlegen.**
   > *I have to think about that.*

ja

1. **Ja** is frequently used when stating facts that are known or when making assertions with confidence. **Ja** either remains untranslated or remarks such as "you know," "as is known," are added.

   > **Das ist ja kein Geheimnis.**
   > *That's no secret, you know.*

   > **Das weiß ja jeder.**
   > *Everybody knows that.*

2. **Ja** conveys admonition in imperatives.

   > **Vergiß das (nur) ja nicht!**
   > *Be sure not to forget that.*

   > **Machen Sie das (nur) ja nicht wieder!**
   > *Don't ever do that again.*

   Ja is stressed in these cases; **nur** is frequently added for reinforcement (see below).

nur, bloß

Colloquially, **bloß** is frequently used instead of **nur**.

1. **Nur (bloß)** may express intense interest in learning the answer to some puzzling question.

> **Warum hat er nur (bloß) gelogen?**
> *Why did he lie? (I'd really like to know.)*

> **Wie konntest du nur (bloß) soviel Geld verschwenden?**
> *How on earth could you waste so much money?*

2. In imperative sentences **nur** may express encouragement and reassurance.

> **Kommen Sie nur herein!**
> *Do come in.*

> **Haben Sie nur keine Angst!**
> *Don't be afraid.*

It may also express admonition, frequently reinforcing **ja.**

> **Beleidige ihn nur nicht!** ⎫
> **Beleidige ihn nur ja nicht!** ⎭ *Don't insult him. (by all means)*

schon

1. **Schon** may express reassurance that something will be so, although it may seem to be doubtful.

> **Du wirst es schon schaffen.**
> *Don't worry, you'll make it.*

> **Wir werden schon eine Lösung finden.**
> *Don't worry, we'll find a solution.*

2. **Schon** may express a concession.

> **Das ist schon richtig, aber das ist nicht die ganze Wahrheit.**
> *That's correct, I admit (I grant you), but that's not the whole truth.*

> In den Ferien hast du doch genug Zeit zum Schreiben.—**Das schon, aber ich habe keine Lust dazu.**
> *During vacation you do have enough time to write. - That's true, I admit, but I don't have the urge to.*

As the above sentences illustrate, this concessive use can easily be recognized by the conjunction **aber** introducing a qualifying remark, frequently a counter-argument.

3. **Schon** is used in rhetorical questions in the sense of *after all, but then.*

> Ich habe nichts gesagt. **Was kann man schon in so einem Fall sagen?**
> *I said nothing. After all, what can one say in such a case?*

> Natürlich ist das eine herrliche Jacht. **Aber wer kann sich schon so einen Luxus leisten?**
> *Of course, that is a magnificent yacht. But then, who can afford such a luxury?*

§5   COMMON GERMAN MEASUREMENTS AND THEIR ENGLISH EQUIVALENTS*

Most measures (except those ending in **-e**) add no ending in the plural when they follow a numeral.

das Pfund, -e	zwei Pfund	*two pounds*
der Grad,-e	zwei Grad	*two degrees*
die Meile,-n	zwei Meilen	*two miles*
die Gallone,-n	zwei Gallonen	*two gallons*

German	English Equivalents	English	German equivalents
1 Zentimeter (1 cm)	0.4 inch	1 inch	2,5 Zentimeter
1 Meter (1 m)	3.3 feet	1 foot	0,3 Meter
	or: 1.1 yard	1 yard	0,9 Meter
1 Kilometer (1 km)	0.62 mile	1 mile	1,6 Kilometer

Illustration of how many miles correspond to 1-500 km:

Mile	0.6 1.8 3.1 4.9 6.2 9.3	12.4	15.5	18.6	21.7	24.8	27.9	31.0	62.1	93.1	124.2	155.2	186.4	217.4	248.5	279.5	310.6
Kilometer	1 3 5 8 10	15	20	25	30	35	40	45	50	100	150	200	250	300	350	400	450	500

1 Quadratmeter (1 qm)
  = 10.8 square feet
1 Quadratkilometer (1 qkm)
  =0.39 square mile
	1 square foot
	  = 0,092 Quadratmeter (qm)
	1 square mile
	  =2.6 Quadratkilometer (qkm)

1 Liter (1 l) = 2.1 U.S. pints 1.05 U.S. quarts	1 U.S. pint = 0,47 Liter (l) 1 U.S. quart = 0,94 Liter (l) 1 U.S. gallon = 3,76 Liter (l)
1 Gramm (1 g) = 0.04 ounce 1 Pfund (1 Pfd) = 1.1 pounds 1 Kilogramm (1 kg) = 2.2 pounds or: Kilo	1 ounce = 28 Gramm (g) 1 pound = 454 Gramm (g)

Some practical hints:

A **Meter** is a little more than a yard.
A **Pfund** is a little more than a pound.
A **Liter** is a little more than a quart. **3 3/4 Liter** = 1 gallon.
A **Kilometer** is 5/8 of a mile. **5 Kilometer** = approx. 3 miles.

When you weigh yourself on a German scale, your weight is 10 percent less than on an American scale; for example, Barbara weighs 120 pounds in America, but **108 Pfund** in Germany.

---

* Data and illustrations from "These Strange German Ways," courtesy Atlantik-Brücke e. V., Hamburg.

Fahrenheit and Centigrades (Celsius)

> Wieviel Grad haben wir heute?
> Heute haben wir zehn Grad Celsius. (written: 10 C)

If you have the centigrade reading and want to find out the temperature in Fahrenheit, multiply the centigrades by 9, divide by 5, and add 32.

Formula: $F = \dfrac{9C}{5} + 32$

If you have the Fahrenheit reading and want to find out the temperature in centigrade, deduct 32 from the Fahrenheit reading, multiply by 5, and divide by 9.

Formula: $C = \dfrac{5(F-32)}{9}$

The dual scales on the thermometer shown below give you some equivalents.

Conversion Tables

SKIRTS, DRESSES, COATS		SHIRTS		SHOES	
U.S.	EUROPE	U.S.	EUROPE	U.S.	EUROPE
10	38	14	36	6	37
12	40	14 1/2	37	7	38
14	42	15	38	8	39
16	44	15 1/2	39	9	40
18	46	16	41	10	41
20	48	16 1/2	42	11	42
		17	43	12	43
				13	44

	SUITS			BLOUSES			HATS	
U.S.	EUROPE		U.S.	EUROPE		U.S.	EUROPE	
36	46		30	38		7	57	
38	48		32	40		7 1/8	58	
40	50		34	42		7 1/4	59	
42	52		36	44		7 3/8	60	
44	54		38	46		7 1/2	61	
46	56		40	48				
48	58							

KITCHEN HINTS	
U.S	EUROPE
1 cup sugar	200 g
1 cup flour	150 g
1 tsp.	5 g
1 tbsp.	12 g

§6   PUNCTUATION

The following punctuation rules differ from English usage.

The comma

1. In enumerations the last item is not set off by a comma if preceded by **und** or **oder**.

> Klaus, Margot, und Renate haben einen Preis gewonnen.
> *Klaus, Margot, and Renate won a prize.*

> Klaus Margot oder Renate haben den ersten Preis gewonnen.
> *Klaus, Margot or Renate won first prize.*

2. Main clauses joined by **und** or **oder** are more often separated by commas than in English.

> Helga las die Zeitung, und ihre Schwester schrieb Briefe.
> *Helga read the newspaper and her sister wrote letters.*

> Das Eis auf dem See taut schon, oder es wird bald tauen.
> *The ice on the lake is thawing already or it is going to thaw soon.*

But if the clauses share one or more elements, no comma is used.

> Das Eis auf dem See taut schon oder wird bald tauen.
> *The ice on the lake is thawing already or is going to thaw soon.*

Das Eis is the subject of both **taut** and **wird…tauen**.

3. The conjunctions **aber** and **sondern** are preceded by a comma if the following element is a phrase or clause.

> Sie ist sehr intelligent, aber leider etwas faul.
> *She is very intelligent but unfortunately a little lazy.*

> Er wohnt nicht in Bonn, sondern in Köln.
> *He doesn't live in Bonn but in Cologne.*

4. All dependent clauses are set off by commas.

> Ich weiß daß er jetzt zu Hause ist.
> *I know that he is at home now.*
>
> Ich weiß, er ist jetzt zu Hause.
> *I know he is at home now.*
>
> Das ist ein Film, der mir gefällt.
> *That's a film I like.*
>
> Die Schallplatte, die ich gestern gekauft habe, ist verschwunden.
> *The record I bought yesterday has disapppeared.*

5. Infinitive phrases are set off by commas unless they consist only of **zu** + infinitive.

> Ich versuche zu arbeiten.
> *I'm trying to work.*
>
> Ich versuche, mich zu konzentrieren.
> *I'm trying to concentrate.*
>
> Ich versuche, mich auf meine Arbeit zu konzentrieren.
> *I'm trying to concentrate on my work.*

6. Adverbs and prepositional phrases are normally not set off by commas.

> Natürlich weiß er das.
> *Of course, he knows that.*
>
> Zum Glück war Margot zu Hause.
> *Luckily, Margot was at home.*
>
> Nach vielen Jahren schwerer Arbeit ist mein Vater endlich in den Ruhestand getreten.
> *After many years of hard work, my father finally retired.*

7. The comma is used as a decimal point (cf. Chap. 11, §1).

> 3,50 (read: drei Komma fünf null) = 3.50 (three point five O)

Keep in mind: German leaves a space or uses a period to separate thousands and millions (cf. Chap. 11, §1).
10 000 or 10.000 = English 10,000
1 000 000 or 1.000.000 = English 1,000,000

Punctuation of direct quotations

> Er sagte: „Ich habe keine Zeit."
> *He said, "I don't have time."*

Direct quotations are preceded by a colon. Except in typing, the opening quotation mark is set on the line. As in English, the end quote follows a period, question mark, or exclamation point, but in contrast to English it precedes a comma.

„Ich habe keine Zeit", sagte er. "I have no time," he said.

Typewriters and computers that do not have the opening quotation mark use the end quote instead:

"Ich habe keine Zeit", sagte er.

The exclamation point

Bitte kommen Sie!
or: Bitte kommen Sie ⟶ *Please come.*

Imperative sentences end with an exclamation point or, if there is no special emphasis, with a period.

The hyphen in compounds

German often omits an element belonging to two different compound nouns. The hyphen is then used to show where it has been omitted.

Er ist Mathematik- und Physikprofessor.
(for: Mathematikprofessor und Physikprofessor)
Ich habe einen Sonnenaufgang und -untergang fotografiert.
(for: Sonnenaufgang und Sonnenuntergang)

§7   WRITING LETTERS AND ADDRESSES

For writing the date, see Chapter 11, §4, 5.

Formal letter

Sehr geehrter Herr Krause,
ich danke Ihnen für Ihren Brief vom 23. August. Ich verstehe natürlich, daß….
Mit freundlichen Grüßen

Maria Schreiber

The salutation **Sehr geehrter Her Krause** (lit. *Very esteemed Mr. Krause*) corresponds to English *Dear Mr. Krause*. When the letter is directed to a company, it may begin with **Sehr geehrte Herren** or no salutation.

Some people hesitate to begin a letter with **ich** because it might be considered impolite. They begin with another element and use inversion:

Sehr geehrter Herr Krause,
für Ihren Brief vom 23. August danke ich Ihnen…

Note that there are no indentations.

Informal letters

Note that the personal pronouns of the familiar address and the corresponding possessives are capitalized:

> Liebe Monika,
>
> lange habe ich nichts von Dir und Deiner Familie gehört.
> Hast Du meinen Brief vom. 1 September nicht erhalten?…
>
> Mit herzlichen Grüßen
Deine

Sabine

> Liebe Barbara und lieber Dietmar,
>
> lange habe ich nichts von Euch gehört. Habt Ihr meinen Brief vom 30. Juli nicht erhalten?…
>
> Beste Grüße
von Eurem

Klaus

Addresses

Familie	Frau
Martin Schramm	Dr. Käte Wolf
Beethovenstraße 21	D-040209 Leipzig
D-6000 Frankfurt/Main	Ringstraße 171
Fräulein	Herrn
Maria Renner	Professor Dr. H. Spörli
Schubertring 2	Mainaustr. 12
A-1011 Wien	CH-8008 Zürich

Note: a. The house number follows the street.
      b. The ZIP code precedes the city name.
      c. Letters sent to another country have a country symbol prefixed to the ZIP code. Some of the common ones are:

D	Federal Republic of Germany
A	Austria
CH	Switzerland

§8   THE GERMAN ALPHABET

Modern German books and newspapers use the same type fonts as are used in English, and German handwriting is similar to ours. Until the second quarter of the twentieth century Gothic type (Fraktur) was commonly used in Germany. Since you may encounter this type in older books, the following table provides Roman and Gothic styles, together with handwritten Gothic forms.

ROMAN TYPE		GOTHIC TYPE AND GERMAN SCRIPT		PRONUNCIATION OF LETTER NAME
A	a			ah
B	b			beh
C	c			tseh
D	d			deh
E	e			eh
F	f			eff
G	g			geh
H	h			hah
I	i			ee
J	j			yot
K	k			kah
L	l			ell
M	m			em
N	n			en
O	o			oh
P	p			peh
Q	q			coo
R	r			err
S	s			ess
T	t			teh
U	u			oo
V	v			fow (as in fowl)
W	w			veh
X	x			iks
Y	y			üpsilon
Z	z			tset

UMLAUTE

Ä	ä			ah umlaut
Ö	ö			oh umlaut
Ü	ü			oo umlaut

DIPTHONGS

Au	au	**Au**		au = ow (as in owl)
Äu	äu	**Äu**		äu = ow umlaut
Eu	eu	**Eu**		eu = oy (as in boy)
Ai	ai	**Ai**		ai
Ei	ei	**Ei**		ei } = eye

GERMAN SCRIPT

GOTHIC TYPE

Herbstlied

Bunt sind schon die Wälder,
Gelb die Stoppelfelder,
Und der Herbst beginnt.
Und die Blätter fallen,
Und die Nebel wallen,
Kühler weht der Wind.

—Salis-Seewis.

EXAMPLE IN ROMAN TYPE

Herbstlied

Bunt[1] sind schon die Wälder,
Gelb die Stoppelfelder,[2]
Und der Herbst beginnt.
Und die Blätter fallen,
Und die Nebel[3] wallen,[4]
Kühler weht[5] der Wind.

—Salis-Seewis

1 bunt	many-colored
2 das Stoppelfeld. -er	stubble field
3 der Nebel. -	fog
4 wallen	to surge
5 wehen	to blow

German-English Vocabulary

With the exception of numerals and personal pronouns, all vocabulary items that appear in the exercises are included. The number in parentheses indicates the chapter in which each vocabulary item is introduced. A second number indicates that the word in question is reintroduced in a subsequent chapter with additional information about its use.

The nouns are given in the nominative singular and plural:

die Stadt, -ë =	nom. sing.	**die Stadt**
	nom. pl.	**die Städte**
der Lehrer, – =	nom. sing.	**der Lehrer**
	nom. pl.	**die Lehrer**

Irregular plurals are written out:

das Drama, die Dramen

Weak nouns (cf. Chap. 5, §5) are listed as follows:

der Student (*weak*), **-en**

The genitive singular is added when it is irregular:

der Name (*weak*; *gen.* **-ns**), **-n**

Adjectival nouns (cf. Chap. 9, §12-§13) are listed as follows:

der Fremde (*adj. noun*)

Only the infinitive is provided for weak verbs; (**ist**) after the infinitive indicates that the present perfect and past perfect tenses require the auxiliary **sein**:

reisen (ist)

The principal parts are given for all strong and irregular verbs:

geben (gibt), gab, gegeben
gehen, ging, ist gegangen

ab•brechen (bricht ab), brach ab, abgebrochen (14) to break off
der Abend, -e (11) evening. night
   (*before bedtime*)
   zu Abend essen (19) to have dinner
   (*evening meal*)
   aber (1,12) but, however, nevertheless

ab•hängen (hängt ab), hing ab, abgehangen von (*dat.*) (20) to depend on
ab•holen (2) to pick up
ab•lehnen (15) to decline
ab•nehmen (nimmt ab), nahm ab, abgenommen (2,3) to decrease, lose weight
ab•sagen (18) to call off

ab•schalten (16) to turn off

ach so (4) oh, I see

die Ahnung: keine Ahnung haben (2) to have no idea

die Aktentasche, -n (7) briefcase

der Alkohol, -e (4) alcohol

alle (*pl.*) (6) all

allein (20) alone

Allwissend: Dr. Allwissend (14) Dr. know-it-all

als (10) than

als (*sub. conj.*) (12) when

alt (10) old

altmodisch (9) old-fashioned

amerikanisch (9) American

an (acc./dat.) (7) on (*vertically*), by, at the edge of

die Ananasbowle, -n (20) pineapple punch

an•bauen (18) to grow, cultivate, plant

ändern (14) to change: **das läßt sich nicht ändern** (18) that cannot be helped

anders (18) different(ly)

der Anfang, ¨e (5) beginning

an•fangen (fängt an), fing an, angefangen (2,3) to begin, start

die Angabe (14) showing off, bragging

an•geben (gibt an), gab an, angegeben (2, 3) to show off, brag, put on airs

das Angebot, -e (4) offer: **das Angebot an•nehmen (nimmt an), nahm an, angenommen** to accept the offer

der Angestellte (*adj. noun*) (9) employee

an•greifen, griff an, angegriffen (20) to attack

die Angst, ¨e (2) fear: **Angst haben vor** (*dat.*) (2,8) to be afraid of; **keine Angst!** (10) don't be afraid, don't worry

an•kommen, kam an, ist angekommen (7) to arrive; **an•kommen auf** (acc) (8) to depend on; **es kommt (ganz) darauf an** it (all) depends

an•nehmen (nimmt an), nahm an, angenommen (2,3) to accept; to assume

die Anordnung, -en (18) regulation, rule

an rufen, rief an, angerufen (1,3) to call (*by phone*)

sich (*dat*) etwas an•schauen (17) to (take a) look at

sich (dat.) etwas an sehen(sieht an), sah an, angesehen (17) to (take a) look at

die Ansichtskarte, -n (18) picture postcard

anstatt (*gen.*) (7) instead

antik (16) antique

antworten (dat.) (5) to answer someone; **antworten auf** (acc.) (8) to answer something

an•ziehen, zog an, angezogen (9) to put on

der Anzug, ¨e (5) suit

applaudieren (2) to applaud

der April (11) April

die Arbeit, -en (2) work

arbeiten an (dat.) (1,8) to work on

der Arbeiter,—(5) worker

ärgern (15) to annoy

der Arme (adj. noun) (9) the poor man

das Aroma, die Aromen (9) aroma

der Arzt, -¨e (2) male doctor; **der Arzt hat es mir verboten** (4) doctor's orders

die Ärztin, -nen (5) female doctor

die Aspirintablette, -n (1) aspirin (tablet)

der Assistent (*weak*), -en (5) male assistant

die Assistentin, -nen (5) female assistant

atmen (2) to breathe

attraktiv (9) attractive

auch (2) also, too

auf (*acc./dat.*) (7) on (*horizontally*)

auf•geben (gibt auf), gab auf, aufgeben (2,3) to give up

aufgeregt (14) excited, upset

auf•hören (2) to stop, end, cease; **mit einem Kurs auf•hören** (12) to drop a course

auf•machen (2) to open

die Aufnahme, -n (8) picture, photograph; **eine Aufnahme machen** to take a picture

auf•passen (2) to pay attention, watch, keep an eye on

auf•räumen (3) to tidy up, to straighten up

auf•stehen, stand auf, ist aufgestanden (3) to rise, get up

auf•tauchen (20) to emerge, come up

der Augenblick, -e (2) moment

der August (11) August

aus (*dat.*) (7) out of, from

die Ausdauer (13) staying power, perseverance

aus•drücken (18) to express

aus•füllen (4) to fill out

aus•geben: **Geld aus•geben (gibt aus), gab aus, ausgegeben** (3) to spend money aus•gehen, ging aus, ist ausgegangen (2,3) to go out

ausgeschlossen (6) out of the question

ausgezeichnet (9) excellent

aus•kommen, kam aus, ist ausgekommen mit (*dat.*) (12) to get along with

die Auskunft, ̈-e (9) information; **Auskunft geben (gibt), gab, gegeben** to give information

aus•lachen (3) to laugh at

der Ausländer,— (5) male foreigner

die Auslsländerin, -nen (5) female foreigner

ausländisch (9) foreign

aus•nutzen (18) to exploit

die Aussage, -n (14) testimony

aus•sehen (sieht aus), sah aus, ausgesehen (2,3) to appear, look

außer (dat.) (7) except, besides

außer sich (*dat.*) sein (17) to be beside oneself

außerdem (8) besides, aside from that

die Ausrede, -n (20) excuse, pretext

aus•reden lassen (20) to let finish (*talking*)

aus•steigen, stieg aus, ist ausgestiegen (3) to get off (*a vehicle*)

die Auswahl (16) selection, choice

der Ausweg, -e (18) way out

auswendig lernen (19) to learn by heart

der Ausweis, -e (5) identification card

des Auto, s (1) car

automatisch (18) automatic

der Autoschlüssel, — (1) car key

der Autounfall, -ë (14) car accident

das Baby, -s (5) baby

die Bäckerei, -en (7) bakery

das Bad (das Badezimmer, —) (20) bathroom

baden (2) to bathe

der Bahnhof, ̈-e (1) railway station

bald (10) soon

der Ball, -ë (2) Ball

die Bank, -en (7) bank

der Bankrott, -e (18) bankruptcy

bankrott machen (14) to go bankrupt

bannen (11) to excommunicate

bar bezahlen (4) to pay cash

der Beamte (*adj. noun*) (14) official

bedeuten (1) to mean

bedienen (18) to wait on

sich (*acc.*) bedienen (17) to help *or* serve oneself

beenden (3) to finish

befehlen (befiehlt), befahl, befohlen (8) to order, give orders

beförden (18) to promote

befreundet sein mit (*dat.*) (16) to be friends with

begeistert sein von (dat.) (8) to be enthusiastic about

beginnen, begann, begonnen (1, 3) to begin

begraben (begräbt), begrub, begraben (2) to bury; **die Sache begraben** to bury the matter

begrüßen (14) to welcome

behalten (behält), behielt, behalten (4) to keep

behandeln (12) to treat, deal with

behaupten (14) to claim, assert

bei (*dat.*) (7) at, near, at someone's place; **bei sich** (*dat.*) **haben: ich habe kein Geld bei mir** (17) I have no money on me

beide (6) both

das Beispiel, -e (9) example

beißen, biß, gebissen (9) to bite

bekommen, bekam, bekommen (2,3) to get, receive

beleidigen (2) to insult

die Beleidigung, -en (9) insult

beliebt (9) popular

bellen (9) to bark; **bellend** barking

die Bemerkung, -en (2) remark, observation

benachrichtigen (18) to notify

beneiden (2) to envy

bequem (10) comfortable

der Bericht, -e (19) report

berühmt (8) famous

die Bescheidenheit (17) modesty

besetzt: die Leitung ist besetzt (12) the line is busy

besprechen (bespricht), besprach, besprochen (19) to discuss

bestehen: die Prüfung bestehen, bestand, bestanden (3) to pass the exam

sich (*dat.*) bestellen (17) to order for oneself

bestimmt (3) certain(ly), definate(ly)

besuchen (1) to visit

betonen (14) to emphasize

betrugen, betrog, betrogen (15) to cheat

das **Bett. -en** (7) bed
bevor (*sub. conj.*) (12) before
beweisen, bewies, bewiesen (5) to prove
der **Bewerber, —** (9) application
die **Bewerbung,-en** (18) application
bewundern (2) to admire
bezahlen (1) to pay
die **Bibliothek, -en** (1) library
das **Bild, -er** (6) picture
billig (10) cheap, inexpensive
die **Billion, -en** (11) trillion
die **Biographie, -en** (9) biography
bis (*acc.*) (7) until *or* as far as, to, up to (*location*)
bis jetzt (2) until now, so far
bißchen; ein bißchen (9) a little (bit)
bitten, bat, gebeten um (*acc.*) (2,3,8) to ask for, request
bleiben, blieb, ist geblieben (3) to stay, remain
der **Blinde** (*adj. noun*) (9) the blind man
der **Boden, -**(7) floor
böse sein auf (*acc.*) *or* **mit** (*dat.*) (1,6,8) to be angry with
brauchen (4) to need: **etwas nicht zu machen brauchen** (4) not to have to do something
braun (9) brown
brechen (bricht), brach, gebrochen (17) to break, **sich** (*dat.*) **den Arm brechen** to break one's arm
die **Bremse, -n** (2) brake
brennen, brannte, gebrannt (3) to burn; **es brennt** there is a fire
der **Brief, -e** (1) letter
der **Briefkasten, -**(7) mailbox
die **Briefmarke, -n** (2) stamp
die **Briefmarkensammlung, -en** (7) stamp collection
die **Brieftasche, -n** (7) wallet
die **Brille, -n** (4) (eye) glasses
bringen, brachte, gebracht (3) to bring; **nach Hause bringen** to bring *or* take home
der **Bruder, -** (5) brother
das **Brüderchen** (*diminutive*) (5) little brother
brummen (4) to grumble
die **Buchhhandlung, -en** (7) bookstore
das **Bücherregal, -e** (5) book shelf
der **Bügel, der Kleiderbügel, —** (20) (clothes)hanger

bügeln (4) to iron, press
der **Bummel, —** (7) stroll; **einen Bummel machen** to go for *or* take a stroll
der **Bürgermeister, —** (5) mayor
das **Büro,-s** (1) office
der **Bus, -se** (2) bus
die **Bushaltestelle, -n** (7) bus stop

die **Chance, -n** (5) chance
charmant (9) charming
der **Charme** (9) charm
der **Chef, -s** (1) male boss
die **Chefin, -nen** (5) female boss

da (12) then *or* there; **da drüben** (19) over there; **da** (*sub. conj.*) (12) since (*stating reason*), because
das **Dach, -er** (2) roof
damit (*sub. conj.*) (12) so that, in order that
der **Dampfer, —** (19) steamship
danken (*dat.*) **für** (*acc.*) (5,8) to thank for
dann (12) then
das (1) that
daß (*sub. conj.*) (1) that
das **Datum, die Daten** (5) date
die **Dauerwelle, -n** (20) permanent; **sich** (*dat.*) **eine Dauerwelle machen lassen** to get a permanent
die **Debatte, -n** (14) debate
der **Dekan, -e** (5) dean
denken, dachte, gedacht an (*acc.*) (3,8) to think of
denn (12) for, because
deprimiert (6) depressed
deshalb (8) bacause of that, therefore
deswegen (8) because of that, therefore
der **Deutsche** (*adj. noun*) (9) the German
die **Deutschstunde, -n** (7) German class
der **Dezember** (11) December
das **Dia, -s** (short for **das Diapositiv, -e**) (6) slide
der **Diamantring, -e** (6) diamond ring
dick (2) fat
der **Dieb, -e** (18) thief
der **Dienstag, -e** (3) Tuesday
dieser, dieses, diese (1) this
diplomatisch (14) diplomatic
dirigieren (20) to conduct (music)
die **Disko, -s** (short for **die Diskothek, -en**) (7) disco

der Donnerstag, -e (11) Thursday
das Dorf, ̈-e (5) village
   dort (2) there
das Drama, die Dramen (5) drama
der Dreck (10) dirt; die Dreckarbeit dirty
      work
   dringend (10) urgent
   drohen (dat.) (18) to threaten; mit
      Entlassung drohen to threaten with
      dismissal
   dumm (3) stupid, silly, dumb
die Dummheit, -en (8) stupidity
der Dummkopf, -̈e (male and female) (7)
      dumbell
   dunkel (9) dark
   dünn (2) thin
   durch (acc.) (3) through
   durch•fahren (fährt durch), fuhr durch,
      ist durchgefahren (2) to go nonstop
   durchfahren (durchfährt), durchfuhr,
      hat durchfahren (2) to run through
      (figuratively); ein großer Schreck durch-
      fährt die Menge a feeling of great
      horror runs through the crowd
   durch•fallen (fällt durch), fiel durch, ist
      durchgefallen (3) to flunk (exam)
   dürfen (darf), durfte, gedurft (4) may, to
      be allowed to
   Durst haben (3) to be thirsty

die Ecke, -n (7) corner
   egoistisch (10) egotistical
   ehe (sub. conj.) (12) before
das Ehepaar, -e (16) (married) couple
das Ehrenwort (6) word of honor
das Ei, -er (9) egg
   eilig, es eilig haben (2) to be in a hurry
   einander (17) each other; one another
   ein•biegen, bog ein, ist eingebogen (20)
      to turn into (a street)
   einfach (4) simple, simply
   eingebildet (14) conceited
   ein•gehen, ging ein, ist eingegangen auf
      (acc.) (16) to go into (question, point)
   sich (acc.) einigen (14) to come to an
      agreement
   einkaufen gehen (7) to go shopping
   ein•laden (lädt ein), lud ein, eingeladen
      (2, 3) to invite
die Einladung, -en (2) invitation; die Einla-
      dung an•nehmen (nimmt an), nahm

an, angenommen to accept the invitation
   ein•lösen; den Scheck ein lösen (6) to
      cash the check
   ein•reichen (4) to hand in
   ein•schlafen (schläft ein), schlief ein, ist
      eingeschlafen (3) to fall asleep
   ein•steigen, stieg ein, ist eingestiegen (3)
      to climb in, get on, board a vehicle
die Einzelheit, -en (16) detail
   einzig (20) single; nicht eine einzige
      Tasse Kaffee not a single cup of coffee
das einzige (16) the only thing
das Eis (2) ice, ice cream
   elegant (9) elegant
die Eltern (1) parents
   empfehlen (empfiehlt), empfahl,
      empfohlen (2,6) to recommend
   englisch (9) English
   entlang (acc.) (7) along
   entlassen (entläßt), entließ, entlassen (2)
      to dismiss, fire
die Entlassung, -en (18) dismissal; mit
      Entlassung drohen to threaten with
      dismissal
die Entscheidung, -en (20) decision
   entschuldigen (2) to excuse
   sich (acc.) entschuldigen bei (dat.) (17,19)
      to apologize to
   enttäuschen (4) to disappoint
die Enttäuschung, -en (18) disappointment
   entwickeln (20) to develop
die Entwicklung, -en (18) development
   erben (16) to inherit
der Erfinder, — (5) male inventor
die Erfinderin, -nen (5) female inventor
die Erfindung, -en (5) invention
der Erfolg, -e (3) success
   erhöhen (5) to raise
   sich (acc.) erinnern an (acc.) (17) to
      remember
   sich (acc.) erkälten (17) to catch a cold
die Erkältung, -en (5) cold
   erkennen, erkannte, erkannt (12) to
      recognize
   erklären (2) to explain
die Erlaubnis: die Erlaubnis erteilen (18) to
      give permission; um Erlaubnis bitten
      (4) to ask for permission
   erledigen (2) to take care of, settle
   ernst nehmen (nimmt), nahm, genommen
      (12) to take seriously

erreichen (8, 11) to achieve, to reach contact

der Erwaschsene (*adj. noun*) (9) adult

erwähnen (18) to mention

erzählen (4) to tell, relate

das Essen, (5) meal

essen (ißt), aß, gegessen (2,3,) to eat

etwas (2,16) a little; something

das Experiment,-e (2) experiment

die Fabrik, -en (5) factory

die Fahne, -n (2) flag

fahren (fährt), fuhr, ist gefahren (1, 3) to drive, ride, go

der Fahrer, - (6) driver

der Fahrgast, ¨e (20) passenger

das Fahrrad, ¨er (6) bicycle

der Fall, ¨er (9) case

fallen (fällt), fiel, ist gefallen (3) to fall

falsch (16) false, wrong

die Familie, -n (8) family

faulenzen (18) to loaf

der Faulenzer,—(5) male lazybones

die Faulenzerin, -nen (5) female lazybones

der Februar (11) February

der Fehler,—(1) mistake

feiern (18) to celebrate

der Feind, -e (5) enemy

das Fenster,—(3) window

die Ferne (18) distance; in der Ferne in the distance

fern•sehen (sieht fern), sah fern, ferngesehen (4) to watch television

der Fernseher,—(6) TV set

feucht (12) humid

das Fieber (1) fever

die Figur, -en (7) figure

der Film, -e (5) film

finanzieren (18) to finance

finden, fand, gefunden (2, 3) to find

die Firma, die Firmen (7) company, firm

der Fisch, -e (3) fish

fit bleiben, blieb, ist geblieben (12) to stay fit

die Fleischerei, -en (17) butcher's shop

fliegen, flog, ist geflogen (1) to fly

die Flitterwochen (pl.) (6) honeymoon; die Flitterwochen verbringen, verbrachte, verbracht (6) to spend the honeymoon

die Flöte, -n (20) flute

der Flughafen, ¨ (4) airport

der Flugplatz, ¨e (3) airport

das Flugzeug, -e (15) airplane

der Fluß, ¨sse (7) river

die Folge, -n (6) consequence

folgen (ist) (*dat.*) (3) to follow

folgend (9) following

das Formular, -e (4) form

formulieren (14) to formulate, phrase

das Foto, -s (20) photo(graph)

die Frage, -n (5) question; eine Frage stellen (14) to ask a question

fragen (1) to ask; sich (*acc.*) fragen (17) to ask oneself

französisch (9) French

die Frau, -en (2, 4) woman; wife; Frau... Mrs....

frech (2) fresh, impudent

die Freiheit, -en (5) freedom, liberty

der Freitag, -e (2) Friday

der Fremde (*adj. noun*) (9) stranger

sich (*acc.*) freuen auf (*acc.*) (17) to look forward to

sich (*acc.*) freuen über (*acc.*) (17) to be happy about

der Freund, -e (1) male friend; der feste Freund (9) steady boyfriend

die Freundin, -nen (1) female friend

freundlich (1) friendly

die Freundlichkeit, -en (5) friendliness

der Friede (*weak; gen.* -ns) (5) peace

der Friseur, -e (19) hairdresser

die Frisur, -en (20) hairdo

froh sein über (*acc.*) (3, 8) to be glad about

früher (10) earlier, before, in the past

frühestens (10) at the earliest

der Frühling, -e (11) spring

der Führerschein, -e (5) driver's licence

funktionieren (1) to function, work

für (*acc.*) (1, 7) for

fürchten (3) to fear, be afraid of

Fuß: zu Fuß gehen (3) to go on foot, to walk

die Fußballmannschaft, -en (1) soccer team

das Fußballspiel, -e soccer game

der Fußballspieler,—(3) soccer player

der Fußballtrainer,—(5) soccer coach

der Fußboden, ¨ (20) floor

gähnen (3) to yawn

ganz (2) whole

gar nicht (14) not at all

die Garage, -n (3) garage

der Garten, ⸚ (5) garden

das Gebäude,—(9) building

geben (gibt), gab, gegeben (2, 3) to give; es gibt (*acc.*) (9, 15) there is, there are

gebrauchen (9) to use; ein gebrauchter Wagen a used car; gebrauchte Bücher second-hand books

der Geburtstage, -e (3) birthday; ich habe Geburtstag (11) it is my birthday

das Gedächtnis (12) memory

das Gedicht, -e (16) poem

die Geduld (4) patience

die Gefahr, -en (14) danger gefährlich (7) dangerous

der Gefallen,—(8) favor; um einen Gefallen bitten to ask for a favor gefallen (gefällt), gefiel, gefallen (*dat.*) (1, 3, 5) to like sich (*dat.*) gefallen (17) to like oneself

das Gefängnis, -se (5) prison gegen (acc.) (7) against gegenüber (*dat.*) (7) across from

der Gegner,— (20) opponent

die Gehaltserhöhung, -en (8) salary raise gehen, ging, ist gegangen (1, 3) to go; *idiom:* es geht nach mir, dir, ihm, *etc.* (13) it is up to me, you, him, *etc.*

das Geheimnis, -se (5) secret gehören (*dat.*) (5) to belong to

das Geld (1) money

der Geldbeutel, — (9) purse, pocketbook

die Gelegenheit, -en (18) opportunity, chance

der Gelehrte (*adj. noun*) (9) scholar genau (2) exact(ly), precise(ly) genial (9) ingenious genug (1) enough genügen (8) to suffice, be enough

das Gepäck (2) luggage

der Gepäckträger,—(5) porter gerade (4) just (now)

das Gericht, -e (19) court; vor Gericht in court gern (2) gladly; etwas gern tun (2, 20) to like doing something; gern haben (12, 20) to be fond of

der Geruch, ⸚e (9) smell

das Gerücht, -e (6) rumor

das Geschenk, -e (7) gift, present

die Geschichte, -n (5) story

geschieden sein (7) to be divorced

das Geschirr (12) dishes; das Geschirr spülen to do the dishes

der Geschmack, ⸚e (9) taste

die Geschwister (9) brothers and sisters

das Gesetz, -e (2) law

die Geste, -n (2) gesture gestern (1) yesterday

die Gesundheit (9) health gewinnen, gewann, gewonnen (2, 3) to win

das Gewitter,—(15) thunderstorm sich (*acc.*) gewöhnen an (*acc.*) (17) to get used or accustomed to

die Glatze, -n (6) bald head; eine Glatze bekommen to go bald

der Glaube (*weak; gen.* -ns) (5) faith glauben (1) to believe gleich: es ist mir (ganz) gleich (15) it is (all) the same to me

das Glück (12) luck; großes Glück haben to be very lucky; zum Glück (9) luckily glücklich sein über (*acc.*) (8) to be happy about

das Gold (5) gold

die Grammatik, -en (1) grammar gratulieren (*dat.*) zu (*dat.*) (5, 8) to congratulate on grausam (16) cruel

die Grippe, -n (1) flu groß (3, 10) big, large, tall (*referring to a person's height*) großartig (6) great

die Großeltern (7) grandparents grün (9) green

der Grund, ⸚e (7) reason; aus diesem Grund for this reason

der Grundsatz, ⸚e (20) principle

der Gruß, ⸚e (10) greeting grüßen (17) to greet, say hello gut (10) good

das Haar, -e (20) hair; sich (*dat.*) die Haare schneiden lassen to get a haircut haben, hatte, gehabt (1, 3) to have

der Haken,—(7) hook

die Hälfte, -n (11) half

das Hallenbad, ⸚er (12) indoor swimming pool halten (hält), hielt, gehalten (2, 3) to hold; stop

die Haltung, -en (16) attitude

die **Hand**, ⸚e (3) hand
handeln von (*dat.*) (8) to deal with, be about
die **Handschrift**, -en (9) handwriting
der **Handschuh**, -e (5) glove
hängen (20) to hang (*activity*)
hängen, hing, gehangen (20) to hang (*condition*)
hassen (2) to hate
das **Hauptfach**, ⸚er (6) major
das **Haus**, ⸚er (2) house; **zu Hause sein** (1) to be at home; **zu Hause bleiben** (13) to stay at home; **nach Hause gehen** (7) to go home
die **Hausaufgaben** (*pl.*) (1) homework
der **Hausmann**, ⸚er (17) house husband
der **Hausmeister**,—(5) janitor
die **Hautcreme** (2) skin cream
heben, hob, gehoben (3) to raise, lift
heiraten (1) to marry, get married
der **Heiratsantrag**, ⸚e (12) marriage proposal; **einen Heiratsantrag machen** to propose marriage
heiß (10) hot
heißen, hieß, geheißen (1) to be called, be named
der **Held** (*weak*), -en (5) hero
die **Heldin**, -nen (5) heroine
helfen (hilft), half, geholfen (dat.) (2, 3) to help
hell (9) light, light-colored
der **Herbst**, -e (11) fall
der **Herr** (weak; -n), -en (5) gentleman; **Herr...Mr....**
herrlich (18) magnificent
das **Herz** (weak; gen. -ns), -en (3, 5) heart
heute (1) today; **heute abend** (11) tonight (before bedtime); **heute nacht** tonight (after bedtime)
hier (2) here
die **Hilfe**, -n (8) help
hinten (19) behind, in the back; **nach hinten gehen** to go to the back
hinter (*acc./dat.*) (7) behind
das **Hobby**, -s (5) hobby
hoch (10) high
höchstens (10) at the most
hoffen (2) to hope
hoffentlich (1) hopefully, I hope
die **Hoffnung**, -en (2) hope
hoffnungslos (9) hopeless

höflich (9) polite
der **Höhepunkt**, -e (5) high point
holen (2) to (go and) get, fetch; **sich** (dat.) **etwas holen** (17) to get something for oneself
das **Holz**, ⸚er (7) wood
hören (4) to hear
der **Hörsaal, die Hörsäle** (11) lecture hall
das **Hotel**, -s (6) hotel
hübsch (10) pretty
der **Hund**, -e (9) dog
der **Hunger** (3) hunger; **Hunger haben** to be hungry

die **Idee**, -n (9) idea
immer (2) always
importieren (18) to import
in (*acc./dat.*) (7) in, into, to
indem (*sub. conj.*) (12) by (*doing something*)
die **Information**, -en (5) information
das **Inserat**, -e (20) ad, advertisement; **ein Inserat in die Zeitung setzen** to put an ad in the newspaper
intelligent (10) intelligent
die **Intelligenz** (9) intelligence
interessant (2) interesting
sich (*acc.*) **interessieren für** (*acc.*) (17) to be interested in
investieren (4) to invest
sich (*acc.*) **irren** (17) to be mistaken
irritieren (2) to irritate
der **Irrtum**, ⸚er (20) error
das **Italien** (3) Italy
italienisch (1) Italian
die **Jacke**, -n (14) jacket
das **Jahr**, -e (2) year
die **Jahreszeit**, -en (11) season
das **Jahrhundert**, -e (11) century
der **Januar** (11) January
jeder, jedes, jede (6) every, each
jemals (11) ever
jemand (4) somebody, someone
jener, jenes, jene (6) that
jetzig (11) present
jetzt (1) now
der **Job**, -s (3) job
der **Journalist** (*weak*), -en male journalist
die **Journalistin**, -nen (5) female journalist
der **Juli** (11) July
jung (10) young

der Junge (*weak*), -n (5) boy
der Juni (1) June

der Kaffee (4) coffee; Kaffee kochen (10) to
    make coffee
der Kalender, -(5) calendar
    kalt (1) cold
die Kälte: bei dieser Kälte (¨) in this cold
die Kamera, -s (5) camera
das Kapitel, - (5) chapter
    kaputt sein (6) to be broken (*not working*)
die Karriere, -n (6) career
der Käse (9) cheese
der Katalog, -e (5) catalogue
die Karte, -n (1) card; Karten spielen (3) to
    play cards
der Kassettenrecorder, - (1) cassette recorder
die Katastrophe, -n (18) catastrophe
    kaufen (1) to buy; sich (*dat.*) etwas
        kaufen (17) to buy something for
        oneself
der Kaviar (9) caviar
    kein (1) no, not a, not any
    kennen, kannte, gekannt (1, 3) to know,
        be acquainted with
    kennenlernen (4) to get to know, meet
        (*for the first time*)
das Kind, -er (2) child
das Kino, -s (1) movie theater
der Klapperkasten, ¨ (9) boneshaker
    klären (16) to clarify
der Klatsch (5) gossip
    klatschen (4) to gossip
das Klavier, -e (6) piano; Klavier spielen to
    play the piano
das Kleid, -er (5) dress
    klein (10) small, little, short (*referring to
    a person's height*)
    kleinlich (13) petty
    klingeln (15) to ring the bell; es klingelt
        the bell is ringing
    klingen, klang, geklungen (14) to sound
    klopfen (15) to knock; es klopft there is
        a knock at the door
    klug (16) smart
das Klügste (16) the smartest thing
    kochen (4) to cook; Kaffee kochen to
        make coffee; selbst (selber) kochen
        (17) to do one's cooking
der Koffer,—(3) suitcase
die Kombination, -en (14) combination

kommen, kam, ist gekommen (1, 3) to
    come; wie kommt es? (9) how come?
das Kompliment, -e (2) compliment
    kompliziert (2) complicated
der Kompromiß, -sse (12) compromise; einen
    Kompromiß schließen, schloß, ge-
    schlossen to make a compromise, to
    compromise
die Konditorei, -en (5) pastry shop
    können (kann), konnte, gekonnt (4) can,
        to be able to; ich kann nicht anders I
        can't help it
die Konstruktion, -en (16) construction; die
    grammatische Konstruktion the gram-
    matical construction
    sich (*acc.*) konzentrieren auf (*acc.*) (17)
    to concentrate on
das Konzert, -e (1) concert
der Konzertsaal, die Konzertsäle (5) concert
    hall
der Kopf, ¨e (5) head
der Kopfschmerz, -en (1) headache
    korrigieren (2) to correct
    kosten (1) to cost
die Krabbe, -n (20) shrimp
    krank (2) ill, sick; schwer krank sein
        (14) to be seriously ill
das Krankenhaus, ¨er (2) hospital
die Krankheit, -en (5) illness, sickness
    disease
der Krieg, -e (8) war
    kritisieren (2) to criticize
der Kuchen,—(4) cake
der Kugelschreiber,—(6) ballpoint pen
der Kühlschrank, ¨e (9) refrigerator
der Kunde (*weak*), -n (5) customer
der Künstler, - (20) artist
der Kurs, -e (12) course; mit einem Kurs
    auf•hören to drop a course
    kurz (10) short
der Kuß, ¨sse (2) kiss

    lächeln (2) to smile
    lachen über (*acc.*) (1, 8) to laugh at *or*
    about
der Laden, ¨ (18) shop, store
    laden (lädt), lud, geladen (2) to load
die Lampe, -n (7) lamp
das Lampenfieber (3) stage fright
das Land, ¨er (13) country; aufs Land ziehen,
    zog, ist gezogen to move to the country

landen (ist) (3) to land
lang (10) long
lange (2) a long time
langsam (10) slow
sich (*acc.*) langweilen (17) to be bored,
    get bored
langweilig (3) boring
der Lärm (3) noise
lassen (läßt), ließ, gelassen (3) to let leave
der Lastwagen,—(20) truck
laufen (läuft), lief, ist gelaufen (2, 3)
    to run
die Laune (1) mood; gute/ schlechte
    Laune haben to be in a good/ bad mood
laut (10) loud
das Leben (13) life
die Lebenshaltungskosten (*pl.*) (20) cost of
    living
das Leder (7) leather
ledig (13) single
legen (20) to put (*in a lying position*), lay,
    make lie
der Lehrer,—(5) male teacher
die Lehrerin, -nen (5) female teacher
leicht (3) easy
leider (1) unfortunately
leihen, lieh, geliehen (14) to lend
die Leine, -n (15) line, rope; an der Leine
    führen to keep on a leash
leise (3) soft, low (*tone, voice*)
sich (*dat.*) etwas leisten (17) to treat
    oneself to something; sich etwas
    leisten können to be able to afford
    something
die Leistung, -en (16) achievement
die Leiter, -n (2) ladder
lernen (2) to learn
lesen (liest), las gelesen (2) to read
leugnen (20) to deny
die Leute (*pl.*) (1) people
die Liebe (5) love
lieben (1) to love
die Liebesgeschichte, -n (6) love story
der Liebling, -e (*male or female*) (8) darling
das Lied, -er (9) song
liederlich (10) sloppy
liegen, lag, gelegen (3) to lie, be situated
loben (18) to praise
der Löffel,—(5) spoon
logisch (10) logical
die Lohnerhöhung, -en (20) wage increase

lösen (4) to solve
die Lösung, -en (10) solution
die Lotterie, -n (13) lottery
die Lüge, -n (4) lie
    lügen, log, gelogen (14) to lie, tell a lie
    (keine) Lust haben zu (*dat.*) (7) (not) to
    be in the mood to, (not) to feel like

machen (2) to make; das macht nichts
    (6) that doesn't matter
das Mädchen,—(5) girl
der Magister (12) the Master's; den Magister
machen to get one's Master's degree
der Mai (11) May
    Mal: dieses Mal (3) this time
    mancher, manches, manche (6) many a:
        pl. some, a few
    manchmal (1) sometimes
    manipulieren (2) to manipulate
der Mantel, ¨ (5) coat
die Mappe, -n (7) folder
das Märchen,—(5) fairy tale
der Marktplatz, ¨e (7) marketplace
    marschieren (ist) (3) to march
der März (11) March
die Maschine, -n (20) machine, plane
die Medaille, -n (9) medal
    mehr (1) more
    meinen (2) to mean
    meinetwegen (7) as far as I am
        concerned, for all I care
die Meinung, -en (5) opinion; meiner
    Meinung nach (7) in my opinion
    meistens (9) mostly, usually
der Mensch (weak), -en (9) man, human
        being
der Menschenverstand (9) human under-
        standing; gesunder Menschenverstand
        common sense
    merken (3) to notice
die Methode, -n (9) method
    mies (12) crummy
der Miesepeter,—(male or female) (2) grouch
die Miete, -n (9) rent
    mieten (3) to rent
der Mieter,—(10) tenant
die Milch (9) milk
die Milliarde, -n (11) billion
die Million, -en (5) million
der Millionär, -e (6) millionaire
    mindestens (10) at least

die **Minute, -n** (11) minute
miserabel (9) miserable
mißachten (2) to disregard
mißverstehen, mißverstand, mißver-
standen (2, 3) to misunderstand
mit (*dat.*) with
der **Mitarbeiter,—**(14) collaborator
mit•bringen, brachte mit, mitgebracht
(2, 3) to bring along
mit-fahren (fährt mit), fuhr mit, ist mitge-
fahren (3) to ride with someone
das **Mitglied, -er** (6) member
mit•kommen, kam mit, ist mitgekommen
(2) to come along
mit•nehmen (nimmt mit), nahm mit,
mitgenommen (2, 3) to take along
der **Mittag, -e** (11) noon; **zu Mittag essen** (19)
to have lunch
die **Mitternacht** (11) midnight
der **Mittwoch, -e** (11) Wednesday
mögen (mag), mochte, gemocht (4) to
like; **ich möchte** I would like
möglich (1) possible
die **Möglichkeit, -en** (5) possibility
der **Monat, -e** (2) month
der **Mond, -e** (20) moon
der **Montag, -e** (1) Monday
der **Morgen,—**(11) morning
morgen (1, 11) tomorrow
das **Motel, -s** (5) motel
das **Motorrad, ̈-er** (3) motorcycle
müde (2) tired
das **Museum, die Museen** (5) museum
die **Musik** (5) music
das **Musikinstrument, -e** (6) musical instrument
müssen (muß), mußte, gemußt (4) must,
to have to
mysteriös (9) mysterious

nach (*dat.*) (7) after, to, according to
der **Nachbar, -n** (2) male neighbor
die **Nachbarin, -nen** (2) female neighbor
die **Nachbarschaft, -en** (20) neighborhood
nachdem (*sub. conj.*) (3, 12) after
nach•geben (gibt nach), gab nach, nach-
gegeben (2, 3) to give in, yield
nach•gehen, ging nach, ist nachgegangen
(11) to be slow (clock)
nachher (19) afterwards
der **Nachmittag, -e** (11) afternoon

die **Nachricht, -en** (8) news
die **Nacht, ̈-e** (11) night (*after bedtime*)
der **Nachtisch, -e** (16) dessert
nächst- (1) nearest, next
nahe (10) near
der **Name** (*weak; gen.* **-ns**), **-n** (1, 5) name
die **Nase, -n** (4) nose; **die Nase ins Buch**
stecken to hit the books
naß (20) wet
natürlich (1) naturally, of course
neben (*acc./dat.*) (7) next to, beside
das **Nebenfach, ̈-er** (6) minor
das **Nebenzimmer, -** (9) adjoining room
nehmen (nimmt), nahm, genommen
(2, 3) to take
nennen, nannte, genannt (3) to call, name
der **Nerv, -en** (1) nerve; **diese Leute gehen**
mir auf die Nerven (9) these people are
getting on my nerves
der **Nervenzusammenbruch, ̈-e** (3) nervous
breakdown
nervös (2) nervous
nett (1) nice
neu (1) new
neuerdings (20) recently; **erst neuerdings**
only recently
die **Neugierde** (13) curiosity; **vor Neugierde**
sterben to die of curiosity
neugierig (9) curious, nosy
nicht (1) not; **nicht mehr** (9) not anymore
nichts (2) nothing
nie (2) never
niemand (2) nobody
noch nicht (2) not yet
die **Note, -n** (1) grade
die **Notiz, -en** (6) note
der **November** (11) November
die **Nummer, -n** (5) number
nur (13) only

ob (*sub. conj.*) (1, 12) whether, if
oben (19) at the top, upstairs, **nach oben**
gehen to go upstairs
obgleich (*sub. conj.*) (12) although
das **Obst** (9) fruit
obwohl (*sub. conj.*) (12) although
oder (12) or
öffnen (2) to open
oft (2) often
ohne (acc.) (7) without
der **Oktober** (11) October

die Olympischen Spiele (11) Olympic Games
die Oper, -n (7) opera
die Operation, -en (5) operation
    optimistisch (14) optimistic
der Orangensaft, ⸚e (10) orange juice
    ordentlich (10) orderly, neat
    organisieren (2) to organize
der Osten (5) east

    paar; ein paar (2) a few, some
das Paket, -e (5) parcel
der Park, -s (3) park
    parken (4) to park
der Parkplatz, ⸚e (12) parking space, parking
    lot
die Party, -s (5) party
    passieren (ist) (3) to happen
der Patient (weak), -en (2) patient
die Pause, -n (2) recess, break; eine
    Pause machen to take a break
    peinlich (9) embarassing
die Perle, -n (8) pearl; sie ist eine Perle she is
    a gem
die Pfeife, -n (8) pipe
das Picknick, -e or -s (8) picnic
der Plan, ⸚e (14) plan
der Plattenspieler, - (4) record player
das Plätzchen,—(4) cookie
    platzen (ist) (12) to blow out, burst
    pleite sein (3) to be broke
    plötzich (19) suddenly, all of a sudden
die Polizei (5) police
der Polizeiwagen (3) police car
der Polizist (weak), -en (5) policeman
die Polizistin, -nen (5) policewoman
    portugiesisch (9) Portuguese
die Post (2) mail; die Post nachschicken (19)
    to forward the mail
das Postamt, ⸚er (2) post office
    praktisch (10) practical
der Präsident (weak), -en (5) president
der Preis, -e (2) prize; (9) price
der Preisträger,—(20) prize winner
das Problem, -e (5) problem
    problematisch (3) problematic
der Professor (weak), -en (5) male professor
die Professorin, -nen (6) female professor
das Programm, -e (5) program
das Projekt, -e (3) project
    prophezeien (14) to prophesy, predict
der Protest, -e (5) protest

der Prozeß, -sse (14) trial; den Prozeß ver-
    lieren, verlor, verloren to lose the case
die Prüfung, -en (2) exam, test
der Punkt, -e (16) point
    pünktlich (1) punctual, on time
    putzen (17, 20) to clean; das Fenster
    putzen to wash the window; sich (dat.)
    die Zähne putzen to brush one's teeth

die Qual, -en (16) pain

das Rad, ⸚er (5) wheel
das Radio, -s (6) radio
der Rahmen, - (6) frame
der Rasen, -n (20) lawn; den Rasen mähen
    to mow the lawn
    sich (acc.) rasieren (17) to shave
    raten (rät), riet, geraten (2, 3) to advise
    rauchen (1) to smoke
das Raumschiff, -e (20) spaceship
    reagieren auf (acc.) (8) to react to
die Rechnung, -en (1) bill
    recht haben (2) to be right
der Rechtsanwalt, ⸚e (6) male lawyer
die Rechtsanwältin, -nen (14) female lawyer
die Rede, -n (19) speech; eine Rede halten
    (hält), hielt, gehalten to make a speech
    reden (2) to speak, talk
der Redner,—(3) speaker
das Referat, -e (8) seminar paper (oral
    presentation)
das Regal, -e (5) shelf
der Regenschirm, -e (20) umbrella
das Regenwetter (5) rainy weather
    regnen (2) to rain
der Reifen,—(12) tire
die Reihe, -n (2) row; in der ersten Reihe in
    the first row
die Reihenfolge, -n (7) sequence, order
    reinigen lassen (20) to have dry-cleaned
die Reinigung (5) cleaning; in die Reinigung
    bringen to take to the cleaners
die Reise, -n (13) trip; eine Reise um die Welt
    machen to take a trip around the world
der Reiseleiter,—(5) male travel guide
die Reiseleiterin, -nen female travel guide
    reisen (ist) (2, 3) to travel
der Reisende (adj. noun) (9) traveler
    reiten, ritt, ist geritten (3) to ride, go on
    horseback
    reizend (20) charming

die Reklame, -n (7) advertisement; **Reklame machen** to advertise

die Reklamesendung, -en (5) commercial (*radio, television*)

die Religion, -en (5) religion

rennen, rannte, ist gerannt (3) to run

das Rennpferd, -e (20) racehorse

reparieren (4) to repair

der Reporter, — (5) male reporter

die Reporterin, -nen (5) female reporter

die Republik, -en (5) republic

das Restaurant, -s (5) restaurant

das Resultat, -e (16) result

der Richter, — (14) judge

richtig (6) right, correct

riechen, roch, gerochen nach (dat.) (9, 15) to smell of

der Ring, -e (1) ring

der Roman, -e (3) novel

der Rücktritt, -e (14) resignation

die Ruhe (20) quiet, peace; **in Ruhe lassen (läßt), ließ, gelassen** to leave alone

russisch (9) Russian

der Saal, die Säle (5) hall

die Sache, -n (2) matter, thing

sagen (1) to say; **sagen wir ...** (7) let's say ...

der Salat, -e (9) salad

sammeln (2) to collect

der Samstag, -e (11) Saturday

der Satz, ⁻e (2) sentence

das Saubermachen (8) cleaning (*generally house cleaning*)

sauer (9) sour

der Schach (19) chess; **Schach spielen** to play chess

schade sein (1) to be a pity

schade (2) too bad

das Schaf, -e (9) sheep; **das schwarze Schaf sein** to be the black sheep

die Schallplatte, -n (3) record; *short*: **die Platte, -n**

das Schaufenster, — (17) shop window; **sich** (*dat.*) **die Schaufenster an-sehen (sieht an), sah an, angesehen** to window-shop

der Schauspieler, — (5) male actor

die Schauspielerin, -nen (5) actress

der Scheck, -s (5) check

schenken (3) to give (*as a gift*)

schick (2) chic

schicken (16) to send

das Schicksal, -e (8) destiny, fate

schief•gehen, ging schief, ist schiefgegangen (15) to go wrong

das Schild, -er (18) sign

schlafen (schläft), schlief, geschlafen (2, 3) to sleep

der Schlager, — (3) pop song

die Schlagsahne (4) whipped cream

schlank (10) slim

die Schlankheitskur, -en (4) slimming diet; **eine Schlankheitskur machen** to be *or* go on a diet

der Schlaukopf, ⁻e (7) male or female whiz kid, smarty

schlecht (10) bad

schließen, schloß, geschlossen (2) to close

das Schließfach, ⁻er (20) locker

das Schloß, ⁻sser (18) castle

schneien (3) to snow

schnell (1) fast

schockierend (9) shocking

schockiert sein (1) to be shocked

schon (2) already

schreiben, schrieb, geschrieben (1, 3) to write

die Schreibmaschine, -n (13) typewriter

der Schreibtisch, -e (7) desk

schreien, schrie, geschrie(e)n (7, 15) to scream, cry out; **vor Schmerzen schreien** to cry out in pain

schüchtern (14) shy

der Schuh, -e (5) shoe

die Schuld, -en (3) debt; **die Schuld** (18) guilt

schuld sein an (*dat.*) (14) to be to blame for

der Schürzenjäger, — (20) womanizer

schwänzen (2) to cut *or* skip class

schwarz (9) black

schweigen, schwieg, geschwiegen (12) to remain silent

schwer (4, 9) heavy; difficult, hard

die Schwester, -n (5) sister

die Schwierigkeit, -en (8) difficulty; **Schwierigkeiten haben mit** (*dat.*) to have trouble with

das Schwimmbad, ⁻er (2) swimming pool

der See, -n (19) lake

sehen (sieht), sah, gesehen (2, 3) to see

sehr (1) very

sein, war, ist gewesen (2, 3) to be
seit (*dat.*) (2, 7) since; seitdem (8) since (*referring to time*)
die Sekunde, -n (11) second
selbst (17) oneself; even
der Selbstmord, -e (16) suicide; Selbstmord begehen, beging, begangen to committ suicide
das Semester, — (4) semester, term
die Semesterarbeit, -en (4) term paper
senden, sandte, gesandt (3) to send
die Sendung, -en (5) broadcast
der September (11) September
die Serviette, -n (5) napkin
der Sessel, — (7) armchair
setzen (20) to put, set, make sit
sich (*acc.*) setzen (17) to sit down
siegesbewußt (14) confident of victory
das Silber (5) silver
singen, sang, gesungen (3) to sing
der Sinn, -e (7) sense, mind
sitzen, saß, gesessen (2, 3) to sit
die Sitzung, -en (14) session
der Skandal, -e (3) scandal
so... wie (10) as...as
sobald (*sub. conj.*) (12) as soon as
sofort (2) immediately, at once
sogar (9) even
solange (*sub. conj.*) (12) as long as
solcher, solches, solche (6) such a; pl. such
sollen, sollte, gesollt (4) to be supposed to, expected to, should
der Sommer, — (11) summer
die Sommerferien (*pl.*) summer vacation
das Sommerkleid, -er (5) summer dress
sondern (12) but, rather
der Sonnabend, -e (11) Saturday
der Sonnenuntergang, ⸚e (6) sunset
der Sonntag, -e (1) Sunday
die Sorge, -n (10) worry
soviel (2) so much; soviel ich weiß (15) as far as I know
das Spanien (9) Spain
spanisch (9) Spain
die Spannung, -en (14) tension
sparsam (11) thrifty, economical
der Spaß (3) fun; es macht mir Spaß it's fun to me, I enjoy it; zum Spaß sagen (14) to say as a joke
spät (2) late; zu spät kommen (3) to be late

der Spaziergang, ⸚e (7) walk
spazieren•gehen, ging spazieren, ist spazierengegangen (3) to go for a walk
die Spezialität, -en (5) specialty
spielen (1) to play
der Sport (12) sport; viel Sport treiben, trieb getrieben to do a lot of sport
die Sporthalle, -n (7) gymnasium
sprechen (spricht), sprach, gesprochen mit (*dat.*) (1, 3, 8) to speak with *or* to; sprechen von (*dat.*) (8) to talk of *or* about; von sich (*dat.*) sprechen to talk of oneself
die Sprechstunde, -n (11) consultation (hour); Sprechstunde haben to have office hours
die Stadt, ⸚e (1) city, town
der Stadtrat, ⸚e (14) male town councilor
die Stadträtin, -nen (14) female town councilor
der Stadtteil, -e (10) part of town
stark (9) strong
statt (*gen.*) (7) instead; statt dessen (8) instead of that
das Statussymbol, -e (6) status symbol
stehen, stand, gestanden (3) to stand
stehen•bleiben, bliebstehen, ist stehengeblieben (11) to stop (clock)
stehlen (stiehlt), stahl, gestohlen (9) to steal; der gestohlene Wagen the stolen car
steigen, stieg, ist gestiegen (3) to climb, go up
die Stelle, -n (3) position, job
stellen (20) to put (*in an upright position*)
das Stellenangebot, -e (16) job offer
sterben (stirbt), starb, ist gestorben (3) to die; vor Angst sterben (13) to die of fear
die Steuer, -n (2) tax
das Stiefkind, -er (18) stepchild
die Stimme, -n (19) voice; mit lauter (leiser) Stimme in a loud (low) voice
stimmen (9) to be correct; das stimmt *or* stimmt that's correct *or* correct
das Stipendium, die Stipendien (2) scholarship
der Stoff, -e (4) material, fabric
stolz sein auf (*acc.*) (8) to be proud of
stören (2) to disturb
stoßen (stößt), stieß, gestoßen (2,3) to push
stottern (20) to stutter

die Strafe, -n (4) fine
der Strafzettel, — (3) traffic ticket
strahlen (14) to beam
streichen, strich, gestrichen (20 to paint (*house*)
streiken (9) to strike, be on strike
der Strikende (*adj. noun*) (9) striker
der Streit (12) quarrel, fight
streng (1) strict
der Strumpf, ¨e (15) stocking
das Stück, -e (4) piece
der Student (*weak*), -en (5) male student
die Studentin, -nen (5) female student
das Studentenheim, -e (4) dormitory
studieren (2) to study
das Studium, die Studien (11) study; **mit dem Studium auf•hören** (13) to drop out of school (*higher education*); **mit dem Studium fertig werden** to graduate
stumm (17) silent(ly)
die Stunde, -n (5, 7) hour; class (*instruction*);
die Deutschstunde German class
stur (4) stubborn
suchen (9) to seek, to look for
der Supermarkt (12) supermarket
das Symbol, -e (5) symbol
sympathisch sein (20) to be likeable, pleasant

die Tablette, -n (11) tablet, pill; **eine Tablette ein•nehmen (nimmt ein), nahm ein, eingenommen** to take a tablet, pill
tadeln (10) to reprimand
der Tag, -e (5) day
taktlos (9) tactless
die Tankstelle, -n (1) gas station
tanzen (2) to dance
die Tasche, -n (10) bag
die Tasse, -n (15) cup
die Tatsache, -n (20) fact
sich (*acc.*) täuschen (17) to deceive oneself
das Taxi, -s (6) taxi
der Taxifahrer, — (6) taxi driver
der Tee, -s (9) tea
das Telefon, -e (7) telephone; **ans Telefon gehen** to go to *or* answer the phone
das Telegramm, -e (3) telegram
der Tennisplatz, ¨e (7) tennis court
das Theater, — (7) theater
das Theaterstück, -e (5) stage play

teuer (9) expensive
tief (2) deep
tippen (13) to type
der Tisch, -e (7) table
die Telefonnummer, -n (5) telephone number
das Thema, die Themen (5) topic, theme
der Tip, -s (5) tip, hint, clue
der Titel, — (5) title
die Tortur, -en (6) torture
tragen (trägt), trug, getragen (3) to carry
der Trainer, — (5) coach
trauen (*dat.*) (5) to trust
der Traum, ¨e (6) dream
die Toilette, -n (1) toilet, lavatory
tolerant (1) tolerant
treten (tritt), trat, getreten (2) to step
treu (4) faithful
trinken, trank, getrunken (3) to drink
das Trinkgeld, -er (5) tip, gratuity
die Trompete, -n (6) trumpet; **die Trompete spielen** to play the trumpet
trotz (*gen.*) (7) in spite of
trotzdem (3) nevertheless, in spite of that
die Trunksucht (8) alcoholism
tun, tat, getan (2,3) to do; **so tun, als ob …** (14) to act as if … pretend
die Tür, -en (2) door

die U-Bahn, -en (*short for* Untergrundbahn) (7) subway
übel•nehmen (nimmt übel), nahm übel, übelgenommen (2,3) to take amiss, resent, take offense
üben (6) to practice
über (*acc./dat.*) (7) above, over, across
der Überblick, -e (20) overview
überglücklich (18) overjoyed
überholen (4) to overtake, pass
der Überlebende (*adj. noun*) survivor
sich (*dat.*) etwas überlegen (17) to think about something
übermorgen (11) the day after tomorrow
übernachten (12) to stay overnight
die Überraschung, -en (6) surprise
überreden (4) to persuade
übersehen (übersieht), übersah, übersehen (16) to overlook
übersetzen (2) to translate
über•setzen (2) to ferry across

Überstunden machen (12) to work over time

überzeugen (3) to convince; überzeugt sein to be convinced

übrigens (16) by the way

die Übung, -en (5) exercise

die Uhr, -en (7) clock, watch; die Uhr stellen (11) to set the clock

um (*acc.*) (7) around

umarmen (17) to embrace, hug

umgehen, umging, umgangen (2) to circumvent, dodge, evade, bypass

um•gehen, ging um, ist umgegangen (2) to go around, circulate

um•ziehen, zog um, (ist) umgezogen (20) to move (*change residence*)

der Umzug, ⁻e (15) move (*change of residence*)

umbedingt (12) absolutely, by all means

und (12) and

der Unfall, ⁻e (3) accident

unfreundlich (2) unfriendly

unhöflich (2) impolite

die Universität, -en (5) university

unsicher (8) insecure

der Unsinn (3) nonsense

unten (19) at the bottom, below, downstairs; nach unten gehen to go downstairs

unter (*acc./dat.*) (7) under

unterbrachen (unterbricht), unterbrach, unterbrochen (18) to interrupt

unterschreiben, unterschrieb, unterschrieben (4) to sign

die Unterschrift, -en (4) signature

untersuchen (18) to investigate

die Untertasse, -n (20) saucer; die fliegende Untertasse flying saucer

die Unzufriedehheit (12) dissatisfaction

der Urlaub, -e (12) vacation (*from a job*)

die Vase, -n (5) vase

der Verbrecher, — (20) criminal

verbreiten (18) to spread

verdienen (3, 9) to earn, deserve

sich (*acc.*) verfahren (verfährt), verfuhr, verfahren (17) to lose one's way (*driving*)

vergessen (vergißt), vergaß, vergessen (2, 3) to forget

Vergessenheit: in Vergessenheit geraten (20) to fall into oblivion, be forgotten

verhaften (18) to arrest

verhandeln (11) to negotiate

verheiratet sein mit (dat.) (8) to be married to

verkaufen (2) to sell

der Verkäufer, — (5) salesman

die Verkäuferin, -nen (3) saleslady

sich (*acc.*) verlaufen (verläuft), verlief, verlaufen (17) to lose one's way (*walking*)

verlegen sein (12) to be embarrassed

verliebt sein in (acc.) (8) to be in love with

verlieren, verlor, verloren (3) to lose

verlobt sein mit (dat.) (8) to be engaged to

der Verlobte (*adj. noun*) (9) fiancé

die Verlobung, -en (8) engagement

vermeiden, vermied, vermieden (12) to avoid

vernachlässigen (11) to neglect

vernünftig (2) sensible, reasonable

verrückt sein auf (*acc.*) to be crazy about

verschieben, verschob, verschoben (14) to postpone

verschlafen (verschläft), verschlief, verschlafen (11) to oversleep

verschwinden, verschwand, ist verschwunden (11) to disappear

die Versicherungsgesellschaft, -en (13) insurance company

Verspätung haben (12) to be late (*train, bus, phone*)

versprechen (verspricht), versprach, versprochen (3) to promise

das Versprechen halten (hält), hielt, gehalten (3) to keep the promise

der Verstand (5) reason, mind; den Verstand verlieren (6) to lose one's mind

verstehen, verstand, verstanden (1, 3) to understand; das versteht sich (von selbst) (18) that is understood, that goes without saying

versteigern (18) to auction off

versuchen (3) to try

die Versuchung, -en (4) temptation; in Versuchung führen to lead into temptation sich (*acc.*) verteidigen (17) to defend oneself

der Vertrag, ⁻e (4) contract

verwandt sein mit (*dat.*) (8) to be related to

der Verwandte (*adj. noun*) (15) relative

verwöhnen (18) to spoil (*someone*)

Verzeihung: um Verzeihung bitten, bat, gebeten (2, 3) to apologize

viel (2) much, a lot

vieles (16) many things

vielleicht (1) perhaps

völlig (20) completely

von (*dat*) (7) from, of, by

vor (*acc./dat.*) (7) in front of, before

voraus•sehen (sieht voraus), sah voraus, vorausgesehen (13) to foresee

vorbei•gehen, ging vorbei, ist vorbeigangen an (*dat.*) (17) to pass by

vor•gehen, ging vor, ist vorgegangen (11) to be fast (*clock*)

vorgestern (11) the day before yesterday

vor•haben, hatte vor, vorgehabt (2) to plan, have plans; **etwas anderes vorhaben** (12) to have something else planned

vorher (19) before

vor•kommen: es kommt mir so vor (14) it seems to me

vor•lesen (liest vor), las vor, vorgelesen (3) to read (*to someone*)

die **Vorlesung, -en** (1) lecture

der **Vormittag, -e** (11) late morning, forenoon

vorn (19) in front; **nach vorn gehen** to go to the front

der **Vorname, -n** (3) first name

der **Vorschlag, ¨e** suggestion

vorsichtig (2) careful

sich (*dat.*) **etwas vor•stellen** (17) to imagine something

der **Vortrag, ¨e** (14) lecture

das **Vorurteil, -e** (13) prejudice

wagen (12) to dare

wahr (2) true

während (*gen.*) (12) during

während (*sub. conj.*) (12) while

die **Wahrheit, -en** (1) truth

wahrscheinlich (3) probably

die **Wand, ¨e** (5) wall

wandern (ist) (3) to wander, hike

die **Wandtafel, -n** *or* die **Tafel, -n** (7) (black)board

wann (1) when

das **Warenhaus, ¨er** (7) department store

warm (10) warm

warnen (3) to warn

die **Warnung, -en** (2) warning

warten auf (*acc.*) (2, 8) to wait for

warum (1) why

was (1) what; **was für (ein)** (6) what kind of (a)

sich (*acc.*) **waschen (wäscht), wusch, gewaschen** (17) to wash (*oneself*)

sich (*dat.*) **die Hände waschen** (17) to wash one's hands

das **Wasser** (9) water

weder ... noch (8) neither ... nor

wegen (*gen.*) (7) because of

weil (*sub. conj.*) (12) because

der **Win, -e** (9) wine

das **Weinglas, ¨er** (5) wine glass

weiter•lesen (liest weiter), las weiter, weitergelesen (2, 3) to continue reading, go on reading

weiter•machen (2) to continue (*doing something*)

weiter•sprechen (spricht weiter), sprach weiter, weitergesprochen (2, 3) to continue talking, go on talking

welcher, welches, welche (6) which

die **Welt, -en** (7) world

das **Weltwunder, —** (9) wonder of the world

wenden, wandte, gewandt (3) to turn

wenig (2) little; **ein wenig** (4) a little

wenn (*sub. conj.*) (12) when, if: **wenn auch** (16) even though

werden (wird), wurde, ist geworden (1, 3) to get, become

wichtig (10) important

widersprechen (widerspricht), widersprach, widersprochen (*dat.*) (4) to contradict

sich (*dat.*) **widersprechen** (14, 17) to contradict oneself

wie (2) how; **wie lange** how long; **wie oft** how often

wieder (1) again; **schon wieder** (2) again (emphatic)

wiederholen (2) to repeat; **die Grammatik wiederholen** to review grammar

wieder•holen (2) to (go and) get something back

wiegen, wog, gewogen (10) to weigh

wieviel (1) how much

die **Willenskraft** (10) willpower

der **Wink, -e** (4) hint; **ein lesser Wink** a subtle hint

winken (20) to wave
der Winter, — (5, 11) winter
der Wintermantel, — (5) winter coat
wirklich (1) real(ly)
die Wirklichkeit (15) reality; in Wirklichkeit
in reality, in actual fact, actually
wirtschaftlich (14) economical
wissen (weiß) wußte, gewußt (1, 3) to
know; ich weiß es nicht mehr (3) I
don't remember
der Witz, -e (6) joke
wo (1) where, at what place
die Woche, -n (3) week
das Wochenende, -n (8) weekend
das Wochenendhaus, ¨er (8) (weekend)
cottage
wohnen (1) to live
die Wohnung, -en (3) apartment
wollen (will), wollte, gewollt, (4) to
want to, intend to; ich wollte gerade I
was on the point of, I was (just) about to
das Wunder, — (2) wonder, miracle; kein
Wunder no wonder
der Wunsch, ¨e (18) wish; einen Wunsch
erfüllen to make a wish come true; auf
eigenen Wunsch (19) at one's own
request

der Zahnarzt, ¨e (7) dentist
der Zahnschmerz, -en (7) toothache
zeichnen (2) to draw
zeigen (5) to show
die Zeit, -en (1) time
die Zeitung, -en (2) newspaper
der Zeitungsstand, ¨e (7) newsstand
die Zeitverschwendung, -en (6) waste of time
zelten (18) to camp (in a tent)
zerreißen, zerriß, zerrissen (2) to tear up
der Zeuge (weak), -n (14) witness
das Zeugnis, -se (8) report card
das Ziel, -e (18) goal; das Ziel erreichen to
reach the goal

die Zigarette, -n (5) cigarette
das Zimmer, — (2) room; in
einem Zimmer wohnen mit (dat.) (16)
to room with
zu (1) too
zu (dat.) (7) to, toward
der Zucker (9) sugar
zuerst (2) at first
der Zufall, ¨e (20) coincidence
zufrieden sein mit (dat.) (8) to be satisfied, content with
der Zug, ¨e (14) train; den Zug verpassen to
miss the train
zu•geben (gibt zu), gab zu, zugegeben
(4) to admit
zu•hören (2) to listen
der Zukunftsplan, ¨e (8) plan for the future
zu•machen (2) to close
zu•nehmen (nimmt zu), nahm zu,
zugenommen (2, 3) to gain weight
zurück•bringen, brachte zurück, zurück-
gebracht (2, 3) to bring back, take back
zurück•fahren (fährt zurück) fuhr
zurück, ist zurückgefahren (2, 3) to
drive back, return
zurück•geben, (gibt zurück), gab zurüc k,
zurückgegeben (2,3) to give back, return
zurück•gehen, ging zurück, ist zurückge-
gangen (2, 3) to go back, return
zurück•treten (tritt zurück, trat zurück,
ist zurückgetreten (14) to resign
zusammen•arbeiten (14) to work together,
collaborate
zusammen•stoßen (stößt zusammen),
stieß zusammen, ist zusammen-
gestoßen (20) to collide
zuviel (2) too much
der Zweck, -e (12) purpose: es hat keinen
Zweck it's no use, there is no point
zwischen (acc./dat.) (7) between

English-German Vocabulary

The explanations at the beginning of the German-English vocabulary apply also to the English-German vocabulary. The following listing contains the vocabulary items of the exercises that require translation from English into German.

to be able to (4) können (kann), konnte, gekonnt
above, over (7) über (*acc./dat.*)
achievement (16) die Leistung, -en
across from (7) gegenüber (*dat.*)
ad, advertisement (20) das Inserat, -e
admire (16) bewundern
to admit (4) zu•geben (gibt zu), gab zu, zugegeben
adult (9) der Erwachsene (*adj. noun*)
afford: to be able to afford something (17) sich (*dat.*) etwas leisten können
after (*prep.*) (7) nach (*dat.*)
after (*sub. conj.*) (12) nachdem
afternoon (11) der Nachmittag, -e
to be afraid (2) Angst haben
against (7) gegen (*acc.*)
airport (6) der Flughafen, ⁻; **to take to the airport** zum Flughafen bringen, brachte, gebracht
alarm clock (11) der Wecker, —; **to set the alarm clock** den Wecker stellen
all (6) alle
to be allowed to (4) dürfen (darf), durfte, gedurft
almost (14)= beinah(e), fast
along (7) entlang (*acc.*)
although (12) obgleich, obwohl (*sub. conbj.*)
always (2) immer
to be angry with (8) böse sein auf (*acc.*) or mit (*dat.*)
to become angry (3) böse weden (wird), wurde, ist geworden
to answer something (7) antworten auf (*acc.*)
antique (16) antik
to apologize (2) um Verzeihung bitten, bat, gebeten; (17) sich (*acc.*) entschuldigen
around (7) um (*acc.*)
artist (20) der Künstler, —
to arrest (18) verhaften
aside from that, besides (8) außerdem
to ask for, request (8) bitten, bat, gebeten um (*acc.*)
assistant (5) der Assistent (*weak*), -en
to asume (2) an•nehmen (nimmt an), nahm an, angenommen
at, at someone's place (6) bei (*dat.*)
attitude (16) die Haltung, -en
to auction off (18) versteigern
auditorium (7) das Auditorium, die Auditorien
to avoid (18) vermeiden, vermied, vermieden

bad: too bad (2) schade
bag (10) die Tasche, -n
ballpoint pen (6) der Kugelschreiber, —
bank (7) die Bank, -en
to bark (9) bellen
beginning (5) der Anfang, ⁻e
because (12) weil (*sub. conj.*)
because of (7) wegen (*gen.*); **because of me** wegen mir or meinetwegen; **because of that, therefore** (8) deswegen, deshalb
bed (7) das Bett, -en
before (*prep.*) (7) vor (*acc./dat.*)
before (*sub. conj.*) (12) bevor, ehe
behind (7) hinter (*acc./dat.*)
to begin (2, 3) an•fangen (fängt an), fing an, angefangen
to believe (10) glauben
bell: the bell is ringing (15) es klingelt
beside (7) neben (*acc./dat.*); **to be beside oneself** (17) außer sich (*dat.*) sein

besides (7) außer (*dat.*)

best: all the best (9) alles Gute!

better: to get better (4) besser werden (wird), wurde, ist geworden

between (7) zwischen (*acc./dat*)

bill (4) die Rechnung, -en

black (10) schwarz

bookstore (7) die Buchhandlung, -en

to be *or* get bored (17) sich (*acc.*) langweilen

boss (5) der Chef, -s; die Chefin, -nen

both (6) beide

to bowl (8) kegeln; to go bowling kegeln gehen, ging, ist gegangen

break: to take a break (2) ein Pause machen

briefcase (7) die Aktentasche, -n

to bring along (12) mit•bringen, brachte mit, mitgebracht

broadcast (6) die Sendung, -en

to be broke (13) pleite sein

brother (5) der Bruder, ∶

brown (10) braun

to bury (2) begraben (begräbt), begrub, begraben

business: that's nobody's business (15) das geht niemand etwas an

but (however, nevertheless) (12) aber

but (*rather*) (12) sondern

to buy (2) kaufen

cake (15) der Kuchen, —

to call (phone) (4) an•rufen, rief an, angerufen

to call off (18) ab•sagen

can (4) können (kann), konnte, gekonnt; I can't help it ich kann nicht anders

camera (5) Kamera, -s

car (1) der Wagen, —; das Auto, -s; to go by car (6) mit dem Wagen (Auto) fahren

car accident (14) der Autounfall, -e

care: to take care of (2) erledigen

career (6) die Karriere, -n

careful(ly) (2) vorsichtig

to cash a check (6) einen Scheck ein•lösen

catalogue (6) der Katalog, -e

to catch a cold (17) sich (acc.) erkälten

chance (6) die Chance, -n

cheap (16) billig

check (8) der Scheck, -s

chess (18) das Schach

child (5) das Kind, -er

child prodigy (20) das Wunderkind, -er

to clarify (18) klären

class: German class (7) die Deutschstunde, -n

to close (4) zu•machen

coach (5) der Trainer, —

coffee (7) der Kaffee; to make coffee (10) Kaffee kochen

coincidence (20) der Zufall, -e

color (10) die Farbe, -n

combination (14) die Kombination, -en

to come along (12) mit•kommen, kam mit, ist mitgekommen

to come in (2) herein•kommen, kam herein, ist hereingekommen

comfortable (10) bequem

commercial (*radio, television*) (5) die Werbesendung, -en

complicated (10) kompliziert

compliment (6) das Kompliment, -e

composition (10) der Aufsatz, ∸e

compromise: to make a compromise (12) einen Kompromiß schließen, schloß, geschlossen

to concentrate on (17) sich (acc.) konzentrieren auf (*acc.*)

concerned: as far as I am concerned (7) meinetwegen

concert (7) das Konzert, -e

to congratulate on (8) gratulieren zu (*dat.*)

consequence (12) die Folge, -n

contract (4) der Vertrag, -e

to contradict (12) widersprechen (widerspricht), widersprach, widersprochen (*dat.*)

contrary: on the contrary (4) im Gegenteil

to convince (12) überzeugen

to cook (17) kochen; to do one's own cooking selbst kochen

cookie (4) das Plätzchen, _

corner (7) die Ecke, -n

to cost (16) kosten

courage (12) der Mut

crazy (8) verrückt; to be crazy about verrückt sein auf (*acc.*); to drive crazy (16) verrückt machen

cruel (6) grausam

crummy (12) mies

to cry (20) weinen

curiosity (13) die Neugierde; to die of curiosity vor Neugierde sterben (stirbt), starb, ist gestorben

customer (5) der Kunde (*weak*), -n

dangerous (12) gefährlich
to dare (12) wagen
darling (8) der Liebling, -e (*male or female*)
date (5) das Datum, die Daten
daughter (5) die Tochter, ⸚
day (11) der Tag, -e
to deal with, be about (7) handeln von (*dat.*)
dean (5) der Dekan, -e
to defend oneself (17) sich (*acc.*) verteidigen
dentist (7) Zahnarzt, -e
department store (7) das Warenhaus, -er
desk (3) der Schreibtisch, -e
destiny, fate (8) das Schicksal, -e
detail (16) Einzelheit, -en
to develop (20) entwickeln
to die (13) sterben (stirbt), starb, ist gestorben;
    to die of fear vor Angst sterben
diet: to be on a diet (4) ein Schlankheitskur
    machen
director (5) der Direktor. -en
to disappoint (4) enttäuschen
disco (7) die Disko, -s
dishes: to do the dishes (12) das Geschirr
    spülen
to disturb (2) stören
to do (3) tun, tat, getan
dog (7) der Hund, -e
dormitory (2) das Studentenheim, -e
drama (5) das Drama, die Dramen
dream (6) Traum, ⸚e
to drink (4) trinken, trank, getrunken
to drive (2) fahren (fährt), fuhr, ist gefahren
driver's license (6) der Führerschein, -e
to drop a course (16) mit einem Kurs auf•
    hören
to dry-clean (20) reinigen; to have something
dry-cleaned etwas reinigen lassen
dumb (10) dumm
during (7) während (*gen.*)

early (10) früh; at the earliest frühestens
easy (12) leicht
to eat out (17) essen gehen, ging, ist gegangen
egotistical (10) egoistisch
embarrassing (16) peinlich
to embrace, hug (17) umarmen
employee (9) der Angestellte (*adj. noun*)
end (6) das Ende, -e
enemy (6) der Feind, -e
engaged (8) verlobt; to be engaged to verlobt
    sein mit (*dat.*)

enough (1) genug
to be enthusiastic about (8) begeistert sein
    von (dat.)
to envy (2) beneiden
error (20) der Irrtum, ⸚er
evening (11) der Abend, -e
every (6) jeder, jedes jede
exam (3) die Prüfung, -en; to pass the exam die
    Prüfung bestehen, bestand, bestanden; to
    flunk the exam in der Prüfung durch•fallen
    (fällt durch), fiel durch, ist durchgefallen
except (7) außer (*dat.*)
excuse, pretext (20) die Ausrede, -n
to excuse (2) entschuldigen
to expect (12) erwarten
expensive (13) teuer
to exploit (18) aus•nutzen
extremely (10) äußerst

to be fair (2) fair sein
faith (5) der Glaube (*weak*; *gen. -ns*), -en
faithful (12) treu
fall (11) der Herbst, -e
to fall asleep (14) ein•schlafen (schläft ein),
    schlief ein, ist eingeschlafen
family (8) die Familie, -n
famous (9) berühmt
fast (10) schnell; to be fast (*clock*) (11) vor•
    gehen, ging vor, ist vorgegangen
fat (12) dick
father (7) der Vater, ⸚
favor: to ask for a favor (12) um einen Gefal-
    len bitten, bat, gebeten
to feel like (12) Lust haben zu (*dat.*)
a few (9) ein paar
fight, quarrel (12) der Streit
film (9) der Film, -e
to find (12) finden, fand, gefunden
to finish (*talking*) (20) aus•reden
fire: there is a fire (15) es brennt
floor (7) der Fußboden, ⸚, *short:* der Boden, ⸚
flower (8) die Blume, -n
to flunk: to flunk the exam (3) in der Prüfung
    durch•fallen (fällt durch), fiel durch, ist
    durchgefallen
flying saucer (20) die fliegende Untertasse, -n
folder (7) die Mappe, -n
to be fond of (20) gern haben
for (*prep.*) (7) für (*acc.*)
for (*coord. conj.*) (12) denn
foreigner (5) der Ausländer, —

to foresee (13) voraus•sehen (sieht voraus), sah voraus, vorausgesehen
to forget (2) vergessen (vergißt), vergaß, vergessen
Friday (11) Freitag, -e
friend (1) der Freund, -e; die Freundin, -nen
friendly (10) freundlich
from (7) aus (*dat.*) or von (*dat.*); **from ... to ...** (11) von ... bis ...

to gain weight (4) zu•nehmen (nimmt zu), nahm zu, zugenommen
garage (7) die Garage, -n
gentleman (5) der Herr (*weak*; -n) -en
to get, become (2,3) werden (wird), wurde, ist geworden
to get, receive (2, 3) bekommen, bekam, bekommen
to get along with (12) aus•kommen, kam aus, ist ausgekommen mit (dat.)
to get one's Master's degree (12) den Magister machen
to get used *or* **accustomed to** (17) sich (*acc.*) gewöhnen an (*acc.*)
gift (8) das Geschenk, -e
girlfriend (1) die Freundin, -nen
to give up (12) auf•geben (gibt auf), gab auf, aufgegeben
glad (3) froh; **to be glad about** (8) froh sein über (*acc.*)
to go (2, 3) gehen, ging, ist gegangen; **to go back** (, 3) zurück•gehen; **to go home** (2) nach Hause gehen; **to go into** (16) ein•gehen auf (*acc.*); **to go on foot** (13) zu Fuß gehen; **to go out** (13) aus•gehen; **to go wrong** (15) schief•gehen
good (3) gut
to gossip (4) klatschen
grade (4) die Note, -n
great (13) großartig
to grumble (4) knurren

haircut: to get a haircut (20) sich (*dat.*) die Haare schneiden lassen
hairdresser (14) der Friseur, -e
to hand in (4) ein•reichen
to handle (*treat*) (12) behandeln
to happen (3) passieren (ist)
to be happy about (8) glücklich sein über (*acc.*); (17) sich (*acc.*) freuen über (*acc.*)
hard, difficult (10) schwer;

the hardest thing (10) das Schwerster
to hate (8) hassen
to have (2) haben (hat), hatte, gehabt
to have to (4) müssen (muß), mußte, gemußt
head: to lose one's head (6) den Kopf verlieren, verlor, verloren
to hear (14) hören
heart (5) das Herz (*weak; gen.* -ns) -en
help (8) die Hilfe, -n
to help (8) helfen (hilft), half, geholfen (*dat.*); **please help yourself** (17) bitte bedienen Sie sich
her (*poss.*) (6) ihr, ihre
hero (5) der Held (*weak*), -en
hint (5) der Tip, -s
his (*poss.*) (6) sein, seine
to hit the books (4) die Nase ins Buch stecken
hobby (5) das Hobby
home: to be at home (1) zu Hause sein; **to go home** (2) nach hause gehen; (14) **to stay at home** (14) zu hause bleiben
hook (7) der Haken, —
hope (14) die Hoffnung; **to give up hope** die Hoffnung auf•geben (gibt auf), gab auf, aufgegeben
to hope (1) hoffen; **I hope** *or* **hopefully** hoffentlich
hot (9) heiß
hotel (5) das Hotel, -s
house (2) das Haus, -er
humid (12) feucht
hurry: to be in a hurry (2) es eilig haben

ID card (17) der Ausweis, -e
idea: to have no idea (2) keine Ahnung haben
if (12) wenn (*subj. conj.*)
to ignore (6) ignorieren
to imagine something (17) sich (*dat.*) etwas vorstellen
impolite (2) unhöflich
important (10) wichtig
to inherit (16) erben
insecure (10) unsicher
to improve, become better (6) besser werden (wird), wurde, ist geworden
in, into, to (7) in (*acc./dat.*)
information: to give information (9) Auskunft geben (gibt), gab, gegeben
in front of (7) vor (*acc./dat.*)
in spite of (7) trotz (*gen.*); **in spite of that** (8) trotzdem

instead (7) anstatt, statt (*gen.*); **instead of that** (8) statt dessen

insurance company (13) die Versicherungs-gesellschaft, -en

to be interested in (17) sich (*acc.*) interessieren für (*acc.*)

interesting (9) interessant

to interrupt (14) unterbrechen (unterbricht), unterbrach, unterbrochen

invention (6) die Erfindung, -en

inventor (6) der Erfinder, —

to invite (2, 3) ein•laden (lädt ein), lud ein, eingeladen

its (*poss.*) (6) sein, seine *or* ihr ihre

janitor (5) der Hausmeister, —

job (5) der Job, -s *or* die Stelle, -n

joke (8) der Witz, -e

just about: I was just about to ... (4) ich wollte gerade (eben) ...

to keep the promise (12) das Versprechen halten (hält), hielt, gehalten

key (3) der Schlüssel, –

to know (*something as a fact*) (3) wissen (weiß), wußte, gewußt; **Dr. know-it-all** (14) Dr. Allwissend

to know (*be aquainted with*) (3) kennen, kannte, gekannt

lady (5) die Dame, -n

to land (3) landen (ist)

late (3) spät; **to be late** zu spät kommen, kam, ist gekommen; **at the latest** (10) spätestens **the latest** (10) das Neu(e)ste

to laugh (2) lachen; **to laugh at** (3) aus•lachen *or* (8) lachen über (*acc.*)

lawyer (6) der Rechtsanwalt, ¨e; (14) die Rechtsanwältin, -nen

lazy (13) faul

lazybones (6) der Faulenzer, —; die Faulenzerin, -nen

to leave alone (20) in Ruhe lassen (läßt), ließ, gelassen

Lebanon (6) der Libanon

at least (10) mindestens

leather (7) das Leder

less (10) weniger

letter (8) der Brief, -e

library (7) die Bibliothek, -en

lie (20) die Lüge, -n

life (10) das Leben

to like (4) mögen; **I would like** ich möchte; (5) gefallen (gefällt), gefiel, gefallen (*dat.*); **like to do something** (20) etwas gern tun

likeable (20) sympathisch; **not likeable** unsympathisch

to listen (3) zu•hören

a little (10) etwas, ein wenig

to live (1) wohnen

logical (10) logisch

as long as (12) solange (sub. conj.)

to look at, take a look at (17) sich (*dat.*) etwas an•schauen *or* an•sehen (sieht an), sah an, angesehen

to look foward to (17) sich (*acc.*) freuen auf.(*acc.*)

to lose (3) verlieren, verlor, verloren

to lose weight (3) ab•nehmen (nimmt ab), nahm ab, abgenommen

to lose one's way (17) (*walking*) sich (*acc.*) ver laufen, verlief, verlaufen; (*driving*) sich (*acc.*) verfahren (verfährt), veruhr, verfahren

a lot (3) viel

loud (14) laut

to be in love with (8) verliebt sein in (*acc.*)

love story (6) die Liebesgeschichte, -n

to be lucky (3) Glück haben, hatte, gehabt

machine (6) die Maschine, -n

to make (3) machen; **to make money** Geld verdienen

man (9) der Mann, ¨er

to manipulate (14) manipulieren

many a (6) mancher, manches, manche

matter (2) die Sache, -n

to marry, get married (13) heiraten

to be married to (8) verheiratet sein mit (*dat.*)

may, to be allowed to (4) dürfen (darf), durfte, gedurft

mayor (5) der Bürgermeister, —; die Bürger-meisterin, -nen

to mean (6) meinen

to meet (*for the first time*) (4) kennen•lernen

to memorize (18) auswendig lernen

message (17) die Nachricht, -en

mind: to lose one's mind (6) den Verstand verlieren, verlor, verloren

mistake (6) der Fehler, —

to be mistaken (17) sich (*acc.*) irren

modern languages (10) Neuere Sprachen

modesty (17) die Bescheidenheit

money (6) das Geld

Monday (11) der Montag, -e
month (11) der Monat, -e
mood: to be in a good/bad mood (1) gute/
   schlechte Laune haben
more (10) mehr
morning (11) der Morgen; **late morning,**
   forenoon der Vormittag, -e
most: at the most (10) höchstens
mostly, most of the time, usually (10) meistens, meist
motel (5) das Motel, -s
mother (7) die Mutter, -
to move to the country (13) aufs Land ziehen,
   zog, ist gezogen
movie (9) der Film, -e; **to go to the movies** (2)
ins Kino gehen, ging, ist gegangen
movie theater (5) das Kino, -s
to mow (20) mähen; **to mow the lawn** (20)
   den Rasen mähen
mistake (9) der Fehler
museum (5) das Museum, die Museen
music (20) die Musik
must (4) müssen (muß), mußte, gemußt
must not (4) nicht dürfen (darf)
my (poss.) (6) mein, meine

name (5) der Name (*weak; gen.* -ns), -n
neat, orderly (10) ordentlich
necessary (2) nötig
neighbor (6) der Nachbar, -n; die Nachbarin,
nervous (2) nervös; **to get nervous** (2, 3)
   nervös werden (wird), wurde,
   ist geworden
never (4) nie, noch nie
news (8) die Nachricht, -en
newspaper (20) die Zeitung, -en
newsstand (7) der Zeitungsstand, ¨-e
next to (7) neben (acc./dat.)
the next one (10) der Nächste; die Nächste
   (*adj. noun*)
night (11) (*before bedtime*) der Abend, -e;
   (*after bedtime*) die Nacht, ¨e **tonight** heute
   abend; heute nacht
no, not a, not any (6) kein, keine
nobody (3) niemand; **nobody else** (15)
   niemand anders
noise (17) der Lärm
noon (11) der Mittag, -e
nosy (10) neugierig
not (1) nicht; **not yet** (8) noch nicht
nothing (12) nichts

to notice (3) merken
to notify (18) benachrichtigen
novel (5) der Roman, -e
nowhere, not anywhere (15) (*motion to a*
   place) nirgend(s) wohin; (*place at which*)
   nirgend(s)wo, nirgends

observation (12) die Bemerkung, -en
of, from (7) von (dat.)
of course (8) natürlich
offense: to take offense (2, 3) übel•nehmen
   (nimmt übel), nahm übel, übelgenommen
office (7) das Büro, -s
often (2) oft
on (7) (*horizontal surface*) auf (acc./dat.);
   (*vertical surface*) an (acc./dat.)
only (9) nur; **not only... but also** (12) nicht
   nur... sondern auch
opinion (7) die Meinung, -en; **in my opinion**
   meiner Meinung nach
or (6) oder
orange juice (1) der Orangensaft, ¨-e
our (*poss.*) (6) unser, uns(e)re
out of (7) aus (*dat.*)
to overlook (16) übersehen (übersieht),
   übersah, übersehen
overnight: to stay overnight (12) übernachten
to oversleep (14) verschlafen (verschläft),
   verschlief, verschlafen
over there (16) da drüben

to paint the house (20) das Haus streichen,
   strich, gestrichen
parents (10) die Eltern; **most parents** die
   meisten Eltern
to park (12) parken
party (5) die Party, -s
to pass the exam (3) die Prüfung bestehen,
   bestand, bestanden
patience (13) die Geduld
to pay (4) bezahlen
peace (5) der Friede (*weak; gen.* -ns)
people (5) die Leute
perhaps (1) vielleicht
permanent: to get a permanent (20) sich (dat.)
   eine Dauerwelle machen lassen
permission: to ask permission (12) um
   Erlaubnis bitten
perseverance (13) die Ausdauer
petty (13) kleinlich
phone (7) das Telefon, -e

piano (6) das Klavier, -e; **to play the piano** Klavier spielen

to pick up (2) ab•holen; **to pick up the mail** (12) die Post ab•holen

picnic (18) das Picknick, -e

pictures: to take pictures (8) Aufnahmen machen

pineapple punch (20) Ananasbowle

pity: it is a pity (4) es ist schade

to plan (12) vor•haben; **to have other plans** etwas anderes vor•haben

plane (3) das Flugzeug, -e

play (*stage*) (5) das Theaterstück, -e

please (2) bitte

poem (16) das Gedicht, -e

point (16) der Punkt, -e

policeman (5) der Polizist (*weak*), -en; **police-woman** die Polizistin, -nen

popular (20) beliebt

possible (1) möglich

to postpone (18) verschieben, verschob, verschoben

practical (10) praktisch

prejudice (13) das Vorurteil, -e

president (5) der Präsident (*weak*), -en

to pretend (14) so tun, als ob

pretty (10) hübsch

prize (14) der Preis, -e; **to win the first prize** den ersten Preis gewinnen

problem (4) das Problem, -e

project (8) das Projekt, -e

to promote (18) befördern

to propose (*marriage*) (18) einen Heiratsantrag machen

to protest (4) protestieren

to be proud of (8) stolz sein auf (*acc.*)

question (8) die Frage, -n

quiet (2) still

railway station (14) der Bahnhof, ̈ e

rain (7) der Regen

rainy weather (5) das Regenwetter

raise (*salary*) (12) die Gehaltserhöhung, -en; **to ask for a raise** (13) um eine Gehaltserhöhung bitten, bat, gebeten

to react to (8) reagieren auf (acc.)

real(ly) (12) wirklich

reason: for this/that reason (7) aus diesem Grund

receiver: **to put down the receiver, to hang up** (12) den Hörer auf•legen

to recognize (8) erkennen, erkannte, erkannt

record (6) die Schallplatte, -n *or* die Platte, -n

record player (6) der Plattenspieler, -

refrigerator (2) der Kühlschrank, ̈ e

to be related to (8) verwandt sein mit (*dat.*)

relative (15) der Verwandte (*adj. noun*)

reliable (12) zuverlässig

to remember (17) sich (*acc.*) erinnern an (*acc.*); **I don't remember** (3) ich weiß es nicht mehr

report card (8) das Zeugnis, -se

reporter (5) der Reporter, —; die Reporterin, -nen

to reprimand (10) tadeln

to resent (3) übel•nehmen (nimmt übel), nahm übel, übelgenommen

restaurant (5) das Restaurant, -s

to be right (2, 3) recht haben, hatte, gehabt

ring (6) der Ring, -e

river (7) der Fluß, ̈ -sse

to room with (16) in einem Zimmer wohnen mit (*dat.*)

rumor (14) Gerücht, -e

to run away (12) davon•laufen, (läuft davon), lief davon, ist davongelaufen

same: the same (9) derselbe, dasselbe, dieselbe; **it's all the same to me** (15) es ist mir ganz gleich

to be satisfied *or* **content with** (8) zufrieden sein mit (*dat.*)

Saturday (11) der Sonnabend, -e *or* der Samstag, -e

to save (*money*) (12) sparen

to say (4) sagen

scholar (9) der *or* die Gelehrte (*adj. noun*)

scholarship (3) das Stipendium, die Stipendien; **to get a scholarship** ein Stipendium bekommen, bekam, bekommen

school (6) die Schule, -n

second-hand (9) gebraucht

secret (6) das Geheimnis, -se

to see (20) sehen (sieht), sah, gesehen

to sell (2) verkaufen

semester (5) das Semester, -

seminar paper (8) das Referat, -e (*oral presentation*)

to send (6) schicken

to set the clock (11) die Uhr stellen

shall (4) sollen

to shave (17) sich (*acc.*) rasieren

shocked (3) schockiert

shoe (10) der Schuh, -e

short (a person's height) (10) klein

to show (6) zeigen

shrimp (20) die Krabbe, -n

shy (14) schüchtern

sick (6) krank

to sign (4) unterschreiben, unterschrieb, unterschrieben

silent: to remain silent (12) schweigen, schwieg, geschwiegen

simple (4) einfach

since (*prep.*) (7) seit (*dat.*)

since (*sub. conj.*) (12) (*referring to time*) seit, seitdem; (*stating reason*) da

since then (18) seitdem

to be single (13) ledig sein

sister (8) die Schwester, -n

to sit down (17) sich (*acc.*) setzen

to skip class (2) schwänzen

to sleep (2, 3) schlafen (schläft), schlief geschlafen

slim (10) schlank

sloppy (10) liederlich

slow (10) langsam; **to be slow** (*clock*) (11) nach•gehen, ging nach, ist nachgegangen

to smoke (13) rauchen

so that, in order that (12) damit (*sub. conj.*)

soccer field (7) der Fußballplatz, ̈e; **soccer game** das Fußballspiel, -e **soccer player** (5) der Fußballspieler,—

to solve the problem (12) das Problem lösen

solution (10) die Lösung, -en

some (9) einige; etwas

somebody (15) jemand; **somebody else** jemand anders

somehow or other (15) irgendwie

something (9) etwas; **something or other** (15) irgend etwas

some time or other (15) irgendwann

somewhere, anywhere (15) (*motion to a place*) irgenwohin; (*place at which*) irgendwo

son (5) der Sohn, ̈e

soon (14) bald; **as soon as** (12) sobald (*sub. conj.*)

Spanish (7) spanisch

to speak (14) sprechen (spricht), sprach, gesprochen

speech: to make a speech (19) eine Rede halten (hält), hielt, gehalten

to spend money (10) Geld aus•geben (gibt aus), gab aus, ausgegeben

sport: to do a lot of sport (12) viel Sport treiben, trieb, getrieben

spring (11) der Frühling, -e

stage fright (20) das Lampenfieber

stamp collection (7) die Briefmarken-sammlung, -en

status symbol (6) das Statussymbol, -e

to stay 913) bleiben, blieb, ist geblieben; **to stay a little longer** etwas länger bleiben; **to stay fit** fit bleiben (12)

to stop, end, cease (2) auf•hören, Schluß machen

story (5) die Geschichte, -n

to straighten up (3) auf•räumen

strict (10) streng

strike (18) der Streik, -s

stubborn (4) stur

student (6) der Student (*weak*), -en; die Studentin, -nen

to study for an exam (4) für eine Prüfung lernen

stupid (9) dumm

subway: to go by subway (6) mit der U-Bahn fahren

success (6) der Erfolg, -e

such a (6) solcher, solches, soche *or* solch ein, solch eine *or* so ein, so eine

suggestion (6) der Vorschlag, ̈e

suitcase (8) der Koffer, -

summer (11) der Sommer,-

Sunday (11) der Sonntag, -e

to be supposed to (4) sollen (soll), sollte, gesollt

surprise (6) die Überraschung, -en

Switzerland (6) die Schweiz

table (7) der Tisch, -e

to take along (12) mit•nehmen (nimmt mit), nahm mit, mitgenommen

to take care of (2) erledigen

to take seriously (12) ernst nehmen (nimmt), nahm, genommen

to talk of *or* **about** (8) sprechen (spricht), sprach, gesprochen von (*dat.*) **to talk with** *or* **to** sprechen mit (*dat.*)

tall (*a person's height*) (10) groß

to taste (10) schmecken

teacher (9) der Lehrer,—

telephone number (5) Telefonnummer

television set (12) der Fernseher

to tell (3) sagen; (*relate*) (6) erzählen

temptation (4) die Versuchung **to lead into temptation** in Versuchung führen

tennis court (7) der Tennisplatz, ̈e

tenor (20) der Tenor, ̈e

term paper (4) die Semesterarbeit, en

terrible (16) schrecklich

to thank for (7) danken für (*acc.*)

that (1) daß (*sub. conj.*)

that, those (6) jener, jenes, jene

their (*poss.*) (6) ihr, ihre

there is, there are (10) es gibt (*acc.*)

thing: the first thing (16) das erste; the last
    thing das letzte; the only thing das einzige;
    many things vieles

to think of *or* about (8) denken, dachte,
    gedacht an (*acc.*); (17) sich (*dat.*) etwas
    überlegen

this, these (6) dieser, dieses, diese

through (7) durch (*acc.*)

thunderstorm (7) das Gewitter, —

Thursday (11) der Donnerstag, -e

time: to be on time (16) pünktlich sein

title (5) der Titel, —

to (*prep.*) (7) zu (*dat.*) nach (*dat.*)

tolerant (1) tolerant

tomorrow (2) morgen

too (13) zu; too bad (3) schade

topic (5) das Thema, die Themen

torture (6) die Tortur, -en

train: to go by train (6) mit dem Zug *or* mit
    der Bahn fahren (fährt), fuhr, ist gefahren

to travel (3) reisen (ist)

traveler's check (6) der Reisescheck, -s

tree (7) der Baum, ⸚e

trip (17) die Reise, -n

trouble: to have trouble with (8)
    Schwierigkeiten haben mit (dat.)

true (3) wahr

to try (3) versuchen; to try again noch einmal
    versuchen

Tuesday (11) der Dienstag, -e

Turkey (6) die Türkei

to type (13) tippen

typewriter (13) die Schreibmaschine, -n

under (7) unter (*acc./dat.*)

to understand (3) verstehen, verstand, ver-
    standen

unfortunately (18) leider

until (2, 12) bis

use: it's no use (12) es hat keinen Zweck

vacation (*from a job*) (12) der Urlaub, -e

very (10) sehr

village (7) das Dorf, ⸚er

violin (6) die Geige *or* die Violine; to play the
    violin Geige/Violine spielen

to visit (2) besuchen

to wait for (8) warten auf (*acc.*)

to want to (4) wollen (will), wollte, gewollt

to warn (4) warnen

warning (6) die Warnung, -en

to wash (*oneself*) (17) sich (*acc.*) waschen
    (wäscht), wusch, gewaschen; to wash one's
    hands sich (*dat.*) die Hände waschen; to
    wash the windows (20) die Fenster putzen

to watch television (4) fern•sehen (sieht fern),
    sah fern, ferngesehen

to wave (20) winken

weather (7) das Wetter; in this weather bei
    diesem Wetter

Wednesday 911) der Mittwoch, -e

week (11) der Woche, -n

weekend (11) das Wochenende, -n

what (2) was; what a (6) welch ein, eine; was
    für ein, eine; what kind of was für

when (12) wann, wenn, als

where (*at what place*) (1) wo; (*to what place*)
    (7) wohin

whether, if (1) ob

which (6) welcher, welches, welche

while (12) während (*sub. conj.*)

who (8) wer

why (1) warum

widow (6) Witwe, -n

wife (8) die Frau, -en

will power (10) die Willenskraft

to window-shop (17) sich (*dat.*) die Schaufen-
    ster an•sehen (sieht an), sah an, angesehen

windy (13) windig

winter (11) der Winter, —

with (7) mit (*dat.*)

without (7) ohne (*acc.*)

word of honor (6) das Ehrenwort

work (17) die Arbeit, -en

to work on (8) arbeiten an (*dat.*)

worker (5) der Arbeiter, -

world (7) die Welt, -en

worse: to get worse (4) schlechter werden
    (wird), wurde, ist geworden

worry (10) die Sorge, -n

wrong (14) falsch

year (11) das Jahr, -e

yesterday (11) gestern

young (9) jung

your (*poss.*) (6) dein, deine (*fam. sing.*) euer
    eu(e)re (*fam. pl.*); Ihr, Ihre (*formal*)

Index